Expert Oracle Exadata

Kerry Osborne
Randy Johnson
Tanel Põder

apress®

Expert Oracle Exadata

ISBN-13 (pbk): 978-1-4302-3392-3

ISBN-13 (electronic): 978-1-4302-3393-0

President and Publisher: Paul Manning
Lead Editor: Jonathan Gennick
Technical Reviewer: Kevin Closson
Editorial Board: Steve Anglin, Mark Beckner, Ewan Buckingham, Gary Cornell, Jonathan Gennick, Jonathan Hassell, Michelle Lowman, Matthew Moodie, Jeff Olson, Jeffrey Pepper, Frank Pohlmann, Douglas Pundick, Ben Renow-Clarke, Dominic Shakeshaft, Matt Wade, Tom Welsh
Coordinating Editor: Adam Heath
Copy Editor: James Compton
Compositor: Bytheway Publishing Services
Indexer: SPI Global
Artist: SPI Global
Cover Designer: Anna Ishchenko

Distributed to the book trade worldwide by Springer Science+Business Media, LLC., 233 Spring Street, 6th Floor, New York, NY 10013. Phone 1-800-SPRINGER, fax (201) 348-4505, e-mail orders-ny@springer-sbm.com, or visit www.springeronline.com.

For information on translations, please e-mail rights@apress.com, or visit www.apress.com.

Apress and friends of ED books may be purchased in bulk for academic, corporate, or promotional use. eBook versions and licenses are also available for most titles. For more information, reference our Special Bulk Sales–eBook Licensing web page at www.apress.com/bulk-sales.

Contents at a Glance

Contents

About the Author

 **Kerry Osborne** began working with Oracle (version 2) in 1982. He has worked as both a developer and a DBA. For the past several years he has been focused on understanding Oracle internals and solving performance problems. He is an OakTable member and an Oracle Ace Director. Kerry is a frequent speaker at Oracle conferences. He is also a co-founder of Enkitec, an Oracle-focused consulting company headquartered in Dallas, Texas. He blogs at `kerryosborne.oracle-guy.com`.

 **Randy Johnson** is a Principal Consultant at Enkitec, a consulting firm specializing in Oracle. Randy has over 18 years of experience with Oracle beginning with Oracle 7 in the early 90s. Much of his career has combined Oracle DBA work with Unix administration duties. Over the last five years he has focused almost exclusively on RAC and ASM. He is also an authority on Oracle backup and recovery via RMAN, having written a popular utility for automating RMAN scripts called Dixie. Randy occasionally blogs at `blog.enkitec.com`.

 **Tanel Põder** is one of the leading Oracle performance specialists in the world, having helped solving complex problems for customers in over 20 countries on five continents. He specializes in advanced performance tuning, end-to-end troubleshooting, and other complex (and therefore interesting) tasks such as migrating VLDBs with very low downtime. Tanel has optimized the performance of Exadata installations starting from Exadata V1, and he plans to go even deeper with his current Exadata performance and troubleshooting research.
He is one of the first Oracle Certified Masters in the world, an Oracle ACE Director and a proud member of the OakTable Network.
Tanel regularly speaks at conferences worldwide and publishes his articles, scripts and tools in his blog at `http://blog.tanelpoder.com`.

About the Technical Reviewer

 **Kevin Closson** is a Technology Director and Performance Architect in the Data Computing Division of EMC. From 2007 through 2011, Kevin was a Performance Architect in Oracle Corporation's Exadata development organization within the Server Technology Group. His 25 year career focus has been system and software performance engineering and architecture, competitive benchmarking, support, and application development on high-end SMP and Clustered Unix and Linux platforms. His work prior to Oracle at HP/PolyServe, Veritas, and IBM/Sequent was focused on scalability and availability enhancements of the Oracle server and platforms that support it. His Oracle port-level work led to his U.S. patents in SMP/NUMA locking and database caching methods (6389513, 6480918). Kevin maintains a very popular technology blog at kevinclosson.wordpress.com.

Acknowledgments

As always, it's the people closest to you that pay the price for your indiscretions. So I'd like to take this opportunity to thank my family for putting up with me while I struggled through this project. It was far more work than I ever expected, but what really surprised me was that there was a sense of impending doom hanging over me every day for almost a year. I joked that everything was measured in paragraphs. I could go out to dinner with my wife, or I could write another two paragraphs. (Actually, I couldn't write them that fast, but you know what I mean.) So again, I'd like to thank my wife Jill and my kids for putting up with the distant stares and the self imposed rain cloud hanging over all of our heads.

Kerry Osborne

I want to say thank you to my kids, Brandon and Charis, who endured the many long nights and weekends I spent at the kitchen table writing this book. They are such an inspiration to me. My daughter Charis, a truly gifted writer, is so creative and bold. My son Brandon, the brilliant scientist and strategic thinker of the family, never gives up. Watching them grow into young adults has taught me the value of creativity and perseverance, especially when the task seems insurmountable. I love you, kids.

To my parents, family, and friends, I'd like to say thank you for all your encouragement and support. You were always there for me when I needed you. I won't try to name everyone here, but you know who you are.

And finally, I'd like to say a special thanks to Kerry for inviting me on this journey with him. A few years ago, if you'd told me I was going to write a book someday, I'd have laughed out loud. But Kerry has a talent for nudging me out of my comfort zone. In addition to being a mentor, over the years he has become a trusted friend.

Randy Johnson

This is the first book I've co-authored, so this acknowledgment is going to be a thank-you note to anyone who has ever helped me with my career and supported my passion for solving problems with data, algorithms, and computers. If you have ever taught me, helped me, or given me advice— thank you! I'd like to give a special thanks to my parents, who strongly supported my interest in technology, electronics, and computers when I was a kid. Additionally, a big thanks to my wife Janika, who, despite not being a computer geek, understands that it's perfectly normal to sometimes stare at a computer screen for 24 hours in a row.

Tanel Põder

Introduction

Thank you for purchasing this book. We worked hard on it for a long time. Our hope is that you find it useful as you begin to work with Exadata. We've tried to introduce the topics in a methodical manner and move from generalizations to specific technical details. While some of the material paints a very broad picture of how Exadata works, some is very technical in nature, and you may find that having access to an Exadata system where you can try some of the techniques presented will make it easier to understand. Note that we've used many undocumented parameters and features to demonstrate how various pieces of the software work. Do not take this as a recommended approach for managing a production system. Remember that we have had access to a system that we could tear apart with little worry about the consequences that resulted from our actions. This gave us a huge advantage in our investigations into how Exadata works. In addition to this privileged access, we were provided a great deal of support from people both inside and outside of Oracle for which we are extremely grateful.

The Intended Audience

This book is intended for experienced Oracle people. We do not attempt to explain how Oracle works except as it relates to the Exadata platform. This means that we have made some assumptions about the reader's knowledge. We do not assume that you are an expert at performance tuning on Oracle, but we do expect that you are proficient with SQL and have a good understanding of basic Oracle architecture.

How We Came to Write This Book

In the spring of 2010, Enkitec bought an Exadata V2 Quarter Rack. We put it in the tiny computer room at our office in Dallas. We don't have a raised floor or anything very fancy, but the room does have its own air conditioning system. It was actually more difficult than you might think to get Oracle to let us purchase one. They had many customers that wanted them, and they were understandably protective of their new baby. We didn't have a top-notch data center to put it in, and even the power requirements had to be dealt with before they would deliver one to us. At any rate, shortly after we took delivery, through a series of conversations with Jonathan Gennick, Randy and I agreed to write this book for Apress. There was not a whole lot of documentation available at that time, and so we found ourselves pestering anyone we could find who knew anything about it. Kevin Closson and Dan Norris were both gracious enough to answer many of our questions at the Hotsos Symposium in the spring of 2010. Kevin contacted me some time later and offered to be the official technical reviewer. So Randy and I struggled through the summer and early fall attempting to learn everything could.

I ran into Tanel at Oracle Open World in September, 2010, and we talked about a client using Exadata that he had done some migration work for. One thing led to another, and eventually he agreed to join the team as a co-author. At Open World, Oracle announced the availability of the new X2 models, so we had barely gotten started and we were already behind on the technology.

In January of 2011, the X2 platform was beginning to show up at customer sites. Enkitec again decided to invest in the technology, and we became the proud parents of an X2-2 quarter rack. Actually, we decided to upgrade our existing V2 quarter rack to a half rack with X2 components. This seemed like a good way to learn about doing upgrades and to see if there would be any problems mixing components from the two versions (there weren't). This brings me to an important point.

A Moving Target

Like most new software, Exadata has evolved rapidly since its introduction in late 2009. The changes have included significant new functionality. In fact, one of the most difficult parts of this project has been keeping up with the changes. Several chapters underwent multiple revisions because of changes in behavior introduced while we were writing the material. The last version we have attempted to cover in this book is database version 11.2.0.2 with bundle patch 6 and cellsrv version 11.2.2.3.2. Note that there have been many patches over the last two years and that there are many possible combinations of database version, patch level, and cellsrv versions. So if you are observing some different behavior than we have documented, this is a potential cause. Nevertheless, we welcome your feedback and will be happy to address any inconsistencies that you find. In fact, this book has been available as part of Apress's Alpha program, which allows readers to download early drafts of the material. Participants in this program have provided quite a bit of feedback during the writing and editing process. We are very thankful for that feedback and somewhat surprised at the detailed information many of you provided.

Thanks to the Unofficial Editors

We have had a great deal of support from a number of people on this project. Having our official technical reviewer actually writing bits that were destined to end up in the book was a little weird. In such a case, who reviews the reviewer's writing? Fortunately, Arup Nanda volunteered early in the project to be an unofficial editor. So in addition to the authors reviewing each other's stuff, and Kevin reviewing our chapters, Arup read and commented on everything, including Kevin's comments. In addition, many of the Oak Table Network members gave us feedback on various chapters throughout the process. Most notably, Frits Hoogland and Peter Bach provided valuable input.

When the book was added to Apress's Alpha Program, we gained a whole new set of reviewers. Several people gave us feedback based on the early versions of chapters that were published in this format. Thanks to all of you who asked us questions and helped us clarify our thoughts on specific issues. In particular, Tyler Muth at Oracle took a very active interest in the project and provided us with very detailed feedback. He was also instrumental in helping to connect us with other resources inside Oracle, such as Sue Lee, who provided a very detailed review of the Resource Management chapter.

Finally I'd like to thank the technical team at Enkitec. There were many who helped us keep on track and helped pick up the slack while Randy and I were working on this project (instead of doing our real jobs). The list of people who helped is pretty long, so I won't call everyone by name. If you work at Enkitec and you have been involved with the Exadata work over the last couple of years, you have contributed to this book. I would like to specifically thank Tim Fox, who generated a lot of the graphics for us in spite of the fact that he had numerous other irons in the fire, including his own book project. We also owe Andy Colvin a very special thanks as a major contributor to the project. He was instrumental in several capacities. First, he was primarily responsible for maintaining our test environment, including upgrading and patching the platform so that we could test the newest features and changes as they became available. Second, he helped us hold down the fort with our customers who were implementing Exadata while Randy and I were busy writing. Third, he was instrumental in helping us figure out how various features worked, particularly with regard to installation, configuration, and connections to external systems. It would have been difficult to complete the project without him.

Who Wrote That?

There are three authors of this book, four if you count Kevin. It was really a collaborative effort among the four of us. But in order to divide the work we each agreed to do a number of chapters. Initially Randy and I started the project and Tanel joined a little later (so he got a lighter load in terms of the assignments, but was a very valuable part of team, helping with research on areas that were not specifically assigned to him). So here's how the assignments worked out:

> Kerry: Chapters 1–6, 10, 16.
> Randy: Chapters 7–9, 14–15, and about half of 13
> Tanel: Chapters 11–12, and about half of 13
> Kevin: Easily identifiable in the "Kevin Says" sections

Online Resources

We used a number of scripts in this book. When they were short or we felt the scripts themselves were of interest, we included their contents in the text. When they were long or just not very interesting, we sometimes left the contents of the scripts out of the text. You can find the source code for all of the scripts we used in the book online at www.ExpertOracleExadata.com. Appendix C also contains a listing of all the diagnostic scripts along with a brief description of their purpose.

A Note on "Kevin Says"

Kevin Closson served as our primary technical reviewer for the book. Kevin was the chief performance architect at Oracle for the SAGE project, which eventually turned into Exadata, so he is extremely knowledgeable not only about how it works, but also about how it should work and why. His duties as technical reviewer were to review what we wrote and verify it for correctness. The general workflow consisted of one of the authors submitting a first draft of a chapter and then Kevin would review it and mark it up with comments. As we started working together, we realized that it might be a good idea to actually include some of Kevin's comments in the book, which provides you with a somewhat unique look into the process. Kevin has a unique way of saying a lot in very few words. Over the course of the project I found myself going back to short comments or emails multiple times, and often found them more meaningful after I was more familiar with the topic. So I would recommend that you do the same. Read his comments as you're going through a chapter, but try to come back and reread his comments after finishing the chapter; I think you'll find that you will get more out of them on the second pass.

How We Tested

When we began the project, the current release of the database was 11.2.0.1. So several of the chapters were initially tested with that version of the database and various patch levels on the storage cells. When

11.2.0.2 became available, we went back and retested. Where there were significant differences we tried to point that out, but there are some sections that were not written until after 11.2.0.2 was available. So on those topics we may not have mentioned differences with 11.2.0.1 behavior. We used a combination of V2 and X2 hardware components for our testing. There was basically no difference other than the X2 being faster.

Schemas and Tables

You will see a couple of database tables used in several examples throughout the book. Tanel used a table called T that looks like this:

```
SYS@SANDBOX1> @table_stats
Owner : TANEL
Table : T
Name                                        Null?    Type
----------------------------------------    -------- ----------------------------------
OWNER                                                VARCHAR2(30)
NAME                                                 VARCHAR2(30)
TYPE                                                 VARCHAR2(12)
LINE                                                 NUMBER
TEXT                                                 VARCHAR2(4000)
ROWNUM                                               NUMBER


========================================================================
    Table Statistics
========================================================================
TABLE_NAME                    : T
LAST_ANALYZED                 : 10-APR-2011 13:28:55
DEGREE                        : 1
PARTITIONED                   : NO
NUM_ROWS                      : 62985999
CHAIN_CNT                     : 0
BLOCKS                        : 1085255
EMPTY_BLOCKS                  : 0
AVG_SPACE                     : 0
AVG_ROW_LEN                   : 104
MONITORING                    : YES
SAMPLE_SIZE                   : 62985999
-----------------

========================================================================
    Column Statistics
========================================================================
Name     Analyzed      NDV      Density  # Nulls   # Buckets   Sample
========================================================================
OWNER    04/10/2011     21      .047619  0         1           62985999
NAME     04/10/2011   5417      .000185  0         1           62985999
TYPE     04/10/2011      9      .111111  0         1           62985999
LINE     04/10/2011  23548      .000042  0         1           62985999
```

TEXT	04/10/2011	303648	.000003	0	1	62985999
ROWNUM	04/10/2011	100	.010000	0	1	62985999

I used several variations on a table called SKEW. The one I used most often is SKEW3, and it looked like this:

```
SYS@SANDBOX1> @table_stats
Owner : KSO
Table : SKEW3
Name                                         Null?     Type
----------------------------------------     --------  ---------------------------
PK_COL                                                 NUMBER
COL1                                                   NUMBER
COL2                                                   VARCHAR2(30)
COL3                                                   DATE
COL4                                                   VARCHAR2(1)
NULL_COL                                               VARCHAR2(10)


===========================================================================
  Table Statistics
===========================================================================
TABLE_NAME            : SKEW3
LAST_ANALYZED         : 10-JAN-2011 19:49:00
DEGREE                : 1
PARTITIONED           : NO
NUM_ROWS              : 384000048
CHAIN_CNT             : 0
BLOCKS                : 1958654
EMPTY_BLOCKS          : 0
AVG_SPACE             : 0
AVG_ROW_LEN           : 33
MONITORING            : YES
SAMPLE_SIZE           : 384000048
-----------------
===========================================================================
  Column Statistics
===========================================================================
Name        Analyzed      NDV    Density  # Nulls     # Buckets  Sample
===========================================================================
PK_COL      01/10/2011 31909888  .000000  12          1          384000036
COL1        01/10/2011   902848  .000001  4           1          384000044
COL2        01/10/2011        2  .500000  12          1          384000036
COL3        01/10/2011  1000512  .000001  12          1          384000036
COL4        01/10/2011        3  .333333  12          1          384000036
NULL_COL    01/10/2011        1 1.000000  383999049   1          999
```

This detailed information should not be necessary for understanding any of our examples, but if you have any questions about the tables, they are here for your reference. Also be aware that we used other tables as well, but these are the ones we used most often.

Good Luck

We have had a blast discovering how Exadata works. I hope you enjoy your explorations as much as we have, and I hope this book provides a platform from which you can build your own body of knowledge. I feel like we are just beginning to scratch the surface of the possibilities that have been opened up by Exadata. Good luck with your investigations and please feel free to ask us questions and share your discoveries with us at `www.ExpertOracleExadata.com`.

CHAPTER 1

What Is Exadata?

No doubt you already have a pretty good idea what Exadata is or you wouldn't be holding this book in your hands. In our view, it is a preconfigured combination of hardware and software that provides a platform for running Oracle Database (version 11g Release 2 as of this writing). Since the Exadata Database Machine includes a storage subsystem, new software has been developed to run at the storage layer. This has allowed the developers to do some things that are just not possible on other platforms. In fact, Exadata really began its life as a storage system. If you talk to people involved in the development of the product, you will commonly hear them refer the storage component as Exadata or SAGE (Storage Appliance for Grid Environments), which was the code name for the project.

Exadata was originally designed to address the most common bottleneck with very large databases, the inability to move sufficiently large volumes of data from the disk storage system to the database server(s). Oracle has built its business by providing very fast access to data, primarily through the use of intelligent caching technology. As the sizes of databases began to outstrip the ability to cache data effectively using these techniques, Oracle began to look at ways to eliminate the bottleneck between the storage tier and the database tier. The solution they came up with was a combination of hardware and software. If you think about it, there are two approaches to minimizing this bottleneck. The first is to make the pipe bigger. While there are many components involved, and it's a bit of an oversimplification, you can think of InfiniBand as that bigger pipe. The second way to minimize the bottleneck is to reduce the amount of data that needs to be transferred. This they did with Smart Scans. The combination of the two has provided a very successful solution to the problem. But make no mistake; reducing the volume of data flowing between the tiers via Smart Scan is the golden goose.

Kevin Says: The authors have provided an accurate list of approaches for alleviating the historical bottleneck between storage and CPU for DW/BI workloads—if, that is, the underlying mandate is to change as little in the core Oracle Database kernel as possible. From a pure computer science perspective, the list of solutions to the generic problem of data flow between storage and CPU includes options such as co-locating the data with the database instance—the "shared-nothing" MPP approach. While it is worthwhile to point this out, the authors are right not to spend time discussing the options dismissed by Oracle.

In this introductory chapter we'll review the components that make up Exadata, both hardware and software. We'll also discuss how the parts fit together (the architecture). We'll talk about how the database servers talk to the storage servers. This is handled very differently than on other platforms, so we'll spend a fair amount of time covering that topic. We'll also provide some historical context. By the end of the chapter, you should have a pretty good feel for how all the pieces fit together and a basic understanding of how Exadata works. The rest of the book will provide the details to fill out the skeleton that is built in this chapter.

▩ **Kevin Says:** In my opinion, Data Warehousing / Business Intelligence practitioners, in an Oracle environment, who are interested in Exadata, must understand Cell Offload Processing fundamentals *before* any other aspect of the Exadata Database Machine. All other technology aspects of Exadata are merely enabling technology in support of Cell Offload Processing. For example, taking too much interest, too early, in Exadata InfiniBand componentry is simply not the best way to build a strong understanding of the technology. Put another way, this is one of the rare cases where it is better to first appreciate the whole cake before scrutinizing the ingredients. When I educate on the topic of Exadata, I start with the topic of Cell Offload Processing. In doing so I quickly impart the following four fundamentals:

Cell Offload Processing: Work performed by the storage servers that would otherwise have to be executed in the database grid. It includes functionality like Smart Scan, data file initialization, RMAN offload, and Hybrid Columnar Compression (HCC) decompression (in the case where In-Memory Parallel Query is not involved).

Smart Scan: The most relevant Cell Offload Processing for improving Data Warehouse / Business Intelligence query performance. Smart Scan is the agent for offloading filtration, projection, Storage Index exploitation, and HCC decompression.

Full Scan or Index Fast Full Scan: The required access method chosen by the query optimizer in order to trigger a Smart Scan.

Direct Path Reads: Required buffering model for a Smart Scan. The flow of data from a Smart Scan cannot be buffered in the SGA buffer pool. Direct path reads can be performed for both serial and parallel queries. Direct path reads are buffered in process PGA (heap).

An Overview of Exadata

A picture's worth a thousand words, or so the saying goes. Figure 1-1 shows a very high-level view of the parts that make up the Exadata Database Machine.

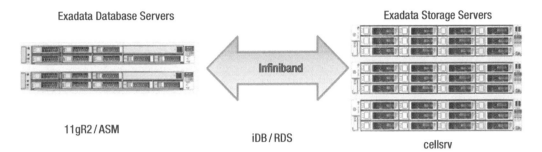

Figure 1-1. *High-level Exadata components*

When considering Exadata, it is helpful to divide the entire system mentally into two parts, the storage layer and the database layer. The layers are connected via an InfiniBand network. InfiniBand provides a low-latency, high-throughput switched fabric communications link. It provides redundancy and bonding of links. The database layer is made up of multiple Sun servers running standard Oracle 11gR2 software. The servers are generally configured in one or more RAC clusters, although RAC is not actually required. The database servers use ASM to map the storage. ASM is required even if the databases are not configured to use RAC. The storage layer also consists of multiple Sun servers. Each storage server contains 12 disk drives and runs the Oracle storage server software (`cellsrv`). Communication between the layers is accomplished via iDB, which is a network based protocol that is implemented using InfiniBand. iDB is used to send requests for data along with metadata about the request (including predicates) to `cellsrv`. In certain situations, `cellsrv` is able to use the metadata to process the data before sending results back to the database layer. When `cellsrv` is able to do this it is called a Smart Scan and generally results in a significant decrease in the volume of data that needs to be transmitted back to the database layer. When Smart Scans are not possible, `cellsrv` returns the entire Oracle block(s). Note that iDB uses the RDS protocol, which is a low-latency protocol that bypasses kernel calls by using remote direct memory access (RDMA) to accomplish process-to-process communication across the InfiniBand network.

History of Exadata

Exadata has undergone a number of significant changes since its initial release in late 2008. In fact, one of the more difficult parts of writing this book has been keeping up with the changes in the platform during the project. Here's a brief review of the product's lineage and how it has changed over time.

■ **Kevin Says:** I'd like to share some historical perspective. Before there was Exadata, there was SAGE—Storage Appliance for Grid Environments, which we might consider V0. In fact, it remained SAGE until just a matter of weeks before Larry Ellison gave it the name Exadata—just in time for the Open World launch of the product in 2008 amid huge co-branded fanfare with Hewlett-Packard. Although the first embodiment of SAGE was a Hewlett-Packard exclusive, Oracle had not yet decided that the platform would be exclusive to Hewlett-Packard, much less the eventual total exclusivity enjoyed by Sun Microsystems—by way of being acquired by Oracle. In fact, Oracle leadership hadn't even established the rigid Linux Operating System requirement for the database hosts; the porting effort of iDB to HP-UX Itanium was in very late stages of development before the Sun acquisition was finalized. But SAGE evolution went back further than that.

V1: The first Exadata was released in late 2008. It was labeled as V1 and was a combination of HP hardware and Oracle software. The architecture was similar to the current X2-2 version, with the exception of the Flash Cache, which was added to the V2 version. Exadata V1 was marketed as exclusively a data warehouse platform. The product was interesting but not widely adopted. It also suffered from issues resulting from overheating. The commonly heard description was that you could fry eggs on top of the cabinet. Many of the original V1 customers replaced their V1s with V2s.

V2: The second version of Exadata was announced at Open World in 2009. This version was a partnership between Sun and Oracle. By the time the announcement was made, Oracle was already in the process of attempting to acquire Sun Microsystems. Many of the components were upgraded to bigger or faster versions, but the biggest difference was the addition of a significant amount of solid-state based storage. The storage cells were enhanced with 384G of Exadata Smart Flash Cache. The software was also enhanced to take advantage of the new cache. This addition allowed Oracle to market the platform as more than a Data Warehouse platform opening up a significantly larger market.

X2: The third edition of Exadata, announced at Oracle Open World in 2010, was named the X2. Actually, there are two distinct versions of the X2. The X2-2 follows the same basic blueprint as the V2, with up to eight dual-CPU database servers. The CPUs were upgraded to hex-core models, where the V2s had used quad-core CPUs. The other X2 model was named the X2-8. It breaks the small 1U database server model by introducing larger database servers with 8×8 core CPUs and a large 1TB memory footprint. The X2-8 is marketed as a more robust platform for large OLTP or mixed workload systems due primarily to the larger number of CPU cores and the larger memory footprint.

Alternative Views of What Exadata Is

We've already given you a rather bland description of how we view Exadata. However, like the well-known tale of the blind men describing an elephant, there are many conflicting perceptions about the nature of Exadata. We'll cover a few of the common descriptions in this section.

Data Warehouse Appliance

Occasionally Exadata is described as a *data warehouse appliance (DW Appliance)*. While Oracle has attempted to keep Exadata from being pigeonholed into this category, the description is closer to the truth than you might initially think. It is, in fact, a tightly integrated stack of hardware and software that Oracle expects you to run without a lot of changes. This is directly in-line with the common understanding of a DW Appliance. However, the very nature of the Oracle database means that it is extremely configurable. This flies in the face of the typical DW Appliance, which typically does not have a lot of knobs to turn. However, there are several common characteristics that are shared between DW Appliances and Exadata.

Exceptional Performance: The most recognizable characteristic of Exadata and DW Appliances in general is that they are optimized for data warehouse type queries.

Fast Deployment: DW Appliances and Exadata Database Machines can both be deployed very rapidly. Since Exadata comes preconfigured, it can generally be up and running within a week from the time you take delivery. This is in stark contrast to the normal Oracle clustered database deployment scenario, which generally takes several weeks.

Scalability: Both platforms have scalable architectures. With Exadata, upgrading is done in discrete steps. Upgrading from a half rack configuration to a full rack increases the total disk throughput in lock step with the computing power available on the database servers.

Reduction in TCO: This one may seem a bit strange, since many people think the biggest drawback to Exadata is the high price tag. But the fact is that both DW Appliances and Exadata reduce the overall cost of ownership in many applications. Oddly enough, in Exadata's case this is partially thanks to a reduction in the number of Oracle database licenses necessary to support a given workload. We have seen several situations where multiple hardware platforms were evaluated for running a company's Oracle application and have ended up costing less to implement and maintain on Exadata than on the other options evaluated.

High Availability: Most DW Appliances provide an architecture that supports at least some degree of *high availability (HA)*. Since Exadata runs standard Oracle 11g software, all the HA capabilities that Oracle has developed are available out of the box. The hardware is also designed to prevent any single point of failure.

Preconfiguration: When Exadata is delivered to your data center, a Sun engineer will be scheduled to assist with the initial configuration. This will include ensuring that the entire rack is cabled and functioning as expected. But like most DW Appliances, the work has already been done to integrate the components. So extensive research and testing are not required.

5

Limited Standard Configurations: Most DW Appliances only come in a very limited set of configurations (small, medium, and large, for example). Exadata is no different. There are currently only four possible configurations. This has repercussions with regards to supportability. It means if you call support and tell them you have an X2-2 Half Rack, the support people will immediately know all they need to know about your hardware. This provides benefits to the support personnel and the customers in terms of how quickly issues can be resolved.

Regardless of the similarities, Oracle does not consider Exadata to be a DW Appliance, even though there are many shared characteristics. Generally speaking, this is because Exadata provides a fully functional Oracle database platform with all the capabilities that have been built into Oracle over the years, including the ability to run any application that currently runs on an Oracle database and in particular to deal with mixed workloads that demand a high degree of concurrency, which DW Appliances are generally not equipped to handle.

■ **Kevin Says:** Whether Exadata is or is not an appliance is a common topic of confusion when people envision what Exadata is. The Oracle Exadata Database Machine is not an appliance. However, the storage grid does consist of Exadata Storage Server cells—which are appliances.

OLTP Machine

This description is a bit of a marketing ploy aimed at broadening Exadata's appeal to a wider market segment. While the description is not totally off-base, it is not as accurate as some other monikers that have been assigned to Exadata. It brings to mind the classic quote:

> *It depends on what the meaning of the word "is" is.*

—Bill Clinton

In the same vein, OLTP (Online Transaction Processing) is a bit of a loosely defined term. We typically use the term to describe workloads that are very latency-sensitive and characterized by single-block access via indexes. But there is a subset of OLTP systems that are also very write-intensive and demand a very high degree of concurrency to support a large number of users. Exadata was not designed to be the fastest possible solution for these write-intensive workloads. However, it's worth noting that very few systems fall neatly into these categories. Most systems have a mixture of long-running, throughput-sensitive SQL statements and short-duration, latency-sensitive SQL statements. Which leads us to the next view of Exadata.

Consolidation Platform

This description pitches Exadata as a potential platform for consolidating multiple databases. This is desirable from a total cost of ownership (TCO) standpoint, as it has the potential to reduce complexity (and therefore costs associated with that complexity), reduce administration costs by decreasing the number of systems that must be maintained, reduce power usage and data center costs through reducing the number of servers, and reduce software and maintenance fees. This is a valid way to view Exadata. Because of the combination of features incorporated in Exadata, it is capable of adequately supporting multiple workload profiles at the same time. Although it is not the perfect OLTP Machine, the Flash Cache feature provides a mechanism for ensuring low latency for OLTP-oriented workloads. The Smart Scan optimizations provide exceptional performance for high-throughput, DW-oriented workloads. Resource Management options built into the platform provide the ability for these somewhat conflicting requirements to be satisfied on the same platform. In fact, one of the biggest upsides to this ability is the possibility of totally eliminating a huge amount of work that is currently performed in many shops to move data from an OLTP system to a DW system so that long-running queries do not negatively affect the latency-sensitive workload. In many shops, simply moving data from one platform to another consumes more resources than any other operation. Exadata's capabilities in this regard may make this process unnecessary in many cases.

Configuration Options

Since Exadata is delivered as a preconfigured, integrated system, there are very few options available. As of this writing there are four versions available. They are grouped into two major categories with different model names (the X2-2 and the X2-8). The storage tiers and networking components for the two models are identical. The database tiers, however, are different.

Exadata Database Machine X2-2

The X2-2 comes in three flavors: quarter rack, half rack, and full rack. The system is built to be upgradeable, so you can upgrade later from a quarter rack to half rack, for example. Here is what you need to know about the different options:

> **Quarter Rack:** The X2-2 Quarter Rack comes with two database servers and three storage servers. The high-capacity version provides roughly 33TB of usable disk space if it is configured for normal redundancy. The high-performance version provides roughly one third of that or about 10TB of usable space, again if configured for normal redundancy.

> **Half Rack:** The X2-2 Half Rack comes with four database servers and seven storage servers. The high-capacity version provides roughly 77TB of usable disk space if it is configured for normal redundancy. The high-performance version provides roughly 23TB of usable space if configured for normal redundancy.

> **Full Rack:** The X2-2 Quarter Rack comes with eight database servers and fourteen storage servers. The high-capacity version provides roughly 154TB of usable disk space if it is configured for normal redundancy. The high performance version provides about 47TB of usable space if configured for normal redundancy.

■ **Note:** Here's how we cam up with the rough useable space estimates. We took the actual size of the disk and subtracted 29GB for OS/DBFS space. Assuming the actual disk sizes are 1,861GB and 571GB for high capacity (HC) and high performance (HP) drives, that leaves 1,833GB for HC and 543GB for HP. Multiply that by the number of disks in the rack (36, 84, or 168). Divide that number by 2 or 3 depending on whether you are using normal or high redundancy to get usable space. Keep in mind that the "usable free mb" that asmcmd reports takes into account the space needed for a rebalance if a failgroup was lost (req_mir_free_MB). Usable file space from asmcmd's lsdg is calculated as follows:

Free_MB / redundancy - (req_mir_free_MB / 2)

Half and full racks are designed to be connected to additional racks, enabling multiple-rack configurations. These configurations have an additional InfiniBand switch called a *spine switch.* It is intended to be used to connect additional racks. There are enough available connections to connect as many as eight racks, although additional cabling may be required depending on the number of racks you intend to connect. The database servers of the multiple racks can be combined into a single RAC database with database servers that span racks, or they may be used to form several smaller RAC clusters. Chapter 15 contains more information about connecting multiple racks.

Exadata Database Machine X2-8

There is currently only one version of the X2-8. It has two database servers and fourteen storage cells. It is effectively an X2-2 Full Rack but with two large database servers instead of the eight smaller database servers used in the X2-2. As previously mentioned, the storage servers and networking components are identical to the X2-2 model. There are no upgrades specific to x2-8 available. If you need more capacity, your option is to add another X2-8, although it is possible to add additional storage cells.

Upgrades

Quarter racks and half racks may be upgraded to add more capacity. The current price list has two options for upgrades, the Half Rack To Full Rack Upgrade and the Quarter Rack to Half Rack Upgrade. The options are limited in an effort to maintain the relative balance between database servers and storage servers. These upgrades are done in the field. If you order an upgrade, the individual components will be shipped to your site on a big pallet and a Sun engineer will be scheduled to install the components into your rack. All the necessary parts should be there, including rack rails and cables. Unfortunately, the labels for the cables seem to come from some other part of the universe. When we did the upgrade on our lab system, the lack of labels held us up for a couple of days.

The quarter-to-half upgrade includes two database servers and four storage servers along with an additional InfiniBand switch, which is configured as a spine switch. The half-to-full upgrade includes four database servers and seven storage servers. There is no additional InfiniBand switch required, because the half rack already includes a spine switch.

There is also the possibility of adding standalone storage servers to an existing rack. Although this goes against the balanced configuration philosophy, Oracle does allow it. Oddly enough, they do not support placing the storage servers in the existing rack, even if there is space (as in the case of a quarter rack or half rack for example).

There are a couple of other things worth noting about upgrades. Many companies purchased Exadata V2 systems and are now in the process of upgrading those systems. Several questions naturally arise with regard to this process. One has to do with whether it is acceptable to mix the newer X2-2 servers with the older V2 components. The answer is yes, it's OK to mix them. In our lab environment, for example, we have a mixture of V2 (our original quarter rack) and X2-2 servers (the upgrade to a half rack). We chose to upgrade our existing system to a half rack rather than purchase another standalone quarter rack with X2-2 components, which was another viable option.

The other question that comes up frequently is whether adding additional standalone storage servers is an option for companies that are running out of space but that have plenty of CPU capacity on the database servers. This question is not as easy to answer. From a licensing standpoint, Oracle will sell you additional storage servers, but remember that one of the goals of Exadata was to create a more balanced architecture. So you should carefully consider whether you need more processing capability at the database tier to handle the additional throughput provided by the additional storage. However, if it's simply lack of space that you are dealing with, additional storage servers are certainly a viable option.

Hardware Components

You've probably seen many pictures like the one in Figure 1-2. It shows an Exadata Database Machine Full Rack. We've added a few graphic elements to show you where the various pieces reside in the cabinet. In this section we'll cover those pieces.

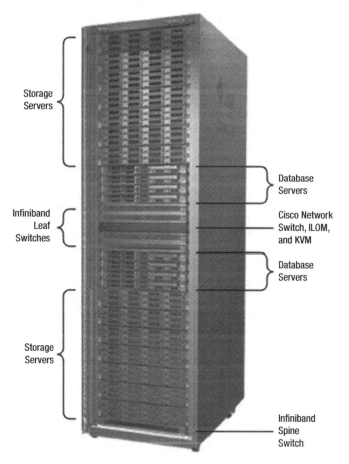

Figure 1-2. *An Exadata Full Rack*

As you can see, most of the networking components, including an Ethernet switch and two redundant InfiniBand switches, are located in the middle of the rack. This makes sense as it makes the cabling a little simpler. There is also a Sun Integrated Lights Out Manager (ILOM) module and KVM in the center section. The surrounding eight slots are reserved for database servers, and the rest of the rack is used for storage servers, with one exception. The very bottom slot is used for an additional InfiniBand "spine" switch that can be used to connect additional racks if so desired. It is located in the bottom of the rack, based on the expectation that your Exadata will be in a data center with a raised floor, allowing cabling to be run from the bottom of the rack.

Operating Systems

The current generation X2 hardware configurations use Intel-based Sun servers. As of this writing all the servers come preinstalled with Oracle Linux 5. Oracle has announced that they intend to support two versions of the Linux kernel—the standard Redhat-compatible version and an enhanced version called the Unbreakable Enterprise Kernel (UEK). This optimized version has several enhancements that are specifically applicable to Exadata. Among these are network-related improvements to InfiniBand using the RDS protocol. One of the reasons for releasing the UEK may be to speed up Oracle's ability to roll out changes to Linux by avoiding the lengthy process necessary to get changes into the standard Open Source releases. Oracle has been a strong partner in the development of Linux and has made several major contributions to the code base. The stated direction is to submit all the enhancements included in the EUK version for inclusion in the standard release.

Oracle has also announced that the X2 database servers will have the option of running Solaris 11 Express. And speaking of Solaris, we are frequently asked about whether Oracle has plans to release a version of Exadata that uses SPARC CPUs. At the time of this writing, there has been no indication that this will be a future direction. It seems more likely that Oracle will continue to pursue the X86-based solution.

Storage servers for both the X2-2 and X2-8 models will continue to run exclusively on Oracle Linux. Oracle views these servers as a closed system and does not support installing any additional software on them.

Database Servers

The current generation X2-2 database servers are based on the Sun Fire X4170 M2 servers. Each server has two × 6 Core Intel Xeon X5670 processors (2.93 GHz) and 96GB of memory. They also have four internal 300GB 10K RPM SAS drives. They have several network connections including two 10Gb and four 1Gb Ethernet ports in addition to the two QDR InfiniBand (40Gb/s) ports. Note that the 10Gb ports are open and that you'll need to provide the correct connectors to attach them to your existing copper or fiber network. The servers also have a dedicated ILOM port and dual hot-swappable power supplies.

The X2-8 database servers are based on the Sun Fire X4800 servers. They are designed to handle systems that require a large amount of memory. The servers are equipped with eight x 8 Core Intel Xeon X7560 processors (2.26 GHz) and 1 TB of memory. This gives the full rack system a total of 128 cores and 2 terabytes of memory.

Storage Servers

The current generation of storage servers are the same for both the X2-2 and the X2-8 models. Each storage server consists of a Sun Fire X4270 M2 and contains 12 disks. Depending on whether you have the high-capacity version or the high-performance version, the disks will either be 2TB or 600GB SAS drives. Each storage server comes with 24GB of memory and two x 6 Core Intel Xeon X5670 processors running at 2.93 GHz. These are the same CPUs as on the X2-2 database servers. Because these CPUs are in the Westmere family, they have built in AES encryption support, which essentially provides a hardware assist to encryption and decryption. Each storage server also contains four 96GB Sun Flash Accelerator F20 PCIe cards. This provides a total of 384GB of flash based storage on each storage cell. The storage servers come pre-installed with Oracle Linux 5.

InfiniBand

One of the more important hardware components of Exadata is the InfiniBand network. It is used for transferring data between the database tier and the storage tier. It is also used for interconnect traffic between the database servers, if they are configured in a RAC cluster. In addition, the InfiniBand network may be used to connect to external systems for such uses as backups. Exadata provides redundant 36-port QDR InfiniBand switches for these purposes. The switches provide 40 Gb/Sec of throughput. You will occasionally see these switches referred to as "leaf" switches. In addition, each database server and each storage server are equipped with Dual-Port QDR InfiniBand Host Channel

Adapters. All but the smallest (quarter rack) Exadata configurations also contain a third InfiniBand switch, intended for chaining multiple Exadata racks together. This switch is generally referred to as a "spine" switch.

Flash Cache

As mentioned earlier, each storage server comes equipped with 384GB of flash-based storage. This storage is generally configured to be a cache. Oracle refers to it as Exadata Smart Flash Cache (ESFC). The primary purpose of ESFC is to minimize the service time for single block reads. This feature provides a substantial amount of disk cache, about 2.5TB on a half rack configuration.

Disks

Oracle provides two options for disks. An Exadata Database Machine may be configured with either high-capacity drives or high-performance drives. As previously mentioned, the high-capacity option includes 2TB, 7200 RPM drives, while the high-performance option includes 600GB, 15000 RPM SAS drives. Oracle does not allow a mixture of the two drive types. With the large amount of flash cache available on the storage cells, it seems that the high-capacity option would be adequate for most read heavy workloads. The flash cache does a very good job of reducing the single-block-read latency in the mixed-workload systems we've observed to date.

Bits and Pieces

The package price includes a 42U rack with redundant power distribution units. Also included in the price is an Ethernet switch. The spec sheets don't specify the model for the Ethernet switch, but as of this writing they are shipping a switch manufactured by Cisco. To date, this is the one piece of the package that Oracle has agreed to allow customers to replace. If you have another switch that you like better, you can remove the included switch and replace it (at your own cost). The X2-2 includes a KVM unit as well. The package price also includes a spares kit that includes an extra flash card, an extra disk drive, and some extra InfiniBand cables (two extra flash cards and two extra disk drives on full racks). The package price does not include SFP+ connectors or cables for the 10GB Ethernet ports. These are not standard and will vary based on the equipment used in your network. The ports are intended for external connections of the database servers to the customer's network.

Software Components

The software components that make up Exadata are split between the database tier and the storage tier. Standard Oracle database software runs on the database servers, while Oracle's relatively new disk management software runs on the storage servers. The components on both tiers use a protocol called iDB to talk to each other. The next two sections provide a brief introduction to the software stack that resides on both tiers.

Database Server Software

As previously discussed, the database servers run Oracle Linux. Of course there is the option to run Solaris Express, but as of this writing we have not seen one running Solaris.

The database servers also run standard Oracle 11g Release 2 software. There is no special version of the database code that is different from the code that is run on any other platform. This is actually a unique and significant feature of Exadata, compared to competing data warehouse appliance products. In essence, it means that any application that can run on Oracle 11gR2 can run on Exadata without requiring any changes to the application. While there is code that is specific to the Exadata platform, iDB for example, Oracle chose to make it a part of the standard distribution. The software is aware of whether it is accessing Exadata storage, and this "awareness" allows it to make use of the Exadata-specific optimizations when accessing Exadata storage.

ASM (Oracle Automatic Storage Management) is a key component of the software stack on the database servers. It provides file system and volume management capability for Exadata storage. It is required because the storage devices are not visible to the database servers. There is no direct mechanism for processes on the database servers to open or read a file on Exadata storage cells. ASM also provides redundancy to the storage by mirroring data blocks, using either normal redundancy (two copies) or high redundancy (three copies). This is an important feature because the disks are physically located on multiple storage servers. The ASM redundancy allows mirroring across the storage cells, which allows for the complete loss of a storage server without an interruption to the databases running on the platform. There is no form of hardware or software based RAID that protects the data on Exadata storage servers. The mirroring protection is provided exclusively by ASM.

While RAC is generally installed on Exadata database servers, it is not actually required. RAC does provide many benefits in terms of high availability and scalability though. For systems that require more CPU or memory resources than can be supplied by a single server, RAC is the path to those additional resources.

The database servers and the storage servers communicate using the Intelligent Database protocol (iDB). iDB implements what Oracle refers to as a *function shipping* architecture. This term is used to describe how iDB ships information about the SQL statement being executed to the storage cells, and then returns processed data (prefiltered, for example), instead of data blocks, directly to the requesting processes. In this mode, iDB can limit the data returned to the database server to only those rows and columns that satisfy the query. The function shipping mode is only available when full scans are performed. iDB can also send and retrieve full blocks when offloading is not possible (or not desirable). In this mode, iDB is used like a normal I/O protocol for fetching entire Oracle blocks and returning them to the Oracle buffer cache on the database servers. For completeness we should mention that it is really not a simple one way or the other scenario. There are cases where we can get a combination of these two behaviors. We'll discuss that in more detail in Chapter 2.

iDB uses the Reliable Datagram Sockets (RDS) protocol and of course uses the InfiniBand fabric between the database servers and storage cells. RDS is a low-latency, low-overhead protocol that provides a significant reduction in CPU usage compared to protocols such as UDP. RDS has been around for some time and predates Exadata by several years. The protocol implements a direct memory access model for interprocess communication, which allows it to avoid the latency and CPU overhead associated with traditional TCP traffic.

■ **Kevin Says:** RDS has indeed been around for quite some time, although not with the Exadata use case in mind. The history of RDS goes back to the partnering between SilverStorm (acquired by Qlogic Corporation) and Oracle to address the requirements for low latency and high bandwidth placed upon the Real Application Clusters node interconnect (via libskgxp) for DLM lock traffic and, to a lesser degree, for Parallel Query data shipping. The latter model was first proven by a 1TB scale TPC-H conducted with Oracle Database 10g on the now defunct PANTASystems platform. Later Oracle aligned itself more closely with Mellanox.

This history lesson touches on an important point. iDB is based on libskgxp, which enjoyed many years of hardening in its role of interconnect library dating back to the first phase of the Cache Fusion feature in Oracle8i. The ability to leverage a tried and true technology like libskgxp came in handy during the move to take SAGE to market.

It is important to understand that no storage devices are directly presented to the operating systems on the database servers. Therefore, there are no operating-system calls to open files, read blocks from them, or the other usual tasks. This also means that standard operating-system utilities like iostat will not be useful in monitoring your database servers, because the processes running there will not be issuing I/O calls to the database files. Here's some output that illustrates this fact:

```
KSO@SANDBOX1> @whoami

USERNAME             SID     SERIAL# PREV_HASH_VALUE SCHEMANAME  OS_PID
---------------- ---------- ---------- ---------------- ---------- -------
KSO                  689        771    2334772408 KSO              23922

KSO@SANDBOX1> select /* avgskew3.sql */ avg(pk_col) from kso.skew3 a where col1 > 0;

...

> strace -cp 23922
Process 23922 attached - interrupt to quit
Process 23922 detached
% time     seconds  usecs/call     calls    errors syscall
------ ----------- ----------- --------- --------- ----------------
 49.75    0.004690           0     10902      5451 setsockopt
 29.27    0.002759           0      6365           poll
 11.30    0.001065           0      5487           sendmsg
  9.60    0.000905           0     15328      4297 recvmsg
  0.08    0.000008           1        16           fcntl
  0.00    0.000000           0        59           read
  0.00    0.000000           0         3           write
  0.00    0.000000           0        32        12 open
  0.00    0.000000           0        20           close
```

```
  0.00    0.000000            0        4           stat
  0.00    0.000000            0        4           fstat
  0.00    0.000000            0       52           lseek
  0.00    0.000000            0       33           mmap
  0.00    0.000000            0        7           munmap
  0.00    0.000000            0        1           semctl
  0.00    0.000000            0       65           getrusage
  0.00    0.000000            0       32           times
  0.00    0.000000            0        1           semtimedop
------  -----------  -----------  ---------  ---------  ----------------
100.00    0.009427                38411     9760  total
```

In this listing we have run `strace` on a user's foreground process (sometimes called a shadow process). This is the process that's responsible for retrieving data on behalf of a user. As you can see, the vast majority of system calls captured by `strace` are network-related (`setsockopt`, `poll`, `sendmsg`, and `recvmsg`). By contrast, on a non-Exadata platform we mostly see disk I/O-related events, primarily some form of the read call. Here's some output from a non-Exadata platform for comparison:

```
KSO@LAB112> @whoami

USERNAME              SID   SERIAL#  PREV_HASH_VALUE  SCHEMANAME   OS_PID
--------------  ----------  --------  ---------------  ----------  -------
KSO                   249     32347       4128301241  KSO            22493

KSO@LAB112> @avgskew

AVG(PK_COL)
-----------
 16093749.8

...

[root@homer ~]# strace -cp 22493
Process 22493 attached - interrupt to quit
Process 22493 detached
% time     seconds  usecs/call     calls    errors  syscall
------  -----------  -----------  ---------  ---------  ----------------
 88.86    4.909365        3860       1272            pread64
 10.84    0.599031          65       9171            gettimeofday
  0.16    0.008766          64        136            getrusage
  0.04    0.002064          56         37            times
  0.02    0.001378         459          3            write
  0.02    0.001194         597          2            statfs
  0.02    0.001150         575          2            fstatfs
  0.02    0.001051         350          3            read
  0.01    0.000385          96          4            mmap2
  0.00    0.000210         105          2            io_destroy
  0.00    0.000154          77          2            io_setup
  0.00    0.000080          40          2            open
  0.00    0.000021          11          2            fcntl64
------  -----------  -----------  ---------  ---------  ----------------
100.00    5.524849                  10638            total
```

15

Notice that the main system call captured on the non-Exadata platform is I/O-related (pread64). The point of the previous two listings is to show that there is a very different mechanism in play in the way data stored on disks is accessed with Exadata.

Storage Server Software

Cell Services (cellsrv) is the primary software that runs on the storage cells. It is a multi-threaded program that services I/O requests from a database server. Those requests can be handled by returning processed data or by returning complete blocks depending in the request. cellsrv also implements the Resource Manager defined I/O distribution rules, ensuring that I/O is distributed to the various databases and consumer groups appropriately.

There are two other programs that run continuously on Exadata storage cells. Management Server (MS) is a Java program that provides the interface between cellsrv and the Cell Command Line Interface (cellcli) utility. MS also provides the interface between cellsrv and the Grid Control Exadata plug-in (which is implemented as a set of cellcli commands that are run via rsh). The second utility is Restart Server (RS). RS is actually a set of processes that is responsible for monitoring the other processes and restarting them if necessary. OSWatcher is also installed on the storage cells for collecting historical operating system statistics using standard Unix utilities such as vmstat and netstat. Note that Oracle does not authorize the installation of any additional software on the storage servers.

One of the first things you are likely to want to do when you first encounter Exadata is to log on to the storage cells and see what's actually running. Unfortunately, the storage servers are generally off-limits to everyone except the designated system administers or DBAs. Here's a quick listing showing the output generated by a ps command on an active storage server:

```
> ps -eo ruser,pid,ppid,cmd

RUSER     PID  PPID CMD
root    12447     1 /opt/oracle/.../cellsrv/bin/cellrssrm -ms 1 -cellsrv 1
root    12453 12447 /opt/oracle/.../cellsrv/bin/cellrsbmt -ms 1 -cellsrv 1
root    12454 12447 /opt/oracle/.../cellsrv/bin/cellrsmmt -ms 1 -cellsrv 1
root    12455 12447 /opt/oracle/.../cellsrv/bin/cellrsomt -ms 1 -cellsrv 1
root    12456 12453 /opt/oracle/.../bin/cellrsbkm
                    -rs_conf /opt/oracle/.../cellsrv/deploy/config/cellinit.ora
                    -ms_conf /opt/oracle/cell
root    12457 12454 /usr/java/jdk1.5.0_15//bin/java -Xms256m -Xmx512m
                    -Djava.library.path=/opt/oracle/.../cellsrv/lib
                    -Ddisable.checkForUpdate=true -jar /opt/oracle/cell11.2
root    12460 12456 /opt/oracle/.../cellsrv/bin/cellrssmt
                    -rs_conf /opt/oracle/.../cellsrv/deploy/config/cellinit.ora
                    -ms_conf /opt/oracle/cell
root    12461 12455 /opt/oracle/.../cellsrv/bin/cellsrv 100 5000 9 5042
root    12772 22479 /usr/bin/mpstat 5 720
root    12773 22479 bzip2 --stdout
root    17553     1 /bin/ksh ./OSWatcher.sh 15 168 bzip2
root    20135 22478 /usr/bin/top -b -c -d 5 -n 720
root    20136 22478 bzip2 --stdout
root    22445 17553 /bin/ksh ./OSWatcherFM.sh 168
root    22463 17553 /bin/ksh ./oswsub.sh HighFreq ./Exadata_vmstat.sh
root    22464 17553 /bin/ksh ./oswsub.sh HighFreq ./Exadata_mpstat.sh
root    22465 17553 /bin/ksh ./oswsub.sh HighFreq ./Exadata_netstat.sh
root    22466 17553 /bin/ksh ./oswsub.sh HighFreq ./Exadata_iostat.sh
```

```
root      22467 17553 /bin/ksh ./oswsub.sh HighFreq ./Exadata_top.sh
root      22471 17553 /bin/bash /opt/oracle.cellos/ExadataDiagCollector.sh
root      22472 17553 /bin/ksh ./oswsub.sh HighFreq
                            /opt/oracle.oswatcher/osw/ExadataRdsInfo.sh
root      22476 22463 /bin/bash ./Exadata_vmstat.sh HighFreq
root      22477 22466 /bin/bash ./Exadata_iostat.sh HighFreq
root      22478 22467 /bin/bash ./Exadata_top.sh HighFreq
root      22479 22464 /bin/bash ./Exadata_mpstat.sh HighFreq
root      22480 22465 /bin/bash ./Exadata_netstat.sh HighFreq
root      22496 22472 /bin/bash /opt/oracle.oswatcher/osw/ExadataRdsInfo.sh HighFreq
```

So as you can see, there are a number of processes that look like cellrsv*XXX*. These are the processes that make up the Restart Server. Also notice the first bolded process; this is the Java program that we refer to as Management Server. The second bolded process is cellsrv itself. Finally, you'll see several processes associated with OSWatcher. Note also that all the processes are started by root. While there are a couple of other semi-privileged accounts on the storage servers, it is clearly not a system that is setup for users to log on to.

Another interesting way to look at related processes is to use the ps –H command, which provides an indented list of processes showing how they are related to each other. You could work this out for yourself by building a tree based on the relationship between the process ID (PID) and parent process ID (PPID) in the previous listing, but the –H option makes that a lot easier. Here's an edited snippet of output from a ps –H command:

```
cellrssrm <= main Restart Server
    cellrsbmt
        cellrsbkm
            cellrssmt
    cellrsmmt
        java - .../oc4j/ms/j2ee/home/oc4j.jar <= Management Server
            cellrsomt
                cellsrv
```

It's also interesting to see what resources are being consumed on the storage servers. Here's a snippet of output from top:

```
top - 18:20:27 up 2 days,  2:09,  1 user,  load average: 0.07, 0.15, 0.16
Tasks: 298 total,   1 running, 297 sleeping,   0 stopped,   0 zombie
Cpu(s):  6.1%us,  0.6%sy,  0.0%ni, 93.30%id,  0.3%wa,  0.0%hi,  0.0%si,  0.0%st
Mem:  24531712k total, 14250280k used, 10281432k free,   188720k buffers
Swap:  2096376k total,        0k used,  2096376k free,   497792k cached

  PID USER      PR  NI  VIRT  RES  SHR S %CPU %MEM    TIME+  COMMAND
12461 root      18   0 17.0g 4.5g  11m S 105.9 19.2 55:20.45 cellsrv
    1 root      18   0 10348  748  620 S  0.0  0.0  0:02.79 init
    2 root      RT  -5     0    0    0 S  0.0  0.0  0:00.14 migration/0
    3 root      34  19     0    0    0 S  0.0  0.0  0:01.45 ksoftirqd/0
    4 root      RT  -5     0    0    0 S  0.0  0.0  0:00.00 watchdog/0
```

The output from top shows that cellsrv is using more than one full CPU core. This is common on busy systems and is due to the multi-threaded nature of the cellsrv process.

Software Architecture

In this section we'll briefly discuss the key software components and how they are connected in the Exadata architecture. There are components that run on both the database and the storage tiers. Figure 1-3 depicts the overall architecture of the Exadata platform.

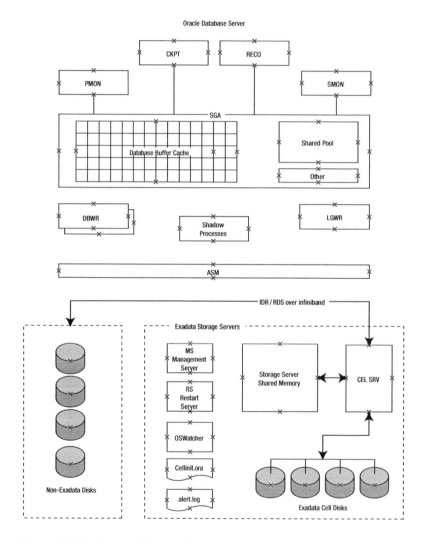

Figure 1-3. *Exadata architecture diagram*

The top half of the diagram shows the key components on one of the database servers, while the bottom half shows the key components on one of the storage servers. The top half of the diagram should look pretty familiar, as it is standard Oracle 11g architecture. It shows the System Global Area (SGA), which contains the buffer cache and the shared pool. It also shows several of the key processes, such as Log Writer (LGWR) and Database Writer (DBWR). There are many more processes, of course, and much more detailed views of the shared memory that could be provided, but this should give you a basic picture of how things look on the database server.

The bottom half of the diagram shows the components on one of the storage servers. The architecture on the storage servers is pretty simple. There is really only one process (cellsrv) that handles all the communication to and from the database servers. There are also a handful of ancillary processes for managing and monitoring the environment.

One of the things you may notice in the architecture diagram is that cellsrv uses an init.ora file and has an alert log. In fact, the storage software bears a striking resemblance to an Oracle database. This shouldn't be too surprising. The cellinit.ora file contains a set of parameters that are evaluated when cellsrv is started. The alert log is used to write a record of notable events, much like an alert log on an Oracle database. Note also that Automatic Diagnostic Repository (ADR) is included as part of the storage software for capturing and reporting diagnostic information.

Also notice that there is a standalone process that is not attached to any database instance (DISKMON), which performs several tasks related to Exadata Storage. Although it is called DISKMON, it is really a network- and cell-monitoring process that checks to verify that the cells are alive. DISKMON is also responsible to propagating Database Resource Manager (DBRM) plans to the storage servers. DISKMON also has a single slave process per instance, which is responsible for communicating between ASM and the database it is responsible for.

The connection between the database server and the storage server is provided by the InfiniBand fabric. All communication between the two tiers is carried by this transport mechanism. This includes writes via the DBWR processes and LGWR process and reads carried out by the user foreground (or shadow) processes.

Figure 1-4 provides another view of the architecture, which focuses on the software stack and how it spans multiple servers in both the database grid and the storage grid.

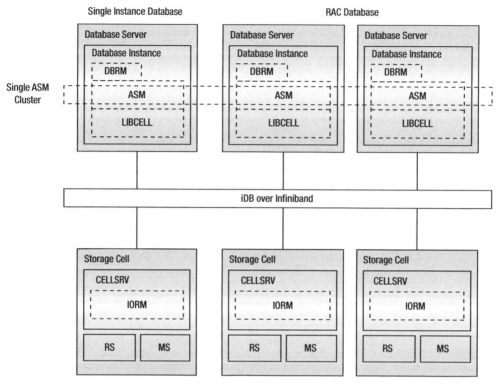

Figure 1-4. *Exadata software architecture*

Restart Server

As we've discussed, ASM is a key component. Notice that we have drawn it as an object that cuts across all the communication lines between the two tiers. This is meant to indicate that ASM provides the mapping between the files and the objects that the database knows about on the storage layer. ASM does not actually sit between the storage and the database, though, and it is not a layer in the stack that the processes must touch for each "disk access."

Figure 1-4 also shows the relationship between Database Resource Manager (DBRM) running on the instances on the database servers and I/O Resource Manager (IORM), which is implemented inside `cellsrv` running on the storage servers.

The final major component in Figure 1-4 is `LIBCELL`, which is a library that is linked with the Oracle kernel. `LIBCELL` has the code that knows how to request data via iDB. This provides a very nonintrusive mechanism to allow the Oracle kernel to talk to the storage tier via network-based calls instead of operating system reads and writes. iDB is implemented on top of the Reliable Datagram Sockets (RDS) protocol provided by the OpenFabrics Enterprise Distribution. This is a low-latency, low-CPU-overhead protocol that provides interprocess communications. You may also see this protocol referred to in some of the Oracle marketing material as the Zero-loss Zero-copy (ZDP) InfiniBand protocol. Figure 1-5 is a basic schematic showing why the RDS protocol is more efficient than using a traditional TCP based protocol like UDP.

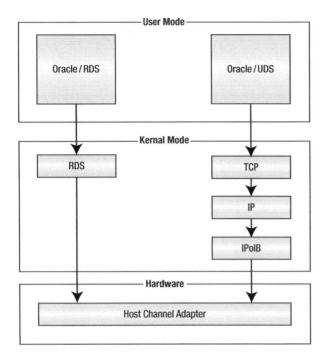

Figure 1-5. RDS schematic

As you can see from the diagram, using the RDS protocol to bypass the TCP processing cuts out a portion of the overhead required to transfer data across the network. Note that the RDS protocol is also used for interconnect traffic between RAC nodes.

Summary

Exadata is a tightly integrated combination of hardware and software. There is nothing magical about the hardware components themselves. The majority of the performance benefits come from the way the components are integrated and the software that is implemented at the storage layer. In the next chapter we'll dive into the offloading concept, which is what sets Exadata apart from all other platforms that run Oracle databases.

CHAPTER 2

Offloading / Smart Scan

Offloading is the secret sauce of Exadata. It's what makes Exadata different from every other platform that Oracle runs on. Offloading refers to the concept of moving processing from the database servers to the storage layer. It is also the key paradigm shift provided by the Exadata platform. But it's more than just moving work in terms of CPU usage. The primary benefit of Offloading is the reduction in the volume of data that must be returned to the database server. This is one of the major bottlenecks of most large databases.

The terms Offloading and Smart Scan are used somewhat interchangeably. Offloading is a better description in our opinion, as it refers to the fact that part of the traditional SQL processing done by the database can be "offloaded" from the database layer to the storage layer. It is a rather generic term, though, and is used to refer to many optimizations that are not even related to SQL processing including improving backup and restore operations.

Smart Scan, on the other hand, is a more focused term, in that it refers only to Exadata's optimization of SQL statements. These optimizations come into play for scan operations (typically Full Table Scans). A more specific definition of a Smart Scan would be any section of the Oracle kernel code that is covered by the Smart Scan wait events. There are actually two wait events that include the term "Smart Scan" in their names, Cell Smart Table Scan and Cell Smart Index Scan. We'll discuss both of these wait events in detail a bit later, in Chapter 10. While it's true that "Smart Scan" has a bit of a marketing flavor, it does have specific context when referring to the code covered by these wait events. At any rate, while the terms are somewhat interchangeable, keep in mind that Offloading can refer to more than just speeding up SQL statement execution.

In this chapter we will focus on Smart Scan optimizations. We'll cover the various optimizations that can come into play with Smart Scans, the mechanics of how they work, and the requirements that must be met for Smart Scans to occur. We'll also cover some techniques that can be used to help you determine whether Smart Scans have occurred for a given SQL statement. The other offloading optimizations will only be mentioned briefly as they are covered elsewhere in the book.

Why Offloading Is Important

We can't emphasize enough how important this concept is. The idea of moving database processing to the storage tier is a giant leap forward. The concept has been around for some time. In fact, rumor has it that Oracle approached at least one of the large SAN manufacturers several years ago with the idea. The manufacturer was apparently not interested at the time and Oracle decided to pursue the idea on its own. Oracle subsequently partnered with HP to build the original Exadata V1, which incorporated the Offloading concept. Fast-forward a couple of years, and you have Oracle's acquisition of Sun Microsystems. This put the company in a position to offer an integrated stack of hardware and software and gives it complete control over which features to incorporate into the product.

Offloading is important because one of the major bottlenecks on large databases is the time it takes to transfer the large volumes of data necessary to satisfy DW-type queries between the disk systems and the database servers (that is, because of bandwidth). This is partly a hardware architecture issue, but the bigger issue is the sheer volume of data that is moved by traditional Oracle databases. The Oracle database is very fast and very clever about how it processes data, but for queries that access a large amount of data, getting the data to the database can still take a long time. So as any good performance analyst would do, Oracle focused on reducing the time spent on the thing that accounted for the majority of the elapsed time. During the analysis, the team realized that every query that required disk access was very inefficient in terms of how much data had to be returned to and processed by the database servers. Oracle has made a living by developing the best cache-management software available, but for really large data sets, it is just not practical to keep everything in memory on the database servers.

▧ **Kevin Says:** The authors make a good point based on a *historical* perspective of Oracle query processing. However, I routinely find myself reminding people that modern commodity x64 servers are no longer architecturally constrained to small memory configurations. For example, servers based on Intel Xeon 7500 processors with Quick Path Interconnect support large numbers of memory channels each with large number of DIMM slots. Commodity-based servers with multiple terabytes of main memory are quite common. In fact, the X2-8 Exadata model supports two terabytes of main memory in the database grid, and that capacity will increase naturally over time. I expect this book to remain relevant long enough for future readers to look back on this comment as arcane, since the trend toward extremely large main memory x64 systems has only just begun. The important thing to remember about Exadata is that it is everything Oracle database offers plus Exadata Storage Servers. This point is relevant because customers can choose to combine deep compression (for example, Exadata Hybrid Columnar Compression) with the In-Memory Parallel Query feature for those cases where ruling out magnetic media entirely is the right solution for meeting service levels.

Imagine the fastest query you can think of: a single column from a single row from a single table where you actually know where the row is stored (rowid). On a traditional Oracle database, at least one block of data has to be read into memory (typically 8K) to get the one column. Let's assume your table stores an average of 50 rows per block. You've just transferred 49 extra rows to the database server that are simply overhead for this query. Multiply that by a billion and you start to get an idea of the magnitude of the problem in a large data warehouse. Eliminating the time spent on transferring completely unnecessary data between the storage and the database tier is the main problem that Exadata was designed to solve.

Offloading is the approach that was used to solve the problem of excessive time spent moving irrelevant data between the tiers. Offloading has three design goals, although the primary goal far outweighs the others in importance:

- Reduce the volume of data transferred from disk systems to the database servers.

- Reduce CPU usage on database servers.

- Reduce disk access times at the storage layer.

Reducing the volume was the main focus and primary goal. The majority of the optimizations introduced by Offloading contribute to this goal. Reducing CPU load is important as well, but is not the primary benefit provided by Exadata and therefore takes a back seat to reducing the volume of data transferred. (As you'll see, however, decompression is a notable exception to that generalization, as it is performed on the storage servers.) Several optimizations to reduce disk access time were also introduced, and while some of the results can be quite stunning, we don't consider them to be the bread-and-butter optimizations of Exadata.

Exadata is an integrated hardware/software product that depends on both components to provide substantial performance improvement over non-Exadata platforms. However, the performance benefits of the software component dwarf the benefits provided by the hardware. Here is an example:

```
SYS@SANDBOX> alter session set cell_offload_processing=false;

Session altered.

Elapsed: 00:00:00.06
SYS@SANDBOX> select count(*) from kso.skew3 where col1 < 0;

  COUNT(*)
----------
         2

1 row selected.

Elapsed: 00:00:51.09
SYS@SANDBOX> alter session set cell_offload_processing=true;

Session altered.

Elapsed: 00:00:00.07
SYS@SANDBOX> select count(*) from kso.skew3 where col1 < 0;

  COUNT(*)
----------
         2

1 row selected.

Elapsed: 00:00:00.15
```

This example shows the performance of a scan against a single table with 384 million rows. We ran it once with Offloading disabled, effectively using all the hardware benefits of Exadata and none of the software benefits. You'll notice that even on Exadata hardware, this query took almost a minute. Keep in mind that this was only spread across three storage servers on our V2 quarter rack and did not utilize the flash cache at all. We then re-enabled Offloading, and the query completed in substantially less than a second. Obviously the hardware in play was the same in both executions. The point is that it's the software's ability via Offloading that made the difference.

A GENERIC VERSION OF EXADATA?

The topic of building a generic version of Exadata comes up frequently. The idea is to build a hardware platform that in some way mimics Exadata, presumably at a lower cost than what Oracle charges for Exadata. Of course, the focus of these proposals is to replicate the hardware part of Exadata, because the software component cannot be replicated. (This realization alone should make you stop and question whether this approach is even feasible.) Nevertheless, the idea of building your own Exadata sounds attractive because the individual hardware components can be purchased for less than the package price Oracle charges. There are a few flaws with this thinking, however:

1. The hardware component that tends to get the most attention is the flash cache. You can buy a SAN or NAS with a large cache. The middle-size Exadata package (1/2 rack) supplies around 2.5 Terabytes of flash cache across the storage servers. That's a pretty big number, but what's cached is as important as the size of the cache itself. Exadata is smart enough not to cache data that is unlikely to benefit from caching. For example, it is not helpful to cache mirror copies of blocks, since Oracle only reads primary copies (unless a corruption is detected). Oracle has a long history of writing software to manage caches. So it should come as no surprise that it does a very good job of not flushing everything out when a large table scan is processed so that frequently accessed blocks would tend to remain in the cache. The result of this database-aware caching is that a normal SAN or NAS would need a much larger cache to compete with Exadata's flash cache. Keep in mind also that the volume of data you will need to store will be much larger on non-Exadata storage because you won't be able to use Hybrid Columnar Compression.

2. The more important aspect of the hardware, which oddly enough is occasionally overlooked by the DIY proposals, is the throughput between the storage and database tiers. The Exadata hardware stack provides a more balanced pathway between storage and database servers than most current implementations. So the second area of focus is generally the bandwidth between the tiers. Increasing the effective throughput between the tiers is not as simple as it sounds, though. Exadata provides the increased throughput via InfiniBand and the Reliable Datagram Sockets (RDS) protocol. Oracle developed the iDB protocol to run across the Infiniband network. The iDB protocol is not available to databases running on non-Exadata hardware. Therefore, some other means for increasing bandwidth between the tiers is necessary. So you can use IPOB on a 10Ge network and use iSCSI or NFS, or you can use high-speed fiber-based connections. In any case you will need multiple interface cards in the servers (which will need to be attached via a fast bus). The storage device (or devices) will also have to be capable of delivering enough output to match the pipe and consumption capabilities (this is what Oracle means when they talk about a balanced configuration). You'll also have to decide which hardware components to use and test the whole thing to make sure that all the various parts you pick work well together without having a major bottleneck at any point in the path from disk to database server.

3. The third component that the DIY proposals generally address is the database servers themselves. The Exadata hardware specifications are readily available, so it is a simple matter to buy exactly the same Sun models. Unfortunately, you'll need to plan for more CPU's since you won't be able to offload any processing to the CPUs on the Exadata storage servers. This in turn will drive up the number of Oracle database licenses.

4. Assuming we could match the Exadata hardware performance in every area, we would still not expect to be able come close to the performance provided by Exadata. That's because it is the software that provides the lion's share of the performance benefit of Exadata. This is easily demonstrated by disabling Offloading on Exadata and running comparisons. This allows us to see the performance of the hardware without the software enhancements. A big part of what Exadata software does is eliminate totally unnecessary work, such as transferring columns and rows that will eventually be discarded, back to the database servers.

As our friend Cary Millsap likes to say, "The fastest way to do anything is to not do it!"

What Offloading Includes

There are many optimizations that can be lumped under the Offloading banner. This chapter focuses on SQL statement optimizations that are implemented via Smart Scans. The big three Smart Scan optimizations are Column Projection, Predicate Filtering, and Storage Indexes. The primary goal of most of the Smart Scan optimizations is to reduce the amount of data that needs to be transmitted back to the database servers during scan execution. However, some of the optimizations also attempt to offload CPU-intensive operations, decompression for example. We won't have much to say about optimizations that are not related to SQL statement processing in this chapter, such as Smart File Creation and RMAN-related optimizations. Those topics will be covered in more detail elsewhere in the book.

▪ **Kevin Says:** This aspect of Offload Processing seems quite complicated. The authors are correct in stating that the primary benefit of Smart Scan is payload reduction between storage and the database grid. And it's true that some CPU-offload benefit is enjoyed by decompressing Exadata Hybrid Columnar Compression units in the storage cells. However, therein lies one case where Offload Processing actually aims to *increase* the payload between the cells and the database grid. The trade-off is important, however. It makes sense to decompress EHCC data in the cells (after filtration) in spite of the fact that more data is sent to the database grid due to the decompression. All technology solutions have trade-offs.

Column Projection

The term *Column Projection* refers to Exadata's ability to limit the volume of data transferred between the storage tier and the database tier by only returning columns of interest (that is, those in the select list or necessary for join operations on the database tier). If your query requests five columns from a 100-column table, Exadata can eliminate most of the data that would be returned to the database servers by non-Exadata storage. This feature is a much bigger deal than you might expect and it can have a very significant impact on response times. Here is an example:

```
SYS@SANDBOX1> alter system flush shared_pool;

System altered.

Elapsed: 00:00:00.12
SYS@SANDBOX1> alter system flush buffer_cache;

System altered.

Elapsed: 00:00:00.13
SYS@SANDBOX1> alter session set "_serial_direct_read"=true;

Session altered.

Elapsed: 00:00:00.00
SYS@SANDBOX1> alter session set cell_offload_processing=false;

Session altered.

Elapsed: 00:00:00.01
SYS@SANDBOX1> select count(col1) from kso.skew3;

COUNT(COL1)
-----------
  384000044

1 row selected.

Elapsed: 00:00:51.32
SYS@SANDBOX1> alter session set cell_offload_processing=true;

Session altered.

Elapsed: 00:00:00.00
SYS@SANDBOX1> select count(col1) from kso.skew3;

COUNT(COL1)
-----------
  384000044

1 row selected.

Elapsed: 00:00:26.27
```

This example deserves a little discussion. First we used a trick to force direct path reads with the _SERIAL_DIRECT_READ parameter (more on that later). Next we disabled Smart Scans by setting CELL_OFFLOAD_PROCESSING to FALSE. You can see that our test query doesn't have a WHERE clause. This means that Predicate Filtering and Storage Indexes cannot be used to cut down the volume of data that must be transferred from the storage tier, because those two optimizations can only be done when there is a WHERE clause (we'll discuss those optimizations shortly). That leaves Column Projection as the only optimization in play. Are you surprised that Column Projection alone could cut a query's response time in half? We were, the first time we saw it, but it makes sense if you think about it. You should be aware that columns in the select list are not the only columns that must be returned to the database server. This is a very common misconception. Join columns in the WHERE clause must also be returned. As a matter of fact, in early versions of Exadata, the Column Projection feature was not as effective as it could have been and actually returned all the columns included in the WHERE clause, which in many cases included some unnecessary columns.

The DBMS_XPLAN package can display information about column projection, although by default it does not. The projection data is stored in the PROJECTION column in the V$SQL_PLAN view as well. Here is an example:

```
SYS@SANDBOX> select count(s.col1),avg(length(s.col4))
  2  from kso.skew s, kso.skew2 s2
  3  where s.pk_col = s2.pk_col
  4  and s.col1 > 0
  5  and s.col2='asddsadasd';

COUNT(S.COL1) AVG(LENGTH(S.COL4))
------------- -------------------
    127999992                   1

1 row selected.

SYS@SANDBOX> select sql_id, child_number, sql_text
  2  from v$sql where sql_text like '%skew%';

SQL_ID        CHILD SQL_TEXT
------------- ------ -------------------------------------------------------------
8xa3wjh48b9ar     0 select count(s.col1),avg(length(s.col4)) from kso.skew s, kso.

1 row selected.

SYS@SANDBOX> select * from
  2  table(dbms_xplan.display_cursor('&sql_id','&child_no','+projection'));
Enter value for sql_id: 8xa3wjh48b9ar
Enter value for child_no:

PLAN_TABLE_OUTPUT
--------------------------------------------------------------------------------
SQL_ID  8xa3wjh48b9ar, child number 0
-------------------------------------
select count(s.col1),avg(length(s.col4)) from kso.skew s, kso.skew2 s2
where s.pk_col = s2.pk_col and s.col1 > 0 and s.col2='asddsadasd'

Plan hash value: 3361152066
```

```
-----------------------------------------------------------------------------------
| Id  | Operation                  | Name  | Rows  | Bytes  |TempSpc| Cost (%CPU)| Time      |
-----------------------------------------------------------------------------------
|   0 | SELECT STATEMENT           |       |       |        |       | 360K(100)|           |
|   1 |  SORT AGGREGATE            |       |     1 |     30 |       |          |           |
|*  2 |   HASH JOIN                |       |   64M |  1836M |  549M |  360K  (1)| 01:12:02 |
|*  3 |    TABLE ACCESS STORAGE FULL| SKEW |   16M |   366M |       | 44585  (2)| 00:08:56 |
|   4 |    TABLE ACCESS STORAGE FULL| SKEW2|  128M |   732M |       |  178K  (1)| 00:35:37 |
-----------------------------------------------------------------------------------
```

Predicate Information (identified by operation id):

```
   2 - access("S"."PK_COL"="S2"."PK_COL")
   3 - storage(("S"."COL2"='asddsadasd' AND "S"."COL1">0))
       filter(("S"."COL2"='asddsadasd' AND "S"."COL1">0))
```

Column Projection Information (identified by operation id):

```
   1 - (#keys=0) COUNT(LENGTH("S"."COL4"))[22], COUNT("S"."COL1")[22],
       SUM(LENGTH("S"."COL4"))[22]
   2 - (#keys=1) "S"."COL4"[VARCHAR2,1], "S"."COL1"[NUMBER,22]
   3 - "S"."PK_COL"[NUMBER,22], "S"."COL1"[NUMBER,22], "S"."COL4"[VARCHAR2,1]
   4 - "S2"."PK_COL"[NUMBER,22]
```

33 rows selected.

```
SYS@SANDBOX> select projection from v$sql_plan
  2   where projection is not null
  3   and sql_id = '8xa3wjh48b9ar';
```

PROJECTION

(#keys=0) COUNT(LENGTH("S"."COL4"))[22], COUNT("S"."COL1")[22], SUM(LENGTH("S"."COL4"))[22]
(#keys=1) "S"."COL4"[VARCHAR2,1], "S"."COL1"[NUMBER,22]
"S"."PK_COL"[NUMBER,22], "S"."COL1"[NUMBER,22], "S"."COL4"[VARCHAR2,1]
"S2"."PK_COL"[NUMBER,22]

4 rows selected.

So as you can see, the plan output shows the projection information, but only if you use the +PROJECTION argument in the call to the DBMS_XPLAN package. Note also that the PK_COL columns from both tables were listed in the PROJECTION section, but that not all columns in the WHERE clause are included. Only those columns that need to be returned to the database (join columns) should be listed. Note also that the projection information is not unique to Exadata but is a generic part of the database code.

The V$SQL family of views contain columns that define the volume of data that may be saved by Offloading (IO_CELL_OFFLOAD_ELIGIBLE_BYTES) and the volume of data that was actually returned by the storage servers (IO_INTERCONNECT_BYTES). Note that these columns are cumulative for all the executions of the statement. We'll be using these two columns throughout the book because they are key indicators of offload processing. Here's a quick demonstration to show that projection does affect the amount of data returned to the database servers and that selecting fewer columns results in less data transferred:

```
SYS@SANDBOX> select /* single col */ avg(pk_col)
  2  from kso.skew3;

AVG(PK_COL)
-----------
 16093750.3

1 row selected.

Elapsed: 00:00:32.13

SYS@SANDBOX> select /* multi col */ avg(pk_col),sum(col1)
  2  from kso.skew3;

AVG(PK_COL)  SUM(COL1)
----------- ----------
 16093750.3 1.9003E+14

1 row selected.

Elapsed: 00:00:45.32
SYS@SANDBOX> set timing off
SYS@SANDBOX> select sql_id,sql_text from v$sql
  2  where sql_text like '%col */ avg(pk_col)%';

SQL_ID        SQL_TEXT
------------- ----------------------------------------------------------------
bb3z4aaa9du7j select /* single col */ avg(pk_col) from kso.skew3
555pskb8aaqct select /* multi col */ avg(pk_col),sum(col1) from kso.skew3

2 rows selected.

SYS@SANDBOX> select sql_id, IO_CELL_OFFLOAD_ELIGIBLE_BYTES eligible,
  2  IO_INTERCONNECT_BYTES actual,
  3  100*(IO_CELL_OFFLOAD_ELIGIBLE_BYTES-IO_INTERCONNECT_BYTES)
  4  /IO_CELL_OFFLOAD_ELIGIBLE_BYTES "IO_SAVED_%", sql_text
  5  from v$sql where sql_id in ('bb3z4aaa9du7j','555pskb8aaqct');

SQL_ID        ELIGIBLE   ACTUAL IO_SAVED_% SQL_TEXT
------------- ---------- ---------- ---------- ------------------------------------
bb3z4aaa9du7j 1.6025E+10 4511552296      71.85 select /* single col */ avg(pk_col)
555pskb8aaqct 1.6025E+10 6421233960      59.93 select /* multi col */ avg(pk_col),s

2 rows selected.

SYS@SANDBOX> @fsx4
Enter value for sql_text: %col */ avg(pk_col)%
Enter value for sql_id:
```

```
SQL_ID          CHILD OFFLOAD IO_SAVED_%    AVG_ETIME SQL_TEXT
------------- ------ ------- ---------- ------------- --------------------
6u7v77c2f8x5r      0 Yes         59.93         45.15 select /* multi col
d43dr7hvmw3yb      0 Yes         71.85         31.94 select /* single col
```

2 rows selected.

Note that the extra column resulted in a great deal of extra time required to complete the query and that the columns in V$SQL verified the increased volume of data that had to be transferred. We've also shown the output of a modified version of the **fsx.sql** script, which we'll discuss in more detail later in this chapter. For now, please just accept that it shows us whether a statement was offloaded or not.

Predicate Filtering

The second of the big three Smart Scan optimizations is *Predicate Filtering*. This term refers to Exadata's ability to return only rows of interest to the database tier. Since iDB includes the predicate information in its requests, this is accomplished by performing the standard filtering operations at the storage cells before returning the data. On databases using non-Exadata storage, filtering is done on the database servers. This generally means that a large number of records that will eventually be discarded will be returned to the database tier. Filtering these rows at the storage layer can provide a very significant decrease in the volume of data that must be transferred to the database tier. While this optimization also results in some savings in CPU usage on the database servers, the biggest advantage is generally the reduction in data transfer.

Here is an example:

```
SYS@SANDBOX> alter session set cell_offload_processing=false;

Session altered.

Elapsed: 00:00:00.01
SYS@SANDBOX> select count(pk_col) from kso.skew3;

COUNT(PK_COL)
-------------
    384000036

Elapsed: 00:00:48.45
SYS@SANDBOX> alter session set cell_offload_processing=true;

Session altered.

Elapsed: 00:00:00.01
SYS@SANDBOX> select count(pk_col) from kso.skew3;

COUNT(PK_COL)
-------------
    384000036

Elapsed: 00:00:26.61
SYS@SANDBOX> -- disable storage indexes
SYS@SANDBOX> alter system set "_kcfis_storageidx_disabled"=true;
```

```
System altered.

Elapsed: 00:00:00.17
SYS@SANDBOX> select count(pk_col) from kso.skew3 where col1 < 0;

COUNT(PK_COL)
-------------
            2

Elapsed: 00:00:08.53
```

First we completely disabled Offloading using the `CELL_OFFLOAD_PROCESSING` parameter and ran a query without a `WHERE` clause. Without the benefit of Offloading this query took about 48 seconds. We then enabled Offloading and re-ran the query. This time the query took only about 27 seconds. The savings of approximately 21 seconds was due strictly to Column Projection (because without a `WHERE` clause for filtering, there were no other optimizations that could come into play). We then used a trick to disable storage indexes by setting the hidden parameter, `_KCFIS_STORAGEIDX_DISABLED`, to `TRUE` (we'll discuss that more in the next section) and added a `WHERE` clause, which reduced the execution time to about 9 seconds. This reduction of an additional 18 seconds or so was thanks to Predicate Filtering. Note that we had to disable storage indexes to be sure that we weren't getting any benefit from that optimization and that all the improvement was due to Predicate Filtering, which brings us to the next topic.

Storage Indexes

Storage Indexes provide the third level of optimization for Smart Scans. Storage Indexes are in-memory structures on the storage cells that maintain a maximum and minimum value for each 1MB disk storage unit, for up to eight columns of a table. Storage Indexes are a little different than most Smart Scan optimizations. The goal of Storage Indexes is not to reduce the amount of data being transferred back to the database tier. In fact, whether they are used on a given query or not, the amount of data returned to the database tier remains constant. On the contrary, Storage Indexes are designed to eliminate time spent reading data from disk on the storage servers themselves. Think of this feature as a pre-filter. Since Smart Scans pass the query predicates to the storage servers, and Storage Indexes contain a map of values in each 1MB storage region, any region that can't possibly contain a matching row can be eliminated without ever being read. You can also think of Storage Indexes as an alternate partitioning mechanism. Disk I/O is eliminated in analogous fashion to partition elimination. If a partition can't contain any records of interest, the partition's blocks will not be read. Similarly, if a storage region cannot contain any records of interest, that storage region need not be read.

Storage Indexes cannot be used in all cases, and there is little that can be done to affect when or how they are used. But in the right situations, the results from this optimization technique can be astounding.

Here is an example:

```
SYS@SANDBOX> -- disable storage indexes
SYS@SANDBOX> alter system set "_kcfis_storageidx_disabled"=true;

System altered.

Elapsed: 00:00:00.22
SYS@SANDBOX> select count(pk_col) from kso.skew3 where col1 < 0;
```

```
COUNT(PK_COL)
-------------
            2

Elapsed: 00:00:08.74
SYS@SANDBOX> -- enable storage indexes
SYS@SANDBOX> alter system set "_kcfis_storageidx_disabled"=false;

System altered.

Elapsed: 00:00:00.03
SYS@SANDBOX> select count(pk_col) from kso.skew3 where col1 < 0;

COUNT(PK_COL)
-------------
            2

Elapsed: 00:00:00.08
```

In this example we disabled storage indexes (using the _KCFIS_STORAGEIDX_DISABLED parameter) to remind you of the elapsed time required to read through 384 million rows using Column Projection and Predicate Filtering. Remember that even though the amount of data returned to the database tier is extremely small in this case, the storage servers still had to read through every block containing data for the SKEW3 table and then had to check each row to see if it matched the WHERE clause. This is where the majority of the 8 seconds was spent. We then re-enabled storage indexes and reran the query, which reduced the execution time to about .08 seconds. This reduction in elapsed time is a result of storage indexes being used to avoid virtually all of the disk I/O and the time spent filtering through those records.

Just to reiterate, Column Projection and Predicate Filtering (and most other Smart Scan optimizations) improve performance by reducing the volume of data being transferred back to the database servers (and thus the amount of time to transfer the data). Storage Indexes improve performance by eliminating time spent reading data from disk on the storage servers and filtering that data. Storage Indexes are covered in much more detail in Chapter 4.

Simple Joins (Bloom Filters)

In some cases, join processing can be offloaded to the storage tier as well. Offloaded joins are accomplished by creating what is called a *bloom filter*. Bloom filters have been around for a long time and have been used by Oracle since Oracle Database Version 10g Release 2. So they are not specific to Exadata. One of the main ways Oracle uses them is to reduce traffic between parallel query slaves. They have the advantage of being very small relative to the data set that they represent. However, this comes at a price— they can return false positives. That is, rows that should not be included in the desired result set can occasionally pass a bloom filter. For that reason, an additional filter must be applied after the bloom filter to ensure that any false positives are eliminated. The interesting thing about bloom filters from an Exadata perspective is that they may be passed to the storage servers and evaluated there. This technique can result in a large decrease in the volume of data that must be transmitted back to database servers.

Here's an example:

```
SYS@SANDBOX> -- disable bloom filter offloading
SYS@SANDBOX> alter session set "_bloom_predicate_pushdown_to_storage"=false;

Session altered.

Elapsed: 00:00:00.82
SYS@SANDBOX> @bloom_join2.sql

COL2                          SUM(A.COL1)
----------------------------- -----------
2342                                  144
asddsadasd                      153598416

2 rows selected.

Elapsed: 00:11:39.39
SYS@SANDBOX> -- enable bloom filter offloading
SYS@SANDBOX> alter session set "_bloom_predicate_pushdown_to_storage"=true;

Session altered.

Elapsed: 00:00:00.82
SYS@SANDBOX> @bloom_join2.sql

COL2                          SUM(A.COL1)
----------------------------- -----------
asddsadasd                      153598416
2342                                  144

2 rows selected.

Elapsed: 00:02:06.13

SYS@SANDBOX> @dplan
Enter value for sql_id: 09m6t5qpgkywx
Enter value for child_no: 0

PLAN_TABLE_OUTPUT
------------------------------------------------------------------------------------------
SQL_ID  09m6t5qpgkywx, child number 0
-------------------------------------
select /*+ bloom join 2  use_hash (skew temp_skew) */ a.col2,
sum(a.col1) from kso.skew3 a, kso.skew2 b where a.pk_col = b.pk_col and
b.col1 = 1 group by a.col2

Plan hash value: 466947137
```

```
----------------------------------------------------------------------------------
| Id  | Operation                       | Name       |   TQ  |IN-OUT| PQ Distrib |
----------------------------------------------------------------------------------
|   0 | SELECT STATEMENT                |            |       |      |            |
|   1 |  PX COORDINATOR                 |            |       |      |            |
|   2 |   PX SEND QC (RANDOM)           | :TQ10002   | Q1,02 | P->S | QC (RAND)  |
|   3 |    HASH GROUP BY                |            | Q1,02 | PCWP |            |
|   4 |     PX RECEIVE                  |            | Q1,02 | PCWP |            |
|   5 |      PX SEND HASH               | :TQ10001   | Q1,01 | P->P | HASH       |
|   6 |       HASH GROUP BY             |            | Q1,01 | PCWP |            |
|*  7 |        HASH JOIN                |            | Q1,01 | PCWP |            |
|   8 |         BUFFER SORT             |            | Q1,01 | PCWC |            |
|   9 |          PX RECEIVE             |            | Q1,01 | PCWP |            |
|  10 |           PX SEND BROADCAST     | :TQ10000   |       | S->P | BROADCAST  |
|  11 |            TABLE ACCESS BY INDEX ROWID| SKEW2 |       |      |            |
|* 12 |             INDEX RANGE SCAN    | SKEW2_COL1 |       |      |            |
|  13 |          PX BLOCK ITERATOR      |            | Q1,01 | PCWC |            |
|* 14 |           TABLE ACCESS STORAGE FULL| SKEW3   | Q1,01 | PCWP |            |
----------------------------------------------------------------------------------
```

Predicate Information (identified by operation id):

```
   7 - access("A"."PK_COL"="B"."PK_COL")
  12 - access("B"."COL1"=1)
  14 - storage(:Z>=:Z AND :Z<=:Z)
       filter(SYS_OP_BLOOM_FILTER(:BF0000,"A"."PK_COL"))
```


36 rows selected.

SYS@SANDBOX> @dplan
Enter value for sql_id: 09m6t5qpgkywx
Enter value for child_no: 1

PLAN_TABLE_OUTPUT

SQL_ID 09m6t5qpgkywx, child number 1
----
select /*+ bloom join 2 use_hash (skew temp_skew) */ a.col2,
sum(a.col1) from kso.skew3 a, kso.skew2 b where a.pk_col = b.pk_col and
b.col1 = 1 group by a.col2

Plan hash value: 466947137


```
------------------------------------------------------------------------------------
| Id  | Operation                       | Name       |   TQ  |IN-OUT| PQ Distrib |
------------------------------------------------------------------------------------
|   0 | SELECT STATEMENT                |            |       |      |            |
|   1 |  PX COORDINATOR                 |            |       |      |            |
|   2 |   PX SEND QC (RANDOM)           | :TQ10002   | Q1,02 | P->S | QC (RAND)  |
```

```
|   3 |       HASH GROUP BY              |          | Q1,02 | PCWP |           |
|   4 |        PX RECEIVE               |          | Q1,02 | PCWP |           |
|   5 |         PX SEND HASH            |:TQ10001  | Q1,01 | P->P | HASH      |
|   6 |          HASH GROUP BY          |          | Q1,01 | PCWP |           |
|*  7 |           HASH JOIN             |          | Q1,01 | PCWP |           |
|   8 |            BUFFER SORT          |          | Q1,01 | PCWC |           |
|   9 |             PX RECEIVE          |          | Q1,01 | PCWP |           |
|  10 |              PX SEND BROADCAST  |:TQ10000  |       | S->P | BROADCAST |
|  11 |               TABLE ACCESS BY INDEX ROWID| SKEW2 |   |      |           |
|* 12 |                INDEX RANGE SCAN |SKEW2_COL1|       |      |           |
|  13 |             PX BLOCK ITERATOR   |          | Q1,01 | PCWC |           |
|* 14 |              TABLE ACCESS STORAGE FULL | SKEW3 | Q1,01 | PCWP |     |
 -------------------------------------------------------------------------
```

Predicate Information (identified by operation id):

```
   7 - access("A"."PK_COL"="B"."PK_COL")
  12 - access("B"."COL1"=1)
  14 - storage(:Z>=:Z AND :Z<=:Z AND SYS_OP_BLOOM_FILTER(:BF0000,"A"."PK_COL"))
       filter(SYS_OP_BLOOM_FILTER(:BF0000,"A"."PK_COL"))
```

36 rows selected.

In this listing we used a hidden parameter, _BLOOM_PREDICATE_PUSHDOWN_TO_STORAGE, to disable this feature for comparison purposes. Notice that our test query ran in about 2 minutes with Offloading and 11.5 minutes without. If you look closely at the Predicate Information of the plans, you will see that the SYS_OP_BLOOM_FILTER(:BF0000,"A"."PK_COL") predicate was run on the storage servers for the second run. The offloaded version ran faster because the storage servers were able to pre-join the tables, which eliminated a large amount of data that would otherwise have been transferred back to the database servers.

Function Offloading

Oracle's implementation of SQL includes many built-in SQL functions. These functions can be used directly in SQL statements. They may be divided into two main groups: single-row functions and multi-row functions. Single-row functions return a single result row for every row of a queried table. These single row functions can be further subdivided into the following general categories:

- Numeric functions (SIN, COS, FLOOR, MOD, LOG, …)

- Character functions (CHR, LPAD, REPLACE, TRIM, UPPER, LENGTH, …)

- Datetime functions (ADD_MONTHS, TO_CHAR, TRUNC, …)

- Conversion functions (CAST, HEXTORAW, TO_CHAR, TO_DATE, …)

Virtually all of these single-row functions can be offloaded to Exadata storage. The second major group of SQL functions operate on a set of rows. There are two subgroups in this multi-row function category:

- Aggregate functions (AVG, COUNT, SUM, …)

- Analytic functions (AVG, COUNT, DENSE_RANK, LAG, …)

These functions return either a single row (aggregate functions) or multiple rows (analytic functions). Note that some of the functions are overloaded and belong to both groups. None of these functions can be offloaded to Exadata. Which makes sense, because many of these functions require access to the entire set of rows, which individual storage cells do not have.

There are some additional functions that don't fall neatly into any of the previously described groupings. These functions are a mixed bag in terms of Offloading. For example, DECODE and NVL are offloadable, but the XML functions are not. Some of the Data Mining functions are offloadable and some are not. Also keep in mind that the list of offloadable functions may change as newer versions are released. The definitive list of which functions are offloadable for your particular version is contained in V$SQLFN_METADATA.

```
SYS@SANDBOX> select distinct name, version, offloadable
  2  from V$SQLFN_METADATA
  3  order by 1,2;

NAME                         VERSION        OFF
---------------------------- -------------- ---
!=                           SQL/DS         YES
!=                           V6 Oracle      YES
<                            SQL/DS         YES
<                            V6 Oracle      YES
<=                           SQL/DS         YES
<=                           V6 Oracle      YES
=                            SQL/DS         YES
=                            V6 Oracle      YES
>                            SQL/DS         YES
>                            V6 Oracle      YES
>=                           SQL/DS         YES
>=                           V6 Oracle      YES
ABS                          V10 Oracle     YES
ABS                          V10 Oracle     YES
ABS                          V6 Oracle      YES
ACOS                         V10 Oracle     YES
ACOS                         V73 Oracle     YES
. . .
VSIZE                        V6 Oracle      YES
WIDTH_BUCKET                 V82 Oracle     NO
XMLCAST                      V11R1 Oracle   NO
XMLCDATA                     V10 Oracle     NO
XMLCOMMENT                   V10 Oracle     NO
XMLCONCAT                    V92 Oracle     NO
XMLDIFF                      V11R1 Oracle   NO
XMLEXISTS2                   V11R1 Oracle   NO
XMLISNODE                    V92 Oracle     NO
XMLISVALID                   V92 Oracle     NO
XMLPATCH                     V11R1 Oracle   NO
XMLQUERY                     V10 Oracle     NO
XMLTOOBJECT                  V11R1 Oracle   NO
```

```
XMLTRANSFORM              V92 Oracle    NO
XMLTRANSFORMBLOB          V10 Oracle    NO
XS_SYS_CONTEXT            V11R1 Oracle NO

921 rows selected.
```

Offloading functions does allow the storage cells to do some of the work that would normally be done by the CPUs on the database servers. However, the saving in CPU usage is generally a relatively minor enhancement. The big gain usually comes from limiting the amount of data transferred back to the database servers. Being able to evaluate functions contained in WHERE clauses allows storage cells to send only rows of interest back to the database tier. So as with most Offloading, the primary goal of this optimization is to reduce the amount of traffic between the storage and database tiers.

Compression/Decompression

One Exadata feature that has received quite a bit of attention is Hybrid Columnar Compression (HCC). Exadata offloads the decompression of data stored in HCC format during Smart Scan operations. That is, columns of interest are decompressed on the storage cells when the compressed data is accessed via Smart Scans. This decompression is not necessary for filtering, so only the data that will be returned to the database tier will be decompressed. Note that all compression is currently done at the database tier, however. Decompression may also be done at the database tier when data is not accessed via a Smart Scan. So to make it simple, Table 2-1 shows where the work is done.

Table 2-1. HCC Compression/Decompression Offloading

Operation	Database Servers	Storage Servers
Compression	Always	Never
Decompression	Non-Smart Scan	Smart Scan

Decompressing data at the storage tier runs counter to the theme of most of the other Smart Scan optimizations. Most of them are geared to reducing the volume of data to be transported back to the database servers. Because decompression is such a CPU-intensive task, particularly with the higher levels of compression, the decision was made to do the decompression on the storage servers. This decision is not be locked in stone, however, as in some situations there may be ample CPU resources available to make decompressing data on the database servers an attractive option (that is, in some situations the reduction in data to be shipped may outweigh the reduction in database server CPU consumption). In fact, as of cellsrv version 11.2.2.3.1, Exadata does have the ability to return compressed data to the database servers when the storage cells are busy.

Kevin Says: The authors are correct to surmise that the delineation of responsibility between the database grid and the storage grid are quite fluid—at least from an architectural standpoint. Allow me to explain. During Smart Scan processing, Exadata Storage Server software performs offload processing (such as filtration, projection, and decompression of EHCC data) on 1MB chunks of data. In true Smart Scan form, the product of Smart Scan (filtered and projected data) flows over iDB into the PGA of the requesting process in the database grid. However, there have always been conditions where Smart Scan is forced to halt intelligent processing within one of these 1MB chunks and return data in original block form. One such case is when Smart Scan encounters a chained row during filtration. Only the database grid can determine the location of the block that contains the chained row. Even if cells were given the intelligence to determine the locale of the chained row, it would most likely not be on the same cell; and cells have no direct communication paths among themselves, anyway. So, with this example in mind, it is easy to see that Smart Scan can revert to a block server when it *needs* to. For that matter, Smart Scan can revert to a block server when it *wants* to. I expect the shelf-life of this book to outlive some of the rigid descriptions we've given regarding roles and the delineation of responsibilities between the database grid and the storage grid of the Exadata Database Machine. Consider a scenario where the cells are servicing a moderately selective query of minimal complexity (for example, few or no joins, and light aggregation and sorting) against deeply compressed data. Given these parameters, the processor utilization would skew heavily toward the storage grid, as the cost of filtering, projecting, and decompressing the data is much greater than the effort being expended in the database grid. We know Smart Scan can revert to a block server when it *needs* to. The scenario I just described may indeed be a case when Smart Scan would *want* to revert to block server for at least some of its payload. Indeed, it's better not to broker work to fully saturated processors if there are other processors near idle.

By the way, there is a hidden parameter that controls whether decompression will be offloaded at all. Unfortunately, it doesn't just move the decompression back and forth between the storage and database tiers. If the `_CELL_OFFLOAD_HYBRIDCOLUMNAR` parameter is set to a value of `FALSE`, Smart Scans will be completely disabled on HCC data.

Encryption/Decryption

Encryption and decryption are handled in a manner very similar to compression and decompression of HCC data. Encryption is always done at the database tier, while decryption can be done by the storage servers or by the database servers. When encrypted data is accessed via Smart Scan, it is decrypted on the storage servers. Otherwise, it is decrypted on the database servers. Note that the X2-2 and x2-8 platforms both use Intel Xeon Westmere chips in the storage servers (X2-2 uses the same chips in the database servers, by the way). These chips contain a special instruction set (Intel AES-NI) that effectively adds a hardware boost to processes doing encryption or decryption. Note that Oracle Database Release 11.2.0.2 is necessary to take advantage of the new instruction set.

Encryption and HCC compression work well together. Since compression is done first, there is less work needed for processes doing encryption and decryption on HCC data. Note that the

CELL_OFFLOAD_DECRYPTION parameter controls this behavior, and that as it does with the hidden parameter _CELL_OFFLOAD_HYBRIDCOLUMNAR, setting the parameter to a value of FALSE completely disables Smart Scans on encrypted data, which also disables decryption at the storage layer.

Virtual Columns

Virtual columns provide the ability to define pseudo-columns that can be calculated from other columns in a table, without actually storing the calculated value. Virtual columns may be used as partition keys, used in constraints, or indexed. Column level statistics can also be gathered on them. Since the values of virtual columns are not actually stored, they must be calculated on the fly when they are accessed. These calculations can be offloaded when access is via Smart Scans.

```
SYS@SANDBOX1> alter table kso.temp_skew add col1_plus_pk as (col1+pk_col);

Table altered.

SYS@SANDBOX1> select col1_plus_pk from kso.temp_skew where rownum < 10;

COL1_PLUS_PK
------------
    27998260
    27998258
    27998256
    27998254
    27998252
    27998250
    27998248
    27998246
    27998244

9 rows selected.

SYS@SANDBOX1> select count(*) from kso.temp_skew where col1_plus_pk=27998244;

  COUNT(*)
----------
         2


SYS@SANDBOX> @fsx4
Enter value for sql_text: select count(*) from kso.temp_skew where col1_plus_pk=27998244
Enter value for sql_id:

SQL_ID        CHILD OFFLOAD   AVG_ETIME IO_SAVED_% SQL_TEXT
------------- ------ ------- ------------- ---------- --------------------
35tqjjq5vzg4b     0 Yes          1.14       99.99 select count(*) from

1 row selected.

SYS@SANDBOX1> @dplan
Enter value for sql_id: 35tqjjq5vzg4b
```

```
Enter value for child_no:

PLAN_TABLE_OUTPUT
---------------------------------------------------------------------------------
SQL_ID  35tqjjq5vzg4b, child number 0
-------------------------------------
select count(*) from kso.temp_skew where col1_plus_pk=27998244

Plan hash value: 725706675

---------------------------------------------------------------------------------
| Id  | Operation                   | Name      | Rows  | Bytes | Cost (%CPU)| Time     |
---------------------------------------------------------------------------------
|   0 | SELECT STATEMENT            |           |       |       | 44804 (100)|          |
|   1 |  SORT AGGREGATE             |           |     1 |    13 |            |          |
|*  2 |   TABLE ACCESS STORAGE FULL | TEMP_SKEW |  320K | 4062K | 44804  (2) | 00:08:58 |
---------------------------------------------------------------------------------

Predicate Information (identified by operation id):
---------------------------------------------------

   2 - storage("COL1"+"PK_COL"=27998244)
       filter("COL1"+"PK_COL"=27998244)


20 rows selected.


SYS@SANDBOX1> alter session set "_cell_offload_virtual_columns"=false;

Session altered.

SYS@SANDBOX1> @flush_sql
Enter value for sql_id: 35tqjjq5vzg4b

PL/SQL procedure successfully completed.

SYS@SANDBOX1> select count(*) from kso.temp_skew where col1_plus_pk=27998244;

  COUNT(*)
----------
         2

1 row selected.

SYS@SANDBOX1> @fsx4
Enter value for sql_text: select count(*) from kso.temp_skew where col1_plus_pk=27998244
Enter value for sql_id:
Enter value for inst_id:

SQL_ID        CHILD OFFLOAD   AVG_ETIME IO_SAVED_% SQL_TEXT
------------- ------ ------- ------------- ---------- --------------------
```

```
35tqjjq5vzg4b          0 Yes                3.00        59.79 select count(*) from

1 row selected.

SYS@SANDBOX1>  alter session set "_cell_offload_virtual_columns"=true;

Session altered.

SYS@SANDBOX1> select count(*) from kso.temp_skew where col1_plus_pk=27998244;

  COUNT(*)
----------
         2

1 row selected.

SYS@SANDBOX1> @fsx4
Enter value for sql_text: select count(*) from kso.temp_skew where col1_plus_pk=27998244
Enter value for sql_id:
Enter value for inst_id:

SQL_ID        CHILD OFFLOAD   AVG_ETIME IO_SAVED_% SQL_TEXT
------------- ------ ------- ------------- ---------- --------------------
35tqjjq5vzg4b     0 Yes          3.00      59.79 select count(*) from
35tqjjq5vzg4b     0 Yes          1.19      99.99 select count(*) from

2 rows selected.
```

This example shows that virtual column evaluation can be offloaded. It also shows that the optimization can be controlled using the _CELL_OFFLOAD_VIRTUAL_COLUMNS parameter. Note that storage indexes are not built on virtual columns. As with Function Offloading, the real advantage of offloading virtual column calculations has more to do with reducing the volume of data returned to the database servers than with reducing CPU usage on the database tier.

Data Mining Model Scoring

Some of the data model scoring functions can be offloaded. Generally speaking this optimization is aimed at reducing the amount of data transferred to the database tier as opposed to pure CPU offloading. As with other function Offloading, you can verify which data mining functions can be offloaded by querying V$SQLFN_METADATA. The output looks like this:

```
SYS@SANDBOX> select distinct name, version, offloadable
  2   from V$SQLFN_METADATA
  3   where name like 'PREDICT%'
  4   order by 1,2;

NAME                          VERSION      OFFLOADABLE
----------------------------- ------------ -----------
PREDICTION                    V10R2 Oracle YES
PREDICTION_BOUNDS             V11R1 Oracle NO
PREDICTION_COST               V10R2 Oracle YES
PREDICTION_DETAILS            V10R2 Oracle NO
```

```
PREDICTION_PROBABILITY        V1oR2 Oracle YES
PREDICTION_SET                V1oR2 Oracle NO

6 rows selected.
```

As you can see, some of the functions are offloadable and some are not. The ones that are offloadable can be used by the storage cells for Predicate Filtering. Here's an example query that should only return records that meet the scoring requirement specified in the WHERE clause:

```
select cust_id
from customers
where region = 'US'
and prediction_probability(churnmod,'Y' using *) > 0.8;
```

This optimization is designed to offload CPU usage as well as reduce the volume of data transferred. However, it is most beneficial in situations where it can reduce the data returned to the database tier, such as in the previous example.

Non-Smart Scan Offloading

There are a few optimizations that are not related to query processing. As these are not the focus of this chapter we will only touch on them briefly.

Smart File Creation

This optimization has a somewhat misleading name. It really is an optimization designed to speed up block initialization. Whenever blocks are allocated, the database must initialize them. This activity happens when tablespaces are created, but it also occurs when files are extended for any number of other reasons. On non-Exadata storage, these situations require the database server to format each block and then write them back to disk. All that reading and writing causes a lot of traffic between the database servers and the storage cells. As you are now aware, eliminating traffic between the layers is a primary goal of Exadata. So as you might imagine, this totally unnecessary traffic has been eliminated. Blocks are formatted by the storage cells themselves without having to send them to the database servers. Time spent waiting on this activity is recorded by the Smart File Creation wait event. This wait event and the operations that invoke it are covered in more detail in Chapter 10.

RMAN Incremental Backups

Exadata speeds up incremental backups by increasing the granularity of block change tracking. On non-Exadata platforms, block changes are tracked for groups of blocks; on Exadata, changes are tracked for individual blocks. This can significantly decrease the number of blocks that must be backed up, resulting in smaller backup sizes, less I/O bandwidth, and reduced time to complete incremental backups. This feature can be disabled by setting the _DISABLE_CELL_OPTIMIZED_BACKUPS parameter to a value of TRUE. This optimization is covered in Chapter 9.

RMAN Restores

This optimization speeds up the file initialization portion when restoring from backup on a cell. Although restoring databases from backups is rare, this optimization can also help speed up cloning of environments. The optimization reduces CPU usage on the database servers and reduces traffic between the two tiers. If the `_CELL_FAST_FILE_RESTORE` parameter is set to a value of `FALSE`, this behavior will be disabled. This optimization is also covered in Chapter 9.

Smart Scan Prerequisites

Smart Scans do not occur for every query run on Exadata. There are three basic requirements that must be met for Smart Scans to occur:

- There must be a full scan of an object.
- The scan must use Oracle's Direct Path Read mechanism.
- The object must be stored on Exadata storage.

There is a simple explanation as to why these requirements exist. Oracle is a C program. The function that performs Smart Scans (`kcfis_read`) is called by the direct path read function (`kcbldrget`), which is called by one of the full scan functions. It's that simple. You can't get to the `kcfis_read` function without traversing the code path from full scan to direct read. And of course, the storage will have to be running Oracle's software in order to process Smart Scans.

We'll discuss each of these requirements in turn.

Full Scans

In order for queries to take advantage of Exadata's Offloading capabilities, the optimizer must decide to execute a statement with a Full Table Scan or a Fast Full Index Scan. Note that I am using these terms somewhat generically. Generally speaking, these terms correspond to `TABLE ACCESS FULL` and `INDEX FAST FULL SCAN` operations of an execution plan. With Exadata, these familiar operations have been renamed slightly to show that they are accessing Exadata storage. The new operation names are `TABLE ACCESS STORAGE FULL` and `INDEX STORAGE FAST FULL SCAN`. Note that there are also some minor variations of these operations, such as `MAT_VIEW ACCESS STORAGE FULL`, that also qualify for Smart Scans. You should, however, be aware that the fact that your execution plan shows a `TABLE ACCESS STORAGE FULL` operation does not mean that your query was performed with a Smart Scan. It merely means that this prerequisite has been satisfied. We'll discuss how to verify whether a statement was actually Offloaded via a Smart Scan a little later in this chapter.

Direct Path Reads

In addition to requiring Full Scan operations, Smart Scans also require that the read operations be executed via Oracle's Direct Path Read mechanism. Direct Path Reads have been around for a long time. Traditionally, this read mechanism has been used by slave processes, which service parallel queries. Because parallel queries were originally expected to be used for accessing very large amounts of data (typically much too large to fit in the Oracle buffer cache), it was decided that the parallel slaves should read data directly into their own memory (also known as the program global area or PGA). The Direct Path Read mechanism completely bypasses the standard Oracle caching mechanism of placing blocks in the buffer cache. This was a very good thing for very large data sets, as it eliminated extra work that was expected to not be helpful (caching full table scan data that would probably not be reused) and kept them from flushing other data out of the cache. And as we previously mentioned, the `kcfis` (kernel file intelligent storage) functions are buried under the `kcbldrget` (kernel block direct read get) function. Therefore, Smart Scans can only be performed if the direct path read mechanism is being used.

45

In addition to parallel slaves, direct path reads are possible for non-parallel SQL statements, when conditions are right. There is a hidden parameter, _SERIAL_DIRECT_READ, which controls this feature. When this parameter is set to its default value (AUTO), Oracle automatically determines whether to use direct path reads for non-parallel scans. The calculation is based on several factors including the size of the object, the size of the buffer cache and how many of the objects blocks are already in the buffer cache. There is also a hidden parameter (_SMALL_TABLE_THRESHOLD) which plays a role in determining how big a table must be before it will be considered for serial direct path reads. The algorithm for determining whether to use the direct path read mechanism on non-parallel scans is not published. While the ability to do serial direct path reads has been around for some time, it has only recently become a relatively common occurrence. Oracle Database 11gR2 has a modified version of the calculations used to determine whether to use direct path reads for non-parallel scans. The new modifications to the algorithm make the direct path read mechanism much more likely to occur than it was in previous versions. This was probably done as a result of Exadata's Smart Scan optimizations and the desire for them to be triggered whenever possible. The algorithm may be somewhat overly aggressive on non-Exadata platforms.

■ **Note**: My Oracle Support Note: 793845.1 contains the following statement:

There have been changes in 11g in the heuristics to choose between direct path reads or reads through buffer cache for serial table scans. In 10g, serial table scans for "large" tables used to go through cache (by default) which is not the case anymore. In 11g, this decision to read via direct path or through cache is based on the size of the table, buffer cache size and various other stats. Direct path reads are faster than scattered reads and have less impact on other processes because they avoid latches.

Exadata Storage

Of course the data being scanned must be stored on Exadata storage in order for Smart Scans to occur. It is possible to create ASM disk groups that access non-Exadata storage on Exadata database servers. And of course it makes sense that any SQL statements accessing objects defined using these non-Exadata diskgroups will not be eligible for Offloading. While it is unusual, it is also possible to create ASM diskgroups using a combination of Exadata and non-Exadata storage. This might be done to facilitate a migration via an ASM rebalance, for example. Queries against objects whose segments reside on these mixed storage diskgroups are also not eligible for Offloading. There is actually an attribute assigned to ASM disk groups (cell.smart_scan_capable) that specifies whether a disk group is capable of processing Smart Scans. This attribute must be set to FALSE before non-Exadata storage can be assigned to an ASM disk group. Here's a listing showing the process of creating a mixed storage disk group and the effects on queries against a table with segments stored in that disk group. Note that we are jumping ahead in this example, so some of the commands may not make a lot of sense yet. Don't worry; we'll cover the details in due time. For now we just want you to see that you can access non-Exadata storage, but that it will disable the Exadata storage-based optimizations.

```
SYS@+ASM> -- Add non-Exadata storage

SYS@+ASM> alter diskgroup SMITHERS add failgroup LOCAL disk '/dev/raw/raw5','/dev/raw/raw6';
```

```
alter diskgroup SMITHERS add failgroup LOCAL disk '/dev/raw/raw5','/dev/raw/raw6'
*
ERROR at line 1:
ORA-15032: not all alterations performed
ORA-15285: disk '/dev/raw/raw5' violates disk group attribute cell.smart_scan_capable
ORA-15285: disk '/dev/raw/raw6' violates disk group attribute cell.smart_scan_capable


SYS@+ASM> alter diskgroup smithers set attribute 'cell.smart_scan_capable' = 'FALSE';

Diskgroup altered.

SYS@+ASM> alter diskgroup SMITHERS add failgroup LOCAL disk '/dev/raw/raw5','/dev/raw/raw6';

Diskgroup altered.

SYS@+ASM> select name, total_mb from v$asm_diskgroup where state='MOUNTED'

NAME                                               TOTAL_MB
------------------------------------------------- --------
SMITHERS                                            512,000
SMITHERS_LOCAL                                        1,562


SYS@+ASM> select g.name "diskgroup", d.path "disk", d.failgroup "failgroup", d.total_mb "disk
size" from v$asm_diskgroup g, v$asm_disk d where g.group_number=d.group_number and
g.state='MOUNTED'

diskgroup       disk                                failgroup               disk size
--------------- ----------------------------------- ----------------------- ---------
SMITHERS        /dev/raw/raw5                       LOCAL                   102,400
SMITHERS        /dev/raw/raw6                       LOCAL                   102,400
SMITHERS        o/192.168.12.3/SMITHERS_CD_05_cell01 ENKCEL01               102,400
SMITHERS        o/192.168.12.4/SMITHERS_CD_05_cell02 ENKCEL02               102,400
SMITHERS        o/192.168.12.5/SMITHERS_CD_05_cell03 ENKCEL03               102,400
SMITHERS_LOCAL  /dev/raw/raw1                       SMITHERS_LOCAL_0000     781
SMITHERS_LOCAL  /dev/raw/raw2                       SMITHERS_LOCAL_0001     781

7 rows selected.
```

We started out with a diskgroup on Exadata storage that contained a table compressed with HCC. When we initially tried to add the non-Exadata storage to that disk group, we got an error saying we had violated the `cell.smart_scan_capable` disk group attribute. Once we changed the attribute, setting it to `FALSE`, we were able to add the non-Exadata storage (of course, changing this setting disables Smart Scans on any object with segments stored in this disk group). We then logged onto the database and tried to access our compressed table:

```
SYS@SMITHERS> select table_name, compression, compress_for
  2  from dba_tables where owner='ACOLVIN';
```

```
TABLE_NAME                      COMPRESS COMPRESS_FOR
------------------------------- -------- ------------
SKEW3                           ENABLED  QUERY HIGH

SYS@SMITHERS> @table_size
Enter value for owner: ACOLVIN
Enter value for table_name: SKEW3
Enter value for type: TABLE

OWNER                SEGMENT_NAME                    TYPE                TOTALSIZE_MEGS TS
-------------------- ------------------------------- ------------------- -------------- -----
ACOLVIN              SKEW3                           TABLE                      1,020.0 USERS
                                                                         --------------
sum                                                                            1,020.0

SYS@SMITHERS> select count(*) from acolvin.skew3 where col1<0;
select count(*) from acolvin.skew3 where col1<0
                             *
ERROR at line 1:
ORA-64307: hybrid columnar compression is only supported in tablespaces residing on Exadata⏎
 storage

SYS@SMITHERS> alter table acolvin.skew3 move nocompress;

Table altered.

SYS@SMITHERS> select /*+ parallel (a 8) */ count(*) from acolvin.skew3 a;

  COUNT(*)
----------
 384000048

Elapsed: 00:03:24.64
SYS@SMITHERS> @fsx4
Enter value for sql_text: select /*+ parallel (a 8) */ count(*) from acolvin.skew3 a
Enter value for sql_id:

SQL_ID        CHILD OFFLOAD IO_SAVED_%    AVG_ETIME SQL_TEXT
------------- ------ ------- ---------- ------------- --------------------
5y9jm9pfbrg7q     0 No            .00        204.58 select /*+ parallel

1 row selected.

SYS@SMITHERS> @table_size
Enter value for owner: ACOLVIN
Enter value for table_name: SKEW3
Enter value for type: TABLE

OWNER                SEGMENT_NAME                    TYPE                TOTALSIZE_MEGS TS
-------------------- ------------------------------- ------------------- -------------- -----
ACOLVIN              SKEW3                           TABLE                     13,814.0 USERS
                                                                         --------------
```

```
sum                                                              13,814.0
```

```
1 row selected.
```

So adding the non-Exadata storage also disabled HCC. We had to decompress the table simply to access it. Once this was done we executed a parallel query on the table and, as you can see, the query was not Offloaded. So all that was to show that you need Exadata storage to do Smart Scans.

Smart Scan Disablers

There are situations where Smart Scans are effectively disabled. The simple case is where they have not been enabled in the code yet, and so Smart Scans don't happen at all. There are other cases where Oracle starts down the Smart Scan path but the storage software either decides, or is forced, to revert to block shipping mode. Generally this decision is made on a block-by-block basis.

Simply Unavailable

During the discussion of Smart Scan optimizations we have covered the prerequisites that must be met to enable Smart Scans. However, even when those conditions are met, there are circumstances that prevent Smart Scans. Here are a few other situations that are not related to specific optimizations, but where Smart Scans simply cannot be used (at least as of `cellsrv` version 11.2.2.2.0).

- Smart Scans cannot be used on clustered tables.

- Smart Scans cannot be used on Index Organized Tables (IOTs).

- Smart Scans cannot be used on tables with ROWDEPENDENCIES enabled.

Reverting to Block Shipping

There are situations where Smart Scans are used, but for various reasons `cellsrv` reverts to block shipping mode. This is a very complex topic, and we struggled with whether to include it in an introductory chapter on offloading. But it is a fundamental concept and so in the end we decided to discuss it here.

We've described how Smart Scans avoid transferring large amounts of data to the database layer by returning prefiltered data directly to the PGA. The key concept to understand here is that Smart Scans can choose (or be forced) to return complete blocks to the SGA. Basically any situation that would cause Oracle to have to read another block to complete a record will cause this to happen. A chained row is perhaps the simplest example. When Oracle encounters a chained row, the head piece will contain a pointer to the block containing the second row piece. Since the storage cells do not communicate directly with each other, and it is unlikely that the chained block resides on the same storage cell, `cellsrv` simply ships the entire block and allows the database layer to deal with it.

So in this very simple case, the Smart Scan is paused momentarily, and a single block read is effectively performed, which motivates another single block read to get the additional row piece. Keep in mind that this is a very simple case. This same behavior comes into play when Oracle must deal with read consistency issues. For example, if Oracle notices that a block is "newer" than the current query, the process of finding an age-appropriate version of the block is left for the database layer to deal with. This effectively pauses the Smart Scan processing while the database does its traditional read consistency processing.

So is this really important, and why should you care? The answer, of course, is that it depends. In most cases you probably won't care. Oracle guarantees that reads will be consistent, even when doing

Smart Scans. This is an important point, by the way. The fact that Oracle behaves exactly the same from the application standpoint, regardless of whether Smart Scans are used or not is a big deal. The fact that Oracle may do some single block reads along with its Smart Scan is of little concern if the results are correct and the performance is not severely impacted, and in most cases it won't be. There are cases, though, where choosing to do a Smart Scan and then reverting to block shipping mode can be painful from a performance standpoint. These are the cases where it's important to understand what's going on under the covers. You'll find more information on this issue in Chapter 16.

Skipping Some Offloading

Another very complex behavior that we will only mention briefly is the ability of cellsrv to refuse to do some of the normal offload processing. This can be done to avoid overloading the CPU resources on the storage cells for example. A good example of this behavior occurs when decompressing HCC data. Decompression is an extremely CPU intensive task, especially for the higher levels of compression. In later versions of the storage software (11.2.2.3.0 and later), cellsrv can choose to skip the decompression step on some portion of the data when the CPUs on the storage cells are very busy and the database host's CPU are not very busy. This effectively moves some of the workload back to the database tier by forcing the database hosts to do the decompression. In this case, some steps such as projection may still be done on the storage cells, despite the fact that the decompression step is skipped. As Kevin has already pointed out, this selective determination of which offload processing to do can make the boundaries between the tiers very fluid and difficult to monitor. Chapter 12 covers some techniques for monitoring this behavior.

How to Verify That Smart Scan is Happening

One of the most important things you can learn about Exadata is how to identify whether a query has been able to take advantage of Smart Scans. This is not as easy as it sounds. Unfortunately, the normal execution plan output produced by the DBMS_XPLAN package will not show you whether a Smart Scan was used or not. Here's an example:

```
PLAN_TABLE_OUTPUT
--------------------------------------------------------------------------------
SQL_ID  05cq2hb1r37tr, child number 0
-------------------------------------
select avg(pk_col) from kso.skew a where col1 > 0

Plan hash value: 568322376


--------------------------------------------------------------------------------
| Id  | Operation                   | Name | Rows  | Bytes | Cost (%CPU)| Time     |
--------------------------------------------------------------------------------
|   0 | SELECT STATEMENT            |      |       |       | 44486 (100)|          |
|   1 |  SORT AGGREGATE             |      |     1 |    11 |            |          |
|*  2 |   TABLE ACCESS STORAGE FULL| SKEW |   32M|  335M| 44486   (1)| 00:08:54 |
--------------------------------------------------------------------------------

Predicate Information (identified by operation id):
---------------------------------------------------
```

```
2 - storage("COL1">0)
    filter("COL1">0)
```

Notice that the optimizer chose a `TABLE ACCESS STORAGE FULL` operation and that the predicate section shows a `storage()` predicate associated with step 2 of the plan. Both of these characteristics indicate that a Smart Scan was possible, but neither provides a definitive verification. In fact, the statement in this listing was *not* executed with a Smart Scan.

▨ **Note:** An interesting feature of the plan output is worth mentioning. Notice that in the predicate section there is a `storage()` clause and there is a matching `filter()` clause that both perform the same comparison. We scratched our heads about this for a while, wondering whether these clauses represented separate parts of the plan or whether it was just a quirk of the XPLAN output. There is actually a very simple explanation for this behavior. The cells have to fall back to regular block I/O in a number of cases. When a Smart Scan hits a chained row, for example, that block must be returned in its entirety to the DB layer. Since there is no such thing as a guaranteed "pure" Smart Scan, a filter operation must be included in the plan in addition to the filtering provided by the storage cells (represented by the `storage()` clause). So the two predicates actually represent two distinct operations. Keep in mind, though, that they will not overlap. The `filter()` operation will be done on rows returned via the block shipping mode, while the `storage()` operation will be performed on the storage cells for the rows that can be returned directly to the PGA via the normal Smart Scan mechanism.

The fact that execution plans do not show whether a Smart Scan was performed is a bit frustrating. However, there are several techniques that we can use to work around this issue. We'll cover a few options in the next several sections.

10046 Trace

One of the most straightforward ways to determine whether a Smart Scan was used is to enable a 10046 trace on the statement in question. Unfortunately, this is a bit cumbersome and doesn't allow you to do any investigation into what has happened with past executions. Nevertheless, tracing is a fairly foolproof way to verify whether a Smart Scan was used or not. If Smart Scan was used, there will be `CELL SMART TABLE SCAN` or `CELL SMART INDEX SCAN` events in the trace file. Here is an excerpt from the trace file collected for the previous statement:

```
PARSING IN CURSOR #47387827351064 len=49 dep=0 uid=0 oct=3 lid=0 tim=1297219338278533
 hv=3279003447 ad='2c8743808' sqlid='05cq2hb1r37tr'
select avg(pk_col) from kso.skew a where col1 > 0
END OF STMT
PARSE #47387827351064:c=57991,e=78256,p=25,cr=199,cu=0,mis=1,r=0,dep=0,
og=1,plh=568322376,tim=12
EXEC #47387827351064:c=0,e=14,p=0,cr=0,cu=0,mis=0,r=0,dep=0,og=1,plh=568322376,tim=1297
WAIT #47387827351064: nam='SQL*Net message to client' ela= 2 . . .
WAIT #47387827351064: nam='cell single block physical read' ela= 487 . . .
WAIT #47387827351064: nam='cell multiblock physical read' ela= 25262 . . .
```

```
*** 2011-02-08 20:42:19.106
WAIT #47387827351064: nam='cell multiblock physical read' ela= 20303 . . .
WAIT #47387827351064: nam='gc cr multi block request' ela= 493 . . .
WAIT #47387827351064: nam='gc cr multi block request' ela= 271 . . .
WAIT #47387827351064: nam='cell multiblock physical read' ela= 2550 . . .

*** 2011-02-08 20:42:20.107
WAIT #47387827351064: nam='cell multiblock physical read' ela= 3095 . . .
WAIT #47387827351064: nam='gc cr multi block request' ela= 548 . . .
WAIT #47387827351064: nam='gc cr multi block request' ela= 331 . . .
WAIT #47387827351064: nam='cell multiblock physical read' ela= 22930 . . .
```

Notice that there are no Smart Scan wait events in the trace file output. For comparison, here is a brief excerpt from a statement using Smart Scan:

```
PARSING IN CURSOR #2 len=32 dep=0 uid=0 oct=3 lid=0 hv=123 ad='196' sqlid='162wjnvwyybhn'
select sum(pk_col) from kso.skew
END OF STMT
PARSE #2:c=2000,e=2424,p=0,cr=0,cu=0,mis=1,r=0,dep=0,og=1,plh=568322376
EXEC #2:c=0,e=34,p=0,cr=0,cu=0,mis=0,r=0,dep=0,og=1,plh=568322376
WAIT #2: nam='SQL*Net message to client' ela= 3 driver id=1650815232 #bytes=1 p3=0 obj#=-1
WAIT #2: nam='ges message buffer allocation' ela= 2 pool=0 request=1 allocated=0 obj#=-1
WAIT #2: nam='KJC: Wait for msg sends to complete' ela= 10 msg=6674450368 dest|rcvr=65536
WAIT #2: nam='reliable message' ela= 1107 channel context=6712270872 channel handle=66967991
WAIT #2: nam='ges message buffer allocation' ela= 1 pool=0 request=1 allocated=0 obj#=-1
WAIT #2: nam='enq: KO - fast object checkpoint' ela= 104 name|mode=126 2=65575 0=1 obj#=-1
WAIT #2: nam='ges message buffer allocation' ela= 1 pool=0 request=1 allocated=0 obj#=-1
WAIT #2: nam='enq: KO - fast object checkpoint' ela= 103 name|mode=126 2=65575 0=2 obj#=-1
WAIT #2: nam='cell smart table scan' ela= 162 cellhash#=2133459483 p2=0 p3=0 obj#=66849
WAIT #2: nam='cell smart table scan' ela= 244 cellhash#=379339958 p2=0 p3=0 obj#=66849
WAIT #2: nam='cell smart table scan' ela= 181 cellhash#=3176594409 p2=0 p3=0 obj#=66849
WAIT #2: nam='cell smart table scan' ela= 1285 cellhash#=2133459483 p2=0 p3=0 obj#=66849
WAIT #2: nam='cell smart table scan' ela= 1327 cellhash#=379339958 p2=0 p3=0 obj#=66849
WAIT #2: nam='cell smart table scan' ela= 1310 cellhash#=3176594409 p2=0 p3=0 obj#=66849
WAIT #2: nam='cell smart table scan' ela= 19755 cellhash#=3176594409 p2=0 p3=0 obj#=66849
WAIT #2: nam='cell smart table scan' ela= 39 cellhash#=3176594409 p2=0 p3=0 obj#=66849
```

As you can see, this trace file contains several CELL SMART TABLE SCAN wait events. There is no doubt that this statement was offloaded. We cover Exadata-specific and -related wait events in detail in Chapter 10.

Performance Statistics (v$sessstat)

Of course, we can also look at some of the performance views such as V$SESSSTAT and V$ACTIVE_SESSION_HISTORY. Tanel Poder's Snapper script provides a great way to see what wait events are being generated while a statement is running; but again, you must catch it in the act to verify what's happening. Active Session History (ASH) is good as well, but since the data is sampled, there is no guarantee that it will catch the wait event you are looking for. Nevertheless, performance statistics provide a reliable source of data as long as you can access the system during the execution of the statement you are investigating. Here's an example using V$MYSTATS, which is simply a version of V$SESSSTAT that limits data to your current session. For this example we'll look at the cell scans statistic, which is incremented when a Smart Table Scan occurs:

```
SYS@dbm1> set echo on
SYS@dbm1> @mystats
SYS@dbm1> select name, value
  2   from v$mystat s, v$statname n
  3   where n.statistic# = s.statistic#
  4   and name like nvl('%&name%',name)
  5   order by 1
  6   /
Enter value for name: cell scans

NAME                                                                   VALUE
---------------------------------------------------------------- ---------------
cell scans                                                               833

1 row selected.

SYS@dbm1> set echo off
SYS@dbm1> select avg(pk_col) from kso.skew2 a where col1 > 0;

AVG(PK_COL)
-----------
 16093748.8

1 row selected.

SYS@dbm1> @mystats
Enter value for name: cell scan

NAME                                                                   VALUE
---------------------------------------------------------------- ---------------
cell scans                                                               834

1 row selected.

SYS@dbm1> alter session set cell_offload_processing=false;

Session altered.

SYS@dbm1> select avg(pk_col) from kso.skew2 a where col1 > 0;

AVG(PK_COL)
-----------
 16093748.8

1 row selected.

SYS@dbm1> @mystats
Enter value for name: cell scans
```

```
NAME                                                                     VALUE
------------------------------------------------------------------- ---------------
cell scans                                                                 834
```

1 row selected.

So as you can see, the first time the statement was executed it was offloaded, and the `cell scans` statistic was incremented from 833 to 834. We then turned off Smart Scans and ran the statement again. This time the statistic was not incremented. So this approach works well as long as we can catch the statements of interest in action. Note that Oracle performance statistics are complementary to the Oracle wait event interface and provide information that is just not available elsewhere. We cover the Exadata-related statistics in detail in Chapter 11.

Offload Eligible Bytes

There is another clue to whether a statement used a Smart Scan or not. As we've already mentioned, the `V$SQL` family of views contain a column called `IO_CELL_OFFLOAD_ELIGIBLE_BYTES`, which shows the number of bytes that are eligible for Offloading. This column can be used as an indicator of whether a statement used a Smart Scan. It appears that this column is set to a value greater than 0 only when a Smart Scan is used. We can make use of this observation to write a little script (`fsx.sql`) that returns a value of YES or NO depending on whether that column in `V$SQL` has a value greater than 0. The output of the script is a little too wide to fit in a book format, so we've used a couple of cut-down versions in our examples. And of course, all of the versions will be available in the online code repository. You've already seen the script in action in several of the previous sections. Here's what's inside the script and an example of its use:

```
SYS@SANDBOX1> !cat fsx.sql
----------------------------------------------------------------------------------------
--
-- File name:    fsx.sql
--
-- Purpose:      Find SQL and report whether it was Offloaded and % of I/O saved.
--
-- Usage:        This scripts prompts for two values.
--
--               sql_text: a piece of a SQL statement like %select col1, col2 from skew%
--
--               sql_id: the sql_id of the statement if you know it (leave blank to ignore)
--
-- Description:
--
--               This script can be used to locate statements in the shared pool and
--               determine whether they have been executed via Smart Scans.
--
--               It is based on the observation that the IO_CELL_OFFLOAD_ELIGIBLE_BYTES
--               column in V$SQL is only greater than 0 when a statement is executed
--               using a Smart Scan. The IO_SAVED_% column attempts to show the ratio of
--               of data received from the storage cells to the actual amount of data
--               that would have had to be retrieved on non-Exadata storage. Note that
--               as of 11.2.0.2, there are issues calculating this value with some queries.
--
--               Note that the AVG_ETIME will not be acurate for parallel queries. The
```

```
--              ELAPSED_TIME column contains the sum of all parallel slaves. So the
--              script divides the value by the number of PX slaves used which gives an
--              approximation.
--
--              Note also that if parallel slaves are spread across multiple nodes on
--              a RAC database the PX_SERVERS_EXECUTIONS column will not be set.
--
--------------------------------------------------------------------------------
set pagesize 999
set lines 190
col sql_text format a70 trunc
col child format 99999
col execs format 9,999
col avg_etime format 99,999.99
col "IO_SAVED_%" format 999.99
col avg_px format 999
col offload for a7

select sql_id, child_number child, plan_hash_value plan_hash, executions execs,
(elapsed_time/1000000)/decode(nvl(executions,0),0,1,executions)/
decode(px_servers_executions,0,1,px_servers_executions/
decode(nvl(executions,0),0,1,executions)) avg_etime,
px_servers_executions/decode(nvl(executions,0),0,1,executions) avg_px,
decode(IO_CELL_OFFLOAD_ELIGIBLE_BYTES,0,'No','Yes') Offload,
decode(IO_CELL_OFFLOAD_ELIGIBLE_BYTES,0,0,
100*(IO_CELL_OFFLOAD_ELIGIBLE_BYTES-IO_INTERCONNECT_BYTES)
/decode(IO_CELL_OFFLOAD_ELIGIBLE_BYTES,0,1,IO_CELL_OFFLOAD_ELIGIBLE_BYTES)) "IO_SAVED_%",
sql_text
from v$sql s
where upper(sql_text) like upper(nvl('&sql_text',sql_text))
and sql_text not like 'BEGIN :sql_text := %'
and sql_text not like '%IO_CELL_OFFLOAD_ELIGIBLE_BYTES%'
and sql_id like nvl('&sql_id',sql_id)
order by 1, 2, 3
/

SYS@SANDBOX1> select avg(pk_col) from kso.skew3 where col1 < 0;

AVG(PK_COL)
-----------
  1849142.5

Elapsed: 00:00:00.07
SYS@SANDBOX1> alter session set cell_offload_processing=false;

Session altered.

Elapsed: 00:00:00.00
SYS@SANDBOX1> select avg(pk_col) from kso.skew3 where col1 < 0;
```

```
AVG(PK_COL)
-----------
  1849142.5

Elapsed: 00:00:49.68
SYS@SANDBOX1> @fsx4
Enter value for sql_text: select avg(pk_col) from kso.skew3 where col1 < 0
Enter value for sql_id:

SQL_ID         CHILD OFFLOAD IO_SAVED_%  AVG_ETIME SQL_TEXT
------------- ------ ------- ---------- ---------- --------------------------------
a6j7wgqf84jvg      0 Yes         100.00        .07 select avg(pk_col) from kso.skew3
a6j7wgqf84jvg      1 No            .00       49.68 select avg(pk_col) from kso.skew3

Elapsed: 00:00:00.04
```

In the fsx script you can see that the OFFLOAD column is just a DECODE that checks to see if the IO_CELL_OFFLOAD_ELIGIBLE_BYTES column is equal to 0 or not. The IO_SAVED_% column is calculated using the IO_INTERCONNECT_BYTES field, and it attempts to show how much data was returned to the database servers. The example shows the same statement run once with Smart Scan enabled and once with Smart Scan disabled. We used the CELL_OFFLOAD_PROCESSING parameter to turn Smart Scans on and off for this purpose. Changing this parameter caused the original cursor to be invalidated because of an optimizer mismatch. This resulted in two child cursors for the statement. In our example, the output of the script shows that one version of the statement was offloaded using Smart Scans and took less than a second. The second execution of the statement though was not Offloaded and took almost a minute.

The technique used by the fsx script seems to work pretty well most of the time. However, in situations where a single child cursor is used repeatedly, it is possible that some executions may be executed using Smart Scans while others are not. While this is an unusual situation, it can cause confusion because the IO_CELL_OFFLOAD_ELIGIBLE_BYTES column contains a cumulative value for all executions. That is to say that each execution adds its eligible bytes count to the running total. When some executions use Smart Scans and some don't, the IO_CELL_OFFLOAD_ELIGIBLE_BYTES column will be greater than 0. This is a fairly rare occurrence and you may never run into it. Nevertheless, here is an example:

```
SYS@SANDBOX1> alter session set "_serial_direct_read"=true;

Session altered.

Elapsed: 00:00:00.01
SYS@SANDBOX1> -- execution 1
SYS@SANDBOX1> select avg(pk_col) from kso.skew a where col1 > 0;

AVG(PK_COL)
-----------
 16093748.8

1 row selected.

Elapsed: 00:00:03.51
SYS@SANDBOX1> @fsx3
Enter value for sql_text: %skew%
Enter value for sql_id:
```

```
SQL_ID        CHILD OFFLOAD EXECS ELIGIBLE_BYTES SQL_TEXT
------------- ------ ------- ----- -------------- --------------------
05cq2hb1r37tr      0 Yes        1       38797312 select avg(pk_col) f

1 row selected.

Elapsed: 00:00:00.01
SYS@SANDBOX1> alter session set "_serial_direct_read"=false;

Session altered.

Elapsed: 00:00:00.00
SYS@SANDBOX1> -- execution 2
SYS@SANDBOX1> select avg(pk_col) from kso.skew a where col1 > 0;

AVG(PK_COL)
-----------
 16093748.8

1 row selected.
```

Elapsed: 00:00:04.71
```
SYS@SANDBOX1> @fsx3
Enter value for sql_text: %skew%
Enter value for sql_id:

SQL_ID        CHILD OFFLOAD EXECS ELIGIBLE_BYTES SQL_TEXT
------------- ------ ------- ----- -------------- --------------------
05cq2hb1r37tr      0 Yes        2       38797312 select avg(pk_col) f

1 row selected.

Elapsed: 00:00:00.01
SYS@SANDBOX1>
SYS@SANDBOX1> alter session set "_serial_direct_read"=true;

Session altered.

Elapsed: 00:00:00.01
SYS@SANDBOX1> -- execution 3
SYS@SANDBOX1> select avg(pk_col) from kso.skew a where col1 > 0;

AVG(PK_COL)
-----------
 16093748.8

1 row selected.
```

Elapsed: 00:00:03.54
```
SYS@SANDBOX1> @fsx3
Enter value for sql_text: %skew%
Enter value for sql_id:
```

```
SQL_ID          CHILD OFFLOAD EXECS ELIGIBLE_BYTES SQL_TEXT
------------- ------ ------- ----- -------------- --------------------
05cq2hb1r37tr     0 Yes         3       58195968 select avg(pk_col) f

1 row selected.

Elapsed: 00:00:00.01
```

In this example we used the _SERIAL_DIRECT_READ parameter to disable Smart Scans. This parameter does not invalidate cursors, so the same cursor was used for all three executions of the statement. If you look at the second execution, you can probably guess that it didn't use a Smart Scan, as it was slower than the previous execution. You can verify that assumption by noting that the Eligible Byte Count did not increase. However, the fsx script simply checks to see if the value of the IO_CELL_OFFLOAD_ELIGIBLE_BYTES column is greater than 0. As you can see, the value of the column remained the same between executions causing the fsx script to report that the statement was offloaded, even though the second execution was not offloaded. So keep in mind that our indicator is a cumulative value for all the executions of this cursor. Note that in the previous example we set up a rather unusual situation where a single cursor is offloaded on one execution and not on another. This rarely happens in real life.

The technique demonstrated by the fsx script provides a very useful alternative to tracing or using session statistics to verify whether Smart Scans are being performed. The biggest advantage is that you don't have to try to catch Smart Scan in real time. The IO_CELL_OFFLOAD_ELIGIBLE_BYTES column is stored in V$SQL and related views, which means it's also captured by AWR. This provides us with a historical view into how statements have been processed in the past. It is one of the main tools that we use for a quick-and-dirty verification of whether a Smart Scan has been used or not.

SQL Monitoring

There is one other tool that is very useful for determining whether a SQL statement was Offloaded. The REPORT_SQL_MONITOR procedure is part of the new Real Time SQL Monitoring functionality that was added with 11g. It is built into the DBMS_SQLTUNE package and provides a great deal of information, not only on whether a statement was offloaded, but also on which steps in a plan were offloaded. Here's an example (first of a statement that was not offloaded and then of the same statement when it was offloaded):

```
SYS@SANDBOX1> alter session set cell_offload_processing=false;

Session altered.

SYS@SANDBOX1> set echo off
SYS@SANDBOX1> @avgskew3

AVG(PK_COL)
-----------
 16093750.2

SYS@SANDBOX1> @fsx4
Enter value for sql_text: %skew3%
Enter value for sql_id:
```

```
SQL_ID          CHILD OFFLOAD IO_SAVED_%  AVG_ETIME SQL_TEXT
------------- ------ ------- ---------- ---------- ----------------------------------------
6uutdmqr72smc     0 No             .00      57.95 select /* avgskew3.sql */ avg(pk_col) fr

SYS@SANDBOX1> @report_sql_monitor
Enter value for sid:
Enter value for sql_id: 6uutdmqr72smc
Enter value for sql_exec_id:

REPORT
-------------------------------------------------------------------------------------
SQL Monitoring Report

SQL Text
------------------------------
select /* avgskew3.sql */ avg(pk_col) from kso.skew3 a where col1 > 0

Global Information
------------------------------
 Status              :  DONE (ALL ROWS)
 Instance ID         :  1
 Session             :  SYS (3:5465)
 SQL ID              :  6uutdmqr72smc
 SQL Execution ID    :  16777216
 Execution Started   :  03/15/2011 15:26:11
 First Refresh Time  :  03/15/2011 15:26:19
 Last Refresh Time   :  03/15/2011 15:27:09
 Duration            :  58s
 Module/Action       :  sqlplus@enkdb01.enkitec.com (TNS V1-V3)/-
 Service             :  SYS$USERS
 Program             :  sqlplus@enkdb01.enkitec.com (TNS V1-V3)
 Fetch Calls         :  1

Global Stats
===================================================================================================
| Elapsed | Cpu    | IO       | Application | Cluster  | Fetch | Buffer | Read  | Read  |
| Time(s) | Time(s)| Waits(s) | Waits(s)    | Waits(s) | Calls | Gets   | Reqs  | Bytes |
===================================================================================================
|      58 |     35 |       23 |        0.00 |     0.00 |     1 |     2M | 15322 |  15GB |
===================================================================================================
```

```
SQL Plan Monitoring Details (Plan Hash Value=2684249835)
===========================================================================================
| Id  |          Operation          |  Name  | ... | Activity |     Activity Detail       |
|     |                             |        |     |   (%)    |      (# samples)          |
===========================================================================================
|  0  |  SELECT STATEMENT           |        |     |          |                           |
|  1  |    SORT AGGREGATE           |        |     |   41.38  |  Cpu (24)                 |
|  2  |      TABLE ACCESS STORAGE FULL | SKEW3 |  |   58.62  |  Cpu (11)                 |
|     |                             |        |     |          |  direct path read (23)    |
===========================================================================================
```

SYS@SANDBOX1> @ss_on
SYS@SANDBOX1> alter session set cell_offload_processing=true;

Session altered.

SYS@SANDBOX1> @avgskew3

AVG(PK_COL)

 16093750.2

SYS@SANDBOX1> @fsx4
Enter value for sql_text: %skew3%
Enter value for sql_id:

```
SQL_ID          CHILD OFFLOAD IO_SAVED_%  AVG_ETIME SQL_TEXT
------------- ------ ------- ---------- ---------- ----------------------------------------
6uutdmqr72smc      0 Yes          71.85      34.54 select /* avgskew3.sql */ avg(pk_col) fr
```

SYS@SANDBOX1> @report_sql_monitor
Enter value for sid:
Enter value for sql_id: 6uutdmqr72smc
Enter value for sql_exec_id:

REPORT

SQL Monitoring Report

SQL Text
----
select /* avgskew3.sql */ avg(pk_col) from kso.skew3 a where col1 > 0

Global Information

 Status   : DONE (ALL ROWS)
 Instance ID   : 1
 Session   : SYS (3:5467)
 SQL ID   : 6uutdmqr72smc
 SQL Execution ID : 16777219
 Execution Started : 03/15/2011 15:36:11

```
First Refresh Time  :  03/15/2011 15:36:15
Last Refresh Time   :  03/15/2011 15:36:45
Duration            :  34s
Module/Action       :  sqlplus@enkdb01.enkitec.com (TNS V1-V3)/-
Service             :  SYS$USERS
Program             :  sqlplus@enkdb01.enkitec.com (TNS V1-V3)
Fetch Calls         :  1
```

Global Stats

```
=====================================================================================
| Elapsed | Cpu     | IO       | Application | Fetch | Buffer | Read  | Read  | Cell    |
| Time(s) | Time(s) | Waits(s) | Waits(s)    | Calls | Gets   | Reqs  | Bytes | Offload |
=====================================================================================
|      35 |      31 |     3.85 |        0.00 |     1 |     2M | 18422 |  15GB | 71.83%  |
=====================================================================================
```

SQL Plan Monitoring Details (Plan Hash Value=2684249835)

```
==========================================================================================
| Id |          Operation        | Name  | | Cell    | Activity |   Activity Detail   |
|    |                           |       | | Offload | (%)      |     (# samples)     |
==========================================================================================
|  0 | SELECT STATEMENT          |       | |         |          |                     |
|  1 |   SORT AGGREGATE          |       | |         |    50.00 | Cpu (17)            |
|  2 |    TABLE ACCESS STORAGE FULL | SKEW3 | |  71.83% |    50.00 | Cpu (12)            |
|    |                           |       | |         |          | cell smart tab... (5) |
==========================================================================================
```

Note that we cut out a number of columns from the report because it is very wide and doesn't fit nicely in book format. Nevertheless, you can see that the report shows which steps were Offloaded (Cell Offload), where the statement spent its time (Activity %), and what it spent time doing (Activity Detail). This can be extremely useful with more complex statements that have multiple steps eligible for offloading. Also note that monitoring occurs automatically on parallelized statements and on statements that the optimizer anticipates will run for a long time. If Oracle is not automatically choosing to monitor a statement that is of interest, you can use the MONITOR hint to tell Oracle to monitor the statement.

Parameters

There are several parameters that apply to Offloading. The main one is CELL_OFFLOAD_PROCESSING, which turns Offloading on and off. There are several others that are of less importance. Table 2-2 shows a list of the non-hidden parameters that affect Offloading (as of Oracle database version 11.2.0.2). Note that we have also included the hidden parameter, _SERIAL_DIRECT_READ, which controls this very important feature.

Table 2-2. Database Parameters Controlling Offloading

Parameter	Default	Description
cell_offload_compaction	ADAPTIVE	This parameter is reserved for future use. The online description says, "Cell packet compaction strategy."

Parameter	Default	Description
cell_offload_decryption	TRUE	Controls whether decryption is offloaded. Note that when this parameter is set to FALSE, Smart Scans are completely disabled on encrypted data.
cell_offload_parameters		This parameter is reserved for future use.
cell_offload_plan_display	AUTO	Controls whether Exadata operation names are used in execution plan output from XPLAN. AUTO means to display them only if the database is using Exadata storage.
cell_offload_processing	TRUE	Turns Offloading on or off.
_serial_direct_read	AUTO	Controls the serial direct path read mechanism. The valid values are AUTO, TRUE, FALSE, ALWAYS and NEVER.

In addition to the normal Oracle-approved parameters, there are a number of so-called hidden parameters that affect various aspects of Offloading. The following listing shows all the cell parameters, including the hidden parameters, along with their descriptions:

```
SYS@POC1> @parmsd
Enter value for parameter: cell
Enter value for isset:
Enter value for show_hidden: Y

NAME                                          DESCRIPTION
-------------------------------------------   ---------------------------------------------
cell_offload_compaction                       Cell packet compaction strategy
cell_offload_decryption                       enable SQL processing offload of encrypted
                                              data to cells

cell_offload_parameters                       Additional cell offload parameters
cell_offload_plan_display                     Cell offload explain plan display
cell_offload_processing                       enable SQL processing offload to cells
_allow_cell_smart_scan_attr                   Allow checking smart_scan_capable Attr
_cell_fast_file_create                        Allow optimized file creation path for Cells
_cell_fast_file_restore                       Allow optimized rman restore for Cells
_cell_file_format_chunk_size                  Cell file format chunk size in MB
_cell_index_scan_enabled                      enable CELL processing of index FFS
_cell_offload_capabilities_enabled            specifies capability table to load
_cell_offload_hybridcolumnar                  Query offloading of hybrid columnar
                                              compressed tables to exadata

_cell_offload_predicate_reordering_enabled    enable out-of-order SQL processing offload to
                                              cells

_cell_offload_timezone                        enable timezone related SQL processing
                                              offload to cells
```

_cell_offload_virtual_columns	enable offload of predicates on virtual columns to cells
_cell_range_scan_enabled	enable CELL processing of index range scans
_cell_storidx_mode	Cell Storage Index mode
_db_check_cell_hints	
_disable_cell_optimized_backups	disable cell optimized backups
_kcfis_cell_passthru_enabled	Do not perform smart IO filtering on the cell
_kcfis_kept_in_cellfc_enabled	Enable usage of cellsrv flash cache for kept objects
_kcfis_nonkept_in_cellfc_enabled	Enable use of cellsrv flash cache for non-kept objects

22 rows selected.

We've used a few of these parameters in the examples in this chapter and we'll use several in the upcoming chapters. There are several other kcfis (kernel file intelligent storage) parameters as well. Here's a listing of them with descriptions:

```
SYS@SMITHERS> @parmsd
Enter value for parameter: kcfis
Enter value for isset:
Enter value for show_hidden: Y
```

NAME	DESCRIPTION
_kcfis_block_dump_level	Smart IO block dump level
_kcfis_caching_enabled	enable kcfis intra-scan session caching
_kcfis_cell_passthru_enabled	Do not perform smart IO filtering on the cell
_kcfis_control1	Kcfis control1
_kcfis_control2	Kcfis control2
_kcfis_control3	Kcfis control3
_kcfis_control4	Kcfis control4
_kcfis_control5	Kcfis control5
_kcfis_control6	Kcfis control6
_kcfis_disable_platform_decryption	Don't use platform-specific decryption on the storage cell
_kcfis_dump_corrupt_block	Dump any corrupt blocks found during smart IO
_kcfis_fast_response_enabled	Enable smart scan optimization for fast response (first rows)
_kcfis_fast_response_initiosize	Fast response - The size of the first IO in logical blocks
_kcfis_fast_response_iosizemult	Fast response - (next IO size = current IO size * this parameter)
_kcfis_fast_response_threshold	Fast response - the number of IOs after which smartIO is used

```
_kcfis_fault_control                    Fault Injection Control
_kcfis_io_prefetch_size                 Smart IO prefetch size for a cell
_kcfis_ioreqs_throttle_enabled          Enable Smart IO requests throttling
_kcfis_kept_in_cellfc_enabled           Enable usage of cellsrv flash cache for kept
                                        objects

_kcfis_large_payload_enabled            enable large payload to be passed to cellsrv
_kcfis_max_cached_sessions              Sets the maximum number of kcfis sessions cached
_kcfis_max_out_translations             Sets the maximum number of outstanding
                                        translations in kcfis

_kcfis_nonkept_in_cellfc_enabled        Enable use of cellsrv flash cache for non-kept
                                        objects

_kcfis_oss_io_size                      KCFIS OSS I/O size
_kcfis_rdbms_blockio_enabled            Use block IO instead of smart IO in the smart IO
                                        module on RDBMS

_kcfis_read_buffer_limit                KCFIS Read Buffer (per session) memory limit in
                                        bytes

_kcfis_spawn_debugger                   Decides whether to spawn the debugger at kcfis
                                        initialize

_kcfis_stats_level                      sets kcfis stats level
_kcfis_storageidx_diag_mode             Debug mode for storage index on the cell
_kcfis_storageidx_disabled              Don't use storage index optimization on the
                                        storage cell

_kcfis_test_control1                    kcfis tst control1
_kcfis_trace_bucket_size                KCFIS tracing bucket size in bytes
_kcfis_trace_level                      sets kcfis tracing level
_kcfis_work_set_appliances              Working Set of appliances in a KCFIS session

34 rows selected.
```

Note that hidden parameters should not be used on production systems without prior discussion with Oracle support. But they do provide valuable clues about how some of the Exadata features work and are controlled.

Summary

Offloading really is the secret sauce of Exadata. While the hardware architecture does a good job of providing more balance between the storage layer's ability to deliver data and the database layer's ability to consume it, the bulk of the performance gains are provided by the software. Smart Scans are largely responsible for these gains. The primary focus of most of these optimizations is to reduce the amount of data transferred between the storage tier and the database tier.

## CHAPTER 3

Hybrid Columnar Compression

Hybrid Columnar Compression (HCC) is probably one of the least understood of the features that are unique to Exadata. The feature was originally rolled out in a beta version of 11gR2 and was enabled on both Exadata and non-Exadata platforms. The production release of 11gR2 restricted the feature to Exadata platforms only. Ostensibly this decision was made because the additional processing power available on the Exadata storage servers. Because the feature is restricted to Exadata, the recent documentation refers to it as Exadata Hybrid Columnar Compression (EHCC).

This chapter will first present basic information on both of Oracle's older row-major format compression methods (BASIC and OLTP). We will then explore in detail the mechanics of Oracle's new HCC feature—how it works, including how the data is actually stored on disk, where and when the compression and decompression occur, and when its use is appropriate. Finally we'll provide some real world examples of HCC usage.

Oracle Storage Review

As you probably already know, Oracle stores data in a block structure. These blocks are typically 8K and from a simplistic point of view they consist of a block header, a row directory, row data and free space. The block header starts at the top of a block and works its way down, while the row data starts at the bottom and works its way up. The free space generally sits in the middle. Figure 3-1 shows a representation of a traditional Oracle block format.

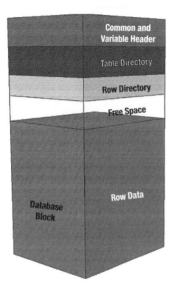

Figure 3-1. The standard Oracle block format (row-major storage)

Rows are stored in no specific order, but columns are generally stored in the order in which they were defined in the table. For each row in a block there will be a row header, followed by the column data for each column. Figure 3.2 shows how the pieces of a row are stored in a standard Oracle block. Note that we called it a *row piece*, because occasionally a row's data may be stored in more than one chunk. In this case, there will be a pointer to the next piece.

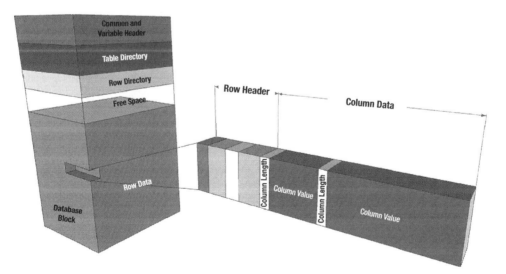

Figure 3-2. The standard Oracle row format (row-major storage)

Note that the row header may contain a pointer to another row piece. We'll come back to this a little later, but for now, just be aware that there is a mechanism to point to another location. Also note that each column is preceded by a separate field indicating the length of the column. Nothing is actually stored in the Column Value field for nulls. The presence of a null column is indicated by a value of 0 in the column length field. Trailing nulls don't even store the column length fields, as the presence of a new row header indicates that there are no more columns with values in the current row.

PCTFREE is a key value associated with blocks; it controls how space is used in a block. Its purpose is to reserve some free space in each block for updates. This is necessary to prevent row migration (moving rows to new blocks) that would be caused by lack of space in the row's original block when a row increases in size. When rows are expected to be updated (with values that require more space), more space is generally reserved. When rows are not expected to increase in size because of updates, values as low as 0 may be specified for PCTFREE. With compressed blocks it is common to use very low values of PCTFREE, because the goal is to minimize space usage and the rows are generally not expected to be updated frequently (if ever). Figure 3-3 shows how free space is reserved based on the value of PCTFREE.

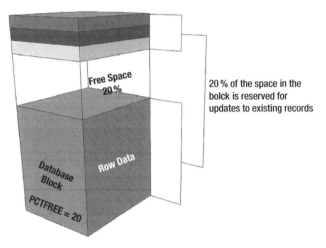

Figure 3-3. *Block free space controlled by PCTFREE*

Figure 3-3 shows a block that reserves 20 percent of its space for updates. A block with a PCTFREE setting of 0 percent would allow inserts to fill the block almost completely. When a record is updated, and the new data will not fit in the available free space of the block where the record is stored, the database will move the row to a new block. This process is called *row migration*. It does not completely remove the row from the original block but leaves a reference to the newly relocated row so that it can still be found by its original rowid (which basically consists of a file number, block number, and row number within the block). This ability of Oracle to relocate rows will become relevant when we discuss what happens if you update a row that has been compressed. Note that the more generic term for storing rows in more than one piece is *row chaining*. Row migration is a special case of row chaining in which the entire row is relocated. Figure 3-4 shows what a block with a migrated row might look like.

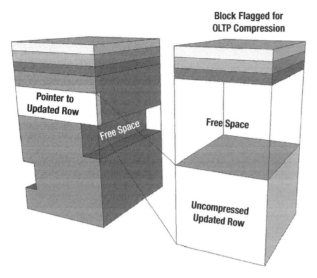

Figure 3-4. *Row migration*

This diagram represents a situation where the entire row has been relocated, leaving behind only a pointer to the new location.

Oracle Compression Mechanisms

Oracle provides several compression mechanisms in addition to HCC. The naming is somewhat confusing due to the common marketing terms and some changes in nomenclature along the way. Here we'll refer to the three main flavors of compression used by Oracle as BASIC, OLTP, and HCC.

BASIC

This compression method is a base feature of Oracle Database 11g Enterprise Edition. It compresses data only on direct path loads. Modifications force the data to be stored in an uncompressed format, as do inserts that do not use the direct path load mechanism. Rows are still stored together in the normal row-major form. The compression unit is a single Oracle block. BASIC is the default compression method, from a syntax standpoint. For example, BASIC compression will be used if you issue the following command:

```
CREATE TABLE … COMPRESS;
```

Basic compression was introduced in Oracle Database version 9i. This form of compression was also referred to as DSS Compression in the past. The syntax COMPRESS FOR DIRECT_LOAD OPERATIONS can still be used to enable BASIC compression, although this syntax has now been deprecated.

OLTP

The OLTP compression method allows data to be compressed for all operations, not just direct path loads. It is part of an extra-cost option called Advanced Compression and was introduced in Oracle

Database version 11g Release 1. The storage format is essentially the same as BASIC, using a symbol table to replace repeating values. OLTP compression attempts to allow for future updates by leaving 10 percent free space in each block via the PCTFREE setting (BASIC compression uses a PCTFREE value of 0 percent). Therefore, tables compressed for OLTP will occupy slightly more space than if they were compressed with BASIC (assuming direct path loads only and no updates). The syntax for enabling this type of compression is

```
CREATE TABLE …  COMPRESS FOR OLTP;
```

Alternatively, the syntax COMPRESS FOR ALL OPERATIONS may be used, although this syntax is now deprecated. OLTP compression is important because it is the fallback method for tables that use HCC compression. In other words, blocks will be stored using OLTP compression in cases where HCC cannot be used (non-direct path loads for example). One important characteristic of OLTP compression is that updates and non-direct path inserts are not compressed initially. Once a block becomes "full" it will be compressed. We'll revisit this issue in the performance section of this chapter.

HCC

HCC is only available for tables stored on Exadata storage. As with BASIC compression, data will only be compressed in HCC format when it is loaded using direct path loads. Conventional inserts and updates cause records to be stored in OLTP compressed format. In the case of updates, rows are migrated to new blocks. These blocks are marked for OLTP compression, so when one of these new blocks is sufficiently full, it will be compressed using the OLTP algorithm.

HCC provides four levels of compression, as shown in Table 3-1. Note that the expected compression ratios are very rough estimates and that the actual compression ratio will vary greatly depending on the data that is being compressed.

Table 3-1. *HCC Compression Types*

Compression Type	Description	Expected Compression Ratio
QUERY LOW	HCC level 1 uses the LZO compression algorithm. This level provides the lowest compression ratios but requires the least CPU for compression and decompression operations. This algorithm is optimized for maximizing speed rather than compression. Decompression is very fast with this algorithm. You may see some documents refer to this level as WAREHOUSE LOW.	4×
QUERY HIGH	HCC level 2 uses the ZLIB (gzip) compression algorithm. Some documents refer to this level as WAREHOUSE HIGH.	6×
ARCHIVE LOW	HCC level 3 uses the ZLIB (gzip) compression algorithm as well, but at a higher compression level than QUERY HIGH. Depending on the data, however, the compression ratios may not be much higher than with QUERY HIGH.	7×

Compression Type	Description	Expected Compression Ratio
ARCHIVE HIGH	HCC level 4 compression uses Bzip2 compression. This is the highest level of compression available but is far and away the most CPU-intensive. Compression times are often several times slower than for levels 2 and 3. But again, depending on the data, the compression ratio may not be that much higher than with ARCHIVE LOW. This level is for situations where the time to compress data is relatively unimportant or where space is in critically short supply.	12×

COMPRESSION ALGORITHMS

The references to the specific algorithms associated with HCC compression (LZO, ZLIB, or BZIP2) are all inferred from the function names used in the Oracle code. The ORADEBUG utility provides a direct interface into the Oracle call stack via the SHORT_STACK command. Operating system utilities such as pstack can also provide the same information. As an example, here is a part of the stack dump for a process doing ARCHIVE HIGH compression.

```
->kgccbzip2pseudodo()
 ->kgccbzip2do()
  ->BZ2_bzCompress()
   ->handle_compress()
    ->BZ2_compressBlock()
```

Tables may be compressed with HCC using the following syntax:

```
CREATE TABLE ... COMPRESS FOR QUERY LOW;
CREATE TABLE ... COMPRESS FOR QUERY HIGH;
CREATE TABLE ... COMPRESS FOR ARCHIVE LOW;
CREATE TABLE ... COMPRESS FOR ARCHIVE HIGH;
```

You may also change a table's compression attribute by using the ALTER TABLE statement. However, this command has no effect on existing records unless you actually rebuild the segment using the MOVE keyword. Without the MOVE keyword, the ALTER TABLE command merely notifies Oracle that future direct path inserts should be stored using HCC. By the way, you can see which form of compression a table is assigned, if any, using a query like this:

```
SYS@SANDBOX1> select owner, table_name, compress_for
  2  from dba_tables
  3  where compression = 'ENABLED'
  4  and compress_for like nvl('&format',compress_for)
  5* order by 1,2;

OWNER                          TABLE_NAME                     COMPRESS_FOR
------------------------------ ------------------------------ ------------
KSO                            SKEW2_BASIC                    BASIC
KSO                            SKEW2_HCC1                     QUERY LOW
```

KSO	SKEW2_HCC2	QUERY HIGH
KSO	SKEW2_HCC3	ARCHIVE LOW
KSO	SKEW2_HCC4	ARCHIVE HIGH
KSO	SKEW2_OLTP	OLTP

6 rows selected.

Of course, the current assignment may have nothing to do with the storage format in use for any or all of the blocks that store data for a given table. Here is a quick example:

```
SYS@SANDBOX1> !cat table_size2.sql
compute sum of totalsize_megs on report
break on report
col owner for a20
col segment_name for a30
col segment_type for a10
col totalsize_megs for 999,999.9
select s.owner, segment_name,
sum(bytes/1024/1024) as totalsize_megs, compress_for
from dba_segments s, dba_tables t
where s.owner = t.owner
and t.table_name = s.segment_name
and s.owner like nvl('&owner',s.owner)
and t.table_name like nvl('&table_name',segment_name)
group by s.owner, segment_name, compress_for
order by 3;

SYS@SANDBOX1> @table_size2
Enter value for owner: KSO
Enter value for table_name: SKEW


OWNER                SEGMENT_NAME                   TOTALSIZE_MEGS COMPRESS_FOR
-------------------- ------------------------------ -------------- ------------
KSO                  SKEW                                  1,460.3
                                                    --------------
sum                                                        1,460.3

1 row selected.

Elapsed: 00:00:00.31
SYS@SANDBOX1> alter table kso.skew compress for ARCHIVE HIGH;

Table altered.

Elapsed: 00:00:00.02
SYS@SANDBOX1> @table_size2
Enter value for owner: KSO
Enter value for table_name: SKEW


OWNER                SEGMENT_NAME                   TOTALSIZE_MEGS COMPRESS_FOR
-------------------- ------------------------------ -------------- ------------
KSO                  SKEW                                  1,460.3 ARCHIVE HIGH
                                                    --------------
```

71

```
sum                                                          1,460.3

1 row selected.

Elapsed: 00:00:00.02
SYS@SANDBOX1> -- It says ARCHIVE HIGH, but obviously the data has not been compressed.
SYS@SANDBOX1>
SYS@SANDBOX1> alter table kso.skew move compress for query low parallel 32;

Table altered.

Elapsed: 00:00:09.60
SYS@SANDBOX1> @table_size2
Enter value for owner: KSO
Enter value for table_name: SKEW

OWNER                SEGMENT_NAME                        TOTALSIZE_MEGS COMPRESS_FOR
-------------------- ----------------------------------- -------------- ------------
KSO                  SKEW                                         301.3 QUERY LOW
                                                         --------------
sum                                                              301.3

Elapsed: 00:00:00.02
```

You could probably guess that the first ALTER command (without the MOVE keyword) didn't really do anything to the existing data. It only took a few hundredths of a second, after all. And as you can see when we looked at the size of the table, it did not compress the existing data, even though the data dictionary now says the table is in ARCHIVE HIGH mode. When we added the MOVE keyword, the table was actually rebuilt with the new compression setting using direct path inserts and as you can see, the data has been compressed from the original 1,406MB to 301MB.

In this section we briefly described each of the three types of compression available in Oracle. Since this chapter is focused on HCC, we won't discuss the other methods further except as they relate to how HCC works.

HCC Mechanics

HCC works by storing data in a nontraditional format—nontraditional for Oracle, anyway. Data stored using HCC still resides in Oracle blocks, and each block still has a block header. But the data storage has been reorganized. In the first place, the blocks are combined into logical structures called *compression units*, or CUs. A CU consists of multiple Oracle blocks (usually adding up to 32K or 64K). Figure 3-5 shows a logical representation of how CUs are laid out.

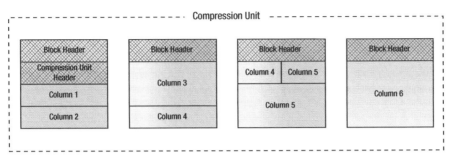

Figure 3-5. *Layout of an HCC Compression Unit*

Notice that the rows are no longer stored together. Instead the data is organized by column within the compression unit. This is not a true column oriented storage format but rather a cross between column oriented and row oriented. Remember that the sorting is done only within a single CU. The next CU will start over with Column 1 again. The advantage of this format is that it allows any row to be read in its entirety by reading a single CU. With a true column oriented storage format you would have to perform a separate read for each column. The disadvantage is that reading an individual record will require reading a multi-block CU instead of a single block. Of course full table scans will not suffer, because all the blocks will be read. We'll talk more about this trade-off a little later but you should already be thinking that this limitation could make HCC less attractive for tables that need to support lots of single row access.

The sorting by column is actually done to improve the effectiveness of the compression algorithms, not to get performance benefits of column oriented storage. This is where the name "Hybrid Columnar Compression" comes from and why Exadata has not been marketed as a column oriented database. The name is actually very descriptive of how the feature actually works.

HCC Performance

There are three areas of concern when discussing performance related to table compression. The first, *load performance*, is how long it takes to compress the data. Since compression only takes place on direct path loads, this is essentially a measurement of the impact of loading data. The second area of concern, *query performance*, is the impact of decompression and other side effects on queries against the compressed data. The third area of concern, *DML performance*, is the impact compression algorithms have on other DML activities such as Updates and Deletes.

Load Performance

As you might expect, load time tends to increase with the amount of compression applied. As the saying goes, "There is no such thing as a free puppy." When you compare costs in terms of increased load time with the benefit provided by increased compression ratio, the two Zlib-based options (QUERY LOW and ARCHIVE HIGH) appear to offer the best trade-off. Here's a listing showing the syntax for generating compressed versions of a 15G table along with timing information.

```
SYS@SANDBOX1> @hcc_build3
SYS@SANDBOX1> set timing on
SYS@SANDBOX1> set echo on
SYS@SANDBOX1> create table kso.skew3_none nologging parallel 8
```

```
  2  as select /*+ parallel (a 8) */ * from acolvin.skew3 a;

Table created.

Elapsed: 00:00:42.76
SYS@SANDBOX1> create table kso.skew3_basic nologging parallel 8 compress
  2  as select /*+ parallel (a 8) */ * from acolvin.skew3 a;

Table created.

Elapsed: 00:01:35.97
SYS@SANDBOX1> create table kso.skew3_oltp nologging parallel 8 compress for oltp
  2  as select /*+ parallel (a 8) */ * from acolvin.skew3 a;

Table created.

Elapsed: 00:01:24.58
SYS@SANDBOX1> create table kso.skew3_hcc1 nologging parallel 8 compress for query low
  2  as select /*+ parallel (a 8) */ * from acolvin.skew3 a;

Table created.

Elapsed: 00:00:56.57
SYS@SANDBOX1> create table kso.skew3_hcc2 nologging parallel 8 compress for query high
  2  as select /*+ parallel (a 8) */ * from acolvin.skew3 a;

Table created.

Elapsed: 00:01:56.49
SYS@SANDBOX1> create table kso.skew3_hcc3 nologging parallel 8 compress for archive low
  2  as select /*+ parallel (a 8) */ * from acolvin.skew3 a;

Table created.

Elapsed: 00:01:53.43
SYS@SANDBOX1> create table kso.skew3_hcc4 nologging parallel 8 compress for archive high
  2  as select /*+ parallel (a 8) */ * from acolvin.skew3 a;

Table created.

Elapsed: 00:08:55.58
SYS@SANDBOX1> set timing off
SYS@SANDBOX1> set echo off
SYS@SANDBOX1> @table_size2
Enter value for owner:
Enter value for table_name: SKEW3
Enter value for type:

OWNER              SEGMENT_NAME                 TYPE               TOTALSIZE_MEGS
------------------ ---------------------------- ------------------ --------------
ACOLVIN            SKEW3                        TABLE                    15,347.5
                                                                  --------------
```

```
sum                                                             15,347.5

1 row selected.

SYS@SANDBOX> !cat comp_ratio.sql
compute sum of totalsize_megs on report
break on report
col owner for a10
col segment_name for a20
col segment_type for a10
col totalsize_megs for 999,999.9
col compression_ratio for 999.9
select owner, segment_name, segment_type type,
sum(bytes/1024/1024) as totalsize_megs,
&original_size/sum(bytes/1024/1024) as compression_ratio
from dba_segments
where owner like nvl('&owner',owner)
and segment_name like nvl('&table_name',segment_name)
and segment_type like nvl('&type',segment_type)
group by owner, segment_name, tablespace_name, segment_type
order by 5;

SYS@SANDBOX1> @comp_ratio
Enter value for original_size: 15347.5
Enter value for owner: KSO
Enter value for table_name: SKEW3%
Enter value for type:

OWNER      SEGMENT_NAME         TYPE          TOTALSIZE_MEGS COMPRESSION_RATIO
---------- -------------------- ------------- -------------- -----------------
KSO        SKEW3_NONE           TABLE             15,370.8                1.0
KSO        SKEW3_OLTP           TABLE             10,712.7                1.4
KSO        SKEW3_BASIC          TABLE              9,640.7                1.6
KSO        SKEW3_HCC1           TABLE              3,790.1                4.0
KSO        SKEW3_HCC3           TABLE                336.9               45.6
KSO        SKEW3_HCC2           TABLE                336.7               45.6
KSO        SKEW3_HCC4           TABLE                274.3               55.9
                                                --------------
sum                                               25,091.4

7 rows selected.
```

The listing shows the commands used to create compressed versions of the SKEW3 table. We also loaded an uncompressed version for a timing reference. Note also that the SKEW3 table is highly compressible due to many repeating values in a small number of columns. It's a little hard to pick out the information from the listing, so Table 3-2 summarizes the data in a more easily digested format.

Table 3-2. HCC Load Times vs.Compression Ratios for SKEW3

Table Name	Compress For	Compression Ratio	Load Time	Load Time Ratio
SKEW3				
SKEW3_NONE		1.0	00:00:42.76	1.0
SKEW3_OLTP	OLTP	1.4	00:01:35.97	2.2
SKEW3_BASIC	BASIC	1.6	00:01:24.58	2.0
SKEW3_HCC1	QUERY LOW	4.0	00:00:56.57	1.3
SKEW3_HCC2	QUERY HIGH	45.6	00:01:56.49	2.7
SKEW3_HCC3	ARCHIVE LOW	45.6	00:01:53.43	2.7
SKEW3_HCC4	ARCHIVE HIGH	55.9	00:08:55.58	12.5

So as you can see, QUERY HIGH and ARCHIVE LOW compression levels resulted in almost exactly the same compression ratios (45.6) for this dataset and took roughly the same amount of time to load. Loading is definitely slower with compression and for this dataset was somewhere between 2 and 3 times slower (with the exception of ARCHIVE HIGH, which we'll come back to). Notice the huge jump in compression between QUERY LOW and QUERY HIGH. While the load time roughly doubled, the compression ratio improved by a factor of 10. For this dataset, this is clearly the sweet spot when comparing load time to compression ratio.

Now let's turn our attention to the ARCHIVE HIGH compression setting. In the previous test we did not attempt to maximize the load time. Our choice of 8 is actually a rather pedestrian setting for parallelism on Exadata. In addition, our parallel slave processes were limited to a single node via the PARALLEL_FORCE_LOCAL parameter (we'll talk more about that in Chapter 6). So our load process was using a total of eight slaves on a single node. Here's some output from the Unix top command showing how the system was behaving during the load:

```
===First HCC4 run (8 slaves)
top - 19:54:14 up 2 days, 11:31,  5 users,  load average: 2.79, 1.00, 1.09
Tasks: 832 total,   9 running, 823 sleeping,   0 stopped,   0 zombie
Cpu(s): 50.5%us,  0.6%sy,  0.0%ni, 48.8%id,  0.1%wa,  0.0%hi,  0.0%si,  0.0%st
Mem:  74027752k total, 29495080k used, 44532672k free,   111828k buffers
Swap: 16771852k total,  2120944k used, 14650908k free, 25105292k cached

  PID USER      PR  NI  VIRT  RES  SHR S %CPU %MEM    TIME+  COMMAND
19440 oracle    25   0 10.1g  86m  55m R 99.9  0.1  0:21.25 ora_p001_SANDBOX1
19451 oracle    25   0 10.1g  86m  55m R 99.9  0.1  0:21.21 ora_p002_SANDBOX1
19465 oracle    25   0 10.1g  86m  55m R 99.9  0.1  0:21.34 ora_p003_SANDBOX1
19468 oracle    25   0 10.1g  87m  55m R 99.9  0.1  0:20.22 ora_p004_SANDBOX1
19479 oracle    25   0 10.1g  86m  55m R 99.9  0.1  0:21.21 ora_p005_SANDBOX1
19515 oracle    25   0 10.1g  86m  54m R 99.9  0.1  0:21.18 ora_p006_SANDBOX1
```

```
19517 oracle    25   0 10.1g  88m  50m R 99.9  0.1   0:27.59 ora_p007_SANDBOX1
19401 oracle    25   0 10.1g  87m  54m R 99.5  0.1   0:21.31 ora_p000_SANDBOX1
```

Clearly, loading data into an ARCHIVE HIGH compressed table is a CPU-intensive process. But notice that we're still only using about half the processing power on the single Database Server. Adding more processors and more servers should make it go considerably faster. By the way, it's usually worthwhile to look at the CPU usage during the uncompressed load for comparison purposes. Here's another snapshot from top taken during the loading of the uncompressed version of the SKEW3 table; in this and similar snapshots, we've highlighted output items of particular interest:

```
===No Compression Load
top - 19:46:55 up 2 days, 11:23,  6 users,  load average: 1.21, 0.61, 1.20
Tasks: 833 total,   2 running, 831 sleeping,   0 stopped,   0 zombie
Cpu(s): 22.3%us,  1.4%sy,  0.0%ni, 75.9%id,  0.1%wa,  0.1%hi,  0.2%si,  0.0%st
Mem:  74027752k total, 29273532k used, 44754220k free,   110376k buffers
Swap: 16771852k total,  2135368k used, 14636484k free, 25074672k cached

  PID USER      PR  NI  VIRT  RES  SHR S %CPU %MEM    TIME+  COMMAND
15999 oracle    16   0 10.0g  72m  64m S 54.8  0.1   0:04.89 ora_p000_SANDBOX1
16001 oracle    16   0 10.0g  72m  64m S 51.5  0.1   0:04.72 ora_p001_SANDBOX1
16024 oracle    16   0 10.0g  69m  61m S 48.5  0.1   0:03.97 ora_p007_SANDBOX1
16020 oracle    16   0 10.0g  70m  61m S 44.6  0.1   0:04.16 ora_p006_SANDBOX1
16003 oracle    16   0 10.0g  71m  62m S 43.6  0.1   0:04.42 ora_p002_SANDBOX1
16014 oracle    16   0 10.0g  71m  62m S 42.9  0.1   0:04.26 ora_p005_SANDBOX1
16007 oracle    16   0 10.0g  69m  61m S 40.9  0.1   0:04.28 ora_p004_SANDBOX1
16005 oracle    15   0 10.0g  72m  64m R 38.3  0.1   0:04.45 ora_p003_SANDBOX1
```

Notice that while the number of active processes is the same (8), the CPU usage is significantly less when the data is not being compressed during the load. The other levels of compression use somewhat less CPU, but are much closer to HCC4 than to the noncompressed load.

To speed up the ARCHIVE HIGH loading we could add more processes or we could allow the slaves to run on multiple nodes. Here's a quick example:

```
SYS@SANDBOX1> alter system set parallel_force_local=false;

System altered.

Elapsed: 00:00:00.09
SYS@SANDBOX1> create table kso.skew3_hcc4 nologging parallel 32 compress for archive high
  2  as select /*+ parallel (a 32) */ * from kso.skew3 a;

Table created.

Elapsed: 00:03:18.96
```

Setting the PARALLEL_FORCE_LOCAL parameter to FALSE allowed slaves to be spread across both nodes. Setting the parallel degree to 32 allowed 16 slaves to run on each of the two nodes in our quarter rack test system. This effectively utilized all the CPU resources on both nodes. Here's one last snapshot of top output from one of the nodes during the load. The other node showed the same basic profile during the load.

```
===Second HCC4 run (32 slaves)
top - 18:32:43 up  2:10,  2 users,  load average: 18.51, 10.70, 4.70
Tasks: 862 total,  19 running, 843 sleeping,   0 stopped,   0 zombie
```

```
Cpu(s): 97.3%us,  0.4%sy,  0.0%ni,  2.2%id,  0.0%wa,  0.0%hi,  0.0%si,  0.0%st
Mem:  74027752k total, 35141864k used, 38885888k free,    192548k buffers
Swap: 16771852k total,        0k used, 16771852k free, 30645208k cached

  PID USER      PR  NI  VIRT  RES  SHR S %CPU %MEM    TIME+  COMMAND
21657 oracle    25   0 10.1g 111m  72m R 99.1  0.2  5:20.16 ora_p001_SANDBOX2
21663 oracle    25   0 10.1g 113m  80m R 99.1  0.2  5:11.11 ora_p004_SANDBOX2
26481 oracle    25   0 10.1g  89m  54m R 99.1  0.1  3:07.37 ora_p008_SANDBOX2
26496 oracle    25   0 10.1g  89m  54m R 99.1  0.1  3:06.88 ora_p015_SANDBOX2
21667 oracle    25   0 10.1g 110m  73m R 98.5  0.2  5:16.09 ora_p006_SANDBOX2
26483 oracle    25   0 10.1g  89m  53m R 98.5  0.1  3:06.63 ora_p009_SANDBOX2
26488 oracle    25   0 10.1g  90m  52m R 98.5  0.1  3:08.71 ora_p011_SANDBOX2
26485 oracle    25   0 10.1g  90m  54m R 97.9  0.1  3:04.54 ora_p010_SANDBOX2
26490 oracle    25   0 10.1g  90m  54m R 97.9  0.1  3:04.46 ora_p012_SANDBOX2
21655 oracle    25   0 10.1g 105m  70m R 97.3  0.1  5:13.22 ora_p000_SANDBOX2
26494 oracle    25   0 10.1g  89m  52m R 97.3  0.1  3:03.42 ora_p014_SANDBOX2
21661 oracle    25   0 10.1g 106m  73m R 95.4  0.1  5:12.65 ora_p003_SANDBOX2
26492 oracle    25   0 10.1g  89m  54m R 95.4  0.1  3:08.13 ora_p013_SANDBOX2
21659 oracle    25   0 10.1g 114m  79m R 94.8  0.2  5:13.42 ora_p002_SANDBOX2
21669 oracle    25   0 10.1g 107m  72m R 90.5  0.1  5:10.19 ora_p007_SANDBOX2
21665 oracle    25   0 10.1g 107m  67m R 86.2  0.1  5:18.80 ora_p005_SANDBOX2
```

Query Performance

Of course, load time is not the only performance metric of interest. Query time is more critical than load time for most systems since the data is only loaded once but queried many times. Query performance is a mixed bag when it comes to compression. Depending on the type of query, compression can either speed it up or slow it down. Decompression certainly adds overhead in the way of additional CPU usage, but for queries that are bottlenecked on disk access, reducing the number of blocks that must be read can often offset and in many cases more than make up for the additional overhead. Keep in mind that depending on the access mechanism used, the decompression can be done on either the storage cells (smart scans) or on the database nodes. Here's an example of running a CPU-intensive procedure:

```
SYS@SANDBOX1> !cat gather_table_stats.sql
begin
  dbms_stats.gather_table_stats(
     '&owner','&table_name',
     degree => 32,
     method_opt => 'for all columns size 1'
  );
end;
/

SYS@SANDBOX1> @gather_table_stats
Enter value for owner: ACOLVIN
Enter value for table_name: SKEW3

PL/SQL procedure successfully completed.

Elapsed: 00:00:12.14
SYS@SANDBOX1> @gather_table_stats
Enter value for owner: KSO
```

```
Enter value for table_name: SKEW3_OLTP

PL/SQL procedure successfully completed.

Elapsed: 00:00:12.75
SYS@SANDBOX1> @gather_table_stats
Enter value for owner: KSO
Enter value for table_name: SKEW3_BASIC

PL/SQL procedure successfully completed.

Elapsed: 00:00:12.60
SYS@SANDBOX1> @gather_table_stats
Enter value for owner: KSO
Enter value for table_name: SKEW3_HCC1

PL/SQL procedure successfully completed.

Elapsed: 00:00:14.21
SYS@SANDBOX1> @gather_table_stats
Enter value for owner: KSO
Enter value for table_name: SKEW3_HCC2

PL/SQL procedure successfully completed.

Elapsed: 00:00:14.94
SYS@SANDBOX1> @gather_table_stats
Enter value for owner: KSO
Enter value for table_name: SKEW3_HCC3

PL/SQL procedure successfully completed.

Elapsed: 00:00:14.24
SYS@SANDBOX1> @gather_table_stats
Enter value for owner: KSO
Enter value for table_name: SKEW3_HCC4

PL/SQL procedure successfully completed.

Elapsed: 00:00:21.33
```

And again for clarity, Table 3-3 shows the timings in a more readable format.

Table 3-3. Statistics Gathering Timing for SKEW3

Table Name	Compress For	Compression Ratio	Run Time	Run Time Ratio
SKEW3			12.14	
SKEW3_OLTP	OLTP	1.4	12.75	1.05

Table Name	Compress For	Compression Ratio	Run Time	Run Time Ratio
SKEW3_BASIC	BASIC	1.6	12.60	1.04
SKEW3_HCC1	QUERY LOW	4.0	14.21	1.17
SKEW3_HCC2	QUERY HIGH	45.6	14.94	1.23
SKEW3_HCC3	ARCHIVE LOW	45.6	14.24	1.17
SKEW3_HCC4	ARCHIVE HIGH	55.9	21.33	1.76

Gathering statistics is a very CPU-intensive operation. Spreading the stat-gathering across 16 slave processes per node almost completely utilized the CPU resources on the DB servers. As you can see, the compression slowed down the processing enough to outweigh the gains from the reduced number of data blocks that needed to be read. This is due to the CPU-intensive nature of the work being done. Here's a snapshot of top output to verify that the system is CPU-bound:

```
top - 14:40:50 up 4 days,  6:17, 10 users,  load average: 10.81, 4.16, 4.53
Tasks: 841 total,  21 running, 820 sleeping,   0 stopped,   0 zombie
Cpu(s): 96.1%us,  0.7%sy,  0.0%ni,  2.9%id,  0.0%wa,  0.0%hi,  0.3%si,  0.0%st
Mem:  74027752k total, 34494424k used, 39533328k free,   345448k buffers
Swap: 16771852k total,   568756k used, 16203096k free, 29226312k cached

  PID USER     PR  NI  VIRT  RES  SHR S %CPU %MEM    TIME+  COMMAND
16127 oracle   25   0 40.3g 146m 106m R 97.6  0.2 10:19.16 ora_p001_POC1
16154 oracle   25   0 40.3g 145m 119m R 97.6  0.2 10:11.75 ora_p014_POC1
16137 oracle   25   0 40.3g 144m 113m R 96.9  0.2 10:14.20 ora_p006_POC1
16125 oracle   25   0 40.3g 139m 108m R 96.6  0.2 10:24.11 ora_p000_POC1
16133 oracle   25   0 40.3g 147m 109m R 96.6  0.2 10:27.14 ora_p004_POC1
16145 oracle   25   0 40.3g 145m 117m R 96.2  0.2 10:20.25 ora_p010_POC1
16135 oracle   25   0 40.3g 154m 112m R 95.9  0.2 10:16.51 ora_p005_POC1
16143 oracle   25   0 40.3g 135m 106m R 95.9  0.2 10:22.33 ora_p009_POC1
16131 oracle   25   0 40.3g 156m 119m R 95.6  0.2 10:16.73 ora_p003_POC1
16141 oracle   25   0 40.3g 143m 115m R 95.6  0.2 10:18.62 ora_p008_POC1
16151 oracle   25   0 40.3g 155m 121m R 95.6  0.2 10:11.54 ora_p013_POC1
16147 oracle   25   0 40.3g 140m 113m R 94.9  0.2 10:17.92 ora_p011_POC1
16139 oracle   25   0 40.3g 155m 114m R 94.6  0.2 10:13.26 ora_p007_POC1
16149 oracle   25   0 40.3g 156m 124m R 93.9  0.2 10:21.05 ora_p012_POC1
16129 oracle   25   0 40.3g 157m 126m R 93.3  0.2 10:09.99 ora_p002_POC1
16156 oracle   25   0 40.3g 141m 111m R 93.3  0.2 10:16.76 ora_p015_POC1
```

Now let's look at a query that is I/O-intensive. This test uses a query without a WHERE clause that spends most of its time retrieving data from the storage layer via cell-smart table scans:

```
SYS@SANDBOX1> @hcc_test3
SYS@SANDBOX1> set timing on
SYS@SANDBOX1> select /*+ parallel (a 32) */ sum(pk_col) from acolvin.skew3 a ;
```

```
SUM(PK_COL)
-----------
 6.1800E+15

1 row selected.
Elapsed: 00:00:06.21
SYS@SANDBOX1> select /*+ parallel (a 32) */ sum(pk_col) from kso.skew3_oltp a ;

SUM(PK_COL)
-----------
 6.1800E+15

1 row selected.
Elapsed: 00:00:05.79
SYS@SANDBOX1> select /*+ parallel (a 32) */ sum(pk_col) from kso.skew3_basic a ;

SUM(PK_COL)
-----------
 6.1800E+15

1 row selected.

Elapsed: 00:00:05.26
SYS@SANDBOX1> select /*+ parallel (a 32) */ sum(pk_col) from kso.skew3_hcc1 a ;

SUM(PK_COL)
-----------
 6.1800E+15

1 row selected.

Elapsed: 00:00:03.56
SYS@SANDBOX1> select /*+ parallel (a 32) */ sum(pk_col) from kso.skew3_hcc2 a ;

SUM(PK_COL)
-----------
 6.1800E+15

1 row selected.

Elapsed: 00:00:03.39
SYS@SANDBOX1> select /*+ parallel (a 32) */ sum(pk_col) from kso.skew3_hcc3 a ;

SUM(PK_COL)
-----------
 6.1800E+15

1 row selected.

Elapsed: 00:00:03.36
SYS@SANDBOX1> select /*+ parallel (a 32) */ sum(pk_col) from kso.skew3_hcc4 a ;
```

```
SUM(PK_COL)
-----------
 6.1800E+15
```

1 row selected.

Elapsed: 00:00:04.78

Table 3-4 shows the timings for the unqualified query in a tabular format.

Table 3-4. *Unqualified Query Timing on SKEW3*

Table Name	Compress For	Compression Ratio	Run Time	Run Time Ratio
SKEW3			6.21	
SKEW3_OLTP	OLTP	1.4	5.79	0.93
SKEW3_BASIC	BASIC	1.6	5.26	0.85
SKEW3_HCC1	QUERY LOW	4.0	3.56	0.57
SKEW3_HCC2	QUERY HIGH	45.6	3.39	0.55
SKEW3_HCC3	ARCHIVE LOW	45.6	3.36	0.54
SKEW3_HCC4	ARCHIVE HIGH	55.9	4.78	0.77

The query does not require a lot of CPU resources on the DB server. As a result, the savings in I/O time more than offset the increased CPU. Note that the rather significant CPU requirements of the ARCHIVE HIGH decompression caused the elapsed time to increase for this test over the less CPU-intensive algorithms. Nevertheless, it was still faster than the uncompressed run. Here's a snapshot of top output while one of these queries was running.

```
top - 15:37:13 up 4 days,  7:14,  9 users,  load average: 5.00, 2.01, 2.50
Tasks: 867 total,   7 running, 860 sleeping,   0 stopped,   0 zombie
Cpu(s): 25.2%us,  0.9%sy,  0.0%ni, 73.4%id,  0.5%wa,  0.0%hi,  0.1%si,  0.0%st
Mem:  74027752k total, 35193896k used, 38833856k free,   346568k buffers
Swap: 16771852k total,   568488k used, 16203364k free, 29976856k cached

  PID USER      PR  NI  VIRT  RES  SHR S %CPU %MEM    TIME+  COMMAND
25414 oracle    16   0 10.0g  40m  31m S 33.0  0.1  0:13.75 ora_p001_SANDBOX1
25474 oracle    15   0 10.0g  39m  30m S 32.4  0.1  0:13.54 ora_p012_SANDBOX1
25472 oracle    15   0 10.0g  37m  29m S 28.8  0.1  0:13.45 ora_p011_SANDBOX1
25420 oracle    16   0 10.0g  35m  28m R 27.8  0.0  0:13.71 ora_p004_SANDBOX1
25418 oracle    15   0 10.0g  39m  31m R 27.4  0.1  0:13.78 ora_p003_SANDBOX1
25435 oracle    15   0 10.0g  38m  30m S 27.4  0.1  0:13.46 ora_p008_SANDBOX1
25478 oracle    15   0 10.0g  38m  30m S 27.1  0.1  0:13.75 ora_p014_SANDBOX1
25428 oracle    15   0 10.0g  38m  31m S 24.8  0.1  0:13.81 ora_p005_SANDBOX1
```

```
25437 oracle    15   0 10.0g  38m   30m R 24.5  0.1   0:13.88 ora_p009_SANDBOX1
25416 oracle    15   0 10.0g  39m   32m S 24.1  0.1   0:13.81 ora_p002_SANDBOX1
25430 oracle    15   0 10.0g  39m   31m R 22.8  0.1   0:13.00 ora_p006_SANDBOX1
25433 oracle    16   0 10.0g  40m   32m S 22.8  0.1   0:12.94 ora_p007_SANDBOX1
25470 oracle    15   0 10.0g  38m   30m R 22.8  0.1   0:13.73 ora_p010_SANDBOX1
25484 oracle    15   0 10.0g  38m   30m S 20.2  0.1   0:13.23 ora_p015_SANDBOX1
25476 oracle    15   0 10.0g  37m   30m S 18.5  0.1   0:13.30 ora_p013_SANDBOX1
25411 oracle    15   0 10.0g  38m   30m R 13.2  0.1   0:12.67 ora_p000_SANDBOX1
```

DML Performance

Generally speaking, records that will be updated should not be compressed. When you update a record in an HCC table, the record will be migrated to a new a block that is flagged as an OLTP compressed block. Of course, a pointer will be left behind so that you can still get to the record via its old rowid, but the record will be assigned a new rowid as well. Since updated records are downgraded to OLTP compression you need to understand how that compression mechanism works on updates. Figure 3-6 demonstrates how non-direct path loads into an OLTP block are processed.

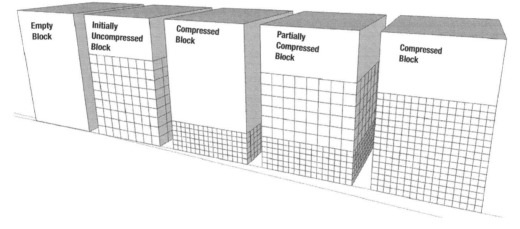

Figure 3-6. The OLTP compression process for non-direct path loads

The progression of states moves from left to right. Rows are initially loaded in an uncompressed state. As the block fills to the point where no more rows can be inserted, the row data in the block is compressed. The block is then placed back on the freelist and is capable of accepting more uncompressed rows. This means that in an OLTP-compressed table, blocks can be in various states of compression. All rows can be compressed, some rows can be compressed, or no rows can be compressed. This is exactly how records in HCC blocks behave when they are updated. A couple of examples will demonstrate this behavior. The first will show how the size of a table can balloon with updates.

```
SYS@SANDBOX1> @table_size2
Enter value for owner: KSO
Enter value for table_name: SKEW
```

```
OWNER                SEGMENT_NAME                  TOTALSIZE_MEGS COMPRESS_FOR
-------------------- ----------------------------- -------------- ------------
KSO                  SKEW                                 1,460.3
                                                   --------------
sum                                                       1,460.3

1 row selected.

SYS@SANDBOX1> create table kso.skew_hcc3 nologging parallel 16 compress for archive low
  2  as select * from kso.skew a;

Table created.

SYS@SANDBOX1> @table_size2
Enter value for owner: KSO
Enter value for table_name: SKEW_HCC3

OWNER                SEGMENT_NAME                  TOTALSIZE_MEGS COMPRESS_FOR
-------------------- ----------------------------- -------------- ------------
KSO                  SKEW_HCC3                              23.0 ARCHIVE LOW
                                                   --------------
sum                                                        23.0

1 row selected.

SYS@SANDBOX1> update /*+ parallel (a 32) */ kso.skew_hcc3 a set col1=col1;

32000004 rows updated.

SYS@SANDBOX1> @table_size2
Enter value for owner: KSO
Enter value for table_name: SKEW_HCC3

OWNER                SEGMENT_NAME                  TOTALSIZE_MEGS COMPRESS_FOR
-------------------- ----------------------------- -------------- ------------
KSO                  SKEW_HCC3                             916.0 ARCHIVE LOW
                                                   --------------
sum                                                       916.0

1 row selected.

SYS@SANDBOX1> -- Check how this compares to direct path load OLTP table.
SYS@SANDBOX1>
SYS@SANDBOX1> create table kso.skew_oltp nologging parallel 16 compress for oltp
  2  as select /*+ parallel (a 16) */ * from kso.skew a;

Table created.

SYS@SANDBOX1> @table_size2
Enter value for owner: KSO
Enter value for table_name: SKEW_OLTP
```

```
OWNER               SEGMENT_NAME                    TOTALSIZE_MEGS COMPRESS_FOR
------------------- ------------------------------- -------------- ------------
KSO                 SKEW_OLTP                                903.1 OLTP
                                                    --------------
sum                                                          903.1

1 row selected.

SYS@SANDBOX1> @comp_ratio
Enter value for original_size: 1460.3
Enter value for owner: KSO
Enter value for table_name: SKEW%
Enter value for type:

OWNER       SEGMENT_NAME         TYPE                TOTALSIZE_MEGS COMPRESSION_RATIO
----------- -------------------- ------------------- -------------- -----------------
KSO         SKEW                 TABLE                      1,460.3               1.0
KSO         SKEW_HCC3            TABLE                        916.0               1.6
KSO         SKEW_OLTP            TABLE                        903.1               1.6
                                                     --------------
sum                                                         3,279.4

3 rows selected.
```

This output shows that updating all the records in an HCC ARCHIVE LOW table expanded it to a slightly larger footprint than an OLTP-compressed (via direct path load) version of the same table. Interestingly enough, the update statement spent most of its time waiting on BUFFER BUSY WAITS. Apparently there is not a specific wait event for when a process is waiting while a block is being compressed. Here is the complete set of events that the update statement waited on (from a 10046 trace file processed with tkprof), along with per-second session statistics (both from one of the parallel slave processes):

```
Elapsed times include waiting on following events:
  Event waited on                          Times   Max. Wait  Total Waited
  ---------------------------------------- Waited  ---------- ------------
  cursor: pin S wait on X                       1        0.01         0.01
  PX Deq: Execution Msg                        16       67.43        68.15
  cell multiblock physical read                14        0.00         0.02
  resmgr:cpu quantum                           90        0.01         0.14
  buffer busy waits                          2077        3.54       139.84
  latch: cache buffers chains                2068        0.34         6.75
  enq: TX - contention                         66        0.27         0.33
  enq: HW - contention                        142        1.55        16.56
  latch: redo allocation                      361        0.25         1.51
  global enqueue expand wait                   19        0.00         0.00
  gc current multi block request               67        0.00         0.03
  KJC: Wait for msg sends to complete          16        0.00         0.00
  log buffer space                            230        0.28        12.44
  latch: enqueue hash chains                   28        0.00         0.01
  latch: ges resource hash list                20        0.01         0.05
  log file switch completion                    5        0.30         0.88
  enq: FB - contention                         61        0.03         0.12
```

enq: US - contention	439	3.98	82.64
Disk file operations I/O	110	0.00	0.02
control file sequential read	720	0.17	1.64
cell single block physical read	131	0.05	0.26
db file single write	72	0.06	0.23
KSV master wait	431	2.10	5.24
ASM file metadata operation	144	0.00	0.01
kfk: async disk IO	36	0.09	0.35
cell smart file creation	4779	0.08	1.05
CSS operation: action	1	0.00	0.00
enq: CF - contention	36	0.19	0.24
control file parallel write	108	0.09	0.95
DFS lock handle	252	0.38	3.06
undo segment extension	163	1.02	9.95
L1 validation	2	0.01	0.01
reliable message	50	0.00	0.05
latch: row cache objects	1	0.00	0.00
gc cr grant 2-way	1	0.00	0.00
gc cr multi block request	4	0.00	0.00
log file switch (checkpoint incomplete)	6	3.29	4.15
latch: undo global data	3	0.00	0.00
latch free	7	0.05	0.07
latch: gc element	4	0.00	0.00
wait list latch free	2	0.00	0.00
log file sync	1	0.00	0.00
latch: object queue header operation	3	0.00	0.00

Stat Name	Events/Sec
HSC OLTP Space Saving	30,485
HSC OLTP Compressed Blocks	10
HSC Compressed Segment Block Changes	8,314
STAT, HSC Heap Segment Block Changes	8,314
STAT, HSC OLTP Non Compressible Blocks	10
STAT, HSC OLTP positive compression	20
HSC OLTP inline compression	20

The second example demonstrates that a row is migrated from an HCC block when it is updated. Basically we'll update a single row, see that its rowid has changed, verify that we can still get to the record via its original rowid, and check to see if the TABLE FETCH CONTINUED ROW statistic gets updated when we access the row via its original rowid.

```
SYS@SANDBOX1> @table_size2
Enter value for owner: KSO
Enter value for table_name: SKEW_HCC3
```

OWNER	SEGMENT_NAME	TOTALSIZE_MEGS	COMPRESS_FOR
KSO	SKEW_HCC3	18.6	ARCHIVE LOW
sum		18.6	

```
SYS@SANDBOX1> select count(*) from kso.skew_hcc3 where pk_col=16367;

  COUNT(*)
----------
         1

SYS@SANDBOX1> select rowid, old_rowid(rowid) old_rowid_format
  2 from kso.skew_hcc3 where pk_col=16367;

ROWID              OLD_ROWID_FORMAT
------------------ --------------------
AAATCBAAIAAF8uSFc9 8.1559442.22333

SYS@SANDBOX1> -- So our row is in file 8, block 1559442, row 22333
SYS@SANDBOX1>
SYS@SANDBOX1> update kso.skew_hcc3 set col1=col1 where pk_col=16367;

1 row updated.

SYS@SANDBOX1> select rowid, old_rowid(rowid) OLD_ROWID_FORMAT
  2 from kso.skew_hcc3 where pk_col=16367;

ROWID              OLD_ROWID_FORMAT
------------------ --------------------
AAATCBAAHAAMGMMAAA 7.3171084.0

SYS@SANDBOX1> -- Ha! The rowid has changed - the row moved to file 7
SYS@SANDBOX1>
SYS@SANDBOX1> -- Let's see if we can still get to it via the original rowid
SYS@SANDBOX1>
SYS@SANDBOX1> select pk_col from kso.skew_hcc3 where rowid = 'AAATCBAAIAAF8uSFc9';

    PK_COL
----------
     16367

SYS@SANDBOX1> -- Yes we can! - can we use the new rowid?
SYS@SANDBOX1>
SYS@SANDBOX1> select pk_col from kso.skew_hcc3 where rowid = 'AAATCBAAHAAMGMMAAA';

    PK_COL
----------
     16367

SYS@SANDBOX1> -- That works too! - It's a migrated Row!
SYS@SANDBOX1> -- Let's verify with "continued row" stat
SYS@SANDBOX1>
SYS@SANDBOX1> @mystats
Enter value for name: table fetch continued row
```

```
NAME                                                                      VALUE
---------------------------------------------------------------- ----------------
table fetch continued row                                                  2947

SYS@SANDBOX1> -- select via the original rowid
SYS@SANDBOX1>
SYS@SANDBOX1> select pk_col from kso.skew_hcc3 where rowid = 'AAATCBAAIAAF8uSFc9';

    PK_COL
 ----------
     16367

SYS@SANDBOX1> @mystats
Enter value for name: table fetch continued row

NAME                                                                      VALUE
---------------------------------------------------------------- ----------------
table fetch continued row                                                  2948

SYS@SANDBOX1> -- Stat is incremented - so definitely a migrated row!
```

So the row has definitely been migrated. Now let's verify that the migrated row is not compressed. We can do this by dumping the block where the newly migrated record resides. But before we look at the migrated row let's have a look at the original block.

```
SYS@SANDBOX1> !cat dump_block.sql
@find_trace
alter system dump datafile &fileno block &blockno;

SYS@SANDBOX1> @dump_block

TRACEFILE_NAME
--------------------------------------------------------------------------------
/u01/app/oracle/diag/rdbms/sandbox/SANDBOX1/trace/SANDBOX1_ora_5191.trc

Enter value for fileno: 7
Enter value for blockno: 3171084

System altered.
```

Now let's look at the trace file produced in the trace directory. Here is an excerpt from the block dump.

```
Block header dump:  0x01f0630c
 Object id on Block? Y
 seg/obj: 0x13081  csc: 0x01.1e0574d4  itc: 3  flg: E  typ: 1 - DATA
     brn: 0  bdba: 0x1f06300 ver: 0x01 opc: 0
     inc: 0  exflg: 0

 Itl           Xid                  Uba         Flag  Lck        Scn/Fsc
 0x01   0x002f.013.00000004  0x00eec383.01f2.44  ----    1  fsc 0x0000.00000000
 0x02   0x0000.000.00000000  0x00000000.0000.00  ----    0  fsc 0x0000.00000000
 0x03   0x0000.000.00000000  0x00000000.0000.00  ----    0  fsc 0x0000.00000000
```

```
bdba: 0x01f0630c
data_block_dump,data header at 0x2b849c81307c
===============
tsiz: 0x1f80
hsiz: 0x14
pbl: 0x2b849c81307c
      76543210
flag=--------
ntab=1
nrow=1
frre=-1
fsbo=0x14
fseo=0x1f60
avsp=0x1f4c
tosp=0x1f4c
0xe:pti[0]        nrow=1  offs=0
0x12:pri[0]       offs=0x1f60
block_row_dump:
tab 0, row 0, @0x1f60
tl: 32 fb: --H-FL-- lb: 0x1  cc: 5
col  0: [ 4]  c3 02 40 44
col  1: [ 2]  c1 02
col  2: [10]  61 73 64 64 73 61 64 61 73 64
col  3: [ 7]  78 6a 07 15 15 0b 32
col  4: [ 1]  59
end_of_block_dump
```

The block is not compressed and conforms to the normal Oracle block format. Notice that there is only one row in the block (nrows=1). Also notice that the data_object_id is included in the block in hex format (seg/obj: 0x13081). The table has five columns. The values are displayed, also in hex format. Just to verify that we have the right block, we can translate the data_object_id and the value of the first column as follows:

```
SYS@SANDBOX1> !cat obj_by_hex.sql
col object_name for a30
select owner, object_name, object_type
from dba_objects
where data_object_id = to_number(replace('&hex_value','0x',''),'XXXXXX');

SYS@SANDBOX1> @obj_by_hex
Enter value for hex_value: 0x13081

OWNER                            OBJECT_NAME                    OBJECT_TYPE
-------------------------------- ------------------------------ -------------------
KSO                              SKEW_HCC3                      TABLE


SYS@SANDBOX1> desc kso.skew_hcc3
 Name                            Null?    Type
 ------------------------------- -------- --------------------
 PK_COL                                   NUMBER
 COL1                                     NUMBER
```

```
        COL2                            VARCHAR2(30)
        COL3                            DATE
        COL4                            VARCHAR2(1)

SYS@SANDBOX1> @display_raw
Enter value for string: c3 02 40 44
Enter value for type: NUMBER

VALUE
--------------------------------------------------
16367
```

As you can see, this is the record that we updated in the SKEW_HCC3 table. Just as an aside, it is interesting to see how the compressed block format differs from the standard uncompressed format. Here is a snippet from the original block in our example that is compressed for ARCHIVE LOW.

```
===============
tsiz: 0x1f80
hsiz: 0x1c
pbl: 0x2b5d7d5cea7c
     76543210
flag=-0------
ntab=1
nrow=1
frre=-1
fsbo=0x1c
fseo=0x30
avsp=0x14
tosp=0x14
        r0_9ir2=0x0
        mec_kdbh9ir2=0x0
                    76543210
        shcf_kdbh9ir2=----------
                76543210
        flag_9ir2=--R-----          Archive compression: Y
                fcls_9ir2[0]={ }
0x16:pti[0]      nrow=1  offs=0
0x1a:pri[0]      offs=0x30
block_row_dump:
tab 0, row 0, @0x30
tl: 8016 fb: --H-F--N lb: 0x2  cc: 1
nrid:  0x0217cbd4.0
col  0: [8004]
Compression level: 03 (Archive Low)
 Length of CU row: 8004
kdzhrh: ------PC CBLK: 2 Start Slot: 00
 NUMP: 02
 PNUM: 00 POFF: 7974 PRID: 0x0217cbd4.0
 PNUM: 01 POFF: 15990 PRID: 0x0217cbd5.0
CU header:
CU version: 0   CU magic number: 0x4b445a30
CU checksum: 0xf0529582
```

```
CU total length: 21406
CU flags: NC-U-CRD-OP
ncols: 5
nrows: 32759
algo: 0
CU decomp length: 17269    len/value length: 1040997
row pieces per row: 1
num deleted rows: 1
deleted rows: 0,
START_CU:
 00 00 1f 44 1f 02 00 00 00 02 00 00 1f 26 02 17 cb d4 00 00 00 00 3e 76 02
 17 cb d5 00 00 00 4b 44 5a 30 82 95 52 f0 00 00 53 9e eb 06 00 05 7f f7 00
```

Notice that this block shows that it is compressed at level 3 (ARCHIVE LOW). Also notice that one record has been deleted from this block (migrated would be a more accurate term, as this is the record that we updated earlier). The line that says deleted rows: actually shows a list of the rows that have been migrated. Remember that we updated the record with rowid 7.3171084.0, meaning file 7, block 3171084, slot 0. So this line tells us that the one deleted row was in slot 0.

▨ **Kevin Says:** I like to remind people to be mindful of the potential performance irregularities that may occur should a table comprised of EHCC data metamorphose into a table that is of mixed compression types with indirection. There should be no expected loss in functionality; however, there is an expected, yet unpredictable, impact to the repeatability of scan performance. The unpredictable nature is due to the fact that it is completely data-dependent.

Expected Compression Ratios

HCC can provide very impressive compression ratios. The marketing material has claimed 10× compression ratios and believe it or not, this is actually a very achievable number for many datasets. Of course the amount of compression depends heavily on the data and which of the four algorithms is applied. The best way to determine what kind of compression can be achieved on your dataset is to test it. Oracle also provides a utility (often referred to as the Compression Advisor) to compress a sample of data from a table in order to calculate an estimated compression ratio. This utility can even be used on non-Exadata platforms as long as they are running 11.2.0.2 or later. This section will provide some insight into the Compression Advisor and provide compression ratios on some sample real world datasets.

Compression Advisor

If you don't have access to an Exadata but still want to test the effectiveness of HCC, you can use the Compression Advisor functionality that is provided in the DBMS_COMPRESSION package. The GET_COMPRESSION_RATIO procedure actually enables you to compress a sample of rows from a specified table. This is not an estimate of how much compression might happen; the sample rows are inserted into a temporary table. Then a compressed version of that temporary table is created. The ratio returned is a comparison between the sizes of the compressed version and the uncompressed version. As of

Oracle Database version 11.2.0.2, this procedure may be used on a non-Exadata platform to estimate compression ratios for various levels of HCC as well as OLTP compression. The Advisor does not work on non-Exadata platforms running Database versions prior to 11.2.0.2, although there may be a patch available to enable this functionality.

The Compression Advisor may also be useful on Exadata platforms. Of course you could just compress a table with the various levels to see how well it compresses, but if the tables are very large this may not be practical. In this case you may be tempted to create a temporary table by selecting the records where rownum < X and do your compression test on that subset of rows. And that's basically what the Advisor does, although it is a little smarter about the set of records it chooses. Here's an example of its use:

```
SYS@SANDBOX1> !cat get_compression_ratio.sql
set sqlblanklines on
set feedback off
accept owner -
 prompt 'Enter Value for owner: '
accept table_name -
 prompt 'Enter Value for table_name: '
accept comp_type -
 prompt 'Enter Value for compression_type (OLTP): ' -
 default 'OLTP'

DECLARE

    l_blkcnt_cmp      BINARY_INTEGER;
    l_blkcnt_uncmp    BINARY_INTEGER;
    l_row_cmp         BINARY_INTEGER;
    l_row_uncmp       BINARY_INTEGER;
    l_cmp_ratio       NUMBER;
    l_comptype_str    VARCHAR2 (200);
    l_comptype     number;
BEGIN

case '&&comp_type'
            when 'OLTP' then l_comptype := DBMS_COMPRESSION.comp_for_oltp;
            when 'QUERY' then l_comptype := DBMS_COMPRESSION.comp_for_query_low;
            when 'QUERY_LOW' then l_comptype := DBMS_COMPRESSION.comp_for_query_low;
            when 'QUERY_HIGH' then l_comptype := DBMS_COMPRESSION.comp_for_query_high;
            when 'ARCHIVE' then l_comptype := DBMS_COMPRESSION.comp_for_archive_low;
            when 'ARCHIVE_LOW' then l_comptype := DBMS_COMPRESSION.comp_for_archive_low;
            when 'ARCHIVE_HIGH' then l_comptype := DBMS_COMPRESSION.comp_for_archive_high;
        END CASE;

    DBMS_COMPRESSION.get_compression_ratio (
        scratchtbsname    => 'USERS',
        ownname           => '&owner',
        tabname           => '&table_name',
        partname          => NULL,
        comptype          => l_comptype,
        blkcnt_cmp        => l_blkcnt_cmp,
        blkcnt_uncmp      => l_blkcnt_uncmp,
        row_cmp           => l_row_cmp,
```

```
        row_uncmp          => l_row_uncmp,
        cmp_ratio            => l_cmp_ratio,
        comptype_str         => l_comptype_str
    );
dbms_output.put_line(' ');
    DBMS_OUTPUT.put_line ('Estimated Compression Ratio using '||l_comptype_str||': '||
round(l_cmp_ratio,3));
dbms_output.put_line(' ');

END;
/
undef owner
undef table_name
undef comp_type
set feedback on

SYS@SANDBOX1> @get_compression_ratio.sql
Enter Value for owner: KSO
Enter Value for table_name: SKEW3
Enter Value for compression_type (OLTP):

Estimated Compression Ratio using "Compress For OLTP": 1.4

Elapsed: 00:00:07.50
SYS@SANDBOX1> @get_compression_ratio.sql
Enter Value for owner: KSO
Enter Value for table_name: SKEW3
Enter Value for compression_type (OLTP): QUERY LOW
Compression Advisor self-check validation successful. select count(*) on both Uncompressed and
EHCC Compressed format = 1000001 rows

Estimated Compression Ratio using "Compress For Query Low": 4

Elapsed: 00:01:04.14
SYS@SANDBOX1> @get_compression_ratio.sql
Enter Value for owner: KSO
Enter Value for table_name: SKEW3
Enter Value for compression_type (OLTP): QUERY HIGH
Compression Advisor self-check validation successful. select count(*) on both Uncompressed and
EHCC Compressed format = 1000001 rows

Estimated Compression Ratio using "Compress For Query High": 42.4

Elapsed: 00:01:01.42
SYS@SANDBOX1> @get_compression_ratio.sql
Enter Value for owner: KSO
Enter Value for table_name: SKEW3
Enter Value for compression_type (OLTP): ARCHIVE LOW
Compression Advisor self-check validation successful. select count(*) on both Uncompressed and
EHCC Compressed format = 1000001 rows
```

```
Estimated Compression Ratio using "Compress For Archive Low": 43.5

Elapsed: 00:01:01.70
SYS@SANDBOX1> @get_compression_ratio.sql
Enter Value for owner: KSO
Enter Value for table_name: SKEW3
Enter Value for compression_type (OLTP): ARCHIVE HIGH
Compression Advisor self-check validation successful. select count(*) on both Uncompressed and
EHCC Compressed format = 1000001 rows

Estimated Compression Ratio using "Compress For Archive High": 54.7

Elapsed: 00:01:18.09
```

Notice that the procedure prints out a validation message telling you how many records were used for the comparison. This number can be modified as part of the call to the procedure if so desired. The get_compression_ratio.sql script prompts for a table and a Compression Type and then executes the DBMS_COMPRESSION.GET_COMPRESSION_RATIO procedure. Once again the pertinent data is a little hard to pick out of the listing, so Table 3-5 compares the actual compression ratios to the estimates provided by the Compression Advisor.

Table 3-5. Compression Advisor Accuracy

Table Name	Compress For	Actual Compression Ratio	Estimated Compression Ratio	Error Percentage
SKEW3_OLTP	OLTP	1.4	1.4	0%
SKEW3_HCC1	QUERY LOW	4.0	4.0	0%
SKEW3_HCC2	QUERY HIGH	45.6	42.4	7%
SKEW3_HCC3	ARCHIVE LOW	45.6	43.5	5%
SKEW3_HCC4	ARCHIVE HIGH	55.9	54.7	2%

The estimates are fairly close to the actual values and while they are not 100 percent accurate, the tradeoff is probably worth it in cases where the objects are very large and a full test would be too time-consuming or take up too much disk space. The ability to run the Compression Advisor on non-Exadata platforms is also a real plus. It should be able to provide you with enough information to make reasonable decisions prior to actually migrating data to Exadata.

Real World Examples

As Yogi Berra once said, you can learn a lot just by watching. Marketing slides and book author claims are one thing, but real data is often more useful. Just to give you an idea of what kind of compression is reasonable to expect, here are a few comparisons of data from different industries. The data should provide you with an idea of the potential compression ratios that can be achieved by Hybrid Columnar Compression.

Custom Application Data

This dataset came from a custom application that tracks the movement of assets. The table is very narrow, consisting of only 12 columns. The table has close to 1 billion rows, but many of the columns have a very low number of distinct values (NDV). That means that the same values are repeated many times. This table is a prime candidate for compression. Here are the basic table statistics and the compression ratios achieved:

```
================================================================================
  Table Statistics
================================================================================
TABLE_NAME              : CP_DAILY
LAST_ANALYZED           : 29-DEC-2010 23:55:16
DEGREE                  : 1
PARTITIONED             : YES
NUM_ROWS                : 925241124
CHAIN_CNT               : 0
BLOCKS                  : 15036681
EMPTY_BLOCKS            : 0
AVG_SPACE               : 0
AVG_ROW_LEN             : 114
MONITORING              : YES
SAMPLE_SIZE             : 925241124
TOTALSIZE_MEGS          : 118019
================================================================================
  Column Statistics
================================================================================
```

Name	Analyzed	Null?	NDV	Density	# Nulls	# Buckets
PK_ACTIVITY_DTL_ID	12/29/2010	NOT NULL	925241124	.000000	0	1
FK_ACTIVITY_ID	12/29/2010	NOT NULL	43388928	.000000	0	1
FK_DENOMINATION_ID	12/29/2010		38	.000000	88797049	38
AMOUNT	12/29/2010		1273984	.000001	0	1
FK_BRANCH_ID	12/29/2010	NOT NULL	131	.000000	0	128
LOGIN_ID	12/29/2010	NOT NULL	30	.033333	0	1
DATETIME_STAMP	12/29/2010	NOT NULL	710272	.000001	0	1
LAST_MODIFY_LOGIN_ID	12/29/2010	NOT NULL	30	.033333	0	1
MODIFY_DATETIME_STAMP	12/29/2010	NOT NULL	460224	.000002	0	1
ACTIVE_FLAG	12/29/2010	NOT NULL	2	.000000	0	2
FK_BAG_ID	12/29/2010		2895360	.000000	836693535	1
CREDIT_DATE	12/29/2010		549	.001821	836693535	1

```
================================================================================
```

```
SYS@POC1> @table_size2
Enter value for owner:
Enter value for table_name: CP_DAILY_INV_ACTIVITY_DTL
```

OWNER	SEGMENT_NAME	TOTALSIZE_MEGS	COMPRESS_FOR
KSO	CP_DAILY_INV_ACTIVITY_DTL	118,018.8	
sum		118,018.8	

```
SYS@POC1> @comp_ratio
Enter value for original_size: 118018.8
Enter value for owner: KSO
Enter value for table_name: CP_DAILY%
Enter value for type:
```

OWNER	SEGMENT_NAME	TYPE	TOTALSIZE_MEGS	COMPRESSION_RATIO
KSO	CP_DAILY_HCC1	TABLE	7,488.1	15.8
KSO	CP_DAILY_HCC3	TABLE	2,442.3	48.3
KSO	CP_DAILY_HCC2	TABLE	2,184.7	54.0
KSO	CP_DAILY_HCC4	TABLE	1,807.8	65.3
sum			13,922.8	

As expected, this table is extremely compressible. Simple queries against these tables also run much faster against the compressed tables, as you can see in this listing:

```
SYS@POC1> select sum(amount) from kso.CP_DAILY_HCC3 where credit_date = '01-oct-2010';

 SUM(AMOUNT)
------------
4002779614.9

1 row selected.

Elapsed: 00:00:02.37
SYS@POC1> select sum(amount) from kso.CP_DAILY where credit_date = '01-oct-2010';

 SUM(AMOUNT)
------------
4002779614.9

1 row selected.

Elapsed: 00:00:42.58
```

This simple query ran roughly 19 times faster using the ARCHIVE LOW compressed table than when it was run against the uncompressed table.

Telecom Call Detail Data

This table contains call detail records for a telecom company. There are approximately 1.5 billion records in the table. Many of the columns in this table are unique or nearly so. In addition, many of the columns contain large numbers of nulls. Nulls are not compressible since they are not stored in the normal Oracle block format. This is not a table we would expect to be highly compressible. Here are the basic table statistics and the compression ratios:

```
=============================================================================
  Table Statistics
=============================================================================
TABLE_NAME              : SEE
LAST_ANALYZED           : 29-SEP-2010 00:02:15
DEGREE                  : 8
PARTITIONED             : YES
NUM_ROWS                : 1474776874
CHAIN_CNT               : 0
BLOCKS                  : 57532731
EMPTY_BLOCKS            : 0
AVG_SPACE               : 0
AVG_ROW_LEN             : 282
MONITORING              : YES
SAMPLE_SIZE             : 1474776874
TOTALSIZE_MEGS          : 455821
=============================================================================


SYS@POC1> @comp_ratio
Enter value for original_size: 455821
Enter value for owner: KSO
Enter value for table_name: SEE_HCC%
Enter value for type:

OWNER       SEGMENT_NAME         TYPE             TOTALSIZE_MEGS COMPRESSION_RATIO
----------  -------------------  ---------------- -------------- -----------------
KSO         SEE_HCC1             TABLE                 168,690.1               2.7
KSO         SEE_HCC2             TABLE                  96,142.1               4.7
KSO         SEE_HCC3             TABLE                  87,450.8               5.2
KSO         SEE_HCC4             TABLE                  72,319.1               6.3
                                                  --------------
sum                                                    424,602.1
```

Financial Data

The next table is made up of financial data, revenue accrual data from an order entry system to be exact. Here are the basic table statistics.

```
=============================================================================
  Table Statistics
=============================================================================
TABLE_NAME              : REV_ACCRUAL
LAST_ANALYZED           : 07-JAN-2011 00:42:47
DEGREE                  : 1
PARTITIONED             : YES
NUM_ROWS                : 114736686
CHAIN_CNT               : 0
```

```
BLOCKS                      : 15225910
EMPTY_BLOCKS                : 0
AVG_SPACE                   : 0
AVG_ROW_LEN                 : 917
MONITORING                  : YES
SAMPLE_SIZE                 : 114736686
TOTALSIZE_MEGS              : 120019
================================================================================
```

So the number of rows is not that great, only about 115 million, but the table is wide. It has 161 columns and the average row length is 917 bytes. It is a bit of a mixed bag with regards to compressibility though. Many of the columns contain a high percentage of nulls. On the other hand, many of the columns have a very low number of distinct values. This table may be a candidate for reordering the data on disk as a strategy to improve the compression ratio. At any rate, here are the compression rates achieved on this table at the various HCC levels.

```
SYS@POC1> @comp_ratio
Enter value for original_size: 120019
Enter value for owner: KSO
Enter value for table_name: REV_ACCRUAL_HCC%
Enter value for type:
```

OWNER	SEGMENT_NAME	TYPE	TOTALSIZE_MEGS	COMPRESSION_RATIO
KSO	REV_ACCRUAL_HCC1	TABLE	31,972.6	3.8
KSO	REV_ACCRUAL_HCC2	TABLE	17,082.9	7.0
KSO	REV_ACCRUAL_HCC3	TABLE	14,304.3	8.4
KSO	REV_ACCRUAL_HCC4	TABLE	12,541.6	9.6
sum			75,901.4	

Retail Sales Data

The final table is made up of sales figures from a retailer. The table contains about 6 billion records and occupies well over half a Terabyte. There are very few columns, and the data is highly repetitive. In fact, there are no unique fields in this table. This is a very good candidate for compression. Here are the basic table statistics:

```
================================================================================
   Table Statistics
================================================================================
TABLE_NAME                  : SALES
LAST_ANALYZED               : 23-DEC-2010 03:13:44
DEGREE                      : 1
PARTITIONED                 : NO
NUM_ROWS                    : 5853784365
CHAIN_CNT                   : 0
BLOCKS                      : 79183862
EMPTY_BLOCKS                : 0
AVG_SPACE                   : 0
AVG_ROW_LEN                 : 93
MONITORING                  : YES
```

```
SAMPLE_SIZE              : 5853784365
TOTALSIZE_MEGS           : 618667
=================================================================================
  Column Statistics
=================================================================================
 Name            Analyzed     Null?    NDV        Density  # Nulls  # Buckets   Sample
=================================================================================
 TRANS_ID        12/23/2010            389808128  .000000  0        1           5853784365
 TRANS_LINE_NO   12/23/2010            126        .007937  0        1           5853784365
 UNIT_ID         12/23/2010            128600     .000008  0        1           5853784365
 DAY             12/23/2010            3          .333333  0        1           5853784365
 TRANS_SEQ       12/23/2010            22932      .000044  0        1           5853784365
 BEGIN_DATE      12/23/2010            4          .250000  0        1           5853784365
 END_DATE        12/23/2010            4          .250000  0        1           5853784365
 UNIT_TYPE       12/23/2010            1          1.000000 0        1           5853784365
 SKU_TYPE        12/23/2010            54884      .000018  0        1           5853784365
 QTY             12/23/2010            104        .009615  0        1           5853784365
 PRICE           12/23/2010            622        .001608  0        1           5853784365
=================================================================================
```

Here are the compression ratios achieved for this table. As expected they are very good.

```
SYS@DEMO1> @comp_ratio
Enter value for original_size: 618667
Enter value for owner: KSO
Enter value for table_name: SALES_HCC%
Enter value for type:

OWNER       SEGMENT_NAME         TYPE               TOTALSIZE_MEGS COMPRESSION_RATIO
----------  -------------------  -----------------  -------------- -----------------
KSO         SALES_HCC1           TABLE                    41,654.6              14.9
KSO         SALES_HCC2           TABLE                    26,542.0              23.3
KSO         SALES_HCC3           TABLE                    26,538.5              23.3
KSO         SALES_HCC4           TABLE                    19,633.0              31.5
                                                    --------------
sum                                                      114,368.1
```

Summary of the Real World Examples

The examples in this section came from real applications. They show a fairly extreme variation in data compressibility. This is to be expected, as the success of compression algorithms is very dependent on the data being compressed. Table 3-6 presents the data from all four examples.

Table 3-6. Real-World Examples Compared

Data Type	Base Table Name	Characteristics	Compression Ratios
Asset Tracking	CP_DAILY	Skinny Table, Many Low NDV Columns	16×-65×
Call Detail Records	SEE	Many NULLs, Many Unique Columns	3×-6×

Data Type	Base Table Name	Characteristics	Compression Ratios
Financial Data	REV_ACCRUAL	Wide Table, Many NULLs, Many Low NDV Columns	4×-10×
Retail Sales Data	SALES	Skinny Table, Mostly Low NDV Columns	15×-32×

Hopefully this data gives you some feel for the range of compression ratios that you can expect from HCC and the types of datasets that will benefit most. Of course the best way to predict how compressible a particular table may be is to actually test it. This fact cannot be overemphasized.

Restrictions/Challenges

There are a few challenges with using HCC. Many of them have to do with the fact that HCC is not available on non-Exadata platforms. This fact poses challenges for recovery and high availability solutions. The other major challenge is that HCC doesn't play well with data that is being actively updated. In particular, systems characterized by lots of single-row updates, which we often describe as OLTP workloads, will probably not work well with HCC.

Moving Data to a non-Exadata Platform

Probably the largest hurdle with using HCC has been moving the data to non-Exadata platforms. For example, while RMAN and Dataguard both support the HCC block format, and will happily restore data to a non-Exadata environment, a database running on such an environment will not be able to do anything with the data until it is decompressed. This can mean a lengthy delay before being able to access the data in a case where a failover to a standby on a non-Exadata platform occurs. The same issue holds true for doing an RMAN restore to a non-Exadata platform. The restore will work but the data in HCC formatted blocks will not be accessible until the data has been moved into a non-HCC format. This can be done with the ALTER TABLE MOVE NOCOMPRESS command, by the way.

■ **Note**: The ability to decompress HCC data on non-Exadata platforms only became available in Oracle database version 11.2.0.2. Attempting this on version 11.2.0.1 would result in an error. (Check with Oracle Support for a patch that may enable this behavior on 11.2.0.1)

In addition to the lengthy delay associated with decompressing data before being able to access it, there is also the issue of space. If HCC is providing a 10× compression factor, you will need to have 10 times the space you are currently using available on the target environment to handle the increased size of the data. For these reasons, Dataguard is rarely set up with a standby on a non-Exadata platform.

Disabling Serial Direct Path Reads

As we discussed in Chapter 2, Serial Direct Path Reads allow nonparallelized scan operations to use the direct path read mechanism, which is a prerequisite for enabling the Smart Scan features of Exadata.

Serial Direct Path Reads are enabled based on a calculation that depends on the size of the object being scanned relative to the available buffer cache. In simplistic terms, only large objects will be considered for Serial Direct Path Reads. HCC's effectiveness can actually work against it here. Since the compression reduces the size of the objects so drastically, it can cause statements that would normally benefit from a Smart Scan to use the standard read mechanism, disabling many of Exadata's optimizations. This is generally not a huge problem, because the number of blocks is considerably reduced by HCC and the database is making this decision at run time. The problem comes in, though, when an object is partitioned. The calculation is based on the size of the object being scanned; in the case of a partitioned object this means the size of the partition. So in cases where partitioning is used with HCC, we often see some partitions using Smart Scans and some unable to use Smart Scans. Keep in mind that this also means decompression cannot be done at the storage layer, as this capability is enabled only when performing Smart Scans.

■ **Kevin Says:** Compression also has a lot to do with the often-overlooked In-Memory Parallel Query feature of Oracle Database 11g. Very effective compression combined with modern large memory servers makes In-Memory Parallel Query a usable feature for production purposes. Customers would do well to consider the best compression technology that suits their DML processing requirements while potentially exploiting the power of In-Memory Parallel Query.

Locking Issues

The Exadata documentation says that updating a single row of a table compressed with HCC locks the entire compression unit containing the row. This can cause extreme contention issues for OLTP-type systems. This is the main reason that HCC is not recommended for tables (or partitions) where the data will be updated. Here's a demonstration of the locking behavior:

```
KSO@SANDBOX1> select rowid, old_rowid(rowid) old_rowid , pk_col from kso.skew_hcc3
  2  where rownum < 10;

ROWID              OLD_ROWID                        PK_COL
------------------ ------------------------------   ----------
AAATCBAAHAAMkyXAAA 7.3296407.0                      27999409
AAATCBAAHAAMkyXAAB 7.3296407.1                      27999408
AAATCBAAHAAMkyXAAC 7.3296407.2                      27999407
AAATCBAAHAAMkyXAAD 7.3296407.3                      27999406
AAATCBAAHAAMkyXAAE 7.3296407.4                      27999405
AAATCBAAHAAMkyXAAF 7.3296407.5                      27999404
AAATCBAAHAAMkyXAAG 7.3296407.6                      27999403
AAATCBAAHAAMkyXAAH 7.3296407.7                      27999402
AAATCBAAHAAMkyXAAI 7.3296407.8                      27999401

9 rows selected.
KSO@SANDBOX1> update kso.skew set col1=col1 where pk_col = 27999409;

1 row updated.
```

```
SYS@SANDBOX1> select col1 from kso.skew_hcc3 where pk_col = 27999409 for update nowait;
select col1 from kso.skew where pk_col = 16858437 for update nowait
                                   *
ERROR at line 1:
ORA-00054: resource busy and acquire with NOWAIT specified or timeout expired


SYS@SANDBOX1> -- Expected because this row has been updated by another process
SYS@SANDBOX1>
SYS@SANDBOX1> select col1 from kso.skew_hcc3 where pk_col = 27999401 for update nowait;
select col1 from kso.skew where pk_col = 16858429 for update nowait
                                   *
ERROR at line 1:
ORA-00054: resource busy and acquire with NOWAIT specified or timeout expired

SYS@SANDBOX1> -- Not normal Oracle locking behavior
```

Clearly this behavior would be disastrous to many OLTP systems. Especially when you consider the large number of records that can be stored in an HCC block. In this case that number is approximately 13,500 rows per block. This means that a single update could lock well over 50,000 rows.

Single Row Access

HCC is built for full table scan access. Decompression is a CPU-intensive task. Smart Scans can distribute the decompression work to the CPU's on the storage cells. This makes the CPU-intensive task much more palatable. However, Smart Scans only occur when Full Scans are performed. This means that other access mechanisms, index access for example, must use the DB server CPUs to perform decompression. This can put an enormous CPU load on DB servers in high volume OLTP-type systems. In addition, since data for a single row is spread across multiple blocks in a CU, retrieving a complete row causes the entire CU to be read. This can have a detrimental effect on the overall database efficiency for systems that tend to access data using indexes, even if the access is read-only.

Common Usage Scenarios

HCC provides such high levels of compression that it has been used as an alternative to traditional ILM strategies, which generally involve moving older historical data off the database entirely. These ILM strategies usually entail some type of date range partitioning and a purge process. This is done to free storage and in some cases to improve performance. Often the data must be retained in some backup format so that it can be accessed if required at some later date. With HCC, it is possible in many cases to retain data indefinitely by compressing the oldest partitions. This approach has many advantages over the traditional approach of moving the data.

First and foremost, the data remains available via the standard application interfaces. No additional work will need to be done to restore a backup of old data before it can be accessed. This advantage alone is often enough to justify this approach. This approach typically entails leaving active partitions uncompressed while compressing old partitions more aggressively. Here's a short example of creating a partitioned table with mixed compression modes.

```
SYS@DEMO1>    CREATE TABLE "KSO"."CLASS_SALES_P"
  2     (    "TRANS_ID" VARCHAR2(30),
  3          "UNIT_ID" NUMBER(30,0),
  4          "DAY" NUMBER(30,0),
```

```
 5          "TRANS_SEQ" VARCHAR2(30),
 6          "END_DATE" DATE,
 7          "BEGIN_DATE" DATE,
 8          "UNIT_TYPE" VARCHAR2(30),
 9          "CUST_TYPE" VARCHAR2(1),
10          "LOAD_DATE" DATE,
11          "CURRENCY_TYPE" CHAR(1)
12      ) PCTFREE 10 PCTUSED 40 INITRANS 1 MAXTRANS 255  NOLOGGING
13     STORAGE(
14     BUFFER_POOL DEFAULT FLASH_CACHE DEFAULT CELL_FLASH_CACHE DEFAULT)
15     TABLESPACE "CLASS_DATA"
16     PARTITION BY RANGE ("BEGIN_DATE")
17     (PARTITION "P1"  VALUES LESS THAN (TO_DATE
18       (' 2008-09-06 00:00:00', 'SYYYY-MM-DD HH24:MI:SS', 'NLS_CALENDAR=GREGORIAN'))
19   SEGMENT CREATION IMMEDIATE
20     PCTFREE 10 PCTUSED 40 INITRANS 1 MAXTRANS 255 NOCOMPRESS NOLOGGING
21     STORAGE(INITIAL 8388608 NEXT 1048576 MINEXTENTS 1 MAXEXTENTS 2147483645
22     PCTINCREASE 0 FREELISTS 1 FREELIST GROUPS 1 BUFFER_POOL DEFAULT
23     FLASH_CACHE DEFAULT CELL_FLASH_CACHE DEFAULT)
24     TABLESPACE "CLASS_DATA" ,
25    PARTITION "P2"  VALUES LESS THAN (TO_DATE
26       (' 2008-09-07 00:00:00', 'SYYYY-MM-DD HH24:MI:SS', 'NLS_CALENDAR=GREGORIAN'))
27   SEGMENT CREATION IMMEDIATE
28     PCTFREE 0 PCTUSED 40 INITRANS 1 MAXTRANS 255 COMPRESS FOR QUERY HIGH NOLOGGING
29     STORAGE(INITIAL 8388608 NEXT 1048576 MINEXTENTS 1 MAXEXTENTS 2147483645
30     PCTINCREASE 0 FREELISTS 1 FREELIST GROUPS 1 BUFFER_POOL DEFAULT
31     FLASH_CACHE DEFAULT CELL_FLASH_CACHE DEFAULT)
32     TABLESPACE "CLASS_DATA" ,
33    PARTITION "P3"  VALUES LESS THAN (TO_DATE
34       (' 2008-09-08 00:00:00', 'SYYYY-MM-DD HH24:MI:SS', 'NLS_CALENDAR=GREGORIAN'))
35   SEGMENT CREATION IMMEDIATE
36     PCTFREE 0 PCTUSED 40 INITRANS 1 MAXTRANS 255 COMPRESS FOR ARCHIVE LOW NOLOGGING
37     STORAGE(INITIAL 8388608 NEXT 1048576 MINEXTENTS 1 MAXEXTENTS 2147483645
38     PCTINCREASE 0 FREELISTS 1 FREELIST GROUPS 1 BUFFER_POOL DEFAULT
39     FLASH_CACHE DEFAULT CELL_FLASH_CACHE DEFAULT)
40     TABLESPACE "CLASS_DATA" ) ;

Table created.

SYS@DEMO1> @part_size2.sql
Enter value for owner: KSO
Enter value for table_name:
```

OWNER	SEGMENT_NAME	PART_NAME	TOTALSIZE_MEGS	COMPRESS_FOR
KSO	CLASS_SALES_P	P1	24.0	
		P2	24.0	QUERY HIGH
		P3	24.0	ARCHIVE LOW
********************	******************		--------------	
sum			72.0	

Summary

Introduced in Oracle 11g R2, Hybrid Columnar Compression provides exceptional compression capabilities that are far beyond anything available in prior releases. This is thanks in large part to the adoption of industry-standard compression algorithms and an increase in the size of the compression unit from a single database block (typically 8K) to a larger unit of 32K or 64K. The feature is only appropriate for data that is no longer being modified, though, because of locking issues and the fact that updated rows are moved into a much less compressed format (OLTP compression format). For this reason, HCC should only be used with data that is no longer being modified (or only occasionally modified). Since compression can be defined at the partition level, it is common to see tables that have a mixture of compressed and uncompressed partitions. This technique can in many cases replace ILM approaches that require moving data to alternate storage media and then purging it from the database.

CHAPTER 4

Storage Indexes

Storage Indexes are the most useful Exadata feature that you never hear about. They are not indexes that are stored in the database like Oracle's traditional B-Tree or bitmapped indexes. In fact, they are not indexes at all in the traditional sense. They are not capable of identifying a set of records that has a certain value in a given column. Rather, they are a feature of the storage server software that is designed to eliminate disk I/O. They are sometimes described as "reverse indexes." That's because they identify locations where the requested records are not, instead of the other way around. They work by storing minimum and maximum column values for disk storage units, which are 1 Megabyte (MB) by default. Because SQL predicates are passed to the storage servers when Smart Scans are performed, the storage software can check the predicates against the Storage Index metadata (maximum and minimum values) before doing the requested I/O. Any storage region that cannot possibly have a matching row is skipped. In many cases, this can result in a significant reduction in the amount of I/O that must be performed. Keep in mind that since the storage software needs the predicates to compare to the maximum and minimum values in the Storage Indexes, this optimization is only available for Smart Scans.

The storage software provides no documented mechanism for altering or tuning Storage Indexes (although there are a few undocumented parameters that can be set prior to starting cellsrv on the storage servers). In fact, there is not even much available in the way of monitoring. For example, there is no wait event that records the amount of time spent when a Storage Index is accessed or updated. Even though there are no commands to manipulate Storage Indexes, they are an extremely powerful feature and can provide dramatic performance improvements. For that reason it is important to understand how they work.

▨ **Kevin Says:** To keep the role of Storage Indexes straight in my mind, I generally picture an optimization that dramatically improves searching for a needle in a haystack as opposed to finding where certain pieces of straw exist in a haystack.

Structure

Storage Indexes consist of a minimum and a maximum value for up to eight columns. This structure is maintained for 1MB chunks of storage (storage regions). Storage Indexes are stored in memory only and are never written to disk.

■ **Kevin Says:** Storage Indexes are stored in the heap of `cellsrv`, so technically speaking they could end up on disk (swap) under insane conditions…so, not never…

Figure 4-1 shows a conceptual view of the data contained in a Storage Index.

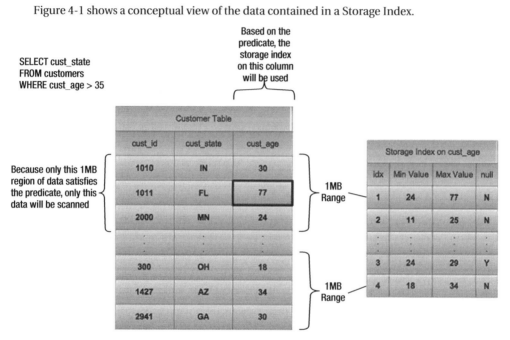

Figure 4-1. Conceptual diagram of a Storage Index

As you can see in the diagram, the first storage region in the Customer table has a maximum value of 77, indicating that it's possible for it to contain rows that will satisfy the query predicate (cust_age >35). The other storage regions in the diagram do not have maximum values that are high enough to contain any records that will satisfy the query predicate. Therefore, those storage regions will not be read from disk.

In addition to the minimum and maximum values, there is a flag to indicate whether any of the records in a storage region contain nulls. The fact that nulls are represented at all is somewhat surprising given that nulls are not stored in traditional Oracle indexes. This ability of Storage Indexes to track nulls may actually have repercussions for design and implementation decisions. There are systems that don't use nulls at all. SAP, for example, uses a single space character instead of nulls. SAP does this simply to insure that records can be accessed via B-Tree indexes (which do not store nulls). At any rate, Storage Indexes provide the equivalent of a bit-mapped index on nulls, which makes finding nulls a very efficient process (assuming they represent a low percentage of the values).

Monitoring Storage Indexes

The ability to monitor Storage Indexes is very limited. The optimizer doesn't know whether a Storage Index will be used for a particular SQL statement. Nor do AWR or ASH capture any information about whether Storage Indexes were used by particular SQL statements. There is a single statistic that tracks Storage Index usage at the database level and an undocumented tracing mechanism.

Database Statistics

There is only one database statistic related to storage indexes. The statistic, `cell physical IO bytes saved by storage index`, keeps track of the accumulated I/O that has been avoided by the use of Storage Indexes. This statistic is exposed in v$sesstat and v$sysstat and related views. It's a strange statistic that calculates a precise value for something it didn't do. Nevertheless, it is the only easily accessible indicator as to whether Storage Indexes have been used. Unfortunately, since the statistic is cumulative, like all statistics in v$sesstat, it must be checked before and after a given SQL statement in order to determine whether Storage Indexes were used on that particular statement. Here is an example:

```
SYS@EXDB1> set echo on
SYS@EXDB1> @si
SYS@EXDB1> col name for a70
SYS@EXDB1> col value for 99999999999999
SYS@EXDB1> select name, value
  2   from v$mystat s, v$statname n
  3   where n.statistic# = s.statistic#
  4   and name like '%storage%';


NAME                                                           VALUE
---------------------------------------------- ---------------
cell physical IO bytes saved by storage index                     0

SYS@EXDB1> select avg(pk_col) from kso.skew2 where col1 is null;

AVG(PK_COL)
-----------
   32000001

SYS@EXDB1> set echo off
SYS@EXDB1> @si

NAME                                                           VALUE
---------------------------------------------- ---------------
cell physical IO bytes saved by storage index            3984949248

SYS@EXDB1> select avg(pk_col) from kso.skew2 where col1 is null;

AVG(PK_COL)
-----------
   32000001
```

```
SYS@EXDB1> @si

NAME                                                    VALUE
---------------------------------------------- ---------------
cell physical IO bytes saved by storage index      7969898496
```

As you can see, the `si.sql` script queries `v$mystat` for a statistic that contains the word "storage." The value for this statistic will be 0 until a SQL statement that uses a Storage Index has been executed in the current session. In our example, the query used a Storage Index that eliminated about 4 billion bytes of disk I/O. This is the amount of additional I/O that would have been necessary without Storage Indexes. Note that `v$mystat` is a view that exposes cumulative statistics for your current session. So if you run the statement a second time, the value should increase to twice the value it had after the first execution. Of course, disconnecting from the session (by exiting SQL*Plus for example) resets most statistics exposed by `v$mystat`, including this one, to 0.

Tracing

There is another way to monitor what is going on with Storage Indexes at the individual storage cell level. The `cellsrv` program has the ability to create trace files whenever Storage Indexes are accessed. This tracing can be enabled by setting the `_CELL_STORAGE_INDEX_DIAG_MODE` parameter to TRUE in the `cellinit.ora` file on one of the storage cells. You will need to restart the `cellsrv` program once this parameter is set. In general this should not cause any interruption to the clusterware or databases running on the database machines, thanks to the redundancy provided by ASM. However, you should be aware that if you have issues on other storage cells, it's possible that restarting a `cellsrv` process could cause an outage. Tracing can also be enabled on all storage servers by setting the hidden database parameter, `_KCFIS_STORAGEIDX_DIAG_MODE` to a value of 2. Since this tracing mechanism is completely undocumented, it should not be used without approval from Oracle support. Better safe than sorry.

Because the `cellsrv` process is multithreaded, the tracing facility creates many trace files. The result is similar to tracing a select statement that is executed in parallel on a database server, in that there are multiple trace files that need to be combined to show the whole picture. The naming convention for the trace files is svtrc_, followed by a process ID, followed by a thread identifier. The process ID matches the operating system process ID of the `cellsrv` process. Since `cellsrv` enables only 100 threads by default, the file names are reused rapidly as requests come into the storage cells. Because of this rapid reuse, it's quite easy to wrap around the thread number portion of the file name. Such wrapping around doesn't wipe out the previous trace file, but rather appends new data to the existing file. Appending happens with trace files on Oracle database servers as well, but is much less common because the process ID portion of the default file name comes from the user's shadow process. So basically each session gets its own number.

There is another related cellsrv parameter, `_CELL_SI_MAX_NUM_DIAG_MODE_DUMPS`, that sets a maximum number of trace files that will be created before the tracing functionality is turned off. The parameter defaults to a value of 20. Presumably the parameter is a safety mechanism to keep the disk from getting filled by trace files, since a single query can create a large number of files.

Here is a snippet from a trace file generated on our test system:

```
Trace file
/opt/oracle/cell11.2.2.2.0_LINUX.X64_101206.2/log/diag/asm/cell/enkcel03/trace/svtrc_13253_100
.trc
ORACLE_HOME = /opt/oracle/cell11.2.2.2.0_LINUX.X64_101206.2
System name:    Linux
Node name:      enkcel03.enkitec.com
Release:        2.6.18-194.3.1.0.3.el5
```

Version: #1 SMP Tue Aug 31 22:41:13 EDT 2010
Machine: x86_64
CELL SW Version: OSS_11.2.0.3.0_LINUX.X64_101206.2

*** 2010-12-17 11:40:41.127
UserThread: LWPID: 13834 userId: 100 kernelId: 100 pthreadID: 0x2aae6b689940
2010-12-17 12:11:26.491971*: FenceMaster: OSS_IOCTL_FENCE_ENTITY is called, host
enkdb02.enkitec.com[pid:8519] number of fencing in progress 1 reid
cid=3cb0d13cdb9cff5eff8b8bfb091c6fe9,icin=171990399,nmn=2,lnid=171990399,gid=23,gin=1,gmn=1,um
emid=1,opid=48,opsn=1,lvl=process hdr=0xfece0100
2010-12-17 12:11:26.497277*: FenceMaster: OSS_IOCTL_FENCE_ENTITY is set, number of fencing in
progress 0 reid
cid=3cb0d13cdb9cff5eff8b8bfb091c6fe9,icin=171990399,nmn=2,lnid=171990399,gid=23,gin=1,gmn=1,um
emid=1,opid=48,opsn=1,lvl=process hdr=0xfece0100
2010-12-17 12:45:25.914281*: FenceMaster: OSS_IOCTL_FENCE_ENTITY is called, host
enkdb01.enkitec.com[pid:9326] number of fencing in progress 1 reid
cid=3cb0d13cdb9cff5eff8b8bfb091c6fe9,icin=171990399,nmn=1,lnid=171990399,gid=-
2147483642,gin=1,gmn=3,umemid=3,opid=42,opsn=3,lvl=process hdr=0xfece0100
2010-12-17 12:45:25.915592*: FenceMaster: OSS_IOCTL_FENCE_ENTITY is set, number of fencing in
progress 0 reid cid=3cb0d13cdb9cff5eff8b8bfb091c6fe9,icin=171990399,nmn=1,lnid=171990399,gid=-
2147483642,gin=1,gmn=3,umemid=3,opid=42,opsn=3,lvl=process hdr=0xfece0100
2010-12-17 12:45:41.118778*: FenceMaster: OSS_IOCTL_FENCE_ENTITY is called, host
enkdb01.enkitec.com[pid:9326] number of fencing in progress 1 reid
cid=3cb0d13cdb9cff5eff8b8bfb091c6fe9,icin=171990399,nmn=1,lnid=171990399,gid=-
2147483642,gin=1,gmn=3,umemid=3,opid=0,opsn=0,lvl=member hdr=0xfece0100
2010-12-17 12:45:41.122256*: FenceMaster: OSS_IOCTL_FENCE_ENTITY is set, number of fencing in
progress 0 reid cid=3cb0d13cdb9cff5eff8b8bfb091c6fe9,icin=171990399,nmn=1,lnid=171990399,gid=-
2147483642,gin=1,gmn=3,umemid=3,opid=0,opsn=0,lvl=member hdr=0xfece0100
2010-12-21 12:12:34.465398*: FenceMaster: OSS_IOCTL_FENCE_ENTITY is called, host
enkdb02.enkitec.com[pid:8519] number of fencing in progress 1 reid
cid=3cb0d13cdb9cff5eff8b8bfb091c6fe9,icin=171990399,nmn=2,lnid=171990399,gid=-
2147483643,gin=1,gmn=1,umemid=1,opid=39,opsn=1,lvl=process hdr=0xfece0100
2010-12-21 12:12:34.471408*: FenceMaster: OSS_IOCTL_FENCE_ENTITY is set, number of fencing in
progress 0 reid cid=3cb0d13cdb9cff5eff8b8bfb091c6fe9,icin=171990399,nmn=2,lnid=171990399,gid=-
2147483643,gin=1,gmn=1,umemid=1,opid=39,opsn=1,lvl=process hdr=0xfece0100
2010-12-23 09:17:38.277822*: RIDX (0x2aae2f29feec) for SQLID 6dx247rvykr72 filter 1
2010-12-23 09:17:38.277822*: RIDX (0x2aae2f29feec) : st 2 validBitMap 7fffffffffffffff tabn 0
id {75759 4 3314771398}
2010-12-23 09:17:38.277822*: RIDX: strt 32 end 2048 offset 533652848640 size 1032192 rgnIdx
508931 RgnOffset 16384 scn: 0x0000.073fd1a7 hist: 0x9
2010-12-23 09:17:38.277822*: RIDX validation history: 0:PartialRead 1:PartialRead 2:Undef
3:Undef 4:Undef 5:Undef 6:Undef 7:Undef 8:Undef 9:Undef
2010-12-23 09:17:38.277822*: Col id [2] numFilt 20 flg 2:
2010-12-23 09:17:38.277822*: lo: c1 2 0 0 0 0 0 0
2010-12-23 09:17:38.277822*: hi: c3 64 51 4b 0 0 0 0
2010-12-23 09:17:38.277822*: Col id [3] numFilt 0 flg 2:
2010-12-23 09:17:38.277822*: lo: 61 73 64 64 73 61 64 61
2010-12-23 09:17:38.277822*: hi: 61 73 64 64 73 61 64 61
2010-12-23 09:17:38.277822*: Col id [5] numFilt 0 flg 2:
2010-12-23 09:17:38.277822*: lo: 4e 0 0 0 0 0 0 0
2010-12-23 09:17:38.277822*: hi: 59 0 0 0 0 0 0 0

. . .

```
2010-12-23 09:17:38.291153*: RIDX (0x2aadfea3d2d0) for SQLID 6dx247rvykr72 filter 1
2010-12-23 09:17:38.291153*: RIDX (0x2aadfea3d2d0) : st 2 validBitMap ffffffffffffffff tabn 0
id {75759 4 3314771398}
2010-12-23 09:17:38.291153*: RIDX: strt 0 end 2048 offset 546303901696 size 1048576 rgnIdx
520996 RgnOffset 0 scn: 0x0000.073fd34b hist: 0x1a
2010-12-23 09:17:38.291153*: RIDX validation history: 0:FullRead 1:PartialWrite 2:Undef
3:Undef 4:Undef 5:Undef 6:Undef 7:Undef 8:Undef 9:Undef
2010-12-23 09:17:38.291153*: Col id [2] numFilt 20 flg 2:
2010-12-23 09:17:38.291153*: lo: c1 2 0 0 0 0 0
2010-12-23 09:17:38.291153*: hi: c3 64 5c 8 0 0 0 0
2010-12-23 09:17:38.291153*: Col id [3] numFilt 0 flg 2:
2010-12-23 09:17:38.291153*: lo: 61 73 64 64 73 61 64 61
2010-12-23 09:17:38.291153*: hi: 61 73 64 64 73 61 64 61
2010-12-23 09:17:38.291153*: Col id [5] numFilt 0 flg 2:
2010-12-23 09:17:38.291153*: lo: 59 0 0 0 0 0 0
2010-12-23 09:17:38.291153*: hi: 59 0 0 0 0 0 0
2010-12-23 09:17:38.292459*: RIDX (0x2aadfea3d3dc) for SQLID 6dx247rvykr72 filter 1
2010-12-23 09:17:38.292459*: RIDX (0x2aadfea3d3dc) : st 2 validBitMap ffffffffffffffff tabn 0
id {75759 4 3314771398}
2010-12-23 09:17:38.292459*: RIDX: strt 0 end 2048 offset 546304950272 size 1048576 rgnIdx
520997 RgnOffset 0 scn: 0x0000.073fd34b hist: 0x1a
2010-12-23 09:17:38.292459*: RIDX validation history: 0:FullRead 1:PartialWrite 2:Undef
3:Undef 4:Undef 5:Undef 6:Undef 7:Undef 8:Undef 9:Undef
2010-12-23 09:17:38.292459*: Col id [2] numFilt 20 flg 2:
2010-12-23 09:17:38.292459*: lo: c1 2 0 0 0 0 0
2010-12-23 09:17:38.292459*: hi: c3 64 27 4f 0 0 0 0
2010-12-23 09:17:38.292459*: Col id [3] numFilt 0 flg 2:
2010-12-23 09:17:38.292459*: lo: 61 73 64 64 73 61 64 61
2010-12-23 09:17:38.292459*: hi: 61 73 64 64 73 61 64 61
2010-12-23 09:17:38.292459*: Col id [5] numFilt 0 flg 2:
2010-12-23 09:17:38.292459*: lo: 59 0 0 0 0 0 0
2010-12-23 09:17:38.292459*: hi: 59 0 0 0 0 0 0
```

Several things are worth pointing out in this trace file:

- The first several lines are the standard trace file header with file name and software version.

- The lines that begin with timestamps are each associated with a single storage region.

- The SQLID of the statement that generated the trace file is identified for each storage region.

- Each line containing the SQLID keyword begins data for a new storage region.

- The line below the SQLID line contains an ID which contains the data_object_id from DBA_OBJECTS for the table being scanned.

- The regionSize fields show that the storage regions really are 1MB.

- It looks like each Storage Index entry occupies 2K of memory based on the strt and end field values.

- For each column evaluated there is an id field that correlates to its position in the table.

- For each column evaluated there is a flg field. It appears that it is the decimal representation of a bit mask. It also appears that the first bit indicates whether nulls are contained in the current column of the storage region. (That is, 1 and 3 both indicate that nulls are present.)

- For each column evaluated there is a lo and a hi value (stored as hex).

- The lo and hi values are only 8 bytes, indicating that the Storage Indexes will be ineffective on columns where the leading portion of the values are not distinct (empirical evidence bears this out, by the way).

While generating and reading trace files is very informative, it is not very easy to do and requires direct access to the storage servers. On top of that, the approach is completely undocumented. It is probably best used for investigations in nonproduction environments.

Monitoring Wrap Up

Neither the database statistic nor the tracing is a particularly satisfying way of monitoring Storage Index usage. It would be nice to be able to track Storage Index usage at the statement level, via a column in V$SQL for example. In the meantime, the cell physical IO bytes saved by storage index statistic is the best option we have.

Controlling Storage Indexes

There is not much you can do to control Storage Index behavior. However, the developers have built in a few hidden parameters that provide some flexibility.

There are three database parameters that deal with Storage Indexes (that we're aware of):

- _kcfis_storageidx_disabled (default is FALSE)

- _kcfis_storageidx_diag_mode (default is 0)

- _cell_storidx_mode (default is EVA)

None of these parameters are documented, so you need to be careful with the methods we discuss in this section. Nevertheless, we'll tell you a little bit about some of these parameters and what they can do.

_kcfis_storageidx_disabled

The _kcfis_storageidx_disabled parameter allows Storage Indexes to be disabled. As with all hidden parameters, it's best to check with Oracle support before setting it, but as hidden parameters go, this one is relatively innocuous. We have used it extensively in testing and have not experienced any negative consequences.

You can set the parameter at the session level with the alter session statement:

```
alter session set "_kcfis_storageidx_disabled"=true;
```

Note that although setting _kcfis_storageidx_disabled to TRUE disables Storage Indexes for reads, the setting does not disable the maintenance of existing Storage Indexes. That is to say that existing

Storage Indexes will still be updated when values in a table are changed, even if this parameter is set to TRUE.

_kcfis_storageidx_diag_mode

The second parameter, __KCFIS_STORAGEIDX_DIAG_MODE, looks eerily like the cellinit.ora parameter _CELL_STORAGE_INDEX_DIAG_MODE, which was discussed earlier. As you might expect, setting this parameter at the database layer causes trace files to be generated across all the affected storage cells. Setting it to a value of 2 enables tracing. Oddly, setting it to a value of 1 disables Storage Indexes. Unfortunately, the trace files are created on the storage cells. But this method of generating them is much less intrusive than restarting the cellsrv process on a storage server.

You can set the parameter at the session level with the alter session statement:

```
alter session set "_kcfis_storageidx_diag_mode"=2;
```

There may be other valid values for the parameter that enable different levels of tracing. Keep in mind that this will produce a large number of trace files on every storage cell that is involved in a query that uses Storage Indexes.

_cell_storidx_mode

The _CELL_STORIDX_MODE parameter was added in the second point release of Oracle Database 11gR2 (11.2.0.2). While this parameter is undocumented, it appears that it controls where Storage Indexes will be applied. There are three valid values for this parameter (EVA,KDST,ALL). EVA and KDST are Oracle kernel function names.

You can set the parameter at the session level with the alter session statement:

```
alter session set "_cell_storidx_mode"=ALL;
```

The effects of this parameter have varied across releases. As of cellsrv version 11.2.2.3.0, EVA (the default) supports all the valid comparison operators. You should note that in older versions, the EVA setting did not support the IS NULL comparison operator. It's also important to keep in mind that the database patching is tied to the storage software patching. Upgrading the version of cellsrv without patching the database software can result in unpredicatable behavior (disabling storage indexes for example).

Storage Software Parameters

In addition to the database parameters, there are also a number of undocumented storage software parameters that are related to Storage Index behavior. These parameters can be modified by adding them to the cellinit.ora file and then restarting cellsrv. Note that cellinit.ora will be discussed in more detail in Chapter 8. Here is a list of the cellinit.ora Storage Index parameters along with their default values.

- _cell_enable_storage_index_for_loads=TRUE
- _cell_enable_storage_index_for_writes=TRUE
- _cell_si_max_num_diag_mode_dumps=20
- _cell_storage_index_columns=0
- _cell_storage_index_diag_mode=FALSE

- `_cell_storage_index_partial_rd_sectors=512`

- `_cell_storage_index_partial_reads_threshold_percent=85`

- `_cell_storage_index_sizing_factor=2`

You've already seen the tracing parameters (`_CELL_STORAGE_INDEX_DIAG_MODE` and `_CELL_SI_MAX_NUM_DIAG_MODE_DUMPS`) in the section "Monitoring Storage Indexes." These two parameters are the most useful in our opinion, although you should get the idea from the list that there is also some built in ability to modify behaviors such as the amount of memory to allocate for storage indexes and the number of columns that can be indexed per table.

Behavior

There is not a lot you can do to control when Storage Indexes are used and when they are not. Other than the parameter for disabling them, there is little you can do. There is no specific hint to enable or disable their use. And unfortunately, the `OPT_PARAM` hint does not work with the `_KCFIS_STORAGEIDX_DISABLED` parameter, either. The fact that there is no way to force the use of a Storage Index makes it even more important to understand when this powerful optimization will and will not be used.

In order for a storage index to be used, a query must include or make use of all the following:

Smart Scan: Storage Indexes can only be used with statements that do Smart Scans. This comes with a whole set of requirements, as detailed in Chapter 2. The main requirements are that the optimizer must choose a full scan and that the I/O must be done via the direct path read mechanism.

At Least One Predicate: In order for a statement to use a Storage Index, there must be a `WHERE` clause with at least one predicate.

Simple Comparison Operators: Storage Indexes can be used with the following set of operators:

`=, <, >, BETWEEN, >=, <=, IN, IS NULL, IS NOT NULL`

If a query meets the requirements of having at least one predicate involving simple comparison operators, and if that query's execution makes use of Smart Scan, then the storage software can make use of storage indexes. They can be applied to any of the following aspects of the query:

Multi-Column Predicates: Storage Indexes can be used with multiple predicates on the same table.

Joins: Storage Indexes can be used on statements accessing multiple tables to minimize disk I/O before the Join operations are carried out.

Parallel Query: Storage Indexes can be used by parallel query slaves. In fact, since direct path reads are required to enable Storage Indexes, parallel queries are very useful for ensuring that Storage Indexes can be used.

HCC: Storage Indexes work with HCC compressed tables.

Bind Variables: Storage Indexes work with bind variables. The values of the bind variables appear to be passed to the storage cells with each execution.

Partitions –Storage Indexes work with partitioned objects. Individual statements can benefit from partition eliminate and storage indexes during the same execution.

Sub-queries: Storage Indexes work with predicates that compare a column to a value returned by a sub-query.

Encryption: Storage Indexes work on encrypted tables.

There are of course limitations. Following are some features and syntax that prevent the use of storage indexes:

CLOBs: Storage Indexes are not created on CLOBs.

!=: Storage Indexes do not work with predicates that use the != comparison operator.

Wildcards: Storage Indexes do not work on predicates that use the % wildcard.

A further limitation is that storage indexes may contain only eight columns. They are created and maintained for eight-columns per table. This does not mean that queries with more than 8 predicates cannot make use of Storage Indexes. In such cases, the storage software can use the indexes that exist, but by default there will be a maximum of eight columns that can be indexed. It does appear that the developers have parameterized this setting, so it may be possible to change this value with help from Oracle support.

Finally, bear in mind that storage indexes are not persisted to disk. The storage cell must rebuild them whenever the cellsrv program is restarted. They are generally created during the first smart scan that references a given column after a storage server has been restarted. They can also be created when a table is created via a CREATE TABLE AS SELECT statement, or during other direct-path loads. And of course, the storage cell will update storage indexes in response to changes that applications make to the data in the tables.

Performance

Storage Indexes provide some of the most dramatic performance benefits available on the Exadata platform. Depending on the clustering factor of a particular column (that is, how well the column's data is sorted on disk), the results can be spectacular. Here's a typical example showing the performance of a query with and without the benefit of Storage Indexes:

```
SYS@EXDB1> alter session set cell_offload_processing=false;

Session altered.

SYS@EXDB1> alter session set "_kcfis_storageidx_disabled"=true;

Session altered.
```

```
SYS@EXDB1> select count(*) from kso.skew3;


  COUNT(*)
----------
 384000048

1 row selected.

Elapsed: 00:01:45.39

SYS@EXDB1> alter session set cell_offload_processing=true;

Session altered.

Elapsed: 00:00:00.00
SYS@EXDB1> select count(*) from kso.skew3;

  COUNT(*)
----------
 384000048

1 row selected.

Elapsed: 00:00:23.70

SYS@EXDB1> select count(*) from kso.skew3 where pk_col = 7000;

  COUNT(*)
----------
        12

Elapsed: 00:00:13.74

SYS@EXDB1> alter session set "_kcfis_storageidx_disabled"=false;

Session altered.

Elapsed: 00:00:00.00

SYS@EXDB1> select count(*) from kso.skew3 where pk_col = 7000;

  COUNT(*)
----------
        12

Elapsed: 00:00:01.06
```

At the start of this demonstration, all offloading was disabled via the database initialization parameter, CELL_OFFLOAD_PROCESSING. Storage Indexes were also disabled, via the hidden parameter _KCFIS_STORAGEIDX_DISABLED. A query without a WHERE clause was run and was completed using direct path reads, but without offloading. That query took 1 minute and 45 seconds to do the full table scan and returned entire blocks to the database grid, just as it would on non-Exadata storage environments. Offloading was then re-enabled and the query was repeated. This time it completed in about 24 seconds. The improvement in elapsed time was primarily due to column projection since the storage layer only had to return a counter of rows, instead of returning any of the column values.

A very selective WHERE clause was then added to the query; it reduced the time to about 14 seconds. This improvement was thanks to predicate filtering. Remember that Storage Indexes were still turned off. A counter for only 12 rows had to be returned to the database machine, but the storage cells still had to read all the data to determine which rows to return. Finally the Storage Indexes were re-enabled, by setting _KCFIS_STORAGEIDX_DISABLED to FALSE, and the query with the WHERE clause was executed again. This time the elapsed time was only about 1 second. While this performance improvement seems extreme, it is relatively common when Storage Indexes are used.

Special Optimization for Nulls

Nulls are a special case for Storage Indexes. There is a separate flag in the Storage Index structure that is used to indicate whether a storage region contains nulls or not. This separate flag makes queries looking for nulls (or the absence of nulls) even more efficient than the normal minimum and maximum comparisons that are typically done. Here's an example comparing typical performance with and without the special null optimization.

```
SYS@EXDB1> set timing on
SYS@EXDB1> select count(*) from kso.skew3 where col1 =10000;

  COUNT(*)
----------
         0

Elapsed: 00:00:14.47
SYS@EXDB1> @si

NAME                                                    VALUE
---------------------------------------------- ---------------
cell physical IO bytes saved by storage index         3915776

Elapsed: 00:00:00.00
SYS@EXDB1> select count(*) from kso.skew3 where col1 is null;

  COUNT(*)
----------
         4

Elapsed: 00:00:00.12
SYS@EXDB1> @si

NAME                                                    VALUE
---------------------------------------------- ---------------
cell physical IO bytes saved by storage index     15954714624

Elapsed: 00:00:00.00
```

In this example you can see that retrieval of a few nulls was extremely fast. This is because there is no possibility that any storage region that doesn't contain a null will have to be read , so no false positives will slow down this query. With any other value (except the minimum or maximum value for a column), there will most likely be storage regions that can't be eliminated, even though they don't actually contain a value that matches the predicates. This is exactly the case in the previous example, where no records were returned for the first query, even though it took 14 seconds to read all the data from disk. Notice also that the amount of I/O saved by the null query is almost 16 gigabytes (GB), while the amount saved by the first query was only about 3MB. That means that the first query found almost no storage regions that it could eliminate.

Physical Distribution of Values

Storage Indexes behave very differently from normal indexes. They maintain a fairly coarse picture of the values that are stored on disk. However, their mechanism can be very effective at eliminating large amounts of disk I/O in certain situations while still keeping the cost of maintaining them relatively low. It's important to keep in mind that the physical distribution of data on disk will have a large impact on how effective the Storage Indexes are. An illustration will make this clearer.

Suppose you have a table that has a column with unique values (that is, no value is repeated). If the data is stored on disk in such a manner that the rows are ordered by that column, then there will be one and only one storage region for any given value of that column. Any query with an equality predicate on that column will have to read at most one storage region. Figure 4-2 shows a conceptual picture of a Storage Index for a sorted column.

idx	Min Value	Max Value	null
1	1	100	N
2	101	200	N
.	.	.	.
3	10,000	10,100	Y
4	10,101	10,200	N

Figure 4-2. A Storage Index on a sorted column

As you can see from the diagram, if you wanted to retrieve the record where the value was 102, you would only have one storage region that could possibly contain that value.

Suppose now that the same data set is stored on disk in a random order. How many storage regions would you expect to have to read to locate a single row via an equality predicate? It depends on the number of rows that fit into a storage region, but the answer is certainly much larger than the 1 storage region that would be required with the sorted data set.

It's just that simple. Storage indexes will be more effective on sorted data. From a performance perspective, the better sorted the data is on disk, the faster the average access time will be when using Storage Indexes. For a column that is completely sorted, the access time should be very fast and there should be little variation in the access time, regardless of what values are requested. For unsorted data the access times will be faster toward the ends of the range of values (because there are not many storage regions that will have ranges of values containing the queried value). The average access times for values in the middle of the distribution will vary widely. Figure 2-3 is a chart comparing access times using Storage Indexes for sorted and unsorted data.

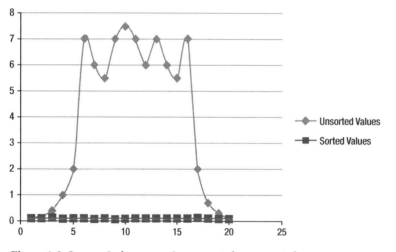

Figure 4-3. Storage Index access times – sorted vs. unsorted

As you can see, sorted data will provide better and more consistent results. While we're on the subject, I should point out that there are many cases where several columns will benefit from this behavioral characteristic of Storage Indexes. It's common in data warehouse environments to have data that is partitioned on a date column. And there are often many other columns that track the partition key such as associated dates (order date, ship date, insert date, return date for example) or sequentially generated numbers like order numbers. Queries against these column are often problematic due the fact that partition eliminate cannot help them. Storage Indexes will provide a similar benefit to partition elimination as long as care is taken to ensure that the data is pre-sorted prior to loading.

Potential Issues

There's no such thing as a free puppy. As with everything in life, there are a few issues with Storage Indexes that you should be aware of.

Incorrect Results

By far the biggest issue with Storage Indexes has been that in early releases of the Exadata Storage Software there were a handful of bugs regarding incorrect results. That is to say that in certain situations, usage of Storage Indexes could eliminate storage regions from consideration that actually contained records of interest. This incorrect elimination could occur due to timing issues with concurrent DML while a Smart Scan was being done using Storage Indexes. These bugs have been addressed in 11.2.0.2 and the latest patches on the storage servers. If you run into this issue, disabling Storage Index use via the hidden parameter, _KCFIS_STORAGEIDX_DISABLED, may be the only option available until the proper patches are applied. This parameter can be set with an alter session command, so that only problematic queries are affected. Of course you should check with Oracle Support before enabling any hidden parameters.

Moving Target

Storage Indexes can be a little frustrating because they don't always kick in when you expect them to. And without any hints to tell Oracle that you really want a Storage Index to be used, there is little you can do other than try to understand why they are not used in certain circumstances so you can avoid those conditions in the future.

In early versions of the storage server software, one of the main reasons that Storage Indexes were disabled was due to implicit data type conversions. Over the years, Oracle has gotten better and better at doing "smart" data type conversions that don't have negative performance consequences. For example, if you write a SQL statement with a WHERE clause that compares a date field to a character string, Oracle will usually apply a to_date function to the character string instead of modifying the date column (which could have the unpleasant side effect of disabling an index). Unfortunately, when the Exadata storage software was relatively new, all the nuances had not been worked out, at least to the degree we're used to from the database side. Dates have been particularly persnickety. Here is an example using cellsrv 11.2.1.2.6:

```
SYS@EXDB1> select count(*) from kso.skew3 where col3 = '20-OCT-05';

  COUNT(*)
----------
         0

Elapsed: 00:00:14.00
SYS@EXDB1> @si

NAME                                              VALUE
--------------------------------------------- ----------------
cell physical IO bytes saved by storage index          0
```

```
Elapsed: 00:00:00.01
SYS@EXDB1> select count(*) from kso.skew3 where col3 = '20-OCT-2005';

  COUNT(*)
----------
         0

Elapsed: 00:00:00.07
SYS@EXDB1> @si

NAME                                             VALUE
---------------------------------------------- ---------------
cell physical IO bytes saved by storage index    15954337792

Elapsed: 00:00:00.01
```

In this very simple example there is a query with a predicate comparing a date column (col3) to a string containing a date. In one case, the string contained a four-digit year. In the other, only two digits were used. Only the query with the four-digit year format used the Storage Index. Let's look at the plans for the statements to see why the two queries were treated differently:

```
SYS@EXDB1> @fsx2
Enter value for sql_text: select count(*) from kso.skew3 where col3 = %
Enter value for sql_id:
Enter value for inst_id:


SQL_ID          AVG_ETIME  PX OFFLOAD IO_SAVED% SQL_TEXT
-------------- ------------- --- ------- --------- --------------------------------------------
2s58n6d3mzkmn         .07   0  Yes        100.00 select count(*) from kso.skew3 where
                                                  col3 = '20-OCT-2005'

fuhmg9hqdbd84       14.00   0  Yes         99.99 select count(*) from kso.skew3 where
                                                  col3 = '20-OCT-05'

2 rows selected.

SYS@EXDB1> select * from table(dbms_xplan.display_cursor('&sql_id','&child_no','typical'));
Enter value for sql_id: fuhmg9hqdbd84
Enter value for child_no:

PLAN_TABLE_OUTPUT
---------------------------------------------------------------------------------------
SQL_ID  fuhmg9hqdbd84, child number 0
------------------------------------
select count(*) from kso.skew3 where col3 = '20-OCT-05'

Plan hash value: 2684249835
```

```
-----------------------------------------------------------------
| Id|Operation                      |Name  | Rows|Bytes|Cost (%CPU)|Time    |
-----------------------------------------------------------------
|  0|SELECT STATEMENT                |      |     |     | 535K(100)|          |
|  1| SORT AGGREGATE                 |      |    1|    8|          |          |
|* 2|  TABLE ACCESS STORAGE FULL|SKEW3 |  384|3072 | 535K  (2)|01:47:04|
-----------------------------------------------------------------

Predicate Information (identified by operation id):
---------------------------------------------------

   2 - storage("COL3"='20-OCT-05')
       filter("COL3"='20-OCT-05')


20 rows selected.

SYS@EXDB1> /
Enter value for sql_id: 2s58n6d3mzkmn
Enter value for child_no:

PLAN_TABLE_OUTPUT
-------------------------------------------------------------------------------------------
SQL_ID  2s58n6d3mzkmn, child number 0
-------------------------------------
select count(*) from kso.skew3 where col3 = '20-OCT-2005'

Plan hash value: 2684249835


---------------------------------------------------------------------------
| Id  | Operation                      | Name  | Rows  | Bytes | Cost (%CPU)| Time       |
---------------------------------------------------------------------------
|   0 | SELECT STATEMENT               |       |       |       | 531K(100)|            |
|   1 |  SORT AGGREGATE                |       |     1 |     8 |          |            |
|*  2 |   TABLE ACCESS STORAGE FULL| SKEW3 |   384 |  3072 | 531K  (1)| 01:46:24 |
---------------------------------------------------------------------------

Predicate Information (identified by operation id):
---------------------------------------------------

   2 - storage("COL3"=TO_DATE(' 2005-10-20 00:00:00', 'syyyy-mm-dd
           hh24:mi:ss'))
       filter("COL3"=TO_DATE(' 2005-10-20 00:00:00', 'syyyy-mm-dd
           hh24:mi:ss'))


22 rows selected.
```

It appears that the optimizer didn't recognize the two-digit date as a date. At the very least, the optimizer failed to apply the to_date function to the literal and so the Storage Index was not used. Fortunately most of these types of data conversion issues have been resolved with the later releases. Here's the same test using cellsrv 11.2.2.2.0:

```
SYS@SANDBOX> @si

NAME                                                              VALUE
------------------------------------------------------------ ---------------
cell physical IO bytes saved by storage index                         0

SYS@SANDBOX> select count(*) from kso.skew3 where col3 = '20-OCT-05';

  COUNT(*)
----------
         0

SYS@SANDBOX> @si

NAME                                                              VALUE
------------------------------------------------------------ ---------------
cell physical IO bytes saved by storage index                16024526848
```

So as you can see, this conversion issue has been resolved. So why bring it up? Well the point is that the behavior of Storage Indexes have undergone numerous changes as the product has matured. As a result, we have built a set of test cases that we use to verify behavior after each patch in our lab. Our test cases primarily verify comparison operators (=,<,like, IS NULL, etc…) and a few other special cases such as LOBs, compression and encryption. Of course it's always a good practice to test application behavior after any patching, but if you have specific cases where Storage Indexes are critical to your application you may want take special care to test those parts of you application.

Partition Size

Storage Indexes depend on Smart Scans, which depend on direct path reads. As we discussed in Chapter 2, Oracle will generally use serial direct path reads for large objects. However, when an object is partitioned, Oracle may fail to recognize that the object is "large," because Oracle looks at the size of each individual segment. This may result in some partitions not being read via the Smart Scan mechanism and thus disabling any Storage Indexes for that partition. When historical partitions are compressed, the problem becomes even more noticeable, as the reduced size of the compressed partitions will be even less likely to trigger the serial direct path reads. This issue can be worked around by not relying on the serial direct path read algorithm and instead specifying a degree of parallelism for the object or using a hint to force the desired behavior.

Incompatible Coding Techniques

Finally, there are some coding techniques that can disable Storage Indexes. Here's an example showing the effect of the trunc function on date columns:

```
SYS@EXDB1> select count(*) from kso.skew3 where trunc(col3) = '20-OCT-2005';

  COUNT(*)
----------
         4
```

1 row selected.

Elapsed: 00:00:57.51
SYS@EXDB1> @fsx2
Enter value for sql_text: select count(*) from kso.skew3 where trunc(col3)%
Enter value for sql_id:

```
SQL_ID          AVG_ETIME  PX OFFLOAD IO_SAVED% SQL_TEXT
-------------  ---------- --- ------- --------- ----------------------------------------
3c1w96cayhut9      56.94   0 Yes         99.99 select count(*) from kso.skew3 where
                                               trunc(col3) = '20-OCT-2005'

3c1w96cayhut9      57.50   0 Yes         99.99 select count(*) from kso.skew3 where
                                               trunc(col3) = '20-OCT-2005'
```

2 rows selected.

Elapsed: 00:00:00.01
SYS@EXDB1> select * from table(dbms_xplan.display_cursor('&sql_id','&child_no','typical'));
Enter value for sql_id: 3c1w96cayhut9
Enter value for child_no:

```
PLAN_TABLE_OUTPUT
--------------------------------------------------------------------------------------------
SQL_ID  3c1w96cayhut9, child number 1
-------------------------------------
select count(*) from kso.skew3 where trunc(col3) = '20-OCT-2005'

Plan hash value: 2684249835

---------------------------------------------------------------------------------
| Id  | Operation                  | Name  | Rows  | Bytes | Cost (%CPU)| Time     |
---------------------------------------------------------------------------------
|   0 | SELECT STATEMENT           |       |       |       | 541K(100)|          |
|   1 |  SORT AGGREGATE            |       |     1 |     8 |          |          |
|*  2 |   TABLE ACCESS STORAGE FULL| SKEW3 |     4 |    32 | 541K  (3)| 01:48:24 |
---------------------------------------------------------------------------------

Predicate Information (identified by operation id):
---------------------------------------------------

   2 - storage(TRUNC(INTERNAL_FUNCTION("COL3"))=TO_DATE(' 2005-10-20
          00:00:00', 'syyyy-mm-dd hh24:mi:ss'))
       filter(TRUNC(INTERNAL_FUNCTION("COL3"))=TO_DATE(' 2005-10-20
          00:00:00', 'syyyy-mm-dd hh24:mi:ss'))

Note
-----
cardinality feedback used for this statement
```

In this example, a function was applied to a date column, which as you might expect, disables the Storage Index. The fact that applying a function to a column disables the Storage Index is not too surprising, but application of the trunc function is a commonly seen coding technique. Many dates have a time component and many queries want data for a specific day. It is well known that truncating a date in this manner will disable normal B-Tree index usage. In the past, that generally didn't matter. Queries in many data warehouse environments were designed to do full scans anyway, so there was really no need to worry about disabling an index. Storage Indexes change the game from this perspective and may force us to re-think some of our approaches. We'll discuss this issue in more detail in Chapter 16.

Summary

Storage Indexes are an optimization technique that is available when the database is able to utilize Smart Table Scans. They can provide dramatic performance improvements. Storage indexes can be thought of as an alternate partitioning strategy, but without the normal restrictions associated with partitioning. They are especially effective with queries that access data via an alternate key that tracks the primary partition key.

How the data is physically stored is an important consideration and has a dramatic impact on the effectiveness of Storage Indexes. Care should be taken when migrating data to the Exadata platform to ensure that the data is clustered on disk in a manner that will allow Storage Indexes to be used effectively.

## CHAPTER 5

Exadata Smart Flash Cache

The marketing guys at Oracle must like the term "smart." They have applied it to a dozen or so different features on the Exadata platform. They also seem to like the term "flash," which is associated with at least a half dozen features as well. To add to the confusion, there are two features in Oracle Database 11g Release 2 that have almost exactly the same names, Database Smart Flash Cache (DBFC) and Exadata Smart Flash Cache (ESFC). While both features make use of flash-based memory devices, they are very different. This chapter is focused on ESFC so we'll only mention DBFC in passing.

Cleary, one of the goals with Exadata V2 (and now X2) was to expand Exadata capabilities to improve its performance with OLTP workloads. ESFC was the key component that was added to the V2 configuration to accomplish this goal. The addition provides over 5TB of cache in a full rack. It's important to understand that this cache is managed by Oracle software that is aware of how the data is being used by the databases that the storage is supporting. Oracle has been working on software for effectively managing database caches for over 30 years. Since the storage software knows what the database is asking for, it has a much better idea of what should and shouldn't be cached than a conventional storage array.

DBFC VS. ESFC

DBFC and ESFC are two completely different things. DBFC is an extension of the buffer cache on the database server. It is a standard part of 11g and is implemented as a tier 2 buffer cache for an instance. It is only supported on Solaris and Oracle Enterprise Linux. It is enabled by adding a flash card to a database server and telling a single instance to use it. If a user needs a block that is not in the buffer cache, it will look in the DBFC to see if it is there before requesting an I/O. When blocks are aged out of the buffer pool, they are moved to the DBFC instead of being simply flushed. ESFC is, of course, the disk cache on the Exadata storage servers. It caches data for all instances that access the storage cell.

Hardware

Each Exadata storage server has 4 Sun Flash Accelerator F20 PCIe cards. Each card holds 96G for a total of 384G on each storage server. These are the numbers that you normally see quoted in the specifications although the amount that's available for use is slightly less. The cards are actually made up of 4 solid-state flash modules (FMods), sometimes called disk on modules (DOMs). Each of the modules contain eight 4GB SLC NAND components. So each of the 4 FMods has 32GB of storage, of which 24GB is addressable. With 4 FMods on each of the 4 cards you have 16 of these modules in each storage server. The modules are presented to the O/S separately. Each module reserves an additional

1.125G of its addressable space for its own purposes, yielding a usable space of 22.875G per module. This yields a total of 366G of usable flash storage per storage cell. That's over a terabyte (TB) on the smallest quarter rack configuration and over 5 TB on a full rack.

The F20 cards also include an energy storage module (ESM), sometimes also referred to as a Super Capacitor. You can think of it as a battery, although it actually uses a capacitor, whereas a traditional battery relies on chemical reactions. At any rate, the purpose of the ESM is to provide enough power to flush any data in its volatile memory to the nonvolatile flash memory in the case of a sudden power loss. The volatile memory consists of 64M of DRAM per FMod and is used to buffer writes to the nonvolatile flash memory. You should note that if the ESM fails, writes will by-pass the DRAM and be sent directly to the flash memory. As a result, write speeds will be significantly decreased in the case of ESM failure. This doesn't present a major issue when the cards are configured as ESFC, since the Oracle storage software treats the ESFC as a write-through cache and therefore writes directly to disk, bypassing the cache. It can be an issue though if the cards are used as Flash Disks. Sun recommends that the ESM modules be replaced every two years as the stored energy degrades over time (like a battery). The ILOM system management firmware monitors ESM usage and issues warnings as the ESM approaches the end of its lifespan. See the Sun Flash Accelerator F20 PCIe Card User's Guide for further details.

According to the Sun documentation, the storage servers allow PCIe cards to be replaced while the system is running. However, the Oracle Exadata Storage Software User's Guide recommends powering down the storage servers before replacing one of these cards. Fortunately, you can accomplish this without experiencing an outage, as ASM redundancy allows entire storage cells to be offline without affecting the databases they are supporting. Note that replacing one of the F20 cards should not require any reconfiguration. Figure 5-1 shows a conceptual diagram of one of the Flash Accelerator cards.

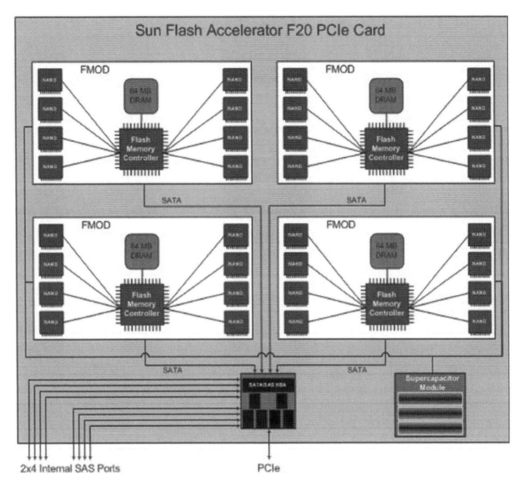

Figure 5-1. Conceptual diagram of the Sun F20 PCIe Flash Card

Cache vs. Flash Disk

The flash memory on the storage servers can be used in two ways. It can be configured as a large disk cache (ESFC), or it can be carved up and presented as solid-state disks (which can be used by ASM for database storage). These two modes are not mutually exclusive. The flash memory can be allocated to either format in whatever percentages are desired. The recommended configuration is to use all the flash memory as cache. This configuration significantly speeds up random access reads. However, it provides no direct benefit to write speeds.

In many systems the approach of allocating all flash memory as cache works very well. However, for systems that are very write-intensive, it may be beneficial to use some of the flash memory as a disk. Keep in mind that depending on the ASM redundancy level used (Normal or High), choosing this option will consume 2 or 3 times the amount of flash storage that the objects actually occupy. This fact alone makes the option less palatable. Also keep in mind that writes to data files are done in the background by the DBWR processes. So choosing to use part of the flash based storage as a disk may not provide as much benefit as you might hope. Fortunately it's pretty easy to reallocate flash storage, so testing your specific situation should not prove too difficult. However, since this chapter focuses on the Exadata Smart Flash Cache feature, we will only briefly cover using the F20's as flash disks.

■ **Note:** A common misconception is that putting online redo logs on flash storage will significantly speed up writes to redo logs and thus increase the throughput of high-transaction systems. While it's true that small random writes are faster on SSD-based storage than on traditional disks, writes to redo logs on high-transaction systems generally do not fall into that bucket and actually do not benefit that much from being stored on SSD storage. In addition, SSD write mechanics cause a lot of variability in individual write times. There may be individual writes that take orders of magnitude longer than the average. This can cause problems on very busy systems as well. So, before you put your online redo logs on to your valuable Exadata Flash storage, you should test to make sure that the benefits outweigh the costs.

Using Flash Memory as Cache

A very simplified description of how a disk cache works goes something like this. When a read request comes in, the I/O subsystem checks the cache to see if the requested data exists in cache. If the data is in the cache, it is returned to the requesting process. If the requested data doesn't reside in the cache, it is read from disk and returned to the requesting process. In the case of uncached data, the data is later copied to the cache (after it is returned to the requesting process). This is done to ensure that the cache doesn't slow down the I/O for the requesting process.

With Exadata, disk caching is not quite as simple as the general case we just described. In an effort to maximize the potential throughput, the cellsrv program may actually fire off async I/O requests to both the disk and the flash cache. Generally speaking, if the requested data is in the cache, the requests will be fulfilled by the flash cache before the disk reads will be able to complete. However, when the system is heavily loaded, it is possible for some requests to be fulfilled by the flash cache while others are fulfilled by the disks. This two-pronged attack effectively increases the amount of throughput that the system can deliver.

■ **Kevin Says:** "The hardware upon which Exadata Storage Server is based offers five high-bandwidth PCI slots for storage attachment. Without attacking both Flash and Hard Disk assets in parallel, each cell would be limited to roughly 1.8 GB/s scan throughput. With cellsrv scanning both Flash and Hard Disk concurrently, the scan throughput increases to roughly 4.8 GB/s.

Figure 5-2 shows the I/O path of reads using Oracle's ESFC.

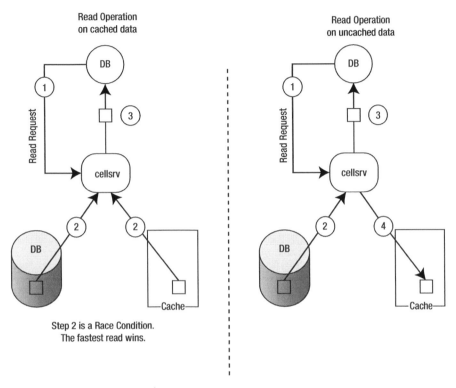

Flash Cache Reads - I / O Path Architecture

Figure 5-2. Conceptual model of read operation I/O path

Since ESFC is a write-through cache, writes bypass the cache and go directly to disk. However, after sending an acknowledgement back to the database server, Oracle's storage software then copies the data into the cache, assuming it is suitable for caching. This is a key point. The metadata that is sent with the write request lets the storage software know if the data is likely to be used again and if so, the data is also written to the cache. This step is done after sending an acknowledgement to the database tier in order to ensure that the write operation can complete as quickly as possible.

Figure 5-3 shows the I/O path of writes using Oracle's ESFC.

Flash Cache Writes - I / O Path Architecture

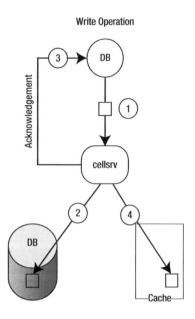

Figure 5-3. Conceptual model of write operation I/O path

As you might guess, Smart Scans generally ignore the ESFC and read directly from disk. However, if the object being scanned has been designated for preferential caching (by setting the storage clause attribute CELL_FLASH_CACHE to KEEP), then even Smart Scans will attempt to read from flash cache. The following example demonstrates this behavior.

```
SYS@EXDB1> @mystats
Enter value for name: cell flash%

NAME                                                         VALUE
------------------------------------------------------------ ---------------
cell flash cache read hits                                   3570

Elapsed: 00:00:00.01
SYS@EXDB1> alter table kso.skew3 storage (cell_flash_cache keep);

Table altered.

Elapsed: 00:00:00.01
SYS@EXDB1> select avg(pk_col) from kso.skew3 where col1 > 1;

AVG(PK_COL)
-----------
 16053318.5
```

```
Elapsed: 00:00:34.35
SYS@EXDB1> @mystats
Enter value for name: cell flash%

NAME                                                        VALUE
------------------------------------------------------ ---------------
cell flash cache read hits                                   3571

Elapsed: 00:00:00.01
SYS@EXDB1> -- nothing in the flash cache the first time, try again
SYS@EXDB1>
SYS@EXDB1> select avg(pk_col) from kso.skew3 where col1 > 1;

AVG(PK_COL)
-----------
 16053318.5

Elapsed: 00:00:27.82    notice that the elapsed time is somewhat faster
SYS@EXDB1> @mystats
Enter value for name: cell flash%

NAME                                                        VALUE
------------------------------------------------------ ---------------
cell flash cache read hits                                  24401

Elapsed: 00:00:00.01
SYS@EXDB1> alter table kso.skew3 storage (cell_flash_cache default);

Table altered.

Elapsed: 00:00:00.05
SYS@EXDB1> select avg(pk_col) from kso.skew3 where col1 > 1;

AVG(PK_COL)
-----------
 16053318.5

Elapsed: 00:00:31.54
SYS@EXDB1> @mystats
Enter value for name: cell flash%

NAME                                                        VALUE
------------------------------------------------------ ---------------
cell flash cache read hits                                  24401

Elapsed: 00:00:00.00
SYS@EXDB1>
SYS@EXDB1> alter table kso.skew3 storage (cell_flash_cache keep);

Table altered.

Elapsed: 00:00:00.01
```

```
SYS@EXDB1> select avg(pk_col) from kso.skew3 where col1 > 1;

AVG(PK_COL)
-----------
 16053318.5

Elapsed: 00:00:27.90
SYS@EXDB1> @mystats
Enter value for name: cell flash%

NAME                                                         VALUE
------------------------------------------------------------ ---------------
cell flash cache read hits                                   45225

Elapsed: 00:00:00.01
```

In the preceding example you can see that the Smart Scan is faster when the CELL_FLASH_CACHE storage clause attribute is set to KEEP and more importantly, that a large number of "cell flash cache read hits" are generated in that case. When the CELL_FLASH_CACHE attribute is set to DEFAULT, the query is slower and no "cell flash cache read hits" are generated.

How ESFC is Created

Storage configuration is covered in detail in Chapter 8, but the basic commands for creating and managing flash cache will be covered briefly in this section as well. The cache is created and managed using the cellcli utility on each storage server (the cellcli command syntax is covered in detail in Appendix A). Alternatively, the dcli utility, which replicates commands across multiple storage cells, can be used. The command to create the cache is CREATE FLASHCACHE. Here's an example.

```
CellCLI> create flashcache all size=300g

Flash cache cell03_FLASHCACHE successfully created
```

This form of the command tells the storage software to spread the cache across all the FMods on all the flash cards. In this case, the size parameter was used to specify that the entire cache should occupy only 300G, leaving roughly 65G available for use as a flash disk. To use all available space for flash cache, simply leave off the size parameter.

```
CellCLI> create flashcache all

Flash cache cell03_FLASHCACHE successfully created
```

This command uses all available storage on all available flash cards. Note that the flash cache is automatically assigned a name that includes the name of the storage cell. To see the size of the flashcache you can issue the LIST FLASHCACHE DETAIL command:

```
CellCLI> list flashcache detail
        name:                   cell03_FLASHCACHE
        cellDisk: FD_15_cell03,FD_02_cell03,FD_14_cell03,FD_10_cell03,FD_01_cell03,
FD_13_cell03,FD_12_cell03,FD_08_cell03,FD_07_cell03,FD_11_cell03,FD_09_cell03,FD_05_cell03,
FD_06_cell03,FD_04_cell03,FD_03_cell03,FD_00_cell03
        creationTime:           2010-11-07T19:45:32-06:00
        degradedCelldisks:
```

```
        effectiveCacheSize:    300G
        id:                    80a40cc9-371c-4c9f-85bf-ffbe580976c1
        size:                  300G
        status:                normal
```

Notice that the flash cache is spread across 16 cell disks. There is one cell disk for each FMod on each flash card. To get more information about the cell disks that make up the flash cache, you can use the LIST CELLDISK command, shown here:

```
CellCLI> list celldisk attributes name, diskType, size where name like 'FD.*'
        FD_00_cell03    FlashDisk    22.875G
        FD_01_cell03    FlashDisk    22.875G
        FD_02_cell03    FlashDisk    22.875G
        FD_03_cell03    FlashDisk    22.875G
        FD_04_cell03    FlashDisk    22.875G
        FD_05_cell03    FlashDisk    22.875G
        FD_06_cell03    FlashDisk    22.875G
        FD_07_cell03    FlashDisk    22.875G
        FD_08_cell03    FlashDisk    22.875G
        FD_09_cell03    FlashDisk    22.875G
        FD_10_cell03    FlashDisk    22.875G
        FD_11_cell03    FlashDisk    22.875G
        FD_12_cell03    FlashDisk    22.875G
        FD_13_cell03    FlashDisk    22.875G
        FD_14_cell03    FlashDisk    22.875G
        FD_15_cell03    FlashDisk    22.875G
```

Since the flash cache sits on top of cell disks, the cell disks must be created before the flash cache. This can be done with the CREATE CELLDISK command:

```
CellCLI> create celldisk all flashdisk
CellDisk FD_00_cell03 successfully created
CellDisk FD_01_cell03 successfully created
CellDisk FD_02_cell03 successfully created
CellDisk FD_03_cell03 successfully created
CellDisk FD_04_cell03 successfully created
CellDisk FD_05_cell03 successfully created
CellDisk FD_06_cell03 successfully created
CellDisk FD_07_cell03 successfully created
CellDisk FD_08_cell03 successfully created
CellDisk FD_09_cell03 successfully created
CellDisk FD_10_cell03 successfully created
CellDisk FD_11_cell03 successfully created
CellDisk FD_12_cell03 successfully created
CellDisk FD_13_cell03 successfully created
CellDisk FD_14_cell03 successfully created
CellDisk FD_15_cell03 successfully created
```

You can also create a flash cache on a limited set of FMods by specifying a specific list of cell disks. In most cases this is not done, but it is possible. Here's an example:

```
CellCLI> create flashcache celldisk='FD_00_cell03, FD_01_cell03', size=40G
Flash cache cell03_FLASHCACHE successfully created
```

```
CellCLI> list flashcache detail
        name:                   cell03_FLASHCACHE
        cellDisk:               FD_01_cell03,FD_00_cell03
        creationTime:           2010-11-09T15:29:28-06:00
        degradedCelldisks:
        effectiveCacheSize:     40G
        id:                     ad56aa9d-0de4-4713-85f2-197134523ebb
        size:                   40G
        status:                 normal
```

Once again, using `cellcli` to manage storage including flash cache is covered in more detail in Chapter 8, but this section should give you a basic understanding of how the flash cache is created.

Controlling ESFC Usage

Generally speaking, objects will be cached in the ESFC based on the storage software's automatic caching policy. However, you can override the automatic policy for individual database objects by using the `CELL_FLASH_CACHE` storage clause attribute. The attribute has three valid values:

> NONE: Never cache this object.

> DEFAULT: The Automatic caching mechanism is in effect. This is the default value.

> KEEP: The object should be given preferential status. Note that this designation also changes the default behavior of Smart Scans, allowing them to read from both the cache and disk.

You can specify the storage clause when an object is created. Some options of the storage clause can be modified using the `ALTER` command as well. Here's an example of changing the `CELL_FLASH_CACHE` storage clause using the `ALTER` command.

```
alter table kso.skew storage (cell_flash_cache keep);
```

You can also see whether objects have been designated for more aggressive caching by looking at the `cell_flash_cache` column of `dba_tables` or `dba_indexes`:

```
SYS@EXDB1> @esfc_keep_tables
SYS@EXDB1> select owner, table_name, status, last_analyzed,
  2  num_rows, blocks, degree, cell_flash_cache
  3  from dba_tables
  4  where cell_flash_cache like nvl('&cell_flash_cache','KEEP')
  5  /
Enter value for cell_flash_cache:

OWNER TABLE_NAME STATUS LAST_ANAL  NUM_ROWS   BLOCKS  DEGREE CELL_FLASH_CACHE
----- ---------- ------ ---------  ---------  ------- ------ ----------------
KSO   SKEW       VALID  18-SEP-10  32000004   162294      1 KEEP
KSO   SKEW3      VALID  14-OCT-10  384000048  1949727     1 KEEP
```

Monitoring

Your options for monitoring ESFC are limited on the database servers. There is only one statistic related to ESFC in v$sysstat and related views (cell flash cache read hits). The storage servers, however, provide a much larger array of diagnostic information via the cellcli utility. Unfortunately, since these metrics are provided by cellcli on individual storage cells, they are limited to that single storage server. There is no comprehensive set of diagnostic information that covers the entire storage grid at this point.

At the Storage Layer

There are a number of statistics that are captured for ESFC usage at the storage cell layer. The cellcli utility allows us to view those metrics. The LIST METRICDEFINITION command provides a description of the various statistics that are collected. For example:

```
CellCLI> LIST METRICDEFINITION attributes name, description WHERE objectType = 'FLASHCACHE'
```

Table 5-1 shows the output of the command. The table provides a brief description for each statistic tracked at the storage layer that you can report on.

Table 5-1. Flash Cache Metric Definitions

Metric	Description
FC_BYKEEP_OVERWR	Number of megabytes pushed out of the flash cache because of space limit for 'keep' objects
FC_BYKEEP_OVERWR_SEC	Number of megabytes per second pushed out of the flash cache because of space limit for 'keep' objects
FC_BYKEEP_USED	Number of megabytes used for 'keep' objects on flash cache
FC_BY_USED	Number of megabytes used on flash cache
FC_IO_BYKEEP_R	Number of megabytes read from flash cache for 'keep' objects
FC_IO_BYKEEP_R_SEC	Number of megabytes read per second from flash cache for 'keep' objects
FC_IO_BYKEEP_W	Number of megabytes written to flash cache for 'keep' objects
FC_IO_BYKEEP_W_SEC	Number of megabytes per second written to flash cache for 'keep' objects
FC_IO_BY_R	Number of megabytes read from flash cache
FC_IO_BY_R_MISS	Number of megabytes read from disks because not all requested data was in flash cache
FC_IO_BY_R_MISS_SEC	Number of megabytes read from disks per second because not all requested data was in flash cache

Metric	Description
FC_IO_BY_R_SEC	Number of megabytes read per second from flash cache
FC_IO_BY_R_SKIP	Number of megabytes read from disks for IO requests with a hint to bypass flash cache
FC_IO_BY_R_SKIP_SEC	Number of megabytes read from disks per second for IO requests with a hint to bypass flash cache
FC_IO_BY_W	Number of megabytes written to flash cache
FC_IO_BY_W_SEC	Number of megabytes per second written to flash cache
FC_IO_ERRS	Number of IO errors on flash cache
FC_IO_RQKEEP_R	Number of read IO requests for 'keep' objects satisfied from flash cache
FC_IO_RQKEEP_R_MISS	Number of read IO requests for 'keep' objects that did not find all data in flash cache
FC_IO_RQKEEP_R_MISS_SEC	Number of read IO requests per second for 'keep' objects that did not find all data in flash cache
FC_IO_RQKEEP_R_SEC	Number of read IO requests for 'keep' objects per second satisfied from flash cache
FC_IO_RQKEEP_R_SKIP	Number of read IO requests for 'keep' objects with a hint to bypass flash cache
FC_IO_RQKEEP_R_SKIP_SEC	Number of read IO requests per second for 'keep' objects with a hint to bypass flash cache
FC_IO_RQKEEP_W	Number of IO requests for 'keep' objects that resulted in flash cache being populated with data
FC_IO_RQKEEP_W_SEC	Number of IO requests per second for 'keep' objects that resulted in flash cache being populated with data
FC_IO_RQ_R	Number of read IO requests satisfied from flash cache
FC_IO_RQ_R_MISS	Number of read IO requests that did not find all data in flash cache
FC_IO_RQ_R_MISS_SEC	Number of read IO requests per second that did not find all data in flash cache
FC_IO_RQ_R_SEC	Number of read IO requests satisfied per second from flash cache

Metric	Description
FC_IO_RQ_R_SKIP	Number of read IO requests with a hint to bypass flash cache
FC_IO_RQ_R_SKIP_SEC	Number of read IO requests per second with a hint to bypass flash cache
FC_IO_RQ_W	Number of IO requests that resulted in flash cache being populated with data
FC_IO_RQ_W_SEC	Number of IO requests per second that resulted in flash cache being populated with data

The metrics in Table 5-1 are cumulative since cellsrv was started. The LIST METRICCURRENT command shows the current values of the metrics for a single storage cell. Following are examples of a couple of cellcli commands showing first all flash cache-related metrics and then only the flash cache metrics that are related to objects designated for aggressive caching (that is, objects whose storage clause specifies CELL_FLASH_CACHE=KEEP).

```
CellCLI> LIST METRICCURRENT WHERE objectType = 'FLASHCACHE'
             FC_BYKEEP_OVERWR            FLASHCACHE      0.0 MB
             FC_BYKEEP_OVERWR_SEC        FLASHCACHE      0.0 MB/sec
             FC_BYKEEP_USED              FLASHCACHE      5,072 MB
             FC_BY_USED                  FLASHCACHE      5,434 MB
             FC_IO_BYKEEP_R              FLASHCACHE      80,288 MB
             FC_IO_BYKEEP_R_SEC          FLASHCACHE      0.0 MB/sec
             FC_IO_BYKEEP_W              FLASHCACHE      11,134 MB
             FC_IO_BYKEEP_W_SEC          FLASHCACHE      0.0 MB/sec
             FC_IO_BY_R                  FLASHCACHE      3,512,908 MB
             FC_IO_BY_R_MISS             FLASHCACHE      944,942 MB
             FC_IO_BY_R_MISS_SEC         FLASHCACHE      0.0 MB/sec
             FC_IO_BY_R_SEC              FLASHCACHE      0.0 MB/sec
             FC_IO_BY_R_SKIP             FLASHCACHE      11,224,781 MB
             FC_IO_BY_R_SKIP_SEC         FLASHCACHE      0.3 MB/sec
             FC_IO_BY_W                  FLASHCACHE      3,547,430 MB
             FC_IO_BY_W_SEC              FLASHCACHE      0.4 MB/sec
             FC_IO_ERRS                  FLASHCACHE      0
             FC_IO_RQKEEP_R              FLASHCACHE      91,231 IO requests
             FC_IO_RQKEEP_R_MISS         FLASHCACHE      11,155 IO requests
             FC_IO_RQKEEP_R_MISS_SEC     FLASHCACHE      0.0 IO/sec
             FC_IO_RQKEEP_R_SEC          FLASHCACHE      0.0 IO/sec
             FC_IO_RQKEEP_R_SKIP         FLASHCACHE      1,532 IO requests
             FC_IO_RQKEEP_R_SKIP_SEC     FLASHCACHE      0.0 IO/sec
             FC_IO_RQKEEP_W              FLASHCACHE      17,794 IO requests
             FC_IO_RQKEEP_W_SEC          FLASHCACHE      0.0 IO/sec
             FC_IO_RQ_R                  FLASHCACHE      420,546,099 IO requests
             FC_IO_RQ_R_MISS             FLASHCACHE      28,959,907 IO requests
             FC_IO_RQ_R_MISS_SEC         FLASHCACHE      0.0 IO/sec
             FC_IO_RQ_R_SEC              FLASHCACHE      0.0 IO/sec
             FC_IO_RQ_R_SKIP             FLASHCACHE      80,970,122 IO requests
             FC_IO_RQ_R_SKIP_SEC         FLASHCACHE      25.4 IO/sec
```

```
           FC_IO_RQ_W                 FLASHCACHE      304,286,158 IO requests
           FC_IO_RQ_W_SEC             FLASHCACHE      22.4 IO/sec

CellCLI> LIST METRICCURRENT WHERE objectType = 'FLASHCACHE' AND name LIKE '.*KEEP.*'
           FC_BYKEEP_OVERWR           FLASHCACHE      0.0 MB
           FC_BYKEEP_OVERWR_SEC       FLASHCACHE      0.0 MB/sec
           FC_BYKEEP_USED             FLASHCACHE      5,072 MB
           FC_IO_BYKEEP_R             FLASHCACHE      80,288 MB
           FC_IO_BYKEEP_R_SEC         FLASHCACHE      0.0 MB/sec
           FC_IO_BYKEEP_W             FLASHCACHE      11,134 MB
           FC_IO_BYKEEP_W_SEC         FLASHCACHE      0.0 MB/sec
           FC_IO_RQKEEP_R             FLASHCACHE      91,231 IO requests
           FC_IO_RQKEEP_R_MISS        FLASHCACHE      11,155 IO requests
           FC_IO_RQKEEP_R_MISS_SEC    FLASHCACHE      0.0 IO/sec
           FC_IO_RQKEEP_R_SEC         FLASHCACHE      0.0 IO/sec
           FC_IO_RQKEEP_R_SKIP        FLASHCACHE      1,532 IO requests
           FC_IO_RQKEEP_R_SKIP_SEC    FLASHCACHE      0.0 IO/sec
           FC_IO_RQKEEP_W             FLASHCACHE      17,794 IO requests
           FC_IO_RQKEEP_W_SEC         FLASHCACHE      0.0 IO/sec
```

In addition to the performance metrics, you can also see what objects are in the cache. The LIST FLASHCACHECURRENT command displays what's in the cache. This command shows a single entry for each cached object, the amount of space it is occupying, and various other statistics. Here's an example of looking at the flash cache content:

```
CellCLI> describe flashcachecontent
        cachedKeepSize
        cachedSize
        dbID
        dbUniqueName
        hitCount
        hoursToExpiration
        missCount
        objectNumber
        tableSpaceNumber
CellCLI> list flashcachecontent where dbUniqueName like 'EXDB' -
> and hitcount > 100 -
> attributes dbUniqueName, objectNumber, cachedKeepSize, -
> cachedSize, hitCount, missCount
           EXDB    2        0           4194304      587     208
           EXDB    40       0           2424832      376     60
           EXDB    383      0           2146304      117     27
           EXDB    471      0           4071424      274     85
           EXDB    475      0           5881856      503     123
           EXDB    503      0           5308416      669     455
           EXDB    6373     0           2539520      122     39
           EXDB    66849    438763520   438763520    420     3322
```

```
EXDB    71497    0              1220608      255    15
EXDB    71775    0              651780096    1263   20868
```

Unfortunately, the object name is not included in the list of attributes. This means you must go back to the database to determine which object is which (by querying dba_objects for example). Note that the ObjectNumber attribute in cellcli is equivalent to the data_object_id in the database views such as dba_objects.

```
SYS@EXDB1> select owner, object_name, object_type
  2 from dba_objects where data_object_id = 66849;

OWNER                            OBJECT_NAME          OBJECT_TYPE
-------------------------------- -------------------- -------------------
KSO                              SKEW                 TABLE
```

At the Database Layer

The database really doesn't provide much visibility into how ESFC is used. There is only one statistic available in v$sysstat and related views regarding its use.

```
SYS@EXDB1> @mystats
Enter value for name: cell flash%

NAME                                                             VALUE
---------------------------------------------------------------- ----------
cell flash cache read hits                                       2188
```

As with all such statistics, "cell flash cache read hits" is cumulative. In v$sysstat the statistic reflects the system total since the instance was started. In v$mystat the statistic reflects the session total since the session was started. So the only real way to make use of the information is to look at the value before and after the execution of a SQL statement of interest:

```
SYS@EXDB1> @mystats
Enter value for name: cell flash%

NAME                                                          VALUE
------------------------------------------------------------ ---------------
cell flash cache read hits                                   769

SYS@EXDB1> set echo on
SYS@EXDB1> @avgskew
SYS@EXDB1> select avg(pk_col) from kso.skew a where col1 > 0
  2 /

AVG(PK_COL)
-----------
 16093750.8

SYS@EXDB1> set echo off
SYS@EXDB1> @mystats
Enter value for name: cell flash%
```

```
NAME                                                           VALUE
------------------------------------------------------------ ---------------
cell flash cache read hits                                      2550
```

Performance

So how much benefit does the Exadata Smart Flash Cache actually provide? Probably one of the most effective measures of the effectiveness of the cache is the single block read times. Here's a snippet from an AWR report for a fairly representative mixed workload production environment.

```
Event                    Waits <1ms <2ms <4ms <8ms <16ms <32ms <=1s >1s
------------------------ ----- ---- ---- ---- ---- ----- ----- ---- ----
cell single block physical 29.4K 96.7  1.5   .2   .4   .4    .3   .4
```

This output was taken from a one-hour snapshot and as you can see, there were almost 30,000 single block reads, of which about 97% took less than 1ms. This is fairly representative of the production systems we've observed and compares favorably with SSD-based systems. Systems that run entirely on SSD storage generally have average single block access times in the 0.4ms range, which is marginally faster than what we generally see on Exadata. However, the SSD systems are usually not capable of scaling the I/O the way Exadata can. Exadata enjoys this advantage primarily because it is designed to be a balanced configuration, meaning that the components in the I/O path are more closely matched than in most conventional storage arrays. Nothing is without limitations, of course, but most storage systems are bottlenecked at various points in the I/O path (at the disk controllers, for example).

An example may be useful in illustrating this point. We recently did a benchmarking exercise pitting an Exadata V2 High Capacity SATA quarter rack system against a Sun M5000 with 32 cores using SSD for all database storage. The test was a batch program that spent most of its time doing what we would typically call OLTP-type processing. There was a large table with a billion plus rows, but it was accessed via B-Tree indexes a row at a time. On the M5000, the process took about 3 hours and on the Exadata it took a little less than an hour. We have had similar experiences with other OLTP-type workloads as well. We generally don't see the enormous performance benefits over other systems that we see on data warehouse oriented workloads, but we have seen the platform turn in improved performance numbers on every system we've compared to date.

So how else could we measure the effectiveness of ESFC? It's tempting to try to calculate a hit ratio for the flash cache. No doubt it would be interesting to know what percentage of requested I/Os are satisfied by the ESFC. But this calculation is not straightforward. Since ESFC caches more than just table and index blocks, it's difficult to get a reasonable estimate. You could argue that other accesses (ESFC buffers control files access as well) are not significant enough to make any difference, and that may be true. But the fact of the matter is there is no easy way to do anything other than make a somewhat educated guess, knowing full well that it won't be completely accurate. Nevertheless, here is a script (esfc_hit_ratio.sql) that makes an attempt. The script adds the single block and multiblock physical reads and compares those with the cell flash cache hits. In many systems this will be reasonably close. You should be aware though that Smart Scans can also access the ESFC for objects that have been designated for aggressive caching via the CELL_FLASH_CACHE storage parameter.

```
SYS@EXDB1> @esfc_hit_ratio
SYS@EXDB1> column c1 heading 'Event|Name'            format a30 trunc
SYS@EXDB1> column c2 heading 'Total|Waits'           format 99,999,999
SYS@EXDB1> column c3 heading 'Seconds|Waiting'       format 9,999,999
SYS@EXDB1> column c5 heading 'Avg|Wait|(ms)' format 9999.9
SYS@EXDB1> column c6 heading 'Flash Cache Hits' for 999,999,999,999
SYS@EXDB1> col hit_ratio heading 'Hit Ratio' for 999.999
```

```
SYS@EXDB1>
SYS@EXDB1> select
  2    'cell single + multiblock reads' c1,
  3    c2, c3, c5, c6,
  4    c6/decode(nvl(c2,0),0,1,c2) hit_ratio
  5  from (
  6  select
  7     sum(total_waits)              c2,
  8     avg(value)                    c6,
  9     sum(time_waited / 100)        c3,
 10     avg((average_wait /100)*1000)     c5
 11  from
 12     sys.v_$system_event, v$sysstat ss
 13  where
 14     event in (
 15  'cell single block physical read',
 16             'cell multiblock physical read')
 17  and
 18      name like 'cell flash cache read hits'
 19  and
 20      event not like '%Idle%')
 21  order by
 22     c3
 23  ;
```

Event Name	Total Waits	Seconds Waiting	Avg Wait (ms)	Flash Cache Hits	Hit Ratio
cell single + multiblock reads	106,642	374	3.5	247,951	2.325

As you can see, the script vastly overestimates the hit ratio on this particular system, coming up with a hit ratio of over 200%. This happens because this system has several objects that are designated for aggressive caching, resulting in many cache hits for Smart Scan events which are not included in the single block and multi-block read statistics . For systems that don't use the KEEP attribute, the numbers should be closer to reality. However, calculated hit ratios are probably not the best approach. It is generally more enlightening to look at the actual single block access times than to try to calculate a hit ratio.

Summary

Exadata Smart Flash Cache provides yet another way to pare down the I/O cost associated with Oracle databases. Most of the optimizations that the Exadata platform provides require the use of Smart Scans (full table or index scans). ESFC does not depend on Smart Scans and in fact is most useful for speeding up access on random reads of single blocks. These operations are generally associated with OLTP workloads, and so ESFC is the key component of Exadata for OLTP or mixed workloads. The fact that ESFC does not provide a write-back cache, though, severely limits its effectiveness with systems that are bottlenecked on writes. Nevertheless, the large cache and the intelligent caching algorithms used by the Oracle storage software allow ESFC to provide read performance similar to solid-state based disk systems. Offloading large portions of random read activity from the disks also provides an indirect benefit to processes attempting to write to those same disks.

While ESFC is generally thought of as an optimization aimed at reducing latency for small reads, it can also be used quite effectively for large DW-type queries. In fact, the large throughput numbers that Oracle quotes depend on disk and flash cache being scanned concurrently. The flash cache actually shoulders the lion's share of the burden in this case. You can enable this ability on specific tables by setting the CELL_FLASH_CACHE attribute on the table to KEEP. This ability should not be overlooked for key tables, as the performance difference can be dramatic.

## CHAPTER 6

Exadata Parallel Operations

Exadata doesn't have a special way of executing parallel operations that is not available on other platforms running 11gR2. However, parallel processing is a key component of Exadata because efficient handling of Data Warehouse workloads was a primary design goal for Exadata. In addition, because Offloading/Smart Scan depends on direct path reads, which are used by parallel query slaves, parallel operations take on a whole new importance. Traditionally, the use of parallel query has required careful control of concurrency in order to maximize the use of available resources without overwhelming the system. Oracle's previous attempts at throttling parallel operations to allow them to be used in multiuser environments have not been entirely successful. 11gR2 provides some new capabilities for controlling parallel operations. In particular, a queuing mechanism has been introduced that allows the number of concurrent parallel processes to be managed more effectively. This approach appears to be much better suited to allowing a high degree of parallelism without overwhelming the available resources than previous attempts. 11gR2 also introduced the ability for Oracle to automatically calculate a degree of parallelism on a statement-by-statement basis.

This chapter is about parallel query. Other forms of parallelism provided by the database, such as recovery parallelism, will not be covered here. We will briefly cover parallel query mechanics and demonstrate specifically how the queuing mechanism and automatic degree of parallelism work with Exadata. This chapter will also briefly cover the new 11gR2 In-Memory Parallel Execution feature and discuss how Exadata storage parallelizes I/O operations. It will not cover all the details of parallel query or parallel DML and assumes that the reader is familiar with basic Oracle parallel concepts. Note also that the discussion and examples will refer to behavior in Oracle Database 11g Release 2 (11.2.0.2). In most cases, the comments apply equally to version 11.2.0.1 as well. Exceptions are explicitly called out.

Parameters

Before describing the various new features and how they apply to Exadata, you should review the parameters that affect how parallel queries are handled by the database. Table 6-1 shows the parameters along with a brief description of each one's purpose.

Table 6-1. Database Parameters Controlling 11gR2 Parallel Features

Parameter	Default	Description
parallel_adaptive_multi_user	TRUE	Old mechanism of throttling parallel statements by downgrading. In most cases, this parameter should be set to FALSE on Exadata, for reasons we'll discuss later in the chapter.
parallel_automatic_tuning	FALSE	Deprecated since 10g. This parameter enabled an automatic DOP calculation on objects for which a parallelism attribute is set.
parallel_degree_limit	CPU	This parameter sets an upper limit on the DOP that can be applied to a single statement. The default means that Oracle will calculate a value for this limit based on the system's characteristics.
parallel_degree_policy	MANUAL	Controls several parallel features including Automatic Degree of Parallelism (auto DOP), Parallel Statement Queuing and In-memory Parallel Execution.
parallel_execution_message_size	16384	The size of parallel message buffers in bytes.
parallel_force_local	FALSE	Determines whether parallel query slaves will be forced to execute only on the node that initiated the query (TRUE), or whether they will be allowed to spread on to multiple nodes in a RAC cluster (FALSE).
parallel_instance_group		Used to restrict parallel slaves to certain set of instances in a RAC cluster.
parallel_io_cap_enabled	FALSE	Used in conjunction with the DBMS_RESOURCE_MANAGER.CALIBRATE_IO function to limit default DOP calculations based on the I/O capabilities of the system.
parallel_max_servers		The maximum number of parallel slave process that may be created on an instance. The default is calculated based on system parameters including CPU_COUNT and PARALLEL_THREADS_PER_CPU. On most systems the value will work out to be $20 \times$ CPU_COUNT.
parallel_min_percent	0	Old throttling mechanism. It represents the minimum percentage of parallel servers that are needed for a parallel statement to execute.

Parameter	Default	Description
parallel_min_servers	0	The minimum number of parallel slave processes that should be kept running, regardless of usage. Usually set to eliminate the overhead of creating and destroying parallel processes.
parallel_min_time_threshold	AUTO	The minimum estimated serial execution time that will be trigger auto DOP. The default is AUTO, which translates to 10 seconds. When the PARALLEL_DEGREE_POLICY parameter is set to AUTO or LIMITED, any statement that is estimated to take longer than the threshold established by this parameter will be considered a candidate for auto DOP.
parallel_server	TRUE/FALSE	Has nothing to do with parallel queries. Set to true or false depending on whether the database is RAC enabled or not. This parameter was deprecated long ago and has been replaced by the CLUSTER_DATABASE parameter.
parallel_server_instances	1 or the number of RAC instances	Has nothing to do with parallel queries. It is set to the number of instances in a RAC cluster.
parallel_servers_target		The upper limit on the number of parallel slaves that may be in use on an instance at any given time if parallel queuing is enabled. The default is calculated automatically.
parallel_threads_per_cpu	2	Used in various parallel calculations to represent the number of concurrent processes that a CPU can support.

Parallelization at the Storage Tier

Exadata has a lot of processing power at the storage layer. Regardless of whether you are using a V2 quarter rack or an X2-8 full rack, you still have more CPU resources available at the storage layer than you have at the database layer. Since Smart Scans offload a lot of processing to the storage cells, every query executed via Smart Scan is effectively parallelized across the CPUs on the storage cells. This type of parallelization is completely independent of the database parallel processing capabilities, by the way. So this kind of parallelization occurs even when the activity is driven by a single process on a single database server. This introduces some interesting issues that should be considered with regard to normal parallelization at the database tier. Since one of the primary jobs of a parallelized query is to allow multiple processes to participate in the I/O operations, and since the I/O operations are already spread across multiple processes, the degree of parallelism required by statements running on the Exadata platform should be smaller than on other platforms.

Auto DOP

One of the major changes to parallel operations in Oracle Database 11g Release 2 was the addition of a feature affectionately known as Auto DOP. It was designed to overcome the problems associated with the fact that there is rarely a single DOP value that is appropriate for all queries touching a particular object. Prior to 11gR2, DOP could be specified at the statement level via hints or at the object level via the DEGREE and INSTANCE settings. Realistically, using hints at the statement level makes more sense in most situations for the reason just mentioned. But it requires that the developers understand the platform that the statements will be running on and the workload that the hardware will be supporting at the time of execution. Getting the settings correct can be a tedious trial-and-error process and unfortunately, DOP cannot be changed while a statement is running. Once it starts, your only options are to let it complete or kill it and try again. This makes fine tuning in a "live" environment a painful process.

Operation and Configuration

When Auto DOP is enabled, Oracle evaluates each statement to determine whether it should be run in parallel and if so, what DOP should be used. Basically any statement that the optimizer concludes will take longer than 10 seconds to run serially will be a candidate to run in parallel. The 10-second threshold can be controlled by setting the PARALLEL_MIN_TIME_THRESHOLD parameter by the way. This decision is made regardless of whether any of the objects involved in the statement have been decorated with a parallel degree setting or not.

Auto DOP is enabled by setting the PARALLEL_DEGREE_POLICY parameter to a value of AUTO or LIMITED. The default setting for this parameter is MANUAL, which disables all three of the new 11gR2 parallel features (Auto DOP, Parallel Statement Queuing, In-memory Parallel Execution). Unfortunately, PARALLEL_DEGREE_POLICY is one of those parameters that control more than one thing. The following list shows the effects of the various settings for this parameter.

> MANUAL: If PARALLEL_DEGREE_POLICY is set to MANUAL, none of the new 11gR2 parallel features will be enabled. Parallel processing will work as it did in previous versions. That is to say, statements will only be parallelized if a hint is used or an object is decorated with a parallel setting.

> LIMITED: If PARALLEL_DEGREE_POLICY is set to LIMITED, only Auto DOP is enabled while Parallel Statement Queuing and In-memory Parallel Execution remain disabled. In addition, only statements accessing objects that have been decorated with the default parallel setting will be considered for Auto DOP calculation.

> AUTO: If PARALLEL_DEGREE_POLICY is set to AUTO, all three of the new features are enabled. Statements will be evaluated for parallel execution regardless of any parallel decoration at the object level.

Although the only documented way to enable Parallel Statement Queuing and In-memory Parallel Execution are via the all-or-nothing setting of AUTO, the developers have thoughtfully provided hidden parameters that provide independent control of these features. Table 6-2 shows the parameters and how the settings of PARALLEL_DEGREE_POLICY alter the hidden parameters.

Table 6-2. Hidden Parameters Affected by PARALLEL_DEGREE_POLICY

Parallel_Degree_Policy	Parameter	Value
MANUAL	_parallel_statement_queuing	FALSE
	_parallel_cluster_cache_policy	ADAPTIVE
LIMITED	_parallel_statement_queuing	FALSE
	_parallel_cluster_cache_policy	ADAPTIVE
AUTO	_parallel_statement_queuing	TRUE
	_parallel_cluster_cache_policy	CACHED

It's pretty obvious what the _PARALLEL_STATEMENT_QUEUING parameter controls. When it is set to TRUE, queuing is enabled. The purpose of the _PARALLEL_CLUSTER_CACHE_POLICY parameter is a little less obvious. It turns out that it controls In-memory Parallel Execution. Setting the value of the _PARALLEL_CLUSTER_CACHE_POLICY parameter to CACHED enables In-memory Parallel Execution. You should note that In-memory Parallel Execution is arguably of less value on the Exadata platform, because the Smart Scan optimizations will not be available when using this feature to scan the buffer cache. We'll discuss that in more detail a little later. In the meantime, here's an example showing Auto DOP in action.

```
SYS@EXDB1> @dba_tables
Enter value for owner: KSO
Enter value for table_name: SKEW

OWNER       TABLE_NAME STATUS   LAST_ANAL   NUM_ROWS    BLOCKS DEGREE
----------  ---------- -------- ---------  ----------  ---------- ----------
KSO         SKEW       VALID    25-NOV-10   32000004    162294            1

SYS@EXDB1> alter system set parallel_degree_policy=auto;

System altered.

SYS@EXDB1> select avg(pk_col) from kso.skew a where col1 > 0;

AVG(PK_COL)
-----------
 16093749.3

1 row selected.

SYS@EXDB1> @fs
Enter value for sql_text: %skew%
Enter value for sql_id:
```

```
SQL_ID          AVG_ETIME    AVG_LIO SQL_TEXT
-------------  ------------  ------- ----------------------------------------
05cq2hb1r37tr       28.77    162,427 select avg(pk_col) from kso.skew a
                                     where col1 > 0

1 rows selected.

SYS@EXDB1> !cat dplan.sql
set lines 150
select * from table(dbms_xplan.display_cursor('&sql_id','&child_no','typical'))
/

SYS@EXDB1> @dplan
Enter value for sql_id: 05cq2hb1r37tr
Enter value for child_no: 2

PLAN_TABLE_OUTPUT

-----------------------------------------------------------------------------------------
SQL_ID  05cq2hb1r37tr, child number 2
-------------------------------------
select avg(pk_col) from kso.skew a where col1 > 0

Plan hash value: 578366071)

----------------------------------------------------------------------------------------
| Id | Operation              | Name     | Rows  | Bytes | Cost (%CPU)| Time     | TQ    |
----------------------------------------------------------------------------------------
|  0 | SELECT STATEMENT       |          |       |       | 6308  (100)|          |       |
|  1 |  SORT AGGREGATE        |          |     1 |    24 |            |          |       |
|  2 |   PX COORDINATOR       |          |       |       |            |          |       |
|  3 |    PX SEND QC (RANDOM) | :TQ10000 |     1 |    24 |            |          | Q1,00 |
|  4 |     SORT AGGREGATE     |          |     1 |    24 |            |          | Q1,00 |
|  5 |      PX BLOCK ITERATOR |          |   32M |  732M | 6308   (1)| 00:01:16 | Q1,00 |
|* 6 |       TABLE ACCESS FULL| SKEW     |   32M |  732M | 6308   (1)| 00:01:16 | Q1,00 |
----------------------------------------------------------------------------------------

Predicate Information (identified by operation id):
---------------------------------------------------

   6 - access(:Z>=:Z AND :Z<=:Z)
       filter("COL1">0)

Note
-----
   - automatic DOP: Computed Degree of Parallelism is 5


28 rows selected. )
```

So as you can see, enabling Auto DOP allowed the statement to be parallelized, even though the table was not decorated with a parallel setting. Also, notice that the plan output produced by DBMS_XPLAN shows that Auto DOP was enabled and the calculated DOP was 5.

Oracle has provided some control over the Automatic DOP calculations as well with the PARALLEL_DEGREE_LIMIT parameter. The default value for this parameter is CPU, which tells Oracle to calculate an "Ideal DOP" based on the amount of data, but then caps it with a formula based on CPU_COUNT, THREADS_PER_CPU, and ACTIVE_INSTANCE_COUNT.

I/O Calibration

Oracle Database version 11.2.0.2 introduced a restriction to Auto DOP requiring that the I/O system be calibrated before statements will be automatically parallelized. The calibration is done by the DBMS_RESOURCE_MANAGER.CALIBRATE_IO procedure, which generates a random read-only workload and spreads it across all instances in a RAC cluster. It runs for several minutes (longer on RAC databases because it must run on each instance). The procedure can put a significant load on the system, and the documentation recommends running it when the system is idle or very lightly loaded. Here's an example of what happens if the calibration procedure has not been run on 11.2.0.2:

```
SYS@LAB11202> @dplan
Enter value for sql_id: 05cq2hb1r37tr
Enter value for child_no:

PLAN_TABLE_OUTPUT
------------------------------------------------------------------------------------
SQL_ID  05cq2hb1r37tr, child number 0
-------------------------------------
select avg(pk_col) from kso.skew a where col1 > 0

Plan hash value: 568322376

-------------------------------------------------------------------------------
| Id  | Operation          | Name | Rows  | Bytes | Cost (%CPU)| Time     |
-------------------------------------------------------------------------------
|   0 | SELECT STATEMENT   |      |       |       | 44298 (100)|          |
|   1 |  SORT AGGREGATE    |      |     1 |    11 |            |          |
|*  2 |   TABLE ACCESS FULL| SKEW |   32M |  335M | 44298   (1)| 00:01:29 |
-------------------------------------------------------------------------------

Predicate Information (identified by operation id):
---------------------------------------------------

   2 - filter("COL1">0)

Note
-----
   - automatic DOP: skipped because of IO calibrate statistics are missing


23 rows selected.
```

As you can see, when the I/O calibration has not been done, Auto DOP is disabled and the optimizer generates a serial execution plan. There are two views that provide additional information about the calibration process. The V$IO_CALIBRATION_STATUS view shows whether the calibration has been done, while the DBA_RSRC_IO_CALIBRATE view shows the results of the procedure. Here's an example showing how to use the procedure:

```
SYS@EXDB1> select * from V$IO_CALIBRATION_STATUS;

STATUS          CALIBRATION_TIME
-------------   ----------------------------------------------------------------
NOT AVAILABLE

1 row selected.

SYS@EXDB1> !cat calibrate_io.sql
SET SERVEROUTPUT ON
DECLARE
  lat  INTEGER;
  iops INTEGER;
  mbps INTEGER;
BEGIN
-- DBMS_RESOURCE_MANAGER.CALIBRATE_IO (<DISKS>, <MAX_LATENCY>, iops, mbps, lat);
   DBMS_RESOURCE_MANAGER.CALIBRATE_IO (&no_of_disks, 10, iops, mbps, lat);

  DBMS_OUTPUT.PUT_LINE ('max_iops = ' || iops);
  DBMS_OUTPUT.PUT_LINE ('latency  = ' || lat);
  dbms_output.put_line('max_mbps = ' || mbps);
end;
/

SYS@EXDB1> set timing on
SYS@EXDB1> @calibrate_io
Enter value for no_of_disks: 36

-- switch to other session on DB server

> top
top - 21:12:32 up 10 days,  9:27,  3 users,  load average: 0.49, 0.44, 0.47
Tasks: 814 total,   1 running, 813 sleeping,   0 stopped,   0 zombie
Cpu(s):  0.4%us,  0.1%sy,  0.0%ni, 99.4%id,  0.1%wa,  0.0%hi,  0.0%si,  0.0%st
Mem:  74027752k total, 52225108k used, 21802644k free,   829336k buffers
Swap: 16771852k total,        0k used, 16771852k free, 43078508k cached

  PID USER      PR  NI  VIRT  RES  SHR S %CPU %MEM    TIME+  COMMAND
14825 oracle    15   0 5225m  22m  19m S  1.7  0.0  0:00.15 ora_cs02_EXDB1
14827 oracle    15   0 5225m  22m  19m S  1.1  0.0  0:00.14 ora_cs03_EXDB1
14831 oracle    15   0 5225m  22m  19m S  1.1  0.0  0:00.14 ora_cs05_EXDB1
11810 oracle    15   0 12.2g  54m  39m S  0.6  0.1 12:44.67 ora_dia0_POC1
14821 oracle    15   0 5225m  22m  19m S  0.6  0.0  0:00.13 ora_cs00_EXDB1
14823 oracle    15   0 5225m  22m  19m S  0.6  0.0  0:00.15 ora_cs01_EXDB1
14829 oracle    15   0 5225m  22m  19m S  0.6  0.0  0:00.12 ora_cs04_EXDB1
15239 osborne   16   0 13268 1648  816 R  0.6  0.0  0:00.03 top
28118 oracle    RT   0  335m 133m  52m S  0.6  0.2 88:21.34
```

```
-- switch to one of the cells

[enkcel01:root] /root > vmstat 2

procs -----------memory---------- ---swap-- -----io---- --system-- -----cpu------
 r  b   swpd    free   buff   cache   si   so    bi    bo    in   cs us sy id wa st
 0  1      0 9147200 311736 1353092    0    0   390   298    1    1  1  1 98  0  0
 0  1      0 9147504 311736 1353092    0    0  2010   233 1732 21385  0  0 94  6  0
 1  1      0 9147504 311736 1353092    0    0  1810   241 1675 21294  0  1 94  5  0
 0  1      0 9148000 311736 1353136    0    0  1917   157 1715 21715  0  0 94  5  0
 0  1      0 9147876 311736 1353140    0    0  2018   357 1770 20928  0  0 94  5  0
 0  1      0 9145776 311736 1353140    0    0  1906   298 1713 20086  0  0 94  5  0

-- switch back to original session)

max_iops = 1004
latency  = 10
max_mbps = 2201

PL/SQL procedure successfully completed.

Elapsed: 00:13:41.27
SYS@EXDB1> set timing off
SYS@EXDB1> @mystats)
Enter value for name: cell flash cache

NAME                                                              VALUE
---------------------------------------------------------- ---------------
cell flash cache read hits                                            0

SYS@EXDB1> select * from V$IO_CALIBRATION_STATUS;

STATUS        CALIBRATION_TIME
------------  ------------------------------------------------------------
READY         10-DEC-10 09.20.11.254 PM

SYS@EXDB1> select to_char(start_time,'dd-mon-yy') start_time ,
  2              MAX_IOPS, MAX_MBPS, MAX_PMBPS, LATENCY, NUM_PHYSICAL_DISKS
  3          from DBA_RSRC_IO_CALIBRATE;

START_TIM   MAX_IOPS   MAX_MBPS   MAX_PMBPS   LATENCY NUM_PHYSICAL_DISKS
---------  ---------  ---------  ---------  ---------  ------------------
11-dec-10       1004       2201        101         10                  36
```

This listing is a little long, so let's walk through what we did:

1. We checked the current status in V$IO_CALIBRATION_STATUS.

2. We ran the DBMS_RESOURCE_MANAGER.CALIBRATE_IO procedure using a script called calibrate_io.sql.

3. We then jumped to another session to see what kind of activity was generated on the database server (using top).

4. Next we created a session on one of the storage servers to see the activity there (using vmstat).

5. We then switched back to the original session and after almost 14 minutes the procedure completed.

6. Finally we checked the status and results in V$IO_CALIBRATION_STATUS and DBA_RSRC_IO_CALIBRATE.

Auto DOP Wrap Up

The end result of setting PARALLEL_DEGREE_POLICY to AUTO is that all kinds of statements will be run in parallel, even if no objects have been specifically decorated with a parallel degree setting. This is truly automatic parallel processing because the database decides what to run in parallel and with how many slaves. On top of that, by default, the slaves may be spread across multiple nodes in a RAC database. Unfortunately this combination of features is a little like the Wild West, with things running in parallel all over the place. But the ability to queue parallel statements does provide some semblance of order, which leads us to the next topic.

Parallel Statement Queuing

I recently attended a Tech Day where one of the speakers recalled the presentation Larry Ellison did when Oracle first announced the Parallel Query feature (Oracle version 7). In the demo, Larry had a multiprocessor computer all to himself. I don't remember how many processors it had, but I remember he had some kind of graphic showing individual CPU utilization on one screen while he fired up a parallel query on another screen. The monitoring screen lit up like a Christmas tree. Every one of the CPUs was pegged during his demo. When the speaker was telling the story he said that he had wondered at the time what would have happened if there had been other users on the system during the demo. Their experience would probably not have been a good one. That's exactly the issue that Parallel Statement Queuing attempts to resolve.

Oracle's parallel capabilities have been a great gift but they have also been a curse because controlling the beast in an environment where there are multiple users trying to share the resources is difficult at best. There have been attempts to come up with a reasonable way of throttling big parallel statements. But to date, I don't think those attempts have been overly successful.

One of the most promising aspects of Exadata is its potential to run mixed workloads (OLTP and DW), without crippling one or the other. In order to do that, Oracle needs some mechanism to separate the workloads and, just as importantly, to throttle the resource intensive parallel queries. Parallel Statement Queuing appears to be just such a tool. And when combined with Resource Manager, it provides a pretty robust mechanism for throttling the workload to a level that the hardware can support.

The Old Way

Before we get to the new Parallel Queuing functionality we should probably review how it was done in previous versions. The best tool we had at our disposal was Parallel Adaptive Multiuser, which provides the ability to automatically downgrade the degree of parallelism for a given statement based on the workload when a query executes. It is actually a powerful mechanism and it is the best approach we've had prior to 11gR2. This feature is enabled by setting the PARALLEL_ADAPTIVE_MULTI_USER parameter to TRUE. This is still the default in 11gR2 by the way, so this is definitely a parameter that you may want to consider changing. The downside of this approach is that parallelized statements can have wildly varying execution times. As you can imagine, a statement that gets 32 slaves one time and then gets downgraded to serial execution the next time will probably not make the users very happy.

The argument for this type of approach is that stuff is going to run slower if the system is busy regardless of what you do, and that users expect it to run slower when the system is busy. The first part of that statement may be true, but I don't believe the second part is (at least in most cases). The bigger problem with the downgrade mechanism though is that the decision about how many slaves to use is based on a single point in time, the point when the parallel statement starts. Recall that once the degree of parallelism (DOP) is set for an execution plan, it cannot be changed. The statement will run to completion with the number of slaves it was assigned, even if additional resources become available while it is running.

So consider the statement that takes one minute to execute with 32 slaves. And suppose that same statement gets downgraded to serial due to a momentarily high load. And say that a few seconds after it starts, the system load drops back to more normal levels. Unfortunately, the serialized statement will continue to run for nearly 30 minutes with its single process, even though on average, the system is not busier than usual. This sort of erratic performance can wreak havoc for those using the system, and for those supporting it.

The New Way

Now let's compare Parallel Adaptive Multi User (the old way), with the new mechanism introduced in 11gR2 that allows parallel statements to be queued. This mechanism separates long running parallel queries from the rest of the workload. The mechanics are pretty simple. Turn the feature on. Set a target number of parallel slaves using the PARALLEL_SERVERS_TARGET parameter. Run stuff. If a statement that requires exceeding the target tries to start, it will be queued until the required number of slaves become available. There are of course many details to consider and other control mechanisms that can be applied to manage the process. So let's look at how it behaves:

```
SYS@EXDB1> alter system set parallel_degree_policy=auto;

System altered.

SYS@EXDB1> alter system set parallel_servers_target=10;

System altered.

SYS@EXDB1> @parms
Enter value for parameter: parallel%
Enter value for isset:
Enter value for show_hidden:
```

```
NAME                            VALUE                           ISDEFAUL
------------------------------- ------------------------------- --------
parallel_adaptive_multi_user    FALSE                           TRUE
parallel_automatic_tuning       FALSE                           TRUE
parallel_degree_limit           8                               FALSE
parallel_degree_policy          AUTO                            FALSE
parallel_execution_message_size 16384                           TRUE
parallel_force_local            TRUE                            FALSE
parallel_instance_group                                         TRUE
parallel_io_cap_enabled         FALSE                           TRUE
parallel_max_servers            320                             TRUE
parallel_min_percent            0                               TRUE
parallel_min_servers            16                              FALSE
parallel_min_time_threshold     2                               TRUE
parallel_server                 TRUE                            TRUE
parallel_server_instances       2                               TRUE
parallel_servers_target         10                              FALSE
parallel_threads_per_cpu        2                               TRUE

16 rows selected.

SYS@EXDB1> !ss.sh avgskew.sql 20 kso/kso

starting 20 copies of avgskew.sql

SYS@EXDB1> set echo on
SYS@EXDB1> @queued_sql
SYS@EXDB1> col sql_text for a60 trunc
SYS@EXDB1> SELECT sid, sql_id, sql_exec_id, sql_text
  2  from v$sql_monitor
  3  WHERE status='QUEUED'
  4  order by 3
  5  /

       SID SQL_ID        SQL_EXEC_ID SQL_TEXT
---------- ------------- ----------- ------------------------------------
       494 05cq2hb1r37tr    16777218 select avg(pk_col) from kso.skew a
                                     where col1 > 0
       541 05cq2hb1r37tr    16777220
       152 05cq2hb1r37tr    16777221
       102 05cq2hb1r37tr    16777222
       106 05cq2hb1r37tr    16777223
       201 05cq2hb1r37tr    16777224
       397 05cq2hb1r37tr    16777225
       250 05cq2hb1r37tr    16777226
       693 05cq2hb1r37tr    16777227
       154 05cq2hb1r37tr    16777228
       444 05cq2hb1r37tr    16777229
       743 05cq2hb1r37tr    16777230
       300 05cq2hb1r37tr    16777231
         5 05cq2hb1r37tr    16777232
        53 05cq2hb1r37tr    16777233
```

```
   642 05cq2hb1r37tr    16777234
   348 05cq2hb1r37tr    16777235
   200 05cq2hb1r37tr    16777236
   251 05cq2hb1r37tr    16777237

19 rows selected.

SYS@EXDB1> @check_px
SYS@EXDB1> select * from V$PX_PROCESS_SYSSTAT where statistic like '%In Use%';

STATISTIC                       VALUE
--------------------------- ----------
Servers In Use                      8

SYS@EXDB1> /

STATISTIC                       VALUE
--------------------------- ----------
Servers In Use                      0

SYS@EXDB1> /

STATISTIC                       VALUE
--------------------------- ----------
Servers In Use                      8

SYS@EXDB1> /

STATISTIC                       VALUE
--------------------------- ----------
Servers In Use                      8

SYS@EXDB1> set echo off
SYS@EXDB1> @snapper ash=sid+event+wait_class,ash1=plsql_object_id+sql_id 5 1 all
Sampling with interval 5 seconds, 1 times...

-- Session Snapper v3.11 by Tanel Poder @ E2SN ( http://tech.e2sn.com )


----------------------------------------------------------------
Active% |  SID | EVENT                   | WAIT_CLASS
----------------------------------------------------------------
   100% |  300 | resmgr:pq queued        | Scheduler
   100% |  348 | resmgr:pq queued        | Scheduler
   100% |  201 | resmgr:pq queued        | Scheduler
   100% |  200 | resmgr:pq queued        | Scheduler
   100% |  743 | resmgr:pq queued        | Scheduler
   100% |  251 | resmgr:pq queued        | Scheduler
   100% |  693 | resmgr:pq queued        | Scheduler
   100% |  642 | resmgr:pq queued        | Scheduler
   100% |    5 | resmgr:pq queued        | Scheduler
   100% |  541 | resmgr:pq queued        | Scheduler
```

```
--------------------------------------
Active% | PLSQL_OBJE | SQL_ID
--------------------------------------
  2152% |            | 05cq2hb1r37tr
     7% |            |
```

-- End of ASH snap 1, end=2010-12-06 19:25:43, seconds=5, samples_taken=42

PL/SQL procedure successfully completed.

There are several things worth mentioning in this listing. To set up the desired conditions we turned on Auto DOP, which also enables Parallel Queuing, and then set the PARALLEL_SERVER_TARGET parameter to a very low number (10) in order to trigger queuing more easily. We then used a shell script (ss.sh) to fire off 20 copies of the avgskew.sql script in rapid succession. Querying V$SQL_MONITOR showed that the statements were indeed queuing. This is an important point. All statements using parallel query will show up in the V$SQL_MONITOR view. If they have a status of QUEUED they are not actually executing but are instead waiting until enough parallel slaves become available. We also queried V$PX_PROCESS_SYSSTAT a few times to see how many parallel slaves were being used. Finally, we ran Tanel Poder's snapper script to see what event the queued statements were waiting on. As you can see, it was the resmgr: pq queued wait event.

⬛ **Note:** There is one other thing you should be aware of with regard to the wait events. There is a wait event change that relates to parallel queuing. This example was created using Oracle Database version 11.2.0.2. If you are using 11.2.0.1 you will see a different set of wait events (there are two). The first is PX Queuing: statement queue. This is the event that a statement waits on when it is next to run. The other is enq: JX - SQL statement queue. This event is what a statement waits on when there are other statements ahead of it in the queue. This scheme seems quite unwieldy, which is probably why it was changed in the later release.

Controlling Parallel Queuing

There are several mechanisms in place for controlling how the Parallel Statement Queuing feature behaves. The basic approach is to use a first-in, first-out queuing mechanism. But there are ways to prioritize work within the queuing framework. It's also possible to completely by-pass the queuing mechanism via a hint. And conversely, it is possible to enable queuing for a statement via a hint even when the parallel Statement Queuing feature is not enabled at the database level. There are also a few parameters that affect the queuing behavior. And finally, Resource Manager has the capability to affect how statements are queued.

Controlling Queuing with Parameters

There are a handful of parameters that affect how Parallel Queuing behaves. The main parameter is PARALLEL_SERVERS_TARGET, which tells Oracle how many parallel server processes to allow before starting to hold statements back in the queue. The default value for this parameter is calculated as follows:

$$((4 \times CPU\_count) \times parallel\_threads\_per\_cpu) \times active\_instances$$

So on an Exadata X2-2 with a database that spans 4 RAC nodes, the default value would be calculated as:

$$((4 \times 12) \times 2) \times 4 = 384$$

This calculated value is almost certainly higher than you would want for most mixed workload systems, as it is geared at completely consuming the available CPU resources with parallel query processes. Allowing long-running parallel statements to consume the server completely means that response-sensitive, OLTP-type statements, could suffer. You should also note that it is possible to have more server processes active than the parameter allows. Since the number of slaves assigned to a query may be twice the DOP, the target can occasionally be exceeded.

The second parameter that deserves some discussion is the hidden parameter, _PARALLEL_STATEMENT_QUEUING, which turns the feature on and off. As already discussed in the Auto DOP section, this parameter is set to TRUE when the PARALLEL_DEGREE_POLICY parameter is set to AUTO. However, the hidden parameter can also be set manually to turn Parallel Queuing off and on independently.

Auto DOP calculations are still a little scary. So it's nice that there is a way to turn on the Parallel Queuing feature without enabling Oracle to take complete control of which statements run in parallel. Of course since this involves setting a hidden parameter you should not do this in a production environment without approval from Oracle support. Nevertheless, here's another quick example showing that queuing can be turned on without enabling Auto DOP or In-memory Parallel Execution:

```
SYS@EXDB1> alter system set parallel_degree_policy=manual;

System altered.

SYS@EXDB1> alter table kso.skew parallel (degree 8);

Table altered.

SYS@EXDB1> @parms
Enter value for parameter: parallel%
Enter value for isset:
Enter value for show_hidden:

NAME                                VALUE                           ISDEFAUL
----------------------------------- ------------------------------- --------
parallel_adaptive_multi_user        FALSE                           TRUE
parallel_automatic_tuning           FALSE                           TRUE
parallel_degree_limit               8                               FALSE
parallel_degree_policy              MANUAL                          FALSE
parallel_execution_message_size     16384                           TRUE
parallel_force_local                TRUE                            FALSE
parallel_instance_group                                             TRUE
parallel_io_cap_enabled             FALSE                           TRUE
parallel_max_servers                320                             TRUE
parallel_min_percent                0                               TRUE
parallel_min_servers                16                              FALSE
parallel_min_time_threshold         2                               TRUE
parallel_server                     TRUE                            TRUE
parallel_server_instances           2                               TRUE
```

```
parallel_servers_target          10                    FALSE
parallel_threads_per_cpu         2                     TRUE

16 rows selected.

SYS@EXDB1>  !ss.sh avgskew.sql 20 kso/kso

starting 20 copies of avgskew.sql

SYS@EXDB1> @queued_sql

no rows selected

SYS@EXDB1> @queued_sql

no rows selected

SYS@EXDB1> @check_px

SYS@EXDB1> /

STATISTIC                    VALUE
---------------------------- --------
Servers In Use                  48

1 row selected.

SYS@EXDB1> /

STATISTIC                    VALUE
---------------------------- --------
Servers In Use                  56

1 row selected.

SYS@EXDB1> /

STATISTIC                    VALUE
---------------------------- --------
Servers In Use                  64

1 row selected.

SYS@EXDB1> /

STATISTIC                    VALUE
---------------------------- --------
Servers In Use                  48

1 row selected.
```

```
SYS@EXDB1> /

STATISTIC                      VALUE
------------------------------ --------
Servers In Use                    56

1 row selected.

SYS@EXDB1> queued_sql

no rows selected

SYS@EXDB1> -- no queuing, lot's of parallel slaves running
SYS@EXDB1>
SYS@EXDB1> alter system set "_parallel_statement_queuing"=true; -- enable Queuing

System altered.

SYS@EXDB1> !ss.sh avgskew.sql 20 kso/kso

starting 20 copies of avgskew.sql

SYS@EXDB1> @queued_sql

 SID SQL_ID         SQL_EXEC_ID SQL_TEXT
---- ------------- ----------- --------------------------------------------
 181 05cq2hb1r37tr    16777363 select avg(pk_col) from kso.skew a
                               where col1 > 0
 216                  16777364
  44                  16777365
 273                  16777366
 234                  16777367
 160                  16777368
 100                  16777369
 233                  16777370
  30                  16777371
 138                  16777372
   7                  16777373
 293                  16777374
 137                  16777375
  83                  16777376
 251                  16777377
  66                  16777378
 123                  16777379
 195                  16777380

18 rows selected.

SYS@EXDB1> -- now we have control of which statements are parallelized and we have queuing
```

This listing shows that you can have Parallel Statement Queuing without turning on Auto DOP. Of course it's using a hidden parameter, so you probably don't want to do this on a production system without discussing it with Oracle Support first.

Controlling Queuing with Hints

There are two hints that can be used to control Parallel Statement Queuing at the statement level. One hint, NO_STATEMENT_QUEUING, allows the queuing process to be completely bypassed, even if the feature is turned on at the instance level. The other hint, STATEMENT_QUEUING, turns on the queuing mechanism, even if the feature is not enabled at the instance level. The STATEMENT_QUEUING hint provides a documented avenue for using the queuing feature without enabling Auto DOP. Here is an example showing how to bypass the queuing by using the NO_STATEMENT_QUEUING hint.

```
SYS@EXDB1> set echo on
SYS@EXDB1> @test_pxq_hint
SYS@EXDB1> -- this should cause queueing, but the hinted statements
SYS@EXDB1> -- should jump the queue
SYS@EXDB1> alter system set "_parallel_statement_queuing"=true;

System altered.

SYS@EXDB1> alter system set parallel_servers_target=32;

System altered.

SYS@EXDB1> !ss.sh test_pxq_hint1.sql 10 kso/kso

starting 10 copies of test_pxq_hint1.sql


SYS@EXDB1> @queued_sql

  SID SQL_ID        SQL_EXEC_ID SQL_TEXT
----- ------------- ----------- --------------------------------------------------------------------
  484 bgcmmcyyyvpg9    16777239 select /*+ parallel (a 16) */ avg(pk_col) from kso.skew3 a
                                where col1 > 0
  774 bgcmmcyyyvpg9    16777240
  584 bgcmmcyyyvpg9    16777241
  199 bgcmmcyyyvpg9    16777242
  679 bgcmmcyyyvpg9    16777243
  391 bgcmmcyyyvpg9    16777244
 1060 bgcmmcyyyvpg9    16777245

7 rows selected.

SYS@EXDB1> !ss.sh test_pxq_hint2.sql 2 kso/kso

starting 2 copies of test_pxq_hint2.sql
```

```
SYS@EXDB1> @queued_sql

  SID SQL_ID         SQL_EXEC_ID SQL_TEXT
----- ------------- ----------- --------------------------------------------------------
  774 bgcmmcyyyvpg9    16777240 select /*+ parallel (a 16) */ avg(pk_col) from kso.skew3 a
                                where col1 > 0
  584 bgcmmcyyyvpg9    16777241
  199 bgcmmcyyyvpg9    16777242
  679 bgcmmcyyyvpg9    16777243
  391 bgcmmcyyyvpg9    16777244
 1060 bgcmmcyyyvpg9    16777245

6 rows selected.

SYS@EXDB1> @as

  SID SQL_ID        CHILD PLAN_HASH_VALUE EXECS  AVG_ETIME SQL_TEXT
----- ------------- ----- --------------- ----- ---------- ------------------------------
    4 5v6grtvwkb836     0      1404581711     2     211.89 select /*+ NO_STATEMENT_QUEUING
 1448 5v6grtvwkb836     0      1404581711     2     211.89 select /*+ NO_STATEMENT_QUEUING
    8 5v6grtvwkb836     0      1404581711     2     211.89 select /*+ NO_STATEMENT_QUEUING
    7 5v6grtvwkb836     0      1404581711     2     211.89 select /*+ NO_STATEMENT_QUEUING
 1446 5v6grtvwkb836     0      1404581711     2     211.89 select /*+ NO_STATEMENT_QUEUING
 1354 5v6grtvwkb836     0      1404581711     2     211.89 select /*+ NO_STATEMENT_QUEUING
 1257 5v6grtvwkb836     0      1404581711     2     211.89 select /*+ NO_STATEMENT_QUEUING
 1253 5v6grtvwkb836     0      1404581711     2     211.89 select /*+ NO_STATEMENT_QUEUING
 1160 5v6grtvwkb836     0      1404581711     2     211.89 select /*+ NO_STATEMENT_QUEUING
 1156 5v6grtvwkb836     0      1404581711     2     211.89 select /*+ NO_STATEMENT_QUEUING
 1065 5v6grtvwkb836     0      1404581711     2     211.89 select /*+ NO_STATEMENT_QUEUING
  969 5v6grtvwkb836     0      1404581711     2     211.89 select /*+ NO_STATEMENT_QUEUING
  201 5v6grtvwkb836     0      1404581711     2     211.89 select /*+ NO_STATEMENT_QUEUING
  297 5v6grtvwkb836     0      1404581711     2     211.89 select /*+ NO_STATEMENT_QUEUING
  393 5v6grtvwkb836     0      1404581711     2     211.89 select /*+ NO_STATEMENT_QUEUING
  394 5v6grtvwkb836     0      1404581711     2     211.89 select /*+ NO_STATEMENT_QUEUING
  486 5v6grtvwkb836     0      1404581711     2     211.89 select /*+ NO_STATEMENT_QUEUING
  488 5v6grtvwkb836     0      1404581711     2     211.89 select /*+ NO_STATEMENT_QUEUING
  585 5v6grtvwkb836     0      1404581711     2     211.89 select /*+ NO_STATEMENT_QUEUING
  586 5v6grtvwkb836     0      1404581711     2     211.89 select /*+ NO_STATEMENT_QUEUING
  778 5v6grtvwkb836     0      1404581711     2     211.89 select /*+ NO_STATEMENT_QUEUING
  868 5v6grtvwkb836     0      1404581711     2     211.89 select /*+ NO_STATEMENT_QUEUING
  869 5v6grtvwkb836     0      1404581711     2     211.89 select /*+ NO_STATEMENT_QUEUING
  872 5v6grtvwkb836     0      1404581711     2     211.89 select /*+ NO_STATEMENT_QUEUING
  965 5v6grtvwkb836     0      1404581711     2     211.89 select /*+ NO_STATEMENT_QUEUING
  967 5v6grtvwkb836     0      1404581711     2     211.89 select /*+ NO_STATEMENT_QUEUING
 1255 bgcmmcyyyvpg9     0      1404581711     4     204.91 select /*+ parallel (a 16) */
  774 bgcmmcyyyvpg9     0      1404581711     4     204.91 select /*+ parallel (a 16) */
  484 bgcmmcyyyvpg9     0      1404581711     4     204.91 select /*+ parallel (a 16) */
  679 bgcmmcyyyvpg9     0      1404581711     4     204.91 select /*+ parallel (a 16) */
  199 bgcmmcyyyvpg9     0      1404581711     4     204.91 select /*+ parallel (a 16) */
  391 bgcmmcyyyvpg9     0      1404581711     4     204.91 select /*+ parallel (a 16) */
 1060 bgcmmcyyyvpg9     0      1404581711     4     204.91 select /*+ parallel (a 16) */
```

```
   584 bgcmmcyyyvpg9        0      1404581711      4      204.91 select /*+ parallel (a 16) */
  1157 bgcmmcyyyvpg9        0      1404581711      4      204.91 select /*+ parallel (a 16) */

35 rows selected.
```

This listing shows that statements using the NO_STATEMENT_QUEUING hint completely bypass the queuing mechanism. The steps we executed were to enable queuing, fire off 10 copies of a select statement that was hinted to use a DOP of 16. These statements were queued as shown by the queued_sql.sql script. We then fired off 2 copies of a statement using the NO_STATEMENT_QUEUING hint. The queued_sql.sql script showed that the new statements were not at the bottom of the queue. In fact, they were not queued at all. They were run immediately. The as.sql script shows active sessions, and as you can see, a side effect of bypassing the queuing is that the number of active slaves can end up being considerably higher than the setting of the PARALLEL_SERVERS_TARGET parameter.

Controlling Queuing with Resource Manager

Oracle's Database Resource Manager (DBRM) provides additional capability to control Parallel Statement Queuing. While a thorough discussion of DBRM is beyond the scope of this chapter, we will cover some specific features related to Parallel Query. Chapter 7 covers DBRM in more detail.

Without DBRM, the parallel statement queue behaves strictly as a first-in, first-out (FIFO) queue. DBRM provides several directive attributes that can be used to provide additional control on a consumer group basis. Many of these controls were introduced in version 11.2.0.2. Table 6-3 contains a list of additional capabilities provided by DBRM.

Table 6-3. DBRM Parallel Statement Queuing Controls

Control	Description
Specify a Timeout	The PARALLEL_QUEUE_TIMEOUT directive attribute can be used to set a maximum queue time for a consumer group. The time limit is set in seconds and once it has expired, the statement will terminate with an error (ORA-07454). Note that this directive did not become available until version 11.2.0.2 of the database.
Specify Maximum DOP	The PARALLEL_DEGREE_LIMIT_P1 directive attribute sets a maximum number of parallel slaves that may be assigned to an individual statement. This is equivalent to the PARALLEL_DEGREE_LIMIT database parameter but is used to set limits for different sets of users based on consumer groups.
Manage Order of Dequeuing	The MGMT_P1, MGMT_P2, … MGMT_P8 directive attributes can be used to alter the normal FIFO processing. This attribute allows prioritization of dequeuing. Each of the eight attributes essentially provides a distinct dequeuing priority level. All statements with an MGMT_P1 attribute will be dequeued prior to any statement with MGMT_P2. In addition to the dequeuing priority, a probability number can be assigned to regulate dequeuing of statements within the same level.

Control	Description
Limit Percentage of Parallel Slaves	The PARALLEL_TARGET_PERCENTAGE directive attribute can be used to limit a consumer group to a percentage of the parallel slaves available to the system. So if a system allowed 64 slaves to be active before starting to queue, and PARALLEL_TARGET_PERCENTAGE was set to 50, the consumer group would only be able to consume 32 slaves. Note that this directive did not become available until version 11.2.0.2 of the database.
Queue Multiple SQLs as a Set	The BEGIN_SQL_BLOCK and END_SQL_BLOCK procedures in DBMS_RESOURCE_MANAGER work with Parallel Statement Queuing by treating individual statements as if they had been submitted at the same time. The mechanism requires surrounding independent SQL statements with calls to the BEGIN and END procedures. Note that this procedure did not become available until version 11.2.0.2 of the database.

The DBRM directives can be quite involved. Here is an example from the *Oracle® Database VLDB and Partitioning Guide 11g Release 2 (11.2)* that shows four directives making use of the Parallel Statement Queuing features.

```
DBMS_RESOURCE_MANAGER.CREATE_PLAN_DIRECTIVE(
    'REPORTS_PLAN', 'SYS_GROUP', 'Directive for sys activity',
    mgmt_p1 => 100);

DBMS_RESOURCE_MANAGER.CREATE_PLAN_DIRECTIVE(
    'REPORTS_PLAN', 'OTHER_GROUPS', 'Directive for short-running queries',
    mgmt_p2 => 70,
    parallel_degree_limit_p1 => 4,
    switch_time => 60,
    switch_estimate => TRUE,
    switch_for_call => TRUE,
    switch_group => 'MEDIUM_SQL_GROUP');

  DBMS_RESOURCE_MANAGER.CREATE_PLAN_DIRECTIVE(
    'REPORTS_PLAN', 'MEDIUM_SQL_GROUP', 'Directive for medium-running queries',
    mgmt_p2 => 20,
    parallel_target_percentage => 80,
    switch_time => 900,
    switch_estimate => TRUE,
    switch_for_call => TRUE,
    switch_group => 'LONG_SQL_GROUP');

  DBMS_RESOURCE_MANAGER.CREATE_PLAN_DIRECTIVE(
    'REPORTS_PLAN', 'LONG_SQL_GROUP', 'Directive for long-running queries',
    mgmt_p2 => 10,
    parallel_target_percentage => 50,
    parallel_queue_timeout => 14400);
```

This example bears some explanation.

7.   The first directive is for sys activity. So sessions in the consumer group SYS_GROUP, will have 100 percent of the highest dequeuing priority (MGMT_P1).

8.   The second directive is for short-running queries. This applies to all sessions in the OTHER_GROUPS consumer group (the default consumer group). This directive specifies that Oracle should evaluate each SQL statement and if the estimated execution time is longer than 60 seconds (SWITCH_TIME), the sessions should be switched to the MEDIUM_SQL_GROUP consumer group. By the way, the session switches back to OTHER_GROUPS when the statement is complete because SWITCH_FOR_CALL=>TRUE. The dequeuing priority (MGMT_P2) is set to 70 percent meaning that statements should be dequeued after any MGMT_P1 statements with a probability of 70 percent when compared with other MGMT_P2 statements. Finally, the maximum DOP is set to 4 by the PARALLEL_DEGREE_LIMIT_P1 attribute.

9.   The third directive is for medium-running queries. It applies to sessions in the MEDIUM_SQL_GROUP consumer group. This directive also includes a switch causing sessions to be moved to the LONG_SQL_GROUP if Oracle estimates a SQL statement will take longer than 15 minutes. Additionally, this directive sets the dequeuing priority to be 20 percent of the second priority group (MGMT_P2). This directive also puts a limit on the percentage of parallel slaves that may be used (PARALLEL_TARGET_PERCENTAGE). In this case, 80 percent of the total slaves allowed on the system is the maximum that may be used by sessions in this consumer group.

10. The last directive is for long-running queries. It applies to sessions in the LONG_SQL_GROUP consumer group. Sessions in this group have a very low dequeuing priority as compared to the others (MGMT_P2=10). It also limits the percentage of parallel slaves to 50 percent. Finally, since statements in this group may be queued for a long time, the PARALLEL_QUEUE_TIMEOUT attribute has been set to 14,400 seconds. So if a statement is queued for 4 hours, it will fail with a timeout error.

Parallel Statement Queuing Wrap Up

This section has been considerably more detailed than the coverage of the other two new parallel features in 11gR2. That's because this feature is a critical component in allowing Exadata to handle mixed workloads effectively. It enables us to effectively handle a mixture of statements that are sensitive to both throughput and response time. Without this feature it would be very difficult to provide adequate resources without severely compromising one or the other.

In-Memory Parallel Execution

The third new feature of 11gR2 related to parallel operations is probably the least well known. Prior to 11gR2, queries that were parallelized totally ignored the buffer cache. Oracle assumed that parallel queries would only be done on very large tables that would probably never have a large percentage of their blocks in the buffer cache. This assumption led to the conclusion that it would be faster to just read the data from disk. In addition, flooding the buffer cache with a large number of blocks from a full table scan was not desirable and so Oracle developed a mechanism called direct path reads, which bypassed the normal caching mechanism in favor of reading blocks directly in to the user's Program Global Area (PGA).

The In-Memory Parallel Execution feature takes a different approach. It attempts to make use of the buffer cache for parallel queries. The feature is cluster-aware and is designed to spread the data across the cluster nodes (that is, the RAC database servers). The data blocks are also affinitized to a single node, reducing the amount of communication and data transfers between the nodes. The goal, of course, is to speed up the parallel query by eliminating disk I/O. This can be a viable technique because many systems now have very large amounts of memory, which of course can provide a significant speed advantage over disk operations. There are some downsides to this approach though. The biggest disadvantage with regard to Exadata is that all the Smart Scan optimizations are disabled by this feature.

░ **Kevin Says:** It is true that In-Memory Parallel Query I/O is buffered in the SGA and remains cached—thus Smart Scan is not involved. This would only be a disadvantage if a query executes faster with Smart Scan than with In-Memory Parallel Query. Comparing the processing dynamic of a query serviced by Smart Scan as opposed to In-Memory Parallel Query is a very complex topic—especially when compressed data is involved. In the same way Smart Scan is able to filter vast amounts of deeply-compressed data (specifically HCC), so is In-Memory Parallel Query. That is, HCC data is filtered in its compressed form regardless of who is doing the filtration. In the case of Smart Scan, however, the data that sifts through filtration must be decompression and sent to the database grid via iDB for data-intensive processing (such as join, sort, or aggregate). With In-Memory Parallel Query there is no data flow over iDB. Furthermore, a table that is accessed frequently by Smart Scan requires the same repetitious physical I/O+filtration+decompression (with the exception of results-cached queries) each time it is accessed. With In-Memory Parallel Query the I/O and iDB effort is eliminated and, as we know, memory is faster than both hard disk and flash. What customers must analyze is whether there are sufficient processor cycles available in the database grid to perform the repetitious filtration and decompression of popular tables. Remember, in the case of Smart Scan that effort is offloaded to the cells. To cap this train of thought, I'll simply say there is no absolute answer in the comparison between In-Memory Parallel Query and Smart Scan. The variables need to be plugged in by the customer using the knowledge gained from reading this book, Oracle documentation and, perhaps, blogs (smiley face).

Note that we haven't actually seen In-memory Parallel Query in the wild on Exadata, which is probably good, since many of the optimizations built into Exadata rely on Offloading, which depends on direct reads. Of course direct reads will not be done if blocks are being accessed in memory on the database servers. On most platforms, memory access would be much faster than direct reads from disk. But with Exadata, eliminating the disk I/O also eliminates a large number of CPUs that could be applied to filtering and other operations. This means that accessing the buffer cache for parallel execution could actually be less efficient than allowing the storage servers to participate in the execution of the SQL statement.

A little demonstration is probably in order at this point. It's worth noting that getting this feature to kick in at all takes quite a bit of effort. Here are the basic steps we had to take in order to get it to work. First we had to find a query that the optimizer estimated would run for longer than the number of seconds specified by the PARALLEL_MIN_TIME_THRESHOLD parameter (assuming the statement wasn't parallelized). The default for this parameter is AUTO, meaning 10 seconds. We set this parameter to 3 seconds to make it easier to trigger the In-memory Parallel behavior. This query also had to be on a table that would almost completely fit in the aggregate buffer cache provided by the combination of all the participating RAC instances. To simplify things, we limited the processing to a single instance by setting the PARALLEL_FORCE_LOCAL parameter to TRUE. Of course we had to set PARALLEL_DEGREE_POLICY to AUTO to enable the feature. We also set very low values for PARALLEL_SERVERS_TARGET and PARALLEL_DEGREE_LIMIT. Here are the parameter settings and pertinent information about the query we used to test the feature:

```
SYS@EXDB1> @parms
Enter value for parameter: parallel
Enter value for isset:
Enter value for show_hidden:

NAME                                 VALUE                ISDEFAUL
------------------------------------ -------------------- --------
fast_start_parallel_rollback         LOW                  TRUE
parallel_adaptive_multi_user         FALSE                TRUE
parallel_automatic_tuning            FALSE                TRUE
parallel_degree_limit                8                    FALSE
parallel_degree_policy               AUTO                 FALSE
parallel_execution_message_size      16384                TRUE
parallel_force_local                 TRUE                 FALSE
parallel_instance_group                                   TRUE
parallel_io_cap_enabled              FALSE                TRUE
parallel_max_servers                 320                  TRUE
parallel_min_percent                 0                    TRUE
parallel_min_servers                 16                   FALSE
parallel_min_time_threshold          3                    FALSE
parallel_server                      TRUE                 TRUE
parallel_server_instances            2                    TRUE
parallel_servers_target              8                    FALSE
parallel_threads_per_cpu             2                    TRUE
recovery_parallelism                 0                    TRUE

18 rows selected.

SYS@EXDB1> @pool_mem

AREA                              MEGS
------------------------------  ----------
free memory                      562.5
fixed_sga                          2.1
log_buffer                         7.5
shared pool                      557.4
large pool                        48.1
buffer_cache                   3,808.0
                               ----------
sum                            4,985.6

6 rows selected.

SYS@EXDB1> @table_size
```

```
Enter value for owner: KSO
Enter value for table_name: SKEW
Enter value for type:

OWNER                 SEGMENT_NAME          TYPE                  TOTALSIZE_MEGS
--------------------  --------------------  --------------------  --------------
KSO                   SKEW                  TABLE                        2,560.0
                                                                  --------------
sum                                                                      2,560.0

1 row selected.

SYS@EXDB1> @dba_tables
Enter value for owner: KSO
Enter value for table_name: SKEW

OWNER    TABLE_NAME     STATUS    LAST_ANAL   NUM_ROWS    BLOCKS DEGREE
-------  -------------  --------  ---------  ----------  ---------- ------
KSO      SKEW           VALID     18-SEP-10   32000004      162294    1

1 row selected.
```

So the buffer cache on this instance is about 3.8G, the table is about 2.5 G. The query we used is simple and will not benefit from storage indexes, as virtually all the records satisfy the single WHERE clause.

```
SYS@EXDB1> !cat avgskew.sql
select avg(pk_col) from kso.skew a where col1 > 0
/

SYS@EXDB1> select count(*) from kso.skew;

  COUNT(*)
----------
  32000004

1 row selected.

SYS@EXDB1> select count(*) from kso.skew where col1 > 0;

  COUNT(*)
----------
  32000000

1 row selected.

SYS@EXDB1> select 32000000/32000004 from dual;

32000000/32000004
-----------------
        .999999875

1 row selected.
```

Now we'll show some statistics before and after executing the statement. You'll be able to see that while the physical reads statistic does not increase, the logical reads statistic shows a large increase. Note that we've done a quick calculation of the total number of logical reads by selecting from dual, and that the number of logical reads (162,715) is very close to the number of blocks that the table occupies as reported by DBA_TABLES.

```
SYS@EXDB1> @flush_pool

System altered.

SYS@EXDB1> @mystats
Enter value for name: reads

NAME                                                             VALUE
-------------------------------------------------------------  ----------
cold recycle reads                                                     0
data blocks consistent reads - undo records applied                   0
lob reads                                                             0
physical reads                                                   4706178
physical reads cache                                                  30
physical reads cache prefetch                                         0
physical reads direct                                           4706148
physical reads direct (lob)                                          0
physical reads direct temporary tablespace                           0
physical reads for flashback new                                     0
physical reads prefetch warmup                                       0
physical reads retry corrupt                                         0
recovery array reads                                                 0
session logical reads                                           7152779
transaction tables consistent reads - undo records applied          0

15 rows selected.

SYS@EXDB1> set timing on
SYS@EXDB1> @avgskew

AVG(PK_COL)
-----------
 16093750.8

1 row selected.

Elapsed: 00:00:00.72
SYS@EXDB1> set timing off
SYS@EXDB1> @mystats
Enter value for name: reads

NAME                                                             VALUE
-------------------------------------------------------------  ------------
cold recycle reads                                                     0
data blocks consistent reads - undo records applied                   0
lob reads                                                             0
```

```
physical reads                                           4706178
physical reads cache                                          30
physical reads cache prefetch                                  0
physical reads direct                                    4706148
physical reads direct (lob)                                    0
physical reads direct temporary tablespace                     0
physical reads for flashback new                               0
physical reads prefetch warmup                                 0
physical reads retry corrupt                                   0
recovery array reads                                           0
session logical reads                                    7315494
transaction tables consistent reads - undo records applied     0

15 rows selected.

SYS@EXDB1> select 7315494-7152779 from dual;

7315494-7152779
---------------
         162715

1 row selected.

SYS@EXDB1> @dplan
Enter value for sql_id: 05cq2hb1r37tr
Enter value for child_no:

PLAN_TABLE_OUTPUT
-------------------------------------------------------------------------------------------
SQL_ID  05cq2hb1r37tr, child number 1
-------------------------------------
select avg(pk_col) from kso.skew a where col1 > 0

Plan hash value: 578366071
```

Id	Operation	Name	Rows	Bytes	Cost (%CPU)	Time
0	SELECT STATEMENT				6139 (100)	
1	SORT AGGREGATE		1	11		
2	PX COORDINATOR					
3	PX SEND QC (RANDOM)	:TQ10000	1	11		
4	SORT AGGREGATE		1	11		
5	PX BLOCK ITERATOR		32M	335M	6139 (1)	00:01:14
* 6	TABLE ACCESS STORAGE FULL	SKEW	32M	335M	6139 (1)	00:01:14

```
Predicate Information (identified by operation id):
---------------------------------------------------

   6 - storage(:Z>=:Z AND :Z<=:Z AND "COL1">0)
       filter("COL1">0)
```

```
Note
-----
automatic DOP: Computed Degree of Parallelism is 8

SYS@EXDB1> @fsx2
Enter value for sql_text: %skew%
Enter value for sql_id:

SQL_ID        AVG_ETIME  PX OFFLOAD IO_SAVED% SQL_TEXT
------------- ---------- --- ------- --------- ------------------------------
05cq2hb1r37tr       .47   8 No           .00 select avg(pk_col) from
                                             kso.skew a where col1 > 0

1 rows selected.
```

So as you can see, the statement was executed in parallel with eight slaves (the PX column in the fsx.sql script output). Note also that the fsx.sql script reports an estimated value for the AVG_ETIME column when parallel slaves are used. This occurs because v$sql reports elapsed time as the sum of the all the elapsed times of the slave processes. Dividing this number by the number of slaves gives an estimate, but that will not be totally accurate as slaves can vary greatly in their elapsed times. If you look back in the listing you'll see that the actual elapsed time of avgskew.sql was 0.72 seconds instead of the estimated average provided by the fsx.sql script (0.47 seconds). Nevertheless, it is a useful metric when comparing between two statements.

Let's now compare our In-memory Parallel Execution to how our system behaves when In-memory Parallel Execution is not in play. We can disable this feature in a couple of ways. The documented way is to set the PARALLEL_DEGREE_POLICY parameter to MANUAL. However, this also disables Auto DOP and Parallel Statement Queuing. The other way is to set the hidden parameter _PARALLEL_CLUSTER_CACHE_POLICY to ADAPTIVE.

```
SYS@EXDB1> alter system set "_parallel_cluster_cache_policy"=adaptive;

System altered.

SYS@EXDB1> @mystats
Enter value for name: reads

NAME                                                        VALUE
----------------------------------------------------- ---------------
cold recycle reads                                              0
data blocks consistent reads - undo records applied            0
lob reads                                                      0
physical reads                                           5193061
physical reads cache                                          31
physical reads cache prefetch                                 0
physical reads direct                                    5193030
physical reads direct (lob)                                   0
physical reads direct temporary tablespace                    0
physical reads for flashback new                              0
physical reads prefetch warmup                                0
physical reads retry corrupt                                  0
recovery array reads                                          0
session logical reads                                    8133835
```

```
transaction tables consistent reads - undo records applied          0

15 rows selected.

SYS@EXDB1> set timing on
SYS@EXDB1> @avgskew

AVG(PK_COL)
-----------
 16093750.8

1 row selected.

Elapsed: 00:00:00.79
SYS@EXDB1> set timing off
SYS@EXDB1> @mystats
Enter value for name: reads

NAME                                                         VALUE
------------------------------------------------------ ---------------
cold recycle reads                                               0
data blocks consistent reads - undo records applied              0
lob reads                                                        0
physical reads                                             5355355
physical reads cache                                            31
physical reads cache prefetch                                    0
physical reads direct                                      5355324
physical reads direct (lob)                                      0
physical reads direct temporary tablespace                       0
physical reads for flashback new                                 0
physical reads prefetch warmup                                   0
physical reads retry corrupt                                     0
recovery array reads                                             0
session logical reads                                      8296342
transaction tables consistent reads - undo records applied       0

15 rows selected.

SYS@EXDB1> select 5355355-5193061 from dual;

5355355-5193061
---------------
         162294

1 row selected.

SYS@EXDB1> @fsx2
Enter value for sql_text: %skew%
Enter value for sql_id:
```

SQL_ID	AVG_ETIME	PX	OFFLOAD	IO_SAVED%	SQL_TEXT
05cq2hb1r37tr	.47	8	No	.00	select avg(pk_col) from kso.skew a where col1 > 0
05cq2hb1r37tr	.58	8	Yes	59.82	select avg(pk_col) from kso.skew a where col1 > 0

2 rows selected.

Notice that with In-memory Parallel Execution disabled, the statistics show that the number of physical reads increased by roughly the number of blocks in the table, as expected. Notice also that the fsx.sql script shows that there is now a new cursor in the shared pool that was executed with eight parallel slaves, but that was offloaded to the storage tier. This is an important point. In-memory Parallel Execution disables the optimizations that Exadata provides via Smart Scans. That should be obvious since the disk I/O was eliminated by the In-memory Parallel Execution feature, but it is the main reason that we believe this feature will not be as useful on the Exadata platform as on other platforms.

As a final demonstration, we'll show a very selective query that benefits more from Offloading than it does from In-memory Parallel Execution.

```
SYS@EXDB1> @parms
Enter value for parameter: para%cache
Enter value for isset:
Enter value for show_hidden: Y

NAME                                     VALUE                 ISDEFAUL
---------------------------------------- --------------------- --------
_parallel_cluster_cache_pct              80                    TRUE
_parallel_cluster_cache_policy           ADAPTIVE              TRUE

2 rows selected.

SYS@EXDB1> -- In-memory Paraellel Execution is off
SYS@EXDB1>
SYS@EXDB1> @flush_pool

System altered.

SYS@EXDB1> set timing on
SYS@EXDB1> select count(*) from kso.skew where col1 is null;

  COUNT(*)
----------
         4

1 row selected.

Elapsed: 00:00:00.26
SYS@EXDB1> alter system set "_parallel_cluster_cache_policy"=cached;

System altered.

Elapsed: 00:00:00.01
```

```
SYS@EXDB1> select count(*) from kso.skew where col1 is null;

  COUNT(*)
----------
         4

1 row selected.

Elapsed: 00:00:00.84
SYS@EXDB1> set timing off
SYS@EXDB1> @fsx2
Enter value for sql_text: %skew%
Enter value for sql_id:

SQL_ID         AVG_ETIME  PX OFFLOAD IO_SAVED% SQL_TEXT
-------------  ---------- --- ------- --------- ------------------------------
4rz0gjuwr9jyq        .14  8   Yes       100.00 select count(*) from kso.skew
                                               where col1 is null
4rz0gjuwr9jyq        .72  8   No           .00 select count(*) from kso.skew
                                               where col1 is null

2 rows selected.
```

In this case, Offloading was more effective (faster) than using In-memory Parallel Execution, primarily because Storage Indexes were able to eliminate an extremely large percentage of the disk I/O. So the comparison came down to reading about 2.5 Gigabytes from the buffer cache on the database server vs. reading the Storage Indexes and a handful of blocks off disk. Granted this is a very simple contrived example, but it illustrates the point that there may be cases where Smart Scan is faster than In-memory Parallel Query.

Summary

Parallel execution of statements is important for maximizing throughput on the Exadata platform. Oracle database 11g Release 2 includes several new features that make the parallel execution a more controllable feature. This is especially important when using the platform with mixed workloads. The new Auto DOP feature is designed to allow intelligent decisions about DOP to be made automatically based on individual statements. In-memory Parallel Execution may not be as useful on Exadata platforms as it is on non-Exadata platforms, because it disables the optimizations that come along with Smart Scans. Of the three new features, Parallel Statement Queuing is the most useful as it allows a mixture of throughput-oriented work to co-exist with response-time–sensitive work. Integration with Oracle Resource Manager further enhances the feature by providing a great deal of additional control over the queuing.

CHAPTER 7

Resource Management

If resources were unlimited, there would be no need to manage them. We see this in all aspects of our daily lives. If yours was the only car on the road, traffic signals wouldn't be necessary. If you were the only customer at the bank, there would be no need for the winding ropes that form orderly lines. But as we all know, this is rarely the case. It is the same for database servers. When the load on the system is light, there is very little need for resource management. Processes complete in a fairly consistent period of time. But when the system gets busy and resources become scarce, we can find ourselves with an angry mob on our hands.

For a number of years now, Oracle's Database Resource Manager (DBRM) has provided an effective way to manage the allocation of critical resources within the database. Without DBRM, all database connections are treated with equal priority, and they are serviced in a sort of round-robin fashion by the operating system scheduler. When the system is under heavy load, all sessions are impacted equally. Low-priority applications receive just as high a priority as business-critical applications. It is not uncommon to see a few poorly written ad-hoc queries degrade the performance of mission-critical applications. If you've been a DBA long enough, especially in data warehouse environments, you're probably familiar with the Unix renice command. It is a root-level command that allows you to influence the CPU priority of a process at the operating-system level. A number of years ago, we worked in a DBA group supporting a particularly heavily loaded data warehouse. The renice command was used frequently to throttle back CPU priority for database sessions that were dominating the system. There were a couple of obvious problems with this approach. First of all, it was a privileged command available only to the root user, and system administrators were reluctant to grant DBAs access to it. The second problem was that automating it to manage CPU resources was difficult at best. Oracle's Database Resource Manager is a much more elegant solution to the problem. It allows DBAs to address resource allocation within the domain of the database itself. It is a well-organized, framework that is automated by design. It ensures that critical system resources like CPU and I/O will be available to your important applications whenever they are needed, even when the system is under a heavy workload. This is done by creating resource allocation schemes that define priorities based on the needs of the business.

Another case for resource management is consolidation. It was inevitable that a platform with the performance, capacity, and scalability of Exadata would be viewed by many as an ideal consolidation platform. But consolidating databases is a challenge, mainly because of the difficulty of managing resources across databases. We've worked with a number of clients who have used Exadata to consolidate multiple database servers onto the Exadata platform. One such client consolidated 29 databases from 17 database servers onto two Exadata full racks. Needless to say, without Oracle's resource management capabilities, it would be extremely difficult, if not impossible, to balance system resources among so many database environments. Until recently there was really no way to prioritize I/O across databases. With Exadata V2, Oracle introduced I/O Resource Manager (IORM), and for the first time we can virtually guarantee I/O service levels within and among databases.

So whether you are consolidating multiple databases onto your Exadata platform or handling resource intensive applications within a single database, effective resource management will play an important role in your success. In this chapter we will review and demonstrate the main components of DBRM and how it is used to manage and allocate CPU resources effectively within a database. We'll also take a look at *instance caging* and how it can be used to set limits on the amount of CPU a database may use in order to provide predictable service levels for multi-tenant database environments. In the last half of the chapter we'll cover the new Exadata-specific feature called I/O Resource Manager, which allocates and prioritizes disk I/O at the storage cell.

Oracle Resource Manager, for all its benefits, has been an infrequently used feature of the database. This is largely due to its complexity and a general lack of understanding among the DBA community. Beyond introducing the new Exadata-specific features of Resource Manager, our goals in presenting this material are twofold. First we want to provide enough detail to demystify Oracle Resource Manager without overwhelming the reader. Second, we intend to demonstrate how to build a fully functional resource management model. These goals present a unique challenge. Provide too little information, and the reader will only be able to set up very simple configurations. Too much detail, and we risk convoluting the topic and losing the audience. The most difficult part of writing this chapter has been striking a balance between the two. As you read through the examples you will notice that we used multi-level resource plans. This is not to suggest that in order to be effective, you must use complex multi-level plans. In fact, simple, single-level resource plans will solve a vast majority of the resource management problems we see in the real world. Moreover, multi-level resource plans can be difficult to design and test. In this chapter we demonstrate multi-level plans because it is important to understand how they work. But if you are considering using Oracle Resource Manager, the best approach is to keep it simple, and add features only as they are needed.

Database Resource Manager

Database Resource Manager (DBRM) has been around for a number of years and is basically geared toward managing CPU resources and I/O (indirectly) at the database tier. Exadata V2 introduced a new feature called I/O Resource Manager (IORM), which, as you might expect, is geared toward managing and prioritizing I/O at the storage cell. When databases on Exadata request I/O from the storage cells, they send additional information along with the request that identifies the database making the request as well as the consumer group making the request. The software on the storage cells (Cellserv or `cellsrv`) knows about the priorities you establish inside the database (DBRM) and/or at the Storage Cell (IORM), and it manages how I/O is scheduled. DBRM and IORM are tightly knit together, so it is important to have a solid understanding of DBRM before IORM is going to make any sense to you. Now, Database Resource Manager is a lengthy topic and could easily justify a book all by itself. So here, we'll focus on the basic constructs that we will need for constructing an effective IORM Resource Plan. If you already have experience with DBRM, you may be able to skip over this topic, but be aware that the examples in this section will be used as we discuss IORM in the last half of the chapter.

Before we begin, let's review the terminology that will be used in this topic. Table 7-1 describes the various components of Database Resource Manager. We'll discuss these in more detail as we go along.

Table 7-1. Resource Manager Components

Name	Description
Resource consumer group Consumer group	These are the various names by which you may see resource consumer groups referred. Resource Manager allocates resources to consumer groups, rather than user sessions. A consumer group is a set of database sessions that may be grouped together based on their priority, and/or resource requirements.
Resource plan directive Plan directive Directive	These are the names by which you may see resource plan directives referred. Resource allocations are not assigned directly to consumer groups. They are defined in a resource plan directive. A consumer group is then assigned to the plan directive so that resource allocations may be enforced.
Resource plan Plan	Resource plans are sometimes referred to simply as "plans", or "the plan." Plan directives are grouped together to create a resource plan, thus defining the overarching allocation of resources to all sessions within the database.

As shown in the table, DBRM consists of three main components: resource consumer groups (consumer groups), resource plan directives (plan directives), and resource plans.

Consumer groups: A consumer group can represent a single database session or a group of sessions. Generally speaking, consumer groups consist of end users or application groups that share a common business priority. Grouping sessions together in this manner allow resources to be assigned and managed collectively. For example, in a mixed-workload database environment, consumer group assignments allow you to collectively assign more CPU and I/O resources to your high-priority business applications while reducing the resources allocated to low-priority applications.

Plan directives: Plan directives are where you define your resource allocations. A plan directive is created using the CREATE_PLAN_DIRECTIVE procedure. In addition to defining the resource allocation itself (percentage of CPU, for example), the procedure also requires you to name one resource plan and one consumer group. In this way, a plan directive "links," or assigns a consumer group to a resource plan. Only one consumer group may be assigned to a directive, and resource plans typically consist of multiple directives. You can say that a consumer group is assigned to a resource plan through the creation of a plan directive.

Resource plan: The resource plan is the collection of directives that determine how and where resources are allocated. Only one plan may be activated in the database instance at any given time. The resource plan is activated by assigning it to the RESOURCE_MANAGER_PLAN instance parameter. For example, the following alter system command activates the resource plan 'myplan':

```
SQL> alter system set resource_manager_plan='myplan';
```

A database's resource plan may be changed at any time, allowing you to reallocate resources at various times of the day, week, or month in order to meet the varying workload requirements of your business. When the resource plan is activated, no resources are allocated to individual user sessions. Instead, resources are allocated to the consumer groups according to the directives in the resource plan.

Consumer Groups

When a resource plan is activated, DBRM examines key attributes of all sessions in the database and assigns them to consumer groups. Sessions are assigned to consumer groups by means of mapping rules that you define. For example, a set of user accounts can be mapped to a consumer group based on their user name or the machine from which they are logging in. A user may belong to many different consumer groups and may be dynamically reassigned from one consumer group to another even in the middle of executing a SQL statement or query. Since database resources are allocated only to consumer groups, reassigning a session to another group immediately changes its resource allocation. All sessions in a consumer group share the resources of that group. For example, if the APPS consumer group is allocated 70% of the total CPU on the server, all sessions belonging to that consumer group will equally share the 70% allocation of CPU. There are two built-in consumer groups in every database: SYS_GROUP and OTHER_GROUPS. These groups cannot be modified or dropped.

> **SYS_GROUP:** This is the default consumer group for the SYS and SYSTEM user accounts. These accounts may be assigned to another consumer group using mapping rules we'll discuss in the next section.

> **OTHER_GROUPS:** This is the default consumer group. Any sessions that belong to a consumer group that is not defined in the currently active resource plan will automatically be mapped to this consumer group. This is Oracle's way of making sure all user sessions are assigned to a consumer group in the active resource plan.

▨ **Note:** We would have preferred a name like OTHER for that last consumer group, but yes, it really is named "OTHER_GROUPS," not OTHER_GROUP, or OTHER. We must have been out of town when Larry called to ask our opinion on this one.

Consumer Group Mapping Rules

All user sessions (except SYS and SYSTEM) are mapped by default to the consumer group OTHER_GROUPS. This behavior can be modified using mapping rules so that sessions are automatically reassigned to other consumer groups. If there is no mapping rule for a session, or if the mapping rules assign the session to a consumer group that is not named in the currently active plan, then it will be automatically assigned to this built-in consumer group. Every resource plan must have the OTHER_GROUPS resource group to handle this condition. The following example shows how a mapping rule is created. This mapping rule calls for the TPODER account to be automatically assigned to the REPORTS consumer group, while anyone logging in using the Payroll.exe application will be mapped to the APPS consumer group:

```
BEGIN
  DBMS_RESOURCE_MANAGER.SET_CONSUMER_GROUP_MAPPING
    (DBMS_RESOURCE_MANAGER.ORACLE_USER, 'TPODER', 'REPORTS');
  DBMS_RESOURCE_MANAGER.SET_CONSUMER_GROUP_MAPPING
    (DBMS_RESOURCE_MANAGER.CLIENT_PROGRAM, 'payroll.exe', 'APPS');
END;
```

There are two types of session attributes that can be used to create mapping rules: *login* attributes and *runtime* attributes. Login attributes are set when the user logs in and do not change during the life of the session. Resource Manager uses login attributes to determine which consumer group the session should initially be assigned to. Runtime attributes are set at runtime and can be changed at any time during the life of the session by the client application. Table 7-2 describes the session attributes Resource Manager can use for creating session-to-consumer-group mapping rules.

Table 7-2. Consumer Group Mapping Rule Attributes

Session Attribute	Type	Description
EXPLICIT	n/a	This attribute refers to the explicit request by a user to switch to another consumer group using one of the following stored procedures in the DBMS_SESSION package: • SWITCH_CURRENT_CONSUMER_GROUP • SWITCH_CONSUMER_GROUP_FOR_SESS • SWITCH_CONSUMER_GROUP_FOR_USER It is a common practice to set the priority of this mapping attribute to the highest level.
ORACLE_USER	Login	This is the USERNAME column from v$session. It is the user name the session used to authenticate to the database during login.
SERVICE_NAME	Login	This is the database service name used to connect to the database. It is the SERVICE_NAME column in the v$session view.
CLIENT_OS_USER	Login	This is the operating system user account of the machine the user is connecting from. It is the OSUSER column from the v$session view.
CLIENT_PROGRAM	Login	This is the executable file the end user is using to connect to the database; for example, sqlplusw.exe. Resource Manager evaluates this value without consideration of case, (upper or lower).

Session Attribute	Type	Description
CLIENT_MACHINE	Login	This is the machine from which the user is connecting to the database. It appears in the MACHINE column of the v$session view.
MODULE_NAME	Runtime	This is the module name set by the application connecting to the database. It is stored in the MODULE column of the v$session view and is set by calling the DBMS_APPLICATION_INFO.SET_MODULE procedure. This is an optional setting, and some applications do not use it.
MODULE_NAME_ACTION	Runtime	This is a concatenation of the module and action in the form *module.action*. The application sets these attributes by calling the following procedures: <ul><li>DBMS_APPLICATION_INFO.SET_MODULE</li><li>DBMS_APPLICATION_INFO.SET_ACTION</li></ul>
SERVICE_MODULE	Runtime	This attribute is the concatenation of the service name used to connect to the database, and the MODULE attribute in the form *service.module*.
SERVICE_MODULE_ACTION	Runtime	This attribute is the concatenation of the service name, module, and action in the form *service.module.action*.
ORACLE_FUNCTION	Runtime	This is a special attribute that is maintained internally by the database. It is set when running RMAN or Data Pump. This attribute can be set to BACKUP, to perform a backup … as backupset, or COPY, to perform a backup … as copy. When Data Pump is used to load data into the database, this attribute is set to DATALOAD. These attributes are automatically mapped to built-in consumer groups such as BATCH_GROUP and ETL_GROUP.

■ **Tip:** SERVICE_MODULE, ACTIVE_SESS_POOL_P1, and QUEUEING_P1 are not commonly used and may be deprecated in future releases. : For attributes other than ORACLE_USER and SERVICE_NAME in Table 7-2, you can also use wildcards such as _ and % for single and multiple characters, respectively.

Conflicts can occur between mapping rules when a user account matches more than one rule. Oracle resolves these conflicts by allowing you to specify the relative priority of each attribute. This way, Oracle can automatically determine which rule (attribute) should take precedence when session attributes satisfy multiple mapping rules. The default priorities for the ORACLE_USER and CLIENT_APPLICATION attributes are 6 and 7, respectively. In the following example, I've promoted the

CLIENT_PROGRAM to position 2, and the ORACLE_USER to position 3. Now the client application establishing a database connection will take precedence over the client's USERNAME.

```
BEGIN
  dbms_resource_manager.clear_pending_area();
  dbms_resource_manager.create_pending_area();
  dbms_resource_manager.set_consumer_group_mapping_pri(
    EXPLICIT              => 1,
    CLIENT_PROGRAM        => 2,
    ORACLE_USER           => 3,
    SERVICE_MODULE_ACTION => 4,
    SERVICE_MODULE        => 5,
    MODULE_NAME_ACTION    => 6,
    MODULE_NAME           => 7,
    SERVICE_NAME          => 8,
    CLIENT_MACHINE        => 9,
    CLIENT_OS_USER        => 10 );
  dbms_resource_manager.submit_pending_area();
END;
```

For example, using the mapping rules and priorities we've created so far, let's say TPODER logs in to the database. According to the ORACLE_USER mapping rule, this user would ordinarily be assigned to the REPORTS consumer group. But if TPODER logs in from the company's Payroll application, his session will be mapped to the APPS consumer group. This is because according to the rule priorities, the CLIENT_APPLICATION mapping rule takes precedence over ORACLE_USER. The following query shows how two different sessions from the same user account get mapped according to the username and client program mapping priorities. Notice how only the Payroll application, payroll.exe, overrides the REPORTS mapping rule.

```
SYS:SCRATCH> select s.username              "User",
                    s.program               "Program",
                    s.resource_consumer_group "Resource Group"
             FROM v$session s, v$process p
             WHERE ( (s.username IS NOT NULL)
               AND (NVL (s.osuser, 'x') <> 'SYSTEM')
               AND (s.TYPE    != 'BACKGROUND') )
               AND (p.addr(+) = s.paddr)
               AND s.username = 'TPODER'
             ORDER BY s.resource_consumer_group, s.username;
```

User	Program	Resource Group
TPODER	payroll.exe	APPS
TPODER	sqlplus@enkdb02.enkitec.com (TNS V1-V3)	REPORTS
TPODER	toad.exe	REPORTS
TPODER	sqlplusw.exe	REPORTS

Plan Directives

DBRM allocates database resources to consumer groups through *plan directives*. A plan directive consists of one consumer group and one or more management attributes. There is a one-to-one relationship between a plan directive and a consumer group, and no two directives may be assigned to the same resource group (within the same plan). A plan directive is made up of a list of management attributes in a *key=value* fashion. For example, the following listing shows how a set of directives may be defined in DBRM:

```
DBMS_RESOURCE_MANAGER.CREATE_PLAN_DIRECTIVE(
    PLAN                     => 'example_plan',
    GROUP_OR_SUBPLAN         => 'APPS',
    COMMENT                  => 'OLTP Application Sessions',
    MGMT_P1                  => 70,
    MAX_UTILIZATION_LIMIT    => 90,
    MAX_EST_EXEC_TIME        => 3600
);
```

MGMT_P*n*

Exadata's IO Resource Manager works with DBRM through plan directives using the CPU management attributes MGMT_P*n*, (where *n* may be 1–8), and MAX_UTILIZATION_LIMIT, so going forward these attributes will be the focus our discussion. CPU is allocated in a level + percentage manner. Usage of the MGMT_P*n* attribute determines the relative priority in which CPU is allocated to consumer groups across the various levels, where 1 is the highest level/priority. The percentage assigned to the MGMT_P*n* attribute determines how available CPU resources (unallocated plus unused) are allocated within a particular level. Whatever CPU is unused or unallocated from level 1 is allocated to level 2. Unused and unallocated CPU from level 2 is then passed to the consumer groups on level 3. If there are two consumer groups on level 2 and one of them doesn't use its allocation, the unused CPU is always passed to the next level in the Plan. The other consumer group on level 2 can't utilize it.

Figure 7-1 shows a simple resource plan and illustrates how this level + percentage method of allocating CPU resources works.

| | | Management Attributes | |
	MGMT_P1	MGMT_P2	MGMT_P3
Consumer Group	Level 1 CPU Allocation	Level 2 CPU Allocation	Level 3 CPU Allocation
APPS	70%		
REPORTS		50%	
MAINTENANCE			50%
OTHER_GROUPS			50%

Figure 7-1. Resource directives

In Figure 7-1 the APPS group is allocated 70% of total CPU available to the database. Sessions in the REPORTS group are the next highest priority at level 2 and will be allocated half of the unallocated CPU (30%) from level 1. Sessions in the resource groups MAINTENANCE and OTHER_GROUPS equally share unallocated CPU (50%) from level 2. This can be expressed in formula form as follows:

$$APPS = 70\% \qquad (100\% \times 70\%)$$

$$REPORTS = 15\% \qquad ((100\% - 70\%) \times 50\%)$$

$$\text{MAINTENANCE} = 7.5\% \qquad (((100\% \ 70\%) \times 50\%) \times 50\%)$$

$$\text{OTHER\_GROUPS} = 7.5\% \qquad (((100\% \ 70\%) \times 50\%) \times 50\%)$$

Resource Manager is designed to maximize CPU utilization. This is important to understand because it means that there are times when consumer groups may actually exceed their allocation. When CPU resources are limited, plan directives define guaranteed service levels for consumer groups. But when extra CPU is available, plan directives also determine how unused CPU resources are allocated among consumer groups. For example, if CPU utilization in the APPS group falls below 70%, half of the unused CPU is redistributed to the REPORTS group on level 2 (mgmt._p2=50%), and half is distributed to the consumer groups on level 3. If the REPORTS group does not fully utilize its allocation of CPU, the unused CPU is also redistributed to the consumer groups on level 3. If you need to set an absolute limit on CPU for a consumer group, use the MAX_UTILIZATION_LIMIT directive.

Resource Plan

A *resource plan* is a collection of plan directives that determine how database resources are to be allocated. You may create any number of resource plans for your database that allow you to meet the specific service levels of your business, but only one may be active at any given time. You may deactivate the current resource plan and activate another plan whenever the needs of the business change. When the active resource plan changes, all current and future sessions will be allocated resources based on directives in the new plan. Switching between various resource plans is commonly done to provide suitable allocations for particular times of the day, week, or month. For example, an after-hours plan may be activated in the evening to favor database backups, batch jobs, extracts, and data-loading activities. Other applications for maintaining multiple plans may include month-end processing, year-end processing, and the like.

The Pending Area

Resource plans in the database cannot be directly modified; nor can you directly define new plan directives or resource groups. Oracle provides a work space called the *pending area* for creating and modifying all the elements of a resource plan. You can think of it as a loading zone where all the elements of your resource plan are staged and validated together before they are submitted to DBRM. There may be only one pending area in the database at any given time. If a pending area is already open when you try to create one, Oracle will display the error message, "ORA-29370: pending area is already active." The pending area is not a permanent fixture in the database. You must explicitly create it before you can create or modify resource plans. The following listing shows the typical process of creating a pending area, validating your changes, and then submitting it. After the pending area is submitted, it is automatically removed and a new one must be created if you want to perform any additional work on DBRM components. The following listing shows how the Pending Area is created, validated, and submitted.

```
BEGIN
  DBMS_RESOURCE_MANAGER.CREATE_PENDING_AREA();        ← Create the pending area
    <create, modify, delete your resource plan>
  DBMS_RESOURCE_MANAGER.VALIDATE_PENDING_AREA();      ← Validate your work
  DBMS_RESOURCE_MANAGER.SUBMIT_PENDING_AREA();        ← Install your work into DBRM
END;
```

Resource Manager Views

Oracle supplies a number of views that report configuration, history, and metrics for Resource Manager. Let's take a look at a few of the views that are useful for reviewing and monitoring resources in your DBRM configuration.

V$RSRC_CONSUMER_GROUP: The V$RSRC_CONSUMER_GROUP view displays information about the active resource consumer groups. It also contains performance metrics that are useful for tuning purposes. We'll take a closer look at this view when we test a resource plan later on in the chapter.

V$RSRC_PLAN: This view displays the configuration of the currently active resource plan.

V$RSRC_PLAN_HISTORY: The V$RSRC_PLAN_HISTORY view shows historical information for your resource plans, including when they were activated and deactivated, and whether they were enabled by the database scheduler or scheduler windows.

V$RSRC_SESSION_INFO: This view shows performance statistics for sessions and how they were affected by the Resource Manager.

V$SESSION: The V$SESSION view is not specifically a Resource Manager view but its RESOURCE_CONSUMER_GROUP field is useful for determining what resource group a session is assigned to.

DBA_RSRC_CATEGORIES: This view displays the resource categories that are configured in the database. Categories are used by the I/O Resource Manager for controlling storage cell I/O allocation within a database.

DBA_RSRC_CONSUMER_GROUPS: This view displays all the consumer groups defined in the database.

DBA_RSRC_CONSUMER_GROUP_PRIVS: This view reports users, and the resource groups to which they have been granted permission. A user must have permission to switch to a consumer group before the session-to-consumer group mapping rules will work.

DBA_RSRC_GROUP_MAPPINGS: This view lists all the various session-to-resource group mapping rules defined in the database.

DBA_RSRC_MAPPING_PRIORITY: This view reports the priority of session attributes used in resolving overlaps between mapping rules.

DBA_RSRC_IO_CALIBRATE: This view displays the I/O performance metrics DBRM uses for I/O resource management. Maximum read rates are captured for I/O operations per second (IOPS), megabytes per second (MBPS), and latencies for data block read requests.

DBA_RSRC_PLANS: This view lists all resource plans and the number of plan directives assigned to each plan in the database.

DBA_RSRC_PLAN_DIRECTIVES: This view lists all resource plan directives, resource allocation percentages, and levels defined in the database.

DBA_USERS: This view is not actually a Resource Manager view but it does display the username and initial resource group assignment, in its INITIAL_RSRC_CONSUMER_GROUP field.

DBA_HIST_RSRC_CONSUMER_GROUP: This view displays historical performance metrics for Resource consumer groups. It contains AWR snapshots of the V$RSRC_CONS_GROUP_HISTORY view.

DBA_HIST_RSRC_PLAN: This is a simple view that displays historical information about resource plans such as when they were activated and deactivated.

The Wait Event: resmgr: cpu quantum

DBRM allocates CPU resources by maintaining an execution queue similar to the way the operating system's scheduler queues processes for their turn on the CPU. The time a session spends waiting in this execution queue is assigned the wait event resmgr: cpu quantum. A CPU quantum is the unit of CPU time (fraction of CPU) that Resource Manager uses for allocating CPU to consumer groups. This event occurs when Resource Manager is enabled and is actively throttling CPU consumption. Increasing the CPU allocation for a session's consumer group will reduce the occurrence of this wait event and increase the amount of CPU time allocated to all sessions in that group. For example, the CPU quantum wait events may be reduced for the APPS resource group (currently 70% at level 1) by increasing the group's CPU allocation to 80%.

DBRM Example

Now that we've discussed the key components of DBRM and how it works, let's take a look at an example of creating and utilizing resource plans. In this example we'll create two resource plans similar to the one in Figure 7-1. One allocates CPU resources suitably for critical DAYTIME processing, and the other favors night-time processing.

Step 1: Create Resource Groups

The first thing we'll do is create the resource groups for our plan. The following listing creates three resource groups, APPS, REPORTS, and MAINTENANCE. Once we have the resource groups created, we'll be able to map user sessions to them.

```
BEGIN
  dbms_resource_manager.clear_pending_area();
  dbms_resource_manager.create_pending_area();
  dbms_resource_manager.create_consumer_group(
    consumer_group => 'APPS',
    comment        => 'Consumer group for critical OLTP applications');
  dbms_resource_manager.create_consumer_group(
    consumer_group => 'REPORTS',
    comment        => 'Consumer group for long-running reports');
  dbms_resource_manager.create_consumer_group(
    consumer_group => 'MAINTENANCE',
    comment        => 'Consumer group for maintenance jobs');
  dbms_resource_manager.validate_pending_area();
```

```
    dbms_resource_manager.submit_pending_area();
END;
```

Step 2: Create Consumer Group Mapping Rules

Okay, so that takes care of our resource groups. Now we'll create our session-to-resource group mappings. The following PL/SQL block creates mappings for three user accounts (KOSBORNE, TPODER, and RJOHNSON), and just for good measure, we'll create a mapping for our TOAD users out there. This will also allow us to see how attribute mapping priorities work.

```
BEGIN
  dbms_resource_manager.clear_pending_area();
  dbms_resource_manager.create_pending_area();
  dbms_resource_manager.set_consumer_group_mapping(
    attribute      => dbms_resource_manager.oracle_user,
    value          => 'KOSBORNE',
    consumer_group => 'APPS');
  dbms_resource_manager.set_consumer_group_mapping(
    attribute      => dbms_resource_manager.oracle_user,
    value          => 'RJOHNSON',
    consumer_group => 'REPORTS');
  dbms_resource_manager.set_consumer_group_mapping(
    attribute      => dbms_resource_manager.oracle_user,
    value          => 'TPODER',
    consumer_group => 'MAINTENANCE');
  dbms_resource_manager.set_consumer_group_mapping(
    attribute      => dbms_resource_manager.client_program,
    value          => 'toad.exe',
    consumer_group => 'REPORTS');
  dbms_resource_manager.submit_pending_area();
END;
```

One more important step is to grant each of these users permission to switch their session to the consumer group you specified in your mapping rules. If you don't, they will not be able to switch their session to the desired resource group and will instead be assigned to the default consumer group, OTHER_GROUPS. So if you find that user sessions are landing in OTHER_GROUPS instead of the resource group specified in your mapping rules, you probably forgot to grant the switch_consumer_group privilege to the user. Remember that this will also happen if the mapping rule assigns a session to a consumer group that is not in the active resource plan. The GRANT_OPITON parameter in the next listing determines whether or not the user will be allowed to grant others permission to switch to the consumer group.

```
BEGIN
  dbms_resource_manager_privs.grant_switch_consumer_group(
    GRANTEE_NAME    => 'RJOHNSON',
    CONSUMER_GROUP  => 'REPORTS',
    GRANT_OPTION    => FALSE);
  dbms_resource_manager_privs.grant_switch_consumer_group(
    GRANTEE_NAME    => 'KOSBORNE',
    CONSUMER_GROUP  => 'APPS',
    GRANT_OPTION    => FALSE);
  dbms_resource_manager_privs.grant_switch_consumer_group(
    GRANTEE_NAME    => 'TPODER',
```

```
      CONSUMER_GROUP =>  'MAINTENANCE',
      GRANT_OPTION   =>   FALSE);
END;
```

▨ **Tip:** If you trust your users and developers not to switch their own session to a higher-priority consumer group, you can grant the switch_consumer_group permission to the public and make things a little easier on yourself.

Step 3: Set Resource Group Mapping Priorities

Since we want to use more than the session's USERNAME to map sessions to resource groups, we'll need to set priorities for the mapping rules. This tells DBRM which rules should take precedence when a session matches more than one rule. The following PL/SQL block sets a priority for the client program attribute higher than that of the database user account:

```
BEGIN
  dbms_resource_manager.clear_pending_area();
  dbms_resource_manager.create_pending_area();
  dbms_resource_manager.set_consumer_group_mapping_pri(
    explicit              => 1,
    client_program        => 2,
    oracle_user           => 3,
    service_module_action => 4,
    service_module        => 5,
    module_name_action    => 6,
    module_name           => 7,
    service_name          => 8,
    client_os_user        => 9,
    client_machine        => 10 );
  dbms_resource_manager.submit_pending_area();
END;
```

Step 4: Create the Resource Plan and Plan Directives

Generally speaking, resource plans are created at the same time as the plan directives. This is because we cannot create an empty plan. A resource plan must have at least one plan directive, for the OTHER_GROUPS resource group. The following listing creates a resource plan called DAYTIME and defines directives for the resource groups: APPS, REPORTS, MAINTENANCE, and, of course, OTHER_GROUPS.

```
BEGIN
 dbms_resource_manager.clear_pending_area();
 dbms_resource_manager.create_pending_area();
 dbms_resource_manager.create_plan(
   plan    => 'daytime',
   comment => 'Resource plan for normal business hours');
 dbms_resource_manager.create_plan_directive(
   plan             => 'daytime',
   group_or_subplan => 'APPS',
```

```
    comment            => 'High priority users/applications',
    mgmt_p1            => 70);
 dbms_resource_manager.create_plan_directive(
    plan               => 'daytime',
    group_or_subplan => 'REPORTS',
    comment            => 'Medium priority for daytime reports processing',
    mgmt_p2            => 50);
 dbms_resource_manager.create_plan_directive(
    plan               => 'daytime',
    group_or_subplan => 'MAINTENANCE',
    comment            => 'Low priority for daytime maintenance',
    mgmt_p3            => 50);
 dbms_resource_manager.create_plan_directive(
    plan               => 'daytime',
    group_or_subplan => 'OTHER_GROUPS',
    comment            => 'All other groups not explicitely named in this plan',
    mgmt_p3            => 50);
 dbms_resource_manager.validate_pending_area();
 dbms_resource_manager.submit_pending_area();
END;
```

Step 5: Create the Night-Time Plan

Organizations typically have different scheduling priorities for after-hours work. The NIGHTTIME plan shifts CPU allocation away from the APPS resource group to the MAINTENANCE group. The next listing creates the NIGHTTIME plan with priorities that favor maintenance processing over applications and reporting. Even so, 50% of CPU resources are reserved for the APPS and REPORTS resource groups to ensure that business applications and reports get sufficient CPU during off-peak hours.

```
BEGIN
 dbms_resource_manager.clear_pending_area();
 dbms_resource_manager.create_pending_area();
 dbms_resource_manager.create_plan(
    plan    => 'nighttime',
    comment => 'Resource plan for normal business hours');
 dbms_resource_manager.create_plan_directive(
    plan               => 'nighttime',
    group_or_subplan => 'MAINTENANCE',
    comment            => 'Low priority for daytime maintenance',
    mgmt_p1            => 50);
 dbms_resource_manager.create_plan_directive(
    plan               => 'nighttime',
    group_or_subplan => 'APPS',
    comment            => 'High priority users/applications',
    mgmt_p2            => 50);
 dbms_resource_manager.create_plan_directive(
    plan               => 'nighttime',
    group_or_subplan => 'REPORTS',
    comment            => 'Medium priority for daytime reports processing',
    mgmt_p2            => 50);
 dbms_resource_manager.create_plan_directive(
```

```
   plan              => 'nighttime',
   group_or_subplan => 'OTHER_GROUPS',
   comment           => 'All other groups not explicitly named in this plan',
   mgmt_p3           => 100);
 dbms_resource_manager.validate_pending_area();
 dbms_resource_manager.submit_pending_area();
END;
```

Step 6: Activate the Resource Plan

Once our resource plans are created, one of them must be activated for DBRM to start managing resources. Resource plans are activated by setting the instance parameter RESOURCE_MANAGER_PLAN, using the ALTER SYSTEM command. If the plan doesn't exist, then DBRM is not enabled.

```
ALTER SYSTEM SET resource_manager_plan='DAYTIME' SCOPE=BOTH SID='SCRATCH';
```

You can automatically set the activate resource plan using scheduler windows. This method ensures that business rules for resource management are enforced consistently. The following listing modifies the built-in scheduler window WEEKNIGHT_WINDOW so that it enables our nighttime resource plan. The window starts at 6:00 PM (hour 18) and runs through 7:00 AM (780 minutes).

```
BEGIN
 DBMS_SCHEDULER.SET_ATTRIBUTE(
   Name      => '"SYS"."WEEKNIGHT_WINDOW"',
   Attribute => 'RESOURCE_PLAN',
   Value     => 'NIGHTTIME');

 DBMS_SCHEDULER.SET_ATTRIBUTE(
  name      => '"SYS"."WEEKNIGHT_WINDOW"',
  attribute => 'REPEAT_INTERVAL',
  value     => 'FREQ=WEEKLY;BYDAY=MON,TUE,WED,THU,FRI;BYHOUR=18;BYMINUTE=00;BYSECOND=0');

 DBMS_SCHEDULER.SET_ATTRIBUTE(
   name=>'"SYS"."WEEKNIGHT_WINDOW"',
   attribute=>'DURATION',
   value=>numtodsinterval(780, 'minute'));

 DBMS_SCHEDULER.ENABLE(name=>'"SYS"."WEEKNIGHT_WINDOW"');
END;
```

Now we'll create a new window that covers normal business hours, called WEEKDAY_WINDOW. This window will automatically switch the active resource plan to our DAYTIME resource plan. The window starts at 7:00 AM (hour 7) and runs until 6:00 PM (660 minutes), at which point our WEEKNIGHT_WINDOW begins.

```
BEGIN
 DBMS_SCHEDULER.CREATE_WINDOW(
  window_name     => '"WEEKDAY_WINDOW"',
  resource_plan   => 'DAYTIME',
  start_date      => systimestamp at time zone '-6:00',
  duration        => numtodsinterval(660, 'minute'),
  repeat_interval => 'FREQ=WEEKLY;BYDAY=MON,TUE,WED,THU,FRI;BYHOUR=7;BYMINUTE=0;BYSECOND=0',
  end_date        => null,
  window_priority => 'LOW',
  comments        => 'Weekday window. Sets the active resource plan to DAYTIME');

 DBMS_SCHEDULER.ENABLE(name=>'"SYS"."WEEKDAY_WINDOW"');
END;
```

Testing a Resource Plan

Before we finish with Database Resource Manager, let's test one of our resource plans to see if it works as advertised. Validating the precise CPU allocation to each of our resource groups is a very complicated undertaking, so we won't be digging into it too deeply. But we will take a look at the V$RSRC_CONSUMER_GROUP view to see if we can account for how the CPU resources were allocated among our consumer groups. For the test, we'll use the SCRATCH database, and the DAYTIME resource plan we created earlier. The results of the test will:

- Verify that sessions map properly to their Resource Groups

- Show how to identify DBRM wait events in a session trace

- Verify that CPU is allocated according to our resource plan

Figure 7-2 shows resource allocation directives for the DAYTIME resource plan we'll be testing.

Resource Allocations								
Group/Subplan	Level 1	Level 2	Level 3	Level 4	Level 5	Level 6	Level 7	Level 8
APPS	70							
MAINTENANCE			50					
OTHER_GROUPS			50					
REPORTS		50						

Figure 7-2. DAYTIME resource plan allocation

If our DAYTIME resource plan is working, CPU will be allocated according to the following formula. Note that the 70%, 15%, 7.5%, and 7.5% allocations reflect the percent of total CPU.

Level 1) APPS = 70% $(100\% \times 70\%)$

Level 2) REPORTS = 15% $((100\% - 70\%) \times 50\%)$

Level 3) MAINTENANCE = 7.5% $(((100\% - 70\%) \times 50\%) \times 50\%)$

Level 3) OTHER_GROUPS = 7.5% $(((100\% - 70\%) \times 50\%) \times 50\%)$

Test Outline

Now that we've created our resource plan, we can test to see how it works. Following are the steps we will follow to test our resource plan.

1. Turn off the Database Resource Manager.

2. Start a session using the RJOHNSON account.

3. Start 20 concurrent CPU intensive queries from each of the user accounts that map to our consumer groups. These user accounts map to resource groups as follows:

   KOSBORNE   → APPS

   RJOHNSON   → REPORTS

   TPODER   → MAINTENANCE

   FRED   → OTHER_GROUPS

4. Check the consumer group assignments in the V$SESSION. RESOURCE_CONSUMER_GROUP view. This column should be null, since DBRM is inactive.

5. Start a 10046 session trace on an RJOHNSON session.

6. Run a CPU intensive query from the RJOHNSON session.

7. Tail the session trace file and watch for resmgr:cpu quantum wait events. There shouldn't be any at this point, because DBRM is inactive.

8. While the load test is still running, activate the DAYTIME resource plan.

9. Check the consumer group assignments again. Now that DBRM is active, sessions should be assigned to their respective consumer groups.

10. Check the RJOHNSON session trace file again. We should see resmgr:cpu quantum wait events now that the DAYTIME resource plan is active.

11. Review the Resource Manager metrics in the V$RSRC_CONSUMER_GROUP view to see how CPU resources were allocated during the test. We should see CPU allocated according to the directives in our resource plan.

Step 1: Deactivate DBRM

Now, we'll begin our test of the resource plan. The first thing we'll do is turn off DBRM by setting the instance database parameter RESOURCE_MANAGER_PLAN to '' (an empty string).

```
SYS:SCRATCH> alter system set resource_manager_plan='';
```

Step 2: Log In as RJOHNSON

Now, we'll start a SQL*Plus session, logging in as RJOHNSON.

```
[enkdb02:rjohnson:SCRATCH] /home/rjohnson/myscripts
> sqlplus rjohnson/x
...
RJOHNSON:SCRATCH>
```

Step 3: Start Load Test

In four separate terminal windows, we'll generate a load on the system by running a shell script that spins up 20 SQL*Plus sessions for each user account. Each session kicks off the following query, which creates a Cartesian product. The skew table has 32,000,000 rows, so the join will create billions of logical I/O operations. That, along with the sum on COL1, should create sufficient CPU load for our tests. The following listing shows the definition of the SKEW table, with indexes on the COL1 and COL2 columns.

```
CREATE TABLE SKEW (
  PK_COL   NUMBER,
  COL1     NUMBER,
  COL2     VARCHAR2(30 BYTE),
  COL3     DATE,
  COL4     VARCHAR2(1 BYTE) );

CREATE INDEX SKEW_COL2 ON SKEW (COL2);
CREATE INDEX SKEW_COL2 ON SKEW (COL2);
```

Now, let's start the test queries and take a look at the CPU utilization. The following listing shows the query we'll be using for the test.

```
-- Test Query --
select a.col2, sum(a.col1)
  from rjohnson.skew a,
       rjohnson.skew b
 group by a.col2;
```

The burn_cpu.sh shell script, shown next, executes 20 concurrent copies of the burn_cpu.sql script. We'll run this script once for each of the user accounts, FRED, KOSBORNE, RJOHNSON, and TPODER. Our test configuration is a single database (SCRATCH), on a quarter rack Exadata V2. Recall that the V2 is configured with two quad-core CPUs.

```
#!/bin/bash
export user=$1
export passwd=$2
export parallel=$3

burn_cpu() {
  sqlplus -s<<EOF
  $user/$passwd
  @burn_cpu.sql
  exit
EOF
}
```

```
JOBS=0
while :; do
  burn_cpu &

  JOBS=`jobs | wc -l`
  while [ "$JOBS" -ge "$parallel" ]; do
    sleep 5
    JOBS=`jobs | wc -l`
  done
done
```

With DBRM disabled, our test sessions put a heavy load on the CPU. Output from the top command shows 26 running processes and user CPU time at 80.8%:

```
top - 22:20:14 up 10 days,  9:38, 13 users,  load average: 13.81, 22.73, 25.98
Tasks: 1233 total,  26 running, 1207 sleeping,   0 stopped,   0 zombie
Cpu(s): 80.8%us,  4.4%sy,  0.0%ni, 14.7%id,  0.0%wa,  0.0%hi,  0.1%si,  0.0%st
```

Step 4: Check Consumer Group Assignments

Let's take a look at our session-to-consumer group mappings. When DBRM is inactive, sessions will show no consumer group assignment. This is another way to verify that Resource Manager is not active.

```
SYS:SCRATCH> SELECT s.username, s.resource_consumer_group, count(*)
             FROM v$session s, v$process p
           WHERE ( (s.username IS NOT NULL)
             AND (NVL (s.osuser, 'x') <> 'SYSTEM')
             AND (s.TYPE <> 'BACKGROUND') )
             AND (p.addr(+) = s.paddr)
             AND s.username not in ('SYS','DBSNMP')
          GROUP BY s.username, s.resource_consumer_group
          ORDER BY s.username;


USERNAME              RESOURCE_CONSUMER_GROUP            COUNT(*)
--------------------  --------------------------------  -----------
FRED                                                           20
KOSBORNE                                                       20
RJOHNSON                                                       21
TPODER                                                         20
```

The query output shows a total of 81 sessions, consisting of twenty sessions per user account, plus one interactive RJOHNSON session that we'll trace in the next step. No sessions are currently mapped to the resource groups, because DBRM is inactive.

Step 5: Start 10046 Session Trace for the interactive RJOHNSON session

Now we'll start a 10046 trace for the interactive RJOHNSON session so we can see the Resource Manager wait events that would indicate DBRM is actively regulating CPU for this session. Remember that DBRM is still inactive, so we shouldn't see any Resource Manager wait events in the trace file yet.

```
RJOHNSON:SCRATCH> alter session set tracefile_identifier='RJOHNSON';
RJOHNSON:SCRATCH> alter session set events '10046 trace name context forever, level 12';
```

Step 6: Execute a Query from the RJOHNSON Session

Next, we'll execute a long-running, CPU-intensive query, from the interactive RJOHNSON session. This is the same query we used for the load test in Step 3.

```
RJOHNSON:SCRATCH> select a.col2, sum(a.col1)
                    from rjohnson.skew a,
                         rjohnson.skew b
                  group by a.col2;
```

Step 7: Examine the Session Trace File

Since our resource plan is not active yet, we don't see any Resource Manager wait events in the trace file at this point.

```
[enkdb02:rjohnson:SCRATCH]
> tail -5000f SCRATCH_ora_2691_RJOHNSON.trc | grep 'resmgr:cpu quantum'
```

Step 8: Activate Resource Manager

Now, while the load test is still running, let's enable DBRM by setting the active resource plan to our DAYTIME plan. When the resource plan is activated, our resource mapping rules should engage and switch the running sessions to their respective consumer groups.

```
SYS:SCRATCH> alter system set resource_manager_plan='DAYTIME';
```

Step 9: Check Consumer Group Assignments

Now, let's run that query again and see what our consumer group assignments look like.

```
SYS:SCRATCH> SELECT s.username, s.resource_consumer_group, count(*)
                FROM v$session s, v$process p
               WHERE ( (s.username IS NOT NULL)
                 AND (NVL (s.osuser, 'x') <> 'SYSTEM')
                 AND (s.TYPE <> 'BACKGROUND') )
                 AND (p.addr(+) = s.paddr)
                 AND s.username not in ('SYS','DBSNMP')
               GROUP BY s.username, s.resource_consumer_group
               ORDER BY s.username;
```

USERNAME	RESOURCE_CONSUMER_GROUP	COUNT(*)
FRED	OTHER_GROUPS	20
KOSBORNE	APPS	20
RJOHNSON	REPORTS	20
TPODER	MAINTENANCE	21

Our user sessions are mapping perfectly. The query shows that all user sessions have been switched to their consumer group according to the mapping rules we defined earlier.

Step 10: Examine the Session Trace File

Now, let's take another look at the session trace we started in step 2 and watch for DBRM wait events (resmgr:cpu quantum). The output from the trace file shows the wait events Oracle used to account for the time our interactive RJOHNSON session spent in the DBRM execution queue, waiting for its turn on the CPU:

```
[enkdb02:rjohnson:SCRATCH] /home/rjohnson
> clear; tail -5000f SCRATCH_ora_17310_RJOHNSON.trc | grep 'resmgr:cpu quantum'
...
WAIT #47994886847368: nam='resmgr:cpu quantum' ela= 120 location=2 consumer group id=78568  =0
obj#=78574 tim=1298993391858765
WAIT #47994886847368: nam='resmgr:cpu quantum' ela= 14471 location=2 consumer group id=78568
=0 obj#=78574 tim=1298993391874792
WAIT #47994886847368: nam='resmgr:cpu quantum' ela= 57357 location=2 consumer group id=78568
=0 obj#=78574 tim=1298993391940561
WAIT #47994886847368: nam='resmgr:cpu quantum' ela= 109930 location=2 consumer group id=78568
=0 obj#=78574 tim=1298993392052259
WAIT #47994886847368: nam='resmgr:cpu quantum' ela= 84908 location=2 consumer group id=78568
=0 obj#=78574 tim=1298993392141914
...
```

As you can see, the RJOHNSON user session is being given a limited amount of time on the CPU. The ela= attrbute in the trace records shows the amount of time (in microseconds) that the session spent in the resmgr:cpu quantum wait event. In the snippet from the trace file, we see that the RJOHNSON session was forced to wait for a total of 266,786 microseconds, or .267 CPU seconds. Note that the output shown here represents a very small sample of the trace file. There were actually thousands of occurrences of the wait event in the trace file. The sum of the ela time in these wait events represents the amount of time the session was forced off the CPU in order to enforce the allocation directives in the DAYTIME plan.

Step 11: Check DBRM Metrics

And finally, if we look at the V$RSRC_CONSUMER_GROUP view, we can see the various metrics that Oracle provides for monitoring DBRM. These counters are reset when a new resource plan is activated. Some accumulate over the life of the active plan, while others are expressed as a percentage and represent a current reading.

> ■ **Tip:** The `V_$RSRCMGRMETRIC` and `V_$RSRCMGRMETRIC_HISTORY` views are also very useful for monitoring the effects that your DBRM resource allocations have on sessions in the database.

Table 7-3 shows the definitions of the CPU-related columns we're interested in.

Table 7-3. CPU-Related Columns in the V$RSRC_CONSUMER_GROUP View

Column	Description
NAME	The resource group name.
ACTIVE_SESSIONS	The number of active sessions in the consumer group.
EXECUTION_WAITERS	The number of active sessions waiting for a time slice in which they can use the CPU.
REQUESTS	The cumulative number of requests made by sessions in the consumer group.
CPU_WAIT_TIME	The cumulative amount of time that Resource Manager made sessions in the Resource Group wait for CPU. This wait time does not include I/O waits, delays from queue or latch contention, or the like. CPU_WAIT_TIME is the sum of the elapsed time allocated to the resmgr:cpu quantum wait event for the consumer group.
CPU_WAITS	The cumulative number of times sessions were made to wait because of resource management.
CONSUMED_CPU_TIME	The total amount of CPU time accumulated (in milliseconds) by sessions in the consumer group.
YIELDS	The cumulative number of times sessions in the consumer group had to yield the CPU to other sessions because of resource management.

The following listing is a report you may use to display the metrics collected in the V$RSRC_CONSUMER_GROUP view. These metrics are a valuable tool for determining the effect our resource allocations had on the consumer groups during the test.

```
col name                format a12          heading "Name"
col active_sessions     format 999          heading "Active|Sessions"
col execution_waiters   format 999          heading "Execution|Waiters"
col requests            format 9,999,999    heading "Requests"
col cpu_wait_time       format 999,999,999  heading "CPU Wait|Time"
```

```
col cpu_waits                    format 99,999,999     heading "CPU|Waits"
col consumed_cpu_time            format 99,999,999     heading "Consumed|CPU Time"
col yields                       format 9,999,999      heading "Yields"

SELECT DECODE(name, '_ORACLE_BACKGROUND_GROUP_', 'BACKGROUND', name) name,
       active_sessions, execution_waiters, requests,
       cpu_wait_time, cpu_waits, consumed_cpu_time, yields
  FROM v$rsrc_consumer_group
ORDER BY cpu_wait_time;
```

Name	Active Sessions	Execution Waiters	Requests	CPU Wait Time	CPU Waits	Consumed CPU Time	Yields
BACKGROUND	34	0	76	0	0	0	0
APPS	30	13	30	87,157,739	11,498,286	47,963,809	365,611
REPORTS	30	27	31	145,566,524	2,476,651	10,733,274	78,950
MAINTENANCE	30	29	30	155,018,913	1,281,279	5,763,764	41,368
OTHER_GROUPS	34	29	131	155,437,715	1,259,766	5,576,621	40,168

In this report you can see how Resource Manager allocated CPU resources to the consumer groups according to our plan directives. Notice the BACKGROUND resource group (named_ORACLE_BACKGROUND_GROUP_). Database background processes are assigned to this special group. Processes included in this group include pmon, smon, dbw, lgwr, and a host of other familiar background processes that manage the database. Assigning performance-critical processes to this group is the way Resource Manager excludes them from resource management. For all other consumer groups, you can see that Resource Manager forced sessions to yield the processor in order to distribute CPU resources according to our resource directives. The number of yields and CPU waits are of interest, but not as telling as the CPU wait time and CPU time consumed. The percentages in Figure 7-3 show how CPU and wait time were allocated among our consumer groups.

Resource Group	Execution Waiters	Requests	CPU Wait Time	CPU Waits	Consumed CPU Time	Yields
BACKGROUND	0	76	0	0	0	0
APPS	13	30	87,157,739	11,498,286	47,963,809	365,611
REPORTS	27	31	145,566,524	2,476,651	10,733,274	78,950
MAINTENANCE	29	30	155,018,913	1,281,279	5,763,764	41,368
OTHER_GROUPS	29	131	155,437,715	1,259,766	5,576,621	40,168
Total	98	298	543,180,891	16,515,982	70,037,468	526,097

Resource Group	% Execution Waiters	% Requests	% Wait Time	% CPU Waits	% Consumed CPU Time	% Yields
APPS	13.27%	10.07%	16.05%	69.62%	68.48%	69.49%
REPORTS	27.55%	10.40%	26.80%	15.00%	15.33%	15.01%
MAINTENANCE	29.59%	10.07%	28.54%	7.76%	8.23%	7.86%
OTHER_GROUPS	29.59%	43.96%	28.62%	7.63%	7.96%	7.64%

Figure 7-3. DAYTIME resource plan allocation

According to Resource Manager, the APPS group consumed 68.48% of the total CPU used by foreground processes, which is very close to the 70% we allocated it in our resource plan. At 15.33%, the REPORTS group was almost a perfect match to the 15% our plan called for. The MAINTENANCE group used 8.23%, which was a little high but still a very good fit with the 7.5% we defined for it. The OTHER_GROUPS used 7.63% CPU, which again was nearly a perfect match with our plan directive of 7.5%. We should mention that at first the allocations in this report were not proportioned very closely to the allocations in our resource plan. We had to let the stress test run for several minutes before DBRM was able to get the numbers fine-tuned to the levels we see in Figure 7-3.

■ **Note:** In order to get CPU utilization to line up with the resource plan, each consumer group must be fully capable of utilizing its allocation. Getting a match between CPU utilization and consumer group CPU allocation is further complicated by multi-level resource plans and the way Resource Manager redistributes unconsumed CPU to other consumer groups. Multi-level resource plans are not common in real-world situations. Most of the time, simple single-level resource plans are sufficient (and much easier to measure).

In conclusion, even though the test results show minor variances between CPU allocated in our plan directives and CPU utilization reported, you can see that DBRM was, in fact, managing CPU resources according to our plan. The test also verified that user sessions properly switched to their respective consumer groups according to our mapping rules when the resource plan was activated.

Database Resource Manager has been available for a number of years now. It is a very elegant, complex, and effective tool for managing the server resources that are the very life blood of your databases. Unfortunately, in our experience, it is rarely used. There are probably several reasons for this. DBAs are continually barraged by complaints that queries run too long and applications seem sluggish. We are often reluctant to implement anything that will slow anyone down. This is often compounded when multiple organizations within the company share the same database or server. It is a difficult task to address priorities within a company where it comes to database performance; and the decision is usually out of the control of DBAs, who are responsible for somehow pleasing everyone. Sound familiar? Our suggestion would be to start small. Separate the most obvious groups within your database by priority. Prioritizing ad-hoc queries from OLTP applications would be a good place to start. With each step you will learn what works and doesn't work for your business. So start small. Keep it simple, and implement resource management in small, incremental steps.

Instance Caging

While Resource Manager plan directives provision CPU usage by consumer group within the database, *instance caging* provisions CPU at the database instance level. Without instance caging, the operating system takes sole responsibility for scheduling processes to run on the CPUs according to its own algorithms. Foreground and background processes among all databases instances are scheduled on the CPUs without respect to business priorities. Without instance caging, sessions from one database can monopolize CPU resources during peak processing periods and degrade performance of other databases on the server. Conversely, processes running when the load on the system is very light tend to perform dramatically better, creating wide swings in response time from one moment to the next. Instance caging allows you to dynamically set an absolute limit on the amount of CPU a database may use. And because instance caging enforces a maximum limit on the CPU available to the instance, it tends to smooth out those wide performance swings and provide much more consistent response times to end users. This is not to say that instance caging locks the database processes down on a specific set of physical CPU cores (a technique called *CPU affinity*); all CPU cores are still utilized by all database background and foreground processes. Rather, instance caging regulates the amount of CPU time (% of CPU) a database may use at any given time.

Instance caging also solves several less obvious problems caused by CPU starvation. Some instance processes are critical to overall health and performance of the Oracle database. For example, if the log writer process (LGWR) doesn't get enough time on the processor, the database can suffer dramatic, system-wide brownouts because all database write activity comes to a screeching a halt while LGWR writes critical recovery information to the online redo logs. Insufficient CPU resources can cause significant performance problems and stability issues if Process Monitor (PMON) cannot get enough time on the CPU. For RAC systems, the Lock Management Server (LMS) process can even cause sporadic node evictions due to CPU starvation, (we've seen this one a number of times).

▪ **Note:** Clusterware was heavily updated in version 11.2 (and renamed Grid Infrastructure). According to our Oracle sources, CPU starvation leading to node eviction is rarely an issue anymore thanks to changes in 11.2.

Instance caging directly addresses CPU provisioning for multitenant database environments, making it a very useful tool for database consolidation efforts. For example, let's say you have four databases, each running on a separate server. These servers each have four outdated CPUs, so consolidating them onto a new server with 16 brand-new CPU cores should easily provide performance that is at least on par with what they currently have. When you migrate the first database, the end users are ecstatic. Queries that used to run for an hour begin completing in less than 15 minutes. You move the second database, and performance slows down a bit but is still much better than it was on the old server. The queries now complete in a little less than 30 minutes. As you proceed to migrate the remaining two databases, performance declines even further. To aggravate the situation, you now find yourself with mixed workloads all competing for the same CPU resources during peak periods of the day. This is a common theme in database consolidation projects. Performance starts off great, but declines to a point where you wonder if you've made a big mistake bringing several databases together under the same roof. And even if overall performance is better than it was before, the perception of the first clients to be migrated is that it is actually worse, especially during peak periods of the day. If you had used instance caging to set the CPU limit for each database to four cores when they were moved, response times would have been much more stable.

Configuring and Testing Instance Caging

Configuring instance caging is very simple. Activating a resource plan and setting the number of CPU cores are all that is required. Recall that the active resource plan is set using the database parameter RESOURCE_PLAN. The number of CPUs is set using the CPU_COUNT parameter, which determines the number of CPUs the instance may use for all foreground and background processes. Both parameters are dynamic, so adjustments can be made at any time. In fact, scheduling these changes to occur automatically is a very useful way to adjust database priorities at various times of the day or week according to the needs of your business. For example, month-end and year-end processing are critical times for accounting systems. If your database server is being shared by multiple databases, allocating additional processing power to your financial database during heavy processing cycles might make a lot of sense.

Now, let's take a look at instance caging in action. For this example we'll use our SCRATCH and SNIFF databases to demonstrate how it works. These are standalone (non-RAC) databases running on an Exadata V2 database server with two quad core CPUs. The Nehalem chipset is hyper-threaded, so the database actually "sees" 16 virtual cores (or CPU threads), as you can see in the following listing.

```
SYS:SCRATCH> show parameter cpu_count

NAME                                 TYPE         VALUE
------------------------------------ ------------ ------------------------------
cpu_count                            integer      16
```

■ **Note:** Many CPU chipsets today implement hyper-threading. When a CPU uses hyper-threading, each CPU thread is seen by the operating system (and subsequently Oracle database instances) as a separate CPU. This is why two quad core chips appear as 16 CPUs, rather than the expected 8. Exadata V2, X2, and X2-8 models feature chipsets that employ hyper-threading, so for purposes of our discussion, we will use the terms *CPU core* and *CPU threads* synonymously.

We'll be using the built-in resource plan, DEFAULT_PLAN, for these tests. Figure 7-4 shows the CPU resource allocation for this plan. Note that under the default_plan, all users other than SYS and SYSTEM will be mapped to the OTHER_GROUPS resource group.

```
SYS:SCRATCH> show parameter resource_plan

NAME                                 TYPE         VALUE
------------------------------------ ------------ ------------------------------
resource_manager_plan                string       DEFAULT_PLAN
```

Resource Allocations								
Group/Subplan	Level 1	Level 2	Level 3	Level 4	Level 5	Level 6	Level 7	Level 8
ORA$AUTOTASK_SUB_PLAN		5						
ORA$DIAGNOSTICS		5						
OTHER_GROUPS		90						
SYS_GROUP	75							

Figure 7-4. DEFAULT_PLAN resource allocation

For this test, we'll use the same script we used for testing our DBRM resource plans in the previous section. Again, the burn_cpu.sh script with a parameter of 20 will spin up 20 concurrent sessions, each running the test query. This should drive the CPU utilization up to approximately 80%. Once the sessions are running, we'll use the top command to see the effect instance caging has on the server CPU load. Let's start out by getting a baseline. To do this, we'll run the test with instance caging and Resource Manager turned off. Recall that these tests are running on a quarter rack Exadata V2, which is configured with two quad-core hyper-threaded CPUs. So the database instances see a CPU_COUNT of 16.

```
> burn_cpu.sh kosborne x 20

top - 18:48:11 up 2 days,  6:53,  4 users,  load average: 15.91, 5.51, 2.09
Tasks: 903 total,  25 running, 878 sleeping,   0 stopped,   0 zombie
Cpu(s): 82.9%us,  1.8%sy,  0.0%ni, 15.1%id,  0.0%wa,  0.1%hi,  0.2%si,  0.0%st
```

As you can see, running the burn_cpu.sh script drove the CPU usage up from a relatively idle 0.3%, to 82.9%, with 25 running processes. Now, let's see what happens when we reset the cpu_count to 8, which is 50% of the total CPU on the server. Notice that the number of running processes has dropped from 25 to 10. The CPU time in user space has dropped to 46.1%, just over half of what it was.

```
SYS:SCRATCH> alter system set cpu_count=8;

top - 19:15:10 up 2 days,  7:20,  4 users,  load average: 4.82, 5.52, 8.80
Tasks: 887 total,  10 running, 877 sleeping,   0 stopped,   0 zombie
Cpu(s): 46.1%us,  0.7%sy,  0.0%ni, 52.3%id,  0.8%wa,  0.0%hi,  0.1%si,  0.0%st
```

Now, we'll set the CPU_COUNT parameter to 4. That is half of the previous setting, so we should see the CPU utilization drop by about 50%. After that, we'll drop the CPU_COUNT to 1 to illustrate the dramatic effect instance caging has on database CPU utilization. Notice that when we set the number of CPUs to 4, our utilization dropped from 46% to 25%. Finally, setting CPU_COUNT to 1 further reduces CPU utilization to 4.8%.

```
SYS:SCRATCH> alter system set cpu_count=4;

top - 19:14:03 up 2 days,  7:18,  4 users,  load average: 2.60, 5.56, 9.08
Tasks: 886 total,  5 running, 881 sleeping,   0 stopped,   0 zombie
Cpu(s): 25.1%us,  0.8%sy,  0.0%ni, 74.1%id,  0.0%wa,  0.0%hi,  0.0%si,  0.0%st

SYS:SCRATCH> alter system set cpu_count=1;

top - 19:19:32 up 2 days,  7:24,  4 users,  load average: 4.97, 5.09, 7.81
Tasks: 884 total,  2 running, 882 sleeping,   0 stopped,   0 zombie
Cpu(s): 4.8%us,  0.8%sy,  0.0%ni, 94.0%id,  0.2%wa,  0.0%hi,  0.1%si,  0.0%st
```

This test illustrated the effect of instance caging on a single database. Now let's configure two databases and see how instance caging controls CPU resources when multiple databases are involved.

In the next two tests we'll add another database to the mix. The SNIFF database is identical to the SCRATCH database we used in the previous test. In the first of the next two tests, we'll run a baseline with instance caging turned off by setting CPU_COUNT set to 16 in both databases. The baseline will run 16 concurrent copies of the test query on each database. We'll let it run for a few minutes and then take a look at the CPU utilization of these databases as well as the readings from the top command. The active resource plan for both databases is set to DEFAULT_PLAN, and CPU_COUNT is set to 16.

```
[enkdb02:SCRATCH] > burn_cpu.sh kosborne x 16

[enkdb02:SNIFF] > burn_cpu.sh kosborne x 16
```

Figure 7-5 shows a summary of our second test. Each line, representing a session foreground process, shows the percentage of one CPU core. This is summed and divided by 16 (CPU cores) to get the percentage of total CPU consumed. As expected, the distribution of CPU between our two databases is approximately equal at 44.6% and 45.3%. Looking at the Total Connection CPU, we can see that the databases accounted for about 90% of total CPU time for the server.

Connection Process	% of 1 Core	Connection Process	% of 1 Core
oracleSCRATCH	35	oracleSNIFF	32.4
oracleSCRATCH	35	oracleSNIFF	37.7
oracleSCRATCH	36.4	oracleSNIFF	37.7
oracleSCRATCH	39.1	oracleSNIFF	39.1
oracleSCRATCH	39.1	oracleSNIFF	39.1
oracleSCRATCH	39.1	oracleSNIFF	40.4
oracleSCRATCH	39.1	oracleSNIFF	41.8
oracleSCRATCH	39.1	oracleSNIFF	44.5
oracleSCRATCH	41.8	oracleSNIFF	44.5
oracleSCRATCH	44.5	oracleSNIFF	45.8
oracleSCRATCH	47.2	oracleSNIFF	47.2
oracleSCRATCH	49.9	oracleSNIFF	51.2
oracleSCRATCH	53.9	oracleSNIFF	51.2
oracleSCRATCH	55.3	oracleSNIFF	56.6
oracleSCRATCH	58	oracleSNIFF	58
oracleSCRATCH	60.7	oracleSNIFF	58
Subtotal	713.2		725.2
% of Total CPU	44.6	% of Total CPU	45.3
System CPU Allocation		Total Connection CPU	89.9
User	90.5	Total Other + Idle CPU	9.9
Kernel	1.3		
Idle	8	SCRATCH %	49.58%
Total CPU	99.8	SNIFF %	50.42%

Figure 7-5. Test summary: two databases, instance caging turned off

The source for the data reflected in this summary was collected as follows:

% of 1 Core: Individual process CPU from the %CPU column from the top command.

% of Total CPU: Result of % of 1 Core / 16 cores (CPU threads).

User: Cpu(s): nn.nn%us from the top command.

Kernel: Cpu(s): nn.nn%sy from the top command.

Idle: Cpu(s): nn.nn%id from the top command.

Total CPU: Sum of User, Kernel, and Idle.

Total Connection CPU: Sum of % of Total CPU for each database.

Total Other + Idle CPU: Total CPU – Total Connection CPU.

SCRATCH %: % of Total CPU(SCRATCH) / Total Connection CPU.

SNIFF %: % of Total CPU(SNIFF) / Total Connection CPU.

The 'SCRATCH %', and 'SNIFF %' numbers are what we're interested in. They represent the percentage of total CPU used by all sessions in each of these databases. As you can see from the summary, the databases were split at approximately 50% each.

Now let's run the same load test with instance caging configured for a 75/25 split on the number of cores assigned to SCRATCH and SNIFF respectively. In this test, SCRATCH gets 12 CPUs (75% of 16 cores), and SNIFF gets 4 CPUs (25% of 16 cores).

```
SYS:SCRATCH> alter system set cpu_count=12;
SYS:SNIFF> alter system set cpu_count=4;
```

Figure 7-6 shows the results of our second test. The split isn't perfect. It is closer to an 80/20 split. Not captured in these tests was the amount of CPU consumed by all the database background processes, so that may account for the some of the difference. It is also important to understand that Oracle's Resource Manager operates in the user space of the O/S process model, rather than the kernel space. So it cannot directly control the amount of CPU a process consumes inside the kernel; it can only influence this by throttling processes in the user space. In our summary, we see that the SCRATCH database sessions consumed 78.79% of total session CPU, while the SNIFF database used 21.21% of total session CPU. Even though the split isn't perfect, it does show that instance caging made a solid effort to manage these databases to the 75/25 split we defined. Now, this is not to say that instance caging locks the database processes down on a specific set of physical CPU cores. All CPU cores are still utilized by all database background and foreground processes. Rather, instance caging regulates the amount of CPU time (% of CPU) a database may use at any given time.

Connection Process	% of 1 Core	Connection Process	% of 1 Core
oracleSCRATCH	78.6	oracleSNIFF	20
oracleSCRATCH	72.9	oracleSNIFF	18.6
oracleSCRATCH	72.9	oracleSNIFF	18.6
oracleSCRATCH	72.9	oracleSNIFF	18.6
oracleSCRATCH	70	oracleSNIFF	18.6
oracleSCRATCH	67.2	oracleSNIFF	17.2
oracleSCRATCH	67.2	oracleSNIFF	17.2
oracleSCRATCH	67.2	oracleSNIFF	17.2
oracleSCRATCH	65.8	oracleSNIFF	17.2
oracleSCRATCH	62.9	oracleSNIFF	17.2
oracleSCRATCH	61.5	oracleSNIFF	17.2
oracleSCRATCH	58.6	oracleSNIFF	17.2
oracleSCRATCH	58.6	oracleSNIFF	17.2
oracleSCRATCH	57.2	oracleSNIFF	17.2
oracleSCRATCH	55.8	oracleSNIFF	15.7
oracleSCRATCH	52.9	oracleSNIFF	15.7
Subtotal	1042.2		280.6
% of Total CPU	65.1	% of Total CPU	17.5
System CPU Allocation		Total Connection CPU	82.7
User	82.4	Total Other + Idle CPU	17.3
Kernel	1.3		
Idle	16.3	SCRATCH %	78.79%
Total CPU	100	SNIFF %	21.21%

Figure 7-6. Test summary: two databases, instance caging, 75% / 25% split

Over-Provisioning

Over-provisioning refers to the practice of allocating more CPUs to the databases than are actually installed in the server. This is useful when your server hosts multiple databases with complementing workload schedules. For example, if all the heavy processing for the SCRATCH database occurs at night, and the SNIFF database is only busy during DAYTIME hours, it wouldn't make sense to artificially limit these databases to 8 CPU threads each (8×8). A better CPU allocation scheme might be more on the order of 12×12. This would allow each database to fully utilize 12 cores during busy periods, while still "reserving" 4 cores for off-peak processing by the other database. DBAs who consolidate multiple databases onto a single server are aware that their databases don't use their full CPU allocation (CPU_COUNT) all of the time. Over-provisioning allows unused CPU to be utilized by other databases rather than sitting idle. Over-provisioning has become a popular way of managing CPU resources in mixed workload environments. Obviously, over-provisioning CPU introduces the risk of saturating CPU resources. Keep this in mind if you are considering this technique. Be sure you understand the workload schedules of each database when determining the most beneficial CPU count for each database.

Instance caging limits the number of CPU cores a database may use at any given time, allowing DBAs to allocate CPU to databases based on the needs and priorities of the business. It does this through the use of the instance parameter CPU_COUNT. Our preference would have been to allocate CPU based on a percentage of CPU rather the number of cores. This would give the DBA much finer-grained control over CPU resources and would be especially useful for server environments that support numerous databases. But CPU_COUNT is tightly coupled with Oracle's Cost Based Optimizer (CBO), which uses the number of CPUs for its internal costing algorithms. It wouldn't make sense to allow the DBA to set the percentage of processing power without matching that with the value the CBO uses for selecting optimal execution plans. It probably would have been a much more difficult effort to implement such a change to the optimizer. Be that as it may, instance caging is a powerful new feature that we've been waiting for, for a long time and is a major advancement database resource management.

I/O Resource Manager

Earlier in this chapter we discussed Oracle's Database Resource Manager, which manages CPU resources within a database through consumer groups and plan directives. Sessions are assigned to resource groups, and plan directives manage the allocation of resources by assigning values such as CPU percentage to resource management attributes such as MGMT_P1..8. DBRM, however, is limited to managing resources within the database.

DBRM manages I/O resources in a somewhat indirect manner by limiting CPU and parallelism available to user sessions (through consumer groups). This is because until Exadata came along, Oracle had no presence at the storage tier. Exadata lifts I/O Resource Management above the database tier and manages I/O at the storage cell in a very direct way. Databases installed on Exadata send I/O requests to cellsrv on the storage cells using a proprietary protocol known as Intelligent Database protocol (iDB). Using iDB, the database packs additional attributes in every I/O call to the storage cells. This additional information is used in a number of ways. For example, IORM uses the type of file (redo, undo, datafile, control file, and so on) for which the I/O was requested to determine whether caching the blocks in flash cache would be beneficial or not. Three other attributes embedded in the I/O request identify the database, the consumer group, and the consumer group's category. These three small bits of additional information are invaluable to Oracle's intelligent storage. Knowing which database is making the request allows IORM to prioritize I/O requests by database. Categories extend the concept of consumer groups on Exadata platforms. Categories are assigned to consumer groups within the database using Database Resource Manager. Common categories, defined in multiple databases, can then be allocated a shared I/O priority. For example, you may have several databases that map user sessions to an

INTERACTIVE category. I/O requests coming from the INTERACTIVE category may now be prioritized over other categories such as REPORTS, BATCH, or MAINTENANCE.

IORM provides three distinct methods for I/O resource management: Interdatabase, Category, and Intradatabase. These methods may be used individually or in combination. Figure 7-7 illustrates the relationship of these three I/O resource management methods.

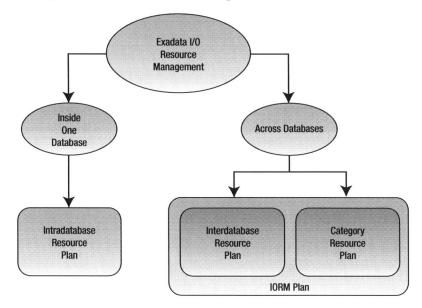

Figure 7-7. Three methods for I/O resource management

Interdatabase IORM (Interdatabase Resource Plan): IORM determines the priority of an I/O request based on the name of the database initiating the request. Interdatabase IORM is useful when Exadata is hosting multiple databases and you need to manage I/O priorities among the databases.

IORM Categories (Category Resource Plan): IORM determines the priority of an I/O request among multiple databases by the category that initiated the request. Managing I/O by category is useful when you want to manage I/O priorities by workload type. For example, you can create categories like APPS, BATCH, REPORTS, MAINTENANCE in each of your databases and then set an I/O allocation for these categories according to their importance to your business. If the APPS category is allocated 70%, then sessions assigned to the APPS category in all databases share this allocation.

Intradatabase IORM (Intradatabase Resource Plan): Unlike Interdatabase and Category IORM, Intradatabase IORM is configured at the database tier using DBRM. DBRM has been enhanced to work in partnership with IORM to provide fine-grained I/O resource management among resource groups within the database. This is done by allocating I/O percentage and priority to consumer groups using the same mechanism used to allocate CPU, the MGMT_Pn attribute. For example, the SALES database may be allocated 50% using Interdatabase IORM. That

50% may be further distributed to the APPS, REPORTS, BATCH, and OTHER_GROUPS
consumer groups within the database. This ensures that I/O resources are available
for critical applications, and it prevents misbehaving or I/O-intensive processes
from stealing I/O from higher-priority sessions inside the database.

How IORM Works

IORM manages I/O at the storage cell by organizing incoming I/O requests into queues according the
database name, category, or consumer group that initiated the request. It then services these queues
according to the priority defined for them in the resource plan. IORM only actively manages I/O
requests when needed. When a cell disk is not fully utilized, cellsrv issues I/O requests to it
immediately. But when a disk is heavily utilized, cellsrv instead redirects the I/O requests to the
appropriate IORM queues and schedules I/O from there to the cell disk queues according to the policies
defined in your IORM plans. For example, using our SCRATCH and SNIFF databases from earlier in this
chapter, we could define a 75% I/O directive for the SCRATCH database, and a 25% I/O directive for the
SNIFF database. When the storage cells have excess capacity available, the I/O queues will be serviced in
a first-in-first-out (FIFO) manner. During off-peak hours, the storage cells will provide maximum
throughput to all databases in an even-handed manner. But when the storage cell begins to saturate, the
SCRATCH queue will be scheduled 75% of the time, and the SNIFF queue will be scheduled 25% of the time.
I/O requests from database background processes are scheduled according to their relative priority to
the foreground processes (client sessions). For example, while the database writer processes (DBWn) are
given priority equal to that of foreground processes, performance critical I/O requests from background
processes that maintain control files, and redo log files are given higher priority.

▨ **Note:** IORM only manages I/O for physical disks. I/O requests for objects in the flash cache or on flash-based
grid disks are not managed by IORM.

IORM Architecture

Figure 7-8 illustrates the architecture of IORM. For each cell disk, cellsrv (Cellserv) maintains an IORM
queue for each consumer group, and each background process (high, medium, and low priority), for
each database accessing the storage cell. By managing the flow of I/O requests between the IORM
queues and the disk queues, cellsrv provides very effective I/O prioritization at the storage cells. I/O
requests sent to the storage cell include tags that identify the database and the consumer group issuing
the request, as well as the type of I/O (redo, control file, and so on). For databases that do not have an
Intradatabase resource plan defined, foreground processes are automatically mapped to the consumer
group OTHER_GROUPS. Three separate queues are maintained for background processes so that cellsrv
may prioritize scheduling according to the type of I/O request. For example, redo and control file I/O
operations are sent to the high-priority queue for background processes. IORM schedules I/O requests
from the consumer group queues according to the I/O directives in your IORM Plan.

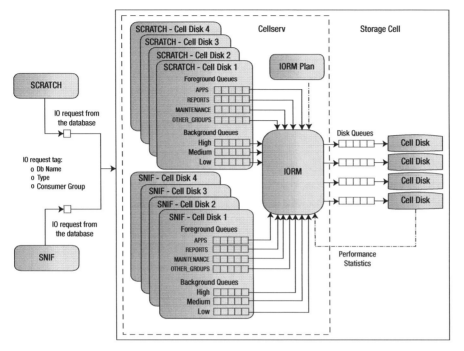

Figure 7-8. *IORM architecture*

Limiting Excess I/O Utilization

Ordinarily, when excess I/O resources are available (allocated but unused by other consumer groups), IORM allows a consumer group to use more than its allocation. For example if the SCRATCH database is allocated 60% at level 1, it may consume I/O resources above that limit if other databases have not fully utilized their allocation. You may choose to override this behavior by setting an absolute limit on the I/O resources allocated to specific databases. This provides more predictable I/O performance for multi-tenant database server environments. The LIMIT IORM attribute is used to set a cap on the I/O resources a database may use even when excess I/O capacity is available. The following listing shows an IORM plan that caps the SCRATCH database at 80%.

```
alter iormplan dbPlan=( -
   (name=SCRATCH,   level=1, allocation=60, limit=80), -
   (name=other,     level=2, allocation=100))
```

By the way, maximum I/O limits may also be defined at the consumer group level, by using the MAX_UTILIZATION_LIMIT attribute in your DBRM resource plans.

▓ **Note:** In most cases, a single-level I/O resource plan is sufficient. As they do with DBRM, multi-level IORM resource plans increase the complexity of measuring the effectiveness of your allocation scheme.

When using multi-level allocation schemes, it's important to understand that I/O resources allocated but unused by a database, category, or consumer group on level 1 are immediately passed to the next level. For example, if you have databases A and B allocated 70%/30% on level 1, and database C is allocated 100% at level 2, then if database A uses only 50% of its allocation, the remaining 20% is passed to database C. Database B cannot capitalize on I/O resources allocated but unused by database A, because A and B are on the same level. This is a subtle but important distinction of multi-level plans. If you are not careful, you can find yourself unintentionally giving excess I/O resources to less important databases at lower levels rather than making those resources available to your higher-priority databases on level 1.

Workload Optimization

To optimize I/O performance, IORM distinguishes between small and large I/O requests. Requests less than 128K in size, typically associated with OLTP transactions, are categorized as small (SM) requests. Requests 128K in size or greater, which are generally associated with DW transactions, are categorized as large (LG) requests. The distinction between small and large I/O requests is important because the algorithms used for optimizing low-latency I/O requests (small requests) and high-throughput I/O requests (large requests) are polar opposites. For OLTP transactions, low latency is most important. For example, consider an end user waiting for a quick ZIP code search to populate the screen. To provide optimized performance for low-latency requests, large I/O requests must be managed in such a way that they don't fully consume the I/O resources of the storage cell. Conversely, DW transactions require high throughput to maximize performance. To optimize I/O for throughput, the storage cell must service many concurrent large I/O requests so that it is fully consumed. By comparing the large (LG) and small (SM) I/O requests in the IORM metrics, you can determine whether your databases lean more toward a DW workload or an OLTP workload. Recently, Oracle added a new attribute to IORM, known as the optimization objective. This attribute determines the optimization mode IORM will use when managing cell disk I/O queues. The optional values for the IORM objective attribute are as follows:

> **low_latency:** This setting provides optimization for applications that are extremely sensitive to I/O latency. It provides the lowest possible I/O latencies, by significantly limiting disk utilization. In other words, throughput-hungry applications will be significantly (negatively) impacted by this optimization objective.

> **high_throughput:** This setting provides the best possible throughput for DW transactions, by attempting to fully utilize the I/O capacity of the storage cells. It is the opposite of low_latency and as such, it will significantly (negatively) impact disk I/O latency.

> **Balanced:** This setting attempts to strike a balance between low latency and high throughput. This is done by limiting disk utilization for large I/O operations to a lesser degree than the low_latency objective described above. Use this objective

when workloads are mixed and you have no applications that require extremely low latency.

Auto: This setting allows IORM to determine the best optimization objective for your workload. Cellsrv continuously monitors the large/small I/O requests and applies the optimization method on a best-fit basis. If 75% or more of the I/O operations from a consumer group are small I/O (less than 128K), then it is considered to be a latency-oriented consumer group and is managed accordingly.

The default setting for an IORM plan objective is '' (an empty string). The objective may be set using the CellCLI alter iormplan objective *objective* command as follows:

```
CellCLI> alter iormplan objective = low_latency
IORMPLAN successfully altered

CellCLI> list iormplan attributes objective
        low_latency
```

Methods for Managing I/O on Exadata

As introduced earlier, there are three methods for managing I/O on the Exadata platform: Interdatabase IORM, Category IORM, and Intradatabase IORM. All three address specific needs for managing I/O. Interdatabase IORM allocates I/O resources by database name, Category IORM allocates I/O resources by common categories among databases, and Intradatabase IORM manages I/O within the database using DBRM resource groups. You can choose to use any one of the methods for managing your I/O resources, or you combine them to implement a more sophisticated resource plan. When these methods are used together, Oracle schedules I/O in the following order: 1) allocation among categories, 2) allocation among databases, and 3) allocation among consumer groups within each category within each database. We'll show how all this works a little later.

Interdatabase I/O Resource Management

Interdatabase I/O resource management refers to the IORM feature that manages I/O priority among multiple databases by database name. Interdatabase IORM allocates I/O resources across multiple databases by means of an IORM plan configured on each storage cell. The IORM plan defines allocation priorities using I/O directives. Each storage cell manages its own I/O queues based on the local IORM plan defined in the cell. IORM plans should be identical for all storage cells in the storage grid. If you have split your Exadata storage cells into multiple storage grids, then IORM plans may differ from grid to grid, but they should still be identical among storage cell members within each storage grid. We discuss configuring multiple storage grids in Chapter 14. Figure 7-9 illustrates how I/O allocation policies are organized within the IORM plan.

I/O Resource Plan

	Database	Level 1 I/O Allocation	Level 2 I/O Allocation	Level 3 I/O Allocation
	SCRATCH	60%		
	SNIFF		80%	
	OTHER			100%

I/O Resource Directives

Figure 7-9. Interdatabase IORM plan

In Figure 7-9, our SCRATCH database, the highest-priority database, is guaranteed 60% of the total I/O on level 1. On level 2, our SNIFF database takes its 80% slice of the remaining 40% of unallocated I/O from level 1. Any unused I/O from level 1 also cascades down to level 2. In addition to any unconsumed I/O from levels 1 and 2, databases on level 3 will equally share the unallocated 16% of total I/O, (16% = 80% × 20%). Note that any databases that do not explicitly appear in the active I/O resource plan will automatically be assigned to the OTHER group.

Configuring Interdatabase IORM

Interdatabase I/O Resource Manager is configured using an IORM plan. This plan determines the database I/O priorities for the storage cell. IORM plans are created using the CellCLI command ALTER IORMPLAN. There can be only one IORM plan per storage cell, regardless of how many ASM instances (clustered or single instance) use it for storage. Creating an Interdatabase IORM plan is fairly simple. The first step is to determine what your allocation policy should be for each database. You will use these allocation policies to define the directives for your IORM plan. The LEVEL attribute specifies the priority a database should be given relative to other databases in the plan. The ALLOCATION attribute determines the percentage of I/O a database will be given out of the total I/O available on its level. The following example demonstrates how you to create an IORM plan to implement the allocation policies illustrated in Figure 7-9.

```
CellCLI> ALTER IORMPLAN -
  dbPlan=( -
    (name=SCRATCH,   level=1, allocation=60), -
    (name=SNIFF,     level=2, allocation=80), -
    (name=other,     level=3, allocation=100))

IORMPLAN successfully altered
```

The CellCLI command list iormplan detail displays our new IORM plan. Notice that the catPlan attribute is empty. This is a placeholder for the Category IORM plan we'll be looking in the next topic.

```
CellCLI> list iormplan detail
        name:                    enkcel01_IORMPLAN
        catPlan:
        dbPlan:                  name=SCRATCH,level=1,allocation=60
                                 name=SNIFF,level=2,allocation=80
                                 name=other,level=3,allocation=100
        status:                  inactive
```

The aggregate allocation for all databases on a level may not exceed 100%. If the sum of allocations on any level exceeds 100%, CellCLI will throw an error. For example, the following listing shows the error CellCLI produces when over 100% is allocated on level 1:

```
CellCLI> ALTER IORMPLAN -
 dbPlan=( -
   (name=SCRATCH,    level=1, allocation=60), -
   (name=SNIFF,      level=1, allocation=80), -
  (name=other,  level=3, allocation=100))

CELL-00006: IORMPLAN contains an invalid allocation total.
```

Before our Interdatabase IORM Plan can manage I/O resources, it must be activated using the CellCLI command ALTER IORMPLAN ACTIVE. For now, we'll leave it turned off. Later, in the "Understanding IORM Metrics" section of the chapter, we'll test our Interdatabase IORM Plan and discuss how the effects of IORM can be monitored at the storage cells.

Category IORM

The I/O Resource Manager (IORM) extends the concept of resource groups with a new attribute known as a *category*. While resource groups allow DBRM to manage resources within a database, categories provide I/O resource management among multiple databases. For example, suppose our two databases (SCRATCH and SNIFF) have similar workloads. They both host OLTP applications that do short, time-sensitive transactions. During business hours, these transactions must take priority. These databases also do a fair amount of batch processing, such as running reports and maintenance jobs. The batch processing takes a lower priority during business hours. These two workloads can be managed and prioritized using IORM categories. The categories APPS_CATEGORY and BATCH_CATEGORY can be defined in both databases for high-priority applications and long-running, lower-priority activities, respectively. If APPS_CATEGORY is allocated 70% on level 1, then no matter how heavily loaded the storage grid is, sessions assigned to this category, for both databases, will be guaranteed a minimum of 70% of all I/O.

Configuring Category IORM

Setting up Category IORM is fairly straightforward. Once you've created your DBRM consumer groups, you will create categories in the database and assign them to your consumer groups. The final step is to create an IORM plan in the storage cells to establish I/O allocation and priority for each category. You can define as many as eight levels in your Category IORM Plan. Figure 7-10 illustrates the relationship between consumer groups, categories, and the Category IORM Plan.

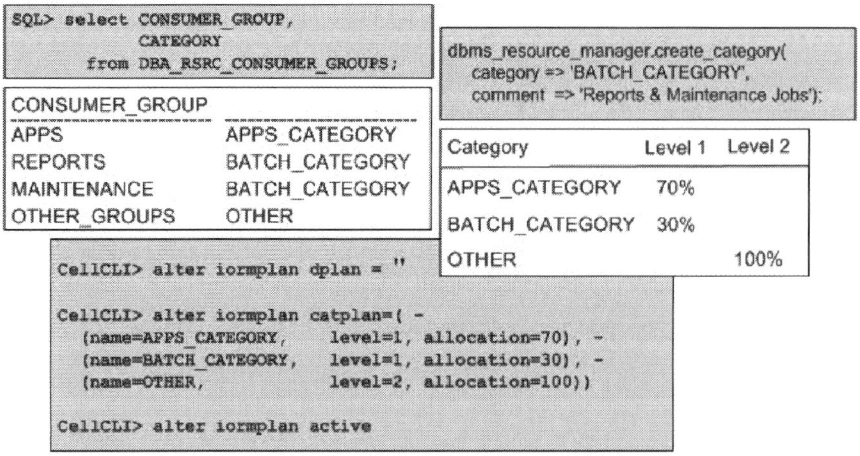

```
SQL> select CONSUMER_GROUP,
            CATEGORY
       from DBA_RSRC_CONSUMER_GROUPS;
```

```
CONSUMER_GROUP
APPS              APPS_CATEGORY
REPORTS           BATCH_CATEGORY
MAINTENANCE       BATCH_CATEGORY
OTHER_GROUPS      OTHER
```

```
dbms_resource_manager.create_category(
    category => 'BATCH_CATEGORY',
    comment  => 'Reports & Maintenance Jobs');
```

Category	Level 1	Level 2
APPS_CATEGORY	70%	
BATCH_CATEGORY	30%	
OTHER		100%

```
CellCLI> alter iormplan dplan = ''

CellCLI> alter iormplan catplan=( -
    (name=APPS_CATEGORY,    level=1, allocation=70), -
    (name=BATCH_CATEGORY,   level=1, allocation=30), -
    (name=OTHER,            level=2, allocation=100))

CellCLI> alter iormplan active
```

Figure 7-10. *IORM resource management by category*

For this exercise, we'll create two new categories, APPS_CATEGORY, and BATCH_CATEGORY, and assign them to the APPS, REPORTS, and MAINTENANCE resource groups we created earlier in the chapter. The following listing creates our new categories and assigns them to the resource groups. Remember that you will need to run these commands on all databases participating in the IORM Category Plan. For illustration purposes, we'll keep the number of categories to two. The REPORTS and MAINTENANCE resource groups will be assigned to the category BATCH_CATEGORY.

```
BEGIN
  dbms_resource_manager.clear_pending_area();
  dbms_resource_manager.create_pending_area();

  -- Create Categories --
  dbms_resource_manager.create_category(
     category => 'APPS_CATEGORY',
     comment  => 'Category for Interactive Applications');
  dbms_resource_manager.create_category(
     category => 'BATCH_CATEGORY',
     comment  => 'Reports & Maintenance Jobs');

  -- Assign Consumer Groups to Categories --
  dbms_resource_manager.update_consumer_group(
     consumer_group => 'APPS',
     new_category   => 'APPS_CATEGORY');
  dbms_resource_manager.update_consumer_group(
     consumer_group => 'REPORTS',
     new_category   => 'BATCH_CATEGORY');
  dbms_resource_manager.update_consumer_group(
     consumer_group => 'MAINTENANCE',
     new_category   => 'BATCH_CATEGORY');
```

```
  dbms_resource_manager.submit_pending_area();
END;
/
```

PL/SQL procedure successfully completed.

To check your resource-group-to-category mappings, query the DBA_RSRC_CONSUMER_GROUPS view as follows. Notice that the OTHER_GROUPS consumer group was assigned to the OTHER category. That mapping is created automatically by Oracle and cannot be altered.

```
SYS:SCRATCH> SELECT consumer_group, category
               FROM DBA_RSRC_CONSUMER_GROUPS
              WHERE consumer_group
                 in ('APPS','REPORTS','MAINTENANCE','OTHER_GROUPS')
              ORDER BY category;

CONSUMER_GROUP                 CATEGORY
------------------------------ ------------------------------
APPS                           APPS_CATEGORY
REPORTS                        BATCH_CATEGORY
MAINTENANCE                    BATCH_CATEGORY
OTHER_GROUPS                   OTHER
```

Now we can create a new Category IORM Plan on the storage cells and set I/O limits on these categories. Before we do, though, we'll drop the Interdatabase IORM Plan we created in the previous example. Remember that each storage cell maintains its own IORM plan, so you will need to run these commands on every cell in your storage grid.

```
CellCLI> alter iormplan dbplan= ''

IORMPLAN successfully altered
```

Now we're ready to create our Category IORM Plan. The following command creates a plan in which APPS_CATEGORY and BATCH_CATEGORY are allocated 70% and 30%, respectively, of the total Cell I/O at level 1. The default category, OTHER, is allocated 100% on level 2.

```
CellCLI> alter iormplan catplan=(                         -
  (name=APPS_CATEGORY,     level=1, allocation=70), -
  (name=BATCH_CATEGORY,    level=1, allocation=30), -
  (name=OTHER,             level=2, allocation=100) -
)

IORMPLAN successfully altered
```

Again, we'll use the CellCLI command list iorm detail and confirm that our Category IORM Plan is configured the way we want it:

```
CellCLI> list iormplan detail
         name:                    enkcel01_IORMPLAN
         catPlan:                 name=APPS_CATEGORY,level=1,allocation=70
                                  name=BATCH_CATEGORY,level=1,allocation=30
                                  name=OTHER,level=2,allocation=100
```

```
dbPlan:
status:                     inactive
```

Because we dropped the Interdatabase plan from the previous exercise, the dbPlan field is empty. We'll reinstall that plan again when we are ready to test our resource plans. Note that the IORM Plan is inactive. We'll leave our Category Plan inactive for now. Later, in the IORM metrics section of the chapter, we'll test our Category IORM Plan and discuss how the effects of IORM can be monitored at the storage cells.

Intradatabase IORM

In the case of Interdatabase I/O resource management, cellsrv identifies I/O requests by a tag containing the database name issuing the request. Category I/O resource management works in a similar way, using a tag in the I/O request to identify the category issuing the request. The third, and final, type of I/O resource management available on the Exadata platform is Intradatabase IORM. Intradatabase I/O resource management is configured in each database using DBRM's management attributes, MGMT_P1..8. You may recall from earlier in the chapter that the MGMT_Pn attributes are what DBRM uses to manage CPU resources. DBRM uses CPU allocation directives to define priorities among consumer groups within the database. By tying I/O allocations to CPU allocations, IORM carries forward these priorities to the storage layer, thus maintaining a consistent provisioning scheme for both.

Configuring Intradatabase IORM

Intradatabase IORM is not terribly difficult to implement. In fact, in a manner of speaking, we have already done so. In the DBRM section of this chapter, we created consumer groups, resource plans, and plan directives that managed CPU resources within the SCRATCH database. On the Exadata platform, when a DBRM resource plan is activated, the database transmits a description of the plan, including MGMT_Pn directives, to all cells in the storage grid. This also happens any time cellsrv is started on the storage cells. So whether you're installing a new cell into the storage grid, rebooting a cell, or bouncing cellsrv services, your Intradatabase resource plan will be pushed to the cell automatically. If IORM is active on the cell, it will generate an Intradatabase Plan and begin managing I/O priorities according to your resource directives. Figure 7-11 illustrates the process of configuring and activating Intradatabase IORM.

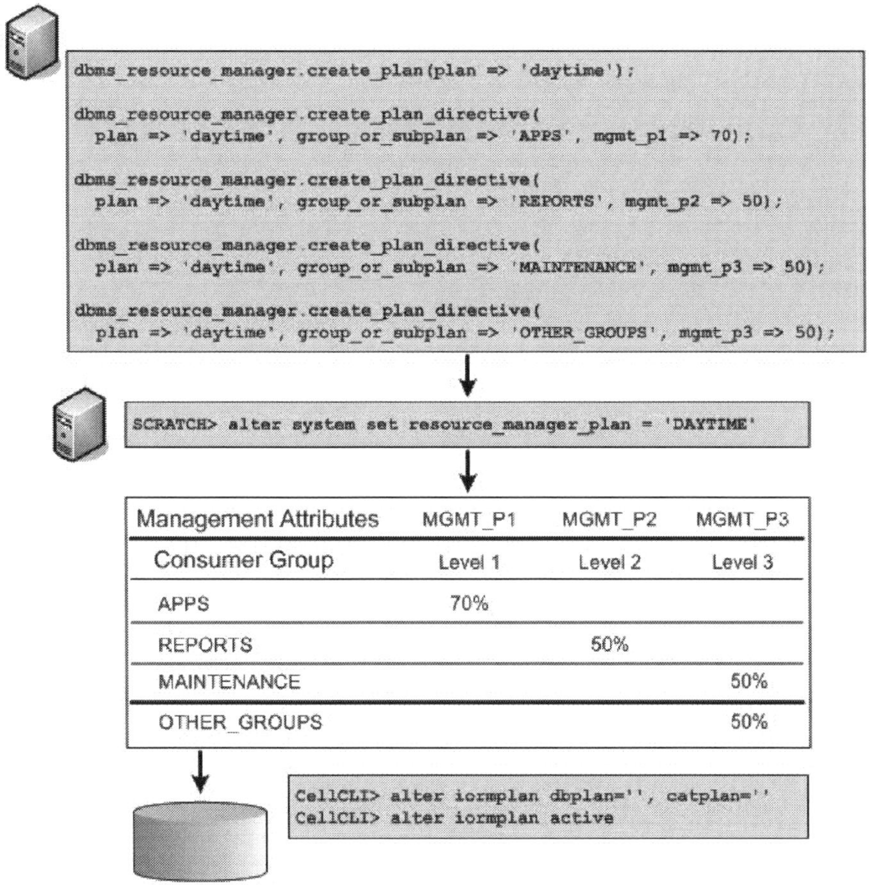

```
dbms_resource_manager.create_plan(plan => 'daytime');

dbms_resource_manager.create_plan_directive(
  plan => 'daytime', group_or_subplan => 'APPS', mgmt_p1 => 70);

dbms_resource_manager.create_plan_directive(
  plan => 'daytime', group_or_subplan => 'REPORTS', mgmt_p2 => 50);

dbms_resource_manager.create_plan_directive(
  plan => 'daytime', group_or_subplan => 'MAINTENANCE', mgmt_p3 => 50);

dbms_resource_manager.create_plan_directive(
  plan => 'daytime', group_or_subplan => 'OTHER_GROUPS', mgmt_p3 => 50);
```

```
SCRATCH> alter system set resource_manager_plan = 'DAYTIME'
```

Management Attributes	MGMT_P1	MGMT_P2	MGMT_P3
Consumer Group	Level 1	Level 2	Level 3
APPS	70%		
REPORTS		50%	
MAINTENANCE			50%
OTHER_GROUPS			50%

```
CellCLI> alter iormplan dbplan='', catplan=''
CellCLI> alter iormplan active
```

Figure 7-11. An Intradatabase I/O resource plan

In Figure 7-11, we see the calls to DBMS_RESOURCE_MANAGER that created our resource plan and plan directives for the SCRATCH and SNIFF databases. These directives are used to assign CPU and I/O allocation for the resource groups APPS, REPORTS, MAINTENANCE, and OTHER_GROUPS. When the DAYTIME plan is activated, its definition is sent to cellsrv on the storage cells. When cellsrv receives the resource plan, it generates an Intradatabase IORM Plan, configures I/O queues for each consumer group, and begins to manage I/O resources.

Bringing It All Together

As discussed earlier, each of the three IORM management methods may be used individually or in combination. Let's take a look at how all three methods work together to manage I/O. Now, this is the part where your college accounting professor would say "each lesson builds on the last, so if you skipped class last week, you may feel a little lost today." In this exercise, we'll be using all of the elements of DBRM and IORM we've discussed in this chapter. To avoid confusion and save you the trouble of thumbing through the pages you've already read, Table 7-4 shows a summary of how we've configured Oracle Resource Manager for the SCRATCH and SNIFF databases in this chapter.

Table 7-4. Summary of DBRM / IORM Resource Allocation

I/O Management Type	Allocation	Assignment
Category IORM		
Categories		**Consumer Groups**
▪ APPS_CATEGORY	70% at level 1	▪ APPS
▪ BATCH_CATEGORY	30% at level 1	▪ REPORTS, MAINTENANCE
▪ OTHER	100% at level 3	▪ OTHER_GROUPS
Interdatabase IORM		
Databases		**Databases**
▪ SCRATCH	60% at level 1	▪ SCRATCH
▪ SNIFF	80% at level 2	▪ SNIFF
▪ OTHER	100% at level 3	▪ All others
Intradatabase IORM		
Consumer Groups		**User Accounts**
▪ APPS	70% at level 1	▪ KOSBORNE
▪ REPORTS	50% at level 2	▪ RJOHNSON
▪ MAINTENANCE	50% at level 3	▪ TPODER
▪ OTHER_GROUPS	50% at level 3	▪ All other user accounts

There is a fixed order of precedence between the three IORM methods we've discussed. As I/O requests traverse the layers of the IORM stack, they are divided and allocated by the next method. At the top of the IORM hierarchy, 100% of I/O resources are available because the storage cell is not saturated by I/O requests. The next level of the hierarchy is Category IORM, which allocates I/O at a 70/30 split between the categories APPS_CATEGORY and BATCH_CATEGORY (at level 1). Any unconsumed I/O between these two groups is available to the OTHER category at level 2.

Next in the IORM hierarchy is the Interdatabase Plan. At the database level, the 70% allocated to the APPS_CATEGORY category is further divided, giving 60% to the SCRATCH database on level 1, and 80% to the SNIFF database at level 2. Any other database receives 20% of the unallocated I/O from level 2, as well as access to any I/O that was not consumed by the SCRATCH and SNIFF databases on levels 1 and 2.

The third and final tier of the IORM hierarchy is Intradatabase IORM. Our Intradatabase plan further divides I/O allocation into the four DBRM consumer groups we created in the databases. The APPS consumer group gets top priority at 70% on level 1. The REPORTS group is allocated 50% at level 2. MAINTENANCE and OTHER_GROUPS share a 50/50 split of I/O that was unallocated or unconsumed at levels 1 and 2.

Now, this is not to imply that all resource management methods must be configured together. You may instead choose to use just one of the methods, or any combination of two, for managing I/O. For example if we had configured Category IORM alone then as illustrated in Figure 7-12, no further restriction of I/O resources would be performed. I/O resources would be split at 70/30 between the categories, APPS_CATEGORY and BATCH_CATEGORY. Similarly, you may choose to implement Interdatabase IORM by itself, in which case I/O will be allocated strictly at a 60/80 split between sessions in the SCRATCH and SNIFF databases, respectively. If you have only one database and need to manage differing workloads, then Intradatabase IORM is your only option. When Intradatabase IORM is used by itself, I/O is managed according to your DBRM Plan directives alone. Figure 7-12 shows how I/O calls are allocated as they filter through each layer of IORM.

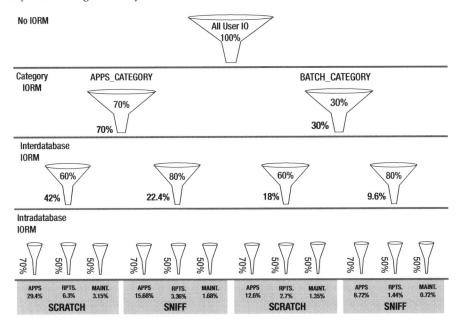

Figure 7-12. IORM method heirarchy

In Figure 7-12, allocations for the default consumer group OTHER_GROUPS and the default category OTHER are not shown, because of space constraints. In Figures 7-13, 14, and 15 we see the calculations used to allocate I/O resources as shown in Figure 7-12. The OTHER_GROUPS consumer group and OTHER category are shown here along with their allocation. Figures 7-13 through 7-15 shows a tabular representation of the resource plans along with their allocation percentage. Also displayed in these examples are the formulas used to calculate the allocation.

	A	B	C	D	E
5	**Category IORM**				
6					
7	Total IO	100.00%			
8	Category	Allocation	Level	% of Total	Formula
9	APPS_CATEGORY	70.00%	1	70.0%	=B7*B9
10	BATCH_CATEGORY	30.00%	1	30.00%	=B2*B10
11	OTHER	100.00%	2	0.00%	=(B2-(B9+B10))*B11

Figure 7-13. Category IORM calculations

	A	B	C	D	E
14	**Interdatabase IORM**				
15					
16	APPS_CATEGORY	70.00%			
17	Database	Allocation	Level	% of Total	Formula
18	SCRATCH	60.00%	1	42.00%	=B16*B18
19	SNIFF	80.00%	2	22.40%	=(B16-D18)*B19
20	OTHER	100.00%	3	5.60%	=(B16-(SUM(D18,D19)))*B20
22					
23	BATCH_CATEGORY	30.00%			
24	Database	Allocation	Level	% of Total	Formula
25	SCRATCH	60.00%	1	18.00%	=B23*B25
26	SNIFF	80.00%	2	9.60%	=(B23-D25)*B26
27	OTHER	100.00%	3	2.40%	=(B23-(SUM(D25,D26)))*B27

Figure 7-14. Interdatabase IORM calculations

	A	B	C	D	E
30	**Intradatabase IORM**				
31					
32	**APPS_CATEGORY: SCRATCH**	**42.00%**			
33	**Consumer Group**	**Allocation**	**Level**	**% of Total**	**Formula**
34	APPS	70.00%	1	29.40%	=B32*B34
35	REPORTS	50.00%	2	6.30%	=(B32-D34)*B35
36	MAINTENANCE	50.00%	3	3.15%	=(B32-(SUM(D34,D35)))*B36
37	OTHER_GROUPS	100.00%	4	3.15%	=(B32-(SUM(D34:D36)))*B37
39					
40	**APPS_CATEGORY: SNIFF**	**22.40%**			
41	**Consumer Group**	**Allocation**	**Level**	**% of Total**	**Formula**
42	APPS	70.00%	1	15.68%	=B40*B42
43	REPORTS	50.00%	2	3.36%	=(B40-D42)*B43
44	MAINTENANCE	50.00%	3	1.68%	=(B40-(SUM(D42,D43)))*B44
45	OTHER_GROUPS	100.00%	4	1.68%	=(B40-(SUM(D42:D44)))*B45
47					
48	**BATCH_CATEGORY: SCRATCH**	**18.00%**			
49	**Consumer Group**	**Allocation**	**Level**	**% of Total**	**Formula**
50	APPS	70.00%	1	12.60%	=B48*B50
51	REPORTS	50.00%	2	2.70%	=(B48-D50)*B51
52	MAINTENANCE	50.00%	3	1.35%	=(B48-(SUM(D50,D51)))*B52
53	OTHER_GROUPS	100.00%	4	1.35%	=(B48-(SUM(D50:D52)))*B53
55					
56	**BATCH_CATEGORY: SNIFF**	**9.60%**			
57	**Consumer Group**	**Allocation**	**Level**	**% of Total**	**Formula**
58	APPS	70.00%	1	6.72%	=B56*B58
59	REPORTS	50.00%	2	1.44%	=(B56-D58)*B59
60	MAINTENANCE	50.00%	3	0.72%	=(B56-(SUM(D58,D59)))*B60
61	OTHER_GROUPS	100.00%	4	0.72%	=(B56-(SUM(D58:D60)))*B61

Figure 7-15. Intradatabase IORM calculations

IORM Monitoring and Metrics

I/O performance metrics are collected and maintained for IORM in the storage cell. These metrics may be used to determine the effects your IORM plan has on the databases, categories, and resource group resource directives you defined in your environment. For example, you can see how much I/O a particular database is using compared to other databases. By observing the actual I/O distribution for your IORM consumer groups, you can determine whether adjustments need to be made to provide adequate I/O resources for applications using your databases. In this section we'll look at how these metrics are organized and tap into the valuable information stored there.

Understanding IORM Metrics

When an IORM plan is defined in the storage cell, cellsrv creates I/O consumer groups corresponding to the I/O directives defined in the Intradatabase, Category, and Intradatabase IORM Plans. For example, the following I/O consumer groups were created in the storage cells from our IORM plan for the SCRATCH and SNIFF databases:

Interdatabase: SCRATCH,

SNIFF

OTHER

Category: APPS_CATEGORY

BATCH_CATEGORY

OTHER

Intradatabase: APPS

REPORTS

MAINTENANCE

OTHER_GROUPS

Every 60 seconds, cellsrv collects key performance metrics from the I/O queues and stores them in the METRICCURRENT object. Note that we said *object*, not *table* or *file*. Cellsrv is a Java program, written by Java developers, not SQL developers. So unfortunately, these metrics are not stored in the familiar tabular format DBAs have come to know and love. Instead of tables, columns, and rows, these metrics are stored in objects and attributes. The following listing shows the structure of the METRICCURRENT object along with a few sample records.

```
CellCLI> describe metriccurrent
        name
        alertState
        collectionTime
        metricObjectName
        metricType
        metricValue
        objectType

CellCLI> LIST METRICCURRENT -
        WHERE name = 'CT_IO_RQ_LG' -
          AND objecttype = 'IORM_CATEGORY' -
   ATTRIBUTES name, objecttype, metricObjectName, metricValue

Name           objectType      metricObjectName  metricValue
-------------  --------------  ----------------  ------------------
CT_IO_RQ_LG    IORM_CATEGORY   APPS_CATEGORY     0 IO requests
CT_IO_RQ_LG    IORM_CATEGORY   BATCH_CATEGORY    16,079 IO requests
CT_IO_RQ_LG    IORM_CATEGORY   OTHER             2,498 IO requests
```

■ **Note:** Metrics are collected for I/O requests to flash cache, flash-based grid disks, and physical disks (grid disks). However, IORM only manages I/O resources for physical disks, so metrics for the physical disks will be the focus of this discussion.

When a new collection is run, the previous set of metrics is moved to the METRICHISTORY object, where it is kept for a period of time. Metric history is retained for the number of days specified in the METRICHISTORYDAYS attribute of cell, (the default is 7 days). For example, the next listing shows that cellsrv will maintain a rolling history of 7 days.

```
CellCLI> list cell attributes name, metricHistoryDays
         enkcel01        7
```

If you determine that 7 days is not sufficient history for your needs, you can modify the retention period with the CellCLI command alter cell. The following listing shows how you can change the retention for your storage cells to 14 days.

```
CellCLI> alter cell  metricHistoryDays='14'
Cell enkcel01 successfully altered

CellCLI> list cell attributes name, metricHistoryDays
         enkcel01        14
```

Workload Management

IORM metrics provide insight into how cellsrv is allocating I/O resources among the consumers in your storage grid. Cellsrv keeps track of I/O requests broadly categorized as "small requests" and "large requests." By comparing the large (LG) and small (SM) I/O requests in the IORM metrics, you can determine whether your databases lean more toward a DW workload (high throughput) or an OLTP workload (low latency). Oracle recently added a new option to the IORM plan called objective that tells IORM to optimize the cell disk I/O queues for low latency, high throughput, or something in between. The IORM metric IORM_MODE was added to capture the objective in use during the collection period. By comparing the IORM_MODE with the actual workload on your storage cells, you can determine whether the current IORM objective is appropriate or not. For example, if you find that a majority of I/O operations in the storage cells are greater than 128K and thus large (LG), then IORM should be set to optimize for high throughput (objective=high_throughput). Oracle uses a threshold of 75% large I/O when the IORM objective is set to auto, so that should give you an idea of what is meant by "majority." For more information on the IORM objective and possible settings, refer to the Workload Optimization section earlier in this chapter. The IORM_MODE metric can be observed using the following CellCLI command.

```
CellCLI> list metriccurrent iorm_mode
         IORM_MODE        enkcel01        0
```

Possible settings for the IORM_MODE attribute are as follows:

- 1, IORM objective was set to low_latency,

- 2, IORM objective was set to balanced

- 3, IORM mode was set to high_throughput

An `IORM_MODE` ranging between 1 and 2, or between 2 and 3, indicates the mode was changed during the polling period. It also indicates the proximity to the IORM objective. This might occur, for example, if the objective was set to `auto` and during the polling period the workload shifted significantly from small I/O requests to large I/O requests. By comparing the `IORM_MODE` metric over time, you can determine how volatile your workload is. A constantly changing workload may give insight into where I/O Resource Management is needed the most.

The metrics we're interested in for IORM monitoring have an `objectType` of `IORM_DATABASE`, `IORM_CATEGORY`, and `IORM_CONSUMER_GROUP`. These metrics are further organized by the `name` attribute in the `METRICCURRENT` object. The name of the metric is a concatenation of abbreviations that indicate the type of I/O consumer group, the type of storage device, and a descriptive name. The elements of the `name` attribute appear as follows:

`{consumer_type}_{device type}_{metric}`

Where *consumer_type* represents the IORM resource group and is one of these:

> DB = Interdatabase IORM Plan
>
> CT = Category IORM Plan
>
> CG = Intradatabase IORM Plan

And *device_type* is the type of storage that serviced the I/O request and is one of the following:

> FC = flash cache
>
> FD = Flash-based grid disk
>
> '' = If neither of the above, then the metric represents I/O to physical disks

The last part of the attribute, *{metric}*, is the descriptive name of the metric. The metric name may be further qualified by SM' or LG, indicating that it represents small I/O requests or large I/O requests. For example:

> **CG_FC_IO_RQ_LG:** The total number of large I/O requests serviced from flash cache (FC), for DBRM consumer groups.
>
> **CG_FD_IO_RQ_LG:** The total number of large I/O requests serviced from flash-based grid disks (FD), for DBRM consumer groups.
>
> **CG_IO_RQ_LG:** The total number of large I/O requests serviced from physical disks (grid disks), for DBRM consumer groups.

Table 7-5 describes each of the IORM consumer group performance metrics captured by `cellsrv` using these abbreviations.

Table 7-5. *Description of the Name Attribute of IORM METRICCURRENT*

Name	Description
{CG, CT, DB}_IO_BY_SEC	Megabytes per second scheduled for this I/O consumer.
{CG, CT, DB}_IO_LOAD	Average I/O load for this I/O consumer.
{CG, CT, DB}_IO_RQ_{SM, LG}	The cumulative number of small or large I/O requests from this I/O consumer.
{CG, CT, DB}_IO_RQ_{SM, LG}_SEC	The number of small or large I/O requests per second issued by this I/O consumer.
{CG, CT, DB}_IO_WT_{SM,LG}	The cumulative time (in milliseconds) that I/O requests from the I/O consumer have spent waiting to be scheduled by IORM.
{CG, CT, DB}_IO_WT_{SM,LG}_RQ	Derived from {CG,CT,DB}_IO_WT_{SM,LG} above. It stores the average number of waits (in milliseconds) that I/O requests have spent waiting to be scheduled by IORM in the past minute. A large number of waits indicates that the I/O workload of this I/O consumer is exceeding its allocation. For lower-priority consumers this may be the desired effect. For high-priority consumers, it may indicate that more I/O should be allocated to the resource to meet the objectives of your organization.
{CG, CT, DB}_IO_UTIL_{SM, LG}	The percentage of total I/O resources consumed by this I/O consumer.

All cumulative metrics above are reset to 0 whenever cellsrv is restarted, the IORM plan is enabled, or the IORM plan changes for that I/O consumer group. For example, if the Category IORM plan is changed, the following cumulative metrics will be reset:

    CT_IO_RQ_SM

    CT_IO_RQ_LG

    CT_IO_WT_SM

    CT_IO_WT_LG

These IORM metrics are further categorized using the metricObjectName attribute. Interdatabase resource plan metrics for the SCRATCH, and SNIFF databases are stored in detail records, where metricObjectName is set to the corresponding database name. In a similar fashion, metrics for Category IORM Plans are identified with a metricObjectName matching the Category name. IORM consumer groups are identified by a concatenation of the database name and the name of the DBRM consumer group. For example, the following listing shows how the I/O Resource Groups for our SCRATCH and SNIFF databases would be represented in the METRICCURRENT and METRICHISTORY objects.

```
objectType              metricObjectName
----------------------  ---------------------------
IORM_DATABASE           SCRATCH
IORM_DATABASE           SNIFF
IORM_CATEGORY           APPS_CATEGORY
IORM_CATEGORY           BATCH_CATEGORY
IORM_CATEGORY           OTHER
IORM_CONSUMER_GROUP     SCRATCH.APPS
IORM_CONSUMER_GROUP     SCRATCH.MAINTENANCE
IORM_CONSUMER_GROUP     SCRATCH.REPORTS
IORM_CONSUMER_GROUP     SCRATCH.OTHER_GROUPS
IORM_CONSUMER_GROUP     SNIFF.APPS
IORM_CONSUMER_GROUP     SNIFF.MAINTENANCE
IORM_CONSUMER_GROUP     SNIFF.REPORTS
IORM_CONSUMER_GROUP     SNIFF.OTHER_GROUPS
```

Background Processes

As we discussed earlier, database background processes are automatically assigned to built-in IORM consumer groups according to priority. Table 7-6 shows these special IORM consumer groups, along with a description of what they are used for.

Table 7-6. Built-In Consumer Groups for Background Processes

Consumer Group	Description
ASM	I/O related to Oracle ASM volume management
_ORACLE_BG_CATEGORY_	High-priority I/O requests issued from the database background processes
_ORACLE_MEDPRIBG_CATEGORY_	Medium-priority I/O requests issued from the database background processes
_ORACLE_LOWPRIBG_CATEGORY_	Low-priority I/O requests issued from the database background processes

Mining the Metrics

Now that you have a pretty good idea of what types of metrics are collected by cellsrv, and how to get to them, let's take a look at how this information can be reported and interpreted. First, however, we should mention that as a reporting tool, CellCLI is very limited. For example, multiple filters can be applied to your search criteria using =, LIKE, or AND, but the lack of an OR verb, and the lack of parentheses for setting precedence, make it somewhat cumbersome; if not utterly inadequate for reporting. Also, there is no aggregation functionality. For example, there is no way to roll up the small and large I/O requests for a database and present them as "Total I/O Requests." The long and short of it is, you are better off to just dump out all the rows you are interested in, load them into a database, and use SQL*Plus to report them. Now, let's take a look at some simple LIST commands for extracting IORM metrics along with a sample of the output they generate.

Reporting IORM Database Metrics

This first listing reports I/O metrics for our Database IORM Plan, (name like 'DB_IO_.*'). The objectType = 'IORM_DATABASE' isn't really necessary; we've just included it to illustrate that this is the only objectType stored for this metric.

```
CellCLI> LIST METRICCURRENT -
        WHERE name LIKE 'DB_IO_.*' -
          AND objectType = 'IORM_DATABASE' -
   ATTRIBUTES name, objectType, metricObjectName, metricValue, collectionTime
...
DB_IO_BY_SEC  IORM_DATABASE SCRATCH   453 MB/sec 2011-03-29T07:04:46-05:00
DB_IO_BY_SEC  IORM_DATABASE SMITHERS  17 MB/sec  2011-03-29T07:04:46-05:00
DB_IO_BY_SEC  IORM_DATABASE SNIFF     0 MB/sec   2011-03-29T07:04:46-05:00
DB_IO_LOAD    IORM_DATABASE SCRATCH   7          2011-03-29T07:04:46-05:00
...
```

Reporting IORM Category Metrics

To report I/O metrics for our Category Resource Plan, the name filter is changed to 'CT_IO_.*'. Adding an additional filter on the ObjectName metric (not like '_.*'), eliminates Oracle's automatically maintained categories such as _ASM_, and _ORACLE_BG_CATEGORY_.

```
CellCLI> LIST METRICCURRENT -
        WHERE name LIKE 'CT_IO_.*' -
          AND metricObjectName NOT LIKE '_.*' -
   ATTRIBUTES name, objecttype, metricObjectName, metricValue, collectionTime
...
CT_IO_UTIL_LG IORM_CATEGORY APPS_CATEGORY  0 %  2011-03-29T06:39:45-05:00
CT_IO_UTIL_LG IORM_CATEGORY BATCH_CATEGORY 12 % 2011-03-29T06:39:45-05:00
CT_IO_UTIL_LG IORM_CATEGORY OTHER          13 % 2011-03-29T06:39:45-05:00
CT_IO_UTIL_SM IORM_CATEGORY APPS_CATEGORY  0 %  2011-03-29T06:39:45-05:00
CT_IO_UTIL_SM IORM_CATEGORY BATCH_CATEGORY 0 %  2011-03-29T06:39:45-05:00
CT_IO_UTIL_SM IORM_CATEGORY OTHER          0 %  2011-03-29T06:39:45-05:00
...
```

Reporting IORM Consumer Group Metrics

To report I/O metrics for our consumer groups, we replace the name filter with CG_IO_.*, which displays I/O metrics for consumer groups. The additional filters for metricObjectName remove other databases from the output as well as consumer groups that Oracle creates for background processes, such as _ORACLE_BACKGROUND_GROUP_. The collectionTime was omitted from the sample output because of space constraints.

```
    LIST METRICCURRENT                              -
    WHERE name like 'CG_IO_.*'                      -
        and objectType = 'IORM_CONSUMER_GROUP'      -
        and metricObjectName like 'SCRATCH.*'       -
        and metricObjectName not like 'SCRATCH\._.*'  -
ATTRIBUTES name, objecttype, metricObjectName, metricValue, collectionTime
...
CG_IO_LOAD    IORM_CONSUMER_GROUP    SCRATCH.APPS          0 ...
CG_IO_LOAD    IORM_CONSUMER_GROUP    SCRATCH.MAINTENANCE   4 ...
CG_IO_LOAD    IORM_CONSUMER_GROUP    SCRATCH.OTHER_GROUPS  4 ...
CG_IO_LOAD    IORM_CONSUMER_GROUP    SCRATCH.REPORTS       0 ...
...
```

Testing IORM Plans

Earlier in the chapter, we postponed testing our IORM plans. Now that you understand how to monitor IORM, we can run a stress test and take a look at the metrics collected by cellsrv to see what effect our IORM plans had on performance. For this test, we'll generate a load on the storage cells by running several concurrent full-table scans on our SCRATCH and SNIFF databases. We'll let them run for a few minutes and then collect the database, category, and consumer group metrics for our test databases. As with our DBRM tests earlier in this chapter, validating the precise allocations for each I/O consumer is a very complicated undertaking, because any I/O resources that are allocated but unused are passed to other consumer groups, categories, and databases. This is particularly true when implementing multi-level resource plans. The focus of this test will be to verify that cellsrv is collecting metrics for each database, category, and consumer group, and that the relative I/O utilization numbers for each consumer group are within a reasonable range considering their resource allocations. Refer back to Figures 7-13 through 7-15 for the I/O allocations for each of our resource plans.

Test Outline

Now that we've created our I/O resource plan, we can test to see how it works. Following are the steps we will follow to test our resource plan.

1. Activate the DAYTIME resource plan in the SCRATCH and SNIFF databases. Also, activate the Database and Category IORM plans in each storage cell.

2. In both databases, start three concurrent full table scans from each account that maps to our consumer groups. These user accounts map to the consumer groups as follows:

    KOSBORNE   → APPS

    RJOHNSON   → REPORTS

    TPODER   → MAINTENANCE

    FRED   → OTHER_GROUPS

3. Allow the queries to run for a few minutes, and then, while they are still running, we'll dump the IORM metrics for database, category, and consumer groups to a file. This data will be cleaned up and loaded into an Oracle database for reporting.

Step 1: Activate Resource Manager

Before we start the load test, we need to verify that our DAYTIME resource plan is activated in the databases.

```
SYS:SCRATCH> show parameter resource_manager_plan

NAME                                 TYPE        VALUE
------------------------------------ ----------- -----------------------------
resource_manager_plan                string      DAYTIME

SYS:SNIFF> show parameter resource_manager_plan

NAME                                 TYPE        VALUE
------------------------------------ ----------- -----------------------------
resource_manager_plan                string      DAYTIME
```

We also need to to check our IORM Plan on each storage cell to ensure they are active.

```
CellCLI> list iormplan detail
         name:             enkcel03_IORMPLAN
         catPlan:          name=APPS_CATEGORY,level=1,allocation=70
                           name=BATCH_CATEGORY,level=1,allocation=30
                           name=OTHER,level=2,allocation=100
         dbPlan:           name=SCRATCH,level=1,allocation=60
                           name=SNIFF,level=2,allocation=80
                           name=other,level=3,allocation=100
         objective:        auto
         status:           active
```

Step 2: Start Load Test

Next, we'll start our load test by running the burn_io.sh script in eight separate terminal sessions, one for each user account in the SCRATCH and SNIFF databases. This script is similar to the burn_cpu.sh script we used to test our DBRM resource plan earlier. The script takes three parameters: USERNAME, PASSWORD, and PARALLEL. The PARALLEL parameter determines how many queries will be run concurrently. For our test, we'll run three sessions from each user account. The query is

```
select distinct segment_name from kosborne.bigtab
```

The SQL script turns off output from the query, (set TERMOUT off) to reduce the overhead on the database server. The bigtab table contains 194 million (repeating) rows from the dba_segments view.

```
[enkdb02:SCRATCH] /home/rjohnson/myscripts
> burn_io.sh {kosborne, tpoder, rjohnson, fred} x 3
```

```
[enkdb02:SNIFF] /home/rjohnson/myscripts
> burn_io.sh {kosborne, tpoder, rjohnson, fred} x 3
```

Step 3: Dump IORM Metrics to a File.

We'll allow the stress test to run for a while and then gather the IORM metrics from the storage cells. The following listing shows the CellCLI command for reporting IORM metrics. These metrics are maintained on each cell, so we'll need to run this command on each storage cell and merge the results for further analysis.

```
CellCLI> spool iorm_enkcel01_metrics.dat

CellCLI>  LIST METRICCURRENT -
        WHERE objectType LIKE 'IORM_.*'

CellCLI> spool spool off
```

Analyzing the Results

After cleaning up the output from cellsrv, we can load it into a table in order to run some queries against it. The structure of this table is as follows:

```
SYS:SCRATCH> desc iorm_metrics
 Name                     Null?    Type
 ----------------------- -------- --------------
 CELL_ID                           VARCHAR2(8)
 NAME                              VARCHAR2(19)
 OBJECT_TYPE                       VARCHAR2(19)
 METRIC_NAME                       VARCHAR2(40)
 COLLECTION_TIME                   VARCHAR2(25)
 METRIC_VALUE                      NUMBER
 INC                               VARCHAR2(18)
```

For ease in reporting, we'll create a view for each of our three I/O consumer groups, filtering out activity from ASM, flash cache and flash-based grid disks, and background processes.

```
-- IORM Category View --
CREATE OR REPLACE FORCE VIEW RJOHNSON.CT_IORM_METRICS AS
    SELECT name,
           OBJECT_TYPE,
           METRIC_NAME,
           SUM (METRIC_VALUE) metric_value,
           MAX (INC) inc
      FROM iorm_metrics
     WHERE name LIKE 'CT\_%' ESCAPE '\'            ← IORM Category records
       AND name NOT LIKE 'CT\_FC\_%' ESCAPE '\'    ← Flash Cache records
       AND name NOT LIKE 'CT\_FD\_%' ESCAPE '\'    ← Flash-based grid disks
       AND metric_name NOT LIKE '%\_' ESCAPE '\'   ← ASM, background processes, etc.
  GROUP BY name, OBJECT_TYPE, METRIC_NAME
  ORDER BY name, OBJECT_TYPE, METRIC_NAME;
```

```
-- IORM Database View (interdatabase IORM metrics)
CREATE OR REPLACE FORCE VIEW RJOHNSON.DB_IORM_METRICS AS
    SELECT name,
           OBJECT_TYPE,
           METRIC_NAME,
           SUM (TO_NUMBER (TRIM (METRIC_VALUE))) metric_value,
           MAX (INC) inc
      FROM iorm_metrics
     WHERE name LIKE 'DB\_%' ESCAPE '\'                ← IORM Database records
       AND name NOT LIKE 'DB\_FC\_%' ESCAPE '\'
       AND name NOT LIKE 'DB\_FD\_%' ESCAPE '\'
       AND METRIC_NAME IN ('SCRATCH', 'SNIFF')
  GROUP BY name, OBJECT_TYPE, METRIC_NAME
  ORDER BY name, OBJECT_TYPE, METRIC_NAME;

-- IORM Consumer Group View (intradatabase IORM metrics)
CREATE OR REPLACE FORCE VIEW RJOHNSON.CG_IORM_METRICS AS
    SELECT name,
           OBJECT_TYPE,
           METRIC_NAME,
           SUM (METRIC_VALUE) metric_value,
           MAX (INC) inc
      FROM iorm_metrics
     WHERE name LIKE 'CG\_%' ESCAPE '\'                ← IORM Consumer Group records
       AND name NOT LIKE 'CG\_FC\_%' ESCAPE '\'
       AND name NOT LIKE 'CG\_FD\_%' ESCAPE '\'
       AND (metric_name LIKE 'SCRATCH%' OR metric_name LIKE 'SNIFF%')
       AND metric_name NOT LIKE '%\_' ESCAPE '\'
  GROUP BY name, OBJECT_TYPE, METRIC_NAME
  ORDER BY name, OBJECT_TYPE, METRIC_NAME;
```

You may have noticed the SUM(METRIC_VALUE) function in the view definitions. While it is important to understand the workload mix of your databases, the purpose of this exercise is to verify the effectiveness of our IORM Resource Plan. To that end, we'll subtotal the small and large I/O metrics so that we can see how all I/O is distributed. Importing the IORM metrics from our table into a spreadsheet, we can create pie graphs for each IORM consumer group. The resulting graphs should reflect the proportions for each IORM consumer in our IORM plan. There are several interesting metrics captured in the METRICCURRENT object at the storage cell, but we'll focus on IO_BY_SEC. This metric represents the I/O requests that were sent to the cell disk queues for execution. It should give us a pretty good idea of how I/O requests were prioritized.

One more thing before we take a look at the results of our test. While the filters we applied to our views simplified the output, they also eliminated some I/O from the results. For example, the _ORACLE_BACKGROUND_GROUP_ metric accounted for a measurable amount of I/O in the storage cells but is not reflected in the analysis. That's acceptable, though, because the point of this exercise is not to precisely reconcile the results of our test with the IORM allocations called for in our plan directives (a very tedious process). Rather, the purpose is to show how I/O is actually allocated in the storage cells during peak periods when IORM is active. So while the results are expected to resemble our IORM plans, they are not expected to match precisely.

Category Metrics

IORM prioritizes I/O in a hierarchical manner (illustrated in Figure 7-12). Our Category Plan is at the top of the hierarchy, so that's where we'll start. Recall that our plan allocates I/O for the APPS and BATCH categories at a 70% / 30% ratio on level 1. At level 2, the OTHER category is allocated 100% of the unused I/O from the APPS and BATCH categories. Figure 7-16 shows the ratio of I/O requests serviced per second (in megabytes), on behalf of each category. Remember that the load from each category was the same. Notice that APPS_CATEGORY received approximately 63% of the I/O, while BATCH_CATEGORY received about 30%. The OTHER category received the remaining 8.3% of I/O. You may be surprised at the amount of I/O that OTHER received. This was because of the allocated but unused I/O resources it inherited from the APPS and/or BATCH categories at level 1.

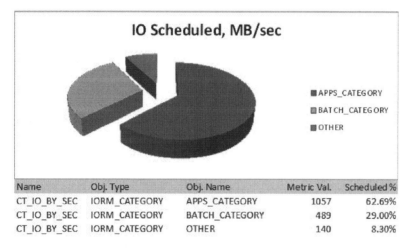

IO Scheduled, MB/sec

■ APPS_CATEGORY
■ BATCH_CATEGORY
■ OTHER

Name	Obj. Type	Obj. Name	Metric Val.	Scheduled %
CT_IO_BY_SEC	IORM_CATEGORY	APPS_CATEGORY	1057	62.69%
CT_IO_BY_SEC	IORM_CATEGORY	BATCH_CATEGORY	489	29.00%
CT_IO_BY_SEC	IORM_CATEGORY	OTHER	140	8.30%

Figure 7-16. *I/O operations scheduled per second, by category*

Database Metrics

Next in the IORM hierarchy is our Interdatabase IORM Plan. This plan calls for the SCRATCH database to be allocated 60% of the I/O at level 1, and the SNIFF database to receive 80% at level 2. Figure 7-17 shows the ratio of I/O requests scheduled on behalf of the SCRATCH and SNIFF databases. Again, the number of requests coming from these databases was the same. According to the metrics collected during our stress test, I/O was allocated to the SCRATCH and SNIFF databases at a ratio of 64% / 36% respectively.

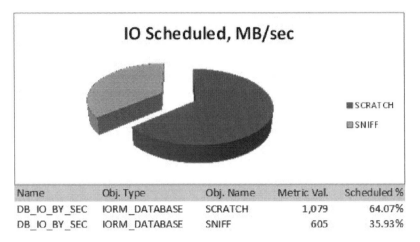

Name	Obj. Type	Obj. Name	Metric Val.	Scheduled %
DB_IO_BY_SEC	IORM_DATABASE	SCRATCH	1,079	64.07%
DB_IO_BY_SEC	IORM_DATABASE	SNIFF	605	35.93%

Figure 7-17. I/O operations scheduled per second, by database

Consumer Group Metrics

The final level in the IORM hierarchy is our Intradatabase IORM Plan. Figure 7-18 shows the allocation directives for IORM consumer groups in our Intradatabase IORM Plan. Remember that our IORM consumer groups are tied to the DBRM consumer groups through the MGMT_P1..8 (CPU) attributes.

	Management Attributes		
	MGMT_P1	MGMT_P2	MGMT_P3
Consumer Group	Level 1 CPU Allocation	Level 2 CPU Allocation	Level 3 CPU Allocation
APPS	70%		
REPORTS		50%	
MAINTENANCE			50%
OTHER_GROUPS			50%

Resource Directives

Figure 7-18. IORM intradatabase plan

Figure 7-19 shows the actual ratio of I/O requests scheduled for our IORM consumer groups during our stress test. A quick glance at the pie chart tells us that our IORM plan was definitely managing I/O resources at the consumer group level. You can see that the APPS consumer group does in fact take priority over all other groups. As expected, I/O is disproportionately allocated to the APPS group in the SCRATCH database (43.87%) compared to the APPS group in the SNIFF database (19.13%). This is because of the influence our Interdatabase Resource Plan has over our Intradatabase Resource Plan. Recall that our Interdatabase Plan grants a higher priority to the SCRATCH database (60% at level 1) than the SNIFF database (80% at level 2). The other IORM consumer groups follow a similar pattern.

231

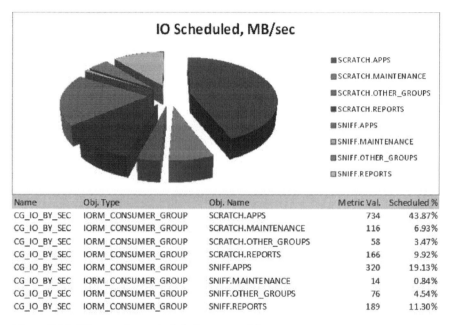

Name	Obj. Type	Obj. Name	Metric Val.	Scheduled %
CG_IO_BY_SEC	IORM_CONSUMER_GROUP	SCRATCH.APPS	734	43.87%
CG_IO_BY_SEC	IORM_CONSUMER_GROUP	SCRATCH.MAINTENANCE	116	6.93%
CG_IO_BY_SEC	IORM_CONSUMER_GROUP	SCRATCH.OTHER_GROUPS	58	3.47%
CG_IO_BY_SEC	IORM_CONSUMER_GROUP	SCRATCH.REPORTS	166	9.92%
CG_IO_BY_SEC	IORM_CONSUMER_GROUP	SNIFF.APPS	320	19.13%
CG_IO_BY_SEC	IORM_CONSUMER_GROUP	SNIFF.MAINTENANCE	14	0.84%
CG_IO_BY_SEC	IORM_CONSUMER_GROUP	SNIFF.OTHER_GROUPS	76	4.54%
CG_IO_BY_SEC	IORM_CONSUMER_GROUP	SNIFF.REPORTS	189	11.30%

Figure 7-19. I/O operations scheduled per second, by consumer group

Other Processes Managed by IORM

There are a few internal processes managed by IORM that don't quite fit anywhere else in this chapter so we'll discuss them here. These internal processes are:

- Fast File Creation

- ETL (extract, transform, load)

- Recovery Manager

Exadata provides a feature called Fast File Creation for creating and extending database datafiles. It provides extremely fast I/O for creating and growing files in the storage grid. Generally speaking, this is a good thing. But how does Exadata manage the priority of certain, low priority, highly I/O intensive processes? The answer is IORM.

Fast File Creation

Exadata provides a feature called *Fast File Creation*, which brings all the I/O resources of the storage cells to bear in order to make quick work of creating and extending tablespace database files. But as you might imagine, if run unchecked, Fast File Creation can steal valuable resources from other database critical, and business critical processes. To prevent this, the FASTFILECRE function, which performs Fast File Creation, is mapped to a hidden IORM consumer group and assigned a priority below that of all other database foreground and background processes. When the storage cells are busy, Fast File

Creation is throttled back so it doesn't degrade other processes. But when the storage cells are not busy, IORM allows it to consume all available I/O resources.

If you want to increase the priority of Fast File Creation, add a new consumer group mapping rule to switch it to another consumer group (with higher priority). The mapping rule must use the mapping attribute DBMS_RESOURCE_MANAGER.ORACLE_FUNCTION with a value set to the name of the Fast File Creation function, FASTFILECRE. For example, we can reassign the FASTFILECRE function to the MAINTENANCE consumer group we created earlier in the chapter as follows.

```
BEGIN
  DBMS_RESOURCE_MANAGER.CREATE_PENDING_AREA();
  DBMS_RESOURCE_MANAGER.SET_CONSUMER_GROUP_MAPPING(
    DBMS_RESOURCE_MANAGER.ORACLE_FUNCTION,
    'FASTFILECRE', 'MAINTENANCE');
  DBMS_RESOURCE_MANAGER.SUBMIT_PENDING_AREA();
END;
/
```

■ **Note:** The priority for extending existing datafiles cannot be modified. The mapping procedure described here only increases priority for creating new tablespaces or adding datafiles to existing tablespaces.

ETL

Depending on the database, extract, transform, and load (ETL) processes may be considered low-priority, or they may be absolutely-mission critical to the business. Oracle provides two built-in DBRM resource plans to manage the priority for typical ETL processes. The ETL_GROUP is set up with lower priority in the built-in DW_PLAN resource plan and, as the name implies, is given a much higher priority in the built-in ETL_CRITICAL_PLAN resource plan. Figures 7-20 and 7-21 show the default settings for these two resource plans.

Resource Allocations

Group/Subplan	Level 1	Level 2	Level 3	Level 4	Level 5	Level 6	Level 7	Level 8
BATCH_GROUP				45				
DSS_CRITICAL_GROUP		75						
DSS_GROUP			75					
ETL_GROUP				45				
ORA$AUTOTASK_SUB_PLAN		5						
ORA$DIAGNOSTICS		5						
OTHER_GROUPS				10				
SYS_GROUP	75							

Figure 7-20. DW_PLAN resource plan

Resource Allocations								
Group/Subplan	Level 1	Level 2	Level 3	Level 4	Level 5	Level 6	Level 7	Level 8
BATCH_GROUP		10						
DSS_CRITICAL_GROUP		35						
DSS_GROUP		10						
ETL_GROUP		35						
ORA$AUTOTASK_SUB_PLAN		3						
ORA$DIAGNOSTICS		3						
OTHER_GROUPS		3						
SYS_GROUP	75							

Figure 7-21. ETL_CRITICAL_PLAN resource plan

Data Pump runs under the built-in `DATALOAD` function, which by default maps to the `ETL_GROUP` consumer group. Other programs, such as SQL Loader, may also be mapped to the `ETL_GROUP` using mapping rules we discussed earlier in the chapter. For example, the SQL Loader command is mapped to the `ETL_GROUP` consumer group as follows:

```
BEGIN
  DBMS_RESOURCE_MANAGER.CREATE_PENDING_AREA();
  DBMS_RESOURCE_MANAGER.SET_CONSUMER_GROUP_MAPPING
    (DBMS_RESOURCE_MANAGER.CLIENT_PROGRAM, 'SQLLDR', 'ETL_GROUP');
  DBMS_RESOURCE_MANAGER.SUBMIT_PENDING_AREA();
END;
/
```

Recovery Manager

Exadata requires ASM for a database to access the storage grid. As such, Recovery Manager (Rman) is the required tool for executing database backup and recovery. Backups are a very I/O-intensive operation. For a number of years now, Rman has provided two ways to manage the load backups put on the I/O subsystem: backup channels and rate. The number of backup channels can be used to increase or decrease performance and load. Finer-grained control is provided through the rate parameter, which controls the rate in bytes per second that Rman streams to the backup channels. Exadata provides IORM management for Rman by mapping backup operations to the `BACKUP` function and copy operations to the `COPY` function. By default, the `BACKUP`, and `COPY` functions map to the built-in `BATCH_GROUP` consumer group. Similar to the `FASTFILECRE` function we described for Fast File Creation, the `BACKUP` and `COPY` functions may be mapped to any other consumer group in order to adjust their IORM priorities. For example, we can remap the `BACKUP` function to our `MAINTENANCE` consumer group as follows:

```
BEGIN
  DBMS_RESOURCE_MANAGER.CREATE_PENDING_AREA();
  DBMS_RESOURCE_MANAGER.SET_CONSUMER_GROUP_MAPPING
    (DBMS_RESOURCE_MANAGER.ORACLE_FUNCTION, 'BACKUP', 'MAINTENANCE');

  DBMS_RESOURCE_MANAGER.SET_CONSUMER_GROUP_MAPPING
    (DBMS_RESOURCE_MANAGER.ORACLE_FUNCTION, 'COPY', 'MAINTENANCE');
DBMS_RESOURCE_MANAGER.SUBMIT_PENDING_AREA();
END;
/
```

Summary

One of the biggest challenges for DBAs is effectively managing system resources to meet business objectives. Over the years Oracle has developed a rich set of features that make resource management a reality. Unfortunately, these features are rarely implemented due to their complexity. But make no mistake, as servers become more powerful and efficient, database consolidation is going to become increasingly common. This is especially true of the Exadata platform. Understanding how to leverage database and I/O resource management is going to become an increasingly important tool for ensuring that your databases meet the demands of your business. The best advice we can offer is to keep things simple. Attempting to make use of every bell and whistle in Oracle Resource Manager can lead to confusion and undesirable results. If you do not have a specific need for multi-level resource plans, then stick to the single-level approach; they are easy to implement and measure, and they work great in most situations. Category plans are another rarely needed feature. A majority of the situations you will face can be resolved by implementing a simple, single-level Interdatabase Resource Plan. So again, start small, keep it simple, and add features as you need them.

CHAPTER 8

Configuring Exadata

Oracle offers an optional service that handles the process of installing and configuring your Exadata Database Machine from start to finish. Many companies purchase this service to speed up their implementation time and reduce the complexity of integrating Exadata into their IT infrastructure. If you're reading this chapter, you may be considering performing the configuration yourself, or perhaps you're just interested in gaining a better understanding of how it's done. The process we'll discuss here closely resembles the installation process Oracle uses, largely because we will be using the same utility Oracle uses to configure Exadata. The utility is called OneCommand. It takes site-specific information you provide and performs the entire configuration from network, to software, to storage. When the process is complete, your Exadata Database Machine will be fully functional, including a starter database.

Exadata Network Components

Oracle database network requirements have evolved over the years, and with Exadata you will notice a few new terms as well as the addition of a new network. Traditionally, Oracle database servers required one public network link to provide administrative access (typically SSH), and database access (SQL*Net). With the introduction of 11gR2 Grid Infrastructure (formerly known as Oracle Clusterware), Oracle coined a new term for this network, the *client access network*. On the Exadata platform, administrative and database traffic have been separated with the creation of a new network for administrative access. This new network is known as the *management network*. The client access network is no longer accessible through SSH and is used only by the Oracle listener for incoming SQL*Net connections. In Exadata terms (and mostly in the context of configuration), these two networks are referred to as NET0 (management network), and NET1 (client access network).

The number and type of Ethernet ports on the compute nodes and storage cells varies between the V2, X2-2, and X2-8 models of Exadata. Hardware specifications for each model are detailed in the *Exadata Database Machine Owner's Guide*. At a minimum, though, all models provide at least four embedded 1 Gigabit Ethernet ports. Oracle identifies these ports as NET0, NET1, NET2, and NET3. As noted, NET0 is used for the management network, and NET1 is used for the client access network. In RAC environments it is a common practice to bond two Ethernet devices together to provide hardware redundancy for the client access network. On Exadata, this is done by bonding the NET1 and NET2 ports together. The NET3 interface is unassigned and available to be configured as an optional network.

The Management Network

Exadata Database Machines have an Ethernet switch mounted in the rack that services the management network. The management network consists of the following links:

- One uplink from the management switch to your company's management network.

- One link to NET0 on each compute node and storage cell

- One link to the ILOM on each compute node and storage cell

- One link for the KVM

- One link for each of the two internal power distribution units (PDUs). This is optional and is only needed if you want to monitor electrical current remotely.

ILOM

In addition to the management network interface (NET0), compute nodes and storage cells come equipped with an Integrated Lights Out Manager (ILOM). The ILOM is an adapter card in each compute node and storage cell that operates independently of the operating system. The ILOM boots up as soon as power is applied to the server and provides Web and SSH access through the management network. The ILOM allows you to perform many of the tasks remotely that would otherwise require physical access to the servers, including gaining access to the console, powering the system off and on, and rebooting or resetting the system. Additionally, the ILOM monitors the configuration and state of the server's internal hardware components. The ILOM is linked via Ethernet port to the management switch within the Exadata enclosure.

KVM

Exadata also features an internal KVM (keyboard, video, and mouse) for managing the system. As you might expect, the KVM is a slide-out tray with a keyboard, touch pad, and flip-up monitor accessible from the front of the rack. The KVM also provides remote Web access to the operating system console of all compute nodes and storage cells. Like the ILOM, the KVM is linked via Ethernet port to the internal management switch.

▓ **Note:** The X2-8 model of Exadata does not come with a KVM. Compute nodes in V2 and X2-2 systems are a 2U form factor and on an Exadata full rack configuration take up a total of eight slots. The compute nodes (2) on the X2-8 occupy five slots each for a total of ten slots in the rack; displacing the 2U KVM switch.

The Client Access Network

The client access network is used by the Oracle listener to provide SQL*Net connectivity to the databases. This network has traditionally been referred to, in RAC terminology, as the *public network*. One or two links (NET1, NET2) from each database server (compute node) connect directly to your corporate switch. Oracle recommends bonding NET1 and NET2 to provide hardware redundancy for client connections. If these ports are bonded, then each link should terminate at a separate switch to provide network redundancy.

The Private Network

The private network is serviced by the internal InfiniBand (IB) switches. This network manages RAC Interconnect traffic (cache fusion, heartbeat), as well as iDB traffic between the database grid and the storage grid. This network is self-contained within the InfiniBand network switch fabric and has no uplink to your corporate network. The network configuration can be found in the ifcfg-ib0 and ifcfg-ib1 configuration files in the /etc/sysconfig/network-scripts directory. They are configured as bonded devices, and the master device file is ifcfg-bondib0. For example, the following listing shows the Infiniband network configuration files from one of the database servers in our lab. Notice how the MASTER parameter is used to map these network devices to the bondib0 device.

```
/etc/sysconfig/network-scripts/ifcfg-bondib0
DEVICE=bondib0
USERCTL=no
BOOTPROTO=none
ONBOOT=yes
IPADDR=192.168.12.6
NETMASK=255.255.255.0
NETWORK=192.168.12.0
BROADCAST=192.168.12.255
BONDING_OPTS="mode=active-backup miimon=100 downdelay=5000 updelay=5000 num_grat_arp=100"
IPV6INIT=no
MTU=65520

/etc/sysconfig/network-scripts/ifcfg-ib0
DEVICE=ib0
USERCTL=no
ONBOOT=yes
MASTER=bondib0
SLAVE=yes
BOOTPROTO=none
HOTPLUG=no
IPV6INIT=no
CONNECTED_MODE=yes
MTU=65520

/etc/sysconfig/network-scripts/ifcfg-ib1
DEVICE=ib1
USERCTL=no
ONBOOT=yes
MASTER=bondib0
SLAVE=yes
BOOTPROTO=none
HOTPLUG=no
IPV6INIT=no
CONNECTED_MODE=yes
MTU=65520
```

Notice that the MTU size for the IB network devices is set to 65,520 (bytes). MTU stands for Maximum Transmission Unit and determines the maximum size of a network packet that may be transmitted across the network. Typical Ethernet networks support an MTU size of up to 1,500 bytes. In recent years, the Jumbo Frames technology has become a popular way to improve database performance by reducing the number of network round trips required for cache fusion between cluster nodes in an Oracle RAC cluster. Conventionally Jumbo Frames supports an MTU of up to 9,000 bytes. But some implementations may support an even larger MTU size.

▪ **Note:** Only the database servers are configured with a 64K MTU. Presumably this is to benefit TCP/IP traffic between the database servers, and between the database servers and any external host that is linked to the IB switch. You may be surprised to know that the IB ports on the storage cells are configured with the standard 1,500 byte MTU size. The large MTU size is not necessary on the storage cells, because I/O between the database grid and the storage grid utilizes the RDS protocol, which is much more efficient for database I/O and bypasses the TCP/IP protocol stack altogether.

About the Configuration Process

Configuring Oracle database servers has always been a manual and somewhat error-prone process, especially for RAC environments. Exadata can be configured manually as well, but the complexities of the platform can make this a risky undertaking. Oracle has greatly simplified the configuration process by providing a utility called OneCommand. This tool uses input parameters you provide, and it carries out all of the low-level tasks for you. Even so, gathering all the right information required by OneCommand will likely be a collaborative effort, especially with the networking components. Figure 8-1 illustrates the Exadata configuration process using OneCommand.

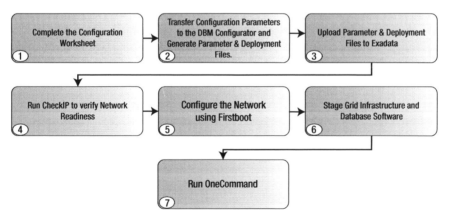

Figure 8-1. The configuration process

As indicated in Figure 8-1, the first step in the process is to fill out the configuration worksheet included in the Exadata documentation set. The purpose of this worksheet is to aid you in gathering all the information you will need to configure your system. When filling in the networking components of the worksheet you will need to enlist the help of your network administrator to reserve IP addresses and register new network names with the domain name server. It's important to understand how these configuration settings are used, so we'll spend a substantial amount of time discussing them in "Step 1: The Configuration Worksheet."

Once you have completed the configuration worksheet, you will transfer that information to the DBM Configurator (`dbm_configurator.xls`). This is an Excel spreadsheet that generates all the parameter and deployment files OneCommand needs for configuring your system. In addition to parameter and deployment files, the DBM Configurator generates the `checkip.sh` script you should use to verify your network settings. This script validates the format of the IP addresses you entered, checks to see if any of them are already in use, and verifies that the network names you specified can be resolved by your DNS server. Once this is done, you are ready to upload these files to Exadata.

Before running OneCommand, you will need to stage the installation media for the Grid Infrastructure and the database (including any Oracle-prescribed patches). The final step of the process is to execute OneCommand. Its operation consists of multiple steps that configure all the components of your Exadata Database Machine. The top-level script that runs OneCommand is called `deploy112.sh` (112 presumably stands for 11gR2). This script can be run end-to-end, executing all of the steps automatically, or you may specify a step to run using command-line options. We strongly recommend running these steps one at a time. Doing so makes it much easier to troubleshoot if a step fails to complete successfully.

■ **Note:** Rather than create an Exadata-specific release of their Grid Infrastructure, ASM, and RDBMS products, Oracle chose to integrate the Exadata specific code right into the same 11gR2 product you would install on non-Exadata platforms. When they did this, Oracle provided a mechanism for releasing Exadata-specific patches that could be managed separately from the mainstream product and coined a new term, *bundle patches*. Bundle patches are Oracle's way of tracking and distributing fixes for their storage cell software as well as Exadata-specific fixes for the Grid Infrastructure, ASM, and database software.

When you take delivery of your Exadata Database Machine, certain tasks will he completed by an Oracle hardware technician. These tasks include connecting all the networked components inside the Exadata rack and configuring IP addresses for the private network (IB switch). When this process is complete, all compute nodes and storage cells will be connected together through the IB switch. OneCommand is only run from the first compute node and uses the private network to execute configuration commands on other servers and storage cells, as well as to install the Grid Infrastructure and RDBMS software on all database servers. There is no place in the configuration worksheet or the DBM Configurator to specify the network address, and the default is 192.168.10. If this network address is already in use elsewhere in your network infrastructure, this may create routing problems later. Be sure to mention this to your Oracle delivery coordinator early in the process so they can negotiate an appropriate network address for your InfiniBand network.

Configuring Exadata

The first step in configuring Exadata is generally to work through the *configuration worksheet*. If you are comfortable with the process, you can opt out of step 1 and enter your parameters directly into the DBM Configurator as you gather them. But don't underestimate the value of the configuration worksheet. It is an integral part of the process Oracle uses; and for good reason. Even experienced Exadata technicians

241

continue to use the configuration worksheet. It is a good communication tool and helps to ensure that the installation goes smoothly.

Step 1: The Configuration Worksheet

The configuration worksheet is provided by Oracle as part of the Exadata documentation set. The documentation is not downloadable from any of the Oracle Web sites. Instead, it is installed in the /usr/share/doc/oracle/Exadata directory of the storage cells. Simply connect to one of the cells as root, celladmin, or cellmonitor and download it to your laptop. Open the welcome.html file in your Web browser and you will see a complete list of all the documents in HTML and PDF format. The one you are looking for is labeled Exadata Database Machine Configuration Worksheets. The worksheet is fairly well documented, but we'll go through it here and talk a little more about some of the parameters and settings you will need to provide. The information collected in the worksheet falls into four general categories:

- Exadata configuration parameters
- Oracle environment parameters
- Network settings
- Cell alert notification parameters

We'll be following a slightly different format here, but we'll discuss all of the configuration settings and parameters from the Oracle documentation and adding some commentary along the way.

Exadata Configuration Parameters

Exadata configuration parameters are system-wide settings, some of which are used for generating yet other parameters used in the configuration process. For example, the Exadata Database Machine Name you provide in the worksheet is used as a host name prefix for all network host names in your Exadata system, including compute nodes, storage cells, network switches, ILOMs, and the KVM. It is also used as a prefix for the cluster name and SCAN name required by Grid Infrastructure.

▓ **Note:** We recently noticed that the new version of the DBM Configurator now appends the Exadata Database Machine Name to the ASM disk group names. For example, if the machine name is 'exa,' then the Configurator generates a disk group name of DATA_EXA, rather than DATA_DG, for the data disk group. This is the default behavior, but it may be overridden before generating your configuration files. We'll talk more about naming your ASM disk groups in "Step 2: The DBM Configurator." You may notice that some of the other chapters of this book, Chapter 15, for example, use the old naming convention.

Table 8-1 shows the Exadata configuration parameters you will enter in the configuration worksheet.

Table 8-1. Exadata Configuration Parameters

Configuration Parameter	Description
Exadata Database Machine name	The machine name (max 4 characters) is used as a prefix for all network host names in your Exadata configuration.
Type of System	This is the type of Exadata configuration. Choose one of the following configurations: X2-8 Full Rack, X2 Full Rack, X2 Half Rack, or X2 Quarter Rack.
Disk Type	This is the type of disk drives your Exadata system is configured with. Choose one of the following configurations: High Performance, High Capacity.
Country	This is the country in which Exadata will reside; for example: United States.
Time Zone	This is the time zone in which Exadata resides. For example: America/Chicago.
Workload Type	This field is used to define the predominant workload type for databases on the system. Choose either DW for data warehouse or OLTP for online transaction processing.
Backup Method	The installation process uses the backup method to determine the sizes for ASM disk groups. Choose between Backups Internal to Oracle and Backups External to Oracle.
Protection Level	This field determines what type of redundancy you wish to use for your ASM disk groups. Choose one of the following: High for ALL, High for DATA, High for RECO, or Normal for ALL.
Exadata Smart Flash Cache	All flash disks are configured as flash cache.

Some of the parameters, like Country and Time Zone, are pretty standard fare when configuring servers. Other parameters are Exadata-specific and will be new to you. One thing you may notice right away is that there is no way to name your ASM disk groups in the configuration worksheet. If you don't like the default names of DATA_{machine_name} and RECO_{machine_name}, you will have the opportunity to change them later in the DBM Configurator. The Exadata configuration parameters are described as follows:

Exadata Database Machine Name: This parameter can be 1–4 characters in length and is used to generate network host names for network endpoints in your Exadata frame. It is also used to name the RAC cluster and the Simple Client Access Name (SCAN) required by RAC. For example, a machine name of exa produces a cluster name of 'exa_cluster' and a SCAN name of exa-scan.ourcompany.com. This parameter is case-sensitive for all but the disk group name postfix, if any, in which case it is forced to uppercase. The following listing shows the management network host names generated for the database servers and storage cells in a quarter rack configuration. In step 2, we'll take a look at a complete listing of the names prefixed with the machine name for a quarter rack configuration.

```
# Management Network
exadb01.ourcompany.com     exadb01
exadb02.ourcompany.com     exadb02
exacel01.ourcompany.com    exacel01
exacel02.ourcompany.com    exacel02
exacel03.ourcompany.com    exacel03
```

If there is a chance you will ever have more than one Exadata system in your data center, consider enumerating your machine name to provide uniqueness. For example a machine name of exa1 allows for future systems to be named exa2, exa3, and so on.

Type of System: The type of system determines how many compute nodes and storage cells are in your configuration. This field is presented as a drop-down list, illustrated in Figure 8-2.

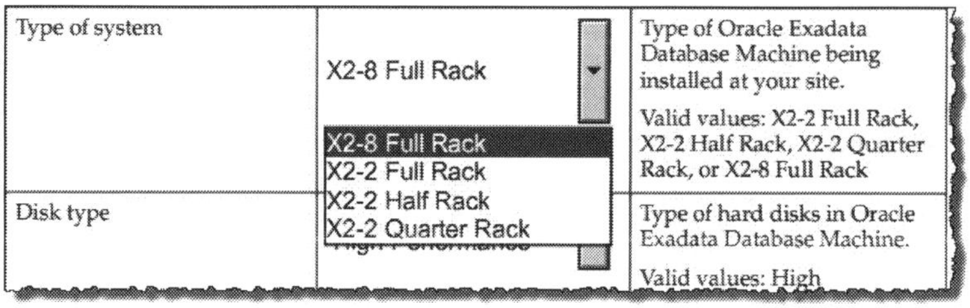

Figure 8-2. The Type of System drop-down

This parameter is used to determine how many compute nodes and storage cells your system has when generating IP addresses and host names. We'll talk more about this later, in the "Network Settings" section, but OneCommand generates sequential IP addresses by starting with a base address for the first host and then incrementing from that address for each host. For example, if your management IPs start at 192.168.8.201, then the following IP addresses will be generated for the compute nodes and storage cells in a quarter rack.

```
192.168.8.201    exadb01.ourcompany.com
192.168.8.202    exadb02.ourcompany.com
192.168.8.203    exacel01.ourcompany.com
192.168.8.204    exacel02.ourcompany.com
192.168.8.205    exacel03.ourcompany.com
```

▓ **Note:** The way OneCommand assigns IP addresses sequentially from a base address can be problematic when adding compute nodes and storage cells to your configuration. We'll talk more about this later in the chapter when we look at upgrading Exadata.

Disk Type: This field is presented as a drop-down list. Exadata X2 models come in two flavors, High Capacity Disks and High Performance Disks. High-capacity disks have a capacity of 2 terabytes, while high performance disks have a capacity of 600 gigabytes. This information is used to calculate cell disk and grid disk sizes for the installation.

Workload Type: Several settings from the configuration worksheet are used to create a starter database during the installation process. These parameters are used to create a database template that is in turn used by the Database Configuration Assistant (dbca) at the end of the installation process. The workload type you specify determines whether your default database is optimized for OLTP or DW workloads. Instance parameters such as SGA_TARGET and PGA_TARGET are sized based on the Workload Type you specified for your database.

Backup Method: This setting determines how your disk groups are sized during the installation process. Disk space is allocated to the DATA and RECO disk groups as follows:

> **Backups Internal to Exadata:** If you plan to use the Fast Recovery Area (FRA) to store online database backups, choose Backups Internal to Oracle. When this allocation scheme is selected, disk space for the DATA and RECO disk groups will be allocated as follows:
>
> DATA: 40%
>
> RECO: 60%
>
> **Backups External to Exadata:** If you are planning to back up your databases directly to tape, NFS, or some other storage external to Exadata, choose Backups External to Exadata. When this allocation scheme is chosen, disk space will be allocated to the DATA and RECO disk groups as follows:
>
> DATA: 80%
>
> RECO: 20%

Protection Level: This determines what level of redundancy will be configured for your ASM disk groups, DATA and RECO. Similar to the Type of System field, this field is presented as a drop-down list from which you can choose the redundancy for your disk groups. Keep in mind that normal redundancy halves the usable space in your disk groups. Normal redundancy is the minimum allowable redundancy level. High redundancy provides the best protection from disk and storage cell failures, but it does so at the cost of reducing available space by two thirds. The following combinations are supported:

High For All: This configuration can significantly reduce available space in your disk groups. According to Oracle, it is best used when the backup method chosen is Backups External to Oracle.

High For DATA: In this configuration, ASM redundancy is set to high for DATA, while RECO is set to normal redundancy. This is best suited for systems that back up the databases to external storage, such as tape, VTL, NFS, and so on.

High For RECO: In this configuration, high redundancy is used for RECO and normal redundancy is used for the DATA disk group. This configuration is best suited for databases that back up to the FRA.

Normal For ALL: This configuration uses normal redundancy for all disk groups. While it provides quite a bit more usable space in the disk groups, keep in mind that the simultaneous loss of one disk drive from two storage cells will cause ASM to dismount your disk groups. If that happens, your databases using those disk groups will also be offline.

As you consider which protection scheme is right for you, think about your pain tolerance where it comes to system outages. Normal redundancy provides more storage and less protection from disk/cell failures. Unless you can afford for your databases to be down for an extended period of time, you should lean toward high redundancy for the DATA disk group. If you can afford an outage while transient disk/cell failures are resolved, or in a worst-case scenario, wait for a full database recovery, then perhaps high redundancy for the RECO disk group is a better fit. If space is very tight and you can tolerate these types of outages, then you may consider setting redundancy for all disk groups to normal.

The redundancy level for your SYSTEM_DG (or DBFS_DG) disk group, which stores the OCR and Voting files, will be automatically set to the maximum level supported by your Exadata rack configuration. High redundancy is not supported on quarter rack configurations, so normal redundancy is the best you can do for them. For half rack and full rack configurations, redundancy will always be set to high for the SYSTEM_DG disk group.

▨ **Kevin Says:** Protection level is a very sensitive and seemingly politically charged topic. The manner in which ASM chooses partner disks leaves any normal redundancy disk group at much greater risk of data loss from a double-disk failure than would be the case with traditional RAID-style protection. While there may be hundreds of disks that *could* fail simultaneously in a double disk failure, it's just a matter of (bad) luck which ones fail. If the "wrong two disks" in a normal redundancy situation happen to fail, the administrator will have to deal with data loss. For this reason, the authors are correct to point out which high-redundancy scheme is recommended based on the backup strategy protecting the system.

The topic of ASM normal redundancy protection from double disk failure scenarios is not Exadata-specific. However, until the advent of Exadata, customers rarely trusted their data to ASM protection—opting instead for external redundancy.

> **Exadata Smart Flash Cache**: There is no mention of the flash cache in the configuration worksheet but there is in the DBM Configurator.

Oracle Environment Parameters

The next set of parameters is used to define the O/S user and group accounts, as well as the location for the Grid Infrastructure (Clusterware) and database software installation. These parameters are well known to DBAs who have been through an Oracle RAC 11gR2 installation or two. Table 8-2 shows the parameters you will need to provide. The parameters in *italics* cannot be modified in the configuration worksheet and are included for informational purposes only. Some of them, however, can be changed when you fill out the DBM Configurator later.

Table 8-2. Oracle Environment Parameters

Environment Parameter	Default Value
Grid Infrastructure user name	oracle
Grid Infrastructure user identifier	1000
RAC home user name	oracle
RAC home identifier	1001
Oracle inventory group name	oinstall
Oracle inventory group identifier	1001
RAC home DBA group name	dba
RAC home DBA group identifier	1002
RAC home OPER group name	racoper
RAC home OPER group identifier	1003
ASM DBA group name	asmdba
ASM DBA group identifier	1004

Environment Parameter	Default Value
ASM ADMIN group name	asmadmin
ASM ADMIN group identifier	1006
Oracle software owner password	*welcome*
Grid Infrastructure (Clusterware) home base directory	*/u01/app/{version}/grid* Where: version is currently 11.2.0
Oracle database home base directory (ORACLE_BASE)	*/u01/app/oracle*
Oracle database home (ORACLE_HOME) directory	*/u01/app/oracle/product{version}/db_home1* Version is currently 11.2.0
Oracle Inventory directory	*/u01/app/oraInventory*
Database name	dbm
Database character set	*AL32UTF8*
Database national character set	*AL16UTF16*
Database block size	*8192*
ASM disk groups	DATA *for the default data file location;* RECO *for the fast recovery area* *Note: Default* DATA *and* RECO *disk group size depends on the type of system (quarter, half, or full rack), the type of disk drives (high capacity or high performance), and the type of backup.*
Starting IP Address for the InfiniBand private network[1]	*192.168.10.1*
Subnet mask for InfiniBand private network	*255.255.252.0*

The InfiniBand private network is more commonly known to DBAs as the *private Interconnect*. This field shows starting IP address for the range of IPs the RAC cluster will use for cluster Interconnect traffic (heartbeat, cache fusion, and so on). If for some reason you have changed the IP addresses for the IB network you will need to also make that adjustment in the DBM Configurator when you transfer the worksheet parameters later.

▪ **Note:** OneCommand does not allow you to modify the character set parameters. So the default database created will use the AL32UTF8 database character set, and AL16UTF16 national character set. After the installation is complete, you may choose to drop the default database and create your own databases that meet the specific requirements of your environment. Keep in mind that Oracle recommends using Unicode for all new database implementations.

Network Settings

The final set of configuration parameters is where you specify the network settings for Exadata. OneCommand supports the configuration of up to four networks, identified as NET0 through NET3. NET0 and NET1 are required and are used for the management network and client access network, respectively. NET2 and NET3 are optional networks you may choose to configure if needed. Table 8-3 shows all the network settings used to configure Exadata.

Table 8-3. Network Settings

Network Setting	Description
Domain name	Your network domain name. For example: ourcompany.com
IP address of the name server(s)	The IP address of one or more of your network name servers.
IP address of the Network Time Protocol (NTP) server(s)	The IP address of one or more NTP servers for server time synchronization.
Management Network (NET0) Starting IP address	The starting IP address for the management network. IP addresses for all management network end-points will derive sequentially from this IP address. This network must be separate from all other networks on Exadata.
Management Network (NET0) Subnet mask	The subnet mask for the management network.
Management Network (NET0) Gateway IP address	The IP address of the gateway for the management network.
Client Access Network (NET1) Starting IP address	The client access network is configured on the compute nodes. It is the interface used by the database SCAN listeners. Client applications connect to the database through the NET1 interface. This network must be separate from all other networks on Exadata.
Client Access Network (NET1) Subnet mask	The subnet mask for the Client Access Network.

Network Setting	Description
Client Access Network (NET1) Gateway IP address	The gateway for the Client Access Network.
Client Access Network (NET1) Channel bonding	Oracle recommends the Client Access Network Ethernet devices (eth1 and eth2) be bonded to provide redundancy for client connections to the database. Yes or No in this field determines whether or not NET1 will be configured for channel bonding. If it is, it will be bonded to with the NET2 interface.
Additional Network (NET2) Starting IP address	If channel bonding is not used for the Client Access Network, then NET2 is available as an additional network interface (eth2). This field is the starting IP address for the range of IPs assigned to NET2 across the database servers. If configured, this network must be separate from all other networks on Exadata.
Additional Network (NET2) Subnet mask	The subnet mask for the NET2 network interface.
Additional Network (NET2) Gateway IP address	The IP address of the gateway used by the NET2 network.
Additional Network (NET2) Network host name suffix	This suffix is appended to the host name on each of the database servers to identify the NET2 network.
Additional Network (NET3) Starting IP address	NET3 is an optional network available on the database servers. This is the IP address for the sequential range of IPs for the NET3 network. This network must be separate from all other networks on the system.
Additional Network (NET3) Subnet mask	The subnet mask for the NET3 network.
Additional Network (NET3) Gateway IP address	The IP address of the gateway for the NET3 network.
Additional Network (NET3) Network host name suffix	This suffix is appended to the host name on each of the database servers to identify the NET3 network.
PDU-A IP address	The power distribution unit (PDU) has an Ethernet interface (eth0) and can be configured on the network by assigning it an IP address. This field defines the IP address for the PDU.

Network Setting	Description
PDU-B IP address	Exadata is equipped with a redundant PDU that can also be configured on the network by assigning it an IP address. This field defines the network for the PDU.

The domain name, DNS server, and NTP server settings are all standard network settings. These should be specified as you would for any other Oracle database server on your network. The remaining network settings are described as follows:

Management Network (NET0): The management network is used for administrative access to the database servers and storage cells. You can think of this network as your SSH entry point for logging into the compute nodes, storage cells, and IB switches. The management network is serviced by the internal Cisco network switch. Only one network drop is required to uplink the Cisco management switch to your company network. The management network also includes the ILOM interfaces on the compute nodes and storage cells.

Client Access Network (NET1): The client access network provides SQL*Net access to the database. This is the network used by the SCAN Listeners to establish client connections to the database. Only the database servers use this network; storage cells are not assigned an IP address on this network. And even though the database servers have an IP on this network, you cannot connect to these IP addresses using SSH, because SSH is not configured to listen on this network. One network drop (minimum) is required for each database server to provide access through your company network. If channel bonding is used to provide hardware redundancy, you will need two drops per database server. The cable pairs from the database servers should be connected to redundant network switches to provide full network redundancy. If channel bonding is configured for the client access network, OneCommand configures these devices in the ifcfg-eth1 and ifcfg-eth2 configuration files in the /etc/sysconfig/network-scripts directory. They are bonded to the bondeth0 device defined in the ifcfg-bondeth0 file. For example, the following listing shows how the master bond device is referenced by the eth1 and eth2 slave devices.

```
# egrep 'DEVICE|MASTER|SLAVE' ifcfg-bondeth0 ifcfg-eth1 ifcfg-eth2
ifcfg-bondeth0:DEVICE=bondeth0
ifcfg-eth1:DEVICE=eth1
ifcfg-eth1:MASTER=bondeth0
ifcfg-eth1:SLAVE=yes
ifcfg-eth2:DEVICE=eth2
ifcfg-eth2:MASTER=bondeth0
ifcfg-eth2:SLAVE=yes
```

Channel Bonding (NET1): Oracle recommends that you configure NIC bonding for the client access network to provide network redundancy. If you choose to bond the client access network, OneCommand will use NET2 as the secondary network device.

Additional Network (NET2): If channel bonding is not configured for the client access network, NET2 is may be used to configure an additional network.

Additional Network (NET3): The NET3 device is available as an additional network if needed.

■ **Tip:** In addition to the network devices we've discussed here, each Exadata X2-2 compute node features two 10 gigabit Ethernet (10gE) network ports. These ports are not ready to be used right out of the box. You must first purchase and install SFP transceiver modules in order to connect them to your network switch. Each Exadata X2-8 compute node has eight of these 10gE ports. If your backup media server supports 10gE, then this network could be used to improve the performance of your database backups.

Cell Alert Notification Parameters

The `cellsrv` management service (on each storage cell) monitors the health of the storage cells and is capable of sending out SMTP and SNMP notifications if problems arise. Configuring email and SNMP alert notifications for the storage cells is optional but highly recommended. Table 8-4 describes the various parameters used to configure Cell Alert Notifications.

Table 8-4. *Cell Alert Notification Parameters*

Configuration Parameter	Description
SMTP Server	This is the name of the SMTP server the storage cells will use for routing email alert notifications. For example: `mail.corporate.com`.
SMTP Port	This is the SMTP email port used for routing email notifications. For example: 25, or 465.
smtpUseSSL	This field indicates whether or not your email server requires secure connections using SSL. Valid responses are Yes and No.
smtpToAddr	This field should be filled in with a comma-delimited list of email addresses for distributing email alerts. For example: `dba@corporate.com,john.doe@corporate.com`.
smtpFromAddr	This is the return address for email alerts. For example: `exadata@corporate.com`.
smtpFrom	This email address appears in the "From" field of email alerts. For example: `Exadata Database Machine`.

Configuration Parameter	Description
smtpUser	This is the user name the storage cell will use for logging in to the SMTP server.
smtpPwd	This password is used to establish sessions with your SMTP server. If your SMTP server does not require authentication, this field may be left blank.
snmpSubscriber	This is the host, port, and community for receiving SNMP alert notifications. The port and community attributes are optional. The default port is 162, and the default community is 'public'. For example: `snmp.corporate.com,162,public`. You may enter only one target here, but additional SNMP targets can be added after the installation is complete.

Step 2: The DBM Configurator

Once you've completed the configuration worksheet, the information you gathered can be transferred to the DBM (Database Machine) Configurator. The DBM Configurator is an Excel spreadsheet (`dbm_configurator.xls`) that generates all the input files OneCommand will need to carry out the installation process. The spreadsheet is located in the `/opt/oracle.SupportTools/onecommand` directory on every compute node. The DBM Configurator is heavily documented in the Exadata *Database Machine Owner's Guide*, so we won't be discussing all of the fields here. But we will take a look at how a few of them are used in the installation process. Table 8-5 describes a few of the key data-entry fields from the spreadsheet.

Table 8-5. DBM Configurator

Field	Description
Customer Name	This field is used when creating the base directory for the output files generated by the Configurator. For example if the customer name is "OurCompany" then a directory named `C:\dbmachine_OurCompany` will be created to store the output files.
Exadata Database Machine Name	As we discussed earlier, the machine name is used as a prefix for network host names and as a suffix for ASM disk group names. Additionally, it is also used for the target directory name (inside the base directory mentioned above) for storing the output files. This allows the Configurator to manage the configuration of multiple Database Machine configurations.

Field	Description
Data Diskgroup Name	The name for the ASM DATA disk group is generated automatically in the form: DATA_*{machine_name}*. The default name can be changed here, as needed, before generating your parameter files.
Reco Diskgroup Name	The name for the ASM RECO disk group is generated automatically in the form: RECO_*{machine_name}*. The default name can be changed here, before generating your parameter files.

The DBM Configurator process is as follows:

1. Enter the configuration parameters from the configuration worksheet into the DBM Configurator.

2. Click the Generate button on the right side of the spreadsheet. A brief report showing the topology of your system is generated at the bottom of the spreadsheet. Scroll down to review your settings and make corrections to the output as needed. When you are finished making changes, you are ready to create the output files.

3. The last step is to click the Create Config Files button. This generates the parameter and deployment files used by OneCommand. It also creates an *installation template* in a separate spreadsheet tab in the Configurator. The information in the template consists mostly of the input parameters you provided in an easy-to-read format. Review the template carefully and make changes in the data entry or topology report areas as needed. If you must go back and make any changes, you should click the Generate and Create Config Files buttons again so that your changes are written to the output files.

■ **Caution:** Be careful when filling out the spreadsheet. It's very easy for a typo to slip through and cause you problems later. The topology report generated below the data entry fields is useful for catching errors in the host names and IP addresses you entered. This report is created when you click the Generate button.

Step 3: Upload Parameter and Deployment Files

The DBM Configurator generates a number of files that will be used to configure your Exadata Database Machine. These files are saved in the C:\dbmachine_*{company_name}**{machine_name}* directory. The files are primarily used by OneCommand to perform the installation and configuration process. But a few of the files are used by other processes. For example, the checkip.sh script uses the dbm.dat file to perform network readiness tests prior to running OneCommand. These files will be needed for various tasks going forward in the configuration, and they must be uploaded to the first compute node on your Exadata platform.

There are a couple of ways to transfer the parameter and deployment files to Exadata. One method involves setting up temporary network access to the first compute node. This network configuration will be replaced with permanent network settings by Firstboot or ApplyConfig in subsequent steps. The other option is to save the files to a portable USB flash drive and then, using the USB port on the front panel of the first compute node, copy the files to the OneCommand directory. We'll talk about where that directory is in the following example. The USB approach is as follows:

1.   Connect the USB flash drive to your laptop and copy the directory containing your configuration files to the USB drive. For example:

```
mkdir e:\exa
copy C:\dbmachine_OurCompany\exa e:\exa

C:\> copy dbmachine_OurCompany\exa e:\exa
dbmachine_OurCompany\exa\all_group
dbmachine_OurCompany\exa\all_ib_group
dbmachine_OurCompany\exa\all_nodelist_group
dbmachine_OurCompany\exa\cell_group
dbmachine_OurCompany\exa\cell_ib_group
dbmachine_OurCompany\exa\checkip.sh
dbmachine_OurCompany\exa\config.dat
dbmachine_OurCompany\exa\databasemachine.xml
dbmachine_OurCompany\exa\dbm.dat
dbmachine_OurCompany\exa\dbmachine.params
dbmachine_OurCompany\exa\dbMachine_exa
dbmachine_OurCompany\exa\dbs_group
dbmachine_OurCompany\exa\dbs_ib_group
dbmachine_OurCompany\exa\hosts.sample
dbmachine_OurCompany\exa\preconf-11-2-1-1-0.csv
dbmachine_OurCompany\exa\preconf-11-2-1-2-2.csv
dbmachine_OurCompany\exa\preconf-11-2-2-1-0.csv
dbmachine_OurCompany\exa\preconf.csv
dbmachine_OurCompany\exa\priv_ib_group
        19 file(s) copied.
```

2.   Remove the USB flash drive from your laptop and connect it to the USB port on the front panel of the first compute node in your system. The servers are numbered from bottom to top in the rack, so the bottom-most compute node is the one you are looking for.

3.   Using the Exadata KVM, log in to the first compute node as root and check the /var/log/dmesg file to determine the device name assigned to the USB flash drive. For example, you should see a message something like the following:

```
… Attached scsi removable disk sdb
```

You can confirm the partition and device name using the fdisk command as follows:

```
# fdisk -l /dev/sdb

Disk /dev/sdb: 2038 MB, 2038431744 bytes
251 heads, 62 sectors/track, 255 cylinders
Units = cylinders of 15562 * 512 = 7967744 bytes
```

255

```
      Device Boot  Start   End    Blocks  Id  System
   /dev/sdb1    *      1    256   1990624   c  W95 FAT32 (LBA)
```

4. Create a directory you can use as a mount point for the USB flash drive. For example, /mnt/usb.

5. Mount the USB device using the following command.

    ```
    # mount -t vfat /dev/sdb1 /mnt/usb
    ```

6. Copy the files to the onecommand directory as follows:

    ```
    # cp /mnt/sdb1/exa/* /opt/oracle.SupportTools/onecommand
    ```

7. Unmount the USB flash drive as follows:

    ```
    # umount /mnt/usb
    ```

8. You can now remove the USB flash drive from the compute node.

Table 8-6 describes what these files are and how they are used in the installation and configuration process.

Table 8-6. Parameter and Deployment Files

File Name	Description
dbs_ib_group	This file contains the private network IP address, long network host name, and short network host name for all compute nodes. The format is similar to what you would see in the /etc/hosts file, in the form: *ip_address long_name short_name*
cell_ib_group	This file contains information similar to that of the dbs_ib_group file, but the information pertains to the storage cells.
priv_ib_group	This file is a combination of the dbs_ib_group and cell_ib_group files and is used for to populate the /etc/hosts file.
all_group	This file contains the host names for all database servers and storage cells in the Exadata Database Machine; For example, exadb01, exacel01
all_ib_group	This file contains the private host names for all servers and storage cells in the configuration. For example: exadb01-priv and exacel01-priv.
all_nodelist_group	This file is a combination of the all_group and all_ib_group files.

File Name	Description
cell_group	This file contains a list of the host names for all storage cells in your configuration. For example: exace101, exace102, exace103, and so on.
dbs_group	This file contains a list of the host names for all compute nodes in your configuration. For example: exadb01, exadb02, exadb03, and so on.
hosts.sample	This is a sample hosts file that is installed in /etc/hosts when there is no DNS server available.
checkip.sh	This is the network validation script you will run before running the OneCommand utility. Among other things, it verifies access to the NTP server, checks name resolution using your DNS server, and checks to see if any of the IP addresses in your configuration are already in use. We'll talk more about checkip.sh in step 4.
dbm.dat	This file contains your network host names and IP addresses. It is used by the checkip.sh script to validate the network settings you specified. When you are running the checkip.sh script, this file must be in the same directory.
config.dat	This file contains all the configuration parameters and network settings from the DBM Configurator in a *name=value* format.
dbmachine.params	This is the input parameter file used by OneCommand to configure your system.
dbMachine_{machine_name}	This file is used to generate the Installation Template, which shows up in a separate spreadsheet tab in the DBM Configurator after you click the Create Config Files button.
preconf.csv	This is the [1]Firstboot configuration file used by release 11.2.2.1.0 and later of the cell software image.
preconf-11-2-1-1-0.csv	This is the [1]Firstboot configuration file used by releases 11.2.1.2.3, and 11.2.1.2.6 of the cell software image.
preconf-11-2-1-2-2.csv	The [1]Firstboot configuration file used by release 11.2.1.3
preconf-11-2-2-1-0.csv	This is the [1]Firstboot configuration file used by releases 11.2.2.1 and later.

[1]*Firstboot is run before OneCommand and performs the initial configuration of the servers. We'll talk more about Firstboot later in this chapter.*

In addition to the files listed in this table, OneCommand also creates a database template (dbmDBTemplate) used for creating your starter database. The template contains database parameters that should be used whenever creating databases on Exadata, such as these:

```
_file_size_increase_increment
_kill_diagnostics_timeout
_lm_rcvr_hang_allow_time
```

The template file, dbmDBTemplate.dbt, is installed in the $ORACLE_HOME/assistants/dbca/templates directory during the OneCommand installation process.

Step 4: CheckIP (checkip.sh)

One of the files the DBM Configurator generates is a shell script used to validate your network settings. The checkip.sh (CheckIP) script reads your network configuration settings from its parameter file (dbm.dat, also generated by the Configurator) and runs a variety of tests to verify network readiness before, during, and after the configuration process. CheckIP tests the network to confirm that the following conditions are met:

- IP addresses that should respond to a ping, do.

- IP addresses that should not respond to a ping, do not.

- Host names that must be registered in DNS can be both forward and reverse resolved using the first DNS server specified in the dbm.dat file.

Before running OneCommand, the checkip.sh script (CheckIP) should be run to validate the readiness of your corporate network. The script has several modes of operation that validate your network configuration at various points of the configuration process. At this point, you should run CheckIP in pre_applyconfig mode from a server, external to Exadata platform. The server you choose to run CheckIP from must have the same network visibility as your Exadata system will have. For example, the server must have access to the same DNS server and NTP server, and it must be able to ping the IP addresses you listed in your network settings for Exadata. Ideally, the server you choose should run the Linux operating system, but Unix servers may work as well. CheckIP uses the Bash shell, which is popular on the Linux platform but also available on most versions of Unix. The O/S commands required by CheckIP include host, ping, ntpdate, tr, cut, sed, wc, grep, and head. Be aware that even if these commands are available on your Unix server, they may produce incompatible output and cause false failures in the output. The checkip.sh script and the dbm.dat parameter file are created in Linux/Unix format, so when you upload them from your laptop, be sure to transfer them in binary mode. If you want to be sure, you can use the dos2unix command after uploading them to ensure that the format is correct before executing the script. Upload the checkip.sh and dbm.dat files to a server on your network and run the following command as the root user:

```
./checkip.sh -m pre_applyconfig
```

CheckIP will print its progress out to the screen as well as build a dbm.out report file. The following listing shows sample output from the CheckIP script:

```
Running in mode pre_applyconfig
Using name server 192.168.10.15 found in dbm.dat for all DNS lookups
Processing section #
Processing section
Processing section DOMAIN
```

```
ourcompany.com
...
Processing section GATEWAY
GOOD : 10.34.96.1 pings successfully
GOOD : 10.34.97.1 pings successfully
GOOD : 10.34.97.1 pings successfully
GOOD : 10.34.98.1 pings successfully

Processing section SCAN
GOOD : exa-scan.ourcompany.com resolves to 3 IP addresses
GOOD : exa-scan.ourcompany.com forward resolves to 10.34.97.36
GOOD : 10.34.97.36 reverse resolves to ex01-scan.ourcompany.com.
GOOD : 10.34.97.36 does not ping
GOOD : exa-scan.your.ourcompany.com forward resolves to 10.34.97.37
GOOD : 10.34.97.37 reverse resolves to ex01-scan.ourcompany.com.
GOOD : 10.34.97.37 does not ping
GOOD : exa-scan.ourcompany.com forward resolves to 10.34.97.38
GOOD : 10.34.97.38 reverse resolves to ex01-scan.ourcompany.com.
GOOD : 10.34.97.38 does not ping
...
Processing section COMPUTE
GOOD : exadb01.ourcompany.com forward resolves to 10.34.96.20
GOOD : 10.34.96.20 reverse resolves to exadb01.ourcompany.com.
GOOD : 10.34.96.20 does not ping
GOOD : exadb02.ourcompany.com forward resolves to 10.34.96.21
GOOD : 10.34.96.21 reverse resolves to exadb02.ourcompany.com.
GOOD : 10.34.96.21 does not ping
...
Processing section CELL
GOOD : exacel01.ourcompany.com forward resolves to 10.34.96.28
GOOD : 10.34.96.28 reverse resolves to exacel01.ourcompany.com.
GOOD : 10.34.96.28 does not ping
GOOD : exacel02.ourcompany.com forward resolves to 10.34.96.29
GOOD : 10.34.96.29 reverse resolves to exacel02.ourcompany.com.
GOOD : 10.34.96.29 does not ping
...
Processing section SWITCH
...
Processing section VIP
...
Processing section NET3
...
Processing section SMTP
```

The output report generated in the dbm.out file contains the same information as we see in the display. If any validation errors occur, they are prefixed with ERROR,' and a message describing the failure indicates the problem encountered, and what the expected results should be. For example:

```
Processing section SCAN
GOOD : exa-scan.ourcompany.com resolves to 3 IP addresses
ERROR : exa-scan. ourcompany.com forward resolves incorrectly to 144.77.43.182 144.77.43.181
144.77.43.180 , expected 144.77.43.87
…
Processing section COMPUTE
GOOD : exadb01.ourcompany.com forward resolves to 10.80.23.1
GOOD : 10.80.23.1 reverse resolves to exadb01.ourcompany.com.
ERROR : 10.80.23.1 pings
```

The output from CheckIP must contain no errors. If you see any errors in the output, they must be corrected before running OneCommand. Check the dbm.dat file and make sure you didn't enter an IP address incorrectly, or mistype a hostname before opening a discussion with your network administrator. Sometimes a simple correction to a data entry field on the DBM Configurator is all that is needed. If everything looks in order from your side, then send the dbm.out file to your network administrator for remediation.

Step 5: Firstboot

When the Oracle hardware engineers complete their installation, you are ready to boot up the compute nodes and storage cells for the first time. When you are ready to begin configuring Exadata, open up the internal KVM and power up one compute node or storage cell at a time. It's not important which order you follow. The Firstboot process is not documented in the Oracle manuals, so we'll take a minute to talk through the boot process and what happens the first time you boot the servers and storage cells.

Every time a server boots up, the /etc/init.d/precel script is called at run level 3. This script calls the /opt/oracle.cellos/cellFirstboot.sh (Firstboot) script. Firstboot determines whether or not the network settings have been configured. This is undocumented, but it appears that it is triggered by the existence of the /opt/oracle.cellos/cell.conf file. This file is created and maintained by the /opt/oracle.cellos/ipconf.pl script (IPConf) and contains all the information about your network configuration. If the file exists, it is assumed that the system is already configured and the boot cycle continues. But if the file is not found, Firstboot calls IPConf and you are lead, interactively, through the network configuration process. IPConf is used to set the following network settings for your compute nodes and storage cells:

- Name Server (DNS)

- Time Server (NTP)

- Country Code

- Local Time Zone

- Hostname

- IP address, netmask, gateway, *type*, and hostname for all network devices. The *type* is required and used for internal documentation in the cell.conf file. Valid types are Private, Management, SCAN, and Other.

For example, the following listing shows the prompts for configuring the management network:

```
Select interface name to configure or press Enter to continue: eth0
Selected interface. eth0
IP address or none: 192.168.8.217
Netmask: 255.255.252.0
Gateway (IP address or none) or none: 192.168.10.1

Select network type for interface from the list below
1: Management
2: SCAN
3: Other
Network type: 1
Fully qualified hostname or none: exadb03.ourcompany.com
```

When you have finished entering all your network settings, IPConf generates a new `cell.conf` file and reboots the system. Once the system has finished rebooting, it is ready for the O/S configuration and software installation performed by OneCommand.

ApplyConfig

For quarter rack and half rack configurations, it's a fairly trivial task to enter all your network settings using the Firstboot process. For full rack configurations, however, it can be a time-consuming and error-prone process. The `applyconfig.sh` script (ApplyConfig) automates the process. ApplyConfig is found in the `/opt/oracle.SupportTools/firstconf` directory of all compute nodes and storage cells. It is basically a wrapper script for the IPConf script we discussed earlier, for Firstboot). In step 3, we discussed the various parameter and deployment files generated by the DBM Configurator. Among these files was the `preconf.csv` parameter file, (see also `preconf-11-2-1-1-0.csv`, `preconf-11-2-1-2-2.csv`, and `preconf-11-2-2-1-0.csv`). The `preconf.csv` file contains all the network settings IPConf needs to create a `cell.conf` file for each compute node and storage cell.

IPConf may be run interactively (as we saw in the Firstboot example), allowing you to enter your network settings manually. IPConf may also be run non-interactively, taking its input from the `preconf.csv` parameter file. When run in this mode, IPConf creates a full set of `cell.conf` files, one for each compute node and storage cell. For example, the following command creates all the required `cell.conf` files for an Exadata half rack configuration:

```
[root@exadb01 root]# cd /opt/oracle.SupportTools/firstconf
[root@exadb01 firstconf]# /opt/oracle.cellos/ipconf \
  -preconf /opt/oracle.SupportTools/onecommand/{company_name}/preconf.csv \
  -generateall \
  -generateorder /opt/oracle.SupportTools/firstconf/half
```

That last parameter (`half`) is a reference to a parameter file containing the factory default private IP address for all compute nodes and storage cells in an Exadata half rack configuration. The files generated by IPConf are saved in the `/tmp/ipconf` directory as follows:

```
[root@exadb01 firstconf]# ls -1 /tmp/ipconf
cell.conf.exacel01.ourcompany.com
cell.conf.exacel02.ourcompany.com
cell.conf.exacel03.ourcompany.com
cell.conf.exacel04.ourcompany.com
cell.conf.exacel05.ourcompany.com
```

```
cell.conf.exacel06.ourcompany.com
cell.conf.exacel07.ourcompany.com
cell.conf.exadb01.ourcompany.com
cell.conf.exadb02.ourcompany.com
cell.conf.exadb03.ourcompany.com
cell.conf.exadb04.ourcompany.com
```

ApplyConfig calls IPConf to generate these files and installs them as /opt/oracle.cellos/cell.conf in each compute node and storage cell. To run ApplyConfig, log in as root to the first compute node in your system and run applyconfig.sh as follows:

```
[root@exadb01 root]# cd /opt/oracle.SupportTools/firstconf
[root@exadb01 firstconf]# ./applyconfig.sh half \
  /opt/oracle.SupportTools/onecommand/preconf.csv
```

Once the cell.conf files have been installed on all servers, ApplyConfig uses the dcli command to run the cleanup_n_reboot.sh script on all servers. As the name implies, this script performs cleanup tasks and reboots the servers. Once the servers complete the boot cycle, Exadata should be ready to be configured using OneCommand.

Whether you choose to configure the Exadata network components manually, using Firstboot, or by running ApplyConfig, you should verify the network configuration once again before proceeding with the installation process. Run the CheckIP post_applyconfig process to verify your configuration as follows:

```
# cd /opt/oracle.SupportTools/onecommand
[root@exadb03 onecommand]# ./checkip.sh -m post_applyconfig

Exadata Database Machine Network Verification version 1.9
Network verification mode post_applyconfig starting ...
Saving output file from previous run as dbm.out_8385
Using name server 192.168.10.19 found in dbm.dat for all DNS lookups
Processing section DOMAIN   : SUCCESS
Processing section NAME     : SUCCESS
Processing section NTP      : SUCCESS
Processing section GATEWAY  : SUCCESS
Processing section SCAN     : SUCCESS
Processing section COMPUTE  : SUCCESS
Processing section CELL     : SUCCESS
Processing section ILOM     : SUCCESS
Processing section SWITCH   : SUCCESS
Processing section VIP      : SUCCESS
Processing section SMTP     : SMTP "Email Server Settings" mail.ourcompany.com 25:0 SUCCESS
```

Again, the output from all tests must be SUCCESS before continuing with the installation. If errors occur, you can review the dbm.out file for the reason of the failure.

Step 6: Staging the Installation Media

The last step before running OneCommand is to make sure you have the necessary Oracle install media properly staged on the first compute node. OneCommand will handle unzipping the installation files to a working directory and perform the entire installation automatically. My Oracle Support (MOS) note 888828.1 contains a complete list of Oracle software and patches supported for the Exadata Database

Machine. However, the version of OneCommand that came with your Exadata system only supports automatic installation of certain software versions and patches.

The *Exadata Owner's Guide* that came with your system specifies the RDBMS and Grid Infrastructure installation media OneCommand needs for the installation. The patches and install media required by OneCommand tends to change as new versions of OneCommand are released. Currently, the following media is required by OneCommand:

- Oracle RDBMS & Grid Infrastructure 11.2.0.2 (patch 10098816)

    - `p10098816_112020_Linux-x86-64_1of7.zip`

    - `p10098816_112020_Linux-x86-64_2of7.zip`

    - `p10098816_112020_Linux-x86-64_3of7.zip`

The Readme file included within the `onecommand` directory states which bundle patches are supported by the version of OneCommand installed on your system. For example, we recently installed a quarter rack X2-2 system in our lab. The following listing shows the patches supported by it in the Readme file:

```
# egrep 'PATCHES|bundle patch' /opt/oracle.SupportTools/onecommand/README
PATCHES Applied with this version
Bug 10252487 - 11.2.0.2 db machine bundle patch 1
```

Checking MOS note 888828.1, we see that Bundle Patch 1 for 11.2.0.2 is patch 10252487.

- Bundle Patch 1 (patch 10252487)

    - p10252487_112020_Linux-x86-64.zip

The install media (zip files) listed above may already be installed on the first compute node of your Exadata Database Machine. So it's worth a look, and it may save you some time to check before downloading the installation files. If necessary, download and stage the installation files in the `/opt/oracle.SupportTools/onecommand` directory on the first compute node.

Step 7: Running OneCommand

Although Exadata can be configured manually, OneCommand is the preferred method. OneCommand is an Oracle-provided utility consisting of several configuration steps, (31 as of this writing). OneCommand provides two very important benefits to Exadata customers and Oracle's support staff. First, it creates a limited number of standardized (and well known) configurations, which makes the platform much easier to support. After all, who wants to hear "oh, I've never seen it configured that way before" when we finally get a support tech on the phone? This is one of Exadata's key strengths. Second, it provides a simplified and structured mechanism for configuring Exadata from start to finish. This means that with very little knowledge of Exadata internals, an experienced technician can install and configure Exadata in a matter of hours. It's unclear whether Oracle originally intended to provide support for OneCommand externally, but about the same time the X2 began shipping, Oracle added it to the *Exadata Owner's Guide*. The instructions in the Owner's Guide are not very extensive, but the Readme included with the utility does a fairly good job of explaining how to run it, and what to watch out for. OneCommand comes preinstalled in the `/opt/oracle.SupportTools/onecommand` directory on your compute nodes. If you need access to the latest version of OneCommand, it is available for download from Oracle's Technology Network. The download link is password-protected however, and you will need to open a service request with Oracle Support to request temporary access to download it.

OneCommand is a multiple-step process that is run from a shell script called `deploy112.sh`. These steps can be run end-to-end or one at a time. Table 8-7 shows each step in the OneCommand process along with a brief description of what the step does.

Table 8-7. OneCommand Steps

File Name	Description
Step 0	Validates the compute node from which you are running the installation. It verifies the network configuration of the server, verifies and unzips the installation media, verifies the `cell.conf` file, and verifies that all parameter and deployment files can be found in the `onecommand` directory.
Step 1	Creates SSH keys for the root account on all compute nodes and storage cells for trusted SSH authentication.
Step 2	Validates the `cell.conf` file on all compute nodes and storage servers and verifies that all storage cells are installed with the same version of cell software.
Step 3	Unzips the DBMS, Grid Infrastructure, and bundle patch files.
Step 4	Updates the `/etc/hosts` files.
Step 5	Creates the `cellip.ora` file on the compute nodes, and the `cellinit.ora` file on the storage cells.
Step 6	Validates the hardware on all servers and cells using the `CheckHWnFWProfile` command.
Step 7	Verifies the InfiniBand network.
Step 8	Validates the storage cells by running various CellCLI commands. For example: `cellcli -e list physicaldisk`
Step 9	Checks RDS using the `/usr/bin/rds-ping` command.
Step 10	Check cell disks using the CellCLI `calibrate` command. This command tests the performance characteristics of your cell disks.
Step 11	Validates the date, time, and NTP synchronization across all computed nodes and storage cells. The NTP service is started if necessary.
Step 12	Updates the following files on the database servers, adding settings typical for an Oracle database server environment: `/etc/security/limits.conf` `/etc/profile`

File Name	Description
Step 13	Creates the Oracle Linux user and group accounts. For example, `oracle`, `oinstall`, `dba`, and so on.
Step 14	Configures SSH equivalency for the user accounts created in Step 13.
Step 15	Creates the `ORA_CRS_HOME` and `ORACLE_HOME` directories for the Grid Infrastructure and database software.
Step 16	Creates all cell disks, grid disks, and the flash cache (if enabled on the DBM Configurator spreadsheet).
Step 17	Performs a silent installation of Grid Infrastructure.
Step 18	Runs the root scripts (`root.sh`) for post-installation of the Grid Infrastructure. When this step is complete, your OCR and Voting disks will be created and the cluster should be running.
Step 19	Performs a silent installation of the database software.
Step 20	Creates the default Oracle Listener.
Step 21	Runs asmca and creates your ASM disk groups. For example: `DATA`, and `RECO`.
Step 22	Shuts down the cluster and opens permissions on the `ORA_CRS_HOME` using the `rootcrs.pl -unlock` command.
Step 23	Installs Bundle Patch 1 (patch 10252487) for the Grid Infrastructure and database software, and relinks the Oracle software stack.
Step 24	Configures the RDS protocol for the cluster Interconnect.
Step 25	Locks down the permissions for the Grid Infrastructure (`ORA_CRS_HOME`) directories and restarts the cluster stack.
Step 26	Configures cell alert notification on the storage cells. At the end of this step the CellCLI command `alter cell validate mail` generates test alert messages. If you configured email alerts, then you should get a test message from each cell.
Step 27	Runs `dbca` in silent mode and creates your starter database.
Step 28	Sets up Enterprise Manager Grid Control.
Step 29	Applies security fixes for in the starter database. For example, it drops unsecured user accounts such as `XS$NULL`, `MGMT_VIEW`, and `DIP`. This step will shut down and restart the cluster.

File Name	Description
Step 30	Secures the Exadata environment. This step is optional. It removes the SSH authentication keys for the root user account. If you run this step, you will not be able to run remote commands on the compute nodes and storage cells from the root account without entering the password.

The main script used to run OneCommand is deploy112.sh (Deploy112). The 31 installation steps may be listed by running Deploy112 as follows:

```
[root@exadb01 onecommand]# ./deploy112.sh -i -l
The steps in order are...
Step 0  =  ValidateThisNodeSetup
Step 1  =  SetupSSHForRoot
Step 2  =  ValidateAllNodes
Step 3  =  UnzipFiles
Step 4  =  UpdateEtcHosts
Step 5  =  CreateCellipnitora
Step 6  =  ValidateHW
Step 7  =  ValidateIB
Step 8  =  ValidateCell
Step 9  =  PingRdsCheck
Step 10 =  RunCalibrate
Step 11 =  ValidateTimeDate
Step 12 =  UpdateConfig
Step 13 =  CreateUserAccounts
Step 14 =  SetupSSHForUsers
Step 15 =  CreateOraHomes
Step 16 =  CreateGridDisks
Step 17 =  InstallGridSoftware
Step 18 =  RunGridRootScripts
Step 19 =  Install112DBSoftware
Step 20 =  Create112Listener
Step 21 =  RunAsmCa
Step 22 =  UnlockGIHome
Step 23 =  ApplyBP
Step 24 =  RelinkRDS
Step 25 =  LockUpGI
Step 26 =  SetupCellEmailAlerts
Step 27 =  RunDbca
Step 28 =  SetupEMDbControl
Step 29 =  ApplySecurityFixes
Step 30 =  ResecureMachine
```

■ **Note:** OneCommand is constantly changing to improve the installation process and to support additional bundle patches. The number of steps and what they do is very likely to change with each version of Exadata. So be sure to review the README file for instructions on how to run OneCommand on your system before you begin.

There are number of ways Deploy112 may be used. For example, the following command-line options process all 31 steps of the installation process, only stopping if a step failes:

```
[root@exadb01 onecommand]# ./deploy112.sh -i -r 0-30
```

Each step must complete successfully before you can proceed to the next. Oracle recommends running the steps one at a time, reviewing the output at the end of each before proceeding on to the next. Deploy112 provides this capability with the -s command line option. For example, the installation procedure would look something like the following:

```
[root@exadb01 onecommand]# ./deploy112.sh -i -s 0
```

Check output for errors…

```
[root@exadb01 onecommand]# ./deploy112.sh -i -s 1
```

Check output for errors…

```
[root@exadb01 onecommand]# ./deploy112.sh -i -s 2
```

Check output for errors…

```
[root@exadb01 onecommand]# ./deploy112.sh -i -s 3
```

and so on…

Deploy112 takes as input the parameters from the files you generated earlier using the DBM Configurator. Log files are created each time Deploy112 is called to execute a configuration step, and for some steps, it dynamically generates and executes a shell script that carries out all the tasks required. Reviewing these files can be very useful in determining why a step failed. The log files and dynamically generated shell scripts are stored in the onecommand/tmp directory.

The output generated by the various installation steps varies quite a bit. But in general, Deploy112 displays some header information telling you what step it is running, where to find the log file, and whether it completed successfully. For example, the following output was generated by running step 1 on the quarter rack system in our lab:

```
Script started, file is /opt/oracle.SupportTools/onecommand/tmp/STEP-1-exadb01-
20110513110841.log
=========== 1 SetupSSHForRoot Begin ===============
Setting up ssh for root on ALL nodes....
Checking nodes in /opt/oracle.SupportTools/onecommand/all_group
......
INFO: We're running... /opt/oracle.SupportTools/onecommand/setssh-Linux.sh -s -c Y -h
/opt/oracle.SupportTools/onecommand/all_group -p welcome1 -n N -x
...................................setssh-Linux.sh Done.
SUCCESS: Running SetSSH completed successfully...Return Status: 0 Step# 1
exadb01: Fri May 13 11:09:50 CDT 2011
exadb02: Fri May 13 11:09:50 CDT 2011
```

```
exadb03: Fri May 13 11:09:50 CDT 2011
exadb04: Fri May 13 11:09:50 CDT 2011
exacel01: Fri May 13 11:09:50 CDT 2011
exacel02: Fri May 13 11:09:50 CDT 2011
exacel03: Fri May 13 11:09:50 CDT 2011
exacel04: Fri May 13 11:09:50 CDT 2011
exacel05: Fri May 13 11:09:50 CDT 2011
exacel06: Fri May 13 11:09:50 CDT 2011
exacel07: Fri May 13 11:09:50 CDT 2011
SUCCESS: Running dcli completed successfully...Return Status: 0 Step# 1
INFO: Copying required files to all nodes...please wait...
INFO: Waiting for copies to complete...

INFO: Did SSH setup correctly...
Time spent in step 1 SetupSSHForRoot = 69 seconds
=========== 1 SetupSSHForRoot completed ===============
Running single step at a time....Exiting now
Exiting...
Script done, file is /opt/oracle.SupportTools/onecommand/tmp/STEP-1-exadb01-20110513110841.log
```

Upgrading Exadata

With all the companies out there adopting the Exadata platform, we expect hardware upgrades to be an increasingly popular topic in the near future. Our foray into the Exadata space began over a year ago with an Exadata V2 Quarter Rack configuration. A couple of months ago we upgraded our system to a half rack. Of course, the V2s are no longer in production, so our upgrade came in the form of two X2-2 database servers, and four storage cells. The configuration options we considered were as follows:

- Configure the new X2 equipment as a separate RAC cluster and storage grid, creating two somewhat asymmetric quarter rack configurations within the same Exadata enclosure. Oracle refers to this as a "split rack" configuration.

- Add the new X2 equipment to our existing quarter rack cluster; effectively upgrading it to a half rack.

Creating a New RAC Cluster

The DBM Configurator doesn't directly support upgrading a system in this manner, but with a few adjustments it can be used to generate all the files OneCommand needs to perform the installation. Once the parameter and deployment files are uploaded to Exadata, you should have no problem running through all of the configuration steps without impacting your existing cluster. One coworker actually used this process to create a separate Exadata configuration on the new equipment while leaving the existing system untouched.

For the most part, you simply fill in the DBM Configurator spreadsheet as if you are creating a typical quarter rack configuration. The tricky part is making sure the sequentially assigned network IP addresses don't conflict with your current system. There are a few items you will need to consider when using the DBM Configurator for this type of Exadata upgrade:

> **Name Prefixes:**– It is not required, but you may want to set your Database Machine Name, Database Server Base Name, and Storage Servers Base Names values to match your existing Exadata configuration. That way, if you ever

decide to merge these servers into your old cluster, you won't have to make changes to the host names. For example, our quarter rack configuration had database host names of enkdb01 and enkdb02. Adding the new servers continued with the names enkdb03, and enkdb04. Likewise, the storage cell host names continued with enkcel04 through enkcel07.

Client Access SCAN Name: This procedure will be creating a new RAC cluster, so you will need a new SCAN name for it. You will also need to see that it and all of the other new host names are properly registered in your company's DNS server (just as you did when your existing Exadata system was installed).

Country Code / Time Zone: Of course, these settings should match your existing Exadata system.

NTP and DNS Servers: These should also match your existing Exadata environment.

Oracle Database Machine Model: This setting determines how many compute nodes and storage cells the Configurator will use when creating host names and IP addresses. You will want to set this to X2-2 Quarter Rack, since it is the closest choice to what you are actually configuring. Remember, though, that upgrading from a quarter to half rack adds four storage cells, not three.

Oracle Exadata Storage Server Nodes: You will need to adjust this number to reflect the actual number of storage cells in the upgrade. The default number of storage cells in a quarter rack configuration is 3. But since you are upgrading to a half rack, you will need to set this to 4.

Network IP Addresses: You should continue to use the networks you configured for the Exadata rack you are upgrading. As you enter the starting IP addresses for hosts in the DBM Configurator, take care that you are not creating any address conflicts with existing hardware on your network.

O/S User & Group Accounts: It is not required, but you should use the same user/group names and user/group IDs when configuring your new cluster. This is especially true if there is any chance these user accounts will ever interact between the new system and the old system. OneCommand will not establish user equivalency between the old and new servers for you. So that must be done manually after the upgrade is complete.

When you are finished entering your settings, click the Generate button on the right side of the spreadsheet. This creates a network topology report below the data entry area of the spreadsheet. This report area of the spreadsheet is a place where you can manually override some of the settings generated in the data entry area of the spreadsheet. You will need to scroll down and adjust a few settings in this area before you are ready to create your parameter files and upload them to Exadata. You will notice that the topology report shows incorrect host names for the compute nodes and storage cells. Of course, this is because the DBM Configurator assumes this is a new configuration, not an upgrade. The host names for the compute nodes are postfixed with 01–02, and the storage cells are postfixed with 01–03. Make the necessary changes to the host names in the report, so they reflect compute node names of 03–04 and storage cell host names of 04–07. Once you've made all the necessary changes, click the Create Config Files button to generate your parameter and deployment files. Take a few minutes to review contents of the files to be sure they are correct before you upload them to the /opt/oracle.SupportTools/onecommand directory of the first new compute node, *{machine_name}*db03.

From this point forward, the process is no different than it is for a fresh install. First you will need to configure the network components using Firstboot or ApplyConfig as we discussed earlier. Then simply log in to the first new compute node as root and run through the Deploy112 configuration steps. When you are finished, you will have a new RAC cluster, complete with starter database.

Upgrading the Existing Cluster

If you're upgrading your Exadata to a half or full rack configuration and want to integrate the new servers and cells into your existing RAC cluster, you must configure the new servers and cells manually. The *Exadata Owner's Guide* has a section called "Configuring the Replacement Database Server" that discusses the process in detail. First, we'll take a look at the basic steps for configuring the new database. Then we'll take a look at how you can add the new cells to your existing storage grid.

■ **Caution:** The steps in this section are not intended to be a comprehensive guide and are subject to change. Refer to your Exadata documentation for details specific to your version of Exadata.

Configuring Database Servers

The process for configuring the new database servers are as follows:

1. Upgrade the firmware on your IB Switch to the current release or latest patch. The Oracle hardware technician who installed your new hardware can do this for you or you can download the latest patch and install it yourself. Recommended firmware patches can be found in MOS note: 888828.1.

2. If possible, update the Oracle Grid Infrastructure, and database software to the most current bundle patch for the version of the software your existing system is running. Ideally, the software should be running at the latest release and bundle patch.

3. Use the DBM Configurator to generate IP addresses, and host names for the new compute nodes and storage cells.

4. Register the new host names and IP addresses in your DNS server.

5. Boot your new compute nodes one at a time. The first time they are booted, IPConfig will start automatically, allowing you to enter your network settings.

6. On the database servers, copy the following files from one of your existing database servers to the new database servers:

   - `/etc/security/limits`
     This file is the same on all compute nodes.

   - `/etc/profile`
     This file is the same on all compute nodes.

   - `/etc/oracle/cell/network-config/cellip.ora`
     This file is the same on all compute nodes.

- `/etc/oracle/cell/network-config/cellinit.ora`
  The `cellinit.ora` file should be updated with the private InfiniBand IP address of the compute node where the file is installed. Each compute node will have a unique version of this file.

7. Update the `/etc/hosts` file with the contents of the `priv_ib_group` file generated from DBM Configurator. Use the hosts file on one of your other compute nodes as a guide. It is very important not to remove comments such as the following:

   `#### BEGIN Generated by Exadata. DO NOT MODIFY ####`

8. Update the `/opt/oracle.SupportTools/onecommand/*.group` files on all compute nodes, adding the nodes to the configuration.

9. Create the O/S users and groups as they are defined on the other compute nodes. The `finger` command may be used to compare user account definitions as follows.

10. Set up SSH user equivalency between the new and old compute nodes for the Oracle software owner.

11. Follow the steps in the Owner's Guide for cloning the Grid Infrastructure and database homes to a replacement server. That section of the Owner's Guide is discussing the replacement of a failed database server. Of course you will not be replacing a server so you can skip over any steps having to do with removing a failed server from the cluster.

■ **Note:** The Exadata platform consists of multiple software and hardware components that require periodic updates. These updates come in three forms: Storage Server patches, Database Server patches (bundle patches), and InfiniBand Switch updates. Considering the complexity of Exadata, it is more important than ever to keep your system fairly current with the latest software and firmware patches. A word of caution though, we recommend that you wait at least a month after a patch is available before installing it on a production system. Even for test and development systems, we recommend you wait at least 2–3 weeks after a patch is available before installing it. Oracle maintains a document on My Oracle Support (MOS) containing a list of all supported software and patches available for Exadata, starting with version 11.2. The document is continually updated with useful information, instructions and links to the latest patches as they become available. The document is MOS note 888828.1 "Database Machine and Exadata Storage Server Release 2 (11.2) Supported Versions". See Appendix B for a list of other useful MOS notes relating to the Exadata platform.

Configuring Storage Cells

Adding new cells to your existing storage grid is a fairly simple process. There may be other ways to simplify the process by cloning an existing storage cell, but we'll take a look at the manual process so you can see the commands and files involved. The process is as follows:

1. Your new storage cells will come with the latest version of the Exadata cell software installed. Before you begin, check the version of software on the new cells and upgrade your old cells to match. The imageinfo command can be used to display this information.

2. Locate the cellinit.ora file on one of your old cells and copy it over to the new cells. Modify the cellinit.ora file on the new cells and change the ipaddress1 field to the private InfiniBand address of the cell. Login as the root account when configuring the storage cell. The $OSSCONF environment variable should point to the location of the correct cellinit.ora file.

3. Update the /etc/hosts file with the contents of the priv_ib_group file generated from DBM Configurator. Use the hosts file on one of your other storage cells as a guide. It is very important not to remove comments such as the following:

   ```
   #### BEGIN Generated by Exadata. DO NOT MODIFY ####
   ```

4. Reboot the new cells and verify that they restart properly.

5. Verify that the cell services are running using the CellCLI command list cell. If the cell services are down you may see an error such as this:

   ```
   CELL-01514: Connect Error. Verify that Management Server is listening
   at the specified HTTP port: 8888.
   ```

   ```
   Cell Services must be stopped and started from the root or celladmin
   user accounts. The following commands may be used to manually shutdown
   and startup the services:
   ```

   ```
   CellCLI> alter cell shutdown services all;
   CellCLI> alter cell startup services all;
   ```

6. Configuring the storage cell is done using the ALTER CELL command. For example storage cell alert notification can be configured using the following command:

   ```
   ALTER CELL smtpServer='mail.ourcompany.com', -
     smtpFromAddr='Exadata@ourcompany.com', -
     smtpFrom='Exadata', -
     smtpToAddr=''all.dba@ourcompany.com,all.sa@ourcompany.com'', -
     notificationPolicy='critical,warning,clear', -
     notificationMethod='mail,snmp'
   ```

7. Your current cell configuration may be displayed using the LIST CELL DETAIL command. Once you are finished configuring the cell, stop and restart the cell services to pick up the new settings.

8. Configure the cell smart flash cache using the CREATE FLASHCACHE ALL command.

9. Configure all cell disks using the CREATE CELLDISK ALL command.

10. Using one of your old storage cells for reference, create your grid disks using the CREATE GRIDDISK command. We discuss using this command in Chapter 14. Be sure you create your grid disks in the proper order, as this will impact the performance of the disks. If you still have the original create scripts generated and run by OneCommand on the first compute node of your existing cluster, you will find all the commands you need for creating your grid disks in the proper order. The scripts are createocrvotedg.sh and CreateGridDisk.sh and should be located in the /opt/oracle.SupportTools/tmp directory. If these files are not available, you can use the size and offset attributes of the LIST GRIDDISK DETAIL command to determine the proper size and creation order for the grid disks.

11. Once you are finished configuring the cells and creating your grid disks, you can add the cell to the storage grid. This is done on the compute nodes by adding the cell's private InfiniBand network IP address to the /etc/oracle/cell/network-config/cellip.ora file on each database server.

Summary

Configuring Exadata is a very detailed process, and some things tend to change somewhat as new versions of the software become available. This chapter discussed some of the main points of configuring Exadata compute nodes and storage cells, but it is not intended to be a substitute for the official Oracle documentation. Oracle has done an excellent job of documenting the platform, and you will find the *Owner's Guide* and *User's Guide* to be invaluable assets when learning the ins and outs of configuring Exadata. There is some overlap in subject matter covered in this chapter with the topics discussed in Chapters 9 and 15, so you might find them helpful as a cross reference for some of the configuration tasks discussed here.

CHAPTER 9

Recovering Exadata

You may have heard the saying "disk drives spin, and then they die." It's not something we like to think about, but from the moment you power up a new system, your disk drives begin aging. Disk drives have come a long way in the past 30 years, and typical life expectancy has improved dramatically. At the end of the day, though, it's a matter of "when" a disk will fail, not "if." And we all know that many disk drives fail long before they should. Knowing how to diagnose disk failures and what to do when they occur has generally been the responsibility of the system administrator or storage administrator. For many DBAs, Exadata is going to change that. Many Exadata systems out there are being managed entirely by the DBA staff. Whether or not this is the case in your data center, the procedure for recovering from a disk failure on Exadata is going to be a little different than you are used to.

Oracle database servers have traditionally required two types of backup: operating system backups and database backups. Exadata adds storage cells to the mix, and with that comes a whole new subsystem that must be protected and, on occasion, restored. The storage cell is a fairly resilient piece of hardware that employs Linux software RAID to protect the operating system volumes. As such, it is unlikely that a disk failure would necessitate an operating system restore. The more likely causes would be human error, a failed patch install, or a bug. Remember that these physical volumes also contain grid disks (database volumes), so a loss one of these disks will most likely mean a loss of database storage as well. Oracle has engineered several features into Exadata to protect your data and reduce the impact of such failures. This chapter will discuss some of the more common storage failure scenarios, how to diagnose them, and how to recover with minimal downtime.

▨ **Note:** One of the most challenging aspects of writing this chapter is the rapidly changing nature of the commands and scripts we will be discussing. In many cases, recovery tasks will have you working very closely with the hardware layer of Exadata. So as you read this chapter, keep in mind that with each new version of Exadata hardware and software, the commands and scripts discussed in this chapter may change. Be sure to check the Oracle documentation for the latest updates to the commands and scripts discussed here.

Exadata Diagnostic Tools

Exadata is a highly complex blend of hardware and software that work together to produce an incredibly resilient delivery platform. The complexity of the platform can be a bit daunting at first. There are simply a lot of moving parts that one must understand in order to maintain the platform effectively. Oracle provides a wealth of diagnostic tools that can be used to verify, analyze, and report important information about the configuration and health of the system. In this section, we'll discuss some of those tools and how to use them.

Sun Diagnostics: sundiag.sh

Installed on every Exadata database server and storage cell is the `sundiag.sh` script, located in the `/opt/oracle.SupportTools` directory. If for some reason you don't find it installed on your system, you can download it from My Oracle Support. Refer to MOS Doc ID 761868.1. This script is run from the root account and collects diagnostic information needed for troubleshooting disk failures. The files it collects are bundled in the familiar `tar` format and then compressed using bzip2.

sundiag.sh Output

The log files produced by `sundiag.sh` are named using the host name of the server, followed by a descriptive name, and postfixed with the date and time of the report. For example, running the script on our lab system produced an output file (created by the `demsg` command) named as follows:

`enkdb01_dmesg_2011_01_28_09_42.out`

Now, let's take a look at the diagnostic files collected by `sundiags.sh`.

messages: This is a copy of the `/var/log/messages` file from your system. The messages file is rotated and aged out automatically by the operating system. If your system has been running for a while, you will have several of these files enumerated in ascending order from current (`messages`) to oldest (`messages.4`). This file is maintained by the `syslog` daemon and contains important information about the health and operation of the operating system.

dmesg: This file is created by the `dmesg` command and contains diagnostic kernel-level information from the *kernel ring buffer*. The kernel ring buffer contains messages sent to or received from external devices connected to the system, such as disk drives, keyboard, video, and so on.

lspci: This file contains a list of all the PCI buses on the system.

lsscsi: The `lsscsi` file contains a list of all the SCSI drives on the system.

fdisk-l: The `fdisk-l` file contains a listing of all disk device partitions in your system.

sel-list: The `sel-list` file contains output from the `ipmitool sel elist` command. IPMI stands for Intelligent Platform Management Interface and is part of the ILOM (Integrated Lights Out Management) component. The `ipmitool` command taps into the ILOM and extracts sensor readings on all IPMI enabled devices such as memory and CPU.

megacli64: The `sundiags.sh` script runs the `MegaCli64` command with various options that interrogate the MegaRAID controller for information on the configuration and status of your disk controller and attached disk drives. There is a wealth of information collected by the MegaRAID controller that can be easily tapped into using the `MegaCli64` command. For example, the following listing shows a summary of the RAID configuration of the disk drives on our lab system:

```
Slot 00 Device 11 (HITACHI H103014SCSUN146GA2A81017FAJW9E ) status is: Online
Slot 01 Device 10 (HITACHI H103014SCSUN146GA2A81017FBAY8E ) status is: Online
Slot 02 Device 09 (HITACHI H103014SCSUN146GA2A81017FAK0BE ) status is: Online
Slot 03 Device 08 (HITACHI H103014SCSUN146GA2A81017FB8PHE ) status is: Hotspare
```

Information in these files includes an event log and a status summary of your controller and disk drives. For example, the following listing shows a summary of the state of the physical disk drives attached to one of our database servers:

```
Checking RAID status on enkdb01.enkitec.com
Controller a0:  LSI MegaRAID SAS 9261-8i
No of Physical disks online : 3
Degraded : 0
Failed Disks : 0
```

It is hard to say whether Exadata uses the MegaCli64 command to monitor predictive failure for disk drives or if the developers have tapped into SMART metrics through an API, but this information is all available to you at the command line. There isn't a lot of information about MegaCli64 out there, but the sundiag.sh script is a good place to start if you are interested in peeking under the hood and getting a closer look at some of the metrics Exadata collects to determine the health of your disk subsystem.

If you run the sundiag.sh script on your storage cells, additional data is collected about the cell configuration, alerts, and special log files that do not exist on the database server. The following list describes these additional log files collected by sundiag.sh.

cell-detail: The cell-detail file contains detailed site-specific information about your storage cell. This is output from the CellCLI command LIST CELLDISK DETAIL.

celldisk-detail: This file contains a detailed report of your cell disks. The report is created using the CellCLI command LIST CELLDISK DETAIL. Among other things, it shows the status, logical unit number (LUN), and physical device partition for your cell disks.

lun-detail: This report is generated using the CellCLI command LIST LUN DETAIL. It contains detailed information about the underlying LUNs on which your cell disks are configured. Included in this report are the names, device types, and physical device names (like /dev/sdw) of your LUNs.

physicaldisk-detail: The physicaldisk-detail file contains a detailed report of all physical disks and FMODs used by the storage cell for database type storage, and Flash Cache. It is generated using the CellCLI command LIST PHYSICALDISK DETAIL, and it includes important information about these devices such as the device type (hard disk or flash disk), make and model, slot address, and device status.

physicaldisk-fail: This file contains a listing of all physical disks (including flash disks) that do not have a status of Normal. This would include disks with a status of Not Present, which is a failed disk that has been replaced but not yet removed from the configuration. When a physical disk is replaced, its old configuration remains in the system for 7 days, after which it is automatically purged.

griddisk-detail: This file contains a detailed report of all grid disks configured on the storage cell. It is created using the CellCLI command LIST GRIDDISK DETAIL and includes, among other things, the grid disk name, cell disk name, size, and status of all grid disks you have configured on the storage cell.

flashcache-detail: This report contains the list of all FMODs that make up the cell flash cache. It is the output of the CellCLI command LIST FLASHCACHE DETAIL and includes the size and status of the flash cache. Also found in this report is a list of all flash cache cell disks that are operating in a degraded mode.

alerthistory: The alerthistory file contains a detailed report of all alerts that have occurred on the storage cell. It is created using the CellCLI command LIST ALERTHISTORY.

fdom-1: This report contains detailed information about the four flash cache cards and flash cache modules (FDOMs) on your storage cell. It is created by running the /usr/bin/flash_dom -l command on the storage cell and includes information like firmware version, address, and device name of each of the FDOMs. For example:

```
D#  B___T  Type   Vendor Product         Rev   Operating System Device Name
1.  0   0  Disk   ATA    MARVELL SD88SA02 D20Y  /dev/sdu    [3:0:0:0]
2.  0   1  Disk   ATA    MARVELL SD88SA02 D20Y  /dev/sdv    [3:0:1:0]
3.  0   2  Disk   ATA    MARVELL SD88SA02 D20Y  /dev/sdw    [3:0:2:0]
4.  0   3  Disk   ATA    MARVELL SD88SA02 D20Y  /dev/sdx    [3:0:3:0]
```

alert.log: The alert.log file is written to by the cellsrv process. Similar to a database or ASM alert log file, the storage cell alert.log contains important runtime information about the storage cell and the status of its disk drives. This file is very useful in diagnosing problems with cell storage.

ms-odl.trc: The ms-odl.trc contains detailed runtime, trace-level information from the cell's management server process.

ms-odl.log: This file is written to by the cell's management server process. It is not included in the collection created by the sundiag.sh script, but we have found it very useful in diagnosing problems that occur in the storage cell. It also contains normal, day-to-day operational messages. Storage cells maintain their log files by rotating them, similar to the way the operating system rotates the system log (/var/log/messages). The ms-odl.log file records these tasks as well as more critical tasks like disk failures.

HealthCheck

HealthCheck is a set of shell scripts developed by Oracle that you can use to verify your configuration. These scripts are not included in your Exadata installation but are readily available for download from My Oracle Support under Article ID: 1070954.1, "Oracle Database Machine HealthCheck." The scripts are well documented and produce a staggering amount of information about your Exadata Database Machine, so we won't go through all the gory details here. HealthCheck reports the current configuration of key hardware and software components of Exadata. Oracle recommends that you routinely run HealthCheck as a normal part of maintaining your database machine. The output should be compared with bulletins and best practices published by Oracle Corporation to ensure optimal performance and manageability of the platform. Health checks are fairly lightweight, and all except one can be run during normal business operations. The exception is the CheckHWnFWProfile test. This test is not executed by default and should only be run immediately following a fresh installation of the Exadata software.

HealthCheck is made up of two main scripts, the ASM health check (run_os_commands_as_oracle.sh) and the O/S health check (run_os_commands_as_root.sh). The ASM health check should only take a few seconds to execute, while the O/S health check will run for around 3–5 minutes depending on your specific Exadata configuration (V2, X2-2, X2-8) and system load. The output from these tests is stored in files named with a "date+time"pattern, stored in the output directory under the HealthCheck home directory. For example, after running HealthCheck on a couple different occasions, our "output_files" directory shows the following:

```
[enkdb01:oracle:DEMO1] /u01/app/HealthCheck/output_files
> ls -ltr
total 324
-rw-rw-r-- 1 oracle dba     5683 Dec 30 14:59 asm_output_012811_145938.lst
-rw-r--r-- 1 root   root 148341 Dec 30 16:00 os_output_123010_145931.lst
-rw-rw-r-- 1 oracle dba     5683 Jan 28 15:01 asm_output_012811_150122.lst
-rw-r--r-- 1 root   root 153205 Jan 28 15:44 os_output_012811_154236.lst
```

The thing we really like about the HealthCheck is that instead of simply reporting what it finds, it gives a short description of what the expected readings should be and what to do if your results are outside the norm. Another nice thing about the HealthCheck is that it is all written in shell scripts with callouts to programs like sqlplus and MegaCli64. This means that in addition to being a very useful auditing and verification tool, it is also a very good learning tool because you can easily see some of the commands that Oracle support analysts would use to diagnose your Exadata Database Machine.

CellCLI

The cellsrv process on each storage cell collects important information about the current state of the storage cell and components such as CPU, flash cache modules, cell disks, grid disks, and more. These cell metrics are in turn received by the Management Service (MS) process. Once an hour, the MS process writes the cell metrics to its Automatic Diagnostics Repository (ADR) similar to the way 11g databases record alerts to the ADR on the database servers. Exadata monitors the metrics it collects and triggers alerts when key thresholds are exceeded, hardware errors occur, or software errors occur in the cellsrv process. The CellCLI program is your primary interface for configuring and managing the storage cells. CellCLI also provides convenient access to the metrics and alerts recorded in the ADR. The information in the ADR can also be accessed with the adrci command, just as you would on the database servers (for database alerts). The ADR has been around for several years and is well documented, so we won't be discussing adrci here. Instead, we'll be focusing our attention on CellCLI and how it can be used to tap into the diagnostic information stored in the ADR.

Cell Metrics

Cell metrics are key measurements collected from various components in the storage cell. These metrics can be retrieved using the LIST METRICDEFINITION command. For example, the following report shows the definition for the CL_RUNQ metric, which tracks run queue information from the operating system:

```
CellCLI> list metricdefinition where name = CL_RUNQ detail
        name:                   CL_RUNQ
        description:            "Average number (over the preceding minute) of processes in
                                the Linux run queue marked running or uninterruptible (from
                                /proc/loadavg)."
        metricType:             Instantaneous
        objectType:             CELL
        unit:                   Number
```

At the time of this writing, the storage cell maintains 165 specific metrics. The DESCRIBE METRICCURRENT command displays the attributes of the metriccurrent object, as shown in the following listing.

```
CellCLI> describe metriccurrent
        name
        alertState
        collectionTime
        metricObjectName
        metricType
        metricValue
        objectType
```

The LIST METRICCURRENT command can be used to report current readings of these metrics. The report generated by this command is very lengthy so you will want to apply filters to limit the report to the components you are interested in. The following list shows the object types stored in the ADR.

- CELL

- CELLDISK

- CELL_FILESYSTEM

- FLASHCACHE

- GRIDDISK

- HOST_INTERCONNECT

- IORM_CATEGORY

- IORM_CONSUMER_GROUP

- IORM_DATABASE

Understanding the naming convention used for the metric name will help you focus the report on the specific metrics you are interested in. The metric name is a concatenation of abbreviations for the type of component, delimited by the underscore character (_). The first part of the metric name is an abbreviation for the object type. This can be used as shorthand for filtering the report output. Table 9-1 shows the metric name prefixes and what each one represents.

Table 9-1. Metric Name Prefixes

Name Prefix	Description
CL_	Cell level metrics
CD_	Cell disk metrics
GD_	Grid disk metrics
FC_	Flash Cache metrics
DB_	Database metrics
CG_	IORM Consumer group metrics
CT_	IORM Categories
N_	Network (InfiniBand network interconnect)

For I/O-related metrics, the metric name continues with one of the values listed in Table 9-2.

Table 9-2. I/O Metric Abbreviations

Abbreviation	Description
IO_RQ	Number of I/O requests
IO_BY	Number of megabytes
IO_TM	I/O Latency
IO_WT	I/O Wait time

For I/O-related metrics, the next part of the metric name may be R (for reads) or W (for writes) followed by SM or LG for small or large reads and writes. The last abbreviation in the metric name will be either SEC for seconds or RQ for requests. For example, the following command shows the number of small I/O write operations per second for all grid disks on the storage cell.

```
CellCLI> list metriccurrent where name = GD_IO_RQ_W_SM_SEC
        GD_IO_RQ_W_SM_SEC       DATA_CD_00_cell01       0.8 IO/sec
        GD_IO_RQ_W_SM_SEC       DATA_CD_01_cell01       0.9 IO/sec
        GD_IO_RQ_W_SM_SEC       DATA_CD_02_cell01       1.4 IO/sec
        GD_IO_RQ_W_SM_SEC       DATA_CD_03_cell01       1.6 IO/sec
...
```

The default retention for metric detail is 7 days, after which it will be summarized by min, max, and average (at which time the detail records will be purged). The DESCRIBE METRICHISTORY command shows the structure of the metrichistory object.

```
CellCLI> describe metrichistory
        name
        alertState
        collectionTime
        metricObjectName
        metricType
        metricValue
        metricValueAvg
        metricValueMax
        metricValueMin
        objectType
```

The LIST METRICHISTORY command provides a summarized report of the full history of cell metrics stored in the ADR. Usually you will want to apply filters to specify a date range and possibly a metric type for this report. To do this, provide a WHERE clause with the metric name and a date filter, as in this example:

```
CellCLI> list metrichistory -
        where name like 'CL_.*' -
            and collectiontime > '2011-01-01T08:00:00-08:00'
```

Cell Alerts

In addition to tracking metrics for storage cell components, Exadata also evaluates these metrics and applies thresholds to verify that the components are running within normal parameters. When a metric crosses one of these operational thresholds, an alert is generated. Some of the alerts generated by Exadata include cell temperature, cell disk read/write errors, and software failures. Exadata tracks over 70 alert types in the storage cell. Additional alerts may be defined using Grid Control's monitoring and alerting features. Alert severities fall into four categories: Information, Warning, Critical, and Clear. These are used to manage alert notifications. For example, you may choose to get an email alert notification for critical alerts only. The Clear severity is used to notify you when a component has returned to Normal status. The LIST METRICHISTORY DETAIL command can be used to generate a detailed report of the alerts generated by the system. The following listing is an example of an alert generated by the storage cell:

```
        name:                209_1
        alertMessage:        "All Logical drives are in WriteThrough caching mode.
                             Either battery is in a learn cycle or it needs to be
                             replaced. Please contact Oracle Support"
        alertSequenceID:     209
        alertShortName:      Hardware
        alertType:           Stateful
        beginTime:           2011-01-17T04:42:10-06:00
        endTime:             2011-01-17T05:50:29-06:00
        examinedBy:
        metricObjectName:    LUN_CACHE_WT_ALL
        notificationState:   1
        sequenceBeginTime:   2011-01-17T04:42:10-06:00
```

```
        severity:            critical
        alertAction:         "Battery is either in a learn cycle or it needs
                             replacement. Please contact Oracle Support"
```

When the battery subsequently returns to Normal status, a follow-up alert is generated with a severity of Clear, indicating that the component has returned to normal operating status:

```
        name:                209_2
        alertMessage:        "Battery is back to a good state"
        ...
        severity:            clear
        alertAction:         "Battery is back to a good state. No Action Required"
```

When you review alerts, you should get in the habit of setting the examinedBy attribute of the alert so you can keep track of which alerts are already being investigated. If you set the examinedBy attribute, you can use it as a filter on the LIST ALERTHISTORY command to report all alerts that are not currently being attended to. By adding the severity filter you can further reduce the output to just critical alerts. For example:

```
LIST ALERTHISTORY WHERE severity = 'critical' AND examinedBy = '' DETAIL
```

To set the examinedBy attribute of the alert, use the ALTER ALERTHISTORY command and specify the name of the alert you wish to alter. For example, we can set the examinedBy attribute for the Battery alert just shown as follows:

```
CellCLI> alter alerthistory 209_1 examinedBy="rjohnson"
Alert 209_1 successfully altered

CellCLI> list alerthistory attributes name, alertMessage, examinedby where name=209_1 detail
        name:                209_1
        alertMessage:        "All Logical drives are in WriteThrough caching mode.
                             Either battery is in a learn cycle or it needs to be
                             replaced. Please contact Oracle Support"
        examinedBy:          rjohnson
```

There is quite a bit more to say about managing, reporting, and customizing Exadata alerts. An entire chapter would be needed to cover the subject in detail. In this section we've only touched on the basics. Fortunately, once you get email configured for alert notification, very little must be done to manage these alerts. In many environments, email notification is all that is used to catch and report critical alerts.

Exadata is one of the best-instrumented and self-documented systems we've ever worked on. It is also one of the most complex. This section has discussed three very helpful tools that provide the kind of diagnostic information you must have in order to resolve Exadata problems. Sun Diagnostics and HealthCheck are wrapper scripts that call other commands and scripts to tap into key hardware and software component metrics. If you are brave enough, it is well worth the time to crack these scripts open and become familiar with what they are doing. CellCLI provides an excellent way of producing reports detailing alerts that affect the normal operations of your system. There is a lot to be learned about where configuration and diagnostic information is stored so you can quickly go straight to the source when problems arise. In this section we've tried to touch on some of the more important areas you should be aware of.

Backing Up Exadata

When we took delivery of our Exadata system, one of our primary concerns was, "how can we back up everything so we can restore it to working order if something goes horribly wrong?" When our Exadata arrived in May of 2010, the latest version of the Cell software was 11.2.0.1.0. And at the time, the only way to back up a database server was to use third-party backup software or standard Linux commands like tar. Oracle is constantly developing new features for Exadata and less than a year later, Exadata X-2 database servers come configured with the native Linux Logical Volume Manager (LVM). This is a big step forward, because the LVM has built-in snapshot capabilities that provide an easy method of taking backups of the operating system. Storage cells use a completely different, proprietary, method for backup and recovery. In this section we'll take a look at the various methods Oracle recommends for backing up Exadata database servers and storage cells. We'll also take a brief look at Recovery Manager (RMAN) and some of the features Exadata provides that improve the performance of database backup and recovery. After that, we'll take a look at what it takes to recover from some of the more common types of system failure. It may surprise you, but the focus of this chapter is not database recovery. There are very few Exadata-specific considerations for database backup and recovery. A majority of the product-specific backup and recovery methods pertain to backup and recovery of the system volumes containing the operating system and Exadata software, so we'll spend a quite a bit of time discussing recovery, from the loss of a cell disk, to the loss of a system volume on the database servers or storage cells.

Backing Up the Database Servers

Recently, Oracle began shipping Exadata with the Linux LVM configured for managing file system storage on the database servers. Logical volume managers provide an abstraction layer for physical disk partitions similar to the way ASM does for its underlying physical storage devices. LVMs have volume groups comparable to ASM disk groups. These volume groups are made up of one or more physical disks (or disk partitions), as ASM disk groups are made up of one or more physical disks (or disk partitions). LVM volume groups are carved up into logical volumes in which file systems can be created. In a similar way, databases utilize ASM disk groups for creating tablespaces that are used for storing tables, indexes, and other database objects. Abstracting physical storage from the file systems allows the system administrator to grow and shrink the logical volumes (and file systems) as needed. There are a number of other advantages to using the LVM to manage storage for the Exadata database servers, but our focus will be the new backup and restore capabilities the Linux LVM provides, namely LVM snapshots. In addition to their convenience and ease of use, LVM snapshots eliminate many of the typical challenges we face with simple backups using the tar command or third-party backup products. For example, depending on the amount of data in the backup set, file system backups can take quite a while to complete. These backups are not consistent to a point in time, meaning that if you must restore a file system from backup, the data in your files will represent various points in time from the beginning of the backup process to its end. Applications that continue to run during the backup cycle can hold locks on files, causing them to be skipped (not backed up). And once again, open applications will inevitably make changes to data during the backup cycle. Even if you are able to back up these open files, you have no way of knowing if they are in any usable state unless the application is shut down before the backup is taken. LVM snapshots are instantaneous because no data is actually copied. You can think of a snapshot as an index of pointers to the physical data blocks that make up the contents of your file system. When a file is changed or deleted, the original blocks of the file are written to the snapshot volume. So even if it takes hours to complete a backup, it will still be consistent with the moment the snapshot was created. Now, let's take a look at how LVM snapshots can be used to create a consistent file system backup of the database server.

System Backup Using LVM Snapshots

Creating file system backups using LVM snapshots is a pretty simple process. First you need to create a destination for the final copy of the backups. This can be SAN or NAS storage or simply an NFS file system shared from another server. If you have enough free space in the volume group to store your backup files, you can create a temporary LVM partition to stage your backups before sending them off to tape. This can be done using the lvcreate command. Before creating a new LVM partition, make sure you have enough free space in your volume group using the vgdisplay command:

```
[root@enkdb01 ~]# vgdisplay
  --- Volume group ---
  VG Name              VGExaDb
...
  VG Size              556.80 GB
  PE Size              4.00 MB
  Total PE             142541
  Alloc PE / Size      45824 / 179.00 GB
  Free  PE / Size      96717 / 377.80 GB
...
```

The vgdisplay command shows the size of our volume group, physical extents (PE) currently in use, and the amount of free space available in the volume group. The Free PE/Size attribute indicates that we have 377.8GB of free space remaining in the volume group. This is plenty of room for us to create a new 25GB LVM partition to store our backup images.

First we'll use the lvcreate command to create a new 25GB LVM partition:

```
[root@enkdb01 ~]# lvcreate -L 25G -n /dev/VGExaDb/sysback
  Logical volume "sysback" created
```

Now we can create a new file system on the sysback partition:

```
 [root@enkdb01 ~]# mkfs.ext3 -m 0 -b 4096 /dev/VGExaDb/sysback
mke2fs 1.39 (29-May-2006)
...
Writing inode tables: done
Creating journal (32768 blocks): done
Writing superblocks and filesystem accounting information: done
...
```

Next we'll create a target directory and mount the new file system:

```
[root@enkdb01 ~]# mkdir /mnt/sysback
[root@enkdb01 ~]# mount /dev/VGExaDb/sysback /mnt/sysback
[root@enkdb01 ~]# df -k /mnt/sysback
```

The fdisk command displays our new file system and the logical volumes we want to include in our system backup, VGExaDb-LVDbSys1 (root file system), and VGExaDb-LVDbOra1 (/u01 file system). Notice that the /boot file system does not use the LVM for storage. This file system must be backed up using the tar command. This isn't a problem, because the /boot file system is fairly small and static so we aren't concerned with these files being modified, locked, or open during the backup cycle.

```
[root@enkdb01 ~]# df -h
Filesystem                      Size  Used Avail Use% Mounted on
/dev/mapper/VGExaDb-LVDbSys1     30G  9.3G   19G  33% /
/dev/sda1                       124M   16M  102M  14% /boot
```

```
/dev/mapper/VGExaDb-LVDbOra1      99G   14G   80G   15% /u01
tmpfs                            81G  200M   81G    1% /dev/shm
/dev/mapper/VGExaDb-sysback       25G  173M   25G    1% /mnt/sysback
```

Now that we have a place to stage our backup images and we know the logical volumes we want to back up, we're ready to create snapshots for the / and /u01 file systems. Using the Linux time command we can see that it took just over 1 second to create a snapshot for the root volume:

```
[root@enkdb01 ~]# time lvcreate -L1G -s -n root_snap /dev/VGExaDb/LVDbSys1
  Logical volume "root_snap" created
real    0m1.066s
user    0m0.005s
sys     0m0.013s

[root@enkdb01 ~]# lvcreate -L5G -s -n u01_snap /dev/VGExaDb/LVDbOra1
  Logical volume "u01_snap" created
```

Notice the –L1G and -L5G options we used to create these snapshots. The –L parameter determines the size of the snapshot volume. When data blocks are modified or deleted after the snapshot is created, the original copy of the block is written to the snapshot. It is important to size the snapshot sufficiently to store an original copy of all changed blocks. If the snapshot runs out of space, it will be deactivated. Now that we have snapshots tracking changes to the / and /u01 file systems, we are ready to take a backup. To prove that these snapshots are consistent, we'll copy the /etc/hosts file to a test file in the /root directory. If snapshots work as they are supposed to, this file will not be included our backup, because it was created after the snapshot was created. The command looks like this:

```
[root@enkdb01 ~]# cp /etc/hosts /root/test_file.txt
```

Mount the snapshots as you would any other file system. First, we'll create a directory to use as a mount point for our snapshots. Then we'll mount the root and u01 snapshots.

```
[root@enkdb01 ~]# mkdir /mnt/snap
[root@enkdb01 ~]# mount /dev/VGExaDb/root_snap /root/mnt/snap
[root@enkdb01 ~]# mount /dev/VGExaDb/u01_snap /mnt/snap/u01
```

Now that the snapshots are mounted, we can browse them just like any other file system. They look and feel just like the original file systems, with one exception. If we look in the mounted snapshot for the test file we created, we don't see it. It's not there because it was created after the snapshots were created and started tracking changes to the file system:

```
[root@enkdb01 ~]# ls -l /root/testfile
-rw-r--r-- 1 root root 1023 Jan 23 13:30 /root/test_file.txt   <- the test file we created

[root@enkdb01 ~]# ls -l /mnt/snap/root/test_file.txt
ls: /mnt/snap/root/testfile: No such file or directory    <- no test file in the snapshot
```

Once the snapshots are mounted, they can be backed up using any standard Linux backup software. For this test, we'll use the tar command to create a tarball backup of the / and /u01 file systems. Since we are backing up a snapshot, we don't have to worry about files that are open, locked, or changed during the backup. Notice that we've also included the /boot directory in this backup.

```
[root@enkdb01 ~]# cd /mnt/snap
[root@enkdb01 snap]# tar -pjcvf /mnt/sysback/enkdb01_system_backup.tar.bz2 * /boot \
  --exclude /mnt/sysback/enkdb01_system_backup.tar.bz2 \
   >/tmp/ enkdb01_system_backup.stdout 2>/tmp/enkdb01_system_backup.stderr
```

When the backup is finished, you should check the error file, enkdb01_system_backup.stderr, for any issues logged during the backup. If you are satisfied with the backup, you can unmount and drop the snapshots. You will create a new set of snapshots each time you run a backup. After you copy the backup image off to tape you can optionally unmount and drop the temporary partition you created to store it.

```
[root@enkdb01 snap]# cd /

[root@enkdb01 /]# umount /mnt/snap/u01
[root@enkdb01 /]# rmdir /mnt/snap/u01

[root@enkdb01 /]# umount /mnt/snap
[root@enkdb01 /]# rmdir /mnt/snap

[root@enkdb01 /]# lvremove /dev/VGExaDb/root_snap
Do you really want to remove active logical volume root_snap? [y/n]: y
  Logical volume "root_snap" successfully removed

root@enkdb01 /]# lvremove /dev/VGExaDb/u01_snap
Do you really want to remove active logical volume u01_snap? [y/n]: y
  Logical volume "u01_snap" successfully removed

[root@ricudb01 /]# lvremove /dev/VGExaDb/sysback
Do you really want to remove active logical volume sysback? [y/n]: y
  Logical volume "sysback" successfully removed

[root@enkdb01 /]# umount /mnt/sysback
[root@enkdb01 /]# rmdir /mnt/sysback

[root@ricudb01 /]# lvremove /dev/VGExaDb/sysback
Do you really want to remove active logical volume sysback? [y/n]: y
  Logical volume "sysback" successfully removed
```

As discussed in the opening paragraph, early models of Exadata V2 did not implement LVM for managing file system storage. Without LVM snapshots, getting a clean system backup would require shutting down the applications on the server (including the databases), or purchasing third-party backup software. Even then, there would be no way to create a backup in which all files are consistent with the same point in time. LVM snapshots fill an important gap in the Exadata backup and recovery architecture and offer a simple, manageable strategy for backing up the database servers. Later in this chapter we'll discuss how these backups are used for restoring the database server when file systems are lost or damaged.

Backing Up the Storage Cell

The first two disks in a storage cell contain the Linux operating system. These Linux partitions are commonly referred to as the *system volumes*. Backing up the system volumes using industry standard Linux backup software is not recommended. So how do you back up the system volumes? Well, the answer is that you don't. Exadata automatically does this for you through the use of an internal USB drive called the *CELLBOOT USB flash drive*. If you are the cautious sort, you can also create your own cell recovery image using an external USB flash drive. In addition to the CELLBOOT USB flash drive, Exadata also maintains, on a separate set of disk partitions, a full copy of the system volumes as they were before the last patch was installed. These backup partitions are used for rolling back a patch. Now let's take a look at how these backup methods work.

CELLBOOT USB Flash Drive

You can think of the internal CELLBOOT USB flash drive as you would any external USB drive you would plug into your laptop. The device can be seen using the fdisk command as follows:

```
[enkcel01:root] /root
> fdisk -l /dev/sdac

Disk /dev/sdac: 4009 MB, 4009754624 bytes
124 heads, 62 sectors/track, 1018 cylinders
Units = cylinders of 7688 * 512 = 3936256 bytes

    Device Boot      Start         End      Blocks   Id  System
/dev/sdac1               1        1017     3909317   83  Linux
```

Just for fun, we mounted the internal USB flash drive to take a peek at what Oracle included in this backup. The following listing shows the contents of this device:

```
[enkcel01:root] /root
mount /dev/sdac1 /mnt/usb

[enkcel01:root] /mnt/usb
> ls -l
total 48200
-r-xr-x--- 1 root root      2048 Dec  7 07:58 boot.cat
-r-xr-x--- 1 root root        16 Dec  7 07:55 boot.msg
drwxr-xr-x 2 root root      4096 Dec 17 11:44 cellbits
drwxr-xr-x 2 root root      4096 Dec 17 11:44 grub
-rw-r--r-- 1 root root        16 Dec 17 11:44 I_am_CELLBOOT_usb
-r-xr-x--- 1 root root       854 Dec 17 11:13 image.id
-r-xr-x--- 1 root root       441 Dec 17 11:14 imgboot.lst
-rw-rw-r-- 1 root root   6579844 Dec  7 07:50 initrd-2.6.18-194.3.1.0.2.el5.img
-rw-r--r-- 1 root root   6888101 Dec 17 11:44 initrd-2.6.18-194.3.1.0.3.el5.img
-r-xr-x--- 1 root root  29747008 Dec 17 11:14 initrd.img
-r-xr-x--- 1 root root     10648 Dec  7 07:55 ISOlinux.bin
-r-xr-x--- 1 root root        97 Dec  7 07:55 ISOlinux.cfg
-rw-r--r-- 1 root root        23 Dec 17 11:44 kernel.ver
drwxr-xr-x 4 root root      4096 Dec 17 11:43 lastGoodConfig
drwxr-xr-x 2 root root      4096 Dec 17 11:45 log
drwx------ 2 root root     16384 Dec 17 11:42 lost+found
-r-xr-x--- 1 root root     94600 Dec  7 07:55 memtest
-r-xr-x--- 1 root root      7326 Dec  7 07:55 splash.lss
-r-xr-x--- 1 root root      1770 Dec  7 07:55 trans.tbl
-r-xr-x--- 1 root root   1955100 Dec  7 07:55 vmlinuz
-rw-r--r-- 1 root root   1955100 May 27  2010 vmlinuz-2.6.18-194.3.1.0.2.el5
-rw-r----- 1 root root   1955100 Dec 17 11:23 vmlinuz-2.6.18-194.3.1.0.3.el5
```

In this backup we see the Linux boot images and all the files required to boot Linux and restore the operating system. Notice that you also see a directory called lastGoodConfig. This directory is a backup of the /opt/oracle.cellos/iso directory on our storage cell. There is also a directory called cellbits containing the Cell Server software. So not only do we have a complete copy of everything needed to recover our storage cell to a bootable state on the internal USB drive, but we also have an online backup of all of our important cell configuration files and Cell Server binaries.

External USB Drive

In addition to the built-in CELLBOOT USB flash drive, Exadata also provides a way to create your own external bootable recovery image using a common 1–8GB USB flash drive you can buy at the local electronics store. Exadata will create the rescue image on the first external USB drive it finds, so before you create this recovery image you must remove all other external USB drives from the system or the script will throw a warning and exit.

Recall that Exadata storage cells maintain two versions of the operating system and cell software: active and inactive. These are managed as two separate sets of disk partitions for the / and /opt/oracle file systems as can be confirmed using the imageinfo command, as follows:

```
> imageinfo | grep device
Active system partition on device: /dev/md6
Active software partition on device: /dev/md8
Inactive system partition on device: /dev/md5
Inactive software partition on device: /dev/md7
```

The imageinfo command shows the current (Active), and previous (Inactive) system volumes on the storage cell. Using the df command we can see that we are indeed currently using the Active partitions (/dev/md6 and /dev/md8) identified in the output from the imageinfo command.

```
> df | egrep 'Filesystem|md6|md8'

Filesystem          1K-blocks      Used Available Use% Mounted on
/dev/md6            10317752    6632836   3160804  68% /
/dev/md8             2063440     654956   1303668  34% /opt/oracle
```

By default, the make_cellboot_usb command will create a rescue image of your active configuration (the one you are currently running). The –inactive option allows you to create a rescue image from the previous configuration. The inactive partitions are the system volumes that were active when the last patch was installed.

The make_cellboot_usb command is used to create a bootable rescue image. To create an external rescue image, all you have to do is plug a USB flash drive into one of the USB ports on the front panel of the storage cell and run the make_cellboot_usb command.

■ **Caution:** The rescue image will be created on the first external USB drive found on the system. Before creating an external rescue image, remove all other external USB drives from the system.

For example, the following listing shows the process of creating an external USB rescue image. The output from the make_cellboot_usb script is fairly lengthy, a little over 100 lines, so we won't show all of it here. Some of the output excluded from the following listing includes output from the fdisk command that is used to create partitions on the USB drive, formatting of the file systems, and the many files that are copied to create the bootable rescue disk.

```
[enkcel01:root] /opt/oracle.SupportTools
> ./make_cellboot_usb
...
Candidate for the Oracle Exadata Cell start up boot device     : /dev/sdad
```

```
Partition on candidate device                                    : /dev/sdad1
The current product version                                      : 11.2.1.2.6
...
Setting interval between checks to 0 seconds
Copying ./imgboot.lst to /mnt/usb.make.cellboot/. ...
Copying ./boot.cat to /mnt/usb.make.cellboot/. ...
Copying ./boot.msg to /mnt/usb.make.cellboot/. ...
Copying ./image.id to /mnt/usb.make.cellboot/. ...
Copying ./initrd.img to /mnt/usb.make.cellboot/. ...
Copying ./isolinux.bin to /mnt/usb.make.cellboot/. ...
Copying ./isolinux.cfg to /mnt/usb.make.cellboot/. ...
Copying ./memtest to /mnt/usb.make.cellboot/. ...
Copying ./splash.lss to /mnt/usb.make.cellboot/. ...
Copying ./trans.tbl to /mnt/usb.make.cellboot/. ...
Copying ./vmlinuz to /mnt/usb.make.cellboot/. ...
Copying ./cellbits/cell.bin to /mnt/usb.make.cellboot/./cellbits ...
Copying ./cellbits/cellboot.tbz to /mnt/usb.make.cellboot/./cellbits ...
Copying ./cellbits/cellfw.tbz to /mnt/usb.make.cellboot/./cellbits ...
Copying ./cellbits/cellrpms.tbz to /mnt/usb.make.cellboot/./cellbits ...
...
Copying ./lastGoodConfig/cell.conf to /mnt/usb.make.cellboot/./lastGoodConfig ...
Copying ./lastGoodConfig/cell/cellsrv/deploy/config/cell_disk_config.xml to
...
Copying ./lastGoodConfig/etc/ssh/ssh_host_key.pub to
/mnt/usb.make.cellboot/./lastGoodConfig/etc/ssh ...
Copying ./lastGoodConfig/etc/ssh/ssh_host_dsa_key to
/mnt/usb.make.cellboot/./lastGoodConfig/etc/ssh ...
Copying ./lastGoodConfig/root_ssh.tbz to /mnt/usb.make.cellboot/./lastGoodConfig ...
Copying ./lastGoodConfig/cellmonitor_ssh.tbz to /mnt/usb.make.cellboot/./lastGoodConfig ...
Running "tar -x -j -p -C /mnt/usb.make.cellboot -f
//opt/oracle.cellos/iso/cellbits/cellboot.tbz grub/" ...
Copying //opt/oracle.cellos/tmpl/USB_grub to /mnt/usb.make.cellboot/grub/grub.conf ...
Copying //opt/oracle.cellos/tmpl/oracle.xpm.gz to /mnt/usb.make.cellboot/grub/oracle.xpm.gz
...
    GNU GRUB  version 0.97  (640K lower / 3072K upper memory)

 [ Minimal BASH-like line editing is supported.  For the first word, TAB
   lists possible command completions.  Anywhere else TAB lists the possible
   completions of a device/filename.]
grub> root (hd0,0)
 Filesystem type is ext2fs, partition type 0x83
grub> setup (hd0)
 Checking if "/boot/grub/stage1" exists... no
 Checking if "/grub/stage1" exists... yes
 Checking if "/grub/stage2" exists... yes
 Checking if "/grub/e2fs_stage1_5" exists... yes
 Running "embed /grub/e2fs_stage1_5 (hd0)"...  15 sectors are embedded.
succeeded
 Running "install /grub/stage1 (hd0) (hd0)1+15 p (hd0,0)/grub/stage2 /grub/grub.conf"...
succeeded
Done.
grub>
```

Here you can see that the make_cellboot_usb script copies over all of the storage cell software (cellbits), and configuration files (lastGoodConfig) it needs to recover the storage cell. Finally, you see that the Grub boot loader is installed on the USB drive so you can boot the system from it. When the script completes, you can remove the external USB disk from the system. This rescue disk can later be used for restoring your storage cell to working condition should the need arise.

Active and Inactive System Volumes

Exadata has three modes for installing software: first time install, patch (or *in-partition patch*), and an *out-of-partition upgrade*. A journal of your installation history can be seen using the imagehistory command:

```
> imagehistory
Version                     : 11.2.1.2.3
Image activation date       : 2010-05-15 20:07:07 -0700
Imaging mode                : fresh
Imaging status              : success

Version                     : 11.2.1.2.6
Image activation date       : 2010-06-03 09:10:08 -0700
Imaging mode                : patch
Imaging status              : success
...
Version                     : 11.2.2.2.0.101206.2
Image activation date       : 2010-12-17 11:45:17 -0600
Imaging mode                : out of partition upgrade
Imaging status              : success
```

The -all option can be used to show much more detail about your software installation history.

In-Partition Patches

As discussed earlier, Exadata maintains two sets of system volumes, Active, and Inactive. In-partition patches are rare. But when an in-partition patch is performed, the patch is applied to the Active system image. Exadata saves a copy of the files and settings that were changed during the installation process so you can back out the patch later if needed.

Out-of-Partition Upgrades

When an out-of-partition upgrade is performed, Exadata installs the software into the Inactive system volumes. If the installation fails, the cell will continue to boot from the current (Active) system image. This is how Exadata ensures that a failed upgrade does not cause an extended outage. If the upgrade completes successfully, Exadata sets the upgraded volumes to Active status and changes the old Active volumes to Inactive. It then updates the /boot/grub/grub.conf file with the device name of the newly activated root file system and reboots. During the boot process, the Grub boot loader reads the grub.conf file to find the device it will use for mounting the root file system. A quick look at the grub.conf file shows that our Active partition for the root file system is /dev/md6.

```
> grep kernel /boot/grub/grub.conf | cut -c1-53 | head -1
      kernel /vmlinuz-2.6.18-194.3.1.0.3.el5 root=/dev/md6
```

The imageinfo command displays everything we need to know about our Active and Inactive system images, including the partition device names, when the image was created (installed), when it was activated, and whether or not you can roll back to it (switch it to the Active image). Also notice that the internal CELLBOOT USB flash drive we discussed earlier is listed (/dev/sdac1).

```
> imageinfo -all

Kernel version: 2.6.18-194.3.1.0.3.el5 #1 SMP Tue Aug 31 22:41:13 EDT 2010 x86_64
Cell version: OSS_11.2.0.3.0_LINUX.X64_101206.2
Cell rpm version: cell-11.2.2.2.0_LINUX.X64_101206.2-1

Active image version: 11.2.2.2.0.101206.2
Active image created: 2010-12-07 05:55:51 -0800
Active image activated: 2010-12-17 11:45:17 -0600
Active image type: production
Active image status: success
Active internal version:
Active image label: OSS_11.2.0.3.0_LINUX.X64_101206.2
Active node type: STORAGE
Active system partition on device: /dev/md6
Active software partition on device: /dev/md8

In partition rollback: Impossible

Cell boot usb partition: /dev/sdac1
Cell boot usb version: 11.2.2.2.0.101206.2

Inactive image version: 11.2.2.1.1.101105
Inactive image created: 2010-11-05 15:50:21 -0700
Inactive image activated: 2010-11-18 14:48:49 -0600
Inactive image type: production
Inactive image status: success
Inactive internal version: 101105
Inactive image label: OSS_11.2.2.1.1_LINUX.X64_101105
Inactive node type: STORAGE
Inactive system partition on device: /dev/md5
Inactive software partition on device: /dev/md7

Boot area has rollback archive for the version: 11.2.2.1.1.101105
Rollback to the inactive partitions: Possible
```

Exadata storage cells are an elegant blend of Linux commands and proprietary programs. The more we poke around through their scripts, processes, and documentation, the greater our appreciation of the architecture and what Oracle has done to build in software redundancy and recovery. The storage cells maintain a bootable cell recovery image on an internal USB flash disk as well as an online copy of everything Exadata needs to create an external bootable recovery image. This secondary copy of your configuration provides a convenient way to restore individual files if needed. These are all in addition to Exadata's ability to roll back patches and upgrades conveniently. All these built-in features provide convenient recovery from various user errors and protection from issues that can arise when patching or upgrading the storage cell.

Backing Up the Database

Exadata represents a leap forward in capacity and performance. Just a few years ago, large databases were described in terms of gigabytes. Today it's not uncommon to find databases measured in terabytes. It wasn't long ago when a table was considered huge if it contained tens of millions of rows. Today, we commonly see tables that contain tens of billions of rows. This trend makes it clear that we will soon see databases measured in exabytes. As you might imagine, this creates some unique challenges for backup and recovery. The tools for backing up Exadata databases have not fundamentally changed, and the need to complete backups in a reasonable period of time is becoming increasingly difficult to achieve. Some of the strategies we'll discuss here will not be new. But we will be looking at ways to leverage the speed of the platform so backup performance can keep pace with the increasing volume of your databases.

Disk-Based Backups

Oracle 10g introduced us to a new feature called the *Flash Recovery Area*, which extended Recovery Manager's structured approach to managing backups. Recently this feature has been renamed to the *Fast Recovery Area (FRA)*. The FRA is a storage area much like any other database storage. It can be created on raw devices, block devices, file systems, and of course, ASM. Since the FRA utilizes disk-based storage, it provides a very fast storage medium for database recovery. This is especially true when using Exadata's high-performance storage architecture. Eliminating the need to retrieve backups from tape can shave hours and sometimes days off the time it takes to recover your databases. And, since the FRA is an extension of the database, Oracle automatically manages that space for you. When files in the FRA are backed up to tape they are not immediately deleted. They are instead kept online as long as there is enough free space to do so. When more space is needed, the database deletes (in a FIFO manner) enough of these files to provide the needed space.

Tape-Based Backups

Using the FRA for disk-based backups can greatly improve the time it takes to recover your databases, but it does not eliminate the need for tape backups. As a matter of fact, tape-based backups are required for backing up the FRA. Moving large quantities of backup data to tape can be a challenge, and with the volume of data that can be stored on Exadata, the need for high-performance tape backups is critical. Exadata V2 comes equipped with Gigabit Ethernet (GigE) ports that are each capable of delivering throughput up to 1000 megabits per second. Exadata X2-2 comes with two 10 Gigabit Ethernet ports, each capable of delivering up to 10 times the throughput of the GigE ports of the V2. The problem is that even the 10 GigE ports between Exadata and the tape library's media server may not be fast enough to keep up.

A common solution to this problem is to install a 40 Gbps QDR InfiniBand card (or two) into the media server, allowing it to be linked directly into the spare ports on the Exadata InfiniBand network switch. Figure 9-1 illustrates a common backup configuration that leverages the high-speed InfiniBand network inside the Exadata rack to provide high-speed backups to tape.

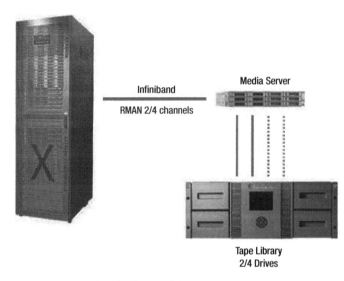

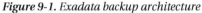

Figure 9-1. *Exadata backup architecture*

For very large databases, one InfiniBand card may not provide the throughput needed to complete backups in a reasonable time. For Oracle RAC databases, backups can be parallelized and distributed across any or all nodes in the RAC cluster. For Exadata full rack configurations, this means you can have up to 8 nodes (in a single rack) participating in the backup workload. Installing additional InfiniBand cards into the media server allows you to increase the throughput in 40 Gbps increments (3.2GB effective) up to the limits of the media server. An additional media server can be added to the configuration and load-balanced to extend performance even further. Oracle's MAA group published a very good white paper entitled "Backup and Recovery Performance and Best Practices for Exadata Cell and the Sun Oracle Database Machine," in which they reported backup rates of up to 2,509 MB/sec or 8.6 TB/hr for tape backups.

Backup from Standby Database

If you are planning to set up a disaster recovery site using Data Guard, you have the option of offloading your database backups to the standby database. This is not in any way an Exadata feature, so we will only touch briefly on the subject. The main purpose of the standby database is to take over the production load in the event that the primary database experiences a total failure. However, using a physical standby database also provides an additional backup for your primary database. If a datafile from the primary database is lost, a replacement datafile from the standby database can be used to replace it. Once the file has been restored to the primary database, archived redo logs are used to recover the datafile up to the current SCN of the database. The standby database is typically mounted (but not open) during normal operations. Cold backups can be made from the standby to the Fast Recovery Area (FRA) and then to tape. Backups from the standby database can be restored directly to the primary database. This provides three levels of recovery to choose from before deciding whether a failover to the standby is necessary.

It is best to use an Exadata platform for your standby database. This is because although tables that use Hybrid Columnar Compression (HCC) will replicate to non-Exadata databases just fine, you will not be able to read from them. The database kernel on non-Exadata databases cannot read HCC-compressed data. For example, the following error is returned when you select from an HCC table on a standard 11.2.x database:

```
SQL> select distinct segment_name from bigtab_arch_high;
 select distinct segment_name from small_table_arch_high
                     *
ERROR at line 1:
ORA-64307: hybrid columnar compression is only supported in tablespaces residing on Exadata
storage
```

Your compressed data is still intact. You just cannot read it unless you first uncompress it. HCC-compressed tables can be uncompressed on non-Exadata databases using the ALTER TABLE MOVE command as follows:

```
SQL> alter table BIGTAB_ARCHIVE_HIGH move nocompress;
```

Partitioned tables can be uncompressed in a similar manner, and the operation can be parallelized using the parallel option, as you can see in the following command:

```
SQL> alter table BIGTAB_ARCHIVE_HIGH move partition JAN_2011 nocompress parallel;
```

Once the table is uncompressed, it can be read from a non-Exadata database. Keep in mind that with the high degree of compression HCC provides, you must take into consideration the additional disk storage that will be required by the uncompressed table or partition, which can be quite substantial.

Exadata Optimizations for RMAN

When RMAN performs an incremental backup on the Exadata platform, cellsrv filters out unwanted blocks and sends back only those that have changed since the last level 0 or level 1 backup. This improves the performance of incremental backups and reduces the workload on the database server. But even when only a relatively small number of blocks have changed, discovering them is a very I/O-intensive process, because every block in the database must be examined to determine which ones have changed since the last incremental backup. This is true for both Exadata and non-Exadata databases. The only difference is where the work is done; on the database server, or on the storage cells. A few years ago, Oracle 10g introduced *block change tracking* (BCT) to address this problem. Of course this was long before Exadata came onto the scene. This feature maintains a bitmap structure in a file called the block change tracking file. Each bit in the BCT file (1 bit per 32K of data) represents a group of blocks in the database. When a data block is modified, Oracle flips a bit in the BCT file representing the group of blocks in which the changed block resides. When an incremental backup is taken, RMAN retrieves the whole group of blocks (represented by a flipped bit in the BCT file), and examines them to determine which one changed. Block change tracking introduces minimal overhead on the database server and is a very efficient way to track changed blocks. And, since it greatly reduces the number of blocks that must be examined during a backup, it improves backup performance while reducing the workload on the database server and storage grid.

For the Exadata platform, you may choose to allow cellsrv to do all of the block filtering for incremental backups, or use it in tandem with block change tracking. Block change tracking seems to provide the most benefit when fewer than 20 percent of the blocks in the database have changed since the last level 0 or level 1 backup. If your database is close to that threshold, you should do some testing to determine whether or not BCT improves incremental backup performance. The BLOCKS_SKIPPED_IN_CELL column of the V$BACKUP_DATAFILE view shows the number of blocks that were read and filtered out at the storage cell. This offloading is transparent and requires no user intervention or special parameters to be set ahead of time.

Wait Events

There are two Exadata-specific wait events that are triggered by database backup and recovery operations on the Exadata platform; `cell smart incremental backup`, and `cell smart restore from backup`. These wait events are covered in more detail in Chapter 10.

> **`cell smart incremental backup`:** This wait event occurs when Exadata offloads incremental backup processing to the storage cells. The P1 column of the `V$SESSION_WAIT` view contains the cell hash number. This hash value can be used to compare the relative backup performance of each storage cell and determine if there is a performance problem on any of the cells.

> **`cell smart restore from backup`:** This wait event occurs during restore operations when Exadata offloads the task of initializing a file to the storage cells. The P1 column of `V$SESSION_WAIT` contains the cell hash number. This hash value can be used to compare the relative restore performance of each storage cell and determine if there is a performance problem on any of the cells.

Recovering Exadata

A better title for this section might be, "When Things Go Wrong." After all, that's usually about the time we realize how little practical experience we have recovering our systems. As corporate America continues to squeeze every drop of productive time out of our work week, DBAs and System Administrators spend most if not all of their waking hours (and sometimes sleeping hours) just "keeping the wheels on." So actually practicing system recovery is more often than not treated like the proverbial "red-headed step child"—seldom thought about, and rarely attended to. And even if we find ourselves in the enviable position of having the time to practice system recovery, it's rare to have the spare equipment to practice on. So kudos to you if you are reading this and nothing is actually broken. In this section we'll be discussing Exadata system recovery using the backup methods we covered in the "Backing Up Exadata" section of this chapter.

Restoring the Database Server

Backing up and restoring the database servers can be done using third-party backup software or homegrown scripts using familiar commands like `tar` and `zip`. Recently Oracle began configuring the Exadata database servers with the Linux Logical Volume Manager (LVM), which provides snapshots for creating point-in-time, `tar`-based backup sets. The procedure for recovering Exadata database servers is a very structured process that is specific to Exadata. In this section we'll be stepping through this procedure presuming the backup was taken using the backup procedure discussed earlier in this chapter. So, if you haven't read through that section of this chapter, you might want to take a look at it before continuing.

Recovery Using LVM Snapshot-Based Backup Images

Restoring the database server using the LVM snapshot backup procedure we discussed earlier in this chapter is a fairly straightforward process. The backup image we will use in this procedure, `enkdb01_system_backup.tar.bz2`, is the one we created earlier in this chapter and includes the /, /boot, and /u01 file systems. The first thing you need to do is stage the backup image on an NFS file system that can be mounted by the failed database server. The server is then booted from a special diagnostics ISO boot image included on all Exadata servers. When the system boots from the diagnostics ISO, you will be prompted step by step through the recovery process. Let's take a look at the basic steps for recovering a failed database server from the LVM snapshot-based backup we took earlier in this chapter:

1. Place the LVM snapshot backup image on an NFS shared file system that is accessible to the failed server by IP address. The file we'll be working with is named enkdb01_system_backup.tar.bz2.

■ **Note:** This recovery procedure uses a backup image taken using LVM snapshots. Backups that are not snapshot-based can also be used for systems that are not configured with LVM. Without LVM snapshots, the backup image can be created by running the following command from the root directory:

```
tar -pjcvf enkdb01_system_backup.tar.bz2 * /boot  --exclude enkdb01_system_backup.tar.bz2
```

---

2. Attach the /opt/oracle.SupportTools/diagnostics.iso boot image to the failed server through the ILOM. This can be done from any of the other database servers in the rack.

3. Reboot the failed server and select the CD-ROM as the boot device. When the system boots from the diagnostics ISO, it will enter a special server recovery process.

4. From this point on, the recovery process will include step-by-step directions. For example, the following process recovers the database server from the backup image, enkdb01_system_backup.tar.bz2. Answers to the prompts are shown in ***bold_italics***.

```
Choose from following by typing letter in '()':
(e)nter interactive diagnostics shell. Must use credentials from Oracle support to login
(reboot or power cycle to exit the shell),
(r)estore system from NFS backup archive,
Select: r

Are you sure (y/n) [n]: y

The backup file could be created either from LVM or non-LVM based compute node. Versions below
11.2.1.3.1 and 11.2.2.1.0 or higher do not support LVM based partitioning. Use LVM based
scheme(y/n): y

Enter path to the backup file on the NFS server in format:
<ip_address_of_the_NFS_share>:/<path>/<archive_file>

For example, 10.10.10.10:/export/operating_system.tar.bz2

NFS line:nfs_ip: /export/enkdb01_system_backup.tar.bz2
IP Address of this host: 192.168.10.62
```

Netmask of this host: **255.255.255.0**
Default gateway: **192.168.15.1**

5. When all the above information is entered, Exadata will proceed to mount the backup image across the network and recover the system. When the recovery is finished, you will be prompted to log in. Log in as root using the password provided in the Oracle documentation.

6. Detach the diagnostics ISO from the ILOM.

7. Reboot the system using the reboot command. The failed server should be completely restored at this point.

When the system finishes booting you can verify the recovery using the imagehistory command. The following listing shows that the image was created as a restore from nfs backup and was completed successfully:

```
[enkdb01:oracle:EXDB1] /home/oracle
> su -
Password:

[enkdb01:root] /root
> imagehistory
Version                            : 11.2.1.2.3
Image activation date              : 2010-05-15 05:58:56 -0700
Imaging mode                       : fresh
Imaging status                     : success
...

Version                            : 11.2.2.2.0.101206.2
Image activation date              : 2010-12-17 11:51:53 -0600
Imaging mode                       : patch
Imaging status                     : success

Version                            : 11.2.2.2.0.101206.2
Image activation date              : 2010-01-23 15:23:05 -0600
Imaging mode                       : restore from nfs backup
Imaging status                     : success
```

Generally speaking, it's a good idea not to get too creative when it comes to customizing your Exadata database server. Oracle permits you to create new LVM partitions and add file systems to your database servers, but if you do so, your recovery will require some additional steps. They aren't terribly difficult, but if you choose to customize your LVM partitions, be sure to document the changes somewhere and familiarize yourself with the recovery procedures for customized systems in the Oracle documentation.

Reimaging a Database Server

If a database server must be replaced or rebuilt from scratch and there is no backup image to recover from, an image can be created from an install image provided by Oracle Support. It is a lengthy and highly complicated process, but we'll hit the highlights here so you get a general idea of what this process involves.

Before the server can be reimaged it must be removed from the RAC cluster. This is the standard procedure for deleting a node from any 11gR2 RAC cluster. First the listener on the failed server must be shut down and disabled. Then the ORACLE_HOME for the database binaries is removed from the Oracle inventory. The VIP is then stopped and removed from the cluster configuration and the node deleted from the cluster. Finally the ORACLE_HOME for the Grid Infrastructure is removed from the Oracle inventory.

Oracle Support will provide you with a computeImageMaker file that is used for creating an install image from one of the surviving database servers. This image maker file is specific to the version and platform of your Exadata system and will be named as follows:

```
computeImageMaker_{exadata_release}_LINUX.X64_{release_date}.{platform}.tar.zip
```

An external USB flash drive is used to boot the recovery image on the failed server. The USB drive doesn't need to be very big, a 2–4GB thumb drive can be used. The next step is to unzip the image maker file you downloaded from Oracle Support on one of the other Exadata database servers in your rack. A similar recovery processes for storage cells uses the first USB drive found on the system, so before proceeding you should remove all other external USB devices from the system. To create a bootable system image for recovering the failed database server, you will run the makeImageMedia.sh script; it prompts you for system-specific settings it will need to apply to the failed server during the reimaging process. When the makeImageMedia.sh script completes, you are ready to install the image on your failed server. Remove the USB drive from the good server and plug it into the failed server. Login to the ILOM on the failed server and reboot it. When the server boots up it will automatically find the bootable recovery image on the external USB drive and begin the reimaging process. From this point, the process is automated. First it will check the firmware and BIOS versions on the server and update them as needed to match them with your other database servers. Don't expect this to do anything if you are reimaging a server that was already part of your Exadata system, but it is necessary if the damaged server has been replaced with new equipment. Once the hardware components are up to date, a new image will be installed. When the reimaging process is complete you can unplug the external USB drive and power cycle the server to boot up the new system image.

When the reimaging process is complete and the database server is back online it will be set to factory defaults. Depending on the patch level of the install image you downloaded from Oracle Support, you may need to reinstall software patches on the server to make it current with the rest of your Exadata system. You will also need to reconfigure all other site-specific settings such as host name, IP addresses, NTP server, DNS, and user and group accounts. For all intents and purposes you should think of the reimaged server as a brand-new server. Oracle has done an excellent job of improving the product with every release. Perhaps in the near future, we can look forward to a reimaging process that automatically configures most of the site-specific settings for you. Once the operating system is configured, you will need to reinstall the Grid Infrastructure and database software and add the node back into the cluster. This is a well documented process that many RAC DBAs refer to as the "add node" procedure. If you're not familiar with the process, let us reassure you. It's not nearly as daunting or time-consuming as you might think. Once you have the operating system prepared for the install, much of the heavy lifting is done for you by the Oracle Installer. The Exadata Owner's Guide does an excellent job of walking you through each step of the process.

Recovering the Storage Cell

Storage cell recovery is a very broad subject. It can be as simple as replacing an underperforming or failed data disk and as complex as responding to a total system failure such as a malfunctioning chip on the motherboard. In this section we'll be discussing various types of cell recovery including removing and replacing physical disks, failed flash cache modules, and what to do if an entire storage cell dies and must be replaced.

System Volume Failure

Recall that the first two disks in the storage cell contain the Linux operating system and are commonly referred to as the "system volumes." Exadata protects these volumes using software mirroring through the O/S. Even so, certain situations may require you to recover these disks from backup. Some reasons for performing cell recovery would include:

- System volumes (disks 1 and 2) fail simultaneously.

- The boot partition is damaged beyond repair.

- File systems become corrupted.

- A patch installation or upgrade fails.

If you find yourself in any of these situations, it may be necessary, or at least more expedient, to recover the system volumes from backup. As discussed earlier, Exadata automatically maintains a backup of the last good boot configuration using a 4GB internal USB flash drive called the CELLBOOT USB flash drive. Recovering the system volumes using this internal USB flash disk is commonly referred to as the *storage cell rescue procedure*. The steps for performing the cell rescue procedure basically involve booting from the internal USB drive and following the prompts for the type of rescue you want to perform. By the way, since Exadata comes equipped with an ILOM (Integrated Lights Out Management module), you can perform all cell recovery operations remotely, across the network. There is no need to stand in front of the rack to perform a full cell recovery from the internal USB flash disk.

As you might imagine, this type of recovery should not be done without the assistance of Oracle Support. This section is not intended to be a step-by-step guide to cell recovery, so we're not going to go into all the details of cell recovery from the CELLBOOT USB flash disk here. The Oracle documentation should be used for that, but we will take a look at what to consider before starting such a recovery.

> **Cell Disks and Grid Disks**: The rescue procedure restores the Linux system volumes only. Cell disks and their contents are not restored by the rescue procedure. If these partitions are damaged they must be dropped and re-created. Once the grid disks are online, they can be added back to the ASM disk group and a subsequent rebalance will restore the data.

> **ASM Redundancy:** Recovering a storage cell from USB backup can potentially cause the loss of all data on the system volumes. This includes your database data in the grid disks on these disk drives. If your ASM disk groups use Normal redundancy, we strongly recommend making a database backup before performing cell recovery from USB disk. With ASM High redundancy, you have two mirror copies of all your data, so it is safe to perform cell recovery without taking database backups. Even so, we'd still take a backup if at all possible. The recovery process does not destroy data volumes (cell/grid disks) unless you explicitly choose to do so when prompted by the rescue procedure.

> **Software and Patches:** As of version 11.2 of the storage cell software, the rescue procedure will restore the cell to its former state, patches included, when the backup was taken. Also included in the restore are the network settings and SSH keys for the root, celladmin, and cellmonitor accounts. The alert settings and SMTP configuration (including email addresses) for alert notification will not be restored. Reconfiguring these settings is a trivial task and can be done using another cell to determine the correct settings to apply.

Cell Rescue Options

There are two main rescue options, *Partial Reconstruction* and *Full Recovery*. As you might guess, a partial reconstruction attempts to preserve as much of your current configuration as possible, while a full recovery wipes your system and resets it back to the last good configuration it knows about.

>**Partial Reconstruction:** If this option is chosen, the rescue procedure will repair the partitions without damaging the file systems. It scans for file systems on these partitions, and if they are found will try to reboot using them. If the cell reboots successfully, you can use the CellCLI command to check the integrity of the cell configuration. If the cell fails to reboot, a full recovery must be performed to repair the damaged system volumes.

>**Full Recovery:** A full recovery destroys and re-creates all system partitions and re-creates the file systems from scratch. It then restores the system volumes from backup. There are two files that are too big to fit on the internal USB flash drive, the kernel-debuginfo, and kernel-debuginfo-common RPMs. These files must be reinstalled before you can use crash kernel support. If full recovery is performed, you will need to reconfigure the cell alert and SMTP configuration. It is important, so I'll repeat it. Cell and grid disks are not overwritten by this process. You will, however, need to re-import the cell disks before they can be used.

So, what happens if for some reason, the internal CELLBOOT USB flash disk cannot be used for the rescue procedure? If this happens you can boot the storage cell from an external USB drive containing a backup copy of the CELLBOOT USB flash disk. The process is the same as it is for performing cell rescue using the internal CELLBOOT USB flash disk.

Rolling Back a Failed Patch

Exadata storage cells come equipped with what Oracle calls a *validation framework*. This framework is a set of tests that are run at the end of the boot process. The validation script is called vldrun and is called from /etc/rc.local, as can be seen in the following listing:

```
> cat /etc/rc.d/rc.Oracle.Exadata
...
# Perform validations step
/opt/oracle.cellos/vldrun -all
...
```

In addition to the regular validations that are run every time the system boots, other validations are run under certain circumstances. For example, after the cell is patched or upgraded, or the system is recovered using the storage cell rescue procedure, validations are run to ensure that the configuration and software are all intact. The validation framework writes its output to the /var/log/cellos/validations directory, as you can see in the following listing:

```
> ls -l /var/log/cellos/validations
total 184
-rw-r----- 1 root root   685 Dec 17 11:41 beginfirstboot.log
-rw-r----- 1 root root  3982 Dec 31 12:37 biosbootorder.log
-rw-r----- 1 root root  2537 Dec 17 11:26 cellcopymetadata.log
-rw-r----- 1 root root   268 Dec 31 12:37 celldstatus.log
```

```
-rw-r----- 1 root root  3555 Jan 21 21:07 checkconfigs.log
-rw-r----- 1 root root  1612 Dec 31 12:37 checkdeveachboot.log
-rw-r----- 1 root root   257 Dec 17 11:41 createcell.log
-rw-r----- 1 root root  1233 Dec 31 12:37 ipmisettings.log
-rw-r----- 1 root root  3788 Dec 31 12:37 misceachboot.log
-rw-r----- 1 root root 13300 Dec 17 11:26 misczeroboot.log
-rw-r----- 1 root root   228 Dec 31 12:37 oswatcher.log
-rw-r----- 1 root root 34453 Dec 17 11:26 postinstall.log
-rw-r----- 1 root root  4132 Dec 31 12:38 saveconfig.log
-rw-r----- 1 root root    65 Jan 21 12:49 sosreport.log
-rw-r----- 1 root root    75 Dec 17 11:26 syscheck.log
-rw-r----- 1 root root 70873 Dec 17 11:44 upgradecbusb.log
```

As discussed in the "Active and Inactive System Volumes" section of this chapter, Exadata storage cells maintain two sets of system volumes, which contain the Linux operating system and storage cell software. By maintaining separate Active and Inactive system images, Exadata ensures that failed out-of-partition upgrades do not cause an outage to the databases. If the validation tests detect a problem after an out-of-partition upgrade, Exadata will automatically fail back to the last good configuration by switching the Active and Inactive system volumes. For in-partition patches, Exadata will reapply all the settings and files changed by the patch from online backups. Following the first boot-up after installing a patch or upgrade the validation results can be found in the log file, /var/log/cellos/vldrun.first_boot.log. Validation tests will be logged to the /var/log/cellos/validations.log file for all subsequent reboots. The patch rollback procedure can be performed manually, but there is no mention of it in the documentation, so it is probably not something Oracle expects administrators to run without the help of Oracle Support.

Cell Disk Failure

ASM handles the temporary or permanent loss of a cell disk through its redundant failure group technology. So the loss of a cell disk should not cause any interruption to the databases as long as the disk group is defined with Normal redundancy. If High redundancy is used, the disk group can suffer the simultaneous loss of two cell disks within the same failure group. Recall that on Exadata, each storage cell constitutes a separate failure group. This means that with Normal redundancy, you can lose an entire storage cell (12 cell disks) without impact to your databases. With High redundancy you can lose two storage cells simultaneously and your databases will continue to service your clients without interruption. That's pretty impressive. Redundancy isn't cheap, though. For example, consider a disk group with 30 terabytes of usable space (configured for External redundancy). With Normal redundancy, that 30 terabytes becomes 15 terabytes of usable space. With High redundancy, it becomes 10 terabytes of usable storage. Also keep in mind that the database will always read the primary copy of your data unless it is unavailable. Normal and High redundancy provide no performance benefits. They are used strictly for fault tolerance. The key is to choose a redundancy level that strikes a balance between resiliency and budget.

Simulated Disk Failure

In this section we're going to test what happens when a cell disk fails. The system used for these tests was a quarter rack, Exadata V2. We've created a disk group called SCRATCH_DG, defined as follows:

```
SYS:+ASM2> CREATE DISKGROUP SCRATCH_DG NORMAL REDUNDANCY
  FAILGROUP CELL01 DISK 'o/192.168.12.3/SCRATCH_DG_CD_05_cell01'
  FAILGROUP CELL02 DISK 'o/192.168.12.4/SCRATCH_DG_CD_05_cell02'
  FAILGROUP CELL03 DISK 'o/192.168.12.5/SCRATCH_DG_CD_05_cell03'
  attribute 'compatible.rdbms'='11.2.0',
            'compatible.asm'  ='11.2.0',
            'au_size'='4M',
            'cell.smart_scan_capable'='true';
```

Notice that this disk group is created using three grid disks. Following Exadata best practices, we've used one grid disk from each storage cell. It's interesting to note that even if we hadn't specified three failure groups with one disk in each, ASM would have done so automatically. We then created a small, single-instance database called SCRATCH using this disk group. The disk group is configured with normal redundancy (two mirror copies for each block of data), which means our database should be able to suffer the loss of one cell disk without losing access to data or causing a crash. Since each grid disk resides on a separate storage cell, we could even suffer the loss of an entire storage cell without losing data. We'll discuss what happens when a storage cell fails later in the chapter.

In a moment we'll take a look at what happens when a grid disk is removed from the storage cell (a simulated disk failure). But before we do, there are a few things we need to check:

- Verify that no rebalance or other volume management operations are running.

- Ensure that all grid disks for the SCRATCH_DG disk group are online.

- Verify that taking a disk offline will not impact database operations.

- Check the disk repair timer to ensure the disk is not automatically dropped before we can bring it back online again.

There are a couple of ways to verify that volume management activity is not going on. First let's check the current state of the disk groups using asmcmd. The ls -l command shows the disk groups, the type of redundancy, and whether or not a rebalance operation is currently under way. By the way, you could also get this information using the lsdg command, which also includes other interesting information like space utilization, online/offline status, and more. The Rebal column in the following listing indicates that no rebalance operations are executing at the moment.

```
> asmcmd -p
ASMCMD [+] > ls -l
State    Type    Rebal  Name
MOUNTED  NORMAL  N      DATA_DG/
MOUNTED  NORMAL  N      RECO_DG/
MOUNTED  NORMAL  N      SCRATCH_DG/
MOUNTED  NORMAL  N      STAGE_DG/
MOUNTED  NORMAL  N      SYSTEM_DG/
```

Notice that not all volume management operations are shown in the asmcmd commands. If a grid disk has been offline for a period of time, there may be a considerable amount of backlogged data that must be copied to it in order to bring it up to date. Depending on the volume of data, it may take several minutes to finish resynchronizing a disk. Although this operation is directly related to maintaining balance across all disks, it is not technically a "rebalance" operation. As such, it will not appear in the listing. For example, even though the ls -l command in the previous listing showed a status of N for rebalance operations, you can clearly see that a disk is currently being brought online by running the next query:

```
SYS:+ASM2> select dg.name, oper.operation, oper.state
      from gv$asm_operation oper,
           gv$asm_diskgroup dg
     where dg.group_number = oper.group_number
       and dg.inst_id      = oper.inst_id;

NAME                                             OPERATION
------------------------------------------------ ----------
SCRATCH_DG                                       ONLIN
```

Checking for the online/offline state of a disk is a simple matter of running the following query from SQL*Plus. In the listing below you can see that the SCRATCH_CD_05_CELL01 disk is offline by its MOUNT_STATE of MISSING and HEADER_STATUS of UNKNOWN:

```
SYS:+ASM2> select d.name, d.MOUNT_STATUS, d.HEADER_STATUS, d.STATE
 from v$asm_disk d
 where d.name like 'SCRATCH%'
 order by 1;

NAME                                             MOUNT_S HEADER_STATU STATE
------------------------------------------------ ------- ------------ ----------
SCRATCH_CD_05_CELL01                             MISSING UNKNOWN      NORMAL
SCRATCH_CD_05_CELL02                             CACHED  MEMBER       NORMAL
SCRATCH_CD_05_CELL03                             CACHED  MEMBER       NORMAL
```

Still, perhaps a better way of checking the status of all disks in the SCRATCH_DG disk group would be to check the mode_status in V$ASM_DISK_STAT. The following listing shows that all grid disks in the SCRATCH_DG disk group are online:

```
SYS:+ASM2> select name, mode_status from v$asm_disk_stat where name like 'SCRATCH%';

NAME                                             MODE_ST
------------------------------------------------ -------
SCRATCH_CD_05_CELL03                             ONLINE
SCRATCH_CD_05_CELL01                             ONLINE
SCRATCH_CD_05_CELL02                             ONLINE
```

The next thing we'll look at is the disk repair timer. Recall that the disk group attribute disk_repair_time determines the amount of time ASM will wait before it permanently removes a disk from the disk group and rebalances the data to the surviving grid disks when read/write errors occur. Before taking a disk offline we should check to see that this timer is going to give us enough time to bring the disk back online before ASM automatically drops it. This attribute can be displayed using SQL*Plus and running the following query. (By the way, the V$ASM views are visible whether you are connected to an ASM instance or a database instance.)

```
SYS:+ASM2> select dg.name "DiskGoup",
           attr.name,
           attr.value
      from v$asm_diskgroup dg,
           v$asm_attribute attr
     where dg.group_number = attr.group_number
       and attr.name = 'disk_repair_time';
```

DiskGoup	NAME	VALUE
DATA_DG	disk_repair_time	72h
RECO_DG	disk_repair_time	72h
SCRATCH_DG	disk_repair_time	8.5h
STAGE_DG	disk_repair_time	72h
SYSTEM_DG	disk_repair_time	72h

The default value for the disk repair timer is 3.6 hours. In production systems you will want to set the timer high enough for you to resolve transient disk errors. These errors occur when a storage cell is rebooted or when a disk is temporarily taken offline but on rare occasion, they can also occur spontaneously. Sometimes simply pulling a disk out of the chassis and reinserting it will clear unexpected transient errors. Any data that would normally be written to the failed disk will queue up until the disk is brought back online or the disk repair time expires. If ASM drops a disk, it can be manually added back into the disk group but it will require a full rebalance which can be a lengthy process. The following command was used to set the disk repair timer to 8.5 hours for the SCRATCH_DG disk group:

```
SYS:+ASM2> alter diskgroup SCRATCH_DG set  attribute 'disk_repair_time'='8.5h';
```

Now, let's verify whether taking a cell disk offline will affect the availability of the disk group. We can do that by checking the asmdeactivationoutcome and asmmodestatus attributes of our grid disks. For example, the following listing shows the output from the LIST GRIDDISK command when a grid disk in a normal redundancy disk group is taken offline. In this example, we have a SCRATCH_DG disk group consisting of one grid disk from three failure groups (enkcel01, enkcel02, and enkcel03). First we'll check the status of the grid disks when all disks are active:

```
[enkdb02:root] /root
> dcli -g cell_group -l root "su - celladmin -c \"cellcli -e list griddisk \
    attributes name, asmdeactivationoutcome, asmmodestatus \"" | grep SCRATCH
enkcel01: SCRATCH_DG_CD_05_cell01   Yes    ONLINE
enkcel02: SCRATCH_DG_CD_05_cell02   Yes    ONLINE
enkcel03: SCRATCH_DG_CD_05_cell03   Yes    ONLINE
```

Now, we'll deactivate one of these the grid disks at the storage cell and run the command again:

```
CellCLI> alter griddisk SCRATCH_DG_CD_05_cell01 inactive
GridDisk SCRATCH_DG_CD_05_cell01 successfully altered

[enkdb02:root] /root
> dcli -g cell_group -l root "su - celladmin -c \"cellcli -e list griddisk \
    attributes name, asmdeactivationoutcome, asmmodestatus \"" | grep SCRATCH
enkcel01: SCRATCH_DG_CD_05_cell01   Yes    OFFLINE
enkcel02: SCRATCH_DG_CD_05_cell02    "Cannot de-activate due to other offline disks in the
diskgroup"        ONLINE
enkcel03: SCRATCH_DG_CD_05_cell03    "Cannot de-activate due to other offline disks in the
diskgroup"        ONLINE
```

As you can see, the asmmodestatus attribute of the offlined grid disk is now set to OFFLINE, and the asmdeactivationoutcome attribute of the other two disks in the disk group warns us that these grid disks cannot be taken offline. Doing so would cause ASM to dismount the SCRATCH_DG disk group disk group.

> ■ **Note:** Notice that we use the dcli command to run the CellCLI command LIST GRIDDISK ATTRIBUTES on each cell in the storage grid. Basically, dcli allows us to run a command concurrently on multiple nodes. The cell_group parameter is a file containing a list of all of our storage cells.

If the output from the LIST GRIDDISK command indicates it is safe to do so, we can test what happens when we take one of the grid disks for our SCRATCH_DG disk group offline. For this test we will physically remove the disk drive from the storage cell chassis. The test configuration will be as follows:

- For this test we will create a new tablespace with one datafile. The datafile is set to autoextend so it will grow into the disk group as data is loaded.

- Next, we'll generate a considerable amount of data in the tablespace by creating a large table; a couple of billion rows from DBA_SEGMENTS should do it.

- While data is being loaded into the large table, we will physically remove the disk from the cell chassis.

- Once the data is finished loading, we will reinstall the disk and observe Exadata's automated disk recovery in action.

The first order of business is to identify the location of the disk drive within the storage cell. To do this we will use the grid disk name to find the cell disk it resides on, then we'll use the cell disk name to find the slot address of the disk drive within the storage cell. Once we have the slot address we will turn on the service LED on the front panel so we know which disk to remove.

From storage cell 3, we can use the LIST GRIDDISK command to find the name of the cell disk we are looking for:

```
CellCLI> list griddisk attributes name, celldisk where name like 'SCRATCH.*' detail
        name:                   SCRATCH_DG_CD_05_cell03
        cellDisk:               CD_05_cell03
```

Now that we have the cell disk name, we can use the LIST LUN command to find the slot address of the physical disk we want to remove. In the following listing we see the slot address we're looking for, 16:5.

```
CellCLI> list LUN attributes celldisk, physicaldrives where celldisk=CD_05_cell03 detail
        cellDisk:               CD_05_cell03
        physicalDrives:         16:5
```

With the slot address, we can use the MegaCli64 command to activate the drive's service LED on the front panel of the storage cell. Note that the \ characters in the MegaCli64 command below are used to prevent the Bash shell from interpreting the brackets ([]) around the physical drive address. (Single quotes work as well, by the way.)

```
/opt/MegaRAID/MegaCli/MegaCli64 -pdlocate -physdrv \[16:5\] -a0
```

The amber LED on the front of the disk drive should be flashing as can be seen in Figure 9-2.

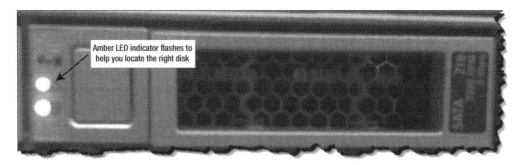

Figure 9-2. Disk drive front panel

And in case you were wondering, the service LED can be turned off again using the stop option of the MegaCli64 command, like this:

```
/opt/MegaRAID/MegaCli/MegaCli64 -pdlocate -stop -physdrv \[16:5\] -a0
```

Now that we've located the right disk, we can remove it from the storage cell by pressing the release button and gently pulling the lever on the front of the disk, as you can see in Figure 9-3.

Figure 9-3. Ejected disk drive

▓ **Note:** All disk drives in the storage cell are hot-pluggable and may be replaced without powering down the storage cell.

Checking the grid disk status in CellCLI, we see that it has been changed from Active to Inactive. This makes the grid disk unavailable to the ASM storage cluster.

```
CellCLI> list griddisk where name = 'SCRATCH_CD_05_cell03';
        SCRATCH_CD_05_cell03     inactive
```

ASM immediately notices the loss of the disk, takes it offline, and starts the disk repair timer. The ASM alert log (alert_+ASM2.log) shows that we have about 8.5 hours (30596/60/60) to bring the disk back online before ASM permanently drops it from the disk group:

```
alert_+ASM1.log
--------------------
Tue Dec 28 08:40:54 2010
GMON checking disk modes for group 5 at 121 for pid 52, osid 29292
Errors in file /u01/app/oracle/diag/asm/+asm/+ASM2/trace/+ASM2_gmon_5912.trc:
ORA-27603: Cell storage I/O error, I/O failed on disk o/192.168.12.5/SCRATCH_CD_05_cell03 at
offset 4198400 for data length 4096
ORA-27626: Exadata error: 201 (Generic I/O error)
WARNING: Write Failed. group:5 disk:3 AU:1 offset:4096 size:4096
...
WARNING: Disk SCRATCH_DG_CD_05_CELL03 in mode 0x7f is now being offlined
WARNING: Disk SCRATCH_DG_CD_05_CELL03 in mode 0x7f is now being taken offline
...
Tue Dec 28 08:43:21 2010
WARNING: Disk (SCRATCH_DG_CD_05_CELL03) will be dropped in: (30596) secs on ASM inst: (2)
Tue Dec 28 08:43:23 2010
```

The status of the disk in ASM can be seen using the following query from one of the ASM instances. Notice that the SCRATCH disk group is still mounted (online):

```
SYS:+ASM2> select dg.name, d.name, dg.state, d.mount_status, d.header_status, d.state
              from v$asm_disk d,
                   v$asm_diskgroup dg
           where dg.name = 'SCRATCH_DG'
             and dg.group_number = d.group_number
           order by 1,2;
```

NAME	NAME	STATE	MOUNT_S	HEADER_STATU	STATE
SCRATCH	SCRATCH_DG_CD_05_CELL01	MOUNTED	CACHED	MEMBER	NORMAL
SCRATCH	SCRATCH_DG_CD_05_CELL02	MOUNTED	CACHED	MEMBER	NORMAL
SCRATCH	SCRATCH_DG_CD_05_CELL03	MOUNTED	MISSING	UNKNOWN	NORMAL

While the disk is offline, ASM continues to poll its status to see if the disk is available. We see the following query repeating in the ASM alert log:

```
alert_+ASM1.log
--------------------
WARNING: Exadata Auto Management: OS PID: 5918 Operation ID: 3015:   in diskgroup  Failed
  SQL   : /* Exadata Auto Mgmt: Select disks in DG that are not ONLINE. */
select name from v$asm_disk_stat
  where
    mode_status='OFFLINE'
      and
    group_number in
      (
        select group_number from v$asm_diskgroup_stat
```

```
    where
      name='SCRATCH_DG'
        and
      state='MOUNTED'
  )
```

Our test database also detected the loss of the grid disk, as can be seen in the database alert log:

```
alert_SCRATCH.log
-----------------------
Tue Dec 28 08:40:54 2010
Errors in file /u01/app/oracle/diag/rdbms/scratch/SCRATCH/trace/SCRATCH_ckpt_22529.trc:
ORA-27603: Cell storage I/O error, I/O failed on disk o/192.168.12.5/SCRATCH_CD_05_cell03 at
offset 26361217024 for data length 16384
ORA-27626: Exadata error: 201 (Generic I/O error)
WARNING: Read Failed. group:5 disk:3 AU:6285 offset:16384 size:16384
WARNING: failed to read mirror side 1 of virtual extent 0 logical extent 0 of file 260 in
group [5.1611847437] from disk SCRATCH_CD_05_CELL03  allocation unit 6285 reason error; if
possible,will try another mirror side
NOTE: successfully read mirror side 2 of virtual extent 0 logical extent 1 of file 260 in
group [5.1611847437] from disk SCRATCH_CD_05_CELL02 allocation unit 224
...
Tue Dec 28 08:40:54 2010
NOTE: disk 3 (SCRATCH_CD_05_CELL03) in group 5 (SCRATCH) is offline for reads
NOTE: disk 3 (SCRATCH_CD_05_CELL03) in group 5 (SCRATCH) is offline for writes
```

Notice that the database automatically switches to the mirror copy for data it can no longer read from the failed grid disk. This is ASM normal redundancy in action.

When we reinsert the disk drive, the storage cell returns the grid disk to a state of Active, and ASM brings the disk back online again. We can see that the grid disk has returned to a state of CACHED and a HEADER_STATUS of NORMAL in the following query:

```
SYS:+ASM2> select dg.name, d.name, dg.state, d.mount_status, d.header_status, d.state
         from v$asm_disk d,
              v$asm_diskgroup dg
       where dg.name = 'SCRATCH'
         and dg.group_number = d.group_number
       order by 1,2;
```

NAME	NAME	STATE	MOUNT_S	HEADER_STATU	STATE	
SCRATCH	SCRATCH_CD_05_CELL01	MOUNTED	CACHED	MEMBER	NORMAL	
SCRATCH	SCRATCH_CD_05_CELL02	MOUNTED	CACHED	MEMBER	NORMAL	
SCRATCH	SCRATCH_CD_05_CELL03	MOUNTED	CACHED	MEMBER	NORMAL	←

It is likely that the disk group will need to catch up on writing data that queued up while the disk was offline. If the duration of the outage was short and the write activity was light, then the rebalance won't take long. It may even go unnoticed. But if the disk has been offline for several hours or days, or if there was a lot of write activity in the disk group during the outage, this could take a while. Generally speaking, the delay is not a problem, because it all happens in the background. During the resilvering process, ASM redundancy allows our databases to continue with no interruption to service.

If this had been an actual disk failure and we actually replaced the disk drive, we would need to wait for the RAID controller to acknowledge the new disk before it could be used. This doesn't take long but you should check the status of the disk to ensure that its status is Normal before using it. The disk status may be verified using the CellCLI command LIST PHYSICALDISK as shown here:

CellCLI> list physicaldisk where diskType=HardDisk AND status=critical detail

When a disk is replaced, the storage cell performs the following tasks automatically:

- The disk firmware is updated to match the other disk drives in the storage cell.

- The cell disk is re-created to match that of the disk it replaced.

- The replacement cell disk is brought online (status set to Normal).

- The grid disk (or grid disks) that were on the failed disk are re-created.

- The grid disk status is set to Active.

Once the replacement grid disks are set to Active, ASM automatically opens the disk and begins the resilvering process. All these tasks are handled automatically by Exadata, making disk replacement a fairly painless process.

When to Replace a Cell Disk

Disk failure can occur abruptly, causing the disk to go offline immediately, or it can occur gradually, manifesting poor I/O performance. Storage cells are constantly monitoring the disk drives. This monitoring includes drive performance, in terms of both I/O and throughput, and SMART metrics such as temperature, speed, and read/write errors. The goal is to provide early warning for disks that are likely to fail before they actually do. When Exadata detects a problem, an alert is generated with specific instructions on how to replace the disk. If the system has been configured for email notification these alerts will be emailed to you automatically.

In the previous section we walked through a simulated drive failure. Had this been an actual disk failure, the procedure for replacing the disk would follow the same steps we used for the simulation. But what happens when Exadata's early warning system determines that a drive is likely to fail soon? When Exadata detects drive problems it sets the physical disk status attribute accordingly. The following CellCLI command displays the status of all disks in the storage cell.

```
CellCLI> list physicaldisk attributes name, status where disktype = 'HardDisk'
        35:0    normal
        35:1    normal
        ...
        35:11   normal
```

Table 9-3 shows the various disk status values and what they mean.

Table 9-3. *Disk Status Definitions*

Status	Description
Normal	The drive is healthy.
Predictive Failure	The disk is still working but likely to fail soon and should be replaced as soon as possible.
Poor Performance	The disk is exhibiting extremely poor performance and should be replaced.

Predictive Failure

If a disk status shows Predictive Failure, ASM will automatically drop the grid disks from the drive and rebalance data to other disks in the disk group according to the redundancy policy of the affected disk groups that use the drive. Once ASM has finished rebalancing and completed the drop operation, you can replace the disk drive. The following listing can be used to track the status of the ASM disk. A status of Offline indicates that ASM has not yet finished rebalancing the disk group. Once the rebalance is complete, the disk will no longer appear in the listing. By the way, tailing the ASM alert log is also an excellent way of checking the progress of the drop.

```
SYS:+ASM2>select name, mode_status
          from v$asm_disk_stat
        where name like 'SCRATCH%'
        order by 1;

NAME                                              MODE_ST
------------------------------------------------- -------
SCRATCH_CD_05_CELL01                              ONLINE
SCRATCH_CD_05_CELL02                              ONLINE
SCRATCH_CD_05_CELL03                              OFFLINE
```

■ **Caution:** The first two physical disks in the storage cell also contain the Linux operating system. The O/S partitions on these two disks are configured as mirrors of one another. If one of these disks fails, the data must be in sync with the mirror disk before you remove it. Use the CellCLI command `alter cell validate configuration` to verify that no `madm` errors exist before replacing the disk.

The CellCLI command VALIDATE CONFIGURATION performs this verification for you:

```
CellCLI> ALTER CELL VALIDATE CONFIGURATION
Cell enkcel01 successfully altered
```

Poor Performance

If a disk exhibits poor performance, it should be replaced. A single poorly performing cell disk can impact the performance of other healthy disks. When a disk begins performing extremely badly, its status will be set to Poor Performance. As is the case with Predictive Failure status, ASM will automatically drop all grid disks (on this cell disk) from the disk groups and begin a rebalance operation. Once the rebalance is complete you can remove and replace the failing disk drive. You can use the CellCLI command CALIBRATE to manually check the performance of all disks in the storage cell. The following listing shows the output of the CALIBRATE command. Ordinarily, cellsrv should be shut down before running CALIBRATE, because it can significantly impact I/O performance for databases using the storage cell. If you cannot shut down cellsrv for the test, you can run CALIBRATE using the FORCE option. As daunting as that sounds, FORCE simply overrides the safety switch and allows you to run CALIBRATE while cellsrv is up and applications are using the cell disks. The following listing shows the output from the CALIBRATE command run on a healthy set of cell disks:

```
CellCLI> calibrate
Calibration will take a few minutes...
Aggregate random read throughput across all hard disk luns: 1025 MBPS
Aggregate random read throughput across all flash disk luns: 3899.18 MBPS
Aggregate random read IOs per second (IOPS) across all hard disk luns: 1707
Aggregate random read IOs per second (IOPS) across all flash disk luns: 145158
Controller read throughput: 1245.08 MBPS
Calibrating hard disks (read only) ...
Lun 0_0  on drive [35:0    ] random read throughput:  83.80 MBPS, and 144 IOPS
Lun 0_1  on drive [35:1    ] random read throughput:  87.85 MBPS, and 145 IOPS
Lun 0_10 on drive [35:10   ] random read throughput:  91.23 MBPS, and 145 IOPS
Lun 0_11 on drive [35:11   ] random read throughput:  91.32 MBPS, and 150 IOPS
Lun 0_2  on drive [35:2    ] random read throughput:  92.07 MBPS, and 147 IOPS
Lun 0_3  on drive [35:3    ] random read throughput:  91.59 MBPS, and 150 IOPS
Lun 0_4  on drive [35:4    ] random read throughput:  93.71 MBPS, and 149 IOPS
Lun 0_5  on drive [35:5    ] random read throughput:  89.86 MBPS, and 147 IOPS
Lun 0_6  on drive [35:6    ] random read throughput:  91.65 MBPS, and 148 IOPS
Lun 0_7  on drive [35:7    ] random read throughput:  88.06 MBPS, and 145 IOPS
Lun 0_8  on drive [35:8    ] random read throughput:  91.00 MBPS, and 149 IOPS
Lun 0_9  on drive [35:9    ] random read throughput:  90.81 MBPS, and 149 IOPS
Calibrating flash disks (read only, note that writes will be significantly slower) ...
Lun 1_0  on drive [[2:0:0:0]] random read throughput: 242.51 MBPS, and 19035 IOPS
Lun 1_1  on drive [[2:0:1:0]] random read throughput: 240.89 MBPS, and 19018 IOPS
Lun 1_2  on drive [[2:0:2:0]] random read throughput: 240.90 MBPS, and 19111 IOPS
Lun 1_3  on drive [[2:0:3:0]] random read throughput: 241.62 MBPS, and 18923 IOPS
Lun 2_0  on drive [[4:0:0:0]] random read throughput: 242.08 MBPS, and 19066 IOPS
Lun 2_1  on drive [[4:0:1:0]] random read throughput: 251.11 MBPS, and 19263 IOPS
Lun 2_2  on drive [[4:0:2:0]] random read throughput: 245.65 MBPS, and 19119 IOPS
Lun 2_3  on drive [[4:0:3:0]] random read throughput: 247.83 MBPS, and 19139 IOPS
Lun 4_0  on drive [[1:0:0:0]] random read throughput: 250.36 MBPS, and 19036 IOPS
Lun 4_1  on drive [[1:0:1:0]] random read throughput: 249.82 MBPS, and 19006 IOPS
Lun 4_2  on drive [[1:0:2:0]] random read throughput: 252.82 MBPS, and 19140 IOPS
Lun 4_3  on drive [[1:0:3:0]] random read throughput: 250.80 MBPS, and 18979 IOPS
Lun 5_0  on drive [[3:0:0:0]] random read throughput: 253.21 MBPS, and 19167 IOPS
Lun 5_1  on drive [[3:0:1:0]] random read throughput: 252.01 MBPS, and 19152 IOPS
Lun 5_2  on drive [[3:0:2:0]] random read throughput: 251.86 MBPS, and 19160 IOPS
Lun 5_3  on drive [[3:0:3:0]] random read throughput: 244.24 MBPS, and 18925 IOPS
```

```
CALIBRATE results are within an acceptable range.

CALIBRATE stress test is now running...
Calibration has finished.
```

Cell Flash Cache Failure

Exadata storage cells come equipped with four F20 PCIe flash cache cards. Each card has four flash cache disks (FDOMs) for a total of 16 flash disks. These flash cache cards occupy slots 1, 2, 3, and 5 inside the storage cell. If a flash cache module fails, performance of the storage cell will be degraded and it should be replaced at your earliest opportunity. If you are using some of your flash cache for flash disk-based grid disks, your disk group redundancy will be affected as well. These flash cache cards are not hot-pluggable, so replacing them will require you to power off the affected cell.

If a flash disk fails, Exadata will send you an email notifying you of the failure. The email will include the slot address of the card, and if a specific FDOM has failed it will include the address of the FDOM on the card (1, 2, 3 or 4). The failed flash cache card can be seen using the CellCLI command LIST PHYSICALDISK as follows:

```
CellCLI> list physicaldisk where disktype=flashdisk and status=normal

        name:               [4:0:3:0]
        diskType:           FlashDisk
        luns:               2_3
        makeModel:          "MARVELL SD88SA02"
        physicalFirmware:   D20Y
        physicalInsertTime: 2010-07-28T20:09:43-05:00
        physicalInterface:  sas
        physicalSerial:     5080020000c7d60FMOD3
        physicalSize:       22.8880615234375G
        slotNumber:         "PCI Slot: 2; FDOM: 3"
        status:             critical
```

The slotNumber attribute here shows you where the card and FDOM are installed. In our case, the card is installed in PCIe slot 2. Once you have this information, you can shut down and power off the storage cell and replace the defective part. Keep in mind that when the cell is offline, ASM will no longer have access to the grid disks. So before you shut down the cell, make sure that shutting it down will not impact the availability of the disk groups it supports. This is the same procedure we described in the "Cell Disk Failure" section of this chapter. Once the part is replaced and the cell reboots, the storage cell will automatically configure the cell disk on the replacement card and, if it was used for flash cache, you will see your flash cache return to its former size.

Cell Failure

There are two main types of cell failure, temporary and permanent. Temporary cell failures can be as harmless as a cell reboot or a power failure. Extended cell failures can also be temporary in nature. For example, if a patch installation fails or a component must be replaced, it could take the cell offline for hours or even days. Permanent cell failures are more severe in nature and require the entire cell chassis to be replaced. In either case, if your system is configured properly, there will be no interruption to ASM or your databases. In this section we'll take a look at what happens when a cell is temporarily offline, and what to do if you ever have to replace one.

Temporary Cell Failure

As discussed in Chapter 14, Exadata storage cells are Sun servers with internal disk drives running Oracle Enterprise Linux 5. If a storage cell goes offline, all the disks on that cell become unavailable to the database servers. This means that all disk groups containing database data (as well as OCR and Voting files) on that storage cell are offline for the duration of the outage. ASM failure groups provide redundancy that allows your cluster and databases to continue to run during the outage, albeit with reduced I/O performance. When grid disks are created in a storage cell they are assigned to a failure group. Each cell constitutes a failure group, as can be seen in the following listing:

```
SYS:+ASM2> select dg.name diskgroup, d.name disk, d.failgroup
             from v$asm_diskgroup dg,
                  v$asm_disk d
            where dg.group_number = d.group_number
              and dg.name like 'SCRATCH%'
            order by 1,2,3;
```

DISKGROUP	DISK	FAILGROUP
SCRATCH_DG	SCRATCH_DG_CD_05_CELL01	CELL01
SCRATCH_DG	SCRATCH_DG_CD_05_CELL02	CELL02
SCRATCH_DG	SCRATCH_DG_CD_05_CELL03	CELL03

Because SCRATCH_DG was created using Normal redundancy, our SCRATCH database should be able to continue even if an entire storage cell dies. In this section we'll be testing what happens when a storage cell goes dark. We'll use the same disk group configuration we used for the disk failure simulation earlier in this chapter. To simulate a cell failure, we'll log in to the ILOM on storage cell 3 and power it off. Because each storage cell constitutes an ASM failure group, this scenario is very similar to losing a single cell disk, I/O performance notwithstanding. The difference, of course, is that we are losing an entire failure group. Just as we did in our cell disk failure tests, we'll generate data in the SCRATCH database during the failure to verify that the database continues to service client requests during the cell outage.

To generate I/O for the tests we'll be repeatedly inserting 23205888 rows from the BIGTAB table into the bigtab2 table:

```
RJOHNSON:SCRATCH> insert /*+ append */ into bigtab2 nologging (select * from bigtab);
RJOHNSON:SCRATCH> commit;
```

While the above inserts are running, let's power off cell03 and take a look at the database alert log. As you can see, the database throws an error when reading from a disk on Cell03, "failed to read mirror side 1." A couple of lines further down in the log you see the database successfully reading the mirror copy of the extent, "successfully read mirror side 2."

```
alert_SCRATCH.log
-----------------------
Fri Jan 14 21:09:45 2011
Errors in file /u01/app/oracle/diag/rdbms/scratch/SCRATCH/trace/SCRATCH_mmon_31673.trc:
ORA-27603: Cell storage I/O error, I/O failed on disk o/192.168.12.5/SCRATCH_CD_05_cell03 at
offset 2483044352 for data length 16384
ORA-27626: Exadata error: 12 (Network error)
...
WARNING: Read Failed. group:3 disk:2 AU:592 offset:16384 size:16384
```

WARNING: failed to read mirror side 1 of virtual extent 2 logical extent 0 of file 260 in
group [3.689477631] from disk SCRATCH_CD_05_CELL03 allocation unit 592 reason error; if
possible,will try another mirror side
NOTE: successfully read mirror side 2 of virtual extent 2 logical extent 1 of file 260 in
group [3.689477631] from disk SCRATCH_CD_05_CELL01 allocation unit 589

Turning to the ASM alert log we see that ASM also noticed the issue with Cell03 and responds by
taking grid disk SCRATCH_CD_05_CELL03 offline. Notice further on that ASM is in the process of taking
other grid disks offline as well. This continues until all grid disks on Cell03 are offline:

```
alert_+ASM2.log
----------------------
--- Test Cell03 Failure --
Fri Jan 14 21:09:45 2011
NOTE: process 23445 initiating offline of disk 2.3915933784 (SCRATCH_CD_05_CELL03) with mask
0x7e in group 3
...
WARNING: Disk SCRATCH_CD_05_CELL03 in mode 0x7f is now being offlined
Fri Jan 14 21:09:47 2011
NOTE: process 19753 initiating offline of disk 10.3915933630 (RECO_CD_10_CELL03) with mask
0x7e in group 2
```

Checking the V$SESSION and V$SQL views we can see that the insert is still running.

```
SID PROG       SQL_ID         SQL_TEXT
----- ---------- ------------- ----------------------------------------
  3 sqlplus@en 9ncczt9qcg0m8  insert /*+ append */ into bigtab2 nologgi
```

So our databases continue to service client requests even when 1/3 of all storage is lost. That's pretty
amazing. Let's power up Cell03 again and observe what happens when this storage is available again.

Looking at Cell03's alert log we see cellsrv bring our grid disks back online again. The last thing we
see in Cell03's alert log is it rejoining the storage grid by establishing a heartbeat with the diskmon (disk
monitor) process on the database servers:

```
Cell03 Alert log
----------------
Storage Index Allocation for GridDisk SCRATCH_DG_CD_05_cell03 successful [code: 1]
CellDisk v0.5 name=CD_05_cell03 status=NORMAL guid=edc5f61e-6a60-48c9-a4a6-58c403a86a7c found
on dev=/dev/sdf
Griddisk SCRATCH_DG_CD_05_cell03  - number is (96)
Storage Index Allocation for GridDisk RECO_CD_06_cell03 successful [code: 1]
Storage Index Allocation for GridDisk SYSTEM_CD_06_cell03 successful [code: 1]
Storage Index Allocation for GridDisk STAGE_CD_06_cell03 successful [code: 1]
Storage Index Allocation for GridDisk DATA_CD_06_cell03 successful [code: 1]
CellDisk v0.5 name=CD_06_cell03 status=NORMAL guid=00000128-e01b-6d36-0000-000000000000 found
on dev=/dev/sdg
Griddisk RECO_CD_06_cell03  - number is (100)
Griddisk SYSTEM_CD_06_cell03  - number is (104)
Griddisk STAGE_CD_06_cell03  - number is (108)
Griddisk DATA_CD_06_cell03  - number is (112)
...
Fri Jan 14 22:51:30 2011
Heartbeat with diskmon started on enkdb02.enkitec.com
Heartbeat with diskmon started on enkdb01.enkitec.com
```

```
Fri Jan 14 22:51:40 2011
...
```

Permanent Cell Failure

So far we've discussed what happens when a cell disk is lost and what happens when a storage cell is temporarily offline. But what do you do when a storage cell completely fails and there is no bringing it back again? Exadata provides a mechanism for removing your good disk drives from a failed storage cell and moving them to a replacement cell.

Believe it or not, replacing a storage cell is not a terribly complicated process. Just about everything you need is contained on those spinning disks inside the cell chassis. As long as your operating system is intact on the system volumes, you have just about everything you need to make the move. Keep in mind that the disk repair timer might need to be readjusted to allow us time for an extended outage. It will, after all, take time to ship a new storage cell to your data center. The process looks something like this.

1. If possible, you should take copies of the configuration files from the failed storage cell. They may come in handy later on.

   - /etc/hosts

   - /etc/modprobe.conf

   - /etc/sysconfig/network

   - /etc/sysconfig/network-scripts

2. Verify that the disk repair timer will give you enough time to complete the procedure:

   ```
   SYS:+ASM2> select dg.name "DiskGoup", attr.name, attr.value
                 from v$asm_diskgroup dg, v$asm_attribute attr
               where dg.group_number = attr.group_number
                 and attr.name = 'disk_repair_time';
   ```

DiskGoup	NAME	VALUE
DATA_DG	disk_repair_time	8h
RECO_DG	disk_repair_time	8h
SCRATCH_DG	disk_repair_time	8h
STAGE_DG	disk_repair_time	8h
SYSTEM_DG	disk_repair_time	8h

   If you need to, you can adjust the disk repair timer for your disk groups by logging in to the ASM instance and using the ALTER DISKGROUP command. For example:

   ```
   [enkdb02:oracle:+ASM2 ] /home/oracle
   > sqlplus / as sysasm
   ...
   SYS:+ASM2> alter diskgroup SCRATCH_DG set attribute 'disk_repair_time'='72h';
   ```

3. Deactivate the grid disks on the failed storage cell and then shut it down. This can be done using the CellCLI and Linux commands as follows:

```
CELLCli> alter griddisk all inactive
```

```
[enkcel03:root] /root
> shutdown -h now
```

4. Once the system is shut down you can power it off using the power button on the front panel.

5. Open the cases of both the failed cell and the replacement cell, and move the following components from the old cell to the new cell:

    a. Flash Cache cards

    b. Disk controller card

    c. USB flash drive

    d. Disk drives

■ **Caution**: It is important that you place the first two disks in the same location on the new storage cell. These are the system volumes that contain the Linux operating system. If you don't, the cell may not boot. Also make sure you install the flash cache modules in the same PCI slots as they were in the failed cell. In general it is a good practice to simply remove each device, one at a time, and reinstall them into the same location on the new storage cell.

---

6. Power on the new cell.

7. Log in to the new cell as root, using either the KVM or ILOM interface.

8. Check the configuration files in the following directories. If they are damaged or otherwise corrupted, replace them with the backup copies you created in step 1.

9. The network settings for your Ethernet devices will remain the same with the exception of the hardware address, or MAC address. Find the new MAC addresses of the network devices eth0, eth1, eth2, and eth3. This can be done using the ifconfig command as follows:

```
[enkcel03:root] /root
> ifconfig eth0

eth0      Link encap:Ethernet  HWaddr 00:21:28:8E:AB:D8
          inet addr:192.168.8.205  Bcast:192.168.11.255  Mask:255.255.252.0
          inet6 addr: fe80::221:28ff:fe8e:abd8/64 Scope:Link
          UP BROADCAST RUNNING MULTICAST  MTU:1500  Metric:1
          RX packets:60238 errors:0 dropped:0 overruns:0 frame:0
          TX packets:22326 errors:0 dropped:0 overruns:0 carrier:0
          collisions:0 txqueuelen:1000
```

```
                    RX bytes:5803074 (5.5 MiB)  TX bytes:4380419 (4.1 MiB)
                    Memory:f8c60000-f8c80000
```

10. Using the MAC addresses from step 9, edit the /etc/sysconfig/network-scripts/ifcfg-eth{0-3} files and replace the old MAC addresses with the new ones. Here is an example using the ifcfg-eth0 file:

```
[enkcel03:root] /etc/sysconfig/network-scripts
> cat ifcfg-eth0
#### DO NOT REMOVE THESE LINES ####
#### %GENERATED BY CELL% ####
DEVICE=eth0
BOOTPROTO=static
ONBOOT=yes
IPADDR=192.168.8.205
NETMASK=255.255.252.0
NETWORK=192.168.8.0
BROADCAST=192.168.11.255
GATEWAY=192.168.10.1
HOTPLUG=no
IPV6INIT=no
HWADDR=00:21:28:8e:ab:d8          ← Replace this MAC address with the new address
```

11. Reboot the new storage cell to pick up the new MAC addresses.

12. After rebooting the cell, you should be able to log in to it using ssh, just as you normally would. Log in and reactivate the grid disks using the CellCLI command 'ALTER GRIDDISK command as follows:

```
CellCLI> alter griddisk all active
```

13. Once the grid disks are activated, ASM will set them to a state of online and begin using them once again. This is only true if the disk repair timer has not expired.

14. The last thing you will need to do is configure the ILOM for ASR. Configuring the ILOM is a little off topic and is covered very well in the Oracle documentation, so we won't be discussing it here.

Summary

Exadata is a highly redundant platform with a lot of moving parts. Businesses don't typically invest in such a platform without expectations of minimal downtime. As such, Exadata is commonly used for hosting mission-critical business applications with very stringent uptime requirements. Knowing what to do when things go wrong is critical to meeting these uptime requirements. In this chapter we've discussed the proper procedures for protecting your applications and customers from component and system failures. Before your system is rolled into production, make it a priority to practice backing up and restoring system volumes, removing and replacing disk drives, and rebooting storage cells, and become familiar with what happens to your databases. Run the diagnostic tools we've discussed in this chapter and make sure you understand how to interpret the output. If you are going to be responsible for maintaining Exadata for your company, now is the time to get comfortable with the topics discussed in this chapter.

## CHAPTER 10

Exadata Wait Events

The Oracle database is a very well instrumented piece of code, and it has been so for quite a while. It keeps track of the amount of time spent in discrete operations via the use of wait events. While the database software is quite complex, wait event analysis allows performance analysts to determine precisely where the database is spending its time. Many difficult performance problems can be resolved by analyzing these wait events. The introduction of Exadata has resulted in the creation of several new wait events to support the unique operations that are performed on the platform. This chapter will focus on describing these new events and how they relate to the activities actually being performed, while contrasting them with the wait events used by the database on non-Exadata platforms. It will also describe a few wait events that aren't specific to Exadata but play an important role on Exadata platforms.

A *wait event* is actually a section of code that is timed and assigned a name. The pieces of code covered by these events are quite often discrete operating system calls such as I/O requests, but some wait events cover considerably larger portions of code. The events may even include sections of code that contain other wait events. The naming of wait events has been somewhat inconsistent over the years, and many events have somewhat misleading names. Even though some of the event names are acknowledged to be potentially misleading, Oracle has been understandably reluctant to change them. The Exadata platform has provided an excuse to rename some of the I/O-related events, and as you'll see shortly, the developers took the opportunity to do just that.

Events Specific to Exadata

There are actually no events that exist exclusively on the Exadata platform. Wait events are built into the database code, and since the compute nodes on Exadata run standard Oracle Database software, all the wait events that are used when invoking Exadata-specific features are available in databases that are running on non-Exadata platforms as well. But because the Exadata features are only available on the Exadata platform, no time is ever allocated to those events on other platforms. By way of proof, consider the following example, which compares the events from V$EVENT_NAME (which exposes the valid wait events) first on an Exadata Database Machine and then on a standard 11gR2 database on a non-Exadata platform:

```
SYS@EXDB> select count(*) from v$event_name;

  COUNT(*)
----------
      1118
```

```
SYS@EXDB> select count(*) from v$event_name@LAB112;

  COUNT(*)
----------
      1118

SYS@EXDB> select name event from v$event_name
  2  minus
  3* select name from v$event_name@LAB112;

no rows selected
```

So there are no differences in the events. This does make it a little difficult to come up with a list of "Exadata Only" events.

The "cell" Events

The *Oracle Exadata Storage Server Software User's Guide 11g Release 2* provides a table of wait events. All of them start with the word "cell." The manual lists nine such events. One of them (cell interconnect retransmit during physical read) doesn't actually exist.

There are also another nine events having the word "cell" in their names that are not included in the documentation. So we'll use the complete list of "cell" events as a starting point. You can query V$EVENT_NAME for that list, and you'll get the following results. Notice that most of the events are in one of the I/O classes. There are only 17 rows, because one of the documented events does not exist in the version of Oracle that we're running (11.2.0.2).

```
SYS@POC2> @valid_events
Enter value for event_name: cell%

EVENT                                 CLASS
------------------------------------- -------------------------
cell list of blocks physical read     User I/O
cell multiblock physical read         User I/O
cell single block physical read       User I/O
cell smart file creation              User I/O
cell smart index scan                 User I/O
cell smart table scan                 User I/O
cell statistics gather                User I/O
cell manager closing cell             System I/O
cell manager discovering disks        System I/O
cell manager opening cell             System I/O
cell smart incremental backup         System I/O
cell smart restore from backup        System I/O
cell manager cancel work request      Other
cell smart flash unkeep               Other
cell worker online completion         Other
cell worker retry                     Other
cell worker idle                      Idle

17 rows selected.
```

The following sections will cover all of these events, along with a couple of additional events that have special applicability to Exadata.

Plan Steps That Trigger Events

First, though, it might be interesting to see what operations (plan steps) cause the "cell" wait events to occur. Here is a query against DBA_HIST_ACTIVE_SESS_HISTORY on an active production system running on an Exadata V2 that shows cell events and the operations that caused them:

```
SYS@EXDB1> select event, operation,  count(*) from (
  2  select sql_id, event, sql_plan_operation||' '||sql_plan_options operation
  3    from DBA_HIST_ACTIVE_SESS_HISTORY
  4    where event like 'cell %')
  5    group by operation, event
  6    order by 1,2,3
  7  /
```

EVENT	OPERATION	COUNT(*)
cell list of blocks physical read		62
	DDL STATEMENT	2
	INDEX FAST FULL SCAN	1
	INDEX RANGE SCAN	3060
	INDEX STORAGE FAST FULL SCAN	7
	INDEX STORAGE SAMPLE FAST FULL SCAN	10
	INDEX UNIQUE SCAN	1580
	INSERT STATEMENT	6
	TABLE ACCESS BY GLOBAL INDEX ROWID	151
	TABLE ACCESS BY INDEX ROWID	5458
	TABLE ACCESS BY LOCAL INDEX ROWID	131
	TABLE ACCESS STORAGE FULL	183
	TABLE ACCESS STORAGE SAMPLE	2
	TABLE ACCESS STORAGE SAMPLE BY ROWID RAN	1
cell multiblock physical read		3220
	DDL STATEMENT	157
	INDEX FAST FULL SCAN	94
	INDEX RANGE SCAN	2
	INDEX STORAGE FAST FULL SCAN	6334
	INDEX STORAGE SAMPLE FAST FULL SCAN	429
	UNIQUE SCAN	2
	VIEW ACCESS STORAGE FULL	634
	MAT_VIEW ACCESS STORAGE SAMPLE	56
	TABLE ACCESS BY GLOBAL INDEX ROWID	5
	TABLE ACCESS BY INDEX ROWID	484
	TABLE ACCESS BY LOCAL INDEX ROWID	3
	TABLE ACCESS STORAGE FULL	41559
	TABLE ACCESS STORAGE SAMPLE	1763
	TABLE ACCESS STORAGE SAMPLE BY ROWID RAN	78
	UPDATE	4

cell single block physical read	181186
BUFFER SORT	1
CREATE TABLE STATEMENT	67
DDL STATEMENT	985
DELETE	11204
DELETE STATEMENT	6
FIXED TABLE FIXED INDEX	352
FOR UPDATE	27
HASH GROUP BY	3
HASH JOIN	14
HASH JOIN RIGHT OUTER	1
INDEX BUILD NON UNIQUE	80
INDEX BUILD UNIQUE	6
INDEX FAST FULL SCAN	9
INDEX FULL SCAN	1101
INDEX RANGE SCAN	17597
INDEX RANGE SCAN (MIN/MAX)	1
INDEX RANGE SCAN DESCENDING	6
INDEX SKIP SCAN	691
INDEX STORAGE FAST FULL SCAN	313
INDEX STORAGE SAMPLE FAST FULL SCAN	72
INDEX UNIQUE SCAN	30901
INSERT STATEMENT	5174
LOAD AS SELECT	120
LOAD TABLE CONVENTIONAL	5827
MAT_VIEW ACCESS STORAGE FULL	3
MAT_VIEW ACCESS STORAGE SAMPLE	1
MERGE	12
PX COORDINATOR	1
SELECT STATEMENT	978
SORT CREATE INDEX	1
SORT GROUP BY	1
SORT JOIN	5
SORT ORDER BY	2
TABLE ACCESS BY GLOBAL INDEX ROWID	5812
TABLE ACCESS BY INDEX ROWID	65799
TABLE ACCESS BY LOCAL INDEX ROWID	4591
TABLE ACCESS BY USER ROWID	464
TABLE ACCESS CLUSTER	57
TABLE ACCESS STORAGE FULL	7168
TABLE ACCESS STORAGE SAMPLE	205
TABLE ACCESS STORAGE SAMPLE BY ROWID RAN	24
UNION-ALL	7
UPDATE	89353
UPDATE STATEMENT	367
WINDOW CHILD PUSHED RANK	2
WINDOW SORT	1
WINDOW SORT PUSHED RANK	1
cell smart file creation	35
DELETE	3
INDEX BUILD NON UNIQUE	5
LOAD AS SELECT	3

```
                                       LOAD TABLE CONVENTIONAL                    1
                                       UPDATE                                     1
cell smart incremental backup                                                   714
cell smart index scan                                                            14
                                       INDEX STORAGE FAST FULL SCAN              42
                                       INDEX STORAGE SAMPLE FAST FULL SCAN       32
cell smart table scan                                                           163
                                       MAT_VIEW ACCESS STORAGE FULL               1
                                       TABLE ACCESS STORAGE FULL              12504
```

Obviously this output does not show all the possible combinations, but it should give you an idea of the relative frequency of events and which operations generally motivate them.

Exadata Wait Events in the User I/O Class

The User I/O Class is far and away the most important for Exadata. The most interesting events in this category are of course the two Smart Scan events (cell smart table scan and cell smart index scan). These are the events that record time for the primary Offloading optimizations provided by Exadata, which include predicate filtering, column projection, and storage index usage. The User I/O Class also contains three events described as *physical I/O* events. These three events actually measure time for physical I/O using the more familiar multi-block and single-block read mechanisms we're used to seeing on non-Exadata platforms, although their names have been changed to something a little more meaningful. Finally, there are two events that don't really seem to belong in the User I/O category at all. One has to do with initialization of blocks when file space is allocated. The other has to do with gathering statistical information from the storage cells. We'll cover each of these wait events in turn in the next several sections, starting with the Smart Scan events.

cell smart table scan

The cell smart table scan event is what Oracle uses to account for time spent waiting for Full Table Scans that are Offloaded. It is the most important new event on the Exadata platform. Its presence or absence can be used to verify whether a statement benefited from Offloading or not. As discussed in Chapter 2, Offloading only occurs when Oracle is able to do direct path reads. Consequently, this event replaces the direct path read event in most cases on Exadata. As with normal direct path reads, data is returned directly to the PGA of the requesting process on the database server (either the user's shadow process or a parallel slave process). Blocks are not returned to the buffer cache.

Event Meaning

Although the mechanism for performing reads across the InfiniBand network is very different from that for normal reads on non-Exadata platforms, the code path driving the smart scans is actually very similar to a direct path read on a non-Exadata platform. The main difference lies in the fact that each request to a storage cell contains a reference to the metadata of the statement, which in the case of Exadata includes the predicates and the list of columns to be returned. Since the storage cells have access to this information, they can apply the filters and do the column projection before returning the data to the requesting process. These optimizations are applied to each set of blocks as they are requested. The processes on the database servers that request the data have access to the ASM extent map and can therefore request the required allocation units (AUs) from each storage cell. The storage cells read the requested AU and apply the predicate filters and, if any rows satisfy the filters, return the projected

323

columns to the requesting process. The process then requests the next AU and the entire routine is repeated until all the data has been scanned. So this event will occur repeatedly in a large scan.

■ **Note:** Column Projection is one of the major optimizations provided by Smart Scans. The feature is slightly misunderstood. It does not pass only columns in the select list back to the database servers; it also passes back some columns from the WHERE clause. Older versions of cellsrv passed all columns specified in a WHERE clause back to the database tier. Later versions have corrected this behavior to include only columns that are involved in join predicates.

Here's a portion of a 10046 trace file showing some of the events. The query generating this trace file did a full table scan which was performed via the direct read mechanism. (Note that we've shortened some of the lines to get them to fit, primarily by stripping off the time values):

```
PARSING IN CURSOR #2 len=32 dep=0 uid=0 oct=3 lid=0 hv=123 ad='196' sqlid='162wjnvwyybhn'
select sum(pk_col) from kso.skew

END OF STMT
PARSE #2:c=2000,e=2424,p=0,cr=0,cu=0,mis=1,r=0,dep=0,og=1,plh=568322376
EXEC #2:c=0,e=34,p=0,cr=0,cu=0,mis=0,r=0,dep=0,og=1,plh=568322376
WAIT #2: nam='SQL*Net message to client' ela= 3 driver id=1650815232 #bytes=1 p3=0 obj#=-1
WAIT #2: nam='ges message buffer allocation' ela= 2 pool=0 request=1 allocated=0 obj#=-1
WAIT #2: nam='KJC: Wait for msg sends to complete' ela= 10 msg=6674450368 dest|rcvr=65536
WAIT #2: nam='reliable message' ela= 1107 channel context=6712270872 channel handle=66967991
WAIT #2: nam='ges message buffer allocation' ela= 1 pool=0 request=1 allocated=0 obj#=-1
WAIT #2: nam='enq: KO - fast object checkpoint' ela= 104 name|mode=126 2=65575 0=1 obj#=-1
WAIT #2: nam='ges message buffer allocation' ela= 1 pool=0 request=1 allocated=0 obj#=-1
WAIT #2: nam='enq: KO - fast object checkpoint' ela= 103 name|mode=126 2=65575 0=2 obj#=-1
WAIT #2: nam='cell smart table scan' ela= 162 cellhash#=2133459483 p2=0 p3=0 obj#=66849
WAIT #2: nam='cell smart table scan' ela= 244 cellhash#=379339958 p2=0 p3=0 obj#=66849
WAIT #2: nam='cell smart table scan' ela= 181 cellhash#=3176594409 p2=0 p3=0 obj#=66849
WAIT #2: nam='cell smart table scan' ela= 1285 cellhash#=2133459483 p2=0 p3=0 obj#=66849
WAIT #2: nam='cell smart table scan' ela= 1327 cellhash#=379339958 p2=0 p3=0 obj#=66849
WAIT #2: nam='cell smart table scan' ela= 1310 cellhash#=3176594409 p2=0 p3=0 obj#=66849
WAIT #2: nam='cell smart table scan' ela= 19755 cellhash#=3176594409 p2=0 p3=0 obj#=66849
WAIT #2: nam='cell smart table scan' ela= 39 cellhash#=3176594409 p2=0 p3=0 obj#=66849
WAIT #2: nam='cell smart table scan' ela= 24 cellhash#=2133459483 p2=0 p3=0 obj#=66849
WAIT #2: nam='cell smart table scan' ela= 847 cellhash#=3176594409 p2=0 p3=0 obj#=66849
WAIT #2: nam='cell smart table scan' ela= 44 cellhash#=2133459483 p2=0 p3=0 obj#=66849
WAIT #2: nam='cell smart table scan' ela= 674 cellhash#=3176594409 p2=0 p3=0 obj#=66849
WAIT #2: nam='cell smart table scan' ela= 32 cellhash#=3176594409 p2=0 p3=0 obj#=66849
WAIT #2: nam='cell smart table scan' ela= 39 cellhash#=2133459483 p2=0 p3=0 obj#=66849
WAIT #2: nam='cell smart table scan' ela= 928 cellhash#=3176594409 p2=0 p3=0 obj#=66849
WAIT #2: nam='cell smart table scan' ela= 37 cellhash#=3176594409 p2=0 p3=0 obj#=66849
WAIT #2: nam='cell smart table scan' ela= 97 cellhash#=379339958 p2=0 p3=0 obj#=66849
```

This portion of the trace file also shows the enq: KO - fast object checkpoint event, which is used to ensure that any dirty blocks for the scanned object are flushed to disk prior to beginning the scan. By the way, the direct path read event is not completely eliminated on Exadata platforms. In fact, we can use a hint to disable Offloading and see how the same statement behaves without Offloading.

```
PARSING IN CURSOR #2 len=84 dep=0 uid=0 oct=3 lid=0 hv=123 ad='196' sqlid='cczz6y6rtz4bn'
select /*+ OPT_PARAM('cell_offload_processing' 'false') */ sum(pk_col) from kso.skew
END OF STMT
PARSE #2:c=26995,e=33582,p=1,cr=100,cu=0,mis=1,r=0,dep=0,og=1,plh=568322376
EXEC #2:c=0,e=20,p=0,cr=0,cu=0,mis=0,r=0,dep=0,og=1,plh=568322376
WAIT #2: nam='SQL*Net message to client' ela= 3 driver id=1650815232 #bytes=1 p3=0 obj#=-1
WAIT #2: nam='ges message buffer allocation' ela= 3 pool=0 request=1 allocated=0 obj#=-1
WAIT #2: nam='KJC: Wait for msg sends to complete' ela= 13 msg=66 dest|rcvr=65536 mtype=12
WAIT #2: nam='reliable message' ela= 1355 channel context=6712270872 channel
    handle=6696795216 broadcast message=6741335856 obj#=-1 tim=1285455676264108
WAIT #2: nam='ges message buffer allocation' ela= 2 pool=0 request=1 allocated=0 obj#=-1
WAIT #2: nam='enq: KO - fast object checkpoint' ela= 172 name|mode=126 2=65573 0=1 obj#=-1
WAIT #2: nam='ges message buffer allocation' ela= 2 pool=0 request=1 allocated=0 obj#=-1
WAIT #2: nam='enq: KO - fast object checkpoint' ela= 221 name|mode=126 2=65573 0=2 obj#=-
WAIT #2: nam='kfk: async disk IO' ela= 14 count=1 intr=0 timeout=4294967295 obj#=66849

WAIT #2: nam='direct path read' ela= 23746 file number=7 first dba=76322 block cnt=94
    obj#=66849
WAIT #2: nam='kfk: async disk IO' ela= 28 count=1 intr=0 timeout=4294967295 obj#=66849
WAIT #2: nam='kfk: async disk IO' ela= 20 count=1 intr=0 timeout=4294967295 obj#=66849
WAIT #2: nam='kfk: async disk IO' ela= 11 count=1 intr=0 timeout=4294967295 obj#=66849
WAIT #2: nam='kfk: async disk IO' ela= 6 count=1 intr=0 timeout=4294967295 obj#=66849
WAIT #2: nam='direct path read' ela= 18566 file number=7 first dba=76800 block cnt=128
    obj#=66849
WAIT #2: nam='kfk: async disk IO' ela= 19 count=1 intr=0 timeout=4294967295 obj#=66849
WAIT #2: nam='kfk: async disk IO' ela= 20 count=1 intr=0 timeout=4294967295 obj#=66849
WAIT #2: nam='kfk: async disk IO' ela= 6 count=1 intr=0 timeout=4294967295 obj#=66849
WAIT #2: nam='direct path read' ela= 35083 file number=7 first dba=77184 block cnt=128
    obj#=66849
WAIT #2: nam='kfk: async disk IO' ela= 19 count=1 intr=0 timeout=4294967295 obj#=66849
WAIT #2: nam='kfk: async disk IO' ela= 22 count=1 intr=0 timeout=4294967295 obj#=66849
WAIT #2: nam='kfk: async disk IO' ela= 7 count=1 intr=0 timeout=4294967295 obj#=66849
WAIT #2: nam='kfk: async disk IO' ela= 5 count=1 intr=0 timeout=4294967295 obj#=66849
```

Note that we still have the enq: KO - fast object checkpoint events for flushing dirty blocks. So it is clear that the cell smart table scan event replaces this event.

Parameters

The parameters for this event are not particularly informative. Only the object ID of the table being scanned and the cell hash number are provided:

P1 - Cell hash number

P2 - Not used

P3 - Not used

obj# - The object number of the table being scanned

You'll notice that the direct path read event (which cell smart table scan replaces) provides additional information including the file number, the offset into the file (first dba) and the number of contiguous blocks read (block cnt). On the other hand, with the direct path read event, there is no indication how the read requests are routed to the individual cells.

▓ **Note:** The Cell hash number reported with many of the wait events can be found in the V$CELL view. This view has only two columns, CELL_PATH and CELL_HASHVAL. The CELL_PATH column actually contains the IP address of the storage cell.

---

cell smart index scan

Time is clocked to the cell smart index scan event when fast full index scans are performed that are Offloaded. This event is analogous to cell smart table scan, except that the object being scanned is an index. It replaces the direct path read event and returns data directly to the PGA of the requesting process as opposed to the buffer cache.

Event Meaning

This event does not show up very often on the systems we have observed, probably for several reasons:

- Exadata is quite good at doing full table scans and so the tendency is to eliminate a lot of indexes when moving to the platform.

- Direct path reads are not done as often on index scans as they are on table scans. One of the important changes to Oracle 11.2 is the aggressiveness with which it does direct path reads on serial table scans. This enhancement was probably pushed forward specifically in order to allow Exadata to do more Smart Full Table Scans, but regardless of that, without this feature, only parallel table scans would be able to take advantage of Smart Scans. The same enhancement applies to index fast full scans. That is, they can also be done via serial direct path reads. However, the algorithm controlling when they happen appears to be less likely to use this technique with indexes (probably because the indexes are usually much smaller than tables).

- In addition, only fast full scans of indexes are eligible for Smart Scans (range scans and full scans are not eligible).

▓ **Kevin says:** A SmartScan on an index is possible without parallelism, but the rules are strict. If you alter the session to disable parallel query and set `_serial_direct_read`=TRUE in the session, and then run your test, you should get a smart, serial, *index fast full scan* (IFFS). If not, then you're looking at a bug. In short, to get a serial IFFS the object needs to be more than five times the size of the SGA.

Gluing range scans to smart index scans can be done, but it's very messy. There isn't likely much to be gained there in terms of completing a query.

As a result of these issues, `cell smart index scans` are fairly rare compared to `cell smart table scans`. It is, of course, possible to encourage the feature with hints (such as `parallel_index`) or by decorating specific indexes with a parallel degree setting of greater than 1. Here's an excerpt from a 10046 trace file showing the event:

```
PARSING IN CURSOR #1 len=112 dep=1 uid=0 oct=3 lid=0 hv=123 ad='197' sqlid='dnmumhk9599p7'
select /*+ parallel_index (a skew2_all 8) index_ffs (a skew2_all) */ sum(pk_col) from
kso.skew2 a where col1 > 1
END OF STMT
PARSE #1:c=0,e=89,p=0,cr=0,cu=0,mis=0,r=0,dep=1,og=1,plh=2801817111,tim=1285372448705192
WAIT #1: nam='PX Deq: Execution Msg' ela= 3124 sleeptime/senderid=268 passes=1 p3=0 obj#=-1
WAIT #1: nam='cell smart index scan' ela= 133 cellhash#=379339958 p2=0 p3=0 obj#=66856
WAIT #1: nam='cell smart index scan' ela= 522 cellhash#=2133459483 p2=0 p3=0 obj#=66856
WAIT #1: nam='cell smart index scan' ela= 277 cellhash#=3176594409 p2=0 p3=0 obj#=66856
WAIT #1: nam='cell smart index scan' ela= 1910 cellhash#=379339958 p2=0 p3=0 obj#=66856
WAIT #1: nam='cell smart index scan' ela= 330 cellhash#=2133459483 p2=0 p3=0 obj#=66856
WAIT #1: nam='cell smart index scan' ela= 348 cellhash#=3176594409 p2=0 p3=0 obj#=66856
WAIT #1: nam='cell smart index scan' ela= 45162 cellhash#=3176594409 p2=0 p3=0 obj#=66856
WAIT #1: nam='cell smart index scan' ela= 13 cellhash#=3176594409 p2=0 p3=0 obj#=66856
WAIT #1: nam='cell smart index scan' ela= 207 cellhash#=379339958 p2=0 p3=0 obj#=66856
WAIT #1: nam='cell smart index scan' ela= 30 cellhash#=379339958 p2=0 p3=0 obj#=66856
WAIT #1: nam='cell smart index scan' ela= 779 cellhash#=3176594409 p2=0 p3=0 obj#=66856
WAIT #1: nam='cell smart index scan' ela= 30 cellhash#=2133459483 p2=0 p3=0 obj#=66856
```

Note that this trace file was produced by one of the parallel slave processes and not the requesting process. The trace produced for the same statement when Offloading is disabled should look familiar. Here's an excerpt:

```
PARSING IN CURSOR #1 len=158 dep=1 uid=0 oct=3 lid=0 hv=338 ad='196' sqlid='g2966dwa2xfm8'
select /*+ OPT_PARAM('cell_offload_processing' 'false') parallel_index (a skew2_all 8)
index_ffs (a skew2_all) */ sum(pk_col) from kso.skew2 a where col1 > 1
END OF STMT
PARSE #1:c=0,e=94,p=0,cr=0,cu=0,mis=0,r=0,dep=1,og=1,plh=2801817111,tim=1285546990415744
WAIT #1: nam='PX Deq: Execution Msg' ela= 2377 sleeptime/senderid=268566527 passes=1 p3=0
WAIT #1: nam='latch: cache buffers chains' ela= 44 address=6636639304 number=150 tries=0
WAIT #1: nam='kfk: async disk IO' ela= 12 count=1 intr=0 timeout=4294967295 obj#=66856
WAIT #1: nam='direct path read' ela= 28957 file number=6 first dba=13 block cnt=124 obj#=66856
WAIT #1: nam='kfk: async disk IO' ela= 32 count=1 intr=0 timeout=4294967295 obj#=66856
WAIT #1: nam='kfk: async disk IO' ela= 24 count=1 intr=0 timeout=4294967295 obj#=66856
```

```
WAIT #1: nam='kfk: async disk IO' ela= 24 count=1 intr=0 timeout=4294967295 obj#=66856
WAIT #1: nam='kfk: async disk IO' ela= 8 count=1 intr=0 timeout=4294967295 obj#=66856
WAIT #1: nam='direct path read' ela= 1410 file number=6 first dba=1304064 block cnt=128
obj#=66856
WAIT #1: nam='kfk: async disk IO' ela= 24 count=1 intr=0 timeout=4294967295 obj#=66856
WAIT #1: nam='kfk: async disk IO' ela= 21 count=1 intr=0 timeout=4294967295 obj#=66856
WAIT #1: nam='kfk: async disk IO' ela= 24 count=1 intr=0 timeout=4294967295 obj#=66856
WAIT #1: nam='kfk: async disk IO' ela= 23 count=1 intr=0 timeout=4294967295 obj#=66856
WAIT #1: nam='kfk: async disk IO' ela= 23 count=1 intr=0 timeout=4294967295 obj#=66856
WAIT #1: nam='kfk: async disk IO' ela= 23 count=1 intr=0 timeout=4294967295 obj#=66856
WAIT #1: nam='kfk: async disk IO' ela= 32 count=1 intr=0 timeout=4294967295 obj#=66856
WAIT #1: nam='kfk: async disk IO' ela= 28 count=1 intr=0 timeout=4294967295 obj#=66856
WAIT #1: nam='kfk: async disk IO' ela= 21 count=1 intr=0 timeout=4294967295 obj#=66856
WAIT #1: nam='kfk: async disk IO' ela= 25 count=1 intr=0 timeout=4294967295 obj#=66856
WAIT #1: nam='kfk: async disk IO' ela= 31 count=1 intr=0 timeout=4294967295 obj#=66856

WAIT #1: nam='kfk: async disk IO' ela= 7 count=1 intr=0 timeout=4294967295 obj#=66856
WAIT #1: nam='direct path read' ela= 16725 file number=6 first dba=1303171 block cnt=125
obj#=66856
WAIT #1: nam='kfk: async disk IO' ela= 24 count=1 intr=0 timeout=4294967295 obj#=66856
WAIT #1: nam='kfk: async disk IO' ela= 27 count=1 intr=0 timeout=4294967295 obj#=66856
WAIT #1: nam='kfk: async disk IO' ela= 8 count=1 intr=0 timeout=4294967295 obj#=66856
```

Again we see the repeating pattern of a single direct path read event followed by several kfk: async disk IO events. The cell smart index scan event replaces both of these events. The enq: KO - fast object checkpoint events for flushing dirty blocks prior to starting the direct path reads are still present (although not shown in this excerpt because they occur in the query coordinator process, not in the parallel slave processes).

Parameters

Just as with the cell smart table scan event, the parameters for cell smart index scan do not contain a lot of details. The cell hash number and the object ID of the segment being scanned are the only information provided.

> P1 - Cell hash number
>
> P2 - Not used
>
> P3 - Not used
>
> obj# - The object number of the index being scanned

cell single block physical read

This event is equivalent to the db file sequential read event used on non-Exadata platforms. Single block reads are used most often for index access paths (both the index block reads and the table block reads via rowids from the index lookups). They can also be used for a wide variety of other operations where it makes sense to read a single block.

Event Meaning

Here is the output of a query that shows the operations that resulted in the cell single block physical read wait event on an active production system:

```
SYS@EXDB1> select event, operation,  count(*) from (
  2   select sql_id, event, sql_plan_operation||' '||sql_plan_options operation
  3     from DBA_HIST_ACTIVE_SESS_HISTORY
  4     where event like 'cell single%')
  5     group by operation, event
  6     order by 1,2,3
  7  /
```

EVENT	OPERATION	COUNT(*)
cell single block physical read		13321
	CREATE TABLE STATEMENT	35
	DDL STATEMENT	118
	DELETE	269
	FIXED TABLE FIXED INDEX	3
	FOR UPDATE	2
	HASH JOIN	4
	HASH JOIN RIGHT OUTER	8
	INDEX FULL SCAN	9283
	INDEX FULL SCAN (MIN/MAX)	1
	INDEX RANGE SCAN	2763
	INDEX STORAGE FAST FULL SCAN	6
	INDEX STORAGE SAMPLE FAST FULL SCAN	13
	INDEX UNIQUE SCAN	1676
	INSERT STATEMENT	1181
	LOAD AS SELECT	6
	LOAD TABLE CONVENTIONAL	92
	MERGE	106
	SELECT STATEMENT	41
	SORT ORDER BY	6
	TABLE ACCESS BY GLOBAL INDEX ROWID	10638
	TABLE ACCESS BY INDEX ROWID	8714
	TABLE ACCESS BY LOCAL INDEX ROWID	10446
	TABLE ACCESS CLUSTER	12
	TABLE ACCESS STORAGE FULL	776
	TABLE ACCESS STORAGE SAMPLE	40
	UPDATE	8116

As you can see, row access via an index is the most common operation that generates this event. You should also be aware that Exadata provides a large amount of flash cache (384G) on each storage cell. For that reason, physical reads (both multi-block and single-block) are considerably faster than on most disk-based storage systems. Here is an excerpt from an AWR report showing a histogram of single block reads for the instance:

```
                              % of Waits
                         -----------------------------------------
              Total
```

```
Event                      Waits <1ms <2ms <4ms <8ms <16ms <32ms <=1s  >1s
-------------------------- ----- ---- ---- ---- ---- ----- ----- ---- ----
cell single block physical 2940K 94.4  3.2   .3   .6    .9    .5   .2   .0
```

Notice that about 95% of the cell single block physical read events take less than 1ms. This is fairly representative of several production systems that we've observed.

Parameters

The cell single block physical read event provides more information than most cell events. The parameters allow you to tell exactly which object was read along with providing the disk and cell where the block was stored.

> P1 - Cell hash number
>
> P2 - Disk hash number
>
> P3 - Total bytes passed during read operation (always 8192 assuming 8K block size)
>
> obj# - The object number of the object being read

cell multiblock physical read

This is another renamed event. It is equivalent to the less clearly named db file scattered read event. On non-Exadata platforms, Oracle Database 11gR2 still uses the db file scattered read event whenever it issues a contiguous multi-block read to the operating system.

Event Meaning

This event is generally used with Full Table Scans and Fast Full Index scans, although it can be used with many other operations. The new name on the Exadata platform is much more descriptive than the older name. This wait event is not nearly as prevalent on Exadata platforms as on non-Exadata platforms, because Exadata handles many full scan operations with Smart Scans that have their own wait events (cell smart table scan and cell smart index scan). The cell multiblock physical read event on Exadata platforms is used for serial Full Scan operations on tables that are below the threshold for serial direct path reads. That is to say, you will see this event used most often on Full Scans of relatively small tables. It is also used for Fast Full Index Scans that are not executed with direct path reads. Here is the output of a query that shows the operations that resulted in the cell multiblock physical read wait event on an active production system:

```
EVENT                          OPERATION                                COUNT(*)
------------------------------ ---------------------------------------- ----------
cell multiblock physical read                                                 764
                               DDL STATEMENT                                    28
                               INDEX FAST FULL SCAN                              2
                               INDEX STORAGE FAST FULL SCAN                    657
                               INDEX STORAGE SAMPLE FAST FULL SCAN            133
                               TABLE ACCESS BY INDEX ROWID                      74
```

```
TABLE ACCESS BY LOCAL INDEX ROWID            1428
TABLE ACCESS STORAGE FULL                    5046
TABLE ACCESS STORAGE SAMPLE                    916
```

Parameters

The `cell multiblock physical read` event also provides more information than most cell events. The parameters in the following list allow you to tell which object was read and identifies the disk and cell where the blocks were stored. The total bytes passed should be a multiple of the block size.

> `P1` - Cell hash number
>
> `P2` - Disk hash number
>
> `P3` - Total bytes passed during read operation
>
> `obj#` - The object number of the object being read

cell list of blocks physical read

This event is a replacement for the `db file parallel read` event. It appears that the developers took the opportunity to rename some of the events that are related to disk operations, and this is one of those events. The new name is actually much more descriptive than the previous name, since the wait event has nothing whatsoever to do with parallel query or parallel DML.

Event Meaning

This event is used for a multi-block read of noncontiguous blocks. This is more effective with async I/O, which is enabled on Exadata by default. This event can be provoked by several operations. The most common are Index Range Scans, Index Unique Scans and Table Access By Index Rowid. The most common reason for the event is index pre-fetching. Here is the output of a query that shows the operations that resulted in this wait event on an active production system:

```
SYS@EXDB1> select event, operation,  count(*) from (
  2  select sql_id, event, sql_plan_operation||' '||sql_plan_options operation
  3    from DBA_HIST_ACTIVE_SESS_HISTORY
  4    where event like 'cell list%')
  5    group by operation, event
  6    order by 1,2,3
  7  /
```

EVENT	OPERATION	COUNT(*)
cell list of blocks physical read		2
	INDEX RANGE SCAN	156
	INDEX STORAGE FAST FULL SCAN	1
	INDEX UNIQUE SCAN	66
	TABLE ACCESS BY GLOBAL INDEX ROWID	90
	TABLE ACCESS BY INDEX ROWID	1273
	TABLE ACCESS BY LOCAL INDEX ROWID	2593

```
                              TABLE ACCESS STORAGE FULL              20
                              TABLE ACCESS STORAGE SAMPLE             1
```

As you can see, the vast majority of these events were motivated by index access paths. By the way, on non-Exadata platforms, noncontiguous multi-block reads still clock time to the old db file parallel read event. It's also possible for this older wait event name to show up on an Exadata platform for some operations.

Parameters

The cell list of blocks physical read event provides more information than most cell events. The following parameters allow you to tell exactly which object was read along with identifying the disk and cell where the block was stored.

> P1 - Cell hash number
>
> P2 - Disk hash number
>
> P3 - Number of blocks read
>
> obj# - The object number of the object being read

cell smart file creation

Exadata has an optimization technique that allows the storage cells to do the initialization of blocks when a data file is created or extended. This occurs when a tablespace is created or a data file is manually added to a tablespace. However, it can also occur when a data file is automatically extended during DML operations.

Event Meaning

We previously stated that this event seemed out of place in the User I/O class. However, if it occurs because of DML operations, it makes sense to have it in this category. At any rate, offloading the block formatting eliminates CPU usage and I/O from the database servers and moves it to the storage tier. When this occurs, time is collected in the cell smart file creation event. This event replaces the Data file init write event that is still used on non-Exadata platforms. Here is the output of a query from a busy production system showing operations that generated this event:

```
SYS@EXDB1> select event, operation,  count(*) from (
  2   select sql_id, event, sql_plan_operation||' '||sql_plan_options operation
  3     from DBA_HIST_ACTIVE_SESS_HISTORY
  4     where event like 'cell smart file%')
  5     group by operation, event
  6     order by 1,2,3
  7  /

EVENT                        OPERATION                  COUNT(*)
-------------------------    -------------------------  --------
cell smart file creation                                      35
                             DELETE                            3
                             INDEX BUILD NON UNIQUE            5
```

```
LOAD AS SELECT              3
LOAD TABLE CONVENTIONAL     1
UPDATE                      1
```

You'll notice that on this particular system, the cell smart file creation event was occasionally generated by a DELETE statement. The fact that a DELETE could cause this event might be a little surprising. But remember that this event is actually timing a section of code that does block formatting, not file creation.

Parameters

The only parameter of interest for this event is P1, which shows which cell was being accessed when this event was generated.

> P1 - Cell hash number

> P2 - Not used

> P3 - Not used

cell statistics gather

The cell statistics gather event records time spent reading from various V$ and X$ tables. Although the event is grouped in the User I/O category, it does not refer to I/O in the sense of reading and writing to and from disk.

Event Meaning

Time is clocked to this event when a session is reading from V$CELL, V$CELL_THREAD_HISTORY (X$KCFISOSSN), V$CELL_REQUEST_TOTALS (X$KCFISOSST), and a few other X$ tables in the same family. The event is miscategorized in our opinion and does not really belong in the User I/O category.

Parameters

The parameters for this event provide no additional information. In fact, values are not even set for the parameters in this event. Here are the parameter definitions:

> P1 - Cell hash number (always 0)

> P2 - Not used

> P3 - Not used

Exadata Wait Events in the System I/O Class

The Exadata wait events that are assigned to the System I/O class are of less importance and do not generally show up as major consumers of time. The backup events are the most interesting as they record time for sections of code that have been optimized on the Exadata platform. The others are simply housekeeping events. The non-backup events are listed in Table 12.1, while the backup events are detailed in the following sections.

Table 10-1. Miscellaneous System I/O Class Events

Event	Description
`cell manager closing cell`	This is a shutdown-related event. The cell hash number is contained in the P1 column of the `v$session_wait` view for this event. The P2 and P3 columns are unused.
`cell manager discovering disks`	This is a startup-related event. The cell hash number is contained in the P1 column of the `v$session_wait` view for this event. The P2 and P3 columns are unused.
`cell manager opening cell`	This is a startup-related event. The cell hash number is contained in the P1 column of the `v$session_wait` view for this event. The P2 and P3 columns are unused.

cell smart incremental backup

This event is used to measure time spent waiting on RMAN when doing an Incremental Level 1 backup. Exadata optimizes incremental backups by offloading much of the processing to the storage tier. This new wait event was added to account for time spent waiting on the optimized incremental backup processing that is offloaded to the storage cells.

Event Meaning

Interestingly, an Incremental Level 0 backup does not result in this wait event even though the word "incremental" is in the RMAN command. That is because the Level 0 backup doesn't actually do an incremental backup at all. It generates a full backup that is flagged as a baseline for future incremental backups. Here's an excerpt from a 10046 trace file generated on a process that was doing an incremental Level 1 backup:

```
WAIT #0: nam='cell smart incremental backup' ela= 27 cellhash#=3176594409 p2=0 p3=0 obj#=-1
WAIT #0: nam='cell smart incremental backup' ela= 54 cellhash#=3176594409 p2=0 p3=0 obj#=-1
WAIT #0: nam='cell smart incremental backup' ela= 119 cellhash#=3176594409 p2=0 p3=0 obj#=-1
WAIT #0: nam='cell smart incremental backup' ela= 603 cellhash#=3176594409 p2=0 p3=0 obj#=-1
WAIT #0: nam='cell smart incremental backup' ela= 120 cellhash#=3176594409 p2=0 p3=0 obj#=-1
WAIT #0: nam='control file sequential read' ela= 378 file#=0 block#=1 blocks=1 obj#=-1
WAIT #0: nam='control file sequential read' ela= 378 file#=1 block#=1 blocks=1 obj#=-1
WAIT #0: nam='control file sequential read' ela= 254 file#=0 block#=15 blocks=1 obj#=-1
WAIT #0: nam='control file sequential read' ela= 332 file#=0 block#=17 blocks=1 obj#=-1
WAIT #0: nam='control file sequential read' ela= 268 file#=0 block#=309 blocks=1 obj#=-1
WAIT #0: nam='control file sequential read' ela= 15794 file#=0 block#=307 blocks=1 obj#=-1
WAIT #0: nam='control file parallel write' ela= 351 files=2 block#=310 requests=2 obj#=-1
WAIT #0: nam='control file parallel write' ela= 404 files=2 block#=18 requests=2 obj#=-1
WAIT #0: nam='control file parallel write' ela= 211 files=2 block#=16 requests=2 obj#=-1
WAIT #0: nam='control file parallel write' ela= 294 files=2 block#=1 requests=2 obj#=-1
```

```
WAIT #0: nam='control file sequential read' ela= 944 file#=0 block#=1 blocks=1 obj#=-1
WAIT #0: nam='KSV master wait' ela= 13352 p1=0 p2=0 p3=0 obj#=-1 tim=1285518586442775
WAIT #0: nam='ASM file metadata operation' ela= 32 msgop=41 locn=0 p3=0 obj#=-1
WAIT #0: nam='kfk: async disk IO' ela= 333 count=1 intr=0 timeout=4294967295 obj#=-1
WAIT #0: nam='Disk file operations I/O' ela= 67 FileOperation=3 fileno=1 filetype=10 obj#=-1
WAIT #0: nam='cell smart incremental backup' ela= 392 cellhash#=3176594409 p2=0 p3=0 obj#=-1
WAIT #0: nam='cell smart incremental backup' ela= 95 cellhash#=3176594409 p2=0 p3=0 obj#=-1
WAIT #0: nam='cell smart incremental backup' ela= 169 cellhash#=3176594409 p2=0 p3=0 obj#=-1
WAIT #0: nam='cell smart incremental backup' ela= 104 cellhash#=3176594409 p2=0 p3=0 obj#=-1
WAIT #0: nam='cell smart incremental backup' ela= 128 cellhash#=3176594409 p2=0 p3=0 obj#=-1
WAIT #0: nam='cell smart incremental backup' ela= 115 cellhash#=3176594409 p2=0 p3=0 obj#=-1
WAIT #0: nam='cell smart incremental backup' ela= 722 cellhash#=3176594409 p2=0 p3=0 obj#=-1
```

Parameters

The only parameter used for this event is P1, which shows which cell was responsible for generating the event.

P1 - Cell hash number

P2 - Not used

P3 - Not used

obj# - Not used

⬛ **Note**: The obj# field is a part of many wait events, even some that are not specifically related to an individual object. Be aware that in some cases, the value may be set by one event and then not cleared appropriately when the wait ends, resulting in meaningless values left in place for the next wait event. In the previous example, the obj# was cleared (set to a value of -1).

---

cell smart restore from backup

This event is used to measure time spent waiting on RMAN when doing a restore. Exadata optimizes RMAN restores by offloading processing to the storage cells.

Event Meaning

The event actually records time related to file initialization during a restore. Here's an excerpt from a 10046 trace file taken while a restore was in progress:

```
The input backup piece
+RECO/test/backupset/2010_09_26/nnndn0_tag20100926t111118_0.1263.730725079 is in BASIC 11.2
compressed format.
```

```
WAIT #0: nam='kfk: async disk IO' ela= 98 count=1 intr=0 timeout=4294967295 obj#=-1
WAIT #0: nam='kfk: async disk IO' ela= 757 count=1 intr=0 timeout=4294967295 obj#=-1
WAIT #0: nam='kfk: async disk IO' ela= 94 count=1 intr=0 timeout=4294967295 obj#=-1
WAIT #0: nam='RMAN backup & recovery I/O' ela= 20 count=1 intr=256 timeout=214748364 obj#=-1
WAIT #0: nam='RMAN backup & recovery I/O' ela= 22 count=1 intr=256 timeout=2147483647 obj#=-
WAIT #0: nam='RMAN backup & recovery I/O' ela= 15 count=1 intr=256 timeout=2147483647 obj#=-
WAIT #0: nam='RMAN backup & recovery I/O' ela= 10 count=1 intr=256 timeout=2147483647 obj#=-
WAIT #0: nam='RMAN backup & recovery I/O' ela= 14 count=1 intr=256 timeout=2147483647 obj#=-
. . .
WAIT #0: nam='RMAN backup & recovery I/O' ela= 1364 count=1 intr=256 timeout=2147483647
WAIT #0: nam='kfk: async disk IO' ela= 16 count=1 intr=0 timeout=4294967295 obj#=-1
WAIT #0: nam='kfk: async disk IO' ela= 30 count=1 intr=0 timeout=4294967295 obj#=-1
WAIT #0: nam='RMAN backup & recovery I/O' ela= 4783 count=1 intr=256 timeout=2147483647
WAIT #0: nam='kfk: async disk IO' ela= 5 count=1 intr=0 timeout=4294967295 obj#=-1
WAIT #0: nam='RMAN backup & recovery I/O' ela= 2952 count=1 intr=256 timeout=2147483647
WAIT #0: nam='kfk: async disk IO' ela= 14 count=1 intr=0 timeout=4294967295 obj#=-1
WAIT #0: nam='kfk: async disk IO' ela= 33 count=1 intr=0 timeout=4294967295 obj#=-1
WAIT #0: nam='kfk: async disk IO' ela= 62 count=1 intr=0 timeout=4294967295 obj#=-1
WAIT #0: nam='kfk: async disk IO' ela= 92 count=1 intr=0 timeout=4294967295 obj#=-1
WAIT #0: nam='kfk: async disk IO' ela= 12 count=1 intr=0 timeout=4294967295 obj#=-1
. . .
WAIT #0: nam='cell smart restore from backup' ela= 43249 cellhash#=379339958 p2=0 p3=0 obj#=
WAIT #0: nam='cell smart restore from backup' ela= 18141 cellhash#=213345948 p2=0 p3=0 obj#=
WAIT #0: nam='cell smart restore from backup' ela= 430 cellhash#=379339958 p2=0 p3=0 obj#=-1
WAIT #0: nam='cell smart restore from backup' ela= 378 cellhash#=213345948 p2=0 p3=0 obj#=-1
WAIT #0: nam='cell smart restore from backup' ela= 15 cellhash#=2133459483 p2=0 p3=0 obj#=-1
WAIT #0: nam='cell smart restore from backup' ela= 1355 cellhash#=213345948 p2=0 p3=0 obj#=-
WAIT #0: nam='cell smart restore from backup' ela= 766 cellhash#=2133459483 p2=0 p3=0 obj#=-
WAIT #0: nam='cell smart restore from backup' ela= 167 cellhash#=379339958 p2=0 p3=0 obj#=-1
WAIT #0: nam='cell smart restore from backup' ela= 199 cellhash#=213345948 p2=0 p3=0 obj#=-1
WAIT #0: nam='cell smart restore from backup' ela= 19 cellhash#=213345948 p2=0 p3=0 obj#=-1
WAIT #0: nam='cell smart restore from backup' ela= 226 cellhash#=379339958 p2=0 p3=0 obj#=-1
WAIT #0: nam='cell smart restore from backup' ela= 127 cellhash#=213345948 p2=0 p3=0 obj#=-1
WAIT #0: nam='cell smart restore from backup' ela= 110 cellhash#=213345948 p2=0 p3=0 obj#=-1
WAIT #0: nam='cell smart restore from backup' ela= 177 cellhash#=379339958 p2=0 p3=0 obj#=-1
WAIT #0: nam='cell smart restore from backup' ela= 160 cellhash#=213345948 p2=0 p3=0 obj#=-1
```

Parameters

The only parameter used for this event is P1, which shows which cell was responsible for generating the event.

P1 - Cell hash number

P2 - Not used

P3 - Not used

Exadata Wait Events in the Other and Idle Classes

These are relatively minor events that occur primarily during startup and shut down of storage cells and fault conditions. You will probably not see them on normally functioning systems. There is one exception to this, the cell smart flash unkeep event. Table 12.2 lists the "cell" wait events in the Other class along with their parameters. A separate section will cover cell smart flash unkeep.

Table 10-2. Miscelaneous Other and Idle Class Events

Event	Description
cell manager cancel work request	This event is not very informative, as all three of the parameters (P1, P2, P3) from the v$session_wait view are unused.
cell worker online completion	This appears to be a startup event. The cell hash number is contained in the P1 column of the v$session_wait view for this event. The P2 and P3 columns are unused.
cell worker retry	The cell hash number is contained in the P1 column of the v$session_wait view for this event. The P2 and P3 columns are unused.
cell worker idle	The P1, P2 and P3 columns from the v$session_wait view are unused in this idle event.

cell smart flash unkeep

This event records the time spent waiting when Oracle must flush blocks out of Exadata Smart Flash Cache. This can occur when a table that has a storage clause designating that it be pinned in Exadata Smart Flash Cache is truncated or dropped.

Event Meaning

Truncating and dropping tables doesn't generally happen very often in most production systems (with some notable exceptions) and therefore this wait event will probably not be seen very often. Here's an excerpt from a 10046 trace file showing the event:

```
WAIT #4: nam='enq: RO - fast object reuse' ela= 393 name|mode=1380909062 2=65581 0=1 obj#=-1
WAIT #4: nam='reliable message' ela= 1548 channel context=6712270872 channel handle=6696807856
broadcast message=6741342984 obj#=-1 tim=1286218926420916
WAIT #4: nam='enq: RO - fast object reuse' ela= 21027 name|mode=1380909 2=65581 0=1 obj#=-1
WAIT #4: nam='ges message buffer allocation' ela= 2 pool=0 request=1 allocated=0 obj#=-1
WAIT #4: nam='enq: RO - fast object reuse' ela= 159 name|mode=1380909057 2=65581 0=2 obj#=-1
WAIT #4: nam='cell smart flash unkeep' ela= 336 cellhash#=379339958 p2=0 p3=0 obj#=-1
WAIT #4: nam='cell smart flash unkeep' ela= 291 cellhash#=2133459483 p2=0 p3=0 obj#=-1
WAIT #4: nam='cell smart flash unkeep' ela= 319 cellhash#=3176594409 p2=0 p3=0 obj#=-1
WAIT #4: nam='cell smart flash unkeep' ela= 418 cellhash#=379339958 p2=0 p3=0 obj#=-1
WAIT #4: nam='cell smart flash unkeep' ela= 1 cellhash#=2133459483 p2=0 p3=0 obj#=-1
```

```
WAIT #4: nam='cell smart flash unkeep' ela= 216 cellhash#=3176594409 p2=0 p3=0 obj#=-1
WAIT #4: nam='cell smart flash unkeep' ela= 222 cellhash#=379339958 p2=0 p3=0 obj#=-1
WAIT #4: nam='cell smart flash unkeep' ela= 196 cellhash#=2133459483 p2=0 p3=0 obj#=-1
WAIT #4: nam='cell smart flash unkeep' ela= 216 cellhash#=3176594409 p2=0 p3=0 obj#=-1
```

Note that the `cell smart flash unkeep` event is preceded by a handful of `enq: RO - fast object reuse` events, which are used to mark time associated with cleaning up the buffer cache after a drop or truncate. The `cell smart flash unkeep` is basically an extension of that event to clean up the Exadata Smart flash cache on the storage server as well.

Parameters

The only parameter used for this event is P1, which shows which cell was responsible for generating the event.

> P1 - Cell hash number
>
> P2 - Not used
>
> P3 - Not used

Old Events

In addition to the new cell events, there are also a few non-Exadata-specific wait events that you should be aware of. These are events that you may already be familiar with from managing Oracle on other platforms. They happen to also be important in an Exadata environment, so they represent cases in which your existing knowledge and skill can carry over and stand you in good stead as you move in to managing Exadata.

direct path read

Direct path reads are used by Oracle to read data directly into PGA memory (instead of into the buffer cache). They are an integral part of Exadata Offloading because SQL processing can only be offloaded to the storage cells when the direct path read mechanism is used. The `direct path read` wait event is actually replaced by the `cell smart table scan` and `cell smart index scan` wait events when a query is offloaded. However, the direct path read mechanism is still used by the code covered by those new wait events. That is, either the plan must include a parallel scan or Oracle must decide to use the serial direct path read mechanism.

Event Meaning

This event records time that Oracle spends waiting on a direct path read to complete. You should know that the direct path read wait event can be very misleading. Both the number of events recorded and the timings associated with them can appear to be inaccurate. This is due to the fact that direct path reads are done in an asynchronous and overlapping fashion. See MOS note 50415.1 for further details about why time recorded by this event can be misleading. It also bears mentioning that 11gR2 contains an enhancement that causes serial direct path reads to occur more frequently than in previous releases. See MOS Note 793845.1, which briefly mentions this change.

By the way, the direct path read wait event does still show up on the Exadata platform for various operations but generally not for full table scans unless the table (or partition is relatively small).

Parameters

The parameters for this event show you exactly which segment (obj) is scanned and which set of blocks were scanned during this event.

> P1 - File number
>
> P2 - First DBA
>
> P3 - Block count
>
> obj# - The object number of the table being scanned

As mentioned in the Cell Smart Table Scan section, the parameters contain specific information about which file and object are being accessed. The offset into the file is also provided in the P2 parameter, along with the number of contiguous blocks read in the P3 parameter.

enq: KO—fast object checkpoint

The enq:KO event has a very strange name. Don't be put off by that. The event is essentially an object checkpoint event. The V$LOCK_TYPE view describes the KO lock as follows:

```
SYS@EXDB1> select type, name, description from v$lock_type
  2* where type = 'KO';

TYPE  NAME                          DESCRIPTION
----- ----------------------------- -------------------------------------------
KO    Multiple Object Checkpoint    Coordinates checkpointing of multiple objects
```

Event Meaning

This event is used when a session is waiting for all dirty blocks to be flushed from the buffer cache for an object prior to starting a direct path read or cell smart table scan or cell smart index scan. This event is important because the time required to do the checkpoint may outweigh the benefit of the direct path reads. This is unlikely on Exadata storage, though, where the additional Smart Scan benefits are only enabled by the direct path read mechanism.

Parameters

The parameters for this event are not overly helpful but the event does show which object is scanned. Here are the parameter definitions:

> P1 - Name/ Mode
>
> P2 - Not used
>
> P3 - Not used
>
> obj# - The object number of the object being checkpointed

reliable message

The reliable message event is used to record time spent communicating with background processes, like the checkpoint process (CKPT). We have included it here because of its close association with the enq: KO - fast object checkpoint event.

Event Meaning

This event is the precursor to the enq: KO - fast object checkpoint event (among others). The communication is done using an inter-process communication channel rather than a more normal post mechanism. This communication method allows the sender to request an ACK before it continues, thus the reason it is called a reliable message. It is generally a very short duration event as it only records time for communicating between processes. Both the users foreground process and the chkpt process will wait on this event as they communicate with each other. Here's an excerpt of a 10046 trace file showing a complete reliable message event:

```
PARSING IN CURSOR #46963980936744 len=50 dep=0 uid=0 oct=3 lid=0 tim=1301885220743528
hv=3032626544 ad='2cf675ff0' sqlid='7y09dtyuc4dbh'
select avg(pk_col) from kso.skew2 a where col1 > 0
END OF STMT
PARSE
#46963980936744:c=1999,e=2122,p=0,cr=0,cu=0,mis=1,r=0,dep=0,og=1,plh=2117817910,tim=1301885220
743527
WAIT #46963980936744: nam='reliable message' ela= 1360 channel context=11888341784 channel
handle=12088585896 broadcast message=12089037216 obj#=75759 tim=1301885220745397
WAIT #469: nam='enq: KO - fast object checkpoint' ela= 183 ... obj#=75759 tim=130
WAIT #469: nam='enq: KO - fast object checkpoint' ela= 144 ... obj#=75759 tim=130
WAIT #469: nam='enq: PS - contention' ela= 200 ... obj#=75759 tim=130
WAIT #469: nam='os thread startup' ela= 58333 p1=0 p2=0 p3=0 obj#=75759 tim=130
WAIT #469: nam='os thread startup' ela= 101705 p1=0 p2=0 p3=0 obj#=75759 tim=130
WAIT #469: nam='enq: PS - contention' ela= 276 ... obj#=75759 tim=130
WAIT #469: nam='os thread startup' ela= 102988 p1=0 p2=0 p3=0 obj#=75759 tim=130
WAIT #469: nam='os thread startup' ela= 103495 p1=0 p2=0 p3=0 obj#=75759 tim=130
WAIT #469: nam='enq: PS - contention' ela= 237 ... obj#=75759 tim=130
WAIT #469: nam='os thread startup' ela= 102655 p1=0 p2=0 p3=0 obj#=75759 tim=130
WAIT #469: nam='os thread startup' ela= 102329 p1=0 p2=0 p3=0 obj#=75759 tim=130
WAIT #469: nam='enq: PS - contention' ela= 313 ... obj#=75759 tim=130
WAIT #469: nam='os thread startup' ela= 102673 p1=0 p2=0 p3=0 obj#=75759 tim=130
```

Parameters

Here are the parameters for the reliable message event.

> P1 - channel context
>
> P2 - channel handle
>
> P3 - broadcast message
>
> obj# - The object number of the object of interest (not always set)

Resource Manager Events

Finally, there are a few Resource Manager events that you should be aware of. While these are not specific to Exadata, Resource Manager provides key functionality for combining mixed workloads on Exadata. There are actually eight separate events as of release 11.2.0.2. The following query against V$EVENT_NAME shows these events and their parameters.

```
SYS@SANDBOX1> @valid_events
Enter value for event_name: resmgr%

EVENT                         CLASS            P1        P2                    P3
----------------------------  ---------------  --------  --------------------  ----
resmgr:internal state change  Concurrency      location
resmgr:sessions to exit                        location

resmgr:internal state cleanup Other            location

resmgr:become active          Scheduler        location
resmgr:cpu quantum                             location  consumer group id
resmgr:large I/O queued                        location
resmgr:pq queued                               location
resmgr:small I/O queued                        location

8 rows selected.
```

There are only two of these events that are of interest.

resmgr:cpu quantum

This event is used to record forced idle time imposed by Database Resource Manager (DBRM) due to competition with higher priority work. Said another way, it is the time a process spent waiting for DBRM to allocate it a time slice.

Event Meaning

DBRM behaves in an analogous manner to CPU scheduling algorithms in that it divides time into units (quantum) and either allows a process to run or not depending on other workload on the system. Unlike CPU scheduling algorithms though, DBRM throttling is interjected at key locations in the Oracle code to eliminate the possibility of a process being kicked off of the CPU when it is holding a shared resource such as a latch. This prevents some nasty behavior that may occur on heavily loaded systems such as priority inversion problems. In effect, the processes voluntarily go to sleep when they are not holding these shared resources. There are multiple locations in the code where these checks are implemented. Here's an excerpt of a 10046 trace file showing the resmgr:cpu quantum event:

```
PARSING IN CURSOR #47046073104400 len=34 dep=0 uid=85 oct=3 lid=85 tim=1301275393323414
hv=3308960238 ad='b3c9faf8' sqlid='c4js15z2mpfgf'
select count(*)
from kso.skew
END OF STMT
PARSE #470460:c=0,e=77,p=0,cr=0,cu=0,mis=0,r=0,dep=0,og=1,plh=937687140,tim=130
EXEC #470460:c=0,e=49,p=0,cr=0,cu=0,mis=0,r=0,dep=0,og=1,plh=937687140,tim=130
WAIT #470460: nam='SQL*Net message to client' ela= 4 driver id=1650815232 #bytes=1 ...
WAIT #470460: nam='resmgr:cpu quantum' ela= 3457 location=3 consumer group id=75525 ...
WAIT #470460: nam='resmgr:cpu quantum' ela= 68126 location=3 consumer group id=75525 ...
WAIT #470460: nam='resmgr:cpu quantum' ela= 68046 location=3 consumer group id=75525 ...
WAIT #470460: nam='resmgr:cpu quantum' ela= 108941 location=3 consumer group id=75525 ...
WAIT #470460: nam='resmgr:cpu quantum' ela= 38234 location=3 consumer group id=75525 ...
WAIT #470460: nam='resmgr:cpu quantum' ela= 103282 location=3 consumer group id=75525 ...
```

Parameters

Here are the parameters for this event. Note that the obj# parameter exists but is not used.

> P1 - Location
>
> P2 - Consumer group id
>
> P3 - Not used
>
> obj# - NA

The location parameter is a numeric value that most likely refers to a location (function) in the Oracle code. There are at least 5 distinct locations that we have observed. Unfortunately, Oracle does not publicly document where in the Oracle kernel these checks are performed.

The consumer group number in the P2 parameter is pretty self-explanatory. It maps to the CONSUMER_GROUP_ID column in the DBA_RSRC_CONSUMER_GROUPS view. This parameter allows you to tell what consumer group a process was assigned to when its CPU usage was curtailed.

resmgr:pq queued

This event is used to record time spent waiting in the parallel query queue.

Event Meaning

The parallel statement queuing feature comes with its own wait event. Statements that are queued due to insufficient parallel server processes or other directives clock time to this event. Here's an excerpt of a 10046 trace file showing the resmgr:pq queued event:

```
PARSING IN CURSOR #47898436021000 len=73 dep=0 uid=0 oct=3 lid=0 tim=1301966072332694
hv=3186480617 ad='2cd2d1cb8' sqlid='bgcmmcyyyvpg9'
select /*+ parallel (a 16) */ avg(pk_col) from kso.skew3 a where col1 > 0
END OF STMT
PARSE #478:c=2000,e=1572,p=0,cr=0,cu=0,mis=1,r=0,dep=0,og=1,plh=1404581711,tim=130
WAIT #478: nam='resmgr:pq queued' ela= 65102047 location=1  =0  =0 obj#=523 tim=130
WAIT #478: nam='enq: KO - fast object checkpoint' ela= 258 ... obj#=523
```

```
WAIT #478: nam='reliable message' ela= 2005 channel context=118 channel handle=120 ...
obj#=523
WAIT #478: nam='enq: KO - fast object checkpoint' ela= 156 ... obj#=523 ...
WAIT #478: nam='PX Deq: Join ACK' ela= 772 sleeptime/senderid=268 passes=1 p3=120 obj#=523 ...
WAIT #478: nam='PX Deq: Join ACK' ela= 932 sleeptime/senderid=268 passes=8 p3=120 obj#=523 ...
WAIT #478: nam='PX Deq: Join ACK' ela= 2 sleeptime/senderid=0 passes=0 p3=0 obj#=523 ...
```

Parameters

Here are the parameters for the resmgr:pq queued event.

> P1 - Location
>
> P2 - Not used
>
> P3 - Not used
>
> obj# - NA

The location parameter is a numeric value that most likely refers to a location (function) in the Oracle code as described above in the resmgr:cpu quantum event.

Summary

The wait interface has been expanded to cover several Exadata-specific features. In this chapter we've covered the new wait events. By far the most interesting of the new events are cell smart table scan and cell smart index scan. These events cover the time spent waiting on an offloadable I/O request to a storage cell. There is a lot of processing that occurs at the storage layer that is lumped together under these events. It's important to understand that these events replace the direct path read event and that the mechanism of returning the data directly to the process PGA employed by the Smart Scan events is analogous to the way it is handled by direct path read.

CHAPTER 11

Understanding Exadata Performance Metrics

Oracle Exadata is a big step forward from the traditional database server architecture; however, it is still running the standard Oracle Database software. Most of the usual database performance rules still apply, with the addition of some that recognize the advantage of Exadata functionality like Smart Scans, cell join filtering and the flash cache. In this chapter we will cover the Exadata-specific and -related performance topics, metrics, and some relevant internals.

Thankfully Oracle, both at the database layer and in cells, provides lots of performance metrics for our use. However, when looking into any metric, you should know *why* you are monitoring this and what numbers are you looking for. In other words, how do you know when everything is OK and no action is needed, and when things are bad and action is needed? And in order to avoid wasting effort on fixing the wrong problem, we really need to measure *what matters!* For database performance, nothing matters more than *response time*, the actual time the end user (or connected system) has to wait for the response. So if we want to make something faster in the database, we should focus on measuring and then optimizing the response time. All the other metrics and indicators, like the number of I/Os or cache hits, are secondary. End users, who are waiting for their report, care about the time they have to wait only, not secondary metrics like CPU utilization or I/O rate. Nevertheless, often these secondary metrics become very useful for understanding and explaining performance issues.

The key metrics for breaking down database *response time* are the Oracle wait interface's wait events. The wait events are discussed in Chapter 10, and we will look into performance monitoring tools that make use of them in the next chapter. However, there are additional useful metrics Exadata provides, such as the number of bytes of data returned by smart scans and the actual amount of I/O avoided thanks to storage indexes, and so on. Such metrics give very important additional info about what's happening in the database and storage cells during SQL execution. In this chapter we will examine these metrics, and you'll learn how to get them and what they mean. Even if you are not interested in knowing what each metric means, we still recommend you read this chapter, as it explains some important internals and design decisions behind Exadata.

The information in this chapter should give you a good understanding about some key internal workings of Exadata databases and cells and prepare you for the next chapter, where we will put this knowledge to use when monitoring and troubleshooting Exadata performance.

Measuring Exadata's Performance Metrics

Before we start looking at Exadata-specific performance metrics, let's examine some internals and review some key elements of Exadata-specific features and metrics. One must understand what the performance numbers actually stand for before trying to monitor or optimize anything with this info.

By now you know that Exadata database nodes don't do physical disk I/O themselves, but ask the cells to do the I/O for them. In the case of smart scans, the cell servers will also process the blocks read, extract their contents, filter rows, and so on. So conceptually, the cells are kind of a black box when viewed from database layer side. The database layer just requests some blocks of data, and the cells do the physical I/O work under the hood and return the requested columns of matching rows. Luckily, Oracle Exadata architects and developers have put decent instrumentation into cells, so the cells keep track of how much work they have done and importantly, they can also *send the metrics back to the database layer* along the results. This allows us—DBAs, developers, and troubleshooters—to have an end-to-end overview of what happened in the database *and* the cells when servicing a user's request or running a query.

For example, when a query is executed via Smart Scan, you will still see statistics like *physical_reads* when you query V$SQLSTATS in the database layer, even though the database layer itself didn't do any physical reads directly. Another example is the *cell physical IO bytes saved by storage index* statistic, which is counted in the cell level and not in the database. These numbers are visible in the database layer thanks to cells sending back useful performance metrics in addition to the data queried.

In addition to the standard Oracle performance tools, we'll use two custom-built tools in this and the next chapter. They are more suitable for flexible and advanced performance analysis and allow you to go beyond the standard wait events and SQL statement level statistics. The first tool, Oracle Session Snapper, is a script containing just an anonymous PL/SQL block, which measures detailed performance metrics from V$SESSION, V$SESSION_EVENT, V$SESS_TIME_MODEL, V$SESSTAT, and so on. The last performance view, V$SESSTAT, is especially important for advanced performance analysis—it contains hundreds of dynamic performance counters (over 600 in Oracle 11.2.0.2) for each session in the instance. In addition to the usual monitoring using wait events, diving into V$SESSTAT gives us a much better idea of what kind of work Oracle sessions are doing, such as how many I/O requests per second they are doing, how many full segment scans per second, how many migrated/chained rows had to be fetched during a scan, and so on.

Revisiting the Prerequisites for Exadata Smart Scans

In this section we will look at the various metrics Oracle Database kernel's instrumentation provides us. We will not go into the details of Exadata wait events here, as these are already explained Chapter 10. We will review how to use these wait events for understanding database performance, and you may find some of the offloading and Smart Scan material already familiar from Chapter 2, but it's important to review some of the concepts here, in the context of monitoring and troubleshooting Exadata performance.

Because the primary performance booster for data warehousing and reporting workloads is the Exadata Smart Scan, and for OLTP workloads it is the use of Exadata Smart Flash Cache, we will see first how to measure whether your workload is benefitting from these features. We will use this knowledge as building blocks for later database and query performance monitoring.

Exadata Smart Scan Performance

Let's start with Smart Scan metrics. Before we talk about any metrics, let's review how the decision to do a Smart Scan is made in Oracle. Note that a Smart Scan can be used on regular table segments and also on materialized view segments – which are physically no different from regular tables. Smart Scans can also be used for full scanning through B*Tree index segments (index fast full scan) and also bitmap index segments (bitmap index fast full scan). Scanning through index segments using the "brute force" multiblock reads approach is very similar to full table scans. The major difference is that inside index segments there are also index branch blocks, which have to be skipped and ignored, in addition to ASSM bitmap blocks, which have to be skipped both in table and index scans. Smart scans on partitions and subpartitions of tables and indexes are internally no different from scans on nonpartitioned objects (a partitioned segment is just a bunch of smaller segments, grouped under their logical parent table or index object). Remember that the Smart Scans can scan a variety of segments.

Regardless of segment type, a Smart Scan always requires direct path reads to be chosen by the SQL execution engine during runtime (this is *not* an optimizer decision). So when troubleshooting why a Smart Scan was not used, you will have to first check whether direct path reads were used or not. You should check the execution plan first, to see whether a full scan is reported there at all. Here you see simple examples showing full segment scans happening on different segment types:

```
SELECT AVG(line) FROM t WHERE owner LIKE 'S%'
```

```
---------------------------------------------------------------------------
| Id | Operation                 | Name | Rows  | Bytes | Cost (%CPU)| Time     |
---------------------------------------------------------------------------
|  0 | SELECT STATEMENT          |      |       |       | 295K(100)|          |
|  1 |  SORT AGGREGATE           |      |     1 |    11 |          |          |
|* 2 |   TABLE ACCESS STORAGE FULL| T    | 5743K|   60M|  295K  (1)| 00:59:01 |
---------------------------------------------------------------------------
```

```
Predicate Information (identified by operation id):
---------------------------------------------------
```

```
   2 - storage("OWNER" LIKE 'S%')
       filter("OWNER" LIKE 'S%')
```

Note that the "STORAGE" in the TABLE ACCESS STORAGE FULL line here does *not* mean that Oracle is attempting to do a Smart Scan. This word merely says that Oracle knows that this segment is residing on a storage cell, not something else like an NFS mount or iSCSI device, and is using the table scan codepath *capable of performing* a Smart Scan.Whether a Smart Scan is actually used depends on multiple other factors, which were discussed in Chapter 2 and will be also demonstrated here. Also, *Smart Scan* is a broad term, covering filtration (which may be able to take advantage of storage indexes), column projection, decompression of HCC-compressed compression units and hash join early elimination with bloom filters— all done in the cells. Even if you are not taking advantage of the filter predicate offloading to storage (filtration), the cells may be able to reduce the amount of data returned to the database. If Smart Scan is used, then the column projection is done in the cells, and they return only the required columns instead of entire blocks containing the full-length rows.

In addition, it is important to check whether a storage() predicate is shown in the "Predicate Information" section below the execution plan. This is a good indicator of whether the execution plan *is capable of* doing a Smart Scan's predicate offload (smart filtration). Unfortunately, this doesn't mean that a Smart Scan predicate offload was actually attempted. There are cases where even the presence of a storage() predicate doesn't guarantee that a predicate offload will take place. (This is where Oracle performance metrics will be helpful, but more about them shortly.) In summary, a full segment scan access path with the STORAGE keyword *and* the storage() predicate must be present in the execution plan in order for it to *be capable of* doing a Smart Scan's predicate offload at all. If you do see the STORAGE lines in execution plan, but no storage() predicates under it, then predicate offload won't be even attempted, but you still may benefit from column projection offload, in which only the required columns are returned by cells. You will probably see multiple storage predicates (and full scan operations) in real-life query plans, as you'll be doing multi-table joins.

In summary, if you see the STORAGE option and storage() predicate in an execution plan, it is capable of doing a Smart Scan and its predicate offload in principle, but it's not guaranteed that a Smart

Scan happens every time you run the query. On the other hand, if you do not see a STORAGE keyword in the execution plan, then there's no way a Smart Scan could happen on a corresponding segment in a given execution plan step. When there's no STORAGE keyword in the execution plan line, it means that this rowsource operator is not capable of using the smart features of the storage cells, and so won't be able to push any storage() predicates into the cell either.

Smart Scans can be done on materialized view segments, too; a materialized view segment is physically exactly the same as any regular table:

```
select count(*) from mv1 where owner like 'S%'
```

```
------------------------------------------------------------------
| Id  | Operation                  | Name  | E-Rows | Cost (%CPU)|
------------------------------------------------------------------
|   0 | SELECT STATEMENT           |       |        | 139K(100)  |
|   1 |  SORT AGGREGATE            |       |     1  |            |
|*  2 |   MAT_VIEW ACCESS STORAGE FULL| MV1  | 2089K | 139K  (1)  |
------------------------------------------------------------------

Predicate Information (identified by operation id):
---------------------------------------------------

   2 - storage("OWNER" LIKE 'S%')
       filter("OWNER" LIKE 'S%')
```

Following are two examples where Smart Scans can be attempted. The first is when scanning through a regular B*Tree index segment:

```
SELECT /*+ INDEX_FFS(t2) */ AVG(LENGTH(owner)) FROM t2 WHERE owner LIKE'S%'
```

```
------------------------------------------------------------------
| Id  | Operation                  | Name  | E-Rows | Cost (%CPU)|
------------------------------------------------------------------
|   0 | SELECT STATEMENT           |       |        | 5165 (100) |
|   1 |  SORT AGGREGATE            |       |     1  |            |
|*  2 |   INDEX STORAGE FAST FULL SCAN| T2_I1 |   597K | 5165  (2)  |
------------------------------------------------------------------

Predicate Information (identified by operation id):
---------------------------------------------------

   2 - storage("OWNER" LIKE 'S%')
       filter("OWNER" LIKE 'S%')
```

The second scans a bitmap index segment:

```
SELECT /*+ INDEX_FFS(t1) */ AVG(LENGTH(owner)) FROM t1 WHERE owner LIKE'S%'
```

```
Plan hash value: 3170056527
```

```
-------------------------------------------------------------------------
| Id  | Operation        | Name     | E-Rows | Cost (%CPU)|
-------------------------------------------------------------------------
|   0 | SELECT STATEMENT |          |        |  505 (100) |
```

```
|   1 |   SORT AGGREGATE                    |            |    1 |          |
|   2 |     BITMAP CONVERSION TO ROWIDS     |            | 597K|  505  (0)|
|*  3 |      BITMAP INDEX STORAGE FAST FULL SCAN| BI_T1_OWNER |     |          |
-------------------------------------------------------------------------------
```

Predicate Information (identified by operation id):

```
   3 - storage("OWNER" LIKE 'S%')
        filter("OWNER" LIKE 'S%')
```

In both cases you see that the segments were scanned using a *fast full scan*, which is just like a full table scan on the index segments, and the presence of the STORAGE option and storage() predicates on the full scan operations shows that a Smart Scan predicate offload can be attempted.

You may wonder why we keep saying, "Smart Scan predicate offload can be *attempted*." It's because there are cases where the Smart Scan either doesn't really get used or is started but does not complete during runtime. Yes, the execution plan structure is capable of using a Smart Scan, but whether the Smart Scan is actually executed depends first on whether a direct path read is chosen to scan the segment or not. We've talked about this earlier in this chapter and also in Chapter 2, on Smart Scan, and Chapter 6, on parallel execution. Moreover, even if a direct path read *is* chosen *and* a Smart Scan is executed, then somewhere during (or at the beginning of) Smart Scan execution, a different decision may be made. This depends on multiple factors, and we will cover some of them here. Luckily, in addition to examining the execution plan, we can look at additional metrics to see what's really happening under the hood.

We can try to achieve a Smart Scan on an Index-Organized Table (IOT) segment first to see how valuable the additional Oracle metrics are. Note that as of the current Oracle version (Database 11.2.0.2 / Cell 11.2.2.3.2), Oracle has *not* implemented Smart Scan functionality on Index Organized Table segments yet, so that's why this is a good example for practicing using the Smart Scan-related metrics.

Check the execution plan shown here; it is from a query using an *index fast full scan* on an Index-Organized Table's index segment:

```
SELECT AVG(LENGTH(owner)) FROM t_iot WHERE owner LIKE '%S%'
```

Plan hash value: 1722440769

```
-------------------------------------------------------------------
| Id  | Operation                | Name     | E-Rows | Cost (%CPU)|
-------------------------------------------------------------------
|   0 | SELECT STATEMENT         |          |        | 2101 (100)|
|   1 |  SORT AGGREGATE          |          |      1 |           |
|*  2 |   INDEX FAST FULL SCAN   | PK_T_IOT | 31493  | 2101   (1)|
-------------------------------------------------------------------
```

```
Predicate Information (identified by operation id):
---------------------------------------------------

   2 - filter("OWNER" LIKE '%S%')
```

Unlike in plans listed earlier, there is no STORAGE option listed in the execution plan row source (line 2), and there is no storage() predicate, indicating an opportunity to push a filter predicate to the storage cells. This plan is not capable of using any Smart Scan functionality; it will do good old block I/O. Looking at additional Exadata and cell metrics isn't really necessary, as the execution plan itself shows that it doesn't even use a Smart Scan-compatible row source codepath.

Understanding Exadata Smart Scan Metrics and Performance Counters

Once you have made an Oracle execution plan use the storage-aware row sources, you still cannot be sure about whether a Smart Scan really is attempted and works as you expect.

One way to determine what's happening is just looking at the wait events your session is waiting for:

- **CPU usage only:** This seems to mean that a buffered data access is used (not direct path), as you won't see I/O wait events if you read through buffer cache and all the data happens to be cached.

- **cell multiblock physical read** : Apparently multiblock reads are used (looks like a full segment scan), but multiblock read waits can be reported also for LOB and SecureFile read operations, where in case of LOBs, the LOB chunk size is bigger than the block size. Otherwise, single-block reads would be reported for LOB access.

- **cell single block physical read:**– Apparently single block reads are used. If these are the only I/O wait events you see (and not together with multiblock reads) then it appears you are not using a full segment scan at all. Of course, sometimes single block reads show up due to other operations in the execution plan (like some index range scan) or due to chained rows in data blocks.

If you see regular "cell multiblock physical read" wait events incremented in your session, then direct path reads were *not* used. This may happen mainly for serially executed operations, as if you are using parallel_degree_policy = MANUAL or LIMITED, Parallel Execution slaves will always do direct path read scans, which will then be offloaded and executed as Smart Scans. Nevertheless, when you are using the new automatic parallel degree policy (parallel_degree_policy = AUTO), Oracle may decide to use reads through buffer cache even for parallel operations.

In addition to these issues, there are more reasons and special cases where Smart Scans just silently aren't used or fall back to regular block I/O mode— potentially making your queries and workload slower than you'd expect. Luckily Oracle is very well instrumented and we can measure what is really happening in the database and also the storage cells.

Exadata Dynamic Performance Counters

While the Oracle wait interface's wait events provide us crucial information about where the database response time is spent, the Exadata dynamic performance counters do take us one step further and explain what kind of operations or tasks the Oracle kernel is performing— and how many of them. Wait events and performance counters complement each other and shouldn't really be used alone. Oracle dynamic performance counters are also known as V$SESSTAT or V$SYSSTAT statistics (or counters), as these views are used for accessing them.

When and How to Use Performance Counters

When troubleshooting performance, one should always start from wait events and SQL_ID-level activity measurements (as they keep track of the *time,* which end users care about) and if additional detail is needed, then proceed to performance counters. If these standard metrics are not enough, the performance counters provide a very detailed insight into what Oracle sessions are doing. For example, if your session seems to be burning lots of CPU, you can see whether the *session logical reads* or *parse count (hard)* counters increase for a session more than normally. Or if you see some unexpected single-block reads during a full table scan, you can check whether the *table fetch continued row* or some statistic like *data blocks consistent reads – undo records applied* increases, which indicate either a chained/migrated row or consistent read (CR) buffer cloning plus rollback overhead. Another useful metric is *user commits,* which gives you an understanding of how many database transactions are done inside an instance (or in chosen sessions). So the next time a session seems to be waiting for a *log file sync* wait event, you can check its *user commits* counter value from V$SESSTAT, to see how frequently this session is committing its work. The following excerpt is just a small example of the kind of statistics Oracle provides:

```
SQL> SELECT name, value FROM v$sysstat WHERE name like 'parse%';

NAME                                                              VALUE
---------------------------------------------------------------- ----------
parse time cpu                                                    154960
parse time elapsed                                               196194
parse count (total)                                              11530118
parse count (hard)                                               30010
parse count (failures)                                           9536
parse count (describe)                                           416
```

Dynamic performance counters provide important clues, which allow us to direct our troubleshooting efforts better. Note that tools like Statspack and AWR reports rely heavily on V$SYSSTAT counters. They just store values from these ever-increasing numbers (since instance start) in their repository tables. So whenever you run a Statspack/AWR report, just deltas between values in chosen snapshots are reported. Statspack and AWR reports are all about showing you deltas between V$SYSSTAT (and other views) numbers from different snapshots of time.

Oracle adds new counters into every new database version. Sometimes new (debug) counters are introduced even with new patch sets. Oracle 11.2.0.2 has 628 different performance counters in V$SYSSTAT:

```
SQL> SELECT COUNT(*) FROM v$sysstat;

  COUNT(*)
----------
       628
```

That's a lot of information!

While the V$SYSSTAT view is fine for monitoring and troubleshooting instance-wide performance (like AWR and Statspack reports do), its problem is that you can't troubleshoot a single session's problem with system-wide statistics, which aggregate all your (potentially thousands of) sessions' metrics together into one set of counters. That's why Oracle also has V$SESSTAT, which keeps track of all these 600+ counters for each session separately! Every single session in the instance has its own 600+ performance counters, keeping track of only its activity. This is a goldmine, as when only a few sessions (or users) have a problem in the instance, we can monitor only their activity and won't be distracted by all the other users' noise in the database.

As said earlier, V$SYSSTAT accumulates instance-wide performance counters; they start from zero and only increase throughout the instance lifetime. Most of the V$SESSTAT counters always increase (cumulative statistics) with some exceptions, like *logons current* and *session pga/uga memory*. In any case, when examining the counter values, you should not just look at the *current* value of a counter, especially if your session has been logged on for a while. The problem is that even if you see a big-looking number for some counter in V$SESSTAT of a long-running connection pool's session, how do you know what portion of that was incremented or added today, right now, when you have the problem, as opposed to a few weeks ago when that session logged on? In other words, when troubleshooting a problem happening right now, you should look at performance for right now only (and a similar rule applies when troubleshooting issues of the past).

This is why coauthor Tanel Poder has written a little helper tool called Oracle Session Snapper, which allows its user to easily display the sessions' current activity from V$SESSTAT and various other session level performance views. An important thing about this tool is that it's just an anonymous PL/SQL block, parsed on the fly— it doesn't require any installation nor DDL privileges whatsoever. The current Snapper version is available online at ExpertOracleExadata.com. Following is one example of how to run Snapper to measure SID 403's activity (for a single 5-second interval). Read the Snapper header for instructions and detailed documentation.

```
SQL> @snapper ash,stats 5 1 403

Sampling SID 403 with interval 5 seconds, taking 1 snapshots...


-- Session Snapper v3.52 by Tanel Poder @ E2SN ( http://tech.e2sn.com )


-------------------------------------------------------------------------------------
  SID, USER   , TYPE, STATISTIC                                            ,    HDELTA
-------------------------------------------------------------------------------------
  403, TANEL , STAT, session logical reads                                ,     1.34M
  403, TANEL , STAT, user I/O wait time                                   ,       411
  403, TANEL , STAT, non-idle wait time                                   ,       411
  403, TANEL , STAT, non-idle wait count                                  ,     8.11k
  403, TANEL , STAT, physical read total IO requests                      ,    10.53k
  403, TANEL , STAT, physical read total multi block requests             ,    10.53k
  403, TANEL , STAT, physical read total bytes                            ,    11.03G
  403, TANEL , STAT, cell physical IO interconnect bytes                  ,      1.6M
  403, TANEL , STAT, consistent gets                                      ,     1.35M
  403, TANEL , STAT, consistent gets direct                               ,     1.35M
  403, TANEL , STAT, physical reads                                       ,     1.35M
  403, TANEL , STAT, physical reads direct                                ,     1.35M
  403, TANEL , STAT, physical read IO requests                            ,    10.52k
  403, TANEL , STAT, physical read bytes                                  ,    11.02G
  403, TANEL , STAT, file io wait time                                    ,   530.73k
  403, TANEL , STAT, cell physical IO bytes eligible for predicate offload,    11.03G
```

```
403, TANEL , STAT, cell physical IO interconnect bytes returned by smart scan,        1.6M
403, TANEL , STAT, cell blocks processed by cache layer                    ,       1.35M
403, TANEL , STAT, cell blocks processed by txn layer                      ,       1.35M
403, TANEL , STAT, cell blocks processed by data layer                     ,       1.35M
403, TANEL , STAT, cell blocks helped by minscn optimization               ,       1.35M
403, TANEL , STAT, cell IO uncompressed bytes                              ,      11.05G
403, TANEL , WAIT, cell smart table scan                                   ,       4.07s
-- End of Stats snap 1, end=2011-04-03 19:07:36, seconds=5
```

```
--------------------------------------------------------------------------------
Active% | SQL_ID          | EVENT                      | WAIT_CLASS
--------------------------------------------------------------------------------
    95% | b7z0fth0asbbt   | cell smart table scan      | User I/O
     5% | b7z0fth0asbbt   | ON CPU                     | ON CPU

-- End of ASH snap 1, end=2011-04-03 19:07:36, seconds=5, samples_taken=42
```

This output shows that during the 5-second monitoring time, the session 403 did 1.34 million logical reads, and it read 11.03GB of data using about 10530 multiblock read I/O requests (large numbers are converted into humanfriendly approximations here, but Snapper can also print out exact figures).

The next example shows how you can use Snapper on a parallel query. Notice the *qc=403* option, which tells Snapper to capture stats for all PX slaves of Query Coordinator SID 403. Also notice the sinclude option, which allows you to list only the metrics of interest using a regular expression:

```
SQL> @snapper ash,stats,gather=s,sinclude=physical.*total.*bytes|cell.*scan 5 1 qc=403

Sampling SID qc=403 with interval 5 seconds, taking 1 snapshots...


-- Session Snapper v3.52 by Tanel Poder @ E2SN ( http://tech.e2sn.com )


---------------------------------------------------------------------------------------------
SID, USER  , TYPE, STATISTIC                                              ,    HDELTA
---------------------------------------------------------------------------------------------
 12, TANEL , STAT, physical read total bytes                             ,     2.86G
 12, TANEL , STAT, cell physical IO interconnect bytes returned by smart scan ,   411.16k
 12, TANEL , STAT, cell scans                                            ,         2
 55, TANEL , STAT, physical read total bytes                             ,     3.05G
 55, TANEL , STAT, cell physical IO interconnect bytes returned by smart scan, 443.54k
 55, TANEL , STAT, cell scans                                            ,         3
113, TANEL , STAT, physical read total bytes                             ,     2.97G
113, TANEL , STAT, cell physical I/O interconnect bytes returned by smart scan , 432.29k
113, TANEL , STAT, cell scans                                            ,         3
159, TANEL , STAT, physical read total bytes                             ,     2.63G
159, TANEL , STAT, cell physical I/O interconnect bytes returned by smart scan , 381.37k
159, TANEL , STAT, cell scans                                            ,         2
-- End of Stats snap 1, end=2011-04-03 19:57:35, seconds=6
```

```
--------------------------------------------------------------------------------
Active% | SQL_ID         | EVENT                        | WAIT_CLASS
--------------------------------------------------------------------------------
   393% | b4kvh3sqsttkw  | cell smart table scan        | User I/O
     7% | b4kvh3sqsttkw  | ON CPU                       | ON CPU

--  End of ASH snap 1, end=2011-04-03 19:57:35, seconds=5, samples_taken=44
```

This output shows that there are apparently four different PX slave sessions (notice the SID column) that have done physical reads during the 5-second Snapper run. The *physical read total bytes* tells us that each slave has read between 2.63 and 3.05GB worth of data blocks from datafiles during the 5-second Snapper run, using cell smart scan, because the *cell scans* statistic has increased for each slave. Moreover, the fact that *cell physical I/O interconnect bytes returned by smart scan* is also non-zero means that a cell smart scan was used and `cellsrv` processes returned some data to the database layer. Note that only around 381–443KB of data was returned to the database layer, while cells scanned through gigabytes of blocks for their "master" PX slave sessions. This is the Smart Scan at its best—parallel brute force scanning in cells at extreme speeds— and return only a small proportion of matching data to the database layer.

The Meaning and Explanation of Exadata Performance Counters

Now, it's time to explore the *meaning* of performance counters. No matter how pretty the charts or pictures a performance tool draws using these metrics, if you don't know what they actually mean, they will be useless for troubleshooting. In this book we will cover mostly Exadata-specific statistics and a few closely related ones. You can find more info about some common performance counters in Appendix E: "Statistics Descriptions," in *Oracle Database Reference guide 11g Release 2 (11.2)*, currently located at

> http://download.oracle.com/docs/cd/E14072_01/server.112/e10820/stats.htm
> .

Here's a script that lists all statistics related to storage cells from v$statname, with the statistic class, which indicates the purposes for which Oracle kernel engineers have expected to use these counters:

```
SQL> SELECT
  2      name
  3  , TRIM(
  4      CASE WHEN BITAND(class,   1) =   1 THEN 'USER  ' END ||
  5      CASE WHEN BITAND(class,   2) =   2 THEN 'REDO  ' END ||
  6      CASE WHEN BITAND(class,   4) =   4 THEN 'ENQ   ' END ||
  7      CASE WHEN BITAND(class,   8) =   8 THEN 'CACHE ' END ||
  8      CASE WHEN BITAND(class,  16) =  16 THEN 'OSDEP ' END ||
  9      CASE WHEN BITAND(class,  32) =  32 THEN 'PARX  ' END ||
 10      CASE WHEN BITAND(class,  64) =  64 THEN 'SQLT  ' END ||
 11      CASE WHEN BITAND(class,128) = 128 THEN 'DEBUG ' END
 12      ) class_name
 13  FROM
 14      v$statname
 15  WHERE
 16      name LIKE '%cell%'
 17  ORDER BY
 18*     name
SQL> /
```

```
NAME                                                          CLASS_NAME
------------------------------------------------------------  ---------------
cell CUs processed for compressed                             SQLT
cell CUs processed for uncompressed                           SQLT
cell CUs sent compressed                                      SQLT
cell CUs sent head piece                                      SQLT
cell CUs sent uncompressed                                    SQLT
cell IO uncompressed bytes                                    SQLT
cell blocks helped by commit cache                            SQLT
cell blocks helped by minscn optimization                     SQLT
cell blocks processed by cache layer                          DEBUG
cell blocks processed by data layer                           DEBUG
cell blocks processed by index layer                          DEBUG
cell blocks processed by txn layer                            DEBUG
cell commit cache queries                                     SQLT
cell flash cache read hits                                    CACHE
cell index scans                                              SQLT
cell num active smart IO sessions                             SQLT
cell num fast response sessions                               SQLT
cell num fast response sessions continuing to smart scan      SQLT
cell num smart IO sessions in rdbms block IO due to big payload  SQLT
cell num smart IO sessions in rdbms block IO due to no cell mem  SQLT
cell num smart IO sessions in rdbms block IO due to user      SQLT
cell num smart IO sessions using passthru mode due to cellsrv  SQLT
cell num smart IO sessions using passthru mode due to timezone  SQLT
cell num smart IO sessions using passthru mode due to user    SQLT
cell num smart file creation sessions using rdbms block IO mode  SQLT
cell physical IO bytes eligible for predicate offload         SQLT
cell physical IO bytes saved by storage index                 CACHE
cell physical IO bytes saved during optimized RMAN file restore  SQLT
cell physical IO bytes saved during optimized file creation   SQLT
cell physical IO interconnect bytes                           SQLT
cell physical IO interconnect bytes returned by smart scan    SQLT
cell scans                                                    SQLT
cell simulated physical IO bytes eligible for predicate offload  SQLT  DEBUG
cell simulated physical IO bytes returned by predicate offload  SQLT  DEBUG
cell smart IO allocated memory bytes                          SQLT
cell smart IO memory bytes hwm                                SQLT
cell smart IO session cache hard misses                       SQLT
cell smart IO session cache hits                              SQLT
cell smart IO session cache hwm                               SQLT
cell smart IO session cache lookups                           SQLT
cell smart IO session cache soft misses                       SQLT
cell smart IO sessions hwm                                    SQLT
cell transactions found in commit cache                       SQLT
chained rows processed by cell                                SQLT
chained rows rejected by cell                                 SQLT
chained rows skipped by cell                                  SQLT
```

With a similar query, we can list all the Exadata Hybrid Columnar Compression (EHCC%) statistics, but we will not cover those in this chapter.

NAME	CLASS_NAME
EHCC Analyze CUs Decompressed	DEBUG
EHCC Analyzer Calls	DEBUG
EHCC Archive CUs Compressed	DEBUG
EHCC Archive CUs Decompressed	DEBUG
EHCC CU Row Pieces Compressed	DEBUG
EHCC CUs Compressed	DEBUG
EHCC CUs Decompressed	DEBUG
EHCC Check CUs Decompressed	DEBUG
EHCC Columns Decompressed	DEBUG
EHCC Compressed Length Compressed	DEBUG
EHCC Compressed Length Decompressed	DEBUG
EHCC DML CUs Decompressed	DEBUG
EHCC Decompressed Length Compressed	DEBUG
EHCC Decompressed Length Decompressed	DEBUG
EHCC Dump CUs Decompressed	DEBUG
EHCC Normal Scan CUs Decompressed	DEBUG
EHCC Pieces Buffered for Decompression	DEBUG
EHCC Query High CUs Compressed	DEBUG
EHCC Query High CUs Decompressed	DEBUG
EHCC Query Low CUs Compressed	DEBUG
EHCC Query Low CUs Decompressed	DEBUG
EHCC Rowid CUs Decompressed	DEBUG
EHCC Rows Compressed	DEBUG
EHCC Rows Not Compressed	DEBUG
EHCC Total Columns for Decompression	DEBUG
EHCC Total Pieces for Decompression	DEBUG
EHCC Total Rows for Decompression	DEBUG
EHCC Turbo Scan CUs Decompressed	DEBUG

All the statistics starting from *cell* are, as the name says, related to storage cells. These stats are measured and maintained by cells themselves and then sent back to the database sessions during any interaction over IDB protocol. Every database session receives the cell statistics along with the replies from their corresponding cell sessions and then updates the relevant database V$ views with it. This is how the Oracle database layer has insight into what's going on in the "black box" of a cell, like the real number of I/O operations done, the number of cell flash cache hits, and so on. Note that there are a few *chained rows [...] cell* statistics, which apparently use a different naming convention, having the "cell" in the end of the statistic name.

Exadata Performance Counter Reference

This section explains some of the more important and interesting statistics in this chapter, although if you are lucky, you won't have to dig down this deep in your troubleshooting; wait events and the SQL monitoring feature are good enough for most basic troubleshooting and performance optimization. Nevertheless, understanding what's behind these statistics and behavior will give you further insight into Exadata internals and enable you to troubleshoot unusual performance problems more effectively. We'll explain the stats in alphabetical order, to make it easier to use this section as a reference.

cell blocks helped by commit cache

During a Smart Scan in the storage cell, the normal data consistency rules still need to be applied, sometimes with help of undo data. Yes, consistent read guarantees must work also for Smart Scans. But the Smart Scan works entirely in the storage cells, where it does not have access to any undo data in the database instances' buffer caches. And remember that a cell never talks to any other cells by design, so it would be unable to read the undo data from undo segments striped across many cells too. So, consistent read buffer cloning and rollbacks, whenever needed, would have to be done inside the database layer. Whenever the Smart Scan hits a row, which still has its lock byte set (the row/block hasn't been cleaned out), it would temporarily have to switch into block I/O mode and send the entire data block back to the database layer for normal consistent read processing— with the help of undo data available there.

Note that when a block is cleaned out correctly (lock bytes cleared) and its cleanout SCN in the block header is from an earlier SCN than the query start time SCN (*snapshot SCN*), then the cell knows that a rollback of that block would not be needed. If the latest change to that block happened earlier than the query start, then the block image in the cell is valid, a good enough block to satisfy the query with the given SCN. How does the cell know the starting SCN of a query executed in the database layer? That is the task of the storage-aware row sources in the execution plans, which communicate the SCN to cells over iDB when setting up Smart Scan sessions for themselves.

Now, when some of the rows do have nonzero lock bytes in the block or when the cleanout SCN in a block header happens to be higher than the query's snapshot SCN, then the cells cannot determine the validity of the block/data version themselves and would need to ship the block back to the database layer for regular, non-Smart Scan processing. This would considerably slow down the Smart Scan processing, if such check had to be done for many locked rows and not cleaned-out blocks.

However, there is an optimization that helps to reduce the number of fallbacks to block I/O processing in the database layer. Whenever a Smart Scan finds a locked row during a segment scan, it will check which transaction locked that row. This can easily be done by reading the transaction's ITL entry in the current data block header, where the locked row's lock byte points. Note that bitmap index segment blocks and HCC compressed blocks don't have a lock byte for each single row in the block, but the idea remains the same— Oracle is able to find out the transaction ID of the locked row(s) from the block at hand itself. Now, the Smart Scan can send that transaction ID back to the database layer (to the database session owning the cell Smart Scan session) and ask the database session to check whether that transaction has already committed or not. If this locking transaction has not committed yet, the Smart Scan falls back to the block I/O mode for that block and the database layer will have to go through the normal consistent read buffer cloning/rollback mechanism and there's no workaround for that. If the transaction *has* already committed, but has left the lock bytes not cleaned out in some blocks (this does usually happen for large DMLs), then the Smart Scan does not have to fall back to block I/O and an in-database, consistent read mechanism. It knows that this row is not really locked anymore, as the locking transaction has committed already, even though the lock byte is still in place.

All of that to read a single locked row! When Smart Scanning, you are probably scanning through millions or billions of rows, and many of these rows may still have their lock bytes set. So, you don't want the Smart Scan to communicate with the database layer every single time it hits another locked row. So, Oracle cells can *cache* the information about transaction statuses in an in-memory structure called "commit cache." It's probably just an in-memory hash-table, organized by transaction ID, and it keeps track of which transactions are committed and which are not. When the cell Smart Scan sees a locked row, it will extract the transaction ID (from the ITL section of the data block) and checks whether there's any info about that transaction in the commit cache. This check will increment the statistic *cell commit cache queries* by one. If there is no such transaction in the commit cache, then the Smart Scan "asks" the status of this transaction from the database layer and stores (caches) the result in the commit cache. Ideally every transaction status is fetched into the cache only once, and all subsequent checks will be satisfied from the commit cache. So every time the Smart Scan opens a new block and realizes that there are some rows locked but manages to avoid having to talk to the database layer thanks to the commit cache, our statistic at hand, *cell blocks helped by commit cache*, would be updated by one.

Seeing this statistic growing, when your sessions are doing a Smart Scan, indicates that the cells have some overhead due to checking whether locked rows are really still locked, but thankfully the commit cache eliminates the need for communicating with the database layer repeatedly. Without this optimization, the whole Smart Scan would get slower as it must repeatedly interact with the database layer. You would also see more logical I/O being done at the database layer (see the statistics starting with *consistent gets from cache*), as opposed to only a single LIO per segment for reading the extent locations and number of blocks under the High Water Mark out from the segment header.

▪ **Note:** A similar optimization actually exists also in the database layer, and in non-Exadata databases. Oracle can cache the committed transaction info in the database session's private memory, so it won't have to perform buffer gets on the undo segment header when hitting many locked rows. Whenever a session caches a committed transaction's state in memory, it increments the *Commit SCN cached* statistic in its V$SESSTAT array. Whenever it does a lookup from that cache, it increments the *Cached Commit SCN referenced* statistic.

If you are not familiar with the delayed block cleanout mechanism in Oracle, you might be wondering how there can be rows with their lock bytes still set, when the transaction has already committed. This is how Oracle is different from most other mainstream commercial RDBMS products. Oracle doesn't have to keep the blocks with noncommitted rows cached in memory; DBWR is free to write them out to disk and release the memory for other data blocks. Now, when committing the transaction, it wouldn't be good to read all the transactions back from the disk just to clean up the lock bytes. If there are many such blocks, then your commit might take ages. Instead, Oracle just marks the transaction complete in its undo segment header slot. Any future block readers can just check whether the transaction in that undo segment header slot is still alive or not. If you perform block I/O to read the data blocks to the database layer later on, then the reading session would clean up the block (clear the lock bytes of rows modified by committed transactions), so no further transaction status checks would be needed in future reads. However, storage cells do not perform block cleanouts, as cells don't change data blocks. This is because database block modifications require writing of redo operations, but how would a cell write to a redo log file that is managed and striped over many cells at the database layer already?

Note that for small transactions, which haven't modified too many blocks and where the blocks are still in buffer cache, Oracle can perform block cleanout right during the commit time. Also, the issues just discussed do not apply to such databases (data warehouses usually) where tables are loaded with direct path load inserts (and index partitions are built after the table partitions are loaded), because in the case of direct loads, the table rows are not locked in the newly formatted table blocks (the same applies to index entries in leaf blocks if an index is created after the data load).

cell blocks helped by minscn optimization

Exadata cell server has another optimization designed to improve consistent read efficiency even more. It's called the Minimum Active SCN optimization and it keeps track of the lowest SCN of any still active (uncommitted) transaction in the database. This allows us to easily compare the SCN in the ITL entries of the locking transactions with the lowest SCN of the "oldest" active transaction in the database. As the

Oracle database is able to send this MinSCN info to the cell when starting a Smart Scan session, the cells can avoid having to talk to the database layer whenever the known minimum active SCN passed to the cell is higher than the SCN in the transaction's ITL entry in the block. Whenever the Smart Scan processes a block and finds a locked row with active transaction in the ITL slot in it but realizes that the transaction must be committed, thanks to the MinSCN passed in by the database session, the *cell blocks helped by minscn optimization* statistic is incremented (once for each block).

Without this optimization, Oracle would have to check the commit cache (described in the *cell blocks helped by commit cache* statistic section) and, if it finds no info about this transaction in the commit cache, then interact with the database layer to find out whether the locking transaction has already committed or not. This optimization is RAC-aware; in fact the Minimum SCN is called Global Minimum SCN, and the MMON processes in each instance will keep track of the MinSCN and keep it synced in an in-memory structure in each node's SGA. You can query the current known global Minimum Active SCN from the x$ktumascn fixed table as shown here (as SYS):

```
SQL> COL min_act_scn FOR 99999999999999999
SQL>
SQL> SELECT min_act_scn FROM x$ktumascn;

       MIN_ACT_SCN
    ------------------
       9920890881859
```

This *cell blocks helped by minscn optimization* statistic is also something you shouldn't be worried about, but it can come in handy when troubleshooting advanced Smart Scan issues, or even bugs, where Smart Scans seem to get interrupted because they have to fall back to block I/O and talk to the database too much.

cell blocks processed by cache layer

The *cell blocks processed by … layer* statistics are good indicators of the *depth* of offload process in the cells. The main point and advantage of the Exadata storage servers is that part of the Oracle kernel code has been ported into the cellsrv executable running in the storage cells. This is what allows the Oracle database layer to offload the data scanning, filtering, and projection work into the cells. In order to do that, the cells must be able to read and understand Oracle data block and row contents, just as the database does. The *cell blocks processed by cache layer* statistic indicates how many data blocks the *cells* have processed (opened, read and used for Smart Scan) as opposed to just passing the blocks read up the database layer.

When a cell just passes the blocks back to the database in block I/O mode, this statistic is not updated. But when the cell itself uses these blocks for Smart Scan, then one of the first things that is done when opening a block (consistent or current read) is to check the block cache layer header. This is to make sure it is the correct block, is not corrupt, and is valid and coherent. These tests are done by cache layer functions (KCB for Kernel Cache Buffer management) and reported back to the database as *cell blocks processed by cache layer*.

In the database layer, with regular block I/O, the corresponding statistics are *consistent gets from cache* and *consistent gets from cache (fastpath)* depending on which buffer pinning code path is used for the consistent buffer get. Note that cellsrv does only consistent mode buffer gets (CR reads) and no current mode block gets. So all the current mode gets you see in stats are done in the database layer and are reported as *db block gets from cache* or *db block gets from cache (fastpath)*. This statistic is a useful and simple measure of how many logical reads the cellsrv does for your sessions.

Note that it is OK to see some database layer I/O processing during a SQL plan execution, as the plan is probably accessing multiple tables (and joining them). So, when doing a 10-table join between a large fact and nine dimension tables, you may well see that all of the dimensions are scanned using regular, cached block I/O (and using some index, if present), and only the large fact table access path will take advantage of the Smart Scan.

cell blocks processed by data layer

While the previous statistic counts all the block gets done by the cache layer (KCB), this statistic is similar, but counts the blocks processed in the cell by the data layer. This statistic applies specifically to reading table blocks or materialized view blocks (which are physically just like table blocks). Information is collected using a data layer module, called KDS for Kernel Data Scan, which can extract rows and columns out of table blocks and pass them on to various evaluation functions for filtering and predicate checks. If the cell Smart Scan can do all of its processing in the cell, without having to fall back to database block I/O mode, then this "processed by data layer" statistic plus the processed by "index layer" statistic should add up to the "processed by cache layer" value. This means that every block actually opened made its way through the cache and transaction layer checks and was passed to the data or index layer for row and column extraction. If the "processed by data layer" plus "processed by index layer" statistics add up to a smaller value than the "processed by cache layer" statistic, it means that the rest of the blocks were not fully processed by the cell and had to be sent back to the database for regular block I/O processing.

cell blocks processed by index layer

This statistic is just like the preceding *cell blocks processed by data layer*, but it is incremented when Smart Scanning through B*Tree or bitmap index segment blocks. The code path for extracting rows out of index blocks is different from The *cell blocks processed by index layer* counts how many index segment blocks were processed by a Smart Scan.

cell blocks processed by txn layer

This statistic shows how many blocks were processed in the cell by the transaction layer. Here is a simplified explanation of the sequence of actions during a consistent read for Smart Scan in a storage cell:

1. The cache layer (KCB) opens the data block and checks its header, last modification SCN, and cleanout status.

2. If the block in the cell has not been modified after the snapshot SCN of the query running the current Smart Scan, this block can be passed to the transaction layer for processing. However, if the block image on disk (cell) has been modified after the query's snapshot SCN, then the cache layer already knows that this block has to be rolled back for consistent read. In this case the block is not passed into the cell transaction layer at all, but the cell falls back to block I/O and passes that block to the database layer for normal CR processing.

3. If the block is passed to the transaction layer (KTR) by the cache layer, then the transaction layer can use the commit cache and MinActiveSCN optimization

to avoid falling back to reduce the amount of communication with the database layer if it hits locked rows and not cleaned out blocks of committed transactions. When there is no need to fall back to block I/O and database-layer consistent reads, then the consistent reads will be performed by the data layer or index layer code inside the storage cell. However, if the consistent read cannot be completed within the cell, then the entire data block at hand must be transported back to the database layer and the consistent read will be performed there.

The point of this explanation is that if the Smart Scans work optimally, they do not have to interrupt their work and talk to the database layer during the Smart Scan processing; ideally all the scanning work is done in the storage cell, and once enough rows are ready to be returned, they're sent to the database in a batch. If this is the case, then the *cell blocks processed by data layer* (or *index layer*) statistic will be as high as the *cell blocks processed by cache layer* (and *txn layer*), showing that all the blocks could be fully processed in the cell and rows extracted from them without having to fall back to database-layer block I/O and consistent reads.

Remember that all this complexity related to consistent reads in storage cells matters only when doing a Smart Scan. When doing regular block I/O, cells just pass the blocks read directly back to the database layer, and the consistent read logic is executed in the database layer as usual. And you shouldn't really worry about these metrics unless you see that your Smart Scan wait events tend to be interspersed with *cell single block physical reads*, consuming a significant part of your query response time.

cell commit cache queries

This is the number of times the cell Smart Scan looked up a transaction status from the cell commit cache hash table. A lookup from commit cache is normally done once per uncommitted transaction found per block scanned by Smart Scan— where the MinActiveSCN optimization hasn't already kicked in and eliminated the need to check for individual transaction statuses. This is closely related to the *cell blocks helped by commit cache* statistic.

cell flash cache read hits

This statistic shows how many I/O requests were satisfied from the cell flash cache, so that a hard disk read was not necessary. Note that we said "hard disk read," not just physical read. That's because the reads from flash cards also require physical reads (system calls resulting in flash card I/O). When you see this number, it means that the required blocks were not in the database layer buffer cache (or the access path chose to use a direct path read), but luckily all the blocks required by an I/O request were in cell flash cache (the official term is Exadata Smart Flash Cache). Note that this number shows the number of I/O requests, not the number of blocks read from cell flash cache. Remember that cell flash cache is usable both by regular block reads and cell Smart Scans. Especially if you run an OLTP database on Exadata, for best performance you should attempt to satisfy most single-block reads from either the database buffer cache or, failing that, the cell flash cache. You can read more about the Exadata Flash Cache in Chapter 5.

cell index scans

This statistic is incremented every time a Smart Scan is started on a B*Tree or bitmap index segment. Note that in order to use Smart Scans on index segments, the *index fast full scan* execution plan row source operator must be used together with direct path reads. This statistic is updated at the start of a Smart Scan session, so if you monitor its value for a session that has been executing a long-running query for a while, then you might not see this statistic incrementing for your session.

When running just a serial session with Smart Scan on a nonpartitioned index segment, this statistic would be incremented by one. However, when running a Smart Scan on a partitioned index segment, then the *cell index scans* statistic would be incremented for each partition scanned using Smart Scan. This is because the Smart Scan is a segment-level decision made at runtime, for each segment (table, index or partition). Because the Smart Scan kicks in only when doing direct path reads to PGA, and the direct path reads decision is made based on the scanned segment size (among other things), different partitions of the same table accessed may be scanned using different methods. You might find that some partitions in your multipartition table or index are not scanned with Smart Scan/direct path reads, as Oracle has decided to use buffered reads for them thanks to their smaller size. In this case, the *cell index scans* statistic would not increment as much and you would see the *cell multiblock physical read* wait event pop up at the table/index scan row source path in an ASH or SQL Monitoring report.

cell IO uncompressed bytes

This statistic shows the *uncompressed* size of the data scanned in the cell. So if you scan through a 10GB compressed segment, *physical read total bytes* statistic would increase by 10GB, but the *cell I/O uncompressed bytes* may well increase by 10 GB if that's the total uncompressed size of the data. This statistic is incremented only when performing a Smart Scan compression offloading, not when you read the compressed blocks directly to the database layer with block I/O.

cell num fast response sessions

This statistic shows how many times Oracle started the Smart Scan code but then chose not to set up the Smart Scan session immediately, but instead to do a few block I/O operations first in hope to find enough rows to satisfy the database session. This optimization is used for FIRST ROWS execution plan options, either when using a FIRST_ROWS_x hint (or equivalent init.ora parameter) or a WHERE rownum < X condition, which may also enable the first rows option in execution plans. The idea is that if fetching only a few rows, Oracle hopes to avoid the overhead of setting up a cell Smart Scan session (with all the cells, thanks to ASM striping), but it will do a few regular block I/O operations first. Following is an example of a first-rows optimization thanks to the ROWNUM predicate:

```
SELECT * FROM t3 WHERE owner like 'S%' AND rownum <= 10

Plan hash value: 3128673074

-----------------------------------------------------------------------
| Id  | Operation                          | Name | E-Rows | Cost (%CPU)|
-----------------------------------------------------------------------
|   0 | SELECT STATEMENT                   |      |        |   4 (100)|
|*  1 |  COUNT STOPKEY                     |      |        |          |
|*  2 |   TABLE ACCESS STORAGE FULL FIRST ROWS | T3   |    11 |   4   (0)|
-----------------------------------------------------------------------
```

```
Predicate Information (identified by operation id):
---------------------------------------------------

   1 - filter(ROWNUM<=10)
   2 - storage("OWNER" LIKE 'S%')
       filter("OWNER" LIKE 'S%')
```

When examining V$SESSION statistics of a Smart Scan of such an execution plan, you are likely to see the *cell num fast response sessions* incremented, as Oracle has tried to avoid the Smart Scan session setup overhead:

```
SQL> SELECT * FROM TABLE(exatest.diff('cell num fast.*'));

NAME                                                             VALUE
---------------------------------------------------------------- ----------
cell num fast response sessions                                       1
cell num fast response sessions continuing to smart scan             0
```

The cell fast response feature is controlled by the *_kcfis_fast_response_enabled* parameter and enabled by default.

cell num fast response sessions continuing to smart scan

This statistic shows how many times the cell Smart Scan fast response session was started, but Oracle had to switch to the real Smart Scan session as it didn't find enough matching rows with the first few I/O operations. The next example query has the first-rows optimization in the execution plan, but the additional predicate on the object_name column ensures that no matching rows are found during first few I/Os from the table:

```
SELECT * FROM t3 WHERE owner like 'S%' AND object_name LIKE '%non-existent%'
AND rownum <= 10

Plan hash value: 3128673074


--------------------------------------------------------------------------
| Id  | Operation                         | Name | E-Rows | Cost (%CPU)|
--------------------------------------------------------------------------
|   0 | SELECT STATEMENT                  |      |        |    9 (100)|
|*  1 |  COUNT STOPKEY                    |      |        |           |
|*  2 |   TABLE ACCESS STORAGE FULL FIRST ROWS| T3   |     10 |    9   (0)|
--------------------------------------------------------------------------

Predicate Information (identified by operation id):
---------------------------------------------------

   1 - filter(ROWNUM<=10)
   2 - storage(("OBJECT_NAME" LIKE '%non-existent%' AND "OWNER" LIKE
              'S%' AND "OBJECT_NAME" IS NOT NULL))
       filter(("OBJECT_NAME" LIKE '%non-existent%' AND "OWNER" LIKE
              'S%' AND "OBJECT_NAME" IS NOT NULL))
```

```
SQL> SELECT * FROM TABLE(exatest.diff('cell num fast.*'));

NAME                                                             VALUE
---------------------------------------------------------------- ----------
cell num fast response sessions                                      1
cell num fast response sessions continuing to smart scan                 1
```

These stats show that a fast response session was invoked, but it had to switch to Smart Scan later on. Interestingly, this optimization causes the Oracle wait interface to report some *db file sequential read* wait events, which we thought were impossible on Exadata cell storage (because regular cell single block reads are reported as *cell single block physical read* wait events).

```
PARSING IN CURSOR #47425277991136 len=93 dep=0 uid=93 oct=3 lid=93 tim=1302602065427828 hv
SELECT * FROM t3 WHERE owner like 'S%' AND object_name LIKE '%non-existent%' AND rownum
<=
END OF STMT
PARSE #47425277991136:c=8999,e=9983,p=2,cr=3,cu=0,mis=1,r=0,dep=0,og=1,plh=3128673074
EXEC #47425277991136:c=0,e=19,p=0,cr=0,cu=0,mis=0,r=0,dep=0,og=1,plh=3128673074
WAIT #47425277991136: nam='SQL*Net message to client' ela= 2 driver id=1413697536 #bytes=1
WAIT #47425277991136: nam='SQL*Net more data to client' ela= 17 driver id=1413697536
WAIT #47425277991136: nam='cell single block physical read' ela= 505 cellhash#=2133459483
WAIT #47425277991136: nam='reliable message' ela= 1473 channel context=11888341784
WAIT #47425277991136: nam='enq: KO - fast object checkpoint' ela= 298 name|mode=1263468550
WAIT #47425277991136: nam='enq: KO - fast object checkpoint' ela= 154 name|mode=1263468545
WAIT #47425277991136: nam='asynch descriptor resize' ela= 2 outstanding #aio=0
WAIT #47425277991136: nam='db file sequential read' ela= 4 file#=0 block#=0 blocks=0
WAIT #47425277991136: nam='db file sequential read' ela= 11592 file#=0 block#=0 blocks=0
WAIT #47425277991136: nam='db file sequential read' ela= 1 file#=0 block#=0 blocks=0
WAIT #47425277991136: nam='db file sequential read' ela= 427 file#=0 block#=0 blocks=0
WAIT #47425277991136: nam='db file sequential read' ela= 1 file#=0 block#=0 blocks=0
WAIT #47425277991136: nam='db file sequential read' ela= 3500 file#=0 block#=0 blocks=0
WAIT #47425277991136: nam='db file sequential read' ela= 2 file#=0 block#=0 blocks=0
WAIT #47425277991136: nam='db file sequential read' ela= 22857 file#=0 block#=0 blocks=0
WAIT #47425277991136: nam='db file sequential read' ela= 2 file#=0 block#=0 blocks=0
WAIT #47425277991136: nam='db file sequential read' ela= 23636 file#=0 block#=0 blocks=0
WAIT #47425277991136: nam='db file sequential read' ela= 3 file#=0 block#=0 blocks=0
WAIT #47425277991136: nam='db file sequential read' ela= 88880 file#=0 block#=0 blocks=0
WAIT #47425277991136: nam='cell smart table scan' ela= 130 cellhash#=2133459483 p2=0 p3=0
WAIT #47425277991136: nam='cell smart table scan' ela= 126 cellhash#=379339958 p2=0 p3=0
WAIT #47425277991136: nam='cell smart table scan' ela= 123 cellhash#=3176594409 p2=0 p3=0
```

cell num smart IO sessions using passthru mode due to *reason*

These three statistics (where *reason* can be either user, cellsrv ,or timezone) indicate how many times Oracle database initiated a Smart Scan, but the cellsrv didn't start a Smart Scan and fell back entirely to block I/O mode. The blocks read are just passed through cellsrv to database, instead of processing them within the cell. This means that while you still see the *cell Smart Scan* wait events and *cell physical IO interconnect bytes returned by smart scan* increasing (which indicates that a Smart Scan is happening), the full power of Smart Scan is not utilized, as the cells just read data blocks and return the blocks back to the database layer. In other words, in passthrough mode, the cells do not open datablocks and extract only the required columns of matching rows, but return all the physical blocks of the segment as they are. Note that the storage indexes (dynamically created in `cellsrv` memory) can be used to eliminate I/O in the passthrough mode too, but these indexes must be populated by a regular Smart Scan, which does actually open and process the data blocks in the cell.

You should not see any passthrough Smart Scans happening on the latest database and Exadata cell versions unless you have problems like cells running out of memory and the like. You can test what happens in a test-environment by setting _*kcfis_cell_passthru_enabled* to TRUE and running a Smart Scan. You will still see *cell smart scan* wait event for your Smart Scans, but they are slower because they are returning all the blocks to the database for processing.

cell physical IO bytes eligible for predicate offload

This performance counter holds one of the most important statistics for understanding cell Smart Scan. When you are Smart Scanning through a segment, this statistic shows how many bytes of that segment the Smart Scan would go through. Essentially, all the bytes from the beginning of the segment all the way to its high water mark will be reported (as the scanning progresses through the entire segment). The catch is that this is the theoretical maximum number of bytes to scan through, but sometimes the cell storage index optimization kicks in, allowing the scan to skip reading some block ranges. Even if the storage index allows you to avoid scanning 80 percent of a 10GB segment, reducing the actual I/O amount to only 2GB, this statistic still shows the *total* size of the segment scanned, regardless of any optimizations. In other words, this statistic shows the total bytes that would have been scanned through, if any cell level optimizations didn't kick in (and often this is the case). Note that this statistic simply counts the physical size of the segment in the data blocks in data files (and not the "eventual" data size after any decompression, filtering, or projection).

If this number does not increase for your session's V$SESSTAT (or Statspack/AWR data when looking at the whole instance), then it's another indicator that Smart Scans aren't being used. Any block ranges scanned through (or even skipped thanks to storage index optimizations) by a Smart Scan session should increment this statistic accordingly. Another thing to know is that when the Smart Scan falls back to passthrough full block shipping mode (described earlier), the *cell physical IO bytes eligible for predicate offload* statistic still gets incremented, although there's no predicate offloading and Smart Scan filtering done in the cell in passthrough mode.

cell physical IO bytes pushed back due to excessive CPU on cell

This statistic is related to the selective fallback to passthrough mode as explained in Kevin's accompanying note. The bigger this number is (compared to the *cell physical I/O bytes eligible for predicate offload* statistic), the more the cell had to send back compressed CUs for decompression and processing in the database layer. This happens when the cell's CPU utilization reaches a threshold and there is enough spare CPU capacity available in the database layer, allowing you to utilize the CPUs of your whole Exadata cluster better.

Note that this performance counter appeared as part of the cell software version 11.2.2.3.0 and database Bundle Patch 6. It was apparently added as a temporary one-off fix, as this statistic replaced the ad-hoc *"spare statistic 1"* counter in the V$ views. In fact, in Oracle 11.2.0.3 (and Exadata Bundle Patch 7), this statistic is renamed to *"cell physical IO bytes sent directly to DB node to balance CPU usage."*

▪ **Kevin Says:** "Regarding passthrough functionality, the authors are correct in asserting that passthrough is generally a sign of problems. However, late releases of Exadata Storage Server software have a feature that tries to mitigate the imbalances between processor utilization in the storage cells and that of database hosts under storage-intensive processing. The definition of "a problem" is subjective. In situations where Smart Scan offload processing is saturating the storage processors—thus creating a bottleneck for data flow—query completion time is severely impacted. That is a problem. Solutions can, sometimes, be problems as well.

In these more recent releases of `cellsrv` there is a hint about database grid processor utilization in the metadata of each Smart Scan I/O request passed over iDB to storage. If storage is significantly busier than the hosts (CPU-wise), `cellsrv` will send data to the foreground processes after no, or very little, offload processing—depending on whether there is HCC involved or not. The term *passthrough* refers to those times when Smart Scan *chooses* to skip offload processing. As of the publication of this book, the only reason Smart Scan *chooses* to skip offload processing is for reasons of processor saturation. There may be other triggers in the future. The infrastructure is in place.

The authors (and I) try to impart the concepts about when a Smart Scan will occur and when a Smart Scan will *need* to revert to block mode processing. Here, on the other hand, we have a case where Smart Scan simply *chooses* to cease offload processing for a significant percentage of the data being read from disk. This middle ground, however, is not a fall-back to block mode processing, because the buffering is still PGA (direct path reads). The term Oracle has chosen for this middle-ground sums it up the best: *passthrough*. To that end, we could say there is now another type of scan: Partially Smart Scan.

So, how much Smart Scan value remains when in passthrough mode? Well, it is still a Smart Scan, so storage indexes can still be of benefit. However, filtration will not occur in storage. Projection, on the other hand, will occur in storage only if the data being scanned is EHCC. You see, projecting EHCC tuples is very inexpensive and, as we know, reducing payload is the critical service Smart Scan aims to deliver. So if payload reduction can occur, that is a good thing.

So what does all this mean? Well, idle processors are a very bad thing with DW/BI workloads, so this new behavior could be a good thing. The only aspect of the feature that makes me wary is that factors external to the query can change the runtime dynamic. Consider, for instance, a query with a good execution plan that takes 10 seconds to complete when processing without other concurrent queries. Suppose further that this query burdens the storage processors to some 75 percent. When executed concurrently with another query that utilizes the remaining 25 percent storage processor bandwidth, Smart Scan will stop offload processing for *some* amount of the data read from disk—for both of these queries. This is a case of hysteresis.

If this new feature stands the test of time, it will add many variables (in multiple dimensions) to performance analysis. In the end, however, the only thing that really matters is whether the users' responsiveness from the system is acceptable. I choose to remain dubious, however, because of the added complexity. It has taken many chapters of this well-written book to explain when Smart Scan, and thus offload processing, will occur. Now we have a Smart Scan situation that doesn't perform offload processing for varying percentages of the data streaming off of storage. It has been said many times that offload processing is the "secret sauce" of Exadata and, of course, Smart Scan is the main agent for delivery. It is yet to be seen how complex workloads behave when Smart Scan sometimes chooses not to do its job.

cell physical IO bytes saved by storage index

This is another important statistic, which shows how many bytes the Smart Scan sessions could simply skip reading from disk thanks to the in-memory storage index in cellsrv. If this statistic, *cell physical IO bytes saved by storage index* is close to *cell physical IO bytes eligible for predicate offload*, it indicates that Smart Scans are greatly benefiting from storage indexes and have avoided disk reads thanks to that.

cell physical IO bytes saved during optimized file creation

This statistic shows how many bytes worth of data file creation and file extension work was done in the cell. Without this optimization, Oracle would format the new data blocks in the database session's PGA and send physical block writes to the cell over interconnect. In Exadata, the file block formatting and writes can be offloaded to the cell, and the database does not have do physical writes itself. In Exadata, you would see a *cell smart file creation* wait event when cells are formatting blocks for new files or when extending files. Without this optimization, you would see the *Data file init write* wait events.

cell physical IO bytes saved during optimized RMAN file restore

This statistic shows how many bytes worth of datafiles were restored within cells, without having to involve the database layer, thanks to offloading the RMAN restore to cells. You should see your recovery sessions waiting for *cell smart restore from backup* wait event when restoring on Exadata *RMAN backup & recovery I/O* wait event.

cell physical IO bytes sent directly to DB node to balance CPU usage

This statistic is the same as the "cell physical IO bytes pushed back due to excessive CPU on cell" statistic earlier, which is used in Oracle 11.2.0.2 with Bundle Patch 6, but in newer Oracle versions and patch levels the current statistic name is used instead.

cell physical IO interconnect bytes

This is a simple, but fundamental statistic, which shows how many bytes worth of any data have been transmitted between the storage cells and your database sessions. This includes all data, both sent and received by the database, the Smart Scan result sets, full blocks read from the cells, temporary I/O reads and writes, log writes (if LGWR), any supplementary iDB traffic, and so on. So, this statistic shows *all traffic bytes*, regardless of its direction, contents or nature.

When measuring the write I/O metrics, don't be surprised when you see that the *cell physical IO interconnect bytes* statistic is two or three times higher than the *physical write total bytes* statistic. This is because the latter statistic is measured at the Oracle database level, but the *cell physical IO interconnect bytes* is measured at the cell level, after ASM mirroring has been done. So if, for example, LGWR writes 1MB to an ASM disk group with high redundancy (triple mirroring), a total of 1.5 MB of data would be sent over the interconnect. Note that there is a bug (#10036425) in Oracle 11.2.0.1 that increments this statistic even on non-Exadata databases, so you can just ignore it on non-Exadata databases.

cell physical IO interconnect bytes returned by smart scan

This statistic is an important one and shows how many bytes of data were returned to the database layer by the Smart Scan. The bytes actually returned should be much less than the bytes scanned / read from disk. This is the main point of the Exadata Smart Scan feature— the cells may read gigabytes of data every second, but as they perform early filtering thanks to predicate offloading, they may send only a small part of the rows back to the database layer. Additionally, thanks to the projection offloading, the Smart Scans only return the requested columns back, not full rows. Of course, if the application uses SELECT * for fetching all the columns of a table, projection offloading would not help, but the early filtering thanks to predicate offloading can still help a lot.

This statistic is a subset of the *cell physical IO interconnect bytes* statistic, but it counts only the bytes (of row sets) that are returned by Smart Scan sessions and no other traffic.

cell scans

This statistic is just like the *cell index scans*, but *cell scans* shows the number of Smart Scans done on table and materialized view segments. With serial execution, this statistic is incremented once in the beginning of every segment scan. So when scanning through a partitioned table, in which each partition is a separate segment, this statistic would be incremented for each partition. With parallel scans, the *cell scans* statistic will increment even more, as parallel slaves perform their scans on block ranges (PX granules) handed over to them by the query coordinator— so the scan on each block range is reported as a separate *cell scan*. The presence of the *table scans (rowid ranges)* statistic indicates that PX scans on block ranges are happening.

Following is an example of a parallel full table scan session's statistics (with two slaves). The 133.8GB table was apparently "split" into 132 rowid ranges and scanned using Smart Scans and thanks to the Smart Scan's offloading features, only 4.54GB worth of resulting data had to be sent to the database.

```
-------------------------------------------------------------------------------
SID, USER  , TYPE, STATISTIC                                        , HDELTA
-------------------------------------------------------------------------------
400, TANEL , STAT, physical read total bytes                        , 133.8G
400, TANEL , STAT, cell physical IO interconnect bytes              ,   4.54G
400, TANEL , STAT, cell smart IO session cache lookups              ,     130
400, TANEL , STAT, cell smart IO session cache hits                 ,     130
400, TANEL , STAT, cell physical IO interconnect bytes returned by smart scan,  4.54G
400, TANEL , STAT, table scans (long tables)                        ,     132
400, TANEL , STAT, table scans (rowid ranges)                       ,     132
400, TANEL , STAT, table scans (direct read)                        ,     132
400, TANEL , STAT, cell scans                                       ,     132
```

cell smart IO session cache hits

This statistic shows how many times a database session managed to reuse a previously initialized Smart Scan session in the cell. This statistic shows up when a single execution plan scans through multiple segments (like with partitioned tables) or revisits the same segment during a single execution.

cell smart IO session cache lookups

This statistic is incremented every time a database session tried to reuse a previously initialized Smart Scan session in the cell. If the *cell smart IO session cache hits* statistic increments too, then the lookup was successful and a previous session can be reused. The smart I/O session caching works only within an execution (and subsequent fetches) of an open cursor. Once the execution finishes, the next executions (even of the same cursor) would have to set up new Smart Scan sessions (and communicate the new consistent read snapshot SCN to the cells too).

cell transactions found in commit cache

This statistic is related to the consistent read mechanism Oracle has to guarantee, even on Exadata. It shows how many times the Smart Scan sessions checked the cell commit cache to decide whether a CR rollback is needed or not; and it finds the transaction status information in the cell commit cache. This avoids a round trip to the database layer to check that transaction's status using undo data available there. There's more information about how the consistent reads work with Exadata Smart Scans in the *cell blocks helped by commit cache* statistic section.

chained rows processed by cell

Before explaining what this specific statistic means, let's look at how Smart Scans deal with chained rows. Chained rows pose a problem for Smart Scans. The chained row's "next" row pieces may be anywhere in the segment; and thanks to the ASM striping, it's not guaranteed that the next row pieces of a chained row are in the same cell where the row head piece is. So a chained row may be physically split across multiple different cells. Given that cells never speak to each other (for scalability and simplicity), how would you be able to construct the full row when needed? The way cellsrv currently solves this problem is that whenever the Smart Scan hits a chained row (and realizes it has to fetch its next row piece), `cellsrv` falls back to regular block I/O for that row and sends the block back to the database layer for normal processing. The database layer can then extract the data block address of the next row piece from the row head piece and issue the block read I/O to the appropriate cell where the ASM striping has physically put that block. The reasoning and fundamental problem behind this optimization is similar to why consistent read rollbacks have to be done in the database layer as opposed to a cell—it's because some of the data blocks required for this operation may just happen to be located in another cell, and cells never talk to other cells.

This behavior means that your Smart Scan performance will drop if it hits a lot of chained rows and has to fetch their next row pieces. If you get lucky and access only the columns that are present in the head piece of the row, then you won't have to fall back to database block I/O mode for these blocks and your Smart Scans will be fast. If you have to fetch the next row pieces, however, then your Smart Scan will be constantly interrupted by the fall-back to block I/O, and the database layer starts doing logical reads (and possibly single-block physical reads as well, if these blocks are not cached in buffer cache). This means that your query ends up waiting most of its time for random single-block reads as opposed to high performance Smart Scanning. Following is the response time profile from a test session hitting many chained rows and spending 86 percent of the response time on *cell single block physical reads* waits. Thankfully, there is a statistic *table fetch continued row* (which is useful also on non-Exadata databases), which counts how many times we had to follow a "next" row piece of a chained row. In the following case around 11320 row pieces had to be fetched using single block reads:

```
--------------------------------------------------------------------------------
 SID, USER , TYPE, STATISTIC                                     ,  HDELTA
--------------------------------------------------------------------------------
 698, TANEL, STAT, table fetch continued row                    , 11.32k
 698, TANEL, TIME, DB time                                      ,  3.96s
 698, TANEL, WAIT, cell smart table scan                        ,  5.82ms
 698, TANEL, WAIT, cell single block physical read              ,  3.93s


--------------------------------------------------------------------------
Active% | SQL_ID         | EVENT                          | WAIT_CLASS
--------------------------------------------------------------------------
    86% | axf3y5zg64vsu  | cell single block physical read | User I/O
    14% | axf3y5zg64vsu  | ON CPU                         | ON CPU
```

Now, this *chained rows processed by cell* statistic indicates that a chained row was hit by Smart Scan *and* was processed within the cell (exactly the opposite of what we just said). This statistic gets incremented in a special case of *intra-block chaining*, in which the next row piece is stored in the same block as the current (head) row piece of a chained row. Intra-block chaining is used for storing rows with more than 255 columns. In such cases the storage cell notices that it just has to fetch the rest of the row from the same block, which it already has opened and can process this chained row without resorting to database block I/O.

> ▨ **Note:** This chained row performance problem applies only to regular data blocks and those compressed with regular block-level compression (LOAD or OLTP). Luckily, it is not a problem for EHCC-compressed tables at all, as in EHCC the rows and columns are physically organized differently. Also, this issue does not apply to migrated rows (where the entire row has moved to another block due to an update, leaving only a stub head piece behind) when full-scanning through a segment. The full scan/Smart Scan just ignores the head pieces of migrated rows, as the entire row is physically elsewhere. Note that updates cause other efficiency issues for HCC-compressed tables, even if chained rows are not a problem.

Another interesting case of row chaining peculiarities is when you have over 255 columns in a table. Even when the total row size is small enough to fit inside a single block, with over 255 columns, Oracle would still do *intra-block chaining*, in which the row is chained but all the row pieces are physically inside the same block. This was needed because Oracle wanted to maintain backward compatibility when they increased the column limit from 255 to 1000 in Oracle 8.0. The "column count" byte in a row piece is just one byte, allowing 255 columns per row piece, but thanks to chaining you can have more columns in next row piece(s). This, however, caused initially some performance problems for Exadata Smart Scans, where even intra-block row chaining resulted in a lot of single block reads. However this bug (#9291589) was fixed in Oracle 11.2 Exadata Patch Bundle 4 (BP4) and you shouldn't see it anymore. It was quite an interesting problem to troubleshoot; if you are interested in seeing more details, including the troubleshooting sequence, you can read Tanel's "Troubleshooting Exadata Smart Scan" article about it:

http://blog.tanelpoder.com/oracle/exadata/troubleshooting/

chained rows rejected by cell

This statistic shows how many chained rows were not processed in the cell. We don't know yet the exact reason for *rejection* as opposed to skipping (as in the next statistic, *chained rows skipped by cell)*. During testing, most of the chained rows will cause the next statistic to be incremented. So far we assume that this rejection is just a special case of not processing the chained row in the cell and falling back to block I/O in database layer.

chained rows skipped by cell

This is one of the main statistics to look at when troubleshooting "forced" single-block read issues in Smart Scans caused by row chaining. Following is a more extended output from the previous test case:

```
--------------------------------------------------------------------------------
 SID, USER , TYPE, STATISTIC                                      , HDELTA
--------------------------------------------------------------------------------
 698, TANEL, STAT, consistent gets                               ,   23.02k
 698, TANEL, STAT, consistent gets from cache                    ,   11.29k
 698, TANEL, STAT, consistent gets from cache (fastpath)         ,    3.78k
 698, TANEL, STAT, consistent gets direct                        ,   11.73k
 698, TANEL, STAT, table fetch continued row                     ,   11.32k
 698, TANEL, STAT, cell blocks processed by cache layer          ,   12.91k
 698, TANEL, STAT, cell blocks processed by txn layer            ,   12.91k
 698, TANEL, STAT, cell blocks processed by data layer           ,   11.44k
 698, TANEL, STAT, chained rows skipped by cell                  ,    6.88k
 698, TANEL, STAT, chained rows rejected by cell                 ,       28
 698, TANEL, TIME, DB time                                       ,    3.96s
 698, TANEL, WAIT, cell smart table scan                         ,   5.82ms
 698, TANEL, WAIT, cell single block physical read               ,    3.93s
```

```
-----------------------------------------------------------------------------
Active% | SQL_ID         | EVENT                        | WAIT_CLASS
-----------------------------------------------------------------------------
   86%  | axf3y5zg64vsu  | cell single block physical read | User I/O
   14%  | axf3y5zg64vsu  | ON CPU                       | ON CPU
```

From these stats you can see how Oracle has skipped about 6880 chained rows in the cell (and has sent these blocks back to the database for regular processing). Another indicator is the *table fetch continued row* statistic, which is significantly higher than *chained rows skipped by cell*. This is because in the example, some of the rows were so big that they didn't even fit into two blocks, but spanned three blocks. Thus for some rows, two fetches of the "next" row pieces had to be done in the database. Also note how the *consistent gets* value, which counts all CR gets done both in the database *and* in cell by Smart Scan, is around 23000. At the same time, the subcounters, *consistent gets from cache* (CR gets done by the database layer, from buffer cache) and *consistent gets direct* (consistent gets done in cell in this case) indicate how much of the CR work was done at the cell level and how much was additionally done at the database level.

As a conclusion about chained rows, the next time you see that your Smart Scan is waiting for lots of *cell single block physical reads* and is doing logical I/O inside the database layer (*consistent gets from cache*), one of the things to check is the abovementioned statistics to see whether you are hitting chained rows and have to process them in the database. Of course, don't forget that the Smart Scans offload only the large segment scan workload, but if your query plan contains other row sources, index range scans or small, cached table scans, then seeing logical I/Os and single-block physical reads is expected. Luckily you can use wait interface data in ASH, V$SESSION or SQL Trace to see against which objects these single block reads accessed. The current_obj# column in ASH and obj# field in raw SQL trace file refer to the object_id of the table (or index or partition) the session is reading from.

physical read requests optimized

This statistic shows how many I/O requests to disk were avoided either by reading the data from flash cache instead of disks or thanks to the storage index I/O elimination. This statistic is also propagated to VSQL/VSQLSTATS and V$SEGMENT_STATISTICS views.

physical read total bytes optimized

This statistic shows how many bytes worth of physical disk drive I/O was avoided either by reading it from flash cache or thanks to storage index I/O elimination. When you also see the statistic *cell physical I/O bytes saved by storage index* equally increase, this means that I/O was completely avoided thanks to storage indexes. If the storage index savings are smaller than the total optimized bytes, then the rest of the I/O was optimized thanks to reading it from flash cache, instead of the good old spinning disks (but I/O to flash cards did still happen internally). Interestingly, this statistic is not propagated to VSQL/VSQLSTATS and V$SEGMENT_STATISTICS views (at least as of Oracle 11.2.0.2).

■ **Kevin Says:** "I've never really agreed with this particular counter. While it is true that a read from Exadata Smart Flash cache is optimized, when compared to a read from a hard disk, it is in no way as optimized as an I/O that didn't happen. In my mind, the savings tracked by this statistic are just too dissimilar to be all that helpful."

---

table fetch continued row

This statistic is not Exadata-specific but is relevant when troubleshooting unexpected single-block reads done by the database, while a Smart Scan is used. This statistic counts how many times Oracle had to fetch a next row piece of a chained row (using a regular single block read).

table scans (direct read)

This statistic is not Exadata-specific; it is seen in any Oracle database that is doing full table scans on table segments using direct path reads. During serial execution, this statistic is incremented in the beginning of the table scan, but with parallel execution, it is incremented each time a slave starts scanning a new rowid range distributed to it. Direct path reads are a prerequisite for Smart Scans to happen, so if you don't get your query to use Smart Scans, check whether a direct path read is used for scanning the table.

table scans (long tables)

This is a similar statistic to the previous one, but it shows whether the table scanned was considered to be large or not. Actually, Oracle considers this separately for each segment. So some partitions of a table may be considered small, some large. If the segment (up to the high water mark) is bigger than 10 percent of the buffer cache, the table is considered large and direct path reads are considered even for serial scans. (But note that this decision logic takes other things into account, like how many blocks of that segment already happen do be in buffer cache.) The 10 percent of the buffer cache rule actually comes from the _small_table_threshold parameter. This parameter defaults to 2 percent of buffer cache size (in blocks), but Oracle uses 5 × _small_table_threshold as its direct-path-scan decision threshold.

Understanding SQL Statement Performance

This section focuses on the SQL statement's performance metrics and understanding where a statement is spending its time and where its bottlenecks are. We will look at the metrics available and when to use them, but we will cover the various SQL performance monitoring tools in the next chapter.

Exadata-specific performance statistics of individual SQL statements may be monitored using the following views:

- V$SQL and V$SQLAREA

- V$SQLSTATS and V$SQLSTATS_PLAN_HASH

- V$SQL_MONITOR and V$SQL_PLAN_MONITOR

- V$ACTIVE_SESSION_HISTORY and the DBA_HIST_ACTIVE_SESS_HISTORY persisted into AWR repository

Note that all the Exadata-specific metrics you see in V$SQL* views are really the same ones you can see from V$SESSTAT views. They come from the same sources but are just accumulated differently. V$SESSTAT accumulates stats for a session, regardless of which SQL statement or command incremented them, while the views with a V$SQL prefix aggregate stats for different SQL statements, regardless of the sessions executing them. So, it is possible to see some Exadata metrics aggregated by a SQL statement.

Here is an example of the V$SQL* view's columns (there are many more columns in V$SQL views, but we'll show those most relevant to our topic at hand):

```
SQL> DESC v$sql

 Name                              Null?    Type
 --------------------------------- -------- ---------------------------
 SQL_TEXT                                   VARCHAR2(1000)
 SQL_ID                                     VARCHAR2(13)
 EXECUTIONS                                 NUMBER
 PLAN_HASH_VALUE                            NUMBER
 CHILD_NUMBER                               NUMBER
 CPU_TIME                                   NUMBER
 ELAPSED_TIME                               NUMBER
 ...
 IO_CELL_OFFLOAD_ELIGIBLE_BYTES             NUMBER
 IO_INTERCONNECT_BYTES                      NUMBER
 PHYSICAL_READ_REQUESTS                     NUMBER
 PHYSICAL_READ_BYTES                        NUMBER
 OPTIMIZED_PHY_READ_REQUESTS                NUMBER
 IO_CELL_UNCOMPRESSED_BYTES                 NUMBER
 IO_CELL_OFFLOAD_RETURNED_BYTES             NUMBER
```

The bold columns are specific to Exadata (although non-Exadata databases also have these columns, thanks to the single database software used both for Exadata and non-Exadata databases).

Table 11.1. V$SQL *Columns and Their Meanings*

Column Name	Metric Meaning
IO_CELL_OFFLOAD_ELIGIBLE_BYTES	How many bytes worth of segment reads were offloaded to the cells. The cells either did read this data or skipped it if storage indexes helped to skip block ranges. This metric corresponds to the *cell physical IO bytes eligible for predicate offload* statistic in V$SESSTAT.
IO_INTERCONNECT_BYTES	The total traffic bytes (read and write) sent between the database node and cells. Note that thanks to the bug 10036425 mentioned earlier, the IO_INTERCONNECT_BYTES column is populated also on non-Exadata platforms, but you can ignore it on these systems.
OPTIMIZED_PHY_READ_REQUESTS	The number of disk IO requests that were either completely avoided thanks to storage indexes or done against cell flash cache cards.
IO_CELL_UNCOMPRESSED_BYTES	The size of uncompressed data the cells have scanned through during a Smart Scan. Note that the cells do not have to actually uncompress all the data to know the uncompressed length. The EHCC compression unit headers store both the compressed and uncompressed CU length info in them. This metric is useful for estimating the I/O reduction from EHCC compression. Note that this metric works for EHCC segments only. For regular block-level compression, this metric just shows the compressed size of data.
IO_CELL_OFFLOAD_RETURNED_BYTES	This metric shows how much data was returned as a result from an offloaded Smart Scan access path. This is a main indicator of smart scan offloading efficiency when compared with IO_CELL_OFFLOAD_ELIGIBLE_BYTES (to measure the IO reduction between cells and database) or IO_CELL_UNCOMPRESSED_BYTES when measuring the total IO reduction thanks to offloading and compression.

Here is example output from a query on an EHCC-compressed table where the table scan was offloaded to the cell. The V$SQL table output is pivoted for better readability:

```
SQL> SELECT SUM(object_id) FROM t4_hcc_query_high WHERE owner LIKE 'S%';

SUM(OBJECT_ID)
--------------
    3.9741E+12


SQL> SELECT * FROM v$sql WHERE sql_id = 'Orv137mgwpnkx';
```

(output pivoted and edited for better readability)

```
IO_CELL_OFFLOAD_ELIGIBLE_BYTES: 6188924928
IO_INTERCONNECT_BYTES         : 720233312
PHYSICAL_READ_REQUESTS        : 6547
PHYSICAL_READ_BYTES           : 6188982272
PHYSICAL_WRITE_REQUESTS       : 0
PHYSICAL_WRITE_BYTES          : 0
OPTIMIZED_PHY_READ_REQUESTS   : 7
LOCKED_TOTAL                  : 1
PINNED_TOTAL                  : 2
IO_CELL_UNCOMPRESSED_BYTES    : 112741585171
IO_CELL_OFFLOAD_RETURNED_BYTES: 720175968
```

In this case the IO_CELL_OFFLOAD_RETURNED bytes is much smaller than the IO_CELL_OFFLOAD_ELIGIBLE bytes; thus, the Smart Scan definitely did help to reduce the data flow between the cells and the database. Furthermore, the IO_CELL_UNCOMPRESSED_BYTES is way bigger than the PHYSICAL_READ_BYTES, which indicates that the EHCC helped to reduce the number of bytes that had to be read from disk by the cells, thanks to compression. Note that the IO_INTERCONNECT_BYTES is not much greater than the IO_CELL_OFFLOAD_RETURNED_BYTES, which indicates that for this SQL, almost all the traffic was due to the data returned by Smart Scans. There was no extra traffic due to other reasons like Temp table space reads/writes thanks to non-optimal sorts, and there were no hash joins or other work-area operations or database block I/Os, thanks to chained rows or in-database consistent read processing.

■ **Note:** Smart Scanning makes data *retrieval* from segments faster, but it doesn't do anything to speed up joining, sorting, and aggregate operations, which are applied after the data has been retrieved from the segments. A notable exception is the Bloom filter pushdown to cells, which allows the cells to filter the data from the probe table using a hash bitmap built based on the driving row source's data in the hash join.

While this example used the V$SQL view, which shows SQL child cursor level statistics, you could also use V$SQL_PLAN_MONITOR (the columns PLAN_LINE_ID, PLAN_OPERATION, and so on) to measure these metrics for each execution plan line. This is useful because a single execution plan usually accesses and joins multiple tables, and different tables may benefit from the Smart Scan offloading differently. We will look at some scripts and tools that use this data in the next chapter.

Summary

The emphasis of this chapter was on understanding Exadata performance and the various related metrics Oracle offers for us. It is important to remember that the Exadata Smart Scan potentially makes your data retrieval scanning faster, but Smart Scans happen only when direct path reads and full segment scans are used. Also, remember that it is not possible to determine whether a Smart Scan actually kicked in just by looking at the execution plan alone. You should always check additional metrics, like whether you see the *cell smart table/index scan* wait events in your session and whether the *IO_CELL_OFFLOAD_ELIGIBLE_BYTES* (in V$SQL) or *cell physical I/O bytes eligible for predicate offload* statistic (in V$SESSTAT) increases while you run your SQL. Many of the other metrics explained here will hopefully be helpful for understanding and troubleshooting advanced performance issues, such as when a Smart Scan kicks in but is throttled by a multitude of special conditions like chained rows, consistent read rollbacks, or just running out of cell server resources. In the next chapter we will see how to use this knowledge in monitoring and troubleshooting Exadata performance, and we will look deeper into the cell-level performance metrics from cellsrv and the operating system, too.

CHAPTER 12

Monitoring Exadata Performance

By now you have learned about the key Exadata performance features and the related performance metrics. Let's see how we can use these for everyday tasks. We will look at standard tools available for database-layer and cell performance monitoring, and how to interpret their output.

Oracle Database and the Exadata cells provide a huge variety of different metrics, but before monitoring any metrics, you should ask yourself why you are monitoring them. Additionally, you should know what your action would be if a metric crosses some threshold. This leads to the follow-up question: which exact threshold should prompt some action from you—and why? In other words, you should know what are you trying to achieve (good response times for users) and how performance metrics relate to that.

The monitoring tasks covered here can be divided into the following categories:

- SQL statement response time monitoring

- Database layer utilization and efficiency monitoring

- Storage cell layer utilization and efficiency monitoring

- Advanced metrics and monitoring for Exadata performance troubleshooting

Note that we will focus on the Exadata-specific performance topics here and not the whole wide range of other Oracle performance topics, like lock contention or general SQL performance issues.

A Systematic Approach

Whatever metrics you monitor, you should have a purpose in mind. In other words, don't collect and display metrics just because they are available; this will lead you nowhere or potentially even mislead you to fixing the wrong problem. Note that the term "performance" is vague—different people may mean different things when they use it. From an IT system user's perspective, performance is ultimately only about one thing— response time. And not some response times of individual wait events measured at a low level; the end users don't care about that. They do care about how much *they* have to wait for their *business task* to complete, like the time it takes from the report submission to actually seeing its output. This time is measured in regular wall-clock time; it's as simple as that.

If your purpose in monitoring is to ensure good response times for your application users, then you should measure what matters—response time as your end-user experiences it. This would be the ideal entry point to performance monitoring. In addition to this entry point, you should measure more detailed lower-level metrics to break the end user response time down into individual components, like time spent in an application server and database time. Your application instrumentation and monitoring tools should keep track of which database sessions were used for which end-user task, so you can report what these exact database sessions were doing when a user experienced unacceptable response times.

■ **Note:** We deliberately said *unacceptable response times* here instead of just "user experienced performance problems." Whenever anyone complains about a performance problem, you should clarify what they actually mean by that and how it was measured. Does any user actually experience far too long response times in their application, or did some monitoring system merely raise an alarm about "too high" CPU utilization or any other secondary metric like that? Your subsequent actions would depend on the problem you're trying to solve. Ideally, you should not use a performance tool or Oracle metric for determining *whether* you have a performance problem. Your starting point should be the users (who report a problem) or application-level metrics, which see the database response time from the application perspective. No matter how good the database metrics look, if the application waits for the report completion for ages, you have a performance problem to drill down into. Conversely, no matter how "bad" your database metrics seem to be, if your application response times are satisfactory, you don't have an acute need to start fixing anything.

When examining performance metrics because of an ongoing problem (of too long response times), you should start by identifying the sessions servicing this slow application or job and then drilling down into that response time. It would be more correct to call this performance troubleshooting, not just monitoring.

Note that there are other kinds of performance monitoring tasks, which you may want to do—for example, proactive utilization and efficiency monitoring. Performing these tasks allows you to keep an eye on the utilization headroom left in the servers and detect any anomalies and sudden spikes in system utilization and low-level response times, possibly even before users notice a response time difference. Yet another reason for collecting and monitoring performance and utilization data is for capacity planning—but capacity planning is outside the scope of this book. Also, because this is a database book, we won't dive into any end-to-end performance measurement topics, which would involve identifying time spent in application servers, on the network, and so on.

We will start by looking at how to identify where a long-running query is spending most of its time. We'll also look at how to tell whether a query is taking full advantage of Exadata's performance features.

Monitoring SQL Statement Response Time

The best tool for monitoring long-running queries is Oracle 11g's SQL Real Time monitoring page. It is able to gather all the key performance information onto a single page, even in the case of parallel execution across multiple RAC instances.

The SQL Monitoring feature requires you to have a Diagnostics and Tuning Pack license. SQL Monitoring kicks in automatically if you run your query with parallel execution or when a serial query consumes more than 5 seconds of I/O and CPU time in total. Additionally, you can control the monitoring feature with MONITOR and NO_MONITOR hints. If you want to monitor your frequently executed short-running queries, the best tool for this would be to use ASH data and list the top wait events and top rowsources from there (using the SQL_PLAN_LINE columns in the V$ACTIVE_SESSION_HISTORY view).

If you are already aware of a performance problem (perhaps your users are already complaining of too long response times), then you should use a top-down approach for monitoring. You should identify the session(s) of the problematic users' applications or reports and drill down into what these sessions are doing with ASH (which gives you the SQL_IDs of the top SQL statements for these sessions) and when needed, then drill down further into the top statements with SQL Monitoring reports.

Monitoring SQL Statements with Real-Time SQL Monitoring Reports

When you click the SQL Monitoring link in the Enterprise Manager performance page, you will see the latest monitored queries. The SQL Monitoring reports are present in Grid Control 11g R1 or 10g R5 (10.2.0.5). If you are not using Grid Control, then you can either use the built-in Enterprise Manager Database Console or run the SQL Monitoring reports manually from SQL*Plus as explained shortly. Note that the SQL Monitoring feature requires Diagnostics and Tuning Pack licenses.

Figure 12-1 shows the entry page to the SQL Monitoring reports. You can get there by clicking the SQL Monitoring link at the bottom of the Performance page in Grid Control. The SQL Monitoring page, as seen in Figure 12-1, lists the currently running, queued, and recently completed monitored SQL executions, with some key performance metrics and details, such as the degree of parallelism.

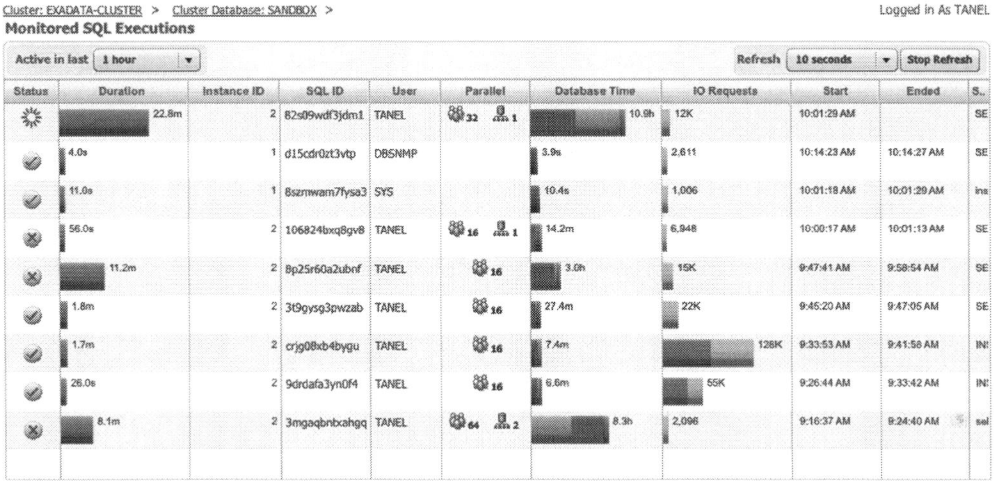

Figure 12-1. Enterprise Manager's overview of Monitored SQL Executions

The Status column shows an icon with one of four statuses—running, done, error, or queued. When you click the status icon, you will be taken to the SQL statement's detailed monitoring page. One of the most important pieces of information is the *Duration* column, showing how long a statement has been active. The duration is the wall-clock time from the start of the statement execution through the finish, or to the current time in the event the statement is still executing. Figure 12-2 illustrates the difference between duration (wall-clock) and CPU time in statement execution.

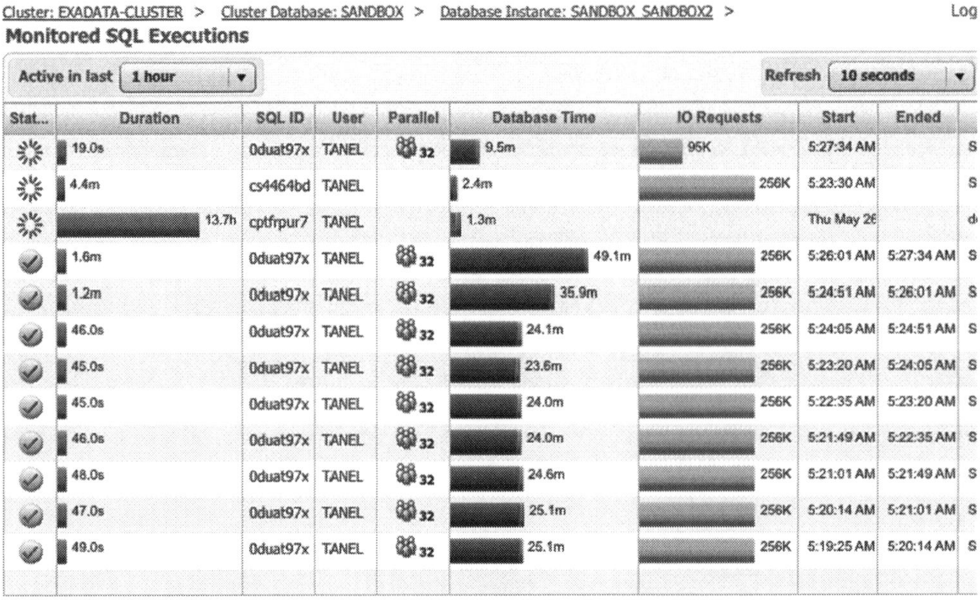

Figure 12-2. Statement Duration compared to Database Time in the SQL Monitoring page

The Duration column shows what users care about, which is the response time of a query since the SQL execution start. This is the time *they* have had to wait for the SQL to complete. Of course, the end users may have had to wait for much longer than the duration of the query, as the page in Figure 12-2 shows only the database response time. Time may have also been spent in the application layer or the network connection in between the user and the application server.

It is important to know that the duration measures time from SQL execution start all the way until the cursor is closed or cancelled (for example, when all data is fetched from it). This means that if your database can process the query in 30 seconds, but then millions of rows are fetched a few at a time, your query will take a long time as far as the application is concerned (thanks to the network ping-pong), but in fact only a little time is spent processing within the database. The Duration column still shows long query "runtime," as the cursor is still kept open for fetching of the data. Remember, the duration measures time from when the cursor is executed all the way to when it is finally closed after all the fetches are done or the application has fetched enough.

This leads us to the next important metric—Database Time, seen in the sixth column in Figure 12-2. The Database Time metric shows the total time your query spent executing *in the database*. So, if you run a serial DML that runs for 60 seconds and spends all of the time executing *inside* the database, you will end up seeing 60 seconds of database time, too. However, if you are running some SELECT statement and are fetching a lot of rows, causing your session to spend (let's say) 50% of its time executing in the database and another 50% waiting for the next fetch command (once it has sent an array of rows back to the application), you would see only half of that total 60-second duration as database time. In other words, you would see 30 seconds of database time, as the database session has been servicing your request only for 30 seconds and the rest of the time it was idle.

Looking at the second entry in Figure 12-2, you see that the *duration* of the query (the time from when the execution phase started) is 4.4 minutes, the query has executed in serial (the fifth column shows that), and it has consumed only 2.4 minutes of *database time*. So this indicates that the executing session has been doing something else for 2 minutes. It was either idle (probably waiting for the next fetch request) or executing some other statement (while the first statement's cursor was still open).

The example we just discussed was about a single serial query. When you run a parallel query, you have multiple sessions executing pieces of the same query for you. Then the database time might end up being much higher than the duration (response time) of your query. If you look at the first entry in Figure 12-2, you see a statement with duration of 19 seconds, but the total time spent in the database is 9.5 minutes. When you look at the *parallel* column, you see that the session was executed with parallel degree 32, which means that you had multiple sessions actively working in the database for your query. All of these parallel sessions' database time plus the query coordinator's time is added into the Database Time column. This database time gives an idea of how much work was done in the database. But because the statement was parallelized, you don't have to wait for that long. If you ran that same query in serial mode, then the database time would be in the ballpark of how much time you might have to wait. (Please take that last statement with a grain of salt, as in practice many other things may happen in SQL execution when switching from parallel execution to serial, so you might have some pleasant or unpleasant surprises in the response time).

Note that these entries in the SQL Monitoring overview page are not SQL *statement*-specific, but SQL statement *execution*-specific. So, if two user sessions were running the same statement, you would see two separate entries in this list. This allows you to examine exactly what the problem is with a specific user (who is complaining) as opposed to looking at statement-level aggregate metrics (like those V$SQL provides) and trying to figure out *your* user's problem from there.

Real-Time Monitoring of Single Long-Running Query

Once you have identified your query of interest from the list of all long-running queries, you can click on its "running" icon in the left side of the list and you will be taken to the Monitored SQL Execution Details page shown in Figure 12-3. This page has a number of sub-tabs, so feel free to explore and see all the information that's available there.

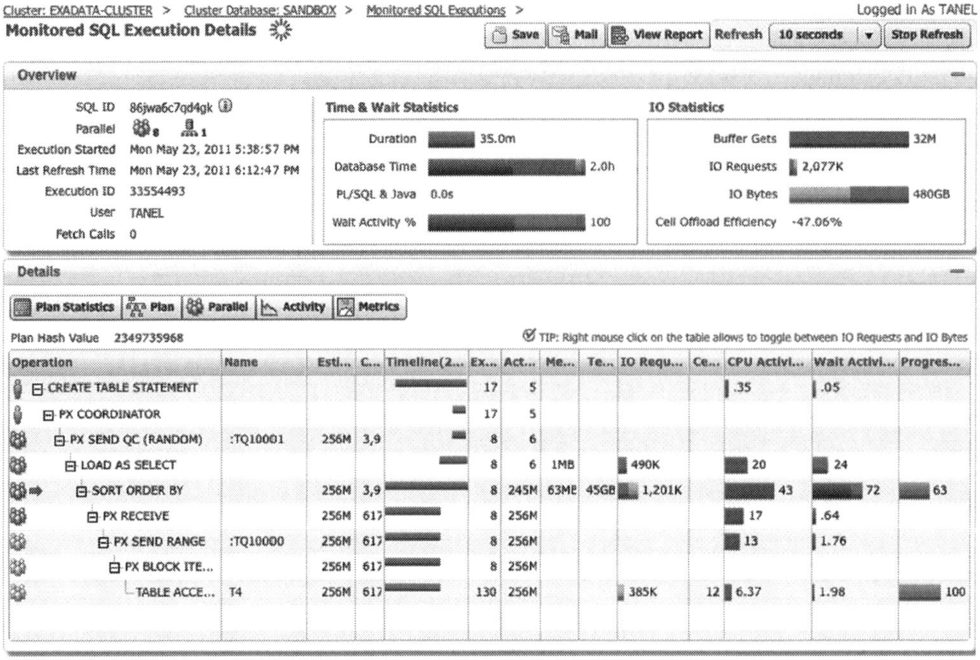

Figure 12-3. Monitored SQL statement execution details

The Monitored SQL Execution Details page has a lot of information in it. This page is pretty self-explanatory if you have read SQL execution plans before, so we won't go through every single detail here, but will focus on the most important metrics. Compared to old-fashioned DBMS_XPLAN output, the SQL Monitoring page is very interactive, so make sure that you hover your mouse over and click on almost everything on the screen, to see the full array of functionality available to you.

Let's start from the top section on the page. At the top of the screen, right after the Monitored SQL Execution Details header, you see a little icon, which shows the status of the selected SQL statement's execution. The little circle will mean that the statement is still being executed (the cursor has not been closed nor cancelled).

The Overview section, illustrated in Figure 12-4, will show some basic details, like which SQL ID is being executed, by whom, and so on. You can see the SQL text when you click on the little *(i)* icon next to the SQL ID. You will see the SQL statement text and, beginning with version 11.2.0.2, you will also see the bind variable values used for the execution. Figure 12-5 shows the display that you get by clicking that *(i)* icon.

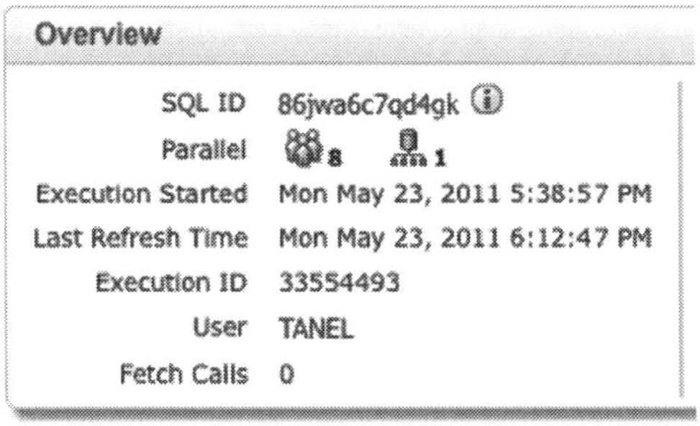

Figure 12-4. SQL Monitoring overivew section

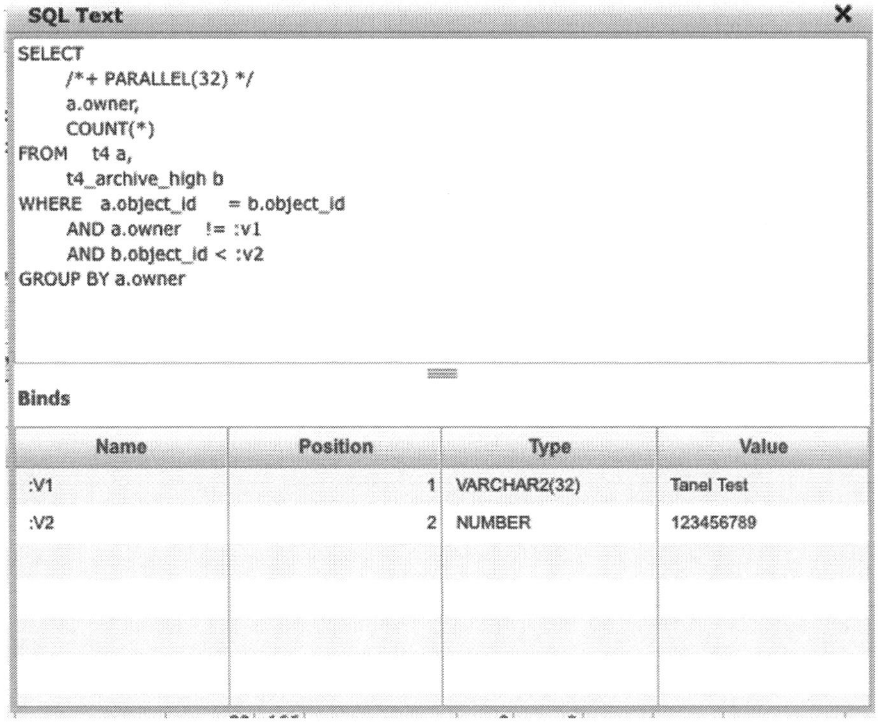

Figure 12-5. Bind variable values in the SQL Monitoring detail page

Of course, whether you should use bind variables for your long-running reports and DW queries is an entirely separate question. You shouldn't use binds for long-running queries in your DW; you'd want to sacrifice some response time for hard-parsing a new query plan for each combination of literal values and possibly get an optimal plan for each variable set. Nevertheless, monitoring bind variable values of an already running query is easy with Oracle 11.2.0.2 and later, because you no longer must resort to the ORADEBUG ERRORSTACK command.

The Time & Wait Statistics section in Figure 12-6 shows the familiar metrics of Duration and Database Time of a statement. Move your mouse over the different database time components to see how much time was spent waiting inside the database compared to running on CPU. The Wait Activity % bar shows the breakdown of wait events. Note that the 100% in this bar means 100% of the *wait time* component of database time, not of the entire database time (which also includes CPU time).

Time & Wait Statistics

Duration		35.2m
Database Time		2.0h
PL/SQL & Java	0.0s	
Wait Activity %		100

Figure 12-6. Time and Wait Statistics in the SQL Monitoring detail page

The IO Statistics section in Figure 12-7a shows some key I/O statistics for statement execution.

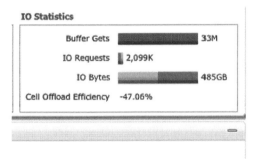

IO Statistics

Buffer Gets		33M
IO Requests	2,099K	
IO Bytes		485GB
Cell Offload Efficiency	-47.06%	

Figure 12-7a. I/O Statistics in the SQL Monitoring detail page

The Buffer Gets bar shows the total number of logical I/Os done in both the database layer and the cells (if Smart Scan kicked in). The IO Requests and IO Bytes statistics are self-explanatory, but note that those metrics show all I/O done for the given statement, which includes the Smart Scan I/O, any regular block I/O, and also TEMP tablespace I/O (done for sorting, hash joins, and for any other work area operations that didn't fit into allowed PGA memory). Now you should begin to understand why the Cell Offload Efficiency is negative for the statement execution in the figure. This metric should ideally show the percentage of disk-to-database-host interconnect traffic that was avoided thanks to the Smart Scans performing filtering and projection early in the cells and returning only a subset of data. However, in a complex execution plan there is much more going on than just a Smart Scan against a single table. You have joins, aggregate operations, sorting, and direct path data loads, which all use extra I/O bandwidth, driving the offload efficiency percentage down. This is a good example of why focusing on only a single ratio is not a good idea. The single percentage value for offload efficiency hides a lot of information, such as where the percentage taken was from and the *real* values behind it. You can move your mouse over the percentage and see the underlying values used for the calculation.

So when moving your mouse over the ratio (see Figure 12-7b), you'll see that the cells did read 486GB from disks, but much more data (715GB) was actually sent back and forth over the interconnect. The metric explanations in Figure 12-7b are actually incorrect. The Bytes Read From Disks actually means total bytes of reads *and* writes that Oracle Database has issued, not just for Smart Scans, but for any reason. And the Bytes Returned From Exadata actually means the total interconnect traffic between the database and the cells, caused by any reason, such as block reads and writes and arrays of returned rows by Smart Scans.

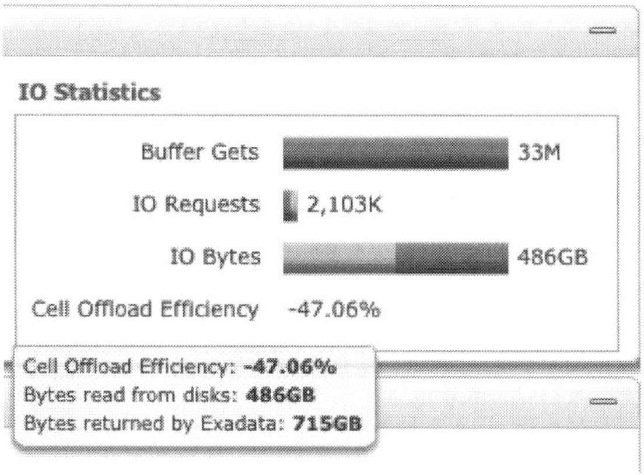

IO Statistics

Buffer Gets		33M
IO Requests		2,103K
IO Bytes		486GB
Cell Offload Efficiency	-47.06%	

Cell Offload Efficiency: **-47.06%**
Bytes read from disks: **486GB**
Bytes returned by Exadata: **715GB**

Figure 12-7b. Cell Offload Efficiency ratio in the SQL Monitoring detail page

If you are wondering why the I/O interconnect bytes is 715GB when the actual database-issued I/O is only 486GB, the explanation is in how these metrics are measured. The database I/O metric (the Bytes Read From Disk in Figure 12-6) is measured by the database layer, while the I/O interconnect bytes is measured by the low-level interconnect/Oracle networking layer. And one of the layers in between is the ASM layer, which manages the software mirroring, among other things. So the interconnect I/O traffic in this case is higher than the database traffic thanks to the write operations done by the SQL statement, which had to be mirrored by the ASM layer. So every MB written by database (whether because of direct path load or some work area operation spilling to temporary tablespace) resulted in the writing of 2MB of data thanks to ASM normal redundancy mirroring.

There are other reasons why the interconnect traffic may be higher than the actual amount of data read. One example is HCC compressed tables. If you have compressed your 10GB partition down to 1GB, then you will have to do 1GB worth of I/O to read it. But now if the Smart Scan uncompresses this data in the cells on the fly and returns all that 10GB of *uncompressed* data back over the interconnect (assuming no projection or filtration in the cell was done), the I/O interconnect bytes will be much higher than the amount of data read from disks. This would drive the Cell Offload Efficiency down to 10% for this example Smart Scan. All this is yet another reason why you shouldn't focus solely on improving just the Cell Offload Efficiency ratio, but should rather look into where response time is spent instead. Time is what end users care about.

Execution Plan Rowsource Details

Now that you have checked the key metrics of your statement execution— duration, database time, parallelism used and how much of the database time is spent running on CPU vs. waiting— it's time to drill down into the details of the execution plan at the row-source level. These are shown in Figure 12-8.

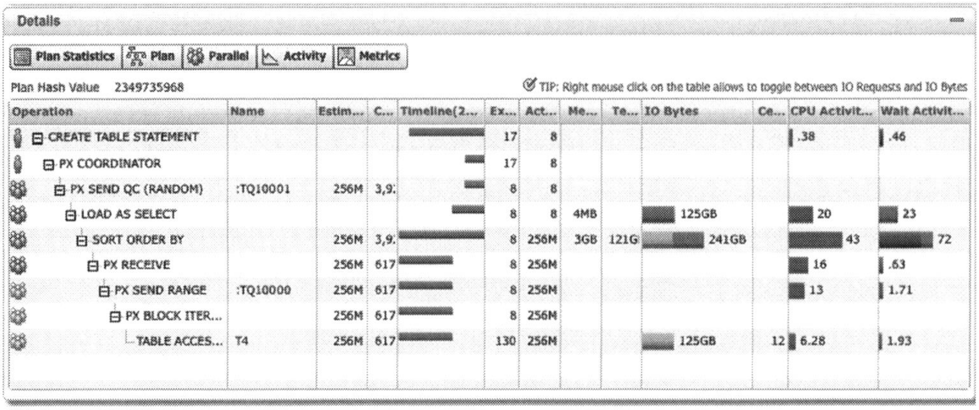

Figure 12-8. Execution plan rowsource activity monitoring in the SQL Monitoring detail page

Let's focus on the right-hand columns of the execution plan output first. The CPU Activity column shows a breakdown of total CPU usage by the statement so far. The longest bar at the SORT ORDER BY line in the execution plan shows that this rowsource consumed 43% of total CPU usage of that statement execution so far. Note that this is 43% of total CPU consumption, not of total duration or database time of the statement execution. You should examine the Time and Wait Statistics section (shown earlier, in Figure 12-4) to see how much of the total database time was consumed by CPU usage and how much by waits.

The Wait Activity column shows a breakdown of which wait events this statement execution waited for. Again, the SORT ORDER BY rowsource has experienced the most waits, 72% of total wait time of that statement execution. Note that this bar consists of two different color bars. If you move your mouse pointer over these bars, you'll see the names of these wait events. In this case these waits were *direct path read temp* and *direct path write temp* events, which you see with multi-pass work area operations such as sorts and hash joins. This column also shows percentages of *total wait time* of this statement execution, not the percentage of total runtime duration, nor total database time.

The IO Bytes column shows how many I/O operations or bytes were read or written by a rowsource. You can right-click on the chart to toggle the display of bytes or I/O operations. In Figure 12-8 you see that the SORT ORDER BY rowsource has done a total of 241GB worth of I/O. When you move your mouse over the different color bars, you'll see the details about how much was written and how much was read (roughly 50/50, as the chart seems to show). The execution plan step LOAD AS SELECT above it has written about 125GB of data to disk. Note that this 125GB of data is measured at the Oracle database level, but the lower-level ASM layer will likely mirror (or triple-mirror, depending on your configuration) these writes, so actually twice as many bytes were written physically to disks. You can check the Cell Physical IO Interconnect Bytes session statistic to see how much data was really sent (and received) over the InfiniBand network; this metric is aware of the ASM mirror write overhead and any other low-level traffic too.

Let's look at a few more columns of the Real Time SQL Monitoring page. The Timeline column you see in Figure 12-9 is one of the most important columns for understanding where the SQL statement spends its time.

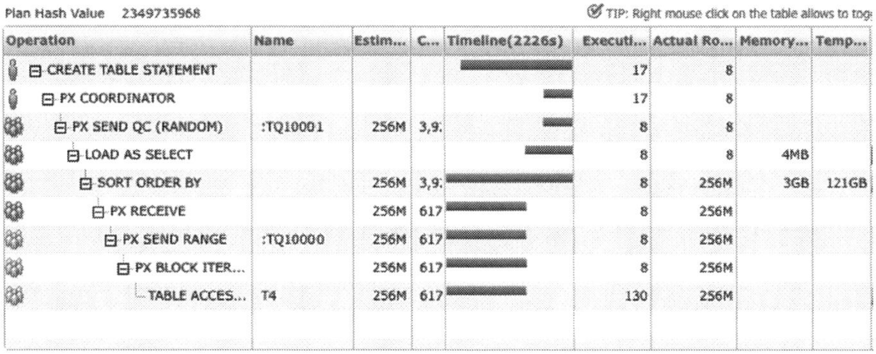

Plan Hash Value	2349735968							
Operation	Name	Estim...	C...	Timeline(2226s)	Executi...	Actual Ro...	Memory...	Temp...
⊟ CREATE TABLE STATEMENT				▬▬▬▬▬▬	17	8		
⊟ PX COORDINATOR				▬	17	8		
⊟ PX SEND QC (RANDOM)	:TQ10001	256M	3,9:	▬	8	8		
⊟ LOAD AS SELECT				▬▬	8	8	4MB	
⊟ SORT ORDER BY		256M	3,9:	▬▬▬▬▬▬▬▬	8	256M	3GB	121GB
⊟ PX RECEIVE		256M	617	▬▬▬▬▬▬	8	256M		
⊟ PX SEND RANGE	:TQ10000	256M	617	▬▬▬▬▬▬	8	256M		
⊟ PX BLOCK ITER...		256M	617	▬▬▬▬▬▬	8	256M		
TABLE ACCES...	T4	256M	617	▬▬▬▬▬▬	130	256M		

TIP: Right mouse click on the table allows to tog...

Figure 12-9. Row-source activity timeline in the SQL Monitoring detail page

The Timeline column in the figure shows a visual timeline of individual execution plan rowsources' activity. It is based on ASH samples; ASH collects SQL execution plan line-level details starting from Oracle 11gR1. Look into the brackets in the Timeline column header. This should show you the total runtime duration of this SQL execution, 2226 seconds in this case (around 37 minutes). So the total width of the timeline column means about 37 minutes of wall-clock runtime. Now it's easy to visually interpret the length and position of these bars in each rowsource in the execution plan. When you look at the TABLE ACCESS (FULL) T4 rowsource at the bottom of the plan, you see that this table scan was active from the beginning of the execution and continued up to around two-thirds of the total Timeline (to around 1400 seconds) and then it completed. So it looks like this table scan was active during most of the execution time.

Oracle execution plans are trees of rowsource functions with strict hierarchy enforced, so a child rowsource can pass its results only to its direct parent. In our case, the TABLE ACCESS FULL against T4 fetched some rows and passed them back to its parent operation, PX BLOCK ITERATOR, which then sent the rows back to the PX SEND RANGE operator, which knows how to send results to other slaves via the PX Table Queue buffers in the SGA. Another set of slaves received these rows using the PX RECEIVE rowsource and passed these rows to their parent, the SORT ORDER BY rowsource, which performed the sorting of these rows. Then the SORT ORDER BY rowsource just repeated its loop and asked for more rows from its child operator PX RECEIVE, which then read (consumed) the table queue buffers for more rows put there by the first set of slaves (producers). We are not going deeper into SQL execution engine internals here, but hopefully this example has illustrated the hierarchical nature of the SQL execution and how the data "flows" upward through the execution plan tree toward the root of the tree (CREATE TABLE STATEMENT in this case).

When you look at the timeline bars, you see that all the bars starting from PX RECEIVE and below it started roughly at the same time and ended roughly at the same time, too. We say roughly, because this data comes from ASH samples, sampled once per second only, so we don't have microsecond accuracy here. And we don't need it anyway, as our query runs for much longer than a second. But anyway, the timeline bars indicate that the table scanning part of the query, including these "data transportation" steps for that data (PX RECEIVE, PX SEND RANGE, and PX BLOCK ITERATOR) took around 66% of the total query response time. If we want to make our query faster, we should probably focus on that part. we should either scan less data, filter more (in cells hopefully), access less partitions or just increase the scanning throughput (by increasing parallelism in this case, because this TABLE ACCESS rowsource wasn't waiting too much for I/O, as shown in Figure 12-8, it's not I/O-bound yet and the database nodes had plenty of CPU resource left).

When you look at the upper rowsources (LOAD AS SELECT and higher), you see that they have only been reported active in the last third of the query response time, extending all the way to the end of execution. So, if we somehow made only this data loading part faster, we would only win up to 33% of the response time back, even if we could make the loading part infinitely fast. The table access and sorting would still take the majority of the response time. The timeline bars are very valuable for quickly understanding in which execution plan tree part (branch) most of the response time is spent.

The timeline bars are just the first thing to check. There are lots of other useful details in the SQL Monitoring report, too. For example, if you look at the SORT ORDER BY line in Figure 12-9, you see that the sort operation has been active throughout the whole execution of this statement. And if you know the basics of sorting, it should make sense—the sorting rowsource was active for the first two-thirds of the time because it was fetching data into sort buffers and sorting it (and spilling some data to temporary tablespace). After the sort itself was complete (the child rowsource returned an "end of data" condition), the sorting rowsource function had still had to be invoked. It is by invoking that function that the sort operation returns the sorted rows to its parent operation. This is why the parent rowsources became active only toward the end of the execution timeline—because *all* the rows had to be fetched and sorted first, before anything could have been returned for further processing. And once all the rows *were* fetched and sorted, there was no reason for the SORT ORDER BY rowsource to visit its child rowsources again. This is why the timeline bar for TABLE ACCESS ended at around two-thirds of the total execution duration timeline.

Manually Querying Real-Time SQL Monitoring Data

All the pretty charts in Grid Control are based on some V$ or DBA_ views internally, so if you don't happen to have access to Grid Control or Enterprise Manager Database Console (or it is just broken), you can get what you want from the V$ views directly. You probably don't have to access the V$ views for your everyday monitoring and tuning tasks, but nevertheless it's useful to know where this information comes from, as it may become handy for custom monitoring and advanced problem troubleshooting. Following are some key views to be aware of:

- The GV$SQL_MONITOR view contains the statement execution-level monitoring data. When multiple sessions are running the same statement, you will have multiple entries in this view. So, make sure that you query the right execution, by using the right search filters. For example, you should pay attention to which SID and INST_ID you are really looking for (or PX_QCSID, PX_QCINST_ID if monitoring a parallel query) and whether the STATUS column still shows EXECUTING if you are trying to troubleshoot a currently running query.

- The GV$SQL_PLAN_MONITOR view contains execution plan line-level metrics, monitored and updated in real time. For example you can query the IO_INTERCONNECT_BYTES and compare it to PHYSICAL_READ_BYTES and PHYSICAL_WRITE_BYTES to determine the offloading efficiency by each individual execution plan line, instead of the whole query efficiency. Note that increasing the offloading efficiency percentage should not be your primary goal of monitoring and tuning – where you spend your response *time*, matters.

- The GV$ACTIVE_SESSION_HISTORY view contains columns like SQL_PLAN_LINE_ID, SQL_PLAN_OPERATION and SQL_PLAN_OPTIONS starting from Oracle 11gR1. You can query these columns, in addition to SQL_ID, to find the top rowsources of an SQL execution plan, too, instead of just listing the top SQL statement.

Reporting Real-Time SQL Monitoring Data with DBMS_SQLTUNE

If you do not have access to Grid Control or Enterprise Manager Database Console for some reason, you can also extract the SQL monitoring details using the DBMS_SQLTUNE.REPORT_SQL_MONITOR package function. You can use the following syntax, but make sure you read the related documentation to see the full power of this feature. Note that the text below is edited, as this function generates very wide output, which wouldn't fit the book pages.

```
SQL> SELECT
        DBMS_SQLTUNE.REPORT_SQL_MONITOR(
            session_id=> &sid,
            report_level=>'ALL',
            type => 'TEXT') as report
    FROM dual
SQL> /
Enter value for sid: 543

REPORT
--------------------------------------------------------------------------
SQL Monitoring Report

SQL Text
------------------------------
SELECT /*+ parallel(32) */ COUNT(*) FROM T4 A

Global Information
------------------------------
 Status              :  EXECUTING
 Instance ID         :  2
 Session             :  TANEL (543:4641)
 SQL ID              :  0duat97xt417k
 SQL Execution ID    :  33555560
 Execution Started   :  05/27/2011 06:59:23
 First Refresh Time  :  05/27/2011 06:59:23
 Last Refresh Time   :  05/27/2011 06:59:59
 Duration            :  36s
 Module/Action       :  SQL*Plus/-
 Service             :  SANDBOX
 Program             :  sqlplus@mac01.lan (TNS V1-V3)
```

Global Stats

```
===============================================================================
| Elapsed | Queuing |   Cpu   |   IO     | Buffer | Read | Read  |  Cell    |
| Time(s) | Time(s) | Time(s) | Waits(s) |  Gets  | Reqs | Bytes | Offload  |
===============================================================================
|    1095 |    0.00 |      17 |     1079 |    11M | 170K |  83GB |  96.60%  |
===============================================================================
```

SQL Plan Monitoring Details (Plan Hash Value=3536567600)

```
===============================================================================
|Id |                Operation             | Name    | Read  | Cell    | Activity |
|   |                                      |         | Bytes | Offload |   (%)    |
===============================================================================
|    0|SELECT STATEMENT                    |         |       |         |          |
|    1|  SORT AGGREGATE                    |         |       |         |          |
|    2|   PX COORDINATOR                   |         |       |         |          |
|    3|    PX SEND QC (RANDOM)             |:TQ10000 |       |         |          |
|-> 4|     SORT AGGREGATE                 |         |       |         |   0.09   |
|-> 5|      PX BLOCK ITERATOR             |         |       |         |          |
|-> 6|       TABLE ACCESS STORAGE FULL    |T4       |  87GB | 96.60%  |  99.91   |
|    |                                    |         |       |         |          |
===============================================================================
```

DBMS_SQLTUNE.REPORT_SQL_MONITOR can also take HTML as a value for the TYPE parameter, instead of TEXT, in which case the output is generated as HTML. If you spool this output into an HTML file and open it in the browser, you will see much nicer output than just text. And starting with Oracle 11.2, you can also use ACTIVE as a parameter and spool that output into an HTML file. Now if you open this file in the browser, you will see the SQL Monitoring page almost exactly as it looks in the Grid Control! And all the data required for displaying that report is self-contained in the spooled HTML file —no database access needed when opening it! So this is very useful if you want to send a detailed self-contained report with some SQL execution problem to someone over the email.

Controlling SQL Monitoring

SQL Monitoring kicks in immediately for all statements executed with parallel execution, no matter how long they run. For serially executed statements, the SQL Monitoring does not kick in immediately, as it's not designed to monitor typical fast OLTP queries, which are executed many times per second. Nevertheless, if a serial query has consumed more than 5 seconds of total CPU and/or I/O wait time, it's considered as a long-running query and the SQL Monitoring is enabled for that statement execution. This happens seamlessly on-the-fly, and statement restart is not needed.

You can also use MONITOR and NO_MONITOR hints to control the SQL monitoring for a statement. V$SQL_HINT shows all the hints available for use and the version when they were introduced. For example:

```
SQL> SELECT name, inverse, version, class, sql_feature
  2  FROM v$sql_hint WHERE name LIKE '%MONITOR%';
```

```
NAME                  INVERSE               VERSION

-------------------   -------------------   ---------------
NO_MONITORING                               8.0.0
MONITOR               NO_MONITOR            11.1.0.6
NO_MONITOR            MONITOR               11.1.0.6
```

Note that the NO_MONITORING hint is something completely different despite the similar name. The NO_MONITORING hint allows you to disable the predicate usage monitoring on table columns (sys.col_usage$), and it has nothing to do with the Real-Time SQL Monitoring option introduced in Oracle 11g.

Monitoring SQL Statements using V$SQL and V$SQLSTATS

The performance monitoring in the "olddays" before-Oracle 10g ASH was usually done using various V$ views, which showed aggregated instance-wide metrics. For example, the Statspack's TOP-5 wait events report section was just a delta between two V$SYSTEM_EVENT view snapshots. The TOP SQL reports were based on V$SQL snapshots, which externalize the execution statistics and resource consumption for each child cursor still in library cache. However, in a large database system (think e-Business Suite or SAP), you can have tens of thousands of cursors in the library cache, so gathering and storing deltas of all of their stats is not feasible. That's why tools like Statspack and AWR store deltas of only some top resource-consuming statements and ignore the insignificant ones. Remember that as these tools gather instance-wide data, they may end up ignoring a long-running statement if there are only a few sessions executing it. A single session running a bad SQL statement may not be "heard" in the noise of all the other sessions in the instance—potentially thousands of them. This instance-wide scope performance data analysis is not as powerful as the session-level ASH data slicing and dicing. With ASH you can drill down into any single session, regardless of how many sessions in total you have making noise in the instance.

If you use Exadata, you must be running at least Oracle 11g R1 on it, so all these superior tools are available, assuming that you have the Diagnostics and Tuning Pack licenses for your Exadata cluster. By the way, we haven't seen an Exadata-using customer without Diagnostics and Tuning Pack licenses yet, so it looks like the vast majority of Exadata users do not have to resort to old tools like Statspack or create a custom ASH-style repository themselves (although it's easily doable with a few lines of PL/SQL code polling V$SESSION or its underlying X$KSUSE view in each instance).

The V$SQL and V$SQLSTATS views still do have some advantage over SQL Monitoring and ASH-style sampled data in a few cases. For example, if you want to measure metrics like the number of executions, buffer gets, parse calls, fetches, or rows returned by the SQL child cursor, you can get this data from both Real-time SQL Monitoring (V$SQL_MONITOR) or the V$SQL/V$SQLSTATS views, but not ASH. But the problem with SQL Monitoring is that it doesn't monitor short-running queries at all, therefore making it unusable for keeping track of OLTP-style small queries executed many times per second. Even adding a MONITOR hint into every query of your application would not help, as the maximum number of monitored plans is limited (controlled by the _sqlmon_max_plan parameter, which defaults to 20 plans per CPU) and you would likely end up with *real-time plan statistics latch* contention as well. The SQL Monitoring feature is not meant to monitor short-running queries executed many times per second.

And this leaves us with V$SQL and V$SQLSTATS. They both maintain similar data, but they are internally different. Whenever you query V$SQL without specifying an exact SQL_ID, Oracle has to traverse through every single library cache hash bucket, and all cursors under it. This may contribute to library cache mutex contention if you have a busy database and lots of cursors in the library cache, because when you traverse the library cache structure and read its objects' contents, you'll have to hold a mutex on the object. Note that starting from Oracle 11g, all library cache latches are gone and are replaced by mutexes. These same mutexes are used for parsing, looking up, and pinning cursors for execution, so if your monitoring queries poll V$SQL frequently, they may end up causing waits for other sessions.

The V$SQLSTATS view, which was introduced in Oracle 10gR2, doesn't have this problem. Starting from Oracle 10gR2, Oracle actually maintains SQL execution statistics in two places— inside the child cursors themselves (V$SQL) and in a separate cursor statistics array stored in a different location in the shared pool. This separation gives the benefit that even if a cursor is flushed out from the shared pool, its stats in this separate array may remain available for longer. Also, when monitoring tools query V$SQLSTATS, they don't have to scan through the entire library cache, thanks to the separate array where stats are stored. This means that your monitoring tools won't cause additional library cache latch (or mutex) contention when they use V$SQLSTATS instead of V$SQL. Both Statspack and AWR do use V$SQLSTATS to collect data for their top SQL reports.

Let's look into V$SQLSTATS (the V$SQL view has pretty much the same columns, by the way). Some of the output here is removed to save space:

```
SQL> @desc v$sqlstats
            Name                                  Null?     Type
            -------------------------------       --------  ----------------------
    1       SQL_TEXT                                        VARCHAR2(1000)
    2       SQL_FULLTEXT                                    CLOB
    3       SQL_ID                                          VARCHAR2(13)
    ...
    6       PLAN_HASH_VALUE                                 NUMBER
    ...
    20      CPU_TIME                                        NUMBER
    21      ELAPSED_TIME                                    NUMBER
    ...
    26      USER_IO_WAIT_TIME                               NUMBER
    ...
    33      IO_CELL_OFFLOAD_ELIGIBLE_BYTES                  NUMBER
    34      IO_INTERCONNECT_BYTES                           NUMBER
    35      PHYSICAL_READ_REQUESTS                          NUMBER
    36      PHYSICAL_READ_BYTES                             NUMBER
    37      PHYSICAL_WRITE_REQUESTS                         NUMBER
    38      PHYSICAL_WRITE_BYTES                            NUMBER
    ...
    41      IO_CELL_UNCOMPRESSED_BYTES                      NUMBER
    42      IO_CELL_OFFLOAD_RETURNED_BYTES                  NUMBER
```

The highlighted rows starting, with IO_CELL, are metrics related to Exadata storage cells (although the IO_INTERCONNECT_BYTES is populated on non-Exadata databases as well, thanks to a bug). You would want to compare these cell metrics to database metrics (like physical_read_bytes) to understand whether this SQL statement is benefitting from Exadata Smart Scan offloading. Note that these metrics, which merely count bytes, should not be used as the primary metric of *performance*; again, the primary metric, the starting point, should always be response time, which you can then break down into individual wait events or into execution plan rowsource activity (with the SQL Monitoring report or ASH). You can learn more about the meaning of the metrics shown here in Chapter 11.

Note that even though the V$SQLSTATS view also contains the PLAN_HASH_VALUE column, it actually does not store separate stats for the same SQL ID with different plan hash values. It aggregates all the stats generated by different plans of the same SQL ID under a single bucket. So you don't really know which plan version consumed the most resources from this view. Luckily in Oracle 11.2 there is a new view, named V$SQLSTATS_PLAN_HASH, which you should query instead. It organizes and reports the stats broken down by SQL ID *and* plan hash value instead of just SQL ID as V$SQLSTATS does.

Monitoring the Storage Cell Layer

Let's look at how to monitor the storage cell layer for utilization and efficiency. As you already know, the storage cells are regular commodity servers with some disks attached to them and running Linux. You can use regular Linux OS monitoring commands and tools to keep an eye on OS metrics like CPU usage or disk I/O activity. The only catch is that Oracle does not allow you to install any additional (monitoring) daemons and software on the cells— if you still want to have a supported configuration.

The good news is that Oracle cell server software and additional OS Watcher scripts do a good job of collecting detailed performance metrics in each cell. The following sections show how to extract, display, and use some of these metrics.

Accessing Cell Metrics in the Cell Layer Using CellCLI

The cell-collected metrics can be accessed using the CellCLI utility. That's in fact how the Exadata storage cell plug-in for Grid Control retrieves its data. You have seen CellCLI used in earlier chapters. Following are a few examples of using CellCLI for retrieving performance metrics. The command names should be fairly self-explanatory - we will cover the CellCLI commands in more detail in Appendix A.

```
$ cellcli
CellCLI: Release 11.2.2.3.1 - Production on Mon May 16 09:22:19 CDT 2011

Copyright (c) 2007, 2009, Oracle.  All rights reserved.
Cell Efficiency Ratio: 163

CellCLI> LIST METRICDEFINITION        ← show metric short names
            CD_IO_BY_R_LG
         CD_IO_BY_R_LG_SEC
         CD_IO_BY_R_SM
         CD_IO_BY_R_SM_SEC
         CD_IO_BY_W_LG
         CD_IO_BY_W_LG_SEC
         CD_IO_BY_W_SM
         CD_IO_BY_W_SM_SEC

    ... lots of output removed ...

         N_MB_RECEIVED
         N_MB_RECEIVED_SEC
         N_MB_RESENT
         N_MB_RESENT_SEC
         N_MB_SENT
         N_MB_SENT_SEC
         N_NIC_KB_RCV_SEC
         N_NIC_KB_TRANS_SEC
         N_NIC_NW
         N_RDMA_RETRY_TM
```

```
CellCLI> LIST METRICDEFINITION CL_CPUT DETAIL;    ← show metric description and details
      name:                   CL_CPUT
      description:            "Percentage of time over the previous minute that the system
CPUs were not idle."
      metricType:             Instantaneous
      objectType:             CELL
      unit:                   %


CellCLI> LIST METRICCURRENT CL_CPUT;              ← list the latest metric snapshot value
CL_CPUT       enkcel01      5.3 %


CellCLI> LIST METRICCURRENT CL_CPUT DETAIL;       ← list latest snapshot in detail
      name:                   CL_CPUT
      alertState:             normal
      collectionTime:         2011-05-16T09:31:53-05:00
      metricObjectName:       enkcel01
      metricType:             Instantaneous
      metricValue:            5.3 %
      objectType:             CELL


CellCLI> LIST METRICHISTORY CL_CPUT;              ← show historical metric snapshots

      CL_CPUT       enkcel01      2.2 %      2011-05-06T12:00:46-05:00
      CL_CPUT       enkcel01      2.4 %      2011-05-06T12:01:49-05:00
      CL_CPUT       enkcel01      2.1 %      2011-05-06T13:00:15-05:00
      CL_CPUT       enkcel01      0.3 %      2011-05-06T13:01:15-05:00
      CL_CPUT       enkcel01      1.4 %      2011-05-06T13:02:15-05:00
      CL_CPUT       enkcel01      0.3 %      2011-05-06T13:03:15-05:00
      CL_CPUT       enkcel01      1.2 %      2011-05-06T13:04:15-05:00
      CL_CPUT       enkcel01      1.2 %      2011-05-06T13:05:15-05:00
```

Accessing Cell Metrics Using the Grid Control Exadata Storage Server Plug-In

If you have configured the System Monitoring plug-in for Exadata Storage Server, you will be able to see some cell-level metrics, reports, and charts in Grid Control. The plug-in installation is out of the scope of this book, but it's well documented in the plug-in's installation guide.

Currently the Exadata Storage Server monitoring plug-in gives only some basic metrics to monitor and is not very sophisticated for systematic cell performance troubleshooting or monitoring. Nevertheless, it will give you a more convenient way for monitoring cell statistics changing over time, compared to running CellCLI's list metrichistory commands manually. When you initially navigate to a storage cell target (or group of cells) in Grid Control, you may not see any charts defined there yet. In Figure 12-10, we have created a group called "cells" from the Exadata Storage Server targets and navigated to the Edit Group page. This is where you can add new charts for collected cell-level metrics.

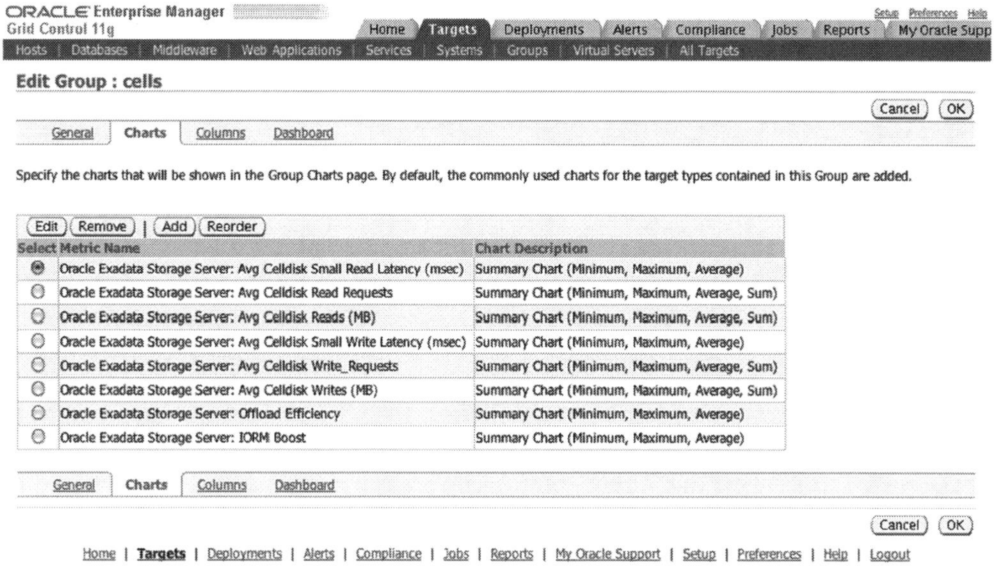

ORACLE Enterprise Manager
Grid Control 11g

Setup Preferences Help

| Home | Targets | Deployments | Alerts | Compliance | Jobs | Reports | My Oracle Supp |

Hosts | Databases | Middleware | Web Applications | Services | Systems | Groups | Virtual Servers | All Targets

Edit Group : cells

(Cancel) (OK)

| General | **Charts** | Columns | Dashboard |

Specify the charts that will be shown in the Group Charts page. By default, the commonly used charts for the target types contained in this Group are added.

(Edit) (Remove) | (Add) (Reorder)

Select	Metric Name	Chart Description
●	Oracle Exadata Storage Server: Avg Celldisk Small Read Latency (msec)	Summary Chart (Minimum, Maximum, Average)
○	Oracle Exadata Storage Server: Avg Celldisk Read Requests	Summary Chart (Minimum, Maximum, Average, Sum)
○	Oracle Exadata Storage Server: Avg Celldisk Reads (MB)	Summary Chart (Minimum, Maximum, Average, Sum)
○	Oracle Exadata Storage Server: Avg Celldisk Small Write Latency (msec)	Summary Chart (Minimum, Maximum, Average)
○	Oracle Exadata Storage Server: Avg Celldisk Write_Requests	Summary Chart (Minimum, Maximum, Average, Sum)
○	Oracle Exadata Storage Server: Avg Celldisk Writes (MB)	Summary Chart (Minimum, Maximum, Average, Sum)
○	Oracle Exadata Storage Server: Offload Efficiency	Summary Chart (Minimum, Maximum, Average)
○	Oracle Exadata Storage Server: IORM Boost	Summary Chart (Minimum, Maximum, Average)

| General | **Charts** | Columns | Dashboard |

(Cancel) (OK)

Home | **Targets** | Deployments | Alerts | Compliance | Jobs | Reports | My Oracle Support | Setup | Preferences | Help | Logout

Figure 12-10. Adding storage cell metrics into Grid Control monitoring charts

All the chart definitions in Figure 12-10 have been manually added for the cell group. You can add charts yourself, by clicking the Add button, which will bring you to the Add Chart page shown in Figure 12-11.

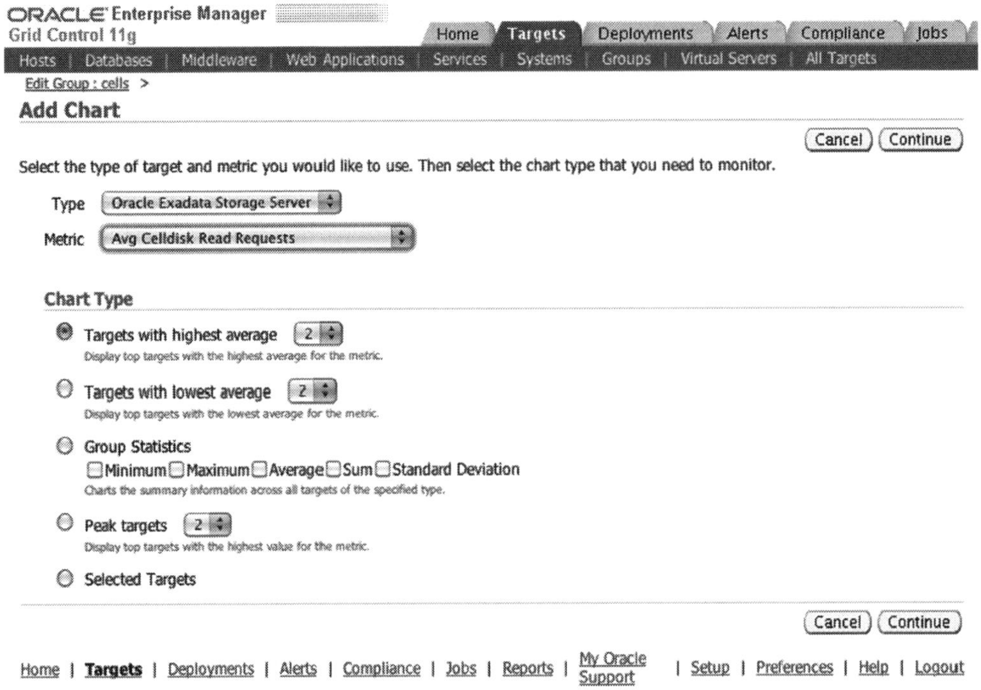

Figure 12-11. Selecting a "highest-average" chart for monitoring cells with highest read I/O requests

To see the cell metrics available, you'll have to select Oracle Exadata Storage Server as the chart type and pick one of the metrics to show. You probably want to use the Group Statistics for monitoring the whole cell group as a starting point, instead of monitoring all 14 storage cells (in a full rack) separately. The group statistics allow you to sum together stats from all the cells in the group (when monitoring total disk I/O throughput, for example) or show minimum, maximum, averages and standard deviation across all cells (when monitoring average disk I/O response times, for example). Pay attention to what the metric means and which aggregation operations make sense for a given metric. For example, it doesn't make much sense to display the *sum* of all average disk I/O response times in a chart. The metrics starting with Avg show average values over multiple objects monitored. For example, the Avg Celldisk Reads (MB) monitors average megabytes read *per celldisk*. On the other hand, the Total Celldisk Reads (MB) metric sums together the MB read by all cell disks in a cell. And now if you use the Group Statistics option to monitor multiple cells, you should use Sum to see the total MB read from cell disks across all cells and Average or Min/Max to see the average *per cell* or a cell with the smallest or biggest MB read cell disk throughput.

If you do want to monitor individual cells— for example, the two storage cells with the worst offload efficiency—then you can either define a separate offloading efficiency chart for each cell (and end up with 14 charts in a full rack configuration) or you can select Targets With Lowest Average as the chart type, as shown in Figure 12-12.

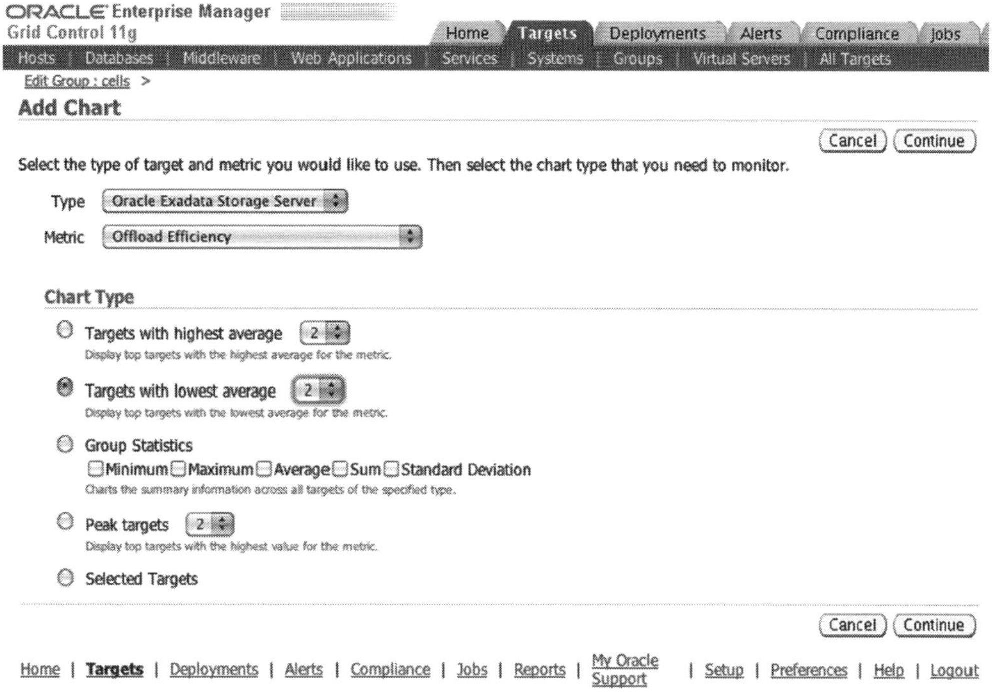

Figure 12-12. Selecting a "lowest average" chart for monitoring cells with worst offload efficiency

You can read more about the meaning of various metrics in the Oracle document *"Enterprise Manager System Monitoring Plug-In Metric Reference Manual for Oracle Exadata Storage Server."*

Now, you can reorder the charts on the cell group dashboard by clicking the Reorder button as shown in Figure 12-10 earlier. This will show you a list of defined charts, which you can then reorder on the screen, as seen in Figure 12-13.

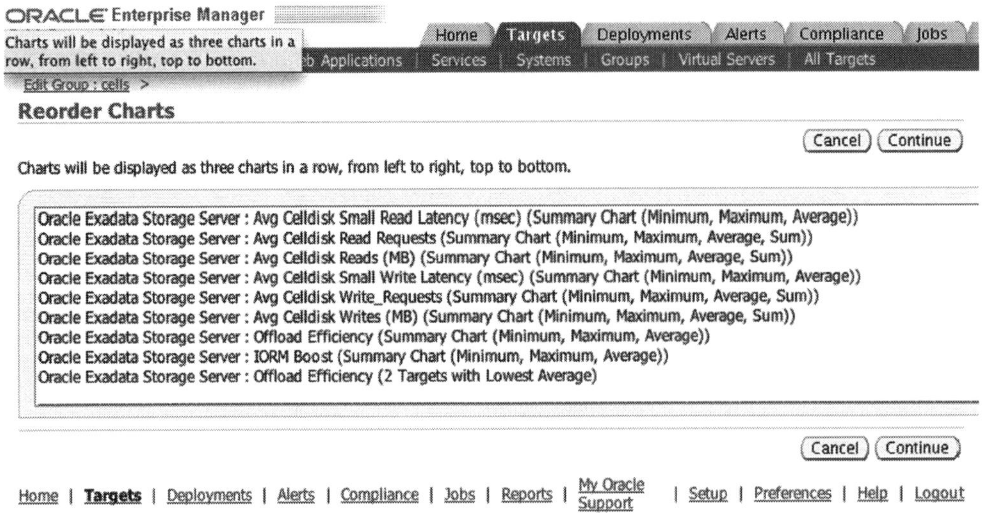

Figure 12-13. Ordering the storage cell metric charts in Grid Control

Now you are ready to view your charts. Depending on how many of them you configured, you should see a screen layout like that in Figure 12-14.

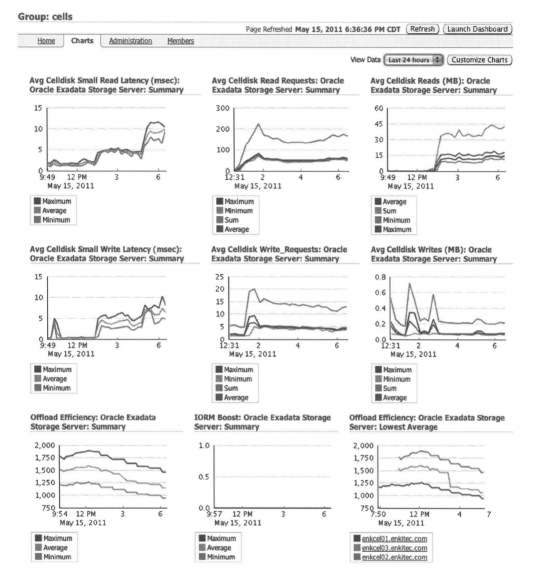

Figure 12-14. Multiple cell-level metrics displayed in Grid Control

Note that when you first configure the charts, they will be empty. If you wait for a few minutes, you should see the first data points appearing, and after a day has passed, the charts should be fully populated (if Last 24 Hours is selected in the View Data drop-down). You can click Customize Charts to modify the chart metrics again.

Now let's look at some of the individual metrics we have put onto the page, as shown in Figure 12-15.

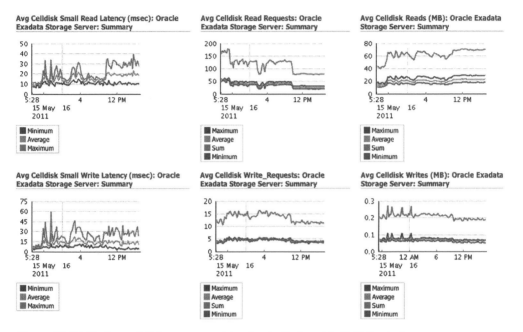

Figure 12-15. *Various celldisk average metrics charts displayed in Grid Control*

In the Avg Celldisk Small Read Latency (msec) chart here, we do see an issue. An hour before 12PM, the average small block I/O (under 256kB) latency has jumped up, probably because more large I/O operations were done in the cell. We can conclude this from the other two metrics in the top row; the Avg Cellidisk Read Requests has significantly dropped, while the Avg Celldisk Reads *(MB)* has remained the same, or actually even increased slightly. So there are more large I/Os being done, perhaps due to more queries using a Smart Scan. The small I/O latency has suffered because of this. Your OLTP database users running on the same cluster may notice that.

This is a place where you should find out what causes all this extra I/O. We will look at it later in this chapter. If you want to avoid situations where large Smart Scans impact small (single-block) IOs, you should consider enabling the I/O Resource Manager (IORM), which allows you to set the IORM goal to optimize random I/O latency as opposed to full scanning throughput. Additionally, you could make sure that your hot segments accessed with single-block reads are cached in flash cache. See Chapter 7 for more about IORM and resource management.

Figure 12-16 shows an example of the total cell disk I/O throughput chart. Note that the metric used starts with "Total," indicating that the throughput MB values are summed over all twelve disks in the cell (as opposed to the Average metrics, which show averages across the disks). This is a very important point. If you are summing together *average* metrics like in the Avg Celldisk Reads section (top right corner) of Figure 12-15, then you will still end up with a sum of the average cell disk read rates, not the total aggregate throughput of all disks in the cell. The cell disks' *average* metrics are good for charting things like the min, max, and cell-level average I/O latencies or disk utilization figures, but not valid for monitoring things like I/O throughput of all cells.

It is valid to *sum* together Total Celldisk metrics to get the total aggregate throughput, so from Figure 12-16 we see that the aggregate disk read throughput across all the cells is around 2000MB/second for the given workload.

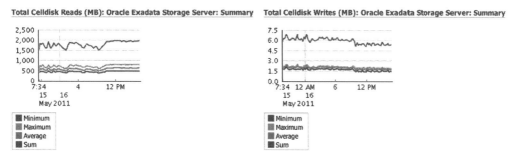

Figure 12-16. *Celldisk-level Total metrics summed together for monitoring total I/O throughput*

Sometimes, especially when the monitoring UI charts don't seem to make sense, you might ask where these charts take their data from. This is easy to find out, as the Grid Control metrics plug-ins are just Perl scripts, which then run command-line utilities like CellCLI or plain SSH clients to fetch their metrics. You can check the directory where you have installed the Exadata Storage Cell Server monitoring plug-in yourself:

```
$ ls /u01/app/oracle/product/middleware/agent11g/sysman/admin/scripts/emx/oracle_cell
```

```
oracle_cell_category_metrics.pl       oracle_cell_griddisk_config.pl
oracle_cell_celldisk_config.pl        oracle_cell_griddisk_metrics.pl
oracle_cell_celldisk_metrics.pl       oracle_cell_interconnect_metrics.pl
oracle_cell_common.pm                 oracle_cell_iormboost_metrics.pl
oracle_cell_config.pl                 oracle_cell_iorm_config.pl
oracle_cell_consumergroup_metrics.pl  oracle_cell_lun_config.pl
oracle_cell_database_metrics.pl       oracle_cell_lun_metrics.pl
oracle_cell_disk_config.pl            oracle_cell_metrics.pl
oracle_cell_disk_metrics.pl           oracle_cell_offload_metrics.pl
oracle_cell_flashcache_metrics.pl     oracle_cell_resp.pl
oracle_cell_fs_metrics.pl
```

Let's take a quick look at one of these Perl scripts, oracle_cell_celldisk_metrics.pl, to see where it gets its data:

...beginning of the script skipped...

```
my $command = "ssh -l cellmonitor $ipaddress cellcli
                  -xml -e 'list metriccurrent where objectType=".'\"CELLDISK\"'."'";

my $xmlout = `$command`;
```

```
my $parser = XML::Parser->new( Handlers => {

                            Start=>\&handle_start,
                            End=>\&handle_end,
                            Char=> \&characterData,
                            });
```

...rest of the script skipped...

As you can see, the Exadata Cell Grid Control plug-in is merely a bunch of Perl scripts, which then log into target cells via SSH and run regular CellCLI commands with XML output mode. The output is then parsed and returned to the Grid Control agent.

Now that we know which actual command the Grid Control plug-in uses for pulling data, we can run it ourselves and see which data it includes. Note that there's an additional filter condition showing only one metric for brevity.

```
CellCLI> LIST METRICCURRENT WHERE objectType = 'CELLDISK' AND name = 'CD_IO_TM_R_SM_RQ'
        CD_IO_TM_R_SM_RQ    CD_00_cell03    25,390 us/request
        CD_IO_TM_R_SM_RQ    CD_01_cell03    11,633 us/request
        CD_IO_TM_R_SM_RQ    CD_02_cell03    6,067 us/request
        CD_IO_TM_R_SM_RQ    CD_03_cell03    11,412 us/request
        CD_IO_TM_R_SM_RQ    CD_04_cell03    20,410 us/request
        CD_IO_TM_R_SM_RQ    CD_05_cell03    2,871 us/request
        CD_IO_TM_R_SM_RQ    CD_06_cell03    30,480 us/request
        CD_IO_TM_R_SM_RQ    CD_07_cell03    22,791 us/request
        CD_IO_TM_R_SM_RQ    CD_08_cell03    2,303 us/request
        CD_IO_TM_R_SM_RQ    CD_09_cell03    12,019 us/request
        CD_IO_TM_R_SM_RQ    CD_10_cell03    2,010 us/request
        CD_IO_TM_R_SM_RQ    CD_11_cell03    15,056 us/request
        CD_IO_TM_R_SM_RQ    FD_00_cell03    464 us/request
        CD_IO_TM_R_SM_RQ    FD_01_cell03    471 us/request
        CD_IO_TM_R_SM_RQ    FD_02_cell03    476 us/request
        CD_IO_TM_R_SM_RQ    FD_03_cell03    473 us/request
        CD_IO_TM_R_SM_RQ    FD_04_cell03    450 us/request
        CD_IO_TM_R_SM_RQ    FD_05_cell03    467 us/request
        CD_IO_TM_R_SM_RQ    FD_06_cell03    469 us/request
        CD_IO_TM_R_SM_RQ    FD_07_cell03    474 us/request
        CD_IO_TM_R_SM_RQ    FD_08_cell03    456 us/request
        CD_IO_TM_R_SM_RQ    FD_09_cell03    459 us/request
        CD_IO_TM_R_SM_RQ    FD_10_cell03    461 us/request
        CD_IO_TM_R_SM_RQ    FD_11_cell03    455 us/request
        CD_IO_TM_R_SM_RQ    FD_12_cell03    467 us/request
        CD_IO_TM_R_SM_RQ    FD_13_cell03    480 us/request
        CD_IO_TM_R_SM_RQ    FD_14_cell03    483 us/request
        CD_IO_TM_R_SM_RQ    FD_15_cell03    471 us/request
```

The grid disk names starting with FD_ indicate that these lines are reported for flash disks (each cell has 4 × 96GB flash cards, but each flash card presents four flash disks to the operating system, totaling 16 flash disks per cell). So, using this exercise we have found out whether the cell-disk metrics include flash disk metrics in addition to regular disk drives— and yes, they do. This makes some of the charts lie, as the flash read times that are an order of magnitude faster will make the average regular disk read times look better as well. In fact, some of the cell disks have a pretty bad small read I/O latency. For example, up to 30 milliseconds per request on average, which is much higher than the average seek + rotational + data transfer latency should be for a modern 15000 RPM disk, even if it is 100% busy with random I/O requests. This probably indicates I/O queueing somewhere, likely in the OS I/O queue, which you can confirm by looking at the `await` and `svctm` columns in `iostat` output (more about `iostat` later in this chapter, but `man iostat` is your friend).

So, ideally you should monitor the flash disks and good old spinning disk drives separately, by either post-processing the returned data or just running two separate CellCLI commands in your monitoring tools. CellCLI allows you to filter its results further using a regular expression, as shown here:

```
CellCLI> LIST METRICCURRENT WHERE objectType = 'CELLDISK'
      AND name = 'CD_IO_TM_R_SM_RQ' AND metricObjectName LIKE 'FD_.*';

      CD_IO_TM_R_SM_RQ      FD_00_cell03      464 us/request
      CD_IO_TM_R_SM_RQ      FD_01_cell03      471 us/request
      CD_IO_TM_R_SM_RQ      FD_02_cell03      476 us/request
      CD_IO_TM_R_SM_RQ      FD_03_cell03      473 us/request
      CD_IO_TM_R_SM_RQ      FD_04_cell03      450 us/request
      CD_IO_TM_R_SM_RQ      FD_05_cell03      467 us/request
      CD_IO_TM_R_SM_RQ      FD_06_cell03      469 us/request
      CD_IO_TM_R_SM_RQ      FD_07_cell03      474 us/request
      CD_IO_TM_R_SM_RQ      FD_08_cell03      456 us/request
      CD_IO_TM_R_SM_RQ      FD_09_cell03      459 us/request
      CD_IO_TM_R_SM_RQ      FD_10_cell03      461 us/request
      CD_IO_TM_R_SM_RQ      FD_11_cell03      455 us/request
      CD_IO_TM_R_SM_RQ      FD_12_cell03      467 us/request
      CD_IO_TM_R_SM_RQ      FD_13_cell03      480 us/request
      CD_IO_TM_R_SM_RQ      FD_14_cell03      483 us/request
      CD_IO_TM_R_SM_RQ      FD_15_cell03      471 us/request
```

Now we see only the flash drives. You can read more about the CellCLI usage and syntax examples in Appendix A of this book and also in the official documentation, *Oracle Exadata Storage Server Software User's Guide*.

Which Cell Metrics to Use?

Which cell metrics to use is an important question. Oracle provides a huge variety of different metrics, from the database level, the host server level, and the Exadata cell level. It is very easy to get lost in them or even worse, get misled and troubleshoot a wrong or non-existent problem. In performance troubleshooting, we should start from what matters—user response time—and drill down from there (as explained in the previous sections of this chapter). But general efficiency monitoring, utilization overview, and capacity planning are sometimes good reasons for examining cell-level aggregated metrics.

This may come as a surprise if you have expected more, but there is no long list of secret and special Exadata metrics you should monitor in your cells. A cell is just a server, with RAM, CPUs, and disks, sending data out over a network link. So the fundamental metrics you would want to monitor at the cell level are the same you'd use in any server: CPU utilization, system load, memory utilization and disk utilization, and I/O throughput and latency. The most important metrics are available in the Grid Control Storage Cell monitoring plug-in, and the rest can be extracted from OS Watcher logfiles. The advanced metrics come into play only when dealing with bugs or some rare, very specific performance issues, so they shouldn't really be actively monitored unless there is a problem.

One topic deserves some elaboration— the CPU usage monitoring, both in the database and cells. The data warehouses and reporting systems, unlike OLTP databases, don't usually require very quick response times for user queries. Of course, the faster a query completes, the better, but in a DW, people don't really notice if a query ran in 35 seconds instead of 30 seconds. But a typical OLTP user would definitely notice if their 1-second query took 6 seconds occasionally. That's one of the reasons why in OLTP servers you would not want to constantly run at 100% CPU utilization. You cannot do that and also maintain stable performance. In an OLTP system you must leave some headroom. In DW servers, however, the small fluctuations in performance would not be noticed, and you can afford to run at 100% of CPU utilization in order to get the most out of your investment.

However, Exadata complicates things. In addition to having multiple database nodes, you also have another whole layer of servers: the cells. Things get interesting especially when running Smart Scans with high parallelism against EHCC tables. That's because offloaded decompression requires a lot of CPU cycles in the cells. Thus it is possible that for some workloads your cells' CPUs will be 100% busy and unable to feed data back to the database layer fast enough. The database layer CPUs may be half idle, while cells could really use some extra CPU capacity.

The risk from cell utilization reaching 100% is the reason Oracle made cellsrv able to skip offload processing for some datablocks and pass these blocks straight back to the database (starting in cellsrv 11.2.2.3.0). The cell checks whether its CPU utilization is over 90% and whether the database CPU utilization (it's sent in based on resource manager stats from the database) is lower than that. And if so, some blocks are not processed in the cells, but passed through to the database directly. The database then will decrypt (if needed) and decompress the blocks and perform projection and filtering in the database layer. This allows you to fully utilize all your CPU capacity in both layers of the Exadata cluster. However, this automatically means that if some blocks are suddenly processed in the database layer (instead of being offloaded to cells), then you may see unexpected CPU utilization spikes in the database layer, when cells are too busy. This shouldn't be a problem on most DW systems, especially with properly configured resource manager, but you would want to watch out for this when running OLTP or other low-latency systems on Exadata.

As usual, Oracle provides good metrics about this pass-through feature. Whenever the offload processing is skipped for some blocks during a Smart Scan and these blocks are sent back to the database layer for processing, the statistic "cell physical IO bytes pushed back due to excessive CPU on cell" gets incremented in V$SESSTAT/V$SYSSTAT and AWR reports. Read more about this feature and statistic in Chapter 11.

Monitoring Exadata Storage Cell OS-level Metrics

Oracle Database and the cellsrv software do a good job of gathering various performance metrics, but there are still cases where you would want to use an OS tool instead. One of the reasons is that usually the V$ views in Oracle tell you what Oracle *thinks* it's doing, but this may not necessarily be what's really happening if you hit a bug or some other limitation of Oracle's built-in instrumentation. One of the limitations is low-level I/O measurement.

Monitoring the Storage Cell Server's I/O Metrics with iostat

Both Oracle Database and the storage cells do measure the I/O Completion Time; in other words, the response time of I/Os. With synchronous I/O operations, Oracle's I/O wait time is merely the system call (like pread) completion time. With asynchronous I/O, the response time measurement is trickier, as an asynchronous I/O submit system call will not block and wait; it will return immediately in microseconds and some I/O reaping system call will be executed later, which will mark the I/O operation as complete. The Exadata storage cells keep track of each asynchronous I/O request (for example, when it was submitted) and once the I/O is successfully reaped, they will check the reaping timestamp against that I/O's submit timestamp and know its duration.

Regardless of this extra cellsrv-level I/O monitoring, the cells still don't break the I/O response time into the two important components: how much time this I/O request spent uselessly *waiting* in the OS I/O queue before it was even sent out to the SCSI device, and how long the actual hardware *service time* was once the I/O request was sent out to the hardware. Comparing the I/O service time to waiting time gives an important clue about whether the storage hardware itself responds slowly, in which case the service time is higher than you would expect from a modern disk drive.

■ **Note:** So what is this normal I/O service time to expect from disks? That depends on which disks you have, what their seek latency is, how far the disk read/write head has to seek from its previous location, what the rotational latency of the disk is, how fast it spins (RPM), and how fast it can transfer the bits just read over the wires (or fiber). There is no magic in calculating what a good service time should be for a disk; it's all based on the physical capabilities of the disk, and these capabilities are documented in the vendor's disk specs. You can read more about the various latencies involved from Wikipedia:
http://en.wikipedia.org/wiki/Hard_disk_drive#Access_time.

Of course, there may be other overhead, like SAN storage network roundtrip times and any extra latency caused by storage controllers, switches, and so on. But remember, Exadata is not connected to SAN storage; the disks are attached directly to the storage cells. Each storage cell has a little LSI MegaRaid controller in it, and the disks are attached to that controller. There are no complex network components between the disks and storage cells, which might drive up latency or fail. More importantly, there are no "other" databases or applications connected to the storage, which you have no control over, but which could suddenly start saturating the disks without a warning. All you would see is that the disk I/O service times suddenly go up as the storage array gets overloaded.

Anyway, a small I/O request (up to 256 KB) against a modern 15000 RPM disk drive should ideally have average service time of 5–7 milliseconds per I/O request. This comes from a 3.5ms average seek latency, 2ms average rotational latency, plus 0.4ms for transferring the 256kB over SAS channels. In theory this average seek latency is a pessimistic figure, assuming that the whole disk is full and the disk read/write heads have to do random seeks across tracks from end to end of the disk cylinders. But you probably have configured your disks into hotter and colder regions (the RECO disk group, for example), and the colder regions are visited much less frequently, driving the real average seek times shorter. So, while you may get these low 2–3ms service times when your disk heads don't have to seek too far, in practice, 10ms average I/O service times are completely OK once you run real production workloads.

▩ **Kevin Says:** I'm often surprised at the lack of focus paid to data placement on physical disks. The authors are correct to point out that so-called short-stroked I/O requests have some, if not all, seek time removed from the service time of the request. However, I'd like to elaborate on this point further. When discussing Exadata we often concentrate on data capacity of enormous proportion. However, it is seldom the case that all data is active in all queries. Most data warehouses have an active subset of the total database. One can easily envision the active portion of a 100TB data warehouse being as small as 1TB. Just one percent? How can this be? Always remember that Oracle Database, combined with Exadata, offers many "lines of defense" in front of the dreaded physical I/O. Before physical I/O there is a results cache miss, SGA buffer cache miss (yes, it has purpose even when Exadata is involved), partition elimination, and finally a storage index miss. Once through these "lines of defense," there is a physical I/O for data that is potentially compressed with a compression ratio of, say, 6:1. To that end, the 1TB active portion is actually 6TB—a sizable amount of data. Seek times are the lion's share of physical I/O service time. In fact, from a current cost perspective, the optimal data warehouse architecture would consist of seek-free rotational hard disk drives. While that may seem absurd, allow me to point out that 1TB is exactly 1 percent of the aggregate surface area of the 168 (600GB) SAS drives offered in a full rack X2 model with high-performance drives. Long seeks are not a fixed cost in modern data warehouses—especially when the active portion is such a small percentage of the whole. If the active portion of the data warehouse remains a fixed percentage, yet service times increase over time, the problem is likely fragmentation. Data scattered over the entirety of round, spinning magnetic media is not optimal regardless of whether Oracle Database is connected to conventional storage or Exadata. Even with Exadata, the fundamentals still apply.

The whole point of this explanation so far is really that it *is* possible to know what the ideal disk *service* times should be for Exadata cells disk drives, and if the service times are constantly much higher than that, then there is some problem with the storage hardware (disks or controllers). With SAN storage, high OS-level service times could also mean that there is some queuing going on inside the SAN network or the storage array (for example, if a thousand other servers are hammering the same storage array with I/O). But as said above, Exadata storage cells have dedicated storage in them; only the current cell OS can access this storage, and all IOs are visible in iostat.

So, what if the service time is OK, but Oracle (cellsrv) still sees bad I/O performance? Well this may mean there is still *queuing* going on inside the cell Linux servers—and iostat can show this information, too. You can have only a limited number of outstanding I/Os in the "on-the-fly" state against your storage controller LUNs. The storage controller needs to keep track of each outstanding I/O (for example, it has to remember where in the host RAM to write the block once it is read from disk and arrives at the controller), and these I/O slots are limited. So the Linux kernel does not allow sending out more I/Os than the storage controller can handle; otherwise a SCSI reset would occur. These throttled I/Os will have to wait in the OS disk device I/O queue— and they are *uselessly* waiting there; they aren't even sent out to the storage controller yet. Only when some previously outstanding I/O operation completes will the first item in the queue be sent to the disks (assuming that the I/O latency deadline hasn't been reached for some request; cellsrv uses the Linux "deadline" I/O scheduler).

If you do have I/O waiting (queueing time) going on, then the await (average I/O completion time) column in iostat will be significantly higher than the svctm (estimated I/O service time) column. Note that the name "await" is somewhat misleading, as it does not show only the wait (queuing) time, it shows the total wait plus service time. Similarly, the avgqu-sz column does not show just the average I/O wait queue length, but rather the average *total* number of not completed I/Os in the I/O request queue, regardless of whether they have already been sent out to storage hardware (are already being serviced) or still waiting in the I/O queue (not yet serviced).

Linux iostat shows statistics for the disk partition and the cell software RAID device (used for cell OS partition mirroring). We can filter out those lines so that only the physical disk stats would be listed. For example:

```
$ iostat -xm 5 | egrep -v "sd.[0-9]|^md"

Linux 2.6.18-194.3.1.0.4.el5 (enkcel03.enkitec.com)    05/22/2011

avg-cpu:  %user   %nice %system %iowait  %steal   %idle
           0.73    0.00    0.75    1.01    0.00   97.51


Device:    r/s    w/s   rMB/s    wMB/s avgrq-sz avgqu-sz   await  svctm  %util
sda      12.56   7.33    9.63     0.26  1018.44     1.39   70.13   3.99   7.94
sdb       8.64   8.75    3.94     0.24   491.94     0.87   49.94   3.16   5.49
sdc       5.99   1.75    3.87     0.14  1062.34     0.63   80.86   5.19   4.02
sdd       5.04   2.89    3.75     0.15  1005.46     0.87  110.01   5.18   4.11
sde      10.84   3.28   10.06     0.20  1488.13     0.94   66.61   4.78   6.74
sdf       1.62   1.83    0.05     0.05    62.18     0.01    3.15   0.92   0.32
sdg       6.62   2.02    6.24     0.15  1515.53     0.49   57.32   5.99   5.17
sdh       4.56   2.50    3.86     0.15  1165.21     0.42   59.70   5.63   3.97
sdi      11.15   3.14    4.58     0.17   681.93     0.66   46.39   4.41   6.30
sdj       4.39   1.66    3.87     0.12  1351.37     0.50   82.55   6.51   3.94
sdk      11.87   3.95   11.09     0.21  1463.66     0.88   55.94   4.64   7.33
sdl      16.60   5.41    9.86     0.15   931.06     0.76   34.68   3.20   7.04
sdm       0.28   0.00    0.01     0.00    47.93     0.00    1.59   1.38   0.04
sdn       2.87   0.30    0.03     0.01    24.42     0.00    0.55   0.34   0.11
sdo       2.84   0.31    0.03     0.01    24.63     0.00    0.57   0.34   0.11
sdp       2.82   0.30    0.03     0.00    24.49     0.00    0.58   0.34   0.10
sdq       2.79   0.45    0.03     0.01    25.05     0.00    0.58   0.33   0.11
sdr       2.89   0.28    0.03     0.00    24.44     0.00    0.60   0.34   0.11
sds       2.94   0.32    0.03     0.01    24.35     0.00    0.56   0.34   0.11
sdt       2.85   0.30    0.03     0.01    24.49     0.00    0.54   0.34   0.11
sdu       2.82   0.29    0.03     0.00    24.64     0.00    0.56   0.34   0.11
sdv       2.86   0.49    0.03     0.01    25.01     0.00    0.55   0.33   0.11
sdw       2.93   0.58    0.03     0.01    25.12     0.00    0.53   0.33   0.11
sdx       2.87   0.35    0.03     0.01    24.37     0.00    0.57   0.33   0.11
sdy       2.84   0.61    0.03     0.01    25.28     0.00    0.52   0.32   0.11
sdz       2.81   0.29    0.03     0.00    24.63     0.00    0.57   0.34   0.10
sdaa      2.86   0.32    0.03     0.01    24.40     0.00    0.60   0.34   0.11
sdab      2.89   0.33    0.03     0.01    24.37     0.00    0.58   0.34   0.11
sdac      2.90   0.29    0.03     0.00    24.36     0.00    0.58   0.34   0.11
```

Wait a minute! Shouldn't we see fewer disks, as each cell has only 12 hard drives in it? We see so many disks because in addition to the 12 hard disks, cells also have their flash cards presented as separate disks. Finally, there's also one USB disk. You can use the lsscsi command in the cell to see all disks detected by the OS:

```
$ lsscsi
[0:2:0:0]    disk    LSI       MR9261-8i          2.12   /dev/sda
[0:2:1:0]    disk    LSI       MR9261-8i          2.12   /dev/sdb
[0:2:2:0]    disk    LSI       MR9261-8i          2.12   /dev/sdc
[0:2:3:0]    disk    LSI       MR9261-8i          2.12   /dev/sdd
[0:2:4:0]    disk    LSI       MR9261-8i          2.12   /dev/sde
[0:2:5:0]    disk    LSI       MR9261-8i          2.12   /dev/sdf
[0:2:6:0]    disk    LSI       MR9261-8i          2.12   /dev/sdg
[0:2:7:0]    disk    LSI       MR9261-8i          2.12   /dev/sdh
[0:2:8:0]    disk    LSI       MR9261-8i          2.12   /dev/sdi
[0:2:9:0]    disk    LSI       MR9261-8i          2.12   /dev/sdj
[0:2:10:0]   disk    LSI       MR9261-8i          2.12   /dev/sdk
[0:2:11:0]   disk    LSI       MR9261-8i          2.12   /dev/sdl
[1:0:0:0]    disk    Unigen    PSA4000            1100   /dev/sdm
[8:0:0:0]    disk    ATA       MARVELL SD88SA02   D20Y   /dev/sdn
[8:0:1:0]    disk    ATA       MARVELL SD88SA02   D20Y   /dev/sdo
[8:0:2:0]    disk    ATA       MARVELL SD88SA02   D20Y   /dev/sdp
[8:0:3:0]    disk    ATA       MARVELL SD88SA02   D20Y   /dev/sdq
[9:0:0:0]    disk    ATA       MARVELL SD88SA02   D20Y   /dev/sdr
[9:0:1:0]    disk    ATA       MARVELL SD88SA02   D20Y   /dev/sds
[9:0:2:0]    disk    ATA       MARVELL SD88SA02   D20Y   /dev/sdt
[9:0:3:0]    disk    ATA       MARVELL SD88SA02   D20Y   /dev/sdu
[10:0:0:0]   disk    ATA       MARVELL SD88SA02   D20Y   /dev/sdv
[10:0:1:0]   disk    ATA       MARVELL SD88SA02   D20Y   /dev/sdw
[10:0:2:0]   disk    ATA       MARVELL SD88SA02   D20Y   /dev/sdx
[10:0:3:0]   disk    ATA       MARVELL SD88SA02   D20Y   /dev/sdy
[11:0:0:0]   disk    ATA       MARVELL SD88SA02   D20Y   /dev/sdz
[11:0:1:0]   disk    ATA       MARVELL SD88SA02   D20Y   /dev/sdaa
[11:0:2:0]   disk    ATA       MARVELL SD88SA02   D20Y   /dev/sdab
[11:0:3:0]   disk    ATA       MARVELL SD88SA02   D20Y   /dev/sdac
```

The LSI disks here are the hard disks presented to the host by the LSI SCSI RAID controller (from devices sda to sdl), the Unigen PSA4000 is the USB disk, and the MARVELL ATA disks are the flash cards. If you compare the average I/O service times (svctm) in iostat, you'll see that the devices belonging to flash cards have a service time an order of magnitude lower than hard disk devices. So, if you want to monitor only the hard-disk devices, you can filter iostat output this way:

```
$ iostat -xm 5 | egrep "Device|^sd[a-l] "
Device:   r/s    w/s  rMB/s    wMB/s avgrq-sz avgqu-sz   await  svctm  %util
sda     11.95 12.22   8.62     1.38   847.59     1.60   66.26   3.76   9.09
sdb      9.79 13.62   4.14     1.36   480.53     1.13   48.12   3.31   7.74
sdc      7.06  6.64   4.07     1.26   796.10     0.63   46.05   3.65   5.00
sdd      6.06  7.89   3.94     1.27   765.02     0.84   60.38   3.74   5.22
sde     10.45  8.20   8.90     1.31  1121.89     0.86   46.02   3.79   7.07
sdf      1.60  1.79   0.05     0.04    55.38     0.01    2.84   1.03   0.35
sdg      7.15  6.93   5.90     1.28  1044.40     0.53   37.76   4.22   5.94
sdh      5.61  7.48   4.06     1.28   835.26     0.49   37.78   3.85   5.04
sdi     12.89  8.11   4.63     1.31   579.09     0.71   33.88   3.50   7.34
```

```
sdj     5.43  6.55   4.07    1.23   906.89    0.56  46.48   4.05  4.85
sdk    11.34  8.86   9.74    1.34  1122.70    0.83  41.18   3.81  7.70
sdl    16.40 10.23   8.80    1.26   773.96    0.75  28.27   2.83  7.53
```

Advanced Cell Monitoring With OS Watcher

While the database-level wait profile and SQL Monitoring should be used as a starting point for performance monitoring and troubleshooting, sometimes these approaches are not enough and you want to drill deeper. This section explains one additional data source for that. Exadata storage cells come with a preinstalled tool called OS Watcher, located in the /opt/oracle.oswatcher/osw directory. This tool is just a set of shell scripts, which then run standard OS tools, like vmstat, iostat and netstat, to collect their data. OS Watcher's benefit is that it runs at OS level, not inside a database, so it is not affected by database hangs and performance issues or cases where the database's V$ views don't show the truth or have enough detail. Additionally, the high-frequency OS Watcher collectors sample data every second or few seconds, allowing it to detect short "hiccups" or bursts of activity.

You can check whether the OS Watcher is running by simply searching for any processes with "OSW" in their name (be sure to search for both upper and lower case):

```
# pgrep -lf "OSW|osw"
10543 /bin/ksh ./oswsub.sh HighFreq ./Exadata_cellsrvstat.sh
26412 /bin/ksh ./OSWatcher.sh 15 168 bzip2
28827 /bin/ksh ./OSWatcherFM.sh 168
28846 /bin/ksh ./oswsub.sh HighFreq ./Exadata_vmstat.sh
28847 /bin/ksh ./oswsub.sh HighFreq ./Exadata_mpstat.sh
28848 /bin/ksh ./oswsub.sh HighFreq ./Exadata_netstat.sh
28849 /bin/ksh ./oswsub.sh HighFreq ./Exadata_iostat.sh
28853 /bin/ksh ./oswsub.sh HighFreq ./Exadata_top.sh
28877 /bin/ksh ./oswsub.sh HighFreq /opt/oracle.oswatcher/osw/ExadataRdsInfo.sh
28910 /bin/bash /opt/oracle.oswatcher/osw/ExadataRdsInfo.sh HighFreq
```

Apparently, the OS Watcher is running in this storage cell and there are a number of Exadata-specific collectors enabled, too. If you want to see the hierarchy of the OS Watcher process daemons, then on Linux you can use either the ps -H command shown in the first chapter or the pstree command as shown here:

```
# pstree -aAhlup `pgrep OSWatcher.sh`

OSWatcher.sh,26412 ./OSWatcher.sh 15 168 bzip2
  |-ExadataDiagColl,28866 /opt/oracle.cellos/ExadataDiagCollector.sh
  |   `-sleep,25718 3
  |-OSWatcherFM.sh,28827 ./OSWatcherFM.sh 168
  |-oswsub.sh,10543 ./oswsub.sh HighFreq ./Exadata_cellsrvstat.sh
  |   `-Exadata_cellsrv,10547 ./Exadata_cellsrvstat.sh HighFreq
  |       |-bzip2,10591 --stdout
  |       `-cellsrvstat,10590 -interval=5 -count=720
  |-oswsub.sh,28846 ./oswsub.sh HighFreq ./Exadata_vmstat.sh
  |   `-Exadata_vmstat.,28850 ./Exadata_vmstat.sh HighFreq
  |       |-bzip2,12126 --stdout
  |       `-vmstat,12125 5 720
  |-oswsub.sh,28847 ./oswsub.sh HighFreq ./Exadata_mpstat.sh
  |   `-Exadata_mpstat.,28852 ./Exadata_mpstat.sh HighFreq
  |       |-bzip2,12627 --stdout
```

```
|         `-mpstat,12626 5 720
|-oswsub.sh,28848 ./oswsub.sh HighFreq ./Exadata_netstat.sh
|    `-Exadata_netstat,28854 ./Exadata_netstat.sh HighFreq
|          `-sleep,25717 15
|-oswsub.sh,28849 ./oswsub.sh HighFreq ./Exadata_iostat.sh
|    `-Exadata_iostat.,28856 ./Exadata_iostat.sh HighFreq
|         |-bzip2,12105 --stdout
|         `-iostat,12104 -t -x 5 720
|-oswsub.sh,28853 ./oswsub.sh HighFreq ./Exadata_top.sh
|    `-Exadata_top.sh,28864 ./Exadata_top.sh HighFreq
|         |-bzip2,13453 --stdout
|         `-top,13452 -b -c -d 5 -n 720
`-oswsub.sh,28877 ./oswsub.sh HighFreq /opt/oracle.oswatcher/osw/ExadataRdsInfo.sh
     `-ExadataRdsInfo.,28910 /opt/oracle.oswatcher/osw/ExadataRdsInfo.sh HighFreq
          `-sleep,25710 10
```

The OS Watcher daemons store their collected data in the /opt/oracle.oswatcher/osw/archive/
directory. It doesn't use any special format for storing the data; it just stores the text output of the
standard OS tools it runs. This makes it easy to use regular text processing utilities, like grep, AWK or
Perl/python scripts to extract and present the information you need. Here's an example:

```
# ls -l /opt/oracle.oswatcher/osw/archive/
total 280
drwxr-s--- 2 root cellusers 28672 May 25 14:00 ExadataDiagCollect
drwxr-s--- 2 root cellusers 20480 May 25 14:00 ExadataOSW
drwxr-s--- 2 root cellusers 20480 May 25 14:00 ExadataRDS
drwxr-s--- 2 root cellusers 45056 May 25 14:00 oswcellsrvstat
drwxr-s--- 2 root cellusers 20480 May 25 14:01 oswiostat
drwxr-s--- 2 root cellusers 20480 May 25 14:00 oswmeminfo
drwxr-s--- 2 root cellusers 20480 May 25 14:00 oswmpstat
drwxr-s--- 2 root cellusers 24576 May 25 14:00 oswnetstat
drwxr-s--- 2 root cellusers  4096 May  6 12:35 oswprvtnet
drwxr-s--- 2 root cellusers 20480 May 25 14:00 oswps
drwxr-s--- 2 root cellusers 20480 May 25 14:00 oswslabinfo
drwxr-s--- 2 root cellusers 20480 May 25 14:00 oswtop
drwxr-s--- 2 root cellusers 20480 May 25 14:01 oswvmstat
```

Each directory contains archive files with corresponding command output:

```
# cd /opt/oracle.oswatcher/osw/archive/oswiostat/
# ls -tr  | tail

enkcel03.enkitec.com_iostat_11.05.25.0500.dat.bz2
enkcel03.enkitec.com_iostat_11.05.25.0600.dat.bz2
enkcel03.enkitec.com_iostat_11.05.25.0700.dat.bz2
enkcel03.enkitec.com_iostat_11.05.25.0800.dat.bz2
enkcel03.enkitec.com_iostat_11.05.25.0900.dat.bz2
enkcel03.enkitec.com_iostat_11.05.25.1000.dat.bz2
enkcel03.enkitec.com_iostat_11.05.25.1100.dat.bz2
enkcel03.enkitec.com_iostat_11.05.25.1200.dat.bz2
enkcel03.enkitec.com_iostat_11.05.25.1400.dat.bz2
enkcel03.enkitec.com_iostat_11.05.25.1300.dat.bz2
```

There is a separate bzipped file saved for each hour, making it easy to manually investigate past performance data or write a quick AWK, grep or Perl script, which extracts only the data of interest. The example below extracts iostat I/O statistics from a bzipped file from 9AM on May 25, 2011:

```
# bzcat enkcel03.enkitec.com_iostat_11.05.25.0900.dat.bz2 | head -15
zzz ***Wed May 25 09:01:43 CDT 2011 Sample interval: 5 secconds
Linux 2.6.18-194.3.1.0.4.el5 (enkcel03.enkitec.com)      05/25/11


Time: 09:01:43
avg-cpu:  %user   %nice %system %iowait  %steal   %idle
           0.76    0.00    0.78    1.37    0.00   97.09


Device:    r/s   w/s   rsec/s    wsec/s avgrq-sz avgqu-sz  await  svctm  %util
sda      12.30 12.66 17968.35   3004.31   840.31     1.27  51.05   3.68   9.18
sda1      0.00  0.00     0.45      0.00   114.13     0.00  12.17   1.57   0.00
sda2      0.00  0.00     0.00      0.00     2.20     0.00   0.62   0.60   0.00
sda3     11.44  7.14 17879.86   2869.85  1116.56     1.21  65.19   4.76   8.84
sda4      0.00  0.00     0.00      0.00     1.14     0.00  18.41  18.41   0.00
sda5      0.25  4.55    14.33    116.28    27.20     0.04   8.01   2.33   1.12
sda6      0.29  0.00    38.61      0.00   131.20     0.01  27.53   0.99   0.03
...
```

The OS Watcher output samples are prefixed by a timestamp line, which starts with "zzz" as you see above. This shows you the exact time, up to the second, when the OS command was executed and what the sample interval was. Note that this "zzz" line will only show you when the monitoring command was executed. Some commands are executed only once per hour, but they keep collecting and dumping data samples throughout that hour. In such case there are monitoring command-specific timestamps printed for each data sample. The following example shows how the cellsrvstat command uses ===Current Time=== to indicate the exact time the performance data below it is from. You can use this prefix in your custom scripts. Here's an example:::

```
# bzcat enkcel03.enkitec.com_cellsrvstat_11.05.25.1300.dat.bz2 | head -30
zzz ***Wed May 25 13:00:00 CDT 2011 Sample interval: 5 secconds
===Current Time===                              Wed May 25 13:00:00 2011

== Input/Output related stats ==
Number of hard disk block IO read requests           0     167987444
Number of hard disk block IO write requests          0     150496829
Hard disk block IO reads (KB)                        0   111186344274
Hard disk block IO writes (KB)                       0    25224016152
Number of flash disk block IO read requests          0      67230332
Number of flash disk block IO write requests         0      15528794
Flash disk block IO reads (KB)                       0     870806808
Flash disk block IO writes (KB)                      0     347337424
Number of disk IO errors                             0             0
Number of reads from flash cache                     0      57890992
Number of writes to flash cache                      0      13119701
Flash cache reads (KB)                               0     870014160
Flash cache writes (KB)                              0     347236056
Number of flash cache IO errors                      0             0
Size of eviction from flash cache (KB)               0             0
Number of outstanding large flash IOs                0             0
Number of latency threshold warnings during job      0         13400
```

```
Number of latency threshold warnings by checker                 0              0
Number of latency threshold warnings for smart IO              0              0
Number of latency threshold warnings for redo log writes       0           6568
Current read block IO to be issued (KB)                         0              0
Total read block IO to be issued (KB)                           0     9066623802
Current write block IO to be issued (KB)                        0              0
Total write block IO to be issued (KB)                          0    25054696317
Current read blocks in IO (KB)                                  0              0
Total read block IO issued (KB)                                 0     9066623802
.... a lot of output removed ....
```

This output is just the first of each 5-second samples dumped by cellsrvstat every hour. The first column shows the cell metric name, and the second column (all zeros) shows the metric value in the *current metric interval* (snapshot). Because the command was just executed (and took its first sample), it shows zero for each metric, as the delta computation starts only after the second snapshot is taken. If you navigate downward in the OS Watcher dumpfile, you will see nonzero values for many metrics, starting from the second snapshot. The last column shows the cumulative value (since the cellsrv process started) for each metric. You probably should just ignore this cumulative value, as it contains information from since the cellsrv start (which may be months ago). Looking at a single cumulative value, accumulating information from such a long time, would not tell you much about what's happening right now or what was happening last Friday at 8AM. Metric deltas over shorter time periods are the way to go, and this is what you see in the second column: the current interval value as of sampling the metrics. Now let's say we are interested only in a single cellsrv metric, Number of Latency Threshold for Redo Log Writes, as the database layer experienced some *log file parallel write* delays (as seen in V$EVENT_HISTOGRAM, for example) earlier. Let's say this happened on May 5, 2011 early in the morning. As the OS Watcher logfiles are named according the date and time (YY.MM.DD and hour in 24-hour format), you can search for specific files only by using regular Unix filesystem wildcards. In the following example we're searching for all hours of May 5, 2011 and using egrep to list both the "current time" and the metric lines from the matching files:

```
# bzcat enkcel03.enkitec.com_cellsrvstat_11.05.25.*.dat.bz2 | \
  egrep "===Current Time===|Number of latency threshold warnings for redo log writes" | \
  head

===Current Time===                                Wed May 25 00:00:03 2011
Number of latency threshold warnings for redo log writes       0           6564
===Current Time===                                Wed May 25 00:00:08 2011
Number of latency threshold warnings for redo log writes       0           6564
===Current Time===                                Wed May 25 00:00:13 2011
Number of latency threshold warnings for redo log writes       0           6564
===Current Time===                                Wed May 25 00:00:18 2011
Number of latency threshold warnings for redo log writes       0           6564
===Current Time===                                Wed May 25 00:00:23 2011
Number of latency threshold warnings for redo log writes       2           6566
```

As it's hard to read the above output, here's a little script which formats the output better and is more convenient to use:

```
#!/bin/bash

# Name:    oswextract.sh
# Purpose: Extract a specific metric from OS Watcher cellsrvstat archives
#
# Usage:
#   ./oswetract.sh "cellsrv metric to grep for" osw_archive_files_of_interest*.dat.bz2
#
# Example:
#   ./oswextract.sh "Number of latency threshold warnings for redo log writes" \
#                                   cell01.example.com_cellsrvstat_11.05.25.*.dat.bz2

METRIC=$1
shift

bzcat -q $* |
  egrep "Current Time|$METRIC" |
  awk '
    BEGIN
      { printf("%-21s %20s %20s\n", "TIME", "CURRENT_VAL", "CUMULATIVE_VAL") }
    /Current/
      { printf("%s %s %s %s", $3, $4, $5, $6, $7) }
    /Number of latency threshold warnings for redo log writes/
      { printf("%20d %20d\n", $10, $11) }

  '

# end of script
```

While this script is meant to make extracting the desired metric history out of the OS Watcher logs easier, the main purpose of listing the script in this book is to show how easy extracting historical OS-level (and other) metrics can be. Investing a day into learning basic AWK or Perl text processing will likely pay off and save time when you need to do unconventional monitoring or troubleshooting tasks. Let's see what it does:

```
# ./oswextract.sh "Number of latency threshold warnings for redo log writes" \
                    enkcel03.enkitec.com_cellsrvstat_11.05.25.*.dat.bz2   | head

TIME                         CURRENT_VAL        CUMULATIVE_VAL
Wed May 25 00:00:03               0                  6564
Wed May 25 00:00:08               0                  6564
Wed May 25 00:00:13               0                  6564
Wed May 25 00:00:18               0                  6564
Wed May 25 00:00:23               2                  6566
Wed May 25 00:00:28               0                  6566
Wed May 25 00:00:33               0                  6566
Wed May 25 00:00:38               0                  6566
Wed May 25 00:00:43               0                  6566
```

The script goes through all the filenames, which match the second expression on the command line and greps for whatever metric is specified as the first parameter (in double quotes). In this case we are looking for Number of Latency Threshold Warnings for Redo Log Writes, which is incremented when I/O operations tagged as redolog file writes take too long to complete in the cell. Apparently there were two I/O operations around the time range between 00:00:18 and 00:00:23 which had response times high enough to be reported.

Using the previous example, you can already generate formatted data good enough for visual inspection or loading into Excel or some charting tool. If you are looking only for some random problem times, then you can do post-processing, such as showing just the lines where the metric value is not zero:

```
# ./oswextract.sh "Number of latency threshold warnings for redo log writes" \
        enkcel03.enkitec.com_cellsrvstat_11.05.*.*.dat.bz2 | grep -v " 0 "
```

TIME	CURRENT_VAL	CUMULATIVE_VAL
Sat May 7 02:00:02	2	2
Sat May 7 06:00:03	10	12
Sat May 7 08:00:02	5	17
Sat May 7 21:28:15	1	18
Sat May 7 22:00:19	1	19
Sat May 7 22:00:29	4	23
Sat May 7 22:00:34	4	27
Sun May 8 02:00:03	10	37
Sun May 8 02:00:09	8	45
Sun May 8 04:00:03	4	49
Sun May 8 06:00:11	11	82
Sun May 8 08:00:05	6	88
Mon May 9 02:00:10	16	104
Mon May 9 04:00:02	4	108

Alternatively, you can sort the output by the metric value in the CURRENT_VAL column to see the worst problem times first. The next example uses sort -nrk5 as we're sorting the fifth column (columns 1–4 are the date column components, as far as the sort utility sees):

```
# ./oswextract.sh "Number of latency threshold warnings for redo log writes" \
        enkcel03.enkitec.com_cellsrvstat_11.05.*.*.dat.bz2 | \
        grep -v " 0 " | sort -nrk5 | head
```

Sat May 14 06:00:03	30	631
Fri May 13 00:00:09	25	432
Tue May 10 02:00:09	22	174
Sat May 14 00:00:11	22	549
Wed May 11 02:00:08	17	215
Mon May 9 02:00:10	16	104
Tue May 10 22:00:09	12	190
Sun May 8 06:00:11	11	82
Mon May 9 22:00:07	11	126
Sun May 8 02:00:03	10	37

Apparently, the most log file write latency problems were detected at 6:00:03 AM May 14. When you look at the other output lines, you probably see an interesting pattern. All these problems are reported from a few seconds after a full hour. Well, this is just because in this particular Exadata testing cluster, we have over ten separate databases installed, but they only run some reports in parallel and usually there is no

OLTP activity doing commits. But is it then doing these commits just after the hour starts? Well, these are default Oracle Database installations with AWR snapshots taking place at the full hour. And there are over 10 databases in the cluster, with an AWR snapshot taken and written in each cluster database instance. Each AWR snapshot write involves multiple commits, and apparently the resulting log file writes have occasionally taken longer than expected. The next step for troubleshooting such low-level I/O issues in a cell would be to look at the OS-level metrics, like iostat. The cells do perform regular block I/O against their disks, after all, so all the OS-level I/O monitoring tools still do apply.

In the following extract from the iostat archive, you see a few interesting things. The await time shows that on average, I/O completion time (queuing plus service time) is over 100ms for almost all the disks. For a couple of disks it is as high as 549 ms and 738 ms on average! The disk's estimated service time (svctm) shows good I/O service times (below 10ms), so the hard disks and lower half of the I/O subsystem seems to work OK. The high response times must have come from I/O queuing waits, which happens when more I/O requests are issued to OS than the storage hardware (and device driver configuration) can accept.

```
Time: 06:00:05
Device:   r/s   w/s    rsec/s    wsec/s avgrq-sz avgqu-sz   await svctm  %util
sda     84.60 15.20 162235.20   1038.40  1636.01    61.35  738.49  9.40  93.84
sdb     68.60 16.80 124716.80   1375.20  1476.49    20.91  253.98  8.37  71.50
sdc     65.00  0.00 130918.40      0.00  2014.13    11.14  171.82  8.94  58.12
sdd     60.00  1.20 120358.40     27.60  1967.09     9.74  167.52  8.56  52.38
sde     60.00  4.80 122752.00    245.60  1898.11    10.41  172.73  8.32  53.92
sdf      1.60  1.20     51.20     28.80    28.57     0.00    0.07  0.07   0.02
sdg     58.00  0.00 118272.00      0.00  2039.17     9.51  173.76  8.53  49.46
sdh     54.60  2.40 110912.00     48.40  1946.67    77.09  549.34  9.08  51.78
sdi     24.20  4.80 133280.00    242.80  1035.06    15.82  125.00  5.24  67.62
sdj     64.20  0.40 130566.40      3.40  2021.20    11.07  171.43  8.68  56.10
sdk     61.20  0.80 124515.20     25.60  2008.72    12.32  202.59  9.32  57.78
sdl     78.40  2.60 131196.80     21.20  1619.98    12.41  153.18  7.55  61.14
```

This case is an example of how low-latency OLTP I/Os (like log file writes for commits) don't go well together with large, massively parallel asynchronous I/O workloads, which drive the disk I/O queue lengths up, possibly making the low-latency I/Os suffer. This is why you should keep the I/O Resource Manager enabled in Exadata cells when running mixed workloads, as IORM is able to throttle the Smart Scan I/O and prioritize important background process I/O, such as log file writes, automatically.

You can read more about the OS Watcher tool in My Oracle Support article "OS Watcher User Guide" (Doc ID 301137.1). In fact, you can download the latest OS Watcher from there and use it for monitoring your other servers too. The My Oracle Support version of OS Watcher does not include the Exadata cell-specific monitoring scripts, but you don't need those for your regular servers, anyway. For Exadata storage cells, you'll have to keep using the original version shipped with the cell software, as Oracle doesn't authorize installation of any additional storage into storage cells if you want to keep the supported configuration.

It pays off to open up and skim through OS Watcher scripts; you might learn some new useful OS-level monitoring commands from there and will have a better overview of which OS metrics are available. You should drill down to these low-level metrics when the more conveniently accessible Oracle Database and Cellcli-level metrics are not enough.

Summary

There are thousands of metrics that Oracle Database and the cells provide us. We've only touched on a small set of them here. This leads to the obvious questions: are all these metrics important? What should be their "good" values? Which ones should we act on? And so on. The general answer to all those questions is that no, you do not need to learn, memorize, and "tune" all of these metrics (it is impossible). You should always measure what matters – and it's usually the response time. Ideally, you should start by measuring the *end user* response time and drill down where needed from there, sometimes to the database, sometimes to the application server or network metrics. It's not always the database that is causing the trouble, you know. However, thanks to the complexity of modern multi-tier applications, this end-to-end diagnosis may not be available (and not feasible to implement).

In such case you would take a step downward and monitor the response time of your database queries and transactions. You just start the top-down approach from a little lower in the application stack, keeping in mind that the problem may still actually be happening somewhere in the application layer or higher. When monitoring the response times of your user reports and DW queries, you should probably start from the SQL Monitoring page (or ASH data), and identify the problem user's query from there so you can drill down into it. Using the top-down approach and following the biggest time consumers in the SQL plan from there is much easier than the opposite bottom-up approach, where you might look at some database-wide top SQL report and hope to figure out what's wrong with your specific user's workload.

Of course, there are cases where you'll be monitoring system-wide aggregated *anonymous* performance data (not tied to any specific user or session), as in capacity planning and utilization monitoring. However, questions like "Is my database performing well?" should never be answered by looking at some system utilization report. None of these tools can tell you whether your database system performs well; only your users can. And if the users are unhappy, you can start from an unhappy user and drill down into the response time from there. Oracle provides all the metrics you need!

CHAPTER 13

Migrating to Exadata

So the day is finally here. Your Exadata Database Machine is installed, configured, tuned, tweaked and ready to go. By now you've probably invested many, many hours learning about Exadata, proving its value to the company, and planning how you will make the most of this powerful database platform. No doubt it has been a long road to travel but you aren't there quite yet. Now the real work begins—migration.

This was a much more difficult chapter to write than we expected. We can't count all the migrations we've been through over the years. But when we considered all the various versions of Oracle, the migration tools available, and how they have changed from one version to the next, it became clear that we needed to narrow the scope somewhat. So to keep this interesting and save a few trees we'll be focusing on version 11.2 Enterprise Edition for a majority of this chapter. Along the way we'll point out ways to make the most of the features available in previous versions of the Oracle database.

There are many methods, tools, and techniques for migrating your database from legacy hardware to Exadata, but generally speaking they fall into two broad categories: physical migration and logical migration. While there are several factors that determine which method is best, the decision making process is usually dominated by one factor, the available down time to complete the move. The good news is that there are several strategies to help you get there. Each method comes with its own pro's and con's. In this chapter we're going to dig into each of these methods. We'll talk about reasons you might use one over the other, the relative advantages and disadvantages, and what common pitfalls you should watch out for.

▧ **Note:** Migrating your applications to Oracle Exadata from non-Oracle platforms is out of the scope of this book, so it won't be covered here.

⬛ **Kevin Says:** During Technical Review I approached this chapter with skepticism. In my thinking, the idea of an entire chapter dedicated to migrating a database to the Exadata Database Machine seemed like a waste of space. Allow me to explain.

I routinely remind people that unless Exadata Hybrid Columnar Compression (EHCC) is being used, there is no difference between data segments stored in Exadata Storage Server cells and those in conventional storage. The Oracle Database software deployed in the Exadata Database Machine is Oracle Database 11g—with a very small amount of code that knows how to compress data into EHCC form and otherwise interface with Exadata via iDB. I conducted my first review pass of this chapter with the mindset of an imaginary customer who, for whatever reason, finds no need for EHCC. With that mindset I expected this chapter to be nothing more than an overview of database migration concepts, an occasional reference to Oracle product documentation, and perhaps, a paragraph or two of special handling considerations for EHCC. However, after my first reading of the chapter I felt compelled to add this note to the reader. Even if you know everything there is to know about database migration, in the context of Oracle database, I encourage you to read this chapter. Having said that, I still wish to reinforce the principle that there is no difference between a database stored in Exadata Storage Server cells and one stored in conventional storage—unless HCC is involved. To end up with an Oracle database stored in Exadata Storage Server cells, you have to flow the data through the database grid using the same tools used for any other migration to Oracle. However, I believe that the principles conveyed in this chapter will be quite helpful in any migration scenario to Oracle. I consider that a bonus!

Migration Strategies

Once you have a good understanding what Exadata is, and how it works, you are ready to start thinking about how you are going to get your database moved. Migration strategies fall into two general categories, logical migration and physical migration. Logical migration involves extracting the data from one database and loading it into another. Physical migration refers to lifting the database, block by block, from one database server and moving it to another. The data access characteristics of your database are a key consideration when deciding which migration method is best. This is primarily because of the way the data is accessed on Exadata. OLTP databases tend to use single block reads and update data across all tables, whereas Data Warehouse (DW) databases are typically optimized for full table scans and only update current data. Exadata uses Flash Cache on the storage cells to optimize single block reads and improve the overall performance for OLTP databases. For DW databases Exadata uses Smart Scan technology to optimize full table scans. The details of these two optimization methods are covered in Chapters 2 and 5. Logical migration allows you the opportunity to make changes to your database to optimize it for the Exadata platform. Such changes might include resizing extents, implementing or redesigning your current partitioning schemes, and compressing tables using HCC. These are all very important storage considerations for large tables and especially so for DW databases. Because OLTP applications tend to update data throughout the database, HCC compression is not a good fit and would actually degrade performance. And while large extents (4MB and 8MB+) are beneficial for DW databases, they are less advantageous for OLTP databases, which use mostly index-based access and "random" single-block reads. Physical migration, by its very nature, allows no changes to be made to the storage parameters for tables and indexes in the database, while logical migration allows much more flexibility in redefining storage, compression, partitioning and more.

Logical Migration

Regardless of the technology used, *logical migration* consists of extracting objects from the source database and reloading them into a target database. Even though logical migration strategies tend to be more complicated than physical strategies, they are usually preferable because of the following advantages:

> **Staged Migration :**Tables and partitions that are no longer taking updates can be moved outside of the migration window, reducing the volume to be moved during the final cut over.

> **Selective Migration:** Often times the source database has obsolete user accounts and database objects that are no longer needed. With the logical method these objects may be simply omitted from the migration. The old database may be kept around for awhile in case you later decide you need something that didn't get migrated.

> **Platform Differences:** Data is converted to target database block size automatically. Big-endian to little-endian conversion is handled automatically.

> Exadata hybrid columnar compression (HCC) can be configured before data is moved. That is the tables may be defined with HCC in the Exadata database so that data is compressed as it is loaded into the new database.

> **Extent Sizing:** Target tables, partitions, and indexes may be pre-created with optimal extent sizes (multiples of 4MB) before the data is moved.

> **Allows Merging of Databases:** This is particularly important when Exadata is used as a consolidation platform. If your Exadata is model V2 or X2-2, memory on the database servers may be a somewhat limiting factor. V2 database servers are configured with 72G of RAM each, while X2-2 comes with 96G RAM per server. This is a lot of memory when dealing with 10 or fewer moderate to large sized databases. But it is becoming fairly common to see 15 or more databases on a server. For example, one of us worked on a project where Exadata was used to host PeopleSoft HR and Financials databases. The implementer requested 15 databases for this effort. Add to this the 10 databases in their plan for other applications and SGA memory became a real concern. The solution of course is to merge these separate databases together allowing them to share memory more efficiently. This may or may not be a difficult task depending on how contained the databases are at the schema level.

> If using the "create table as select" method or "insert into as select" method (CTAS or IAS) over a database link, then the data may also be sorted as it is loaded into the target database to improve index efficiency, optimize for Exadata Storage Indexes and achieve better compression ratios.

There are basically two approaches for logical migration. One involves extracting data from the source database and loading it into the target database. We'll call this the "Extract and Load" method. Tools commonly used in this approach are Data Pump, Export/Import, and CTAS (or IAS) through a database link. The other method is to replicate the source database during normal business operations. When the time comes to switch to the new database, replication is cancelled and client applications are redirected to the new database. We'll refer to this as the "Replication-Based" method. Tools commonly used in the Replication-Based method are Oracle Streams, Oracle Data Guard (Logical Standby), and Oracle Golden Gate. It is also possible to use a combination of physical and logical migration, such as copying (mostly) read only tablespaces over well ahead of the final cut-over and applying changes to them via some replication method like Streams.

Extract and Load

Generally speaking, the Extract and Load method requires the most downtime of all the migration strategies. This is because once the extract begins, and for the duration of the migration, all DML activity must be brought to a stop. Data warehouse environments are the exception to the rule, because data is typically organized in an "age-in/age-out" fashion. Since data is typically partitioned by date range, static data is separated from data that is still undergoing change. This "read only" data may be migrated ahead of time, outside the final migration window; perhaps even during business hours. The biggest advantage of the Extract and Load strategy is its simplicity. Most DBAs have used Data Pump or CTAS for one reason or another, so the tool set is familiar. Another big advantage is the control it gives you. One of the great new features Exadata brings to the table is Hybrid Columnar Compression (HCC). Since you have complete control over how the data is loaded into the target database, it is a relatively simple task to employ HCC to compress tables as they are loaded in. Extract and Load also allows you to implement partitioning or change partitioning strategies. Loading data using CTAS allows you to sort data as it is loaded, which improves the efficiency of Exadata's storage indexes. One could argue that all these things could be done post migration, and that is true. But why move the data twice when it can be incorporated into the migration process itself? In some situations it may not even be possible to fit the data onto the platform without applying compression. In the next few sections we will cover several approaches for performing Extract and Load migrations.

■ **Kevin Says:** The point about ordered loading of data is a very important topic. It is true that this may not always be an option, but the benefit can go even further than the improved storage index efficiency already mentioned. Ordered loading can increase the compression ratio of Exadata Hybrid Columnar Compression as well. In spite of the sophisticated load-time compression techniques employed by the HCC feature, the fundamentals can never be forgotten. In the case of compression, like-values always compress more deeply. It is worth considering whether this approach fits into the workflow and opportunity window for data loading.

Data Pump

Data Pump is an excellent tool for moving large quantities of data between databases. Data Pump consists of two programs, expdp and impdp. The expdp command is used to extract database objects out of the source database. It can be used to dump the contents of an entire database or, more selectively, by schema or by table. Like its predecessor Export (exp), Data Pump extracts data and saves it into a portable data file. This file can then be copied to Exadata and loaded into the target database using the `impdp` command. Data Pump made its first appearance in Oracle 10g, so if your database is version 9i or earlier, you will need to use the old Export/Import (`exp`/`imp`) instead. Export and Import have been around since Oracle 7, and although they are getting a little long in the tooth they are still very effective tools for migrating data and objects from one database to another. And, even though Oracle has been talking about dropping `exp` and `imp` for years now, they are still part of the base 11.2 install. First we'll talk about Data Pump and how it can be used to migrate to Exadata. After that we can take a quick look at ways to migrate older databases using Export and Import. Keep in mind that new features and parameters are added to Data Pump with each major release. Check the Oracle documentation for capabilities and features specific to your database version.

From time to time in this chapter we'll make reference to tests and timings we saw in our lab. Table 13-1 shows some of the relevant characteristics of the servers and databases we used for these tests. The LAB112 database is the source database and EXDB is the target (Exadata) database. It is an Exadata V2 quarter rack configuration.

Table 13-1. Lab Configuration

Database	Db Version	Platform	Processors	CPU Clock
LAB112	11.2.0.1	Red Hat Linux 5, 32 bit	8 Dual Core, Intel Xeon Intel Xeon MP CPU	2.80GHz
EXDB	11.2.0.1	Oracle Enterprise Linux 5, 64 bit	2 Quad Core, Intel Xeon E5540 (Nahalem)	2.53GHz

Here is a breakdown of the segments in my test database.

```
SEGMENT_TYPE              MBYTES
-------------------- ------------
CLUSTER                       63
INDEX                     13,137
INDEX PARTITION              236
LOBINDEX                      48
LOBSEGMENT                   290
TABLE                     20,662
TABLE PARTITION            1,768
TYPE2 UNDO                   142
```

Now, let's take a look at some of the Data Pump parameters you'll want to know about. Here are some of the key parameters that are useful for migrating databases.

> COMPRESSION: Data Pump compression is a relatively new feature. In 10g you had the ability to compress metadata, but in 11g this capability was extended to table data as well. Valid options are ALL, DATA_ONLY, METADATA_ONLY and NONE. Using the COMPRESSION=ALL option Data Pump reduced the size of our export from 13.4G to 2.5G, a compression ratio of over 5 times. That's a pretty significant savings in storage. When we ran the test with compression turned on, we fully expected it to slow down the export, but instead it actually reduced our export time from 39 minutes to just over 9 minutes. This won't always be the case, of course. On our test system the export was clearly I/O-bound. But it does point out that compression can significantly reduce the storage

requirements for exporting your database without necessarily slowing down the process. Unfortunately, the ability to compress table data on the fly was not introduced until release 11gR1. If your database is 10g and you need to compress your dumpfiles before transferring them to Exadata, you will need to do that using external tools like gzip, zip, or compress. Note that the use of the *data* COMPRESSION option in Data Pump requires Oracle Advanced Compression licenses.

FLASHBACK_TIME, FLASHBACK_SCN: Believe it or not, by default Data Pump does not guarantee the read consistency of your export. To export a read-consistent image of your database you must use either the FLASHBACK_SCN or the FLASHBACK_TIME parameter. If you use FLASHBACK_TIME, Data Pump looks up the nearest System Change Number (SCN) corresponding to the time you specified and exports all data as of that SCN. FLASHBACK_TIME can be passed in to Data Pump as follows:

```
FLASHBACK_TIME="to_timestamp('05-SEP-2010 21:00:00','DD-MON-YYYY HH24:MI:SS')"
```

If you choose to use FLASHBACK_SCN, you can get the current SCN of your database by running the following query:

```
SQL> select current_scn from v$database;
```

FULL, SCHEMAS, TABLES: These options are mutually exclusive and specify whether the export will be for the full database, a selection of schemas, or a selection of individual tables. Note that certain schemas, like SYS, MDSYS, CTXSYS, and DBSNMP, are never exported when doing a full database export.

PARALLEL: The PARALLEL parameter instructs Data Pump to split the work up into multiple parts and run them concurrently. PARALLEL can vastly improve the performance of the export process.

NETWORK_LINK: This parameter specifies a database link in the target database to be used for the export. It allows you to export a database from a remote server, pull the data directly through the network via database link (in the target database), and land the files on an Exadata file system. We see this as more of a convenience than anything else, as it saves you the extra step of transporting the dumpfiles manually at the end of the export. It is used by Grid Control to automate the migration process using the "Import From Database" process. Using this method for manual migration doesn't make much sense— if you are going to copy the data over a database link anyway, why not load it to target tables directly, using CTAS or direct-path insert, instead of dumping it to disk and reloading back later on?

Now let's turn our attention to the import process. Schema-level import is usually preferable when migrating databases. It allows you to break the process up into smaller, more manageable parts. This is not always the case, and there are times when a full database import is the better choice. Most of the tasks we will talk about here apply to both schema-level and full database imports, As we go along, we'll note any exceptions you will need to be aware of. If you choose not to do a full database import, be aware that system objects including roles, public synonyms, profiles, public database links, system privileges, and others will not be imported. You will need to extract the DDL for these objects using the SQLFILE parameter and a FULL=Y import. You can then execute the DDL into the target database to create them. Let's take a look at some of the parameters useful for migrating databases.

REMAP_SCHEMA: As the name implies, this parameter tells Data Pump to change the ownership of objects from one schema to another during the course of the import. This is particularly useful for resolving schema conflicts when merging multiple databases into one Exadata database.

REMAP_DATAFILE: Datafiles can be renamed dynamically during the import process using this parameter. This allows ASM to automatically organize and name the datafiles according to Oracle Managed Files (OMF) rules.

REMAP_TABLESPACE: This option changes the tablespace name reference for segments from one tablespace to another. It is useful when you want to physically relocate tables from one tablespace to another during the import.

SCHEMAS: List of schemas to import.

SQLFILE: Instead of importing anything into the database, Object definitions (DDL) are written to an SQL script. This can be quite useful for pre-building objects if you want to make changes to their physical structure, such as partitioning or using HCC compression.

TABLE_EXISTS_ACTION: The action to take if the imported object already exists. Valid keywords are APPEND, REPLACE, [SKIP], and TRUNCATE.

TABLES: A list of tables to import. For example, TABLES=KSO.SKEW, RJOHNSON.TEST

TRANSFORM: This parameter allows you to make changes to segment attributes in object-creation DDL statements, like storage attributes. This provides a convenient way to optimize extent sizes for tables when they are created in Exadata.

Before you begin importing schemas into your Exadata database, be aware that Data Pump only creates tablespaces automatically when a full database import is done. So if you are importing at the schema or table level you will need to create your tablespaces manually. To do this, generate the DDL for tablespaces using the parameters FULL=yes and SQLFILE={your_sql_script}. This produces a script with the DDL for all objects in the dumpfile, (including datafiles). One thing you may notice about the CREATE TABLESPACE DDL is that the datafile file names are fully qualified. This isn't at all what we want, because it circumvents OMF and creates hard-coded file names that cannot be managed by the database. The REMAP_DATAFILE parameter allows you to rename your datafiles to reflect the ASM disk groups in your Exadata database. The syntax looks something like this:

```
REMAP_DATAFILE='/u02/oradata/LAB112/example01.dbf':'+DATA'
```

One final note before we move on to Export/Import. Character set translation between the source and target databases is done automatically with Data Pump. Make sure the character set of the source database is a subset of the target database, or something may be lost in translation. For example, it's okay if your source database is US7ASCII (7 bit) and the target database is WE8ISO8859P1 (8 bit). But migrating between different 8-bit character sets or going from 8 bit to 7 bit may cause special characters to be dropped.

Export and Import

If the database you are migrating to Exadata is a release prior to version 10g, Data Pump won't be an option. Instead you will need to work with its predecessors, Export (exp) and Import (imp). Export/Import features haven't changed much since Oracle 9.2, but if you are migrating from a previous release, you will notice that some features may be missing. Hopefully you aren't still supporting 8i databases, or God forbid 7.x, but not to worry. Even though some options like FLASHBACK_SCN and PARALLEL are not options in these older releases, there are ways to work around these missing features.

PARALLEL is strictly a Data Pump feature but you can still parallelize database exports by running concurrent schema exports. This is a much less convenient way of "parallelizing" your export process. If you have to parallelize your export process in this way you will have to do the work of figuring out which schemas, grouped together, are fairly equal in size to minimize the time it takes for all of them to complete.

COMPRESSION is another feature missing from Export. This has never been much of an issue for DBAs supporting Unix/Linux platforms. These systems provide the ability to redirect the output from Export through the compress or gzip commands by means of a named pipe, something like this (the $ sign is the shell prompt, of course):

```
$ mkfifo exp.dmp
```

```
$ ls -l exp.dmp
prw-rw-r-- 1 rjohnson dba 0 Oct  2 15:17 exp.dmp
```

```
$ cat exp.dmp | gzip -c > my_compressed_export.dmp.gz &
```

```
$ exp system file=exp.dmp owner=rjohnson consistent=y compress=n statistics=none
log=my_compressed_export.log
```

```
$ ls -l my_compressed_export.*
-rw-rw-r-- 1 rjohnson dba 3134148165 Oct  2 22:32 my_compressed_export.dmp.gz
-rw-rw-r-- 1 rjohnson dba       1432 Oct  2 22:32 my_compressed_export.log
```

The REMAP_TABLESPACE parameter is not available in Export/Import. To work around this you will have to generate a SQL file using the INDEXFILE parameter which produces a SQL script like Data Pump's SQLFILE parameter. You can then modify tablespace references and pre-create segments in the new tablespace as needed. Using the IGNORE parameter will allow Import to simply perform an insert into the tables you manually created ahead of time. The REMAP_SCHEMA parameter takes on a slightly different form in Import. To change the name of a schema during import, use the FROMUSER and TOUSER parameters.

There is one limitation with Export/Import that cannot be escaped. Import does not support Exadata Hybrid Columnar Compression (HCC). Our tests show that when importing data using Import, the best table compression you can expect to get is about what you would get with tables compressed for OLTP (also known in 11g as "Advanced Compression"). It doesn't matter if a table is configured for any one of the four HCC compression modes available on Exadata, (Query Low/High and Archive Low/High). This is because HCC compression can only occur if the data is direct-path inserted, using syntax like insert /*+ APPEND */, for example. According the Exadata User's Guide, "Conventional inserts and updates are supported," but "result in a less compressed format, and reduced compression ratio." This "reduced compression ratio" is actually the same as the OLTP compression provided by the Advanced Compression option, which HCC falls back to for normal inserts. By the way, Import will not complain or issue any warnings to this effect. It will simply import the data at a much lower compression rate, silently eating up far more storage than you planned or expected. There is nothing you can do about it other than rebuild the affected tables after the import is complete. The important thing to understand is that you cannot exploit Exadata's HCC compression using Export/Import.

The Export/Import approach also does not support Transparent Data Encryption (TDE). If your database uses TDE you will need to use Data Pump to migrate this data. If you are importing at the schema level, system objects like roles, public synonyms, profiles, public database links, system privileges, and others will not be imported. System objects like these can be extracted by doing a full database import and with the INDEXFILE parameter to extract the DDL to create these objects. This step is where the most mistakes are made. It is a tedious process and careful attention must be given so that nothing falls through the cracks. Fortunately, there are third-party tools that do a very good job of comparing two databases and showing you where you've missed something. Most of these tools, like TOAD and DB Change Manager from Embarcadero, also provide a feature to synchronize the object definitions across to the new database.

If you are still thinking about using Export/Import, note that as the data loading with Import doesn't use direct-path load inserts, it will have much higher CPU usage overhead due to undo and redo generation and buffer cache management. You would also have to use a proper BUFFER parameter for array inserts (you'll want to insert thousands of rows at a time) and use COMMIT=Y (which will commit after every buffer insert) so you wouldn't fill up the undo segments with one huge insert transaction.

When to Use Data Pump or Export/Import

Data Pump and Export/Import are volume-sensitive operations. That is, the time it takes to move your database will be directly tied to its size and the bandwidth of your network. For OLTP applications this is downtime. As such, it is better suited for smaller OLTP databases. It is also well suited for migrating large DW databases, where read-only data is separated from read-write data. Take a look at the downtime requirements of your application and run a few tests to determine whether Data Pump is a good fit. Another benefit of Data Pump and Export/Import is that they allow you to copy over all the objects in your application schemas easily, relieving you from manually having to copy over PL/SQL packages, views, sequence definitions, and so on. It is not unusual to use Export/Import for migrating small tables and all other schema objects, while the largest tables are migrated using a different method.

What to Watch Out for when Using Data Pump or Export/Import

Character-set differences between the source and target databases are supported, but if you are converting character sets make sure the character set of the source database is a subset of the target. If you are importing at the schema level, check to be sure you are not leaving behind any system objects, like roles and public synonyms, or database links. Remember that HCC is only supported in Data Pump. Be sure you use the consistency parameters of Export or Data Pump to ensure that your data is exported in a read-consistent manner. Don't forget to take into account the load you are putting on the network.

Data Pump and Export/Import methods also require you to have some temporary disk space (both in the source and target server) for holding the dumpfiles. Note that using Data Pump's table data compression option requires you to have Oracle Advanced Compression licenses both for the source and target database (only the metadata_only compression option is included in the Enterprise Edition license).

Copying Data over a Database Link

When extracting and copying very large amounts of data—many terabytes—between databases, database links may be your best option. Unlike the DataPump option, with database links you will read your data once (from the source), transfer it immediately over the network, and write it once (into the target database). With Data Pump, Oracle would have to read the data from source, then write it to a dumpfile, and then you'll transfer the file with some file-transfer tool (or do the network copy operation using NFS), read the dumpfile in the target database, and then write it into the target database tables. In addition to all the extra disk I/O done for writing and reading the dumpfiles, you would need extra disk space for holding these dumpfiles during the migration. Now you might say "Hold on, DataPump *does* have the NETWORK_LINK option and the ability to transfer data directly over database links." Yes that's true, but unfortunately when using impdp with database links, Data Pump performs conventional INSERT AS SELECTs, not direct path inserts. And this means that the inserts will be much slower, generate lots of redo and undo, and possibly run out of undo space. And more importantly, conventional path IAS does not compress data with HCC compression (but resorts to regular OLTP compression instead if HCC is enabled for the table). So this makes the DataPump file-less import over database links virtually useless for loading lots of data into Exadata fast. You would have to use your own direct path IAS statements with APPEND hints to get the benefits of direct path loads and maximum performance out of file-less transfer over database links.

■ **Kevin Says:** Add to this list of possible dumpfile transfer techniques the capability known as Injecting Files with Database File System (DBFS). The DBFS client (dbfs_client) has been ported to all Linux and Unix platforms and can be used to copy files into the Exadata Database Machine even if the DBFS file system is not mounted on the hosts of the Exadata Database Machine nor on the sending system. It is a mount-free approach. Oracle Documentation provides clear examples of how to use the built-in copy command that dbfs_client supports. The data flows from the dbfs_client executable over SQL*Net and is inserted directly into SecureFile LOBs. The transfer is much more efficient than the NFS protocol and is secure. Most Exadata Database Machine deployments maintain DBFS file systems, so there is less of a need for local disk capacity used as a staging area.

There are some cases where moving your data through database links may not perform as well as the DataPump approach. If you have a slow network link between the source and target (migrations between remote data centers, perhaps) then you may benefit more from compressing the dumpfiles, while database links over Oracle Net won't do as aggressive compression as, for example, gzip can do. Oracle Net (SQL*Net) does simple compression by de-duplicating common column values within an array of rows when sent over SQL*Net. This is why the number of bytes transferred over SQL*Net may show a smaller value than the total size of raw data.

Transferring the data of a single table over a database link is very easy. In the target (Exadata) database you'll need to create a database link pointing to the source database, then just issue either a CTAS or INSERT SELECT command over the database link:

```
CREATE DATABASE LINK sourcedb
    CONNECT TO source_user
    IDENTIFIED BY source_password
    USING 'tns_alias';

CREATE TABLE fact AS SELECT * FROM fact@sourcedb;
```

This example will create the table structure and copy the data, but it won't create any other objects such as indexes, triggers or constraints for the table. These objects must be manually created later, either by running the DDL scripts or by doing a metadata-only import of the schema objects.

■ **Note:** When creating the database link, you can specify the database link's TNS connect string directly, with a USING clause, like this:

```
CREATE DATABASE LINK ... USING '(DESCRIPTION = (ADDRESS = (PROTOCOL = TCP)(HO/ST = localhost)(PORT = 1521)) (CONNECT_DATA = (SERVER = DEDICATED) (SERVICE_NAME = ORA10G)))'
```

That way, you don't have to set up `tnsnames.ora` entries in the database server.

Another option is to use `INSERT SELECT` for loading data into an existing table structure. We want to bypass the buffer cache, and the undo-generation-and-redo-logging mechanism for this bulk data load, so we can use the `APPEND` hint to make this a direct path load insert:

```
INSERT /*+ APPEND */ INTO fact SELECT * FROM fact@sourcedb;

COMMIT;
```

We're assuming here that the database is in `NOARCHIVELOG` mode during the migration, so we haven't set any logging attributes for the table being loaded. In `NOARCHIVELOG` mode all bulk operations (such as `INSERT APPEND`, index `REBUILD` and `ALTER TABLE MOVE`) are automatically `NOLOGGING`.

If your database must be in `ARCHIVELOG` mode during such data loading, but you still want to perform the loading of some tables without logging, then you can just temporarily turn off logging for those tables for the duration of the load:

```
ALTER TABLE fact NOLOGGING;

INSERT /*+ APPEND */ INTO fact SELECT * FROM fact@sourcedb;

ALTER TABLE fact LOGGING;
```

Of course if your database or tablespace containing this table is marked `FORCE LOGGING`, then logging will still occur, despite any table-level `NOLOGGING` attributes.

Achieving High-Throughput CTAS or IAS over a Database Link

While the previous examples are simple, they may not give you the expected throughput, especially when the source database server isn't in the same LAN as the target. The database links and the underlying TCP protocol must be tuned for high throughput data transfer. The data transfer speed is limited obviously by your networking equipment throughput and is also dependent on the network round-trip time (RTT) between the source and target database.

When moving tens of terabytes of data in a short time, you obviously need a lot of network throughput capacity. You must have such capacity from end to end, from your source database to the target Exadata cluster. This means that your source server must be able to send data as fast as your Exadata cluster has to receive it, and any networking equipment (switches, routers) in between must also be able to handle that, in addition to all other traffic that has to flow through them. Dealing with corporate network topology and network hardware configuration is a very wide topic and out of the scope of this book, but we'll touch the subject of the network hardware built in to Exadata database servers here.

In addition to the InfiniBand ports, Exadata clusters also have built-in Ethernet ports. Table 13-2 lists all the Ethernet and InfiniBand ports.

Table 13-2. Exadata Ethernet and InfiniBand ports in each database server

Exadata Version	Hardware	Ethernet Ports	InfiniBand Ports
V1	HP	2 × 1 Gb/s	2 × 20 Gb/s DDR
V2	Sun	4 × 1 Gb/s	2 × 40 Gb/s QDR
X2-2	Sun	4 × 1 Gb/s 2 × 10 Gb/s	2 × 40 Gb/s
X2-8	Sun	8 × 1 Gb/s 8 × 10 Gb/s	8 × 40 Gb/s

The database servers and cells each have one more administrative Ethernet port for server management (ILOM).

Note that this table shows the number of network ports per database server. So, while Exadata V2 does not have any 10GbE ports, it still has 4 × 1GbE ports per database server. With 8 database servers in a full rack, this would add up to 32 × 1 GbE ports, giving you a maximum theoretical throughput of 32 gigabits per second when using only Ethernet ports. With various overheads, 3 giga*bytes* per second of transfer speed would theoretically still be achievable if you manage to put all of the network ports equally into use and there are no other bottlenecks. This would mean that you have to either bond the network interfaces or route the data transfer of different datasets via different network interfaces. Different dblinks' connections can be routed via different IPs or DataPump dumpfiles transferred via different routes.

This already sounds complicated, that's why companies migrating to Exadata often used the high-throughput bonded InfiniBand links for migrating large datasets with low downtime. Unfortunately, the existing database networking infrastructure in most companies does not include InfiniBand (in old big iron servers). The standard usually is a number of switched and bonded 1 GbE Ethernet ports or 10 GbE ports in some cases. That's why, for Exadata V1/V2 migrations, you would have had to either install an InfiniBand card into your source server or use a switch capable of both handling the source Ethernet traffic and flowing it on to the target Exadata InfiniBand network.

Luckily the new Exadata X2-2 and X2-8 releases both have 10 GbE ports included in them, so you don't need to go through the hassle of getting your old servers InfiniBand-enabled anymore and can resort to 10 GbE connections (if your old servers or network switches have 10GbE Ethernet cards in place). Probably by the time this book comes out, nobody plans large-scale migrations to Exadata V1 and V2 anymore.

■ **Note:** Remember that if you do *not* have huge data transfer requirements within a very low downtime window, then the issues described here may not be problems for you at all. You would want to pick the easiest and simplest data transfer method that gets the job done within the required time window. It's important to know the amount of data to be transferred in advance and test the actual transfer speeds in advance to see whether you would fit into the planned downtime. If your dblink transfer or dumpfile copy operation is too slow, then you can use free tools like iPerf (http://iperf.sourceforge.net) to test out your network throughput between source and target servers. If the dblinks or datapump dumpfile transfer is significantly worse than iPerf's results, there must be a configuration bottleneck somewhere.

This leads us to software configuration topics for high network throughput for database migrations. This chapter does not aim to be a network tuning reference, but we would like to explain some challenges we've seen. Getting the Oracle database links throughput right involves changing multiple settings and requires manual parallelization. Hopefully this section will help you avoid reinventing the wheel when dealing with huge datasets and low downtime requirements.

In addition to the need for sufficient throughput capacity at the network hardware level, there are three major software configuration settings that affect Oracle's data transfer speed:

- Fetch array size (arraysize)

- TCP send and receive buffer sizes

- Oracle Net Session Data Unit (SDU) size

With regular application connections, the fetch array size has to be set to a high value, ranging from hundreds to thousands, if you are transferring lots of rows. Otherwise, if Oracle sends too few rows out at a time, most of the transfer time may end up being spent waiting for SQL*Net packet ping-pong between the client and server.

However, with database links, Oracle is smart enough to automatically set the fetch array size to the maximum—it transfers 32767 rows at a time. So, we don't need to tune it ourselves.

Tuning TCP Buffer Sizes

The TCP send and receive buffer sizes are configured at the operating-system level, so every O/S has different settings for it. In order to achieve higher throughput, the TCP buffer sizes have to be increased in both ends of the connection. We'll cover a Linux and Solaris example here; read your O/S networking documentation if you need to do this on other platforms. We often use the Pittsburgh Supercomputing Center's "Enabling High Performance Data Transfers" page for reference (http://www.psc.edu/networking/projects/tcptune/). First, you'll need to determine the maximum buffer size TCP (per connection) in your system.

On the Exadata servers, just keep the settings for TCP buffer sizes as they were set during standard Exadata install. On Exadata the TCP stack has already been changed from generic Linux defaults. Do *not* configure Exadata servers settings based on generic database documentation (such as the "Oracle Database Quick Installation Guide for Linux").

However, on the source system, which is about to send large amounts of data, the default TCP buffer sizes may become a bottleneck. You should add these lines to /etc/sysctl.conf if they're not there already:

```
net.core.rmem_default = 262144
net.core.rmem_max = 1048576
net.core.wmem_default = 262144
net.core.wmem_max = 4194304
```

Then issue a sysctl -p command to apply these values into the running kernel.

The maximum read and write buffer sizes per TCP connection will be set to 1MB and 4MB respectively, but the default starting value for buffers is 256kB for each. Linux kernels 2.4.27 (and higher) and 2.6.17 (and higher) can automatically tune the actual buffer sizes from default values up to allowed maximums during runtime. If these parameters are not set, Linux kernel (2.6.18) defaults to 128kB buffer sizes, which may become a bottleneck when transferring large amounts of data. The write buffer has been configured bigger as the source data would be sending (writing) the large amounts of data, the amount of data received will be much smaller.

The optimal buffer sizes are dependent on your network roundtrip time (RTT) and the network link maximum throughput (or desired throughput, whichever is lower). The optimal buffer size value can be calculated using the Bandwidth*Delay product (BDP) formula, also explained in the "Enabling High Performance Data Transfers" document mentioned earlier in this section. Note that changing the kernel parameters shown earlier means a global change within the server, and if your database server has a lot of processes running, the memory usage may rise thanks to the increased buffer sizes. So you might not want to increase these parameters until the actual migration happens.

Here's an example from another O/S type. On Solaris 8 and newer versions, the default send and receive buffer size is 48KB. This would result in even poorer throughput compared to Linux's default 128KB. On Solaris you can check the max buffer size and max TCP congestion window with the following commands:

```
$ ndd /dev/tcp tcp_max_buf
1048576
$ ndd /dev/tcp tcp_cwnd_max
1048576
```

This output shows that the maximum (send or receive) buffer size in the Solaris O/S is 1MB. This can be changed with the ndd -set command, but you'll need root privileges for that:

```
# ndd - set/dev/tcp tcp_max_buf 4194304
# ndd - set/dev/tcp tcp_cwnd_max 4194304
```

This, however just sets the *maximum* TCP buffer sizes (and the TCP congestion window) per connection, but not the default buffer sizes, which a new connection would actually get. The default buffer sizes can be read this way:

```
$ ndd /dev/tcp tcp_xmit_hiwat
49152
$ ndd /dev/tcp tcp_recv_hiwat
49152
```

Both the default send buffer (xmit means transmit) and receive buffer sizes are 48KB. To change these defaults to 4MB each, we would run these commands:

```
# ndd -set /dev/tcp tcp_recv_hiwat 4194304
# ndd -set /dev/tcp tcp_xmit_hiwat 4194304
```

Note that these settings are not persistent, they will be lost after a reboot. If you want to persist these settings, you should add a startup script into rc3.d (or some rc.local equivalent), which would re-run the previous commands. Another option would be to put these values to /etc/system, but starting from Solaris 10 the use of the global /etc/system settings is not encouraged. Yet another approach would be to put the values into a Solaris Service Management Framework (SMF) manifest file, but that is out of the scope of this book.

If the source server is still going to be actively in use (in production) during the data transfer, then think twice before increasing the default buffer sizes globally. While you could potentially make the bulk data transfer much faster for everybody with larger buffer sizes, your server memory usage would also grow (TCP buffers live in kernel memory) and you could run into memory shortage issues.

This is where a more sophisticated way for changing buffer sizes becomes very useful. Solaris allows you to set the default send and receive buffer sizes at *route* level. So, assuming that the target server is in a different subnet from most other production servers, you can configure the buffer sizes for a specific route only.

Let's check the current routes first:

```
# netstat -rn
Routing Table: IPv4
  Destination           Gateway              Flags  Ref    Use      Interface
-------------------- -------------------- ----- ----- ---------- ---------
default              192.168.77.2         UG       1         0 e1000g0
default              172.16.191.1         UG       1         1
172.16.0.0           172.16.191.51        U        1         2 e1000g1
192.168.77.0         192.168.77.128       U        1         3 e1000g0
224.0.0.0            192.168.77.128       U        1         0 e1000g0
127.0.0.1            127.0.0.1            UH       1        82 lo0
```

Let's assume that that the target Exadata server uses subnet 192.168.77.0, and one of the servers has IP 192.168.77.123. You can use the route get command in the Solaris machine to see if there are any existing route-specific settings:

```
# route get 192.168.77.123
   route to: 192.168.77.123
destination: 192.168.77.0
       mask: 255.255.255.0
  interface: e1000g0
      flags: <UP,DONE>
 recvpipe  sendpipe  ssthresh    rtt,ms rttvar,ms  hopcount      mtu    expire
        0        0         0         0         0         0      1500        0
```

The recvpipe and sendpipe values are zero; they use whatever are the O/S system-wide defaults. Let's change the route settings now and check the settings with route get again:

```
# route change -net 192.168.77.0 -recvpipe 4194304 -sendpipe 4194304
change net 192.168.77.0
# route get 192.168.77.123
   route to: 192.168.77.123
destination: 192.168.77.0
       mask: 255.255.255.0
  interface: e1000g0
      flags: <UP,DONE>
 recvpipe  sendpipe  ssthresh    rtt,ms rttvar,ms  hopcount      mtu    expire
  4194304   4194304         0         0         0         0      1500        0
```

Now all connections between the source server and that subnet would request both send and receive socket buffer size 4 MB, but connections using other routes would continue using default values.

Note that this route change setting isn't persistent across reboots, so you would need to get the sysadmin to add this command in a Solaris (or SMF service) startup file.

Before you change any of these socket buffer setting at the O/S level, there's some good news if your source database is Oracle 10g or newer. Starting from Oracle 10g, it is possible to make Oracle request a custom buffer size itself (up to the tcp_max_buf limit) when a new process is started. You can do this by changing the listener.ora on the server side (source database) and tnsnames.ora (or the raw TNS connect string in database link definition) in the target database side. The target database acts as the client in the database link connection pointing from target to source. This is well documented in the Optimizing Performance section of the *Oracle Database Net Services Administrator's Guide*, section "Configuring I/O Buffer Size."

Additionally, you can reduce the number of syscalls Oracle uses for sending network data, by increasing the Oracle Net Session Data Unit (SDU) size. This requires either a change in listener.ora or setting the default SDU size in server-side sqlnet.ora. Read the Oracle documentation for more details. Here is the simplest way to enable higher SDU and network buffer in Oracle versions 10g and newer.

Add the following line to the source database's sqlnet.ora:

```
DEFAULT_SDU_SIZE=32767
```

Make sure the source database's listener.ora contains statements like the following example:

```
LISTENER =
  (DESCRIPTION_LIST =
    (DESCRIPTION =
      (ADDRESS = (PROTOCOL = IPC)(KEY = EXTPROC1521))
      (ADDRESS =
        (PROTOCOL = TCP)
        (HO/ST = solaris01)
        (PORT = 1521)
        (SEND_BUF_SIZE=4194304)
        (RECV_BUF_SIZE=1048576)
      )
    )
  )
```

The target Exadata server's tnsnames.ora would then look like this example:

```
SOL102 =
  (DESCRIPTION =
    (SDU=32767)
    (ADDRESS =
      (PROTOCOL = TCP)
      (HO/ST = solaris01)
      (PORT = 1521)
      (SEND_BUF_SIZE=1048576)
      (RECV_BUF_SIZE=4194304)
    )
    (CONNECT_DATA =
      (SERVER = DEDICATED)
```

```
    (SERVICE_NAME = SOL102)
  )
)
```

With these settings, when the database link connection is initiated in the target (Exadata) database, the tnsnames.ora connection string additions will make the target Oracle database request a larger TCP buffer size for its connection. Thanks to the SDU setting in the target database's tnsnames.ora and the source database's sqlnet.ora, the target database will negotiate the maximum SDU size possible—32767 bytes.

▪ **Note:** If you have done SQL*Net performance tuning in old Oracle versions, you may remember another SQL*Net parameter: TDU (Transmission Data Unit size). This parameter is obsolete and is ignored starting with Oracle Net8 (Oracle 8.0).

It is possible to ask for different sizes for send and receive buffers. This is because during the data transfer the bulk of data will move from source to target direction. Only some acknowledgement and "fetch more" packets are sent in the other direction. That's why we've configured the send buffer larger in the source database (listener.ora) as the source will do mostly sending. On the target side (tnsnames.ora), we've configured the receive buffer larger as the target database will do mostly receiving. Note that these buffer sizes are still limited by the O/S-level maximum buffer size settings (net.core.rmem_max and net.core.wmem_max parameters in /etc/sysctl.conf in Linux and tcp_max_buf kernel setting in Solaris).

Parallelizing Data Load

If you choose the extract-load approach for your migration, there's one more bottleneck to overcome in case you plan to use Exadata Hybrid Columnar Compression (EHCC). You probably want to use EHCC to save the storage space and also get better data scanning performance (compressed data means fewer bytes to read from disk). Note that faster scanning may not make your queries significantly faster if most of your query execution time is spent in operations other than data access, like sorting, grouping, joining and any expensive functions called either in the SELECT list or filter conditions. However, EHCC compression requires many more CPU cycles than the classic block-level de-duplication, as the final compression in EHCC is performed with heavy algorithms (LZO, ZLib or BZip, depending on the compression level). Also, while *de*compression can happen either in the storage cell or database layer, the compression of data can happen only in the database layer. So, if you load lots of data into a EHCC-compressed table using a single session, you will be bottlenecked by the single CPU you're using. Therefore you'll need to parallelize the data load to take advantage of all the database layer's CPUs to get the data load done faster.

Sounds simple—we'll just add a PARALLEL flag to the target table or a PARALLEL hint into the query, and we should be all set, right? Unfortunately things are more complex than that. There are a couple of issues to solve; one of them is easy, but the other one requires some effort.

Issue 1—Making Sure the Data *Load* Is Performed in Parallel

The problem here is that while parallel Query and DDL are enabled by default for any session, the parallel DML is not. Therefore, parallel CTAS statements will run in parallel from end to end, but the loading part of parallel IAS statements will be done in serial! The query part (SELECT) will be performed in parallel, as the slaves pass the data to the single Query Coordinator and the QC is the single process, which is doing the data loading (including the CPU-intensive compression).

This problem is simple to fix, though; you'll just need to enable parallel DML in your session. Let's check the parallel execution flags in our session first:

```
SQL> SELECT pq_status, pdml_status, pddl_status, pdml_enabled
  2> FROM v$session WHERE sid = SYS_CONTEXT('userenv','sid');

PQ_STATUS PDML_STATUS PDDL_STATUS PDML_ENABLED
--------- ----------- ----------- ---------------
ENABLED   DISABLED    ENABLED     NO
```

The parallel DML is disabled in the current session. The PDML_ENABLED column is there for backward compatibility. Let's enable PDML:

```
SQL> ALTER SESSION ENABLE PARALLEL DML;

Session altered.

SQL> SELECT pq_status, pdml_status, pddl_status, pdml_enabled
  2> FROM v$session WHERE sid = SYS_CONTEXT('userenv','sid');

PQ_STATUS PDML_STATUS PDDL_STATUS PDML_ENABLED
--------- ----------- ----------- ---------------
ENABLED   ENABLED     ENABLED     YES
```

After enabling parallel DML, the INSERT AS SELECTs are able to use parallel slaves for the loading part of the IAS statements.

Here's one important thing to watch out for, regarding parallel inserts. In the next example we have started a new session (thus the PDML is disabled in it), and we're issuing a parallel insert statement. We have added a "statement-level" PARALLEL hint into both insert and query blocks, and the explained execution plan output (the DBMS_XPLAN package) shows us that parallelism is used. However, this execution plan would be very slow loading into a compressed table, as the parallelism is enabled only for the query (SELECT) part, not the data loading part!

Pay attention to where the actual data loading happens—in the LOAD AS SELECT operator in the execution plan tree. This LOAD AS SELECT, however, resides above the PX COORDINATOR row source (this is the row source that can pull rows and other information from slaves into QC). Also, in line 3 you see the P->S operator, which means that any rows passed up the execution plan tree from line 3 are received by a serial process (QC).

```
SQL> INSERT /*+ APPEND PARALLEL(16) */ INTO t2 SELECT /*+ PARALLEL(16) */ * FROM t1
```

Id	Operation	Name	Rows	TQ	IN-OUT	PQ Distrib
0	INSERT STATEMENT		8000K			
1	**LOAD AS SELECT**	T2				
2	PX COORDINATOR					
3	PX SEND QC (RANDOM)	:TQ10000	8000K	Q1,00	P->S	QC (RAND)
4	PX BLOCK ITERATOR		8000K	Q1,00	PCWC	
5	TABLE ACCESS STORAGE FULL	T1	8000K	Q1,00	PCWP	

Note

   - Degree of Parallelism is 16 because of hint

16 rows selected.

The message "Degree of Parallelism is 16 because of hint" means that a request for running some part of the query with parallel degree 16 was understood by Oracle and this degree was used in CBO calculations, when optimizing the execution plan. However, as explained above, this doesn't mean that this parallelism was used throughout the whole execution plan. It's important to check whether the actual data loading work (LOAD AS SELECT) is done by the single QC or by PX slaves.

Let's see what happens when we enable parallel DML:

```
SQL> ALTER SESSION ENABLE PARALLEL DML;
```

Session altered.

```
SQL> INSERT /*+ APPEND PARALLEL(16) */ INTO t2 SELECT /*+ PARALLEL(16) */ * FROM t1
```

Id	Operation	Name	Rows	TQ	IN-OUT	PQ Distrib
0	INSERT STATEMENT		8000K			
1	PX COORDINATOR					
2	PX SEND QC (RANDOM)	:TQ10000	8000K	Q1,00	P->S	QC (RAND)
3	**LOAD AS SELECT**	T2		Q1,00	PCWP	
4	PX BLOCK ITERATOR		8000K	Q1,00	PCWC	
5	TABLE ACCESS STORAGE FULL	T1	8000K	Q1,00	PCWP	

Note

   - Degree of Parallelism is 16 because of hint

Now, compare this plan to the previous one. They are different. In this case the LOAD AS SELECT operator has moved down the execution plan tree, it's not a parent of PX COORDINATOR anymore. How you can read this simple execution plan is that the TABLE ACCESS STORAGE FULL sends rows to PX BLOCK ITERATOR (which is the row-source who actually calls the TABLE ACCESS and passes it the next range of data blocks to read). PX BLOCK ITERATOR then sends rows back to LOAD AS SELECT, which then immediately loads the rows to the inserted table, without passing them to QC at all. All the SELECT and LOAD work is done within the same slave, there's no interprocess communication needed. How do we know that? It is because the IN-OUT column says PCWP (Parallel operation, Combined With Parent) for both operations, and the TQ value for both of the operations is the same (Q1,00). This indicates that parallel execution slaves do perform all these steps, under the same Table Queue node, without passing the data around between slave sets.

The proper execution plan when reading data from a database link looks like this:

```
SQL> INSERT /*+ APPEND PARALLEL(16) */ INTO tmp
  2> SELECT /*+ PARALLEL(16) */ * FROM dba_source@srcdb
```

```
------------------------------------------------------------------------------------
| Id | Operation              | Name        | Rows  | TQ/Ins |IN-OUT| PQ Distrib |
------------------------------------------------------------------------------------
|  0 | INSERT STATEMENT       |             | 211K  |        |      |            |
|  1 |  PX COORDINATOR        |             |       |        |      |            |
|  2 |   PX SEND QC (RANDOM)   | :TQ10001    | 211K  | Q1,01  | P->S | QC (RAND)  |
|  3 |    LOAD AS SELECT       | TMP         |       | Q1,01  | PCWP |            |
|  4 |     PX RECEIVE          |             | 211K  | Q1,01  | PCWP |            |
|  5 |      PX SEND ROUND-ROBIN| :TQ10000    | 211K  |        | S->P | RND-ROBIN  |
|  6 |       REMOTE            | DBA_SOURCE  | 211K  | SRCDB  | R->S |            |
------------------------------------------------------------------------------------
```

```
Remote SQL Information (identified by operation id):
---------------------------------------------------

   6 - SELECT /*+ OPAQUE_TRANSFORM SHARED (16) SHARED (16) */
          "OWNER","NAME","TYPE","LINE","TEXT"
       FROM "DBA_SOURCE" "DBA_SOURCE" (accessing 'SRCDB' )
```

```
Note
-----
Degree of Parallelism is 16 because of hint
```

In this example, because we enabled parallel DML at the session level, the data loading is done in parallel; the LOAD AS SELECT is a parallel operation (the IN-OUT column shows PCWP) executed within PX slaves and not the QC.

Note that DBMS_XPLAN shows the SQL statement for sending to the remote server over the database link (in the Remote SQL Information section above). Instead of sending PARALLEL hints to the remote server, an undocumented SHARED hint is sent, which is an alias of the PARALLEL hint.

This was the easier issue to fix. If your data volumes are really big, then there is another problem to solve with database links, and it's explained below.

Issue 2—Achieving Fully Parallel Network Data Transfer

Another issue with database links and parallel execution is that even if you manage to run parallel execution on both ends of the link, it is the query coordinators that actually open the database link and do the network transfer. The PX slaves don't somehow magically open their own database link connections to the other database, all traffic flows through the single query coordinator of a query. So you can run your CTAS/IAS statement with hundreds of PX slaves—but you'll still have only a single database link connection doing network transfer. While you can optimize the network throughput by increasing the TCP buffer and SDU sizes, there's still a limit of how much data the QC process (on a single CPU) is able to ingest.

Figure 13-1 illustrates how the data flows through a single query coordinators despite all the parallel execution.

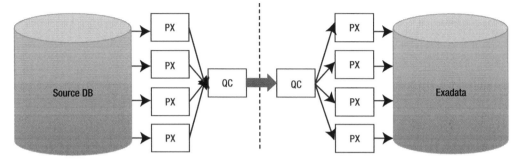

Figure 13-1. *Data flow is single-threaded through query coordinators.*

In addition to the single QC database link bottleneck, sending data (messages) between the QC and PX slaves takes some extra CPU time. This is where fine-tuning the `parallel_execution_message_size` parameter has helped a little in the past, but starting from Oracle 11.2 its value defaults to 16KB anyway, so there probably won't be any significant benefit in adjusting this further. And if you are doing parallel data loads across multiple nodes in a RAC instance, there will still be a single QC per query with a single network connection. So, if QC runs in node 1 and the parallel slaves in node 2, the QC will have to send the data it fetches across the dblink to the PX slaves over the RAC interconnect as PX messages.

So if you choose to use database links with parallel slaves, you should run *multiple separate queries* in different instances and force the PX slaves to be in the same instance as the QC, using the following command:

```
SQL> ALTER SESSION SET parallel_force_local = TRUE;

Session altered.
```

That way you will avoid at least the RAC inter-instance traffic and remote messaging CPU overhead, but the QC to PX slave intra-instance messaging (row distribution) overhead still remains here.

Now, despite all these optimizations and migrating different large tables using parallel queries in different instances, you may still find that a single database link (and query coordinator) does not provide enough throughput to migrate the largest fact tables of your database within your downtime. As stated earlier, the database links approach is best used for the few huge tables in your database, and all the rest can be exported/imported with Data Pump. Perhaps you only have couple of huge fact tables, but if you have eight RAC instances in the full rack Exadata cluster, how could you make all the instances transfer and load data efficiently? You would want to have at least one parallel query with its query coordinator and database link per instance and likely multiple such queries if a single QC process can't pull and distribute data fast enough.

The obvious solution here is to take advantage of partitioning, as your large multi-terabyte tables are likely partitioned in the source database anyway. So you can copy the huge table in multiple separate parts. However there are a couple of problems associated with this approach.

The first issue is that when performing the usual direct path load insert (which is needed for Hybrid Columnar Compression and for `NOLOGGING` loads), your session would lock the table it inserts into exclusively for itself. Nobody else can modify nor insert into that table while there is an uncommitted direct path load transaction active against that table. Note that others can still read that table, as SELECT statements don't take enqueue locks on tables they select from.

So, how to work around this concurrency issue? Luckily Oracle INSERT syntax allows you to specify the exact partition or subpartition where you want to insert, by its name:

```
INSERT /*+ APPEND */
INTO
    fact PARTITION ( Y20080101 )
SELECT
    *
FROM
    fact@sourcedb
WHERE
    order_date >= TO_DATE('20080101 ', 'YYYYMMDD ')
AND order_date < TO_DATE('20080102', 'YYYYMMDD ')
```

With this syntax, the direct-path insert statement would lock only the specified partition, and other sessions could freely insert into other partitions of the same table. Oracle would still perform partition key checking, to ensure that data wouldn't be loaded into wrong partitions. If you attempt to insert an invalid partition key value into a partition, Oracle returns the error message:

```
ORA-14401: inserted partition key is outside specified partition.
```

Note that we did not use the PARTITION (*partition_name*) syntax in the SELECT part of the query. The problem here is that the query generator (unparser), which composes the SQL statement to be sent over the database link, does not support the PARTITION syntax. If you try it, you will get an error:

```
ORA-14100: partition extended table name cannot refer to a remote object.
```

That's why we are relying on the *partition pruning* on the source database side—we just write the filter predicates in the WHERE condition so that only the data in the partition of interest would be returned. In the example just shown, the source table is range-partitioned by order_date column; and thanks to the WHERE clause passed to the source database, the partition pruning optimization in that database will only scan through the required partition and not the whole table.

Note that we are not using the BETWEEN clause in this example, as it includes both values in the range specified in the WHERE clause, whereas Oracle Partitioning option's "values less than" clause excludes the value specified in DDL from the partition's value range.

It is also possible to use subpartition-scope insert syntax, to load into a single subpartition (thus locking only a single subpartition at time). This is useful when even a single partition of data is too large to be loaded fast enough via a single process/database link, allowing you to split your data into even smaller pieces:

```
INSERT /*+ APPEND */
INTO
    fact SUBPARTITION ( Y20080101_SP01 )
SELECT
    *
FROM
    fact@sourcedb
WHERE
    order_date >= TO_DATE('20080101 ', 'YYYYMMDD ')
AND order_date < TO_DATE('20080102', 'YYYYMMDD ')
AND ORA_HASH(customer_id, 63, 0) + 1 = 1
```

In this example the source table is still range-partitioned by order_date, but it is hash partitioned to 64 subpartitions. As it's not possible to send the SUBPARTITION clause through the database link, either, we have used the ORA_HASH function to fetch only the rows belonging to the first hash subpartition of 64 total subpartitions. The ORA_HASH SQL function uses the same kgghash() function internally, which is used for distributing rows to hash partitions and subpartitions. If we had 128 subpartitions, we would change the 63 in the SQL syntax to 127 (n - 1).

As we would need to transfer all the subpartitions, we would copy other subpartitions in parallel, depending on the server load of course, by running slight variations of the above query and changing only the target subpartition name and the ORA_HASH output to corresponding subpartition position.

```
INSERT /*+ APPEND */
INTO
    fact SUBPARTITION ( Y20080101_SP02 )
SELECT
    *
FROM
    fact@sourcedb
WHERE
    order_date >= TO_DATE('20080101 ', 'YYYYMMDD ')
AND order_date  < TO_DATE('20080102', 'YYYYMMDD ')
AND ORA_HASH(customer_id, 63, 0) + 1 = 2
```

And so you'll need to run a total of 64 versions of this script:

```
... INTO fact SUBPARTITION ( Y20080101_SP03 )  ... WHERE ORA_HASH(customer_id, 63, 0) + 1 = 3
...
... INTO fact SUBPARTITION ( Y20080101_SP04 )  ... WHERE ORA_HASH(customer_id, 63, 0) + 1 = 4
...
...
... INTO fact SUBPARTITION ( Y20080101_SP64 )  ... WHERE ORA_HASH(customer_id, 63, 0) + 1 = 64
...
```

If your table's hash subpartition numbering scheme in the subpartition name doesn't correspond to the real subpartition position (the ORA_HASH return value), then you'll need to query DBA_TAB_SUBPARTITIONS and find the correct subpartition_name using the SUBPARTITION_PO/SITION column.

There's one more catch though. While the order_date predicate will be used for partition pruning in the source database, the ORA_HASH function won't—the query execution engine just doesn't know how to use the ORA_HASH predicate for subpartition pruning. In other words, the above query will read all 64 subpartitions of a specified range partition, then the ORA_HASH function will be applied to every row fetched and the rows with non-matching ORA_HASH result will be thrown away. So, if you have 64 sessions, each trying to read one subpartition with the above method, each of them would end up scanning through all subpartitions under this range partition, this means $64 \times 64 = 4096$ subpartition scans.

We have worked around this problem by creating views on the source table in the source database. We would create a view for each subpartition, using a script, of course. The view names would follow a naming convention such as V_FACT_Y2008010_SP01, and each view would contain the SUBPARTITION (xyz) clause in the view's SELECT statement. Remember, these views would be created in the source database, so there won't be an issue with database links syntax restriction. And when it's time to migrate, the insert-into-subpartition statements executed in the target Exadata database would reference appropriate views depending on which subpartition is required. This means that some large fact tables would have thousands of views on them. The views may be in a separate schema, as long as the schema owner has read rights on the source table. Also, you probably don't have to use this trick on all partitions of the table, as if your largest tables are time-partitioned by some order_date or similar, then you can probably transfer much of the old partitions before the downtime window, so you won't need to use such extreme measures.

The techniques just discussed may seem quite complicated and time consuming, but if you have tens or hundreds of terabytes of raw data to extract, transfer, and compress, and all this has to happen very fast, such measures are going to be useful. We have used these techniques for migrating VLDB data warehouses up to 100TB in size (compressed with old-fashioned block compression) with raw data sets exceeding a quarter of a petabyte. However, we need to optimize our own time too, so read the next section about when it is feasible to go with database links and when it is not.

When to Use CTAS or IAS over Database Links

If you have allocated plenty of downtime, and the database to be migrated isn't too big, and you don't want to do major reorganization of your database schemas, then you probably don't have to use data load over database links. A full DataPump export/import is much easier if you have the downtime and disk space available; everything can be exported and imported with a simple command.

However, when you are migrating VLDBs with low downtime windows, database links can provide one performance advantage—with database links you don't have to dump the data to a disk file just to copy it over and reload it back in the other server. Also, you don't need any intermediate disk space for keeping dumps when using database links. With database links you read the data from disk once (in the source database), transfer it over the wire, and write it to disk once in the target.

Transferring lots of small tables may actually be faster with the Export/Import or Data Pump method. Also, the other schema objects (views, sequences, PL/SQL, and so on) have to be somehow migrated anyway. So it's a good idea to transfer only the large tables over database links and use Export/Import or Data Pump for migrating everything else. And by the way, Data Pump has a nice EXCLUDE: parameter you can use for excluding the large manually transferred tables from an export job.

What to Watch Out For When Copying Tables over Database Links

Copying tables during business hours can impact performance on the source database. It can also put a load on the network, sometimes even when dedicated network hardware is installed for reducing the impact of high-throughput data transfer during production time.

Table 13-3 shows a summary of the capabilities of each of these Extract and Load methods.

Table 13-3. When to Use Extract and Load

Requirement	Data Pump	Export/Import	Database Link
Schema Changes	Yes	Yes	Yes
Table/Index Storage Changes	Yes	Yes[1]	Yes
Tablespace Changes	Yes	No	Yes

Requirement	Data Pump	Export/Import	Database Link
Data Is Encrypted (TDE)	Yes	No	Yes
Database Version <9i	No	Yes	Yes[2]
Hybrid Columnar Compression	Yes	No	Yes
Direct path load	Yes	No	Yes

[1] It is possible to change the object creation DDL by running imp with show=y option to extract the DDL statements, modifying the script and creating the objects manually in Sqlplus. Data Pump has made such tasks much easier thanks to its TRANSFORM parameter.

[2] Oracle doesn't support SQL*Net connectivity between Oracle 10g (and newer) and pre-8.1.7.4 database versions. If you attempt such connection, you will receive an error message ORA-03134: Connections to this server version are no longer supported.

Replication-Based Migration

Generally speaking, *replication-based* migration is done by creating a copy of the source database and then keeping it in sync by applying changes to the copy, or "target database." There are two very different methods for applying these changes. *Physical replication* ships archived redo logs to the target where it is applied to the database using its internal recovery mechanisms. This is called "Redo Apply". We'll talk more about how that works in the "Physical Migration" section later in this chapter. With *logical replication*, changes to the source database are extracted as SQL statements and executed on the target database. The technique of using SQL statements to replicate changes from source to target is called *SQL Apply*. Back in the 90,s when Oracle 7 and 8 were all the rage, it was common practice among DBAs to use *snapshots* to keep tables in a remote database in sync with master tables in the source database. These snapshots used triggers to capture changes to the master table and execute them on the target. Snapshot logs were used to queue up these changes when the target tables were unavailable so they could be executed at a later time. It was a simple form of logical replication. Of course, this was fine for a handful of tables but it became unwieldy when replicating groups of tables or entire schemas. In later releases Oracle wrapped some manageability features around this technology and branded it "Simple Replication." Even back in the early days of database replication there were companies that figured out how to mine database redo logs to capture DML more efficiently and less intrusively than triggers could. Today there are several products on the market that do a very good job of using this "log mining" technique to replicate databases. The advantage logical replication has over physical replication is in its flexibility. For example, logical replication allows the target to be available for read access. In some cases it also allows you to implement table compression and partitioning in the target database. In the next few sections we'll discuss several tools that support replication-based migration.

Oracle Streams and Golden Gate

Oracle Streams is included in the base RDBMS product and was introduced as a new feature in version 9i. Golden Gate is a product recently acquired by Oracle. Both products replicate data in much the same way. A copy of the source database is created (the target) and started up. This may be done from a full database backup using Recovery Manager or by using Data Pump to instantiate SELECT schemas. Then changes in the source database are extracted, or mined, from the redo logs. The changes are then converted to equivalent DML and DDL statements and executed in the target database. Oracle calls these steps Capture, Stage, and Apply.

Regardless of which product you use, the target database remains online and available for applications to use while replication is running. New tables may be created in the target schema or in other schemas. Any restrictions on the target are limited to the tables being replicated. This is particularly useful when your migration strategy involves consolidation—taking schemas from multiple source databases and consolidating them into one database. Because of its extremely high performance and scalability, most companies use Exadata for database consolidation to at least some degree, so this is a very useful feature. If you read between the lines, you realize that this means you can migrate multiple databases concurrently.

Another capability of both Streams and Golden Gate is the ability to do data transformation. This is not something we would normally associate with database migration, but it is available should you need it. Since Streams uses SQL Apply to propagate data changes to the target, you can implement changes to the target tables to improve efficiencies. For example, you can convert conventional target tables to partitioned tables. You can also add or drop indexes and change extent sizes to optimize for Exadata. Be aware that even though replication provides this capability, it can get messy. If you are planning a lot of changes to the source tables consider implementing them before you begin replication.

Tables in the target database may be compressed using Exadata HCC. Be prepared to test performance when inserting data and using HCC compression. It is a CPU-intensive process, much more so than Basic and OLTP compression. However, the rewards are pretty significant in terms of storage savings and query performance, depending on the nature of the query of course. If conventional inserts or updates are executed on HCC-compressed tables, Oracle switches to OLTP compression (for the affected rows) and your compression ratio drops significantly. Direct path inserts can be done by implementing the insert append hint as follows:

```
insert /*+ append */ into my_hcc_table select ...;
```

```
insert /*+ append_values */ into my_hcc_table values ( <array of rows> );
```

Note that the append_values hint only works from Oracle 11gR2 onwards.

Also note that as of this writing, Golden Gate does not support *reading* changes of compressed tables yet. There are three bug/enhancement requests outstanding for adding extraction support for tables compressed with regular, OLTP, and HCC compression. As far as *writing* the data to the replication target goes, we ran some tests in our lab and found that we were able to achieve the "reduced" compression ratio by using Golden Gate's direct load feature. It didn't appear to support the higher levels of compression you would expect from bulk inserts. Table 13-4 shows the results of our compression tests.

Table 13-4. Golden Gate Table Compression

Method of Table Load	Table Size (MB)
Uncompressed Table (baseline)	3,443
insert /*+ append */ select * from …	361
GG direct load *	1,722
GG direct load and 'Append' hint on the insert into the source table.	1,722

* Note that Golden Gate has its own meaning for the term "direct load." In Golden Gate terminology, it means that the initial table data copy (instantiation of a table) is done by directly inserting the extracted rows into the target database with array insert *commands. The indirect approach in Golden Gate means that the initially extracted data is dumped to an extract file first and later loaded with other tools like Replicat (initial-load mode) or Oracle's SQL*Loader. This is why we didn't see ideal compression with Golden Gate s "direct load" method as array inserts are not as good as* INSERT SELECT*s for compression.*

As for Streams, the documentation says that direct path inserts are not supported in 10g databases. 11g does provide limited support through the Direct Path API. Once again, make sure you check the Oracle documentation to see what is supported for your database version. If in doubt run a few tests to see whether you do get the level of compression you expect. However, a big improvement in Oracle 11.2 allows Streams to *capture* data from tables compressed with basic table compression and OLTP compression. From Oracle 11.2.0.2 patchset onwards, Streams/XStream can also capture changes to HCC compressed tables. The *Oracle Streams Concepts and Administration Guide* for 11g Release 2 (11.2) explains this in more detail. This feature gives Streams a big advantage over Golden Gate *if* your source tables are compressed *and* the compressed data is updated, thus requiring some sort of change capture unless you want to copy all that data during downtime.

The list of data types Streams does not support is fairly short in version 11gR2. Here is the list from the Oracle documentation:

- BFILE
- ROWID
- User-defined types (including object types, REFs, varrays, and nested tables)
- XMLType stored object relationally or as binary XML
- The following Oracle-supplied types: Any types, URI types, spatial types, and media types

And here is the list of unsupported data types in Golden Gate:

- BFILE
- BLOB
- CFILE

- CLOB

- NCLOB

- NTY

The following is a quick summary of the benefits common to both Oracle Streams and Golden Gate:

- Support for failover (Oracle RAC environments)

- Support for multi-tenant databases

- Support for table partitioning (target tables)

- Support for HCC compression (target tables only for Golden Gate) although you may not get the best loading compression ratio compared to CTAS or IAS

- Support for storage changes for tables and indexes (target tables)

- Ability to change indexing strategy (target tables)

- Read access to the target tables during migration

- Support for endian differences between source and target

- Support for character set differences between source and target

- Support for different database block sizes between source and target

- Support for change Capture on the target server, reducing the performance impact on the source system

- Not difficult to setup

- Database version-agnostic

- Very little downtime to switch over

Disadvantages common to both Streams and Golden Gate:

- Replicated tables must be keyed. If there is no primary key on the source table, you must provide a list of columns that provide uniqueness. If no such combination exists, the table cannot be replicated.

- Some data types are not supported for replication.

- Log mining on the source system can impact performance. Consider moving the change Capture to the target system.

- It's more complex than other migration strategies.

Disadvantages of Streams compared to Golden Gate:

- Data mining can heavily impact performance on the source database.

- It is more complex to set up.

- DDL is supported but problematic.

- If replication breaks, fixing it can be messy. It is often easier to scrap the target and rebuild it.

- SQL Apply is more prone to falling behind the source than Golden Gate.

- Streams tends to require much more CPU resources than Golden Gate.

Advantages of Streams over Golden Gate:

- Streams is included with your database license, while Golden Gate is sold separately

- If the source database is Oracle 11.2 (or higher), Streams supports capturing changes to compressed source tables (basic and OLTP compression). If both the source and target databases are running Oracle version 11.2.0.2 or higher, then the Streams supports capturing changes to HCC compressed tables too.

- All process information is stored in the database, providing convenient remote access.

- There is integration with Grid Control.

So which should you use, Streams or Golden Gate? We've spoken with clients and colleagues who have used both products. In every case they are using the product for simple replication to a remote site much like you would for database migration. The feedback we get is overwhelmingly in favor of Golden Gate. These users cite Golden Gate's ease of use, stability, and performance as the most important reasons. In addition to this, Golden Gate supports non-Oracle database sources. Streams runs inside the Oracle database and has not been ported to any other database platform. As mentioned, Streams is included in your Oracle database license. Golden Gate is not, and the cost based on the total number of cores on the source and target servers is not trivial. If you have need for data replication beyond your Exadata migration, then the investment may be well worth it. If you are faced with a one-time migration, Streams may be a better fit for cost.

When to Use Streams or Golden Gate

Streams and Golden Gate both provide a lot of flexibility with near-zero downtime. They are well suited for migrations that require changes to the target tables. This includes resizing table and index extents, implementing partitioning strategies, and compressing tables. They also allow you to change schemas, tablespaces, and disk groups, among other things.

What to Watch Out for with Streams and Golden Gate

Since Streams and Golden Gate propagate database changes by mining the redo logs, you must account for NOLOGGING operations. This can be done at the tablespace level using alter tablespace force logging or at the database level using alter database force logging.

Here are a few examples of NOLOGGING operations:

- CREATE TABLE newtab NOLOGGING AS select * from …)

- insert /*+ append */ … (for tables in nologging mode)

- Direct path SQL*Loader (for tables in nologging mode)

Note that some large DW databases are designed to use NOLOGGING for large data loads to save CPU and disk space (fewer archive logs generated). These databases rely on incremental backups plus data reloads as a recovery strategy. In such databases, forcing redo logging for everything may cause unacceptable performance degradation and archive log generation. In those cases it makes sense to configure the ETL engine to perform loads to both the old and new DW system during the transition period.

Sequences are not replicated. They must be dropped from the target and recreated from the source database during the final cut-over. Triggers on the target tables must be disabled during replication and re-enabled during the final cut-over (after replication has been shut off).

Logical Standby

Another type of replication useful for database migration is *logical standby*. Logical standby is a built-in feature of the Oracle database. It was introduced in version 9i release 2 as an extension or additional feature of Data Guard (formerly Physical Standby). On the surface, this strategy sounds a lot like Streams and Golden Gate in that it is basically doing the same thing. Changes to the source database are mined from the redo (or archived redo) and converted to SQL statements and executed on the target database. As in other logical replication methods, the database is open and available while replication is running.

Logical standby is far more restrictive than Streams or Golden Gate. Because the logical standby is actually instantiated from a physical, block-for-block, copy of the source database, several rules come into play. The database version must be the same for the source and the target databases, even down to the patch level. With few exceptions, source and target platforms must also match at least within the processor architecture. For example, logical standby does support a source database running on an AMD64 processor architecture while the target database, Exadata in our case, runs on an Intel EM64T processor. The operating system for both source and target must be the same, although different distributions of Linux will work. For example, you could be running Suse Linux on the source system but Oracle Enterprise Linux on the target as long as the Linux kernel is the same.

It might surprise you to know that while indexes and materialized views can be created in the target database, you cannot use logical standby to implement a partitioning strategy there. For example, you can create or drop indexes on a target table, but you cannot pause replication, drop the table, recreate it as a partitioned table, reload it, and resume replication. Table compression is not supported, either. We tried working around that by compressing the table after converting the target database from a physical to a logical standby, but that doesn't work. Remember that HCC compression only works with direct path load, and logical standby applies changes using conventional inserts. Compression and table partitioning are very important performance strategies for Exadata. The lack of support for these features is a significant downside for logical standby.

The list of unsupported data types is the same for logical standby as it is for Streams and Golden Gate:

- BFILE

- ROWID, UROWID

- User-defined types

- Collections (including VARRAYS and nested tables)

- XMLType stored object relationally or as binary XML

- Multimedia data types (including Spatial, Image, and Oracle Text)

There are a lot of steps in configuring and instantiating a logical standby and we won't go into all the details here. But to give you an idea of how a logical standby is set up, here are the high-level steps:

1. Create a physical standby database (we'll talk about this in the "Physical Standby" section).

2. Stop redo apply on the physical standby database.

3. Configure Log Miner in the Primary database.

4. Convert the physical standby database to a logical standby.

5. Open the logical standby database and restart redo apply.

6. Verify that the logical standby database is applying changes from the source.

Logical standby uses SQL Apply technology to replicate changes from the source database to the target. As mentioned earlier, changes in the source database are converted to SQL statements and shipped to the target for execution. Although this may sound fairly straightforward, there are some interesting implications because of how it is implemented. Here are a few things to keep in mind.

Considerations for DML Statements:

- Batch updates are executed one row at a time.

- Direct path inserts are performed in conventional manner.

- Parallel DML is not executed in parallel.

Considerations for DDL Statements:

- Parallel DDL is not executed in parallel.

- CTAS is executed as create table, insert, insert, insert, …

When to Use Logical Standby

Logical standby has a very narrow list of benefits that set it apart from other, more likely, migration methods. It provides full database replication and allows read access to the standby database during replication. As such, the standby may be used to offload resource-intensive reporting operations from the production database until the time you are ready to make the final switch. Tables and materialized views may be created on the standby database, and indexes may be created or dropped to improve performance.

What to Watch Out for with Logical Standby

NOLOGGING operations do not generate redo, which means they will not be replicated to the standby database. Be sure to turn off NOLOGGING operations using the alter database force logging command in SQL*Plus. Considering its lack of support for modifying storage of target tables, compression, and partitioning, you might opt to use the physical standby approach instead. If you don't require full database replication, Streams and Golden Gate are excellent alternatives providing support for many of the capabilities lacking in a logical standby database.

Parallel Load

This is a bit of "roll your own" method for migration. In this strategy data changes are fed to the database through an in-house developed application. As such, it is a small task to configure the application to update Exadata tables in parallel with the current production database. Historical data is then migrated over to Exadata during normal business hours. Depending on the volume, this may take several days to several weeks. Once all tables have been migrated to Exadata, the feed to the old production system is cut and Exadata becomes the new production database.

Non-Oracle Databases

Clearly the list of options will be much smaller for migrating non-Oracle databases. One of our clients is currently migrating thirty or so SQL Server databases to Exadata. To begin with, this type of migration takes us down the logical migration path; essentially extracting every object and row of data from the source database, and inserting it into the target database. If the source database includes code objects such as stored procedures, functions, and triggers, they will need to be converted to PL/SQL or rewritten completely.

Changing database vendors can be a messy and complicated process. There is a lot to consider, plan, and test. Oracle and other vendors have done a pretty good job of providing tools that automate the process (to some degree). Migrating front-end applications to an Oracle database is a much longer discussion, largely because each database vendor has implemented locking and concurrency control differently. An Oracle database tends to do much less locking than many of its competitors. This is a good thing because less aggressive locking means more concurrency, and more concurrency translates to better scalability. However because of this tendency to "under-lock," applications written for non-Oracle databases should be closely reviewed to ensure that they adequately lock rows where serialization is required. Development best practices are beyond the scope of this book but are well documented. Tom Kyte's book *Expert Oracle Database Architecture* (Apress, 2010) is an excellent resource for DBAs and developers making the switch to Oracle. Beware the concept of "database agnostic" applications; it is a myth. If you are migrating a front-end application along with your database, the code should be reviewed and tested thoroughly. Oracle's Migration Workbench can take some of the pain out of the process of converting your non-Oracle databases to Exadata. Better yet, it is free and fully supported. As of this writing the databases it can migrate are these:

- Microsoft SQL Server
- IBM DB2
- Sybase Adaptive Server
- Teradata
- Microsoft Access
- Informix
- MYSQL

Migration Workbench extracts source database objects, stores them in its repository, and converts them to Oracle-compatible objects. Supported objects are tables, views, constraints, primary keys, foreign keys, indexes, stored procedures, functions, triggers, SQL Server identity columns, temporary objects, users, user-defined types, and more. For example, VARCHAR fields with a length greater than 4000 characters are converted to CLOB in Oracle. Data types that Oracle does not directly support are converted to data types with similar characteristics. For example, the MEMO data type will be converted to an Oracle CLOB data type. Oracle handles the notorious IDENTITY data type in SQL Server by converting it to a NUMBER column on the Oracle side and creating a corresponding insert trigger and sequence. Some objects and syntax cannot be converted automatically. For those objects Migration Workbench analyzes and reports, tasks that once required human intervention. Converting code and data types manually is a tedious, time-consuming, and error prone task. Be sure to allow enough time, and test, test, test. If your database stores data structures only such as tables and indexes, other tools like Golden Gate can be effectively used for migrating your database to Exadata.

When to Use Migration Workbench

Migration Workbench is a very useful tool for reducing the time and effort involved in cross-vendor database migration. This is especially true when there is a substantial amount of procedural code inside the database to be migrated. Instead of spending hours in the books trying to figure out which Oracle data types map best to the source database, Migration Workbench generates these mappings automatically. We've also found it to be a real time saver for DBAs and developers who need to learn how built-in data types, packages, and functions translate to PL/SQL.

What to Watch Out for When Migrating from non-Oracle Databases

Do not underestimate the difficulty of cross-vendor database migration. Even among the SQL family of databases on the market there are significant differences in implementation. You will need a thorough understanding of how things like read consistency and locking are done in your source database as well as how they are done in Oracle. The time and effort required for cross-vendor database migration is directly tied to the complexity of your database and the amount of source code for packages, procedures, and functions that must be converted. If user-defined data types are used in the source database, they will need to be converted manually

Logical Migration Wrap Up

In most cases logical migration provides the most flexibility for reconfiguring extent sizes, implementing or modifying partitioning strategies, and compressing tables using HCC. This flexibility comes at the cost of complexity and restrictions that should be weighed and measured against the simplicity of some of the physical migration strategies presented in this chapter. At the end of the day, you will want to properly size extents for large tables, implement a good partitioning strategy, and compress read-only tables using HCC compression. This can be done before you switch over to Exadata using most of the logical migration strategies we've discussed here.

Physical Migration

Physical database migration, as the name implies, is the process of creating a block-for-block copy of the source database (or parts of the database) and moving it to Exadata. Physical migration is a much simpler process than some of the logical migration strategies discussed earlier in this chapter. As you might expect, it does not allow for any changes to be made to the target database, other than choosing not to migrate some unnecessary tablespaces. This means that you will not be able to modify extent sizes for tables and indexes, alter your indexing strategy, implement partitioning, or apply HCC table compression. All these tasks must be done post-migration. However, physical migration is, hands down, the fastest way to migrate your database to Exadata. For all physical migration strategies, except

Transportable Tablespaces (TTS), the new Exadata database starts out as a single-instance database. Post-migration steps are needed to register the database and all its instances with Cluster Ready Services (Grid Infrastructure). Because physical migration creates an exact copy of the source database, the list of restrictions is very short:

- The source Database version must be 11.2.

  This assumes that you will be migrating to Exadata V2 or X2, the old Exadata V1 supports Oracle 11.1 as well.

  One option is to upgrade the production database to version 11.2 before copying it to Exadata. Upgrading is usually a quick process and is not dependent on the size of the database tables, but rather on the number of objects in the database. (The post-upgrade recompilation of PL/SQL packages and views may take a while however.)

- The source platform must be certified for running Oracle 11.2 (OEL5, RHEL5, SLES10 or other certified Linux versions).

- The source platform must be little-endian (ASM rebalance and cross-platform transportable database only). When using a hybrid solution creating a new database on Exadata and using cross-platform transportable tablespaces, the source database can be on different platforms with different endianness (supported platforms are listed in v$transportable_platform view.)

There are three strategies for performing a physical migration: backup and restore, physical standby, and ASM rebalance. In this section we'll discuss these strategies, how they work, and what they are best suited for.

Backup and Restore

The backup and restore strategy uses Oracle's Recovery Manager (RMAN) to create a full backup of the source database and then restore it to the Exadata platform. Unless you plan to shut down the database during this process, the source database must be running in Archivelog mode. The backup and restore process can be done in one pass using a full backup. This is the best way to move smaller databases to Exadata since smaller databases take much less time. Larger databases may take hours to backup and restore. For these databases the process can be done in two passes by taking a full backup followed by an incremental backup.

Full Backup and Restore

RMAN is used to create a full backup of the database to be migrated. The backup files are staged in a file system or tape library accessible to Exadata. The backup is then restored to the Exadata platform. If the source database is on a big-endian platform, the datafiles can be converted during backup or restore process using RMAN's convert database command. The basic steps are:

1. Perform pre-migration tasks:

   a. Create an entry in the tnsnames.ora file for your database on Exadata (optional).

   b. Copy the password file and parameter file (init.ora or spfile) to Exadata.

2. Restrict user and application access to the database.

3. Take a full database backup (optionally convert to little-endian platform).

4. Copy the files to Exadata (not required if backup resides on a shared file system or tape).

5. On Exadata, startup the database in nomount mode.

6. Restore the control file (optionally convert to Linux x86 64-bit platform).

7. Mount the database.

8. Restore the database (optionally convert to Linux x86 64-bit platform).

9. Recover the database. (Note that you cannot *recover* a database with archive- and redo logs from the source database, if the source database is on a different platform than the target database. This means that you can't reduce the migration downtime by restoring and rolling forward an old production backup if the source database is running on a different platform than the target. In such a case the writable source database files should be restored/copied only when they are in their final state (that is, the source database is already shut down). Read-only tablespace files can still be copied/restored in advance.

10. Perform post-migration tasks:

    a. Convert the database to RAC and create service names.

    b. Reconfigure client tnsnames.ora files, configuration files for connecting to the Exadata database.

11. Make the database available to users and applications.

As you can see, this is a fairly straightforward process. After following these steps you have an exact copy of your production database running on Exadata. There are a few things to keep in mind, though. If your source database uses file systems for database storage, or if you are using ASM but the disk group names are different on Exadata, you may redirect the restored files to the new disk group names by changing the db_create_file_dest and db_recovery_file_dest parameters in the init.ora file before starting the restore process. Table 13-5 shows how these parameters can be used to remap disk group names from the source database to Exadata.

Table 13-5. Remap Disk Groups

Init.ora Parameters	Source Database	Exadata Database
db_create_file_dest	'+DATA_FILES'	'+DATA'
db_recovery_file_dest	'+RECOVERY_FILES	'+RECO'

If your database uses multiple ASM disk groups to store your database files, use the RMAN db_file_name_convert command to remap the file names to ASM disk groups. For example:

```
db_file_name_convert= \
  ('+DATA_FILES/exdb/datafile/system.737.729723699','+DATA')
db_file_name_convert= \
  ('+DATA_FILES1/exdb/datafile/sysaux.742.729723701','+DATA')
```

Incremental Backup

If the database you need to migrate is large and the time to migrate is limited you might consider using the incremental backup and restore strategy to reduce downtime for the final switch to Exadata. Alas, the incremental method *does not* support endian format conversion. Here are the basic steps:

1. Perform pre-migration tasks:

    a. Create an entry in the tnsnames.ora file for your database on Exadata (optional).

    b. Copy the password file and parameter file (init.ora or spfile) to Exadata.

2. Make a level 0 backup of the database.

3. Copy the backup files to Exadata (not required if backup resides on a shared file system or tape).

4. On Exadata, start up the database in nomount mode.

5. Restore the control file.

6. Mount the database.

7. Restore the database.

8. Restrict user and application access to the database.

9. Make an incremental level 1 backup of the database.

10. Copy the incremental backup files to Exadata.

11. Recover the database (applying incremental backup and archived redo logs).

12. Perform post-migration tasks:

    a. Convert the database to RAC and create service names.

    b. Reconfigure client tnsnames.ora files.

13. Make the database available to users and applications.

You may notice that the steps for the incremental backup method are almost identical to the full backup method. The important difference is the downtime required. The bulk of the time for migrating the database is in the full backup itself. This could take hours to complete, and with the full backup method that is all database downtime. The incremental backup method uses a level 0 backup instead of a full backup. In actuality the level 0 backup is the same as the full backup except that it has special properties that allow it to be used as a baseline to which incremental backups can be applied. So using the incremental method, the database remains online for users during the longest part of the migration.

Block change tracking must be activated on the source database *before* the incremental level 0 is taken. When block change tracking is turned on, Oracle keeps track of all the blocks that have changed since the last level 0 backup by flipping a bit in a small bitmap file. This means that when you take an incremental level 1 backup, Oracle doesn't have to scan every block in the database to see which ones have changed. I've seen this reduce an incremental backup of a 13T data warehouse from 9 hours to just over 15 minutes. To see if block change tracking is active execute the following query in SQL*Plus:

```
SQL> SELECT status FROM v$block_change_tracking;

STATUS
----------
DISABLED
```

You do not have to shut down the database to activate block change tracking. It can be done at any time. To turn on block change tracking, execute the following command:

```
SQL> ALTER DATABASE ENABLE BLOCK CHANGE TRACKING;
Database altered.
```

By default the block change tracking file is created in the db_create_file_dest location. If this parameter is not set, you will need to set it or specify the file name for the block change tracking file, like this:

```
ALTER DATABASE ENABLE BLOCK CHANGE TRACKING
  USING FILE '/u01/app/oracle/product/11.2.0/dbhome_1/dbs/TEST_bct.ct' {REUSE};
```

Post-migration tasks are necessary to convert your single-instance Exadata database to a multi-instance RAC database. Converting a single-instance database to RAC will be covered at the end of the "Physical Migration" section of this chapter. Once the database is recovered and running on Exadata, you should make a full database backup. Assuming the database is running in Archivelog mode, you can do this after the database is back online and servicing end users and applications.

When to Use Backup and Restore

Executing a simple database backup and recovery using RMAN is something every DBA should be able to do in their sleep. This makes the Backup and Restore a very attractive strategy. It is best suited for OLTP databases that don't require partitioning and HCC compression. It is also suitable for DW databases that already run on a little-endian, 64-bit platform, post-migration steps notwithstanding.

What to Watch Out for when Considering the Backup and Restore Strategy

Incremental backup and restore does not support platform conversion. If this is a requirement, you might be better off using the TTS migration strategy or revisiting some of the logical migration strategies we've discussed in this chapter. Objects will need to be rebuilt after migration to take advantage of Exadata storage features such as HCC.

Transportable Tablespaces (and XTTS)

Transportable tablespaces (TTS) can be used to migrate subsets of the source database to Exadata. To do this you will need a running database on Exadata to host these subsets of your database. We often describe TTS as a sort of "Prune and Graft" procedure. This method allows a set of tablespaces to be copied from a source database, and installed into a live target database. The TTS process is fairly simple but there are a few things you will need to be aware of before beginning.

Restrictions:

- Tablespaces must be put in read-only mode during the process.

- Character sets will, ideally, be the same for the source and target databases. There are exceptions to this rule. See the Oracle documentation if you plan to change character sets during migration.

- Objects with underlying dependencies like materialized views and table partitions are not transportable unless they are contained in the same set. A tablespace set is a way of moving a group of related tablespaces together in one operation.

- Before transporting encrypted tablespaces you must first copy the Oracle wallet to the target system and enable it for the target database. A Database can only have one Oracle wallet. If the database you are migrating to already has a wallet you will need to use Data Pump to export and import table data.

- Tablespaces that do not use block level encryption but have tables that use column encryption cannot be transported with TTS. In this case Data Pump is probably the best alternative.

- Tablespaces that contain XML data types are supported by TTS as of 11gR1, but you will have to use Data Pump to export the metadata. There are other restrictions and caveats to transporting XML data. Refer to the *Oracle XML DB Developer's Guide* for a complete listing. To list tablespaces with XML data types, run the following query:

```
SQL> select distinct p.tablespace_name
      from dba_tablespaces p,
           dba_xml_tables  x,
           dba_users       u,
           all_all_tables  t
    where t.table_name=x.table_name
      and t.tablespace_name=p.tablespace_name
      and x.owner=u.username;
```

- Opaque types such as RAW and BFILE are supported by TTS but are not converted cross-platform. The structure of these types is only known to the application and any differences in endian format must be handled by the application. Types and objects are subject to this limitation whether their use of opaque types is direct or indirect.

- Database version differences are supported as long as the target database is of the same or higher version than the source database.

Cross Platform Transportable Tablespaces (XTTS) supports conversion between most but not all platforms. To determine whether your platform is supported, run the following query:

```
SYS:EXDB1>SELECT * FROM V$TRANSPORTABLE_PLATFORM ORDER BY PLATFORM_NAME;

PLATFORM_ID PLATFORM_NAME                        ENDIAN_FORMAT
----------- ----------------------------------- --------------
          6 AIX-Based Systems (64-bit)          Big
         16 Apple Mac O/S                        Big
         21 Apple Mac O/S (x86-64)                Little
         19 HP IA Open VMS                      Little
         15 HP Open VMS                         Little
          5 HP Tru64 UNIX                       Little
          3 HP-UX (64-bit)                      Big
          4 HP-UX IA (64-bit)                   Big
         18 IBM Power Based Linux               Big
          9 IBM zSeries Based Linux             Big
         10 Linux IA (32-bit)                   Little
         11 Linux IA (64-bit)                   Little
         13 Linux x86 64-bit                    Little
          7 Microsoft Windows IA (32-bit)       Little
          8 Microsoft Windows IA (64-bit)       Little
         12 Microsoft Windows x86 64-bit        Little
         17 Solaris Operating System (x86)      Little
         20 Solaris Operating System (x86-64)   Little
          1 Solaris[tm] OE (32-bit)             Big
          2 Solaris[tm] OE (64-bit)             Big
```

Exadata is little-endian, so if the source database is also little-endian, tablespaces may be transported as if the platform were the same. If the source platform is big-endian, then an additional step is required. To convert a tablespace from one platform to another, use the RMAN CONVERT TABLESPACE or CONVERT DATAFILE command:

You may convert the endian format of files during the backup using the following command:

```
RMAN> CONVERT TABLESPACE payroll_data,payroll_mviews
          TO PLATFORM 'Linux x86 64-bit'
              FORMAT '/u01/shared_files/%U';
```

In this example RMAN converts the datafiles to an endian format compatible with Exadata. The converted datafiles are uniquely named automatically (%U) and saved in the /u01/shared_files directory. This conversion can be done on the source system or the target (Exadata).

The following command converts the endian format during the restore operation on Exadata:

```
RMAN> CONVERT DATAFILE payroll_data.dbf, payroll_mviews.dbf
          FROM PLATFORM 'Solaris[tm] OE (64-bit)'
          DB_FILE_NAME_CONVERT
            '/u01/shared_files/payroll_data.dbf','+DATA',
            '/u01/shared_files/payroll_mviews.dbf','+DATA';
```

A tablespace can be transported individually or as part of a transport set. Transport sets are more common because, more often than not, object dependencies exist across tablespaces. For example, there may be tables in one tablespace and dependent materialized views or indexes in another. In order to transport a tablespace, you must first put it in read-only mode. Tablespace metadata is then exported using Data Pump with the transportable_tablespaces parameter. You should also specify the TRANSPORT_FULL_CHECK parameter to ensure strict containment of the tablespaces being transported. This ensures that no dependent objects (like indexes) exist outside of the transport set. RMAN is then used to take a backup of the tablespaces in the transport set. Conversion between endian formats may be done during the RMAN backup or during the restore on the target system. Here are the steps for transporting tablespaces to Exadata:

1. Identify tablespace object dependencies.

2. Set tablespaces to read-only mode.

3. Export metadata for the transport set using Data Pump.

4. Take an RMAN backup of the tablespaces in the transport set.

5. Copy the export files along with the data file backups to Exadata.

6. Restore the data files from the RMAN backup to your Exadata database. If endian conversion is needed, use the CONVERT DATAFILE command to restore and convert the datafiles simultaneously.

7. Make the tablespaces read/write again.

8. Using Data Pump, import the tablespace metadata into the Exadata database using the transport_datafiles parameter. You can optionally remap the schema of the tablespace contents using the remap_schema parameter.

When to Use Transportable Tablespaces

TTS and XTTS are useful for migrating portions of the source database using the speed of RMAN. If parts of your database are ready to move to Exadata but others are not, TTS may be a good fit.

What to Watch Out for with the Transportable Tablespace Strategy

Check your Oracle documentation for specific restrictions or caveats that may apply to your database. Watch out for tablespace and schema name collisions on the target database. Tablespaces must be put in read-only mode for the move, so this will incur downtime. You can run an RMAN backup of the tablespaces while they are in read/write mode to see how long this operation will take before deciding whether TTS is an appropriate method or not for your migration.

Physical Standby

In the physical standby strategy, the target database is instantiated from a full backup of the source database. The backup is restored to Exadata in the same way you would for the "Backup and Restore" strategy. Once the database is restored to Exadata, it is started in mount mode and kept in a continual state of recovery. As changes occur in the source database, archived redo logs are generated and transmitted to the Standby database where they are applied (Redo Apply). Unlike the "Backup and Restore" strategy this database is kept in recovery mode for a period of time. Because archived redo logs are constantly being applied to the Standby database, conversion from big-endian to little-endian format is not supported. Standby databases have been around since version 7 of Oracle. The capability is inherent in the database architecture. Of course, back then you had to write scripts to monitor the archive log destination on the source system and then copy them (usually via FTP) to the Standby system where another script handled applying them to the Standby database. In version 9i, Oracle introduced a new product called Data Guard to manage and automate many of those tedious tasks of managing and monitoring the Standby environment. Today Data Guard provides the following services:

- Redo Transport Services

  - Handles the transmission of archived redo logs to the target system

  - Resolves gaps in archive redo logs due to network failure

  - Detect and resolve missing or corrupt archived redo logs by retransmitting replacement logs

- Apply Services

  - Automatically applies archived redo logs to the Standby database

  - Allows read-only access to the Standby database during redo apply

  - Provides role transition management: The role of the source and Standby databases may be switched temporarily or permanently.

  - Switchover: Temporarily switches the roles of the source and Standby databases. Useful for failing back a migration.

  - Failover: Permanent change in roles. Useful for finalizing the migration to Exadata. The old source database becomes the standby and is kept in sync with Exadata using Redo Apply.

- Data Guard Broker:

  - Simplifies the configuration and instantiation of the Standby database.

  - Centralized console for monitoring and managing the Standby database environment.

  - Simplifies switchover/failover of the Standby database.

Data Guard provides 3 modes of replication to the Standby database:

Maximum Availability: Transactions in the source database don't commit until all redo necessary to recover the Standby are written to the online redo log and to the standby redo log.

Maximum Performance: Transactions don't commit until they are written to the source online redo logs.

Maximum Protection: Ensures zero data loss at the cost of performance on the source database.

Keep in mind that although Data Guard is an excellent tool for database migration, that is not its only purpose. Data Guard's forte is protecting databases from media corruption, catastrophic media failure, and site failure. It is an integral component in Oracle's Maximum Availability Architecture. So it's no surprise that some of the replication modes mentioned above make no sense in the context of database migration. Maximum Performance is the replication mode most appropriate for migrating databases, because it has no impact on the performance of the source database. In Maximum

Performance mode, the source database continues to function as it always has. Transactions are not delayed by network issues or downstream replication problems. It's also worth mentioning that Data Guard fully supports either a single-instance standby or an Oracle RAC standby. And as of 11gR1, redo can be applied while the Standby database is open in read-only mode. There is also strong integration with Enterprise Manager Grid Control.

When to use Physical Standby

The physical standby database does not allow any changes to the database (other than datafile name changes). Because of this, it is best suited for database migrations where no changes to the target database are required. If changes need to be made they will have to be done post-migration. Generally speaking, this is less of an issue with OLTP databases, because changes like migrating to large table extent sizes, implementing partitioning, and implementing HCC are not as beneficial as they are for larger DW databases. If getting to Exadata as quickly and safely as possible is your goal, then physical standby may be a good fit. With Exadata's performance and scalability, post-migration tasks may take far less time to implement than you might expect.

What to Watch Out for when Considering the Physical Standby Strategy

There aren't many twists or turns with the physical standby strategy. You should keep an eye on network stability and performance. While it is possible to use Oracle's cross-platform physical standby feature for low-downtime migrations between some platforms, you have no opportunity to do such migrations across platforms with different byte order (endian orientation). There are also some Oracle version specific limitations, read more from My Oracle Support note 413484.1 *"Data Guard Support for Heterogeneous Primary and Physical Standbys in Same Data Guard Configuration"*. If a low-downtime migration between incompatible platforms is required, then you should consider the Logical Standby, Streams, or Golden Gate strategies.

ASM Rebalance

This was a difficult topic to cover, because of the lack of documentation available. It is also far and away the most restrictive, and possibly the slowest, method of migrating to Exadata. So why does it merit inclusion in this chapter? It is one of the most interesting topics in this chapter. The ASM Rebalance strategy utilizes ASM's built-in rebalancing feature to literally shift, block-by-block, off of current storage and onto Exadata's high performance storage cell hardware with zero downtime to the database. How is this possible? Before we get to that let's take a look at the restrictions for this migration strategy.

- The platform must be OEL 5 64 bit (RHEL release 5 limited support).

- The database version must be latest patch release of 11gR1 or higher (latest 11gR2 is best).

- There must be current drivers for Oracle RDS/Open Fabrics Enterprise Distribution (OFED).

- It must be connected to the Exadata InfiniBand switch

Oracle recommends the following kernel network parameters for RDS support:

- `net.core.rmem_default = 4194304`

- net.core.wmem_default = 262144

- net.core.rmem_max = 4194304

- net.core.wmem_max = 2097152

- net.ipv4.ip_local_port_range = 9000 65500

So how does it work? Basically, once all platform hardware and software requirements are met, the following steps allow your current production system to join the Exadata storage network and gain access to the storage cells:

1. A familiar pre-migration task is to configure the init.ora, password and oratab files on Exadata to allow you to start up your database on Exadata.

2. Configure the IB network device, giving it an IP address on the Exadata storage network.

3. Create the cellinit.ora file with one line containing the IP address and network mask for server on the storage network:

```
> cat /etc/oracle/cell/network-config/cellinit.ora
ipaddress1=192.168.12.10/24
```

4. Create a cellip.ora file containing the addresses for each of the storage cells:

```
> cat cellip.ora
cell="192.168.12.3"
cell="192.168.12.4"
cell="192.168.12.5"
```

5. Bring the InfiniBand device online:

```
ifconfig ib0 up

ib  0     Link encap:InfiniBand  HWaddr
80:00:00:48:FE:80:00:00:00:00:00:00:00:00:00:00:00:00:00:00
          inet addr:192.168.12.10  Bcast:192.168.12.255  Mask:255.255.255.0
          inet6 addr: fe80::221:2800:13e:eb47/64 Scope:Link
<lines omitted>
```

6. At this point if everything is working you should be able to see the Exadata disks by running the command from the oracle user account: kfod disk=all

```
[enkdb01:oracle:EXDB1] /home/oracle
> kfod disk=all
[enkdb01:oracle:EXDB1] /home/oracle
> kfod disk=all
--------------------------------------------------------------------------------
 Disk        Size Path                                      User      Group
================================================================================
    1:    1313600 Mb o/192.168.12.3/DATA_CD_00_cell01        <unknown> <unknown>
<lines omitted>
   29:      93456 Mb o/192.168.12.3/RECO_CD_00_cell01        <unknown> <unknown>
<lines omitted>
   41:     469136 Mb o/192.168.12.3/STAGE_CD_00_cell01       <unknown> <unknown>
```

```
<lines omitted>
  53:         336 Mb o/192.168.12.3/SYSTEM_CD_00_cell01      <unknown> <unknown>
<lines omitted>
  65:     1313600 Mb o/192.168.12.4/DATA_CD_00_cell02        <unknown> <unknown>
<lines omitted>
  93:       93456 Mb o/192.168.12.4/RECO_CD_00_cell02        <unknown> <unknown>
<lines omitted>
 105:      469136 Mb o/192.168.12.4/STAGE_CD_00_cell02       <unknown> <unknown>
<lines omitted>
 117:         336 Mb o/192.168.12.4/SYSTEM_CD_00_cell02      <unknown> <unknown>
<lines omitted>
 129:     1313600 Mb o/192.168.12.5/DATA_CD_00_cell03        <unknown> <unknown>
<lines omitted>
 157:       93456 Mb o/192.168.12.5/RECO_CD_00_cell03        <unknown> <unknown>
<lines omitted>
 169:      469136 Mb o/192.168.12.5/STAGE_CD_00_cell03       <unknown> <unknown>
<lines omitted>
 181:         336 Mb o/192.168.12.5/SYSTEM_CD_00_cell03      <unknown> <unknown>
<lines omitted>
-----------------------------------------------------------------------------
ORACLE_SID ORACLE_HOME
=============================================================================

    +ASM1 /u01/app/11.2.0/grid
    +ASM2 /u01/app/11.2.0/grid
```

7. Once connectivity is established between the server and the storage cells, the ASM instance on the database server should be able to add Exadata grid disks to its current ASM disk groupdisk groups using the `alter disk group add disk … REBALANCE POWER 5 nowait` command. When the grid disks are added to the current disk groups, ASM will begin rebalancing data onto the new disks at a rate determined by the `power n` parameter of the `add disk` command. A power range of 1–11 represents the number of rebalance processes that will participate in the operation. Nowait causes the command to return you to the prompt rather than hanging until the operation is complete.

8. You can see the current status of the rebalance operation by querying the `v$asm_operation` view from SQL*Plus (connected to the ASM instance).

9. After the rebalance is complete, the old disks can be removed from the disk groups using the `alter disk group drop disk … power 5 nowait` command. Another disk group rebalance will begin moving the remaining data off of the old disks and onto the Exadata storage grid disks.

10. Once all data has been migrated onto Exadata storage, the database is shut down and restarted on Exadata. Before restarting the database, use this opportunity to upgrade the disk groupdisk groups from version11.1 to 11.2 if necessary.

11. Post-migration tasks must be performed to add the database to the Cluster Ready Services configuration.

When to Use ASM Rebalance

ASM Rebalance is an excellent way of leveraging ASM's built-in features to migrate your database with near zero downtime. It is not the fastest way to migrate to Exadata, and there are a lot of very strict configuration requirements, but once the system is configured the migration is fairly automated. It is probably the most reliable and error free method for migrating your database to Exadata.

What to Watch Out for when Using the ASM Rebalance Strategy

This strategy is not well used or well documented. And it is not for the faint of heart (and certainly not for the inexperienced system administrator). It requires strong system administration skills and solid Linux systems experience. Some of the preliminary steps, such as installing and configuring the InfiniBand card and proper RDS/OFED drivers, can be disruptive to production uptime requirements. This method does not create a copy of your database. It migrates your current database at the storage level. As such, storage layout changes like extent sizing, partitioning, and HCC compression must be done post-migration. A downside to the ASM rebalance method is that ASM Allocation Units (AUs) cannot be changed after the disk group is created. Exadata is more efficient at scanning 4MB AUs, so if your disk groups were configured with 1MB AUs, you would eventually want to create new disk groups in Exadata with 4MB AU sizes and migrate your database to them.

Post-Migration Tasks

Because ASM rebalance makes no changes to the database, tasks like resizing extents, partitioning large tables, and compressing tables will all have to be done post-migration. This can be a substantial task that takes anywhere from several days to several weeks to complete. For all physical migration strategies except TTS, you will need to perform some post-migration steps to add the database into the Cluster Ready Services configuration. There is nothing Exadata-specific to this process (other than connecting to the storage cells), it is the same as for any 11gR2 database. The process is well documented and examples are easy to find, so we won't go into the details here, but the basic steps are as follows:

1. Set the following instance parameters in the spfile:

    - `*.cluster_database=true`

    - `*.cluster_database_instances=2`

    - `NEW_PROD1.instance_name=NEW_PROD1`

    - `NEW_PROD2.instance_name=NEW_PROD2`

    - `NEW_PROD1.instance_number=1`

    - `NEW_PROD2.instance_number=2`

    - `NEW_PROD1.thread=1`

    - `NEW_PROD2.thread=2`

    - `NEW_PROD1.undo_tablespace=undo_tbs1`

    - `NEW_PROD2.undo_tablespace=undo_tbs2`

2. Install the RAC system objects by running the `catclust.sql` script as the sys user.

3. Register the new database with Cluster Ready Services (CRS):

   a. Register the database.

   b. Register the instances.

   c. Create Service Names for the database.

4. Create an additional redo thread for each instance. Note that thread 1 is already active for the first instance.

5. Create an Undo tablespace for each database instance. Note that one already exists for the first instance.

Wrap Up Physical Migration Section

Physical migration may prove to be an easy migration option if your application schema is complex enough that you don't want to take any logical path. Also, physical migration can potentially be done with very low downtime, by restoring a production copy to the Exadata database as a *physical* standby database and applying production archivelogs until it's time to switch over and make standby the new production database. However this approach cannot be used between platforms with different endianness and there are a few more Oracle version specific restrictions.

Dealing with Old init.ora Parameters

When migrating from an older version of Oracle, you might be tempted to keep all the old (undocumented) `init.ora` parameters for "tuning" or "stability". The fact is that Oracle has very good default values for its parameters since 10g, especially so in 11.2; which likely runs on your Exadata cluster. Whatever problems were solved by setting these undocumented parameters years ago, are probably fixed in the database code already. Also, moving to Exadata brings a much bigger change than any parameter adjustment can introduce, so the stability point is also moot. As such, it's recommended not to carry over any undocumented parameters from the old databases, unless your application (like Oracle Siebel, SAP) documentation clearly states it as a requirement.

Also, there are some documented parameters which should be unset when migrating to Oracle 11.2, to allow Oracle to pick appropriate values automatically:

> `db_file_multiblock_read_count`: This parameter should be unset, as starting from Oracle 10.2 the database can pick the appropriate values for it automatically. In fact, this way there actually two different multiblock read count parameters used in Oracle, one for costing and one for execution. This arrangement generally works better than leaving the parameter set to some arbitrary value which affects both the costing and the execution.

- `parallel_execution_message_size`: if you have tuned this parameter in past (to reduce PX Qref latch contention or parallel messaging overhead) then you can unset it, as the default value for this parameter is 16kB starting from Oracle 11.2

Planning VLDB Migration Downtime

When you are estimating the downtime or data migration time, you should only rely on actual measurements in your environment, with your data, your network connection, database settings and compression options. While it is possible to load raw data to a full rack at 5TB/hour (Exadata V2) or even 10 TB/hour (Exadata X2-2), you probably won't get such loading speeds when the target tables are compressed with ARCHIVE or QUERY HIGH. No matter which numbers you find from this book or official specs, you will have to test everything out yourself, end to end. There are some temporary workarounds for improving loading rates, for example, if you have enough disk space, you can first load to non-compressed or EHCC QUERY LOW-compressed tables during the downtime window and once in production recompress individual partitions with higher compression rates.

Summary

In this lengthy chapter we looked into the wide range of tools available for migrating your data to Exadata. You should choose the simplest approach you can as this reduces risk and can also save your own time. We recommend you evaluate Data Pump first, as it can transfer the whole database or schema. And it can do the job fast and is even flexible when you want to adjust the object DDL metadata in the process. Often, however, this approach is not fast enough or requires too much temporary disk space. It all depends on how much data you have to transfer and how much downtime you are allowed. When moving VLDBs that are tens or even hundreds of terabytes in size, you may have to get creative and use less straightforward approaches like database links, copying read-only data in advance, or perhaps doing a completely incremental migration using one of the replication approaches.

Every enterprise's database environments and business requirements are different, but you can use the methods explained in this chapter as building blocks. You may need to combine multiple techniques if the migrated database is very large and the allowed downtime is small. No matter which techniques you use, the most important thing to remember is to test everything, the whole migration process from end to end. You will likely find and fix many problems in advance thanks to systematic testing. Good luck!

CHAPTER 14

Storage Layout

In Oracle 10gR1, Oracle introduced Automatic Storage Management (ASM) and changed the way we think of managing database storage. Exadata is tightly integrated with ASM and provides the underlying disks that have traditionally been presented to ASM by the operating system. Looking at all the various intricacies of cell storage can be a little daunting at first. There are several layers of abstraction between physical disks and the ASM disk groups many DBAs are familiar with. If you've never worked with Oracle's ASM product there will be a lot of new terms and concepts to understand there as well. In Chapter 8 we discussed the underlying layers of Exadata storage from the physical disks up through the cell disk layer. This chapter will pick up where Chapter 8 left off, and discuss how cell disks are used to create grid disks for ASM storage. We'll briefly discuss the underlying disk architecture of the storage cell and how Linux presents physical disks to the application layer. From there, we'll take a look at the options for carving up and presenting Exadata grid disks to the database tier. The approach Oracle recommends is to create a few large "pools" of disks across all storage cells. While this approach generally works well from a performance standpoint, there are reasons to consider alternative strategies. Sometimes, isolating a set of storage cells to form a separate storage grid is desirable. This provides separation from more critical systems within the Exadata enclosure so that patches may be installed and tested before they are implemented in production. Along the way we'll take a look at how ASM provides fault resiliency and storage virtualization to databases. Lastly, we'll take a look at how storage security is implemented on Exadata. The storage cell is a highly performant, highly complex, and highly configurable blend of hardware and software. This chapter will take a close look at how all the various pieces work together to provide flexible, high-performance storage to Oracle databases.

Exadata Disk Architecture

When Linux boots up it runs a scan to identify disks attached to the server. When a disk is found, the O/S determines the device driver needed and creates a block device called a LUN for application access. While it is possible for applications to read and write directly to these block devices, it is not a common practice. Doing so subjects the application to changes that are complicated to deal with. For example, because device names are dynamically generated on bootup, adding or replacing a disk can cause all of the disk device names to change. ASM and databases need file permissions to be set that will allow read/write access to these devices as well. In earlier releases of ASM this was managed by the system administrator through the use of native Linux commands like raw and udev. Exadata shields system administrators and DBAs from these complexities through various layers of abstraction. Cell disks provide the first abstraction layer for LUNs. Cell disks are used by cellsrv to manage I/O resources at the storage cell. Grid disks are the next layer of abstraction and are the disk devices presented to the database servers as ASM Disks. Figure 14-1 shows how cell disks and grid disks fit into the overall storage architecture of an Exadata storage cell.

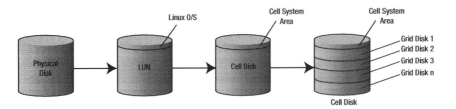

Figure 14-1. The relationship between physical disks and grid disks

With the introduction of ASM, Oracle provided a way to combine many physical disks into a single storage volume called a *disk group*. Disk groups are the ASM replacement for traditional file systems and are used to implement Oracle's SAME (Stripe and Mirror Everything) methodology for optimizing disk performance. As the name implies, the goal of SAME is to spread I/O evenly across all physical disks in the storage array. Virtualizing storage in this way allows multiple databases to share the same physical disks. It also allows physical disks to be added or removed without interrupting database operations. If a disk must be removed, ASM automatically migrates its data to the other disks in the disk group before it is dropped. When a disk is added to a disk group, ASM automatically rebalances data from other disks onto the new disk. In a very basic ASM configuration, LUNs are presented to ASM as ASM disks. ASM disks are then used to create disk groups, which in turn are used to store database files such as datafiles, control files, and online redo logs. The Linux operating system presents LUNs to ASM as native block devices such as /dev/sda1. Exadata virtualizes physical storage through the use of grid disks and ASM disk groups. Grid disks are used for carving up cell disks similar to the way partitions are used to carve up physical disk drives. Figure 14-2 shows the relationship between cell disks, grid disks, and ASM disk groups.

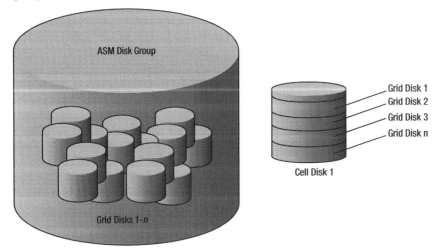

Figure 14-2. ASM disk group with its underlying grid disks, and cell disks

Failure Groups

Before we talk in more detail about grid disks, let's take a brief detour and talk about how disk redundancy is handled in the ASM architecture. ASM uses redundant sets of ASM disks called *failure groups* to provide mirroring. Traditional RAID0 mirroring maintains a block-for-block duplicate of the original disk. ASM failure groups provide redundancy by assigning ASM disks to failure groups and guaranteeing that the original and mirror copy of a block do not reside within the same failure group. It is critically important to separate physical disks into separate failure groups. Exadata does this by assigning the grid disks from each storage cell to a separate failure groups. For example, the following listing shows the fail groups and grid disks for storage cells 1-3. As the names imply, these fail groups correspond to storage cells 1–3. These fail groups were created and named automatically by ASM when the grid disks were created.

```
SYS:+ASM2> select failgroup, name from v$asm_disk order by 1,2

FAILGROUP    NAME
----------   ----------------------
CELL01       DATA_DG_CD_00_CELL01
CELL01       DATA_DG_CD_01_CELL01
CELL01       DATA_DG_CD_02_CELL01
CELL01       DATA_DG_CD_03_CELL01
...
CELL02       DATA_DG_CD_00_CELL02
CELL02       DATA_DG_CD_01_CELL02
CELL02       DATA_DG_CD_02_CELL02
CELL02       DATA_DG_CD_03_CELL02
...
CELL03       DATA_DG_CD_00_CELL03
CELL03       DATA_DG_CD_01_CELL03
CELL03       DATA_DG_CD_02_CELL03
CELL03       DATA_DG_CD_03_CELL03
```

Figure 14-3 shows the relationship between the DATA_DG disk group and the failure groups, CELL01, CELL02, and CELL03. Note that this does not indicate which level of redundancy is being used, only that the DATA_DG disk group has its data allocated across three failure groups.

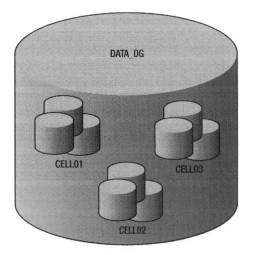

Figure 14-3. ASM failure groups CELL01 – CELL03

There are three types of redundancy in ASM: External, Normal, and High.

External Redundancy: No redundancy is provided by ASM. It is assumed that the storage array, usually a SAN, is providing adequate redundancy; in most cases RAID0, RAID10, or RAID5. This has become the most common method where large storage area networks are used for ASM storage. In the Exadata storage grid, ASM provides the only mechanism for mirroring. If External Redundancy were used, the loss of a single disk drive would mean a catastrophic loss of all ASM diskgroups using that disk. It also means that even the temporary loss of a storage cell (reboot, crash, or the like) would make all disk groups using storage on the failed cell unavailable for the duration of the outage.

Normal Redundancy: Normal Redundancy maintains two copies of data blocks in separate failure groups. Databases will always attempt to read from the primary copy of a data block first. Secondary copies are only read when the primary blocks are unavailable. At least two failure groups are required for Normal Redundancy, but many more than that may be used. For example, an Exadata full rack configuration has 14 storage cells, and each storage cell constitutes a failure group. When data is written to the database, the failure group used for the primary copy of a block rotates from failure group to failure group in a round-robin fashion. This ensures that disks in all failure groups participate in read operations.

High Redundancy: High Redundancy is similar to Normal Redundancy except that three copies of data blocks are maintained in separate failure groups.

Grid Disks

Grid disks are created within cell disks, which you may recall are made up of physical disks and Flash Cache modules. In a simple configuration one grid disk can be created per cell disk. More complex configurations have multiple grid disks per cell disk. The CellCLI command, list griddisk displays the various characteristics of grid disks. For example, the following output shows the relationship between grid disks and cell disks, the type of device on which they are created, and their size.

```
 [enkcel03:root] root
> cellcli
CellCLI: Release 11.2.1.3.1 - Production on Sat Oct 23 17:23:32 CDT 2010

Copyright (c) 2007, 2009, Oracle.  All rights reserved.
Cell Efficiency Ratio: 20M

CellCLI> list griddisk attributes name, celldisk, disktype, size
        DATA_CD_00_cell03        CD_00_cell03      HardDisk      1282.8125G
        DATA_CD_01_cell03        CD_01_cell03      HardDisk      1282.8125G
  ...
        FLASH_FD_00_cell03       FD_00_cell03      FlashDisk     4.078125G
        FLASH_FD_01_cell03       FD_01_cell03      FlashDisk     4.078125G
  ...
```

ASM doesn't know anything about physical disks or cell disks. Grid disks are what the storage cell presents to the database servers (as ASM disks) to be used for Clusterware and database storage. ASM uses grid disks to create disk groups in the same way conventional block devices are used on a non-Exadata platform. To illustrate this, the following query shows what ASM disks look like on a non-Exadata system.

```
SYS:+ASM1> select path, total_mb, failgroup
           from v$asm_disk
           order by failgroup, group_number, path;

PATH            TOTAL_MB FAILGROUP
--------------- ---------- ------------------------------
/dev/sdd1          11444 DATA01
/dev/sde1          11444 DATA02
...
/dev/sdj1           3816 RECO01
/dev/sdk1           3816 RECO02
...
```

The same query on Exadata reports grid disks that have been created at the storage cell.

```
SYS:+ASM1> select path, total_mb, failgroup
           from v$asm_disk
           order by failgroup, group_number, path;

PATH                                     TOTAL_MB FAILGROUP
---------------------------------------- ---------- ------------------------
o/192.168.12.3/DATA_CD_00_cell01          1313600 CELL01
o/192.168.12.3/DATA_CD_01_cell01          1313600 CELL01
o/192.168.12.3/DATA_CD_02_cell01          1313600 CELL01
```

```
...
o/192.168.12.3/RECO_CD_00_cell01                   93456 CELL01
o/192.168.12.3/RECO_CD_01_cell01                   93456 CELL01
o/192.168.12.3/RECO_CD_02_cell01                  123264 CELL01

...
o/192.168.12.4/DATA_CD_00_cell02                 1313600 CELL02
o/192.168.12.4/DATA_CD_01_cell02                 1313600 CELL02
o/192.168.12.4/DATA_CD_02_cell02                 1313600 CELL02

...
o/192.168.12.4/RECO_CD_00_cell02                   93456 CELL02
o/192.168.12.4/RECO_CD_01_cell02                   93456 CELL02
o/192.168.12.4/RECO_CD_02_cell02                  123264 CELL02

...
o/192.168.12.5/DATA_CD_00_cell03                 1313600 CELL03
o/192.168.12.5/DATA_CD_01_cell03                 1313600 CELL03
o/192.168.12.5/DATA_CD_02_cell03                 1313600 CELL03

...
o/192.168.12.5/RECO_CD_00_cell03                   93456 CELL03
o/192.168.12.5/RECO_CD_01_cell03                   93456 CELL03
o/192.168.12.5/RECO_CD_02_cell03                  123264 CELL03
...
```

Tying it all together, Figure 14-4 shows how the layers of storage fit together, from the storage cell to the ASM disk group. Note, that the Linux O/S partitions on the first two cell disks in each storage cell are identified by a dotted line. We'll talk a little more about the O/S partitions later in the chapter, and in much more detail in Chapter 8.

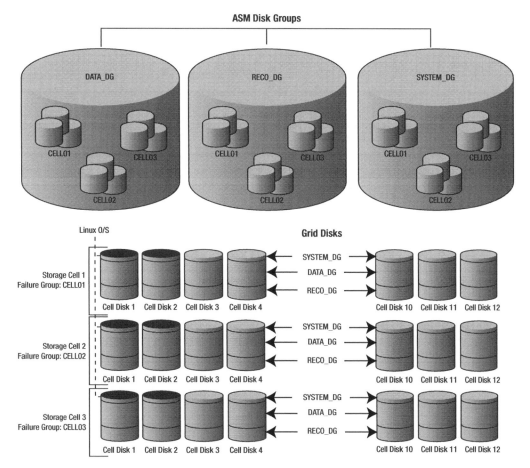

Figure 14-4. *Storage virtualization on Exadata*

Storage Allocation

Disk drives store data in concentric bands called *tracks*. Because the outer tracks of a disk have more surface area, they are able to store more data than the inner tracks. As a result, data transfer rates are higher for the outer tracks and decline slightly as you move toward the innermost track. Figure 14-5 shows how tracks are laid out across the disk surface from fastest to slowest.

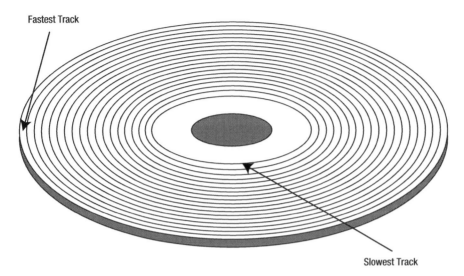

Figure 14-5. Disk tracks

Exadata provides two policies for allocating grid disk storage across the surface of disk drives. The first method is the default behavior for allocating space on cell disks. It has no official name, so for purposes of this discussion I'll refer to it as the *default policy*. The other allocation policy Oracle calls *interleaving*. These two allocation policies are determined when the cell disks are created. Interleaving must be explicitly enabled using the `interleaving` parameter of the `create celldisk` command. For a complete discussion on creating cell disks refer to chapter 8.

Fastest Available Tracks First

The default policy simply allocates space starting with the fastest available tracks first, moving inward as space is consumed. Using this policy, the first grid disk created on each cell disk will be given the fastest storage, while the last grid disk created will be relegated to the slower, inner tracks of the disk surface. When planning your storage grid, remember that grid disks are the building blocks for ASM disk groups. These disk groups will in turn be used to store tables, indexes, online redo logs, archived redo logs, and so on. To maximize database performance, frequently accessed objects (such as tables, indexes, and online redo logs) should be stored in the highest priority grid disks. Low priority grid disks should be used for less performance sensitive objects such as database backups, archived redo logs, and flashback logs. Figure 14-6 shows how grid disks are allocated using the default allocation policy.

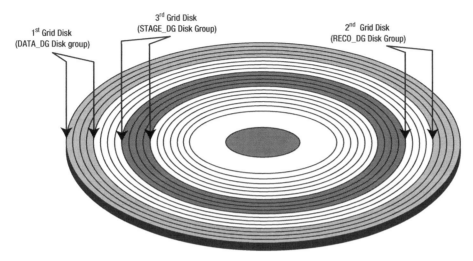

Figure 14-6. The default allocation policy

Table 14-1 shows the performance effect on the ASM disk groups from the first to the last grid disk created when using the default allocation policy. You won't find the term "I/O Performance Rating" in the Oracle documentation. It's a term I'm coining here to describe the relative performance capabilities of each disk group due to its location on the surface of the physical disk drive.

Table 14-1. I/O Performance – Default Allocation Policy

ASM Disk Group	I/O Performance Rating
DATA_DG	1
RECO_DG	2
STAGE_DG	3
Fourth disk group	4
SYSTEM_DG	5

Interleaving

The other policy, interleaving, attempts to even out performance of the faster and slower tracks by allocating space in an alternating fashion between the slower and faster tracks of the disks. This is done by splitting each cell disk into two regions, an outer region and an inner region. Grid disks are slices of cell disks that will be used to create ASM disk groups. For example, the following command creates 12 grid disks (one per physical disk; see Figure 14-4) on Cell03 to be used for the DATA_DG disk group:

```
CellCLI> CREATE GRIDDISK ALL HARDDISK PREFIX=DATA_DG, size=744.6813G
```

These grid disks were used to create the following DATA_DG disk group. Notice how each grid disk was created on a separate cell disk:

```
SYS:+ASM2> select dg.name diskgroup,
                  substr(d.name, 6,12) cell_disk,
                  d.name grid_disk
            from v$asm_diskgroup dg,
                 v$asm_disk d
           where dg.group_number = d.group_number
             and dg.name ='DATA'
             and failgroup = 'CELL03'
           order by 1,2;

DISKGROUP     CELL_DISK      GRID_DISK
----------    ------------   --------------------
DATA_DG       CD_00_CELL03   DATA_DG_CD_00_CELL03
DATA_DG       CD_01_CELL03   DATA_DG_CD_01_CELL03
DATA_DG       CD_02_CELL03   DATA_DG_CD_02_CELL03
DATA_DG       CD_03_CELL03   DATA_DG_CD_03_CELL03

...
DATA_DG       CD_10_CELL03   DATA_DG_CD_10_CELL03
DATA_DG       CD_11_CELL03   DATA_DG_CD_11_CELL03
```

Using interleaving in this example, DATA_DG_CD_00_CELL03 (the first grid disk) is allocated to the outer most tracks of the outer (fastest) region of the CD_00_CELL03 cell disk. The next grid disk, DATA_DG_CD_01_CELL03, is created on the outermost tracks of the slower, inner region of cell disk CD_01_CELL03. This pattern continues until all 12 grid disks are allocated. When the next set of grid disks is created for the RECO_DG disk group, they start with the inner region of cell disk 1 and alternate from inner to outer region until all 12 grid disks are created. Figure 14-7 shows how the interleaving policy would look if two grid disk groups were created.

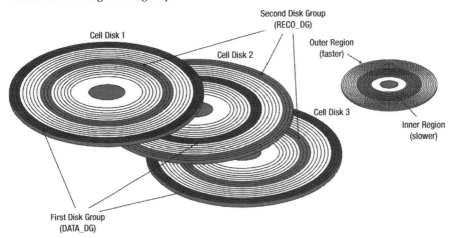

Figure 14-7. The interleaving allocation policy

Table 14-2 shows the performance effect on the ASM disk groups from the first to the last grid disk created when the interleaving allocation policy is used.

Table 14-2. *I/O Performance – Interleaving Policy*

ASM Disk Group	I/O Performance Rating
DATA_DG	1
RECO_DG	1
SYSTEM_DG	2
Fourth disk group	2
Fifth disk group	3

As you can see, the main difference between the default policy and the interleaving policy is that default provides finer-grained control over ASM disks. With the default policy you have the ability to choose which set of grid disks will be given the absolute fastest position on the disk. The interleaving policy has the effect of evening out the performance of grid disks. In practice, this gives the first two sets of grid disks (for DATA_DG and RECO_DG) the same performance characteristics. This may be useful if the performance demands of the first two disk groups are equal. In our experience this is rarely the case. Usually there is a clear winner when it comes to the performance demands of a database environment. Tables, indexes, online redo logs (the DATA_DG disk group) have much higher performance requirements than database backups, archived redo logs, and flashback logs, which are usually stored in the RECO disk group. Unless there are specific reasons for using interleaving, we recommend using the default policy.

Creating Grid Disks

Before we run through a few examples of how to create grid disks, let's take a quick look at some of their key attributes:

- Multiple grid disks may be created on a single cell disk, but a grid disk may not span multiple cell disks.

- Storage for grid disks is allocated in 16M Allocation Units (AUs) and is rounded down if the size requested is not a multiple of the AU size.

- Grid disks may be created one at a time or in groups with a common name prefix.

- Grid disk names must be unique within a storage cell and should be unique across all storage cells.

- Grid disk names should include the name of the cell disk on which they reside.

Once a grid disk is created, its name is visible from ASM in the V$ASM_DISK view. In other words, grid disks = ASM disks. It is very important to name grid disks in such a way that they can easily be associated with the physical disk to which they belong in the event of disk failure. To facilitate this, grid disk names should include both of the following:

- The name of the ASM disk group for which it will be used

- The cell disk name (which includes the name of the storage cell)

Figure 14-8 shows the properly formatted name for a grid disk belonging to the TEST_DG disk group, created on cell disk CD_00_cell03.

TEST_DG_CD_00_cell03

Disk Group   Cell Disk

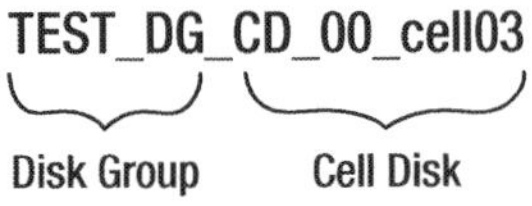

Figure 14-8. Grid disk naming

Creating Grid Disks

The CellCLI command create griddisk is used to create grid disks. It may be used to create individual grid disks one at a time or in groups. If grid disks are created one at a time, it is up to you to provide the complete grid disk name. The following example creates one properly named 96 MB grid disk on cell disk CD_00_cell03. If we had omitted the size=100M parameter, the resulting grid disk would have consumed all free space on the cell disk.

```
CellCLI> create griddisk TEST_DG_CD_00_cell03 -
        celldisk='CD_00_cell03', size=100M

GridDisk TEST_DG_CD_00_cell03 successfully created

CellCLI> list griddisk attributes name, celldisk, size -
        where name='TEST_DG_CD_00_cell03'

        TEST_DG_CD_00_cell03        CD_00_cell03    96M
```

There are 12 drives per storage cell, and the number of storage cells varies from 3, for a quarter rack, to 14, for a full rack. That means you will be creating a minimum of 36 grid disks for a quarter rack, and up to 168 grid disks for a full rack. Fortunately, CellCLI provides a way to create all the grid disks needed for a given ASM disk group in one command. For example, the following command creates all the grid disks for the ASM disk group TEST_DG:

```
CellCLI> create griddisk all harddisk prefix='TEST', size=100M

GridDisk TEST_CD_00_cell03 successfully created
GridDisk TEST_CD_01_cell03 successfully created
...
GridDisk TEST_CD_10_cell03 successfully created
GridDisk TEST_CD_11_cell03 successfully created
```

When this variant of the create griddisk command is used, CellCLI automatically creates one grid disk on each cell disk, naming them with the prefix you provided in the following manner:

{prefix}_{celldisk_name}

The optional size parameter specifies the size of each individual grid disk. If no size is provided, the resulting grid disks will consume all remaining free space of their respective cell disk. The all harddisk parameter instructs CellCLI to use only disk-based cell disks. Just in case you are wondering, Flash Cache modules are also presented as cell disks (of type FlashDisk) and may be used for creating grid disks as well. We'll discuss flash disks later on in this chapter. The following command shows the grid disks created.

```
CellCLI> list griddisk attributes name, cellDisk, diskType, size -
         where name like 'TEST_.*'

         TEST_CD_00_cell03     FD_00_cell03     HardDisk     96M
         TEST_CD_01_cell03     FD_01_cell03     HardDisk     96M
         ...
         TEST_CD_10_cell03     FD_10_cell03     HardDisk     96M
         TEST_CD_11_cell03     FD_11_cell03     HardDisk     96M
```

Grid Disk Sizing

As we discussed earlier, grid disks are equivalent to ASM disks. They are literally the building blocks of the ASM disk groups you will create. The SYSTEM_DG disk group is created when Exadata is installed on a site. It is primarily used to store the OCR and voting files used by Oracle clusterware (Grid Infrastructure). However, there is no reason SYSTEM_DG cannot be used to store other objects such as tablespaces for the Database File System (DBFS). In addition to the SYSTEM_DG, (or DBFS_DG) disk group, Exadata is also delivered with DATA and RECO disk groups to be used for database files and Fast Recovery Areas. But these disk groups may actually be created with whatever names make the most sense for your environment. For consistency, this chapter uses the names SYSTEM_DG, DATA_DG and RECO_DG. If you are considering something other than the "factory defaults" for your disk group configuration, remember that a main reason for using multiple ASM disk groups on Exadata is to prioritize I/O performance. The first grid disks you create will be the fastest, resulting in higher performance for the associated ASM disk group.

■ **Note:** When Exadata V2 rolled out, SYSTEM_DG was the disk group used to store OCR and voting files for the Oracle clusterware. When Exadata X2 was introduced, this disk group was renamed to DBFS_DG, presumably because there was quite a bit of usable space left over that made for a nice location for a moderately sized DBFS file system. Also, the other default disk group names changed somewhat when X2 came out. The Exadata Database Machine name was added as a postfix to the DATA and RECO disk group names. For example, the machine name for one of our lab systems is ENK. So DATA became DATA_ENK, and RECO became RECO_ENK.

By the way, Oracle recommends you create a separate database for DBFS because it requires instance parameter settings that would not be optimal for typical application databases.

Some of the most common ASM disk groups are

SYSTEM_DG: This disk group is the location for clusterware's OCR and voting files. It may also be used for other files with similar performance requirements. For OCR and voting files, normal redundancy is the minimum requirement. Normal redundancy will create 3 voting files, and 3 OCR files. The voting files must be stored is separate ASM failure groups. Recall that on Exadata, each storage cell constitutes a failure group. This means that only normal redundancy may be used for an Exadata quarter rack configuration (3 storage cells/failure groups). Only in half rack and full rack configurations (7 or 14 storage cells/failure groups), are there a sufficient number of failure groups to store the required number of voting and OCR files required by high redundancy. Table 14-3 summarizes the storage requirements for OCR and voting files at various levels of redundancy. Note that External Redundancy is not supported on Exadata. We've included it in the table for reference only.

DATA_DG: This disk group is used for storing files associated with the db_create_file_dest database parameter. These include datafiles, online redo logs, control files, and spfiles.

RECO_DG: This disk group is what used to be called Flash Recovery Area (FRA). Sometime after 11gR1 Oracle renamed it to the "Fast Recovery Area"; rumor has it that the overuse of "Flash" was causing confusion among the marketing team. So to clarify, this diskgroup will be used to store everything corresponding to the db_recovery_file_dest database parameter. It includes online database backups and copies, mirror copies of the online redo log files, mirror copies of the control file, archived redo logs, flashback logs, and Data Pump exports.

Table 14-3. OCR & Voting File Storage Requirements

Redundancy	Min # of Disks	OCR	Voting	Total
External	1	300 MB	300 MB	600 MB
Normal	3	600 MB	900 MB	1.5 GB
High	5	900 MB	1.5 GB	2.4 GB

Recall that Exadata storage cells are actually finely tuned Linux servers with 12 internal disk drives. Oracle could have dedicated two of these internal disks to run the operating system, but doing so would have wasted a lot of space. Instead, they carved off several small partitions on the first two disks in the enclosure. These partitions, about 30 GB each, create a slight imbalance in the size of the cell disks. This imbalance is so small it doesn't affect performance, but it is something that you will have to work with when planning your grid disk allocation strategy. Figure 14-9 illustrates this imbalance.

Figure 14-9. Cell disk layout

This reserved space can be seen by running `fdisk` on one of the storage cells. The `/dev/sda3` partition in the listing is the location of the cell disk. All other partitions are used by the Linux operating system.

```
[enkcel03:root] /root
> fdisk -lu /dev/sda
...
  Device Boot     Start        End      Blocks  Id  System
/dev/sda1    *        63     240974      120456  fd  Linux raid autodetect
/dev/sda2         240975     257039        8032+ 83  Linux
/dev/sda3         257040 3843486989  1921614975  83  Linux
/dev/sda4     3843486990 3904293014    30403012+  f  W95 Ext'd (LBA)
/dev/sda5     3843487053 3864451814    10482381  fd  Linux raid autodetect
/dev/sda6     3864451878 3885416639    10482381  fd  Linux raid autodetect
/dev/sda7     3885416703 3889609604     2096451  fd  Linux raid autodetect
/dev/sda8     3889609668 3893802569     2096451  fd  Linux raid autodetect
/dev/sda9     3893802633 3897995534     2096451  fd  Linux raid autodetect
/dev/sda10    3897995598 3899425319      714861  fd  Linux raid autodetect
/dev/sda11    3899425383 3904293014     2433816  fd  Linux raid autodetect
```

You can see the smaller cell disks in the size attribute when you run the `list celldisk` command:

```
CellCLI> list celldisk attributes name, devicePartition, size -
         where diskType = 'HardDisk'

         CD_00_cell03    /dev/sda3    1832.59375G
         CD_01_cell03    /dev/sdb3    1832.59375G
         CD_02_cell03    /dev/sdc     1861.703125G
         CD_03_cell03    /dev/sdd     1861.703125G
         CD_04_cell03    /dev/sde     1861.703125G
         CD_05_cell03    /dev/sdf     1861.703125G
         CD_06_cell03    /dev/sdg     1861.703125G
         CD_07_cell03    /dev/sdh     1861.703125G
         CD_08_cell03    /dev/sdi     1861.703125G
         CD_09_cell03    /dev/sdj     1861.703125G
         CD_10_cell03    /dev/sdk     1861.703125G
         CD_11_cell03    /dev/sdl     1861.703125G
```

Let's take a look at a fairly typical configuration to illustrate how grid disks are allocated in the storage cell. In this example we'll create grid disks to support three ASM disk groups. SYSTEM_DG is fairly large and will be used for DBFS (clustered file system storage) in addition to the OCR and Voting files.

- DATA_DG
- RECO_DG
- SYSTEM_DG

This storage cell is configured with SATA disks, so the total space per storage cell is 21.76 terabytes. Table 14-4 shows what the allocation would look like. In all cases the physical disk size is 1,861.703125. The sum of the disk sizes is then 22,340.437500.

Table 14-4. I/O Grid Disk Space Allocation (all sizes expressed in gigabytes)

Cell Disk	OS	DATA_DG	SYSTEM_DG	RECO_DG	Total Grid Disk Space
CD_00_cell03	29.109375	744.7	372.340625	715.55	1,832.593750
CD_01_cell03	29.109375	744.7	372.340625	715.55	1,832.593750
CD_02_cell03		744.7	372.340625	744.6625	1,861.703125
CD_03_cell03		744.7	372.340625	744.6625	1,861.703125
CD_04_cell03		744.7	372.340625	744.6625	1,861.703125
CD_05_cell03		744.7	372.340625	744.6625	1,861.703125
CD_06_cell03		744.7	372.340625	744.6625	1,861.703125
CD_07_cell03		744.7	372.340625	744.6625	1,861.703125
CD_08_cell03		744.7	372.340625	744.6625	1,861.703125
CD_09_cell03		744.7	372.340625	744.6625	1,861.703125
CD_10_cell03		744.7	372.340625	744.6625	1,861.703125
CD_11_cell03		744.7	372.340625	744.6625	1,861.703125
Total Per Cell	**58.22**	**8,936.4**	**4,468.087500**	**8,877.73125**	**22,282.218750**

Creating a configuration like this is fairly simple. The following commands create grid disks according to the allocation in Table 14-4.

```
CellCLI> create griddisk all prefix='DATA_DG' size=744.7G

CellCLI> create griddisk all prefix='SYSTEM_DG' size=372.340625G
CellCLI> create griddisk all prefix='RECO_DG'
```

Notice that no size was specified for the RECO_DG grid disks. When size is not specified, CellCLI automatically calculates the size for each grid disk so they consume the remaining free space on the cell disk. For example:

```
CellCLI> list griddisk attributes name, size
        DATA_DG_CD_00_cell03      744.7G
        DATA_DG_CD_01_cell03      744.7G
        ...
        RECO_DG_CD_00_cell03      372.340625G
        RECO_DG_CD_01_cell03      372.340625G
        ...
        SYSTEM_DG_CD_00_cell03    715.55G
        SYSTEM_DG_CD_01_cell03    715.55G
        SYSTEM_DG_CD_02_cell03    744.6625G
        SYSTEM_DG_CD_03_cell03    744.6625G
        ...
```

Creating FlashDisk-Based Grid Disks

Exadata uses offloading features like Smart Scan to provide strikingly fast I/O for direct path reads typically found in DSS databases. These features are only activated for very specific data access paths in the database. To speed up I/O performance for random reads, Exadata V2 introduced solid-state storage called *Flash Cache*. Each storage cell comes configured with four 96G Flash Cache cards (366G usable) to augment I/O performance for frequently accessed data. When configured as Exadata Smart Flash Cache, these devices act like a large, database-aware disk cache for the storage cell. We discussed this in detail in Chapter 5. Optionally, some space from the Flash Cache may be carved out and used like high-speed, solid-state disks. Flash Cache is configured as a cell disk of type FlashDisk, and just as grid disks are created on HardDisk cell disks, they may also be created on FlashDisk cell disks. When FlashDisks are used for database storage, it's primarily to improve performance for highly write-intensive workloads when disk-based storage cannot keep up. FlashDisk cell disks may be seen using the CellCLI list celldisk command, as in the following example:

```
CellCLI> list celldisk attributes name, diskType, size
        CD_00_cell03    HardDisk     1832.59375G
        CD_01_cell03    HardDisk     1832.59375G
        ...
        FD_00_cell03    FlashDisk    22.875G
        FD_01_cell03    FlashDisk    22.875G
        ...
        FD_15_cell03    FlashDisk    22.875G
```

FlashDisk type cell disks are named with a prefix of FD and a diskType of FlashDisk. It is not recommended to use all of your Flash Cache for grid disks. When creating the Flash Cache, use the size parameter to hold back some space to be used for grid disks. The following command creates a Flash Cache of 300GB, reserving 65GB (4.078125GB × 16) for grid disks:

```
CellCLI> create flashcache all size=300g
Flash cache cell03_FLASHCACHE successfully created
```

Note that the create flashcache command uses the size parameter differently than the create griddisk command. When creating the flash cache, the size parameter determines the total size of the cache.

```
CellCLI> list flashcache detail
        name:                   cell03_FLASHCACHE
        cellDisk:               FD_11_cell03,FD_03_cell03,FD_07_cell03, …
        …
        size:                   300G
        status:                 normal

CellCLI> list celldisk attributes name, size, freespace -
        where disktype='FlashDisk'
        FD_00_cell03    22.875G         4.078125G
        FD_01_cell03    22.875G         4.078125G
        …
        FD_15_cell03    22.875G         4.078125G
```

Now we can create 16 grid disks using the remaining free space on the Flash Disks, using the familiar create griddisk command. This time we'll specify flashdisk for the cell disks to use:

```
CellCLI> create griddisk all flashdisk prefix='RAMDISK'
GridDisk RAMDISK_FD_00_cell03 successfully created
…
GridDisk RAMDISK_FD_14_cell03 successfully created
GridDisk RAMDISK_FD_15_cell03 successfully created

CellCLI> list griddisk attributes name, diskType, size -
        where disktype='FlashDisk'

        RAMDISK_FD_00_cell03    FlashDisk       4.078125G
        RAMDISK_FD_01_cell03    FlashDisk       4.078125G
        …
        RAMDISK_FD_15_cell03    FlashDisk       4.078125G
```

Once the grid disks have been created they may be used to create ASM disk groups used to store database objects just as you would any other disk-based disk group. The beauty of Flash Cache configuration is that all this may be done while the system is online and servicing I/O requests. All of the commands we've just used to drop and reconfigure the Flash Cache were done without the need to disable or shutdown databases or cell services.

Storage Strategies

Each Exadata storage cell is an intelligent mini-SAN, operating somewhat independently of the other cells in the rack. Now this may be stretching the definition of SAN a little, but with the Cell Server software intelligently controlling I/O access we believe it is appropriate. Storage cells may be configured in such a way that all Cells in the rack provide storage for all databases in the rack. This provides maximum I/O performance and data transfer rates for each database in the system. Storage cells may also be configured to service specific database servers using the cellip.ora file. In addition, cell security may be used to restrict access to specific databases or ASM instances through use of storage realms. In this section I'll discuss strategies for separating cells into groups that service certain database servers or RAC clusters. To borrow a familiar term from the SAN world, this is where we will talk about "zoning" a set of storage cells to service development, test, and production environments.

Configuration Options

Exadata represents a substantial investment for most companies. For one reason or another, we find that many companies want to buy a full or half rack for consolidating several database environments. Exadata's architecture makes it a very good consolidation platform. These are some of the most common configurations we've seen:

- A full rack servicing development, test, and production

- A full rack servicing several, independent production environments

- A half rack servicing development and test

- Isolating a scratch environment for DBA testing and deploying software patches

For each of these configurations, isolating I/O to specific database servers may be a key consideration. For example, your company may be hosting database environments for external clients that require separation from other database systems. Or your company may have legal requirements to separate server access to data. Another reason for segmenting storage at the cell level may be to provide an environment for DBA training, or testing software patches. There are two ways to isolate Exadata storage cells, by network access and by storage realm.

Isolating Storage Cell Access

Recall that ASM gains access to grid disks through the Infiniband network. This is configured by adding the IP address of storage cells in the cellip.ora file. For example, in a full rack configuration, all 14 storage cells are listed as follows:

```
[enkdb02:oracle:EXDB2] /home/oracle
> cat /etc/oracle/cell/network-config/cellip.ora
cell="192.168.12.9"
cell="192.168.12.10"
cell="192.168.12.11"
cell="192.168.12.12"
cell="192.168.12.13"
cell="192.168.12.14"
cell="192.168.12.15"
cell="192.168.12.16"
cell="192.168.12.17"
cell="192.168.12.18"
cell="192.168.12.19"
cell="192.168.12.20"
cell="192.168.12.21"
cell="192.168.12.22"
```

When ASM starts up it interrogates the storage cells on each of these IP addresses for grid disks it can use for configuring ASM disk groups. We can easily segregate storage cells to service specific database servers by removing the IP address of cells that should not be used. Obviously this is not enforced by any kind of security but it is an effective, simple way of pairing up database servers with the storage cells they should use for storage. Table 14-5 illustrates a configuration that splits a full rack into two database, and storage grids. Production is configured with six database servers and 11 storage cells, while Test is configured for two database servers and three storage cells.

Table 14-5. A Storage Network Configuration

Production Database Servers, 1-6	Production Storage Cells, 1-11	
/etc/oracle/cell/network-config/cellip.ora		
cell="192.168.12.9"	dm01cel01	192.168.12.9
cell="192.168.12.10"	dm01cel02	192.168.12.10
cell="192.168.12.11"	dm01cel03	192.168.12.11
cell="192.168.12.12"	dm01cel04	192.168.12.12
cell="192.168.12.13"	dm01cel05	192.168.12.13
cell="192.168.12.14"	dm01cel06	192.168.12.14
cell="192.168.12.15"	dm01cel07	192.168.12.15
cell="192.168.12.16"	dm01cel08	192.168.12.16
cell="192.168.12.17"	dm01cel09	192.168.12.17
cell="192.168.12.18"	dm01cel10	192.168.12.18
cell="192.168.12.19"	dm01cel11	192.168.12.19
Test Database Servers, 7-8	**Test Storage Cells, 12-14**	
/etc/oracle/cell/network-config/cellip.ora		
cell="192.168.12.20"	dm01cel12	192.168.12.20
cell="192.168.12.21"	dm01cel13	192.168.12.21
cell="192.168.12.22"	dm01cel14	192.168.12.22

Database servers and storage cells can be paired in any combination that best suits your specific needs. Remember that the minimum requirements for Oracle RAC on Exadata requires two database servers and three storage cells, which is basically a quarter rack configuration. Table 14-6 shows the storage and performance capabilities of Exadata storage cells in quarter rack, half rack, and full rack configurations.

If some of your environments do not require Oracle RAC, there is no reason they cannot be configured with stand alone (non-RAC) database servers. If this is done, then a minimum of one storage cell may be used to provide database storage for each database server. In fact a single storage cell may even be shared by multiple standalone database servers. Once again, Exadata is a highly configurable system. But just because you can do something, doesn't mean you should. Storage cells are the workhorse of Exadata. Each cell supports a finite data transfer rate (MBPS) and number of I/O's per second (IOPS). Reducing the storage cell footprint of your database environment directly impacts the performance your database can yield

Table 14-6. Performance Capabilities of Exadata Storage Cells

MBPS & IOPS by Device Type		Quarter Rack	Half Rack	Full Rack
Disk Transfer Bandwidth	SAS	4.5 GB/s	10.5 GB/s	21 GB/s
	SATA	2.5 GB/s	6 GB/s	12 GB/s
Flash Disk Transfer Bandwidth		11 GB/s	25 GB/s	50 GB/s
Disk IOPS	SAS	10,800	25,000	50,000
	SATA	4,300	10,000	20,000
Flash Disk IOPS		225,000	500,000	1,000,000

■ **Note**: Exadata V2 offered two choices for disk drives in the storage cells, SATA, and SAS. With Exadata X2, the SATA option has been replaced with High Capacity SAS drives that have storage and performance characteristics very similar to those of the SATA drives they replaced. So now, with X2, your storage options are High Capacity and High Performance SAS drives.

Cell Security

In addition to isolating storage cells by their network address, Exadata also provides a way to secure access to specific grid disks within the storage cell. An access control list (ACL) is maintained at the storage cell, and grid disks are defined as being accessible to specific ASM clusters and, optionally, databases within the ASM cluster. If you've already logged some time working on your Exadata system, chances are you haven't noticed any such access restrictions. That is because by default, cell security is open, allowing all ASM clusters and databases in the system access to all grid disks. Cell security controls access to grid disks at two levels, by ASM cluster and by database:

> **ASM-Scoped Security:** ASM-scoped security restricts access to grid disks by ASM cluster. This is the first layer of cell security. It allows all databases in the ASM cluster to have access to all grid disks managed by the ASM instance. For example, an Exadata full rack configuration can be split so that four database servers and seven storage cells can be used by Customer-A, and the other four database servers and seven storage cells can be used by Customer-B.

> **Database-Scoped Security:** Once ASM-scoped security is configured, access to grid disks may be further controlled at the database level using database-scoped security. Database-scoped security is most appropriate when databases within the ASM cluster should have access to a subset of the grid disks managed

by the ASM instance. In the earlier example Customer-A's environment could use database-scoped security to separate database environments from one another within its half rack configuration.

Cell Security Terminology

Before we get too far along, let's take a look at some of the new terminology specific to Exadata's cell security.

> **Storage Realm**: Grid disks that share a common security domain are referred to as a *storage realm.*

> **Security Key**: A security key is used to authenticate ASM and database clients to the storage realm. It is also used for securing messages sent between the storage cells and the ASM and database clients. The security key is created using the CellCLI command `create key`. The key is then assigned to grid disks using the CellCLI `assign key` command.

> **cellkey.ora:** The `cellkey.ora` file is stored on the database servers. One `cellkey.ora` file is created for ASM-scoped security and another `cellkey.ora` file is created for each database requiring database-scoped security. The `cellkey.ora` files are used to identify security keys, the storage realm, and the unique name of the ASM cluster or database.

Table 14-7 shows the definitions for the fields in the `cellkey.ora` file.

Table 14-7. The Contents of the Cellkey.ora File

Field	Description
key	This is the security key generated at the storage cell with the `create key` command. This key is used to authenticate the ASM cluster and database to the storage realm.
	For ASM-scoped security, this value must match the key assigned to the ASM cluster using the `assign key` command.
	For database-scoped security this value must match the security key assigned to the database using the `assign key` command.
asm	This is the unique name of the ASM cluster found in the `DB_UNIQUE_NAME` parameter of the ASM instance. It is used to associate the ASM cluster with the `availableTo` attribute of the grid disks in the storage realm. Grid disks are assigned this value using the CellCLI `create griddisk` and `alter grid disk` commands.
realm	This field is optional. If used, the value must match the `realmName` attribute assigned to the storage cells using the CellCLI command `alter cell realmName`.

Cell Security Best Practices

Following Oracle's best practices is an important part of configuring cell security. It will help you avoid those odd situations where things seem to work some of the time or only on certain storage cells. Following these best practices will save you a lot of time and frustration:

- If database-scoped security is used, be sure to use it for all databases in the ASM cluster.

- Make sure the ASM cellkey.ora file is the same on all servers for an ASM cluster. This includes contents, ownership, and permissions.

- Just as you did for the ASM cellkey.ora file, make sure contents, ownership, and permissions are identical across all servers for the database cellkey.ora file.

- Ensure the cell side security settings are the same for all grid disks belonging to the same ASM disk group.

- It is very important that the cellkey.ora files and cell commands are executed consistently across all servers and cells. Use the dcli utility to distribute the cellkey.ora file and reduce the likelihood of human error.

Configuring ASM-Scoped Security

With ASM-scoped security, the ASM cluster is authenticated to the storage cell by its DB_UNIQUE_NAME and a security key. The security key is created at the storage cell and stored in the cellkey.ora file on the database server. An access control list (ACL) is defined on the storage cell that is used to verify the security key it receives from ASM. The availableTo attribute on each grid disk dictates which ASM clusters are permitted access.

Now let's take a look at the steps for configuring ASM-scoped security.

1. Shut down all databases and ASM instances in the ASM cluster.

2. Create the security key using the CellCLI create key command:

   ```
   CellCLI> create key
           3648e2a3070169095b799c44f02fea9
   ```

   This simply generates the key, which is not automatically stored anywhere. The create key command only needs to be run once and can be done on any storage cell. This security key will be assigned to the ASM cluster in the key field of the cellkey.ora file.

3. Next, create a cellkey.ora file and install it in the /etc/oracle/cell/network-config directory for each database server on which this ASM cluster is configured. Set the ownership of the file to the user and group specified during the ASM software installation. Permissions should allow it to be read by the user and group owner of the file. For example:

   ```
   key=3648e2a3070169095b799c44f02fea9
   asm=+ASM
   realm=customer_A_realm

   > chown oracle:dba cellkey.ora
   ```

```
> chmod 640 cellkey.ora
```

Note that if a realm is defined in this file it must match the realm name assigned to the storage cells using the alter cell realm= command.

4. Find the DB_UNIQUE_NAME for your ASM cluster using the show parameter command from one of the ASM instances:

```
SYS:+ASM1>show parameter db_unique_name

NAME                 TYPE         VALUE
-------------------- ----------- ------------------
db_unique_name       string       +ASM
```

5. Use the CellCLI assign key command to assign the security key to the ASM cluster being configured. This must be done on each storage cell to which you want the ASM cluster to have access:

```
CellCLI> ASSIGN KEY -
            FOR '+ASM='66e12adb996805358bf82258587f5050'
```

6. Using the CellCLI create griddisk command, set the availableTo attribute for each grid disk to which you want this ASM cluster to have access. This can be done for all grid disks on the cell as follows:

```
CellCLI> create griddisk all prefix='DATA_DG' -
            size= 1282.8125G availableTo='+ASM'
```

7. For existing grid disks, use the alter grid disk command to set up security:

```
CellCLI> alter griddisk all prefix='DATA_DG' -
            availableTo='+ASM'
```

8. A subset of grid disks may also be assigned, as follows:

```
CellCLI> alter griddisk DATA_CD_00_cell03, -
                        DATA_CD_01_cell03, -
                        DATA_CD_02_cell03, -
                        ...
            availableTo='+ASM'
```

This completes the configuration of ASM-scoped cell security. The ASM cluster and all databases can now be restarted. When ASM starts up it will check for the cellkey.ora file and pass the key to the storage cells in order to gain access to the grid disks.

Configuring Database-Scoped Security

Database-scoped security locks down database access to specific grid disks within an ASM cluster. It is useful for controlling access to grid disks when multiple databases share the same ASM cluster. Before database-scoped security may be implemented, ASM-scoped security must be configured and verified.

When using database-scoped security, there will be one cellkey.ora file per database, per database server, and one ACL entry on the storage cell for each database. The following steps may be used to implement simple database-scoped security for two databases, called HR (Human Resources) and PAY (Payroll)).

1. Shut down all databases and ASM instances in the ASM cluster.

2. Create the security key using the CellCLI create key command:

```
CellCLI> create key
        7548a7d1abffadfef95a53185aba0e98

CellCLI> create key
        8e7105bdbd6ad9fa53d41736a533b9b1
```

The create key command must be run once for each database in the ASM cluster. It can be run from any storage cell. One security key will be assigned to each database within the ASM cluster in the key field of the database cellkey.ora file.

3. For each database, create a cellkey.ora file using the keys created in step 2. Install these cellkey.ora files in the ORACLE_HOME/admin/{db_unique_name}/pfile directories for each database server on which database-scoped security will be configured. Just as you did for ASM-scoped security, set the ownership of the file to the user and group specified during the ASM software installation. Permissions should allow it to be read by the user and group owner of the file. For example:

```
# -- Cellkey.ora file for the HR database --#
key=7548a7d1abffadfef95a53185aba0e98
asm=+ASM
realm=customer_A_realm
# --

> chown oracle:dba $ORACLE_HOME/admin/HR/cellkey.ora
> chmod 640 $ORACLE_HOME/admin/HR/cellkey.ora

# -- Cellkey.ora file for the PAY database --#
key=8e7105bdbd6ad9fa53d41736a533b9b1
asm=+ASM
realm=customer_A_realm
# --

> chown oracle:dba $ORACLE_HOME/admin/PAY/cellkey.ora
> chmod 640 $ORACLE_HOME/admin/PAY/cellkey.ora
```

Note that if a realm is defined in this file, it must match the realm name assigned to the storage cells using the alter cell realm= command.

4. Retrieve the DB_UNIQUE_NAME for each database being configured using the show parameter command from each of the databases:

```
SYS:+HR>show parameter db_unique_name

NAME             TYPE         VALUE
---------------- ------------ ------------------
db_unique_name   string       HR
```

```
SYS:+PAY>show parameter db_unique_name

NAME                 TYPE         VALUE
----------------     ----------   -----------------
db_unique_name       string       PAY
```

5. Use the CellCLI `assign key` command to assign the security keys for each
    database being configured. This must be done on each storage cell you want
    the HR and PAY databases to have access to. The following keys are assigned to
    the DB_UNIQUE_NAME of the)HR and))PAY databases:

```
CellCLI> ASSIGN KEY -
   FOR HR='7548a7d1abffadfef95a53185aba0e98', -
      PAY='8e7105bdbd6ad9fa53d41736a533b9b1'  -

Key for HR successfully created
Key for PAY successfully created
```

6. Verify that the keys were assigned properly:

```
CellCLI> list key
        HR       d346792d6adea671d8f33b54c30f1de6
        PAY      cae17e8fdce7511cc02eb7375f5443a8
```

7. Using the CellCLI `create disk` or `alter griddisk` command, assign access to
    the grid disks to each database. Note that the ASM unique name is included
    with the database unique name in this assignment.

```
CellCLI> create griddisk DATA_CD_00_cell03, -
                          DATA_CD_01_cell03  -
             size=1282.8125G                 -
             availableTo='+ASM,HR'

CellCLI> create griddisk DATA_CD_02_cell03, -
                          DATA_CD_03_cell03  -
             size=1282.8125G                 -
             availableTo='+ASM,PAY'
```

8. The `alter griddisk` command may be used to change security assignments for
    grid disks. For example:

```
CellCLI> alter griddisk DATA_CD_05_cell03, -
                         DATA_CD_06_cell03  -
             availableTo='+ASM,HR'

CellCLI> alter griddisk DATA_CD_01_cell03, -
                         DATA_CD_02_cell03  -
             availableTo='+ASM,PAY'
```

This completes the configuration of database-scoped security for the HR and PAY databases. The
ASM cluster and databases may now be restarted. The human resources database now has access to the
DATA_CD_00_cell03 and DATA_CD_01_cell03 grid disks, while the payroll database has access to the
DATA_CD_02_cell03 and DATA_CD_03_cell03 grid disks.

Removing Cell Security

Once implemented, cell security may be modified as needed by updating the ACL lists on the storage cells, and changing the availableTo attribute of the grid disks. Removing cell security is a fairly straightforward process of backing out the database security settings and then removing the ASM security settings.

The first step in removing cell security is to remove database-scoped security. The following steps will remove database-scoped security from the system.

1. Before database security may be removed, the databases and ASM cluster must be shut down.

2. Remove the databases from the availableTo attribute of the grid disks using the CellCLI command `alter griddisk`. This command doesn't selectively remove databases from the list. It simply redefines the complete list. Notice that we will just be removing the databases from the list at this point. The ASM unique name should remain in the list for now. This must be done for each cell you want to remove security from.

```
CellCLI> alter griddisk DATA_CD_00_cell03, -
                        DATA_CD_01_cell03  -
            availableTo='+ASM'

CellCLI> alter griddisk DATA_CD_02_cell03, -
                        DATA_CD_03_cell03  -
            availableTo='+ASM'
```

Optionally, all the databases may be removed from the secured grid disks with the following command:

```
CellCLI> alter griddisk DATA_CD_00_cell03, -
                        DATA_CD_01_cell03  -
                        DATA_CD_02_cell03  -
                        DATA_CD_03_cell03  -
            availableTo='+ASM'
```

Assuming that these databases have not been configured for cell security on any other grid disks in the cell, the security key may be removed from the ACL list on the storage cell as follows:

```
CellCLI> assign key for HR='', PAY=''

Key for HR successfully dropped
Key for PAY successfully dropped
```

3. Remove the `cellkey.ora` file located in the `ORACLE_HOME/admin/{db_unique_name}/pfile` directory for the database client.

4. Now the `cellkey.ora` file for the HR and PAY databases may be removed from the database servers.

```
> rm $ORACLE_HOME/admin/HR/cellkey.ora
> rm $ORACLE_HOME/admin/PAY/cellkey.ora
```

5. Verify that the HR and PAY databases are not assigned to any grid disks with the following CellCLI command:

```
CellCLI> list griddisk attributes name, availableTo
```

Once database-scoped security has been removed, you can remove ASM-scoped security. This will return the system to open security status. The following steps remove ASM-scoped security. Once this is done, the grid disks will be available to all ASM clusters and databases on the storage network.

1. Before continuing with this procedure, be sure that database-scoped security has been completely removed. The list key command should display the key assignment for the ASM cluster only. No databases should be assigned keys at this point. The list griddisk command should show all the names of the grid disks assignments for the ASM cluster, '+ASM'.

```
CellCLI> list griddisk attributes name, availableTo
```

2. Next, remove the ASM unique name from the availableTo attribute on all grid disks.

```
CellCLI> list griddisk attributes name, availableTo
```

3. Now, remove the ASM security from the ACL by running the following command.

```
CellCLI> alter griddisk all assignTo=''
```

4. The following command removes the ASM cluster assignment for select grid disks:

```
CellCLI> alter griddisk DATA_CD_00_cell03, -
                        DATA_CD_01_cell03  -
                        DATA_CD_02_cell03  -
                        DATA_CD_03_cell03  -
              availableTo=''
```

5. The list griddisk command should show no assigned clients. Verify this by running the list griddisk command.

6. The ASM cluster key may now be safely removed from the storage cell using the CellCLI assign key command:

```
CellCLI> list key detail
        name:    +ASM
        key:     196d7983a9a33fccae276e24e7a9f89

CellCassign key for +ASM=''
Key for +ASM successfully dropped
```

7. Remove the cellkey.ora file from the /etc/oracle/cell/network-config directory on all database servers in the ASM cluster.

This completes the removal of ASM-scoped security. The ASM cluster may now be restarted as well as all the databases it services.

Summary

Understanding all the various layers of the Exadata storage architecture and how they fit together is a key component to properly laying out storage for databases. Understanding the relationship between physical disks, LUNs, cell disks, grid disks, and ASM disk groups is absolutely necessary if you want to carve up disk storage for maximum performance. In this chapter we've discussed what grid disks are, what they are made up of, and how they fit into the ASM storage grid. We've taken a look at how to create disk groups so that IO is prioritized for performance critical datafiles. Carving up storage doesn't end at the disk, so we also discussed methods for partitioning storage by cell and by grid disk within the cell.

## CHAPTER 15

Compute Node Layout

The term *node* is a fairly generic one that has many different meanings in the IT industry. For example, network engineers call any addressable device attached to their network a node. Unix administrators commonly use the term interchangeably with *host* or *server*. Oracle DBAs often refer to a database server that is a member of an RAC cluster as a node. Oracle's documentation uses the term *compute node* when referring to the database server tier of the platform. This chapter is about the various ways in which you can configure your Exadata compute nodes, whether they are members of an RAC cluster (nodes), or nonclustered (database servers).

It's a common misconception that an Exadata rack must be configured as a single Oracle RAC cluster. This couldn't be further from the truth. In its simplest form, the Exadata database tier can be described as a collection of independent database servers hardwired into the same storage and the same management networks. Each of these servers can be configured to run standalone databases completely independent of the others. However, this is not commonly done for a couple of reasons—scalability and high availability. Oracle RAC has historically been used to provide node redundancy in the event of node or instance failure, but Oracle marketing has made it clear all along that the ability to scale-out has been an equally important goal. Traditionally, if we needed to increase database performance and capacity, we did so by upgrading server hardware. This method became so commonplace that the industry coined the phrase "hardware refresh" to describe it. This term can mean anything from adding CPUs, memory, or I/O bandwidth to a complete replacement of the server itself. Increasing performance and capacity in this way is referred to as *scale-up*. With Exadata's ability to provide extreme I/O performance to the database server, bus speed is now the limiting factor for scale-up. So what happens when you reach the limits of single-server capacity? The obvious answer is to add more servers. To continue to scale your application, you must scale-out, using Oracle RAC. Nonetheless, understanding that the database servers are not tied together in some proprietary fashion clarifies the highly configurable nature of Exadata. In Chapter 14 we discussed various strategies for configuring Exadata's storage subsystems to service specific database servers. In this chapter we'll take a look at ways the database tier may be configured to create clustered and nonclustered database environments that are well suited to meet the needs of your business.

Provisioning Considerations

Exadata is an extremely configurable platform. Determining the best configuration for your business will involve reviewing the performance and uptime demands of your applications as well as ensuring adequate separation for development, test, and production systems. Here are a few of the key considerations for determining the most suitable compute node layout to support your database environments:

CPU Resources: When determining the optimal node layout for your databases, keep in mind that Exadata handles the I/O workload very differently from traditional database platforms. On non-Exadata platforms the database server is responsible for retrieving all data blocks from storage to satisfy I/O requests from the applications. Exadata offloads a lot of this work to the storage cells. This can significantly reduce the CPU requirements of your database servers. Figuring out how much less CPU your databases will require is a difficult task because it depends, in part, on how much your database is utilizing parallel query and HCC compression, and how suitable your application SQL is to offloading. Some of the Smart Scan optimizations, such as decryption, predicate filtering, and HCC decompression, will reduce CPU requirements regardless of the type of application. We covered these topics in detail in Chapters 2–6.

Systems requiring thousands of dedicated server connections can overwhelm the resources of a single machine. Spreading these connections across multiple compute nodes reduces the burden on the system's process scheduler and allows the CPU to spend its time more effectively servicing client requests. Load balancing connections across multiple compute nodes also improves the database's capacity for handling concurrent connection requests.

Memory Resources: Systems that require thousands of dedicated server connections can also put a burden on memory resources. Each dedicated server connection requires a slice of memory, whether or not the connection is actively being used. Spreading these connections across multiple RAC nodes allows the database to handle more concurrent connections than a single compute node can manage.

I/O Performance and Capacity: Each compute node and storage cell is equipped with one 40Gbps QDR, dual-port InfiniBand card through which, in practicality, each compute node can transmit/receive a maximum of 3.2 gigabytes per second. If this is sufficient bandwidth, then the decision of moving to a multi-node RAC configuration may be more of an HA consideration. If you have I/O-hungry applications that require more throughput than one compute node can provide, then RAC may be used to provide high availability as well as additional I/O capacity.

Patching and Testing: Another key consideration in designing a stable database environment is providing a separate area where patches and new features can be tested before rolling them into production. For non-Exadata platforms, patching and upgrading generally involves O/S patches and Oracle RDBMS patches. Exadata is a highly complex database platform, consisting of several additional hardware and software layers that must be patched periodically, such as Cell Server, CellCLI, ILOM firmware, InfiniBand switch firmware, InfiniBand network card firmware, and OFED drivers. As such, it is absolutely crucial that a test environment be isolated from critical systems to be used for testing patches.

▨ **Kevin Says:** Regarding I/O Performance and Capacity, it is essential to understand that a producer's ability to send data is metered by the ability of the consumer to ingest the data. There is inherent flow-control in the relationship between the database grid and the storage grid in Exadata architecture. During a Smart Scan, each cell (producer) has the capacity to produce an outbound flow of data via iDB at roughly 3.2 GBps with the X2 models. But the data has to go somewhere. Scaling from this single-cell number is limited to the aggregate ingest bandwidth of the database grid (the consumers), which is 25.6 GBps for a full rack configuration. To put it another way, the X2 models can stream data unimpeded from hard disk to the database grid at full advertised scan rate (25GBps). However, when scanning both flash and hard disk assets concurrently, the full rack scan rate increases to approximately 70 GBps. Where does the excess go? It's clear to see that only about 35% of that 70 GBps can flow into the database grid. The necessary 65% payload reduction is the responsibility of Smart Scan filtration and projection. If the queries are not selective enough to reduce the payload, the result is throttled scan throughput. That leads to a related topic: effective scan rates and data flow.

For EHCC tables, the effective scan rate is equal to the physical scan rate multiplied by the compression ratio. For instance, consider an EHCC table with a compression ratio of 10:1 that fits within the capacity of a full rack Exadata Smart Flash Cache (roughly 5TB). Smart Scan will scan this table at roughly 70 GBps, but the effective scan rate is about 700 GBps. While nobody would argue that 700GBps is a phenomenal scan rate with current technology, the important question must still be asked: How selective are your queries? Considering the aggregate ingest bandwidth of a full rack X2 model, it's clear that the 700GBps effective scan rate has to be filtered down by over 96% (700GB × 25.6GB). If the filtration is not aggressive enough, the scan rate tails off because the consumer throttles the producer. Herein lies a conundrum—the selectivity of your queries must complement the compression factor of your EHCC data. The problem, however, is that query selectivity is a constant, and yet something must give. That something is physical I/O. Consider, for example, a query accessing tables with a combined footprint of 5TB so as to fit within the Exadata Smart Flash capacity of a full rack. Let's say further that this query cites very few columns and is so selective that Smart Scan is able to whittle the payload down by 95%. That would be very effective filtration and, as such, scanning flash and hard disk at a full rack rate of 70 GBps would render an iDB payload of about 3.5 GBps—a rate that doesn't even saturate two database hosts' iDB ingest bandwidth. At 70 GBps the hypothetical query completes in about 70 seconds. Can EHCC reduce the query time? For the sake of example, let's say the data in the hypothetical 5 TB table compresses tenfold with EHCC (down to roughly 500 GB). At a Smart Scan rate of 70 GBps, the query should complete in about 7 seconds, however, the data and query are the same, so the payload reduction remains constant at 95%. EHCC data is decompressed in the storage grid (after filtration and projection), so for a given query the same data flows over iDB whether noncompressed or compressed with EHCC. With payload reduction being constant, can our hypothetical query improve in a manner commensurate with the compression ratio (for example, 1/10th the time)? No, because filtering away 95%, from the effective scan rate of 700 GBps, renders an iDB demand of 35 GBps—about 37%

more than the aggregate ingest bandwidth of the database grid. The scan rate is therefore throttled. The query should indeed run faster than noncompressed, but as we can see there is more to it than simple math. The hypothetical query cannot complete in 1/10th the time. In such a case the physical scan rate for the full rack would be throttled back to roughly 45 GBps, and so the query would complete in approximately 11 seconds—1/6th the time as in the noncompressed case. This example does not take into consideration any other factor that may cause consumers to throttle producers, such as join processing and sorting. It considers only the aggregate iDB ingest bandwidth in the database grid. Other factors, such as database grid CPU-saturation (due to heavy join and sort processing) can further throttle the flow of data over iDB. There is a direct correlation between the selectivity of a query, the host processor utilization level, and the performance improvement delivered by EHCC. I often have to remind people that the concept of compression as a performance feature is quite new, and often misrepresented.

Non-RAC Configuration

Compute nodes may be configured in a number of ways. If your application does not need the high availability or scale-out features of Oracle RAC, then Exadata provides an excellent platform for delivering high performance for standalone database servers. You can manage I/O service levels between independent databases by configuring the IORM. See Chapter 7 for more information about IORM. In a non-RAC configuration each compute node will have its own, non-clustered, ASM instance that provides storage for all databases on that server. Even though your database servers may be independent of one another they can still share Exadata storage (cell disks). This allows each database to make use of the full I/O bandwidth of the Exadata storage subsystem. Note that in this configuration Clusterware is not installed at all. Just like any other standalone database server, multiple databases coexist quite nicely within the same disk groups. For example, let's say you have three databases on your server, called SALES, HR, and PAYROLL. All three databases can share the same disk groups for storage. To do this, all three databases would set their instance parameters as follows:

```
db_create_file_dest='DATA1_DG'
db_recovery_file_dest='RECO1_DG'
```

In Figure 15-1 we see all eight compute nodes in an Exadata full rack configuration running standalone databases. For example, DB1, Node 1, uses the DATA1_DG and RECO1_DG disk groups, which are serviced by the local (nonclustered) ASM instance. Each ASM instance has its own set of ASM disk groups, which consist of grid disks from all storage cells. At the storage cell, these independent ASM instances cannot share grid disks. Each ASM instance will have its own, private set of grid disks.

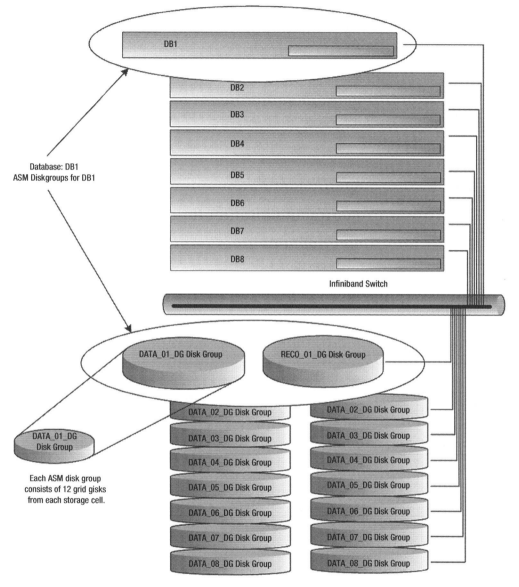

Figure 15-1. *Example of a non-RAC Exadata configuration*

Recall from Chapter 14 that grid disks are actually slices of cell disks. These grid disks are in turn used to create ASM disk groups. For example, each of the following commands creates twelve 200G grid disks on storage cell 1 (one per cell disk). These grid disks are then used to create the DATA1...DATA8, and RECO1...RECO8 disk groups. If all fourteen storage cells of an Exadata full rack configuration are used, it will yield 33.6 terabytes of storage (assuming 2 TB, high-capacity drives) for each disk group, ((14 storage cells × 12 grid disks per cell) × 200G).

```
CellCLI> CREATE GRIDDISK ALL HARDDISK PREFIX=DATA1_DG, size=200G
...
CellCLI> CREATE GRIDDISK ALL HARDDISK PREFIX=DATA8_DG, size=200G

CellCLI> CREATE GRIDDISK ALL HARDDISK PREFIX=RECO1_DG, size=200G
...
CellCLI> CREATE GRIDDISK ALL HARDDISK PREFIX=RECO8_DG, size=200G
```

Table 15-1 is a summary of a storage layout that supports eight standalone databases, each having a 33.6TB DATA disk group and a 33.6TB RECO disk group.

Table 15-1. Grid Disks

Disk Group	Grid Disk	Total GB	Storage Cell	Cell Disk
DATA1	DATA1_DG_CD_00-11	33,600	1–14	1–12
DATA2	DATA2_DG_CD_00-11	33,600	1–14	1–12
DATA3	DATA3_DG_CD_00-11	33,600	1–14	1–12
DATA4	DATA4_DG_CD_00-11	33,600	1–14	1–12
DATA5	DATA5_DG_CD_00-11	33,600	1–14	1–12
DATA6	DATA6_DG_CD_00-11	33,600	1–14	1–12
DATA7	DATA7_DG_CD_00-11	33,600	1–14	1–12
DATA8	DATA8_DG_CD_00-11	33,600	1–14	1–12
RECO1	RECO1_DG_CD_00-11	33,600	1–14	1–12
RECO2	RECO2_DG_CD_00-11	33,600	1–14	1–12
RECO3	RECO3_DG_CD_00-11	33,600	1–14	1–12
RECO4	RECO4_DG_CD_00-11	33,600	1–14	1–12
RECO5	RECO5_DG_CD_00-11	33,600	1–14	1–12
RECO6	RECO6_DG_CD_00-11	33,600	1–14	1–12

Disk Group	Grid Disk	Total GB	Storage Cell	Cell Disk
RECO7	RECO7_DG_CD_00-11	33,600	1–14	1–12
RECO8	RECO8_DG_CD_00-11	33,600	1–14	1–12

By default all ASM instances will have access to all grid disks. The following SQL query run from one of the ASM instances illustrates this. Notice how grid disks from all storage cells are flagged as candidates, that is, available for use.

```
SYS:+ASM1> select substr(path,16,length(path)) griddisk, \
                  failgroup, header_status
             from v$asm_disk
            where substr(path,16,length(path)) like '%DATA%_DG_00%'
               or substr(path,16,length(path)) like '%RECO%_DG_00%'
            order by failgroup, substr(path,16,length(path));

GRIDDISK              FAILGROUP   HEADER_STATUS
--------------------  ----------  --------------
DATA1_CD_00_cell01    CELL01      CANDIDATE
DATA2_CD_00_cell01    CELL01      CANDIDATE
DATA3_CD_00_cell01    CELL01      CANDIDATE
DATA4_CD_00_cell01    CELL01      CANDIDATE
DATA5_CD_00_cell01    CELL01      CANDIDATE
DATA6_CD_00_cell01    CELL01      CANDIDATE
DATA7_CD_00_cell01    CELL01      CANDIDATE
DATA8_CD_00_cell01    CELL01      CANDIDATE
...
DATA1_CD_00_cell02    CELL02      CANDIDATE
DATA2_CD_00_cell02    CELL02      CANDIDATE
DATA3_CD_00_cell02    CELL02      CANDIDATE
...
DATA7_CD_00_cell03    CELL03      CANDIDATE
DATA8_CD_00_cell03    CELL03      CANDIDATE
...
RECO1_CD_00_cell01    CELL01      CANDIDATE
RECO2_CD_00_cell01    CELL01      CANDIDATE
RECO3_CD_00_cell01    CELL01      CANDIDATE
RECO4_CD_00_cell01    CELL01      CANDIDATE
RECO5_CD_00_cell01    CELL01      CANDIDATE
RECO6_CD_00_cell01    CELL01      CANDIDATE
RECO7_CD_00_cell01    CELL01      CANDIDATE
RECO8_CD_00_cell01    CELL01      CANDIDATE
...
RECO1_CD_00_cell02    CELL02      CANDIDATE
RECO2_CD_00_cell02    CELL02      CANDIDATE
RECO3_CD_00_cell02    CELL02      CANDIDATE
...
RECO7_CD_00_cell03    CELL03      CANDIDATE
RECO8_CD_00_cell03    CELL03      CANDIDATE
```

With this many grid disks, (2,688 in this case) visible to all ASM instances, it's easy to see how they can be accidentally misallocated to the wrong ASM disk groups. To protect yourself from mistakes like that, you might want to consider using cell security to restrict the access of each ASM instance so that it only "sees" its own set of grid disks. For detailed steps on how to implement cell security, refer to Chapter 14.

RAC Clusters

Now that we've discussed how each compute node and storage cell can be configured in a fully independent fashion, let's take a look at how they can be clustered together to provide high availability and horizontal scalability using RAC clusters. But before we do that, we'll take a brief detour and establish what high availability and scalability are.

High availability (HA) is a fairly well understood concept, but it often gets confused with fault tolerance. In a truly fault-tolerant system, every component is redundant. If one component fails, another component takes over without any interruption to service. High availability also involves component redundancy, but failures may cause a brief interruption to service while the system reconfigures to use the redundant component. Work in progress during the interruption must be resubmitted or continued on the redundant component. The time it takes to detect a failure, reconfigure, and resume work varies greatly in HA systems. For example, active/passive Unix clusters have been used extensively to provide graceful failover in the event of a server crash. Now, you might chuckle to yourself when you see the words "graceful failover" and "crash" used in the same sentence (unless you work in the airline industry), so let me explain. Graceful failover in the context of active/passive clusters means that when a system failure occurs, or a critical component fails, the resources that make up the application, database, and infrastructure are shut down on the primary system and brought back online on the redundant system automatically with as little downtime as possible. The alternative, and somewhat less graceful, type of failover would involve a phone call to your support staff at 3:30 in the morning. In active/passive clusters, the database and possibly other applications only run on one node at a time. Failover using in this configuration can take several minutes to complete depending on what resources and applications must be migrated. Oracle RAC uses an active/active cluster architecture. Failover on an RAC system commonly takes less than a minute to complete. True fault tolerance is generally very difficult and much more expensive to implement than high availability. The type of system and impact (or cost) of a failure usually dictates which is more appropriate. Critical systems on an airliner, space station, or a life support system easily justify a fault-tolerant architecture. By contrast, a web application servicing the company's retail store front usually cannot justify the cost and complexity of a fully fault-tolerant architecture. Exadata is a high-availability architecture providing fully redundant hardware components. When Oracle RAC is used, this redundancy and fast failover is extended to the database tier.

When CPU, memory, or I/O resource limits for a single server are reached, additional servers must be added to increase capacity. The term "scalability" is often used synonymously with performance. That is, increasing capacity equals increasing performance. But the correlation between capacity and performance is not a direct one. Take, for example, a single-threaded, CPU intensive program that takes 15 minutes to complete on a two-CPU server. Assuming the server isn't CPU-bound, installing two more CPUs is not going to make the process run any faster. If it can only run on one CPU at a time, it will only execute as fast as one CPU can process it. Performance will only improve if adding more CPUs allows a process to have more uninterrupted time on the processor. Neither will it run any faster if we run it on a four-node cluster. As the old saying goes, nine pregnant women cannot make a baby in one month. However, scaling out to four servers could mean that we can run four copies of our program concurrently, and get roughly four times the amount of work done in the same 15 minutes. To sum it up, scaling out adds capacity to your system. Whether or not it improves performance depends on how scalable your application is, and how heavily loaded your current system is. Keep in mind that Oracle

RAC scales extremely well for well written applications. Conversely, poorly written applications tend to scale poorly.

Exadata can be configured as multiple RAC clusters to provide isolation between environments. This allows the clusters to be managed, patched, and administered independently. At the database tier this is done in the same way you would cluster any ordinary set of servers using Oracle Clusterware. To configure storage cells to service specific compute nodes, the `cellip.ora` file on each node lists the storage cells it will use. For example, the following `cellip.ora` file lists seven of the fourteen storage cells by their network address:

```
[enkdb01:oracle:EXDB1] /home/oracle
> cat /etc/oracle/cell/network-config/cellip.ora
cell="192.168.12.9"
cell="192.168.12.10"
cell="192.168.12.11"
cell="192.168.12.12"
cell="192.168.12.13"
cell="192.168.12.14"
cell="192.168.12.15"
```

When ASM starts up, it searches the storage cells on each of these IP addresses for grid disks it can use for configuring ASM disk groups. Alternatively, Cell Security can be used to lock down access so that only certain storage cells are available for compute nodes to use. The `cellip.ora` file and cell security are covered in detail in Chapter 14.

To illustrate what a multi-RAC Exadata configuration might look like, let's consider an Exadata V2 full rack configuration partitioned into three Oracle RAC clusters. A full rack gives us eight compute nodes and fourteen storage cells to work with. Consider an Exadata full rack configured as follows:

- One Production RAC cluster with four compute nodes and seven storage cells

- One Test RAC cluster with two compute nodes and three storage cells

- One Development RAC cluster with two compute nodes and four storage cells

Table 15-2 shows the resource allocation of these RAC clusters, each with its own storage grid. As you read this table, keep in mind that hardware is a moving target. These figures are from an Exadata V2. In this example we used the high-capacity, 2 TB SATA disk drives.

Table 15-2. Cluster Resources

Cluster	Db Servers	Db Memory	Db CPU	Storage Cell	Cell Disks	Raw Storage
PROD_CLUSTER	Prod1-Prod4	72G × 4	8 × 4	1–7	84	152.3T
TEST_CLUSTER	Test1, Test2	72G × 2	8 × 2	8–10	24	65.2T
DEV_CLUSTER	Dev1, Dev2	72G × 2	8 × 2	11–14	48	87.0T

These RAC environments can be patched and upgraded completely independently of one another. The only hardware resources they share are the InfiniBand switch and the KVM switch. If you are considering a multi-RAC configuration like this, keep in mind that patches to the InfiniBand switch will affect all storage cells and compute nodes. This is also true of the KVM switch, which is not needed to run the clusters, ASM instances, or databases; so if an issue takes your KVM switch offline for a few days, it won't impact system performance or availability. Figure 15-2 illustrates what this cluster configuration would look like.

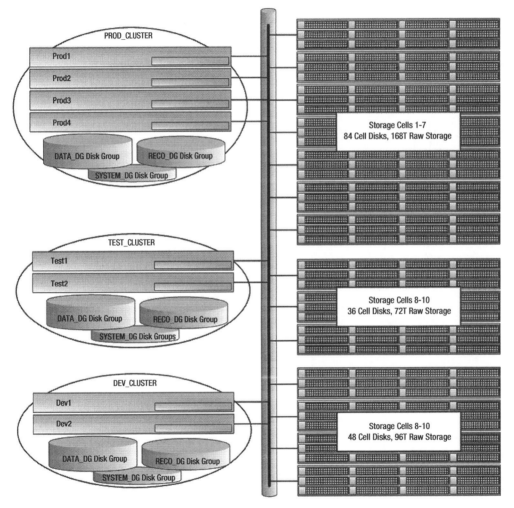

Figure 15-2. An Exadata full rack configured for three RAC clusters

Typical Exadata Configuration

The two configuration strategies we've discussed so far are fairly extreme examples. The "non-RAC Database" configuration illustrated how Exadata can be configured without Clusterware, to create a "shared nothing" consolidation platform. The second example, "RAC Clusters," showed how

Clusterware can be used to create multiple, isolated RAC clusters. Neither of these configurations is typically found in the real world, but they illustrate the configuration capabilities of Exadata. Now let's take a look at a configuration we commonly see in the field. Figure 15-3 shows a typical system with two Exadata half racks. It consists of a production cluster (PROD_CLUSTER) hosting a two-node production database and a two-node UAT database. The production and UAT databases share the same ASM disk groups (made up of all grid disks across all storage cells). I/O resources are regulated and prioritized using Exadata I/O Resource Manager (IORM), discussed in Chapter 7. The production database uses Active Data Guard to maintain a physical standby for disaster recovery and reporting purposes. The UAT database is not considered business-critical, so it is not protected with Data Guard. On the standby cluster (STBY_CLUSTER), the Stby database uses four of the seven storage cells for its ASM storage. On the development cluster (DEV_CLUSTER), the Dev database uses the remaining three cells for its ASM storage. The development cluster is used for ongoing product development and provides a test bed for installing Exadata patches, database upgrades, and new features.

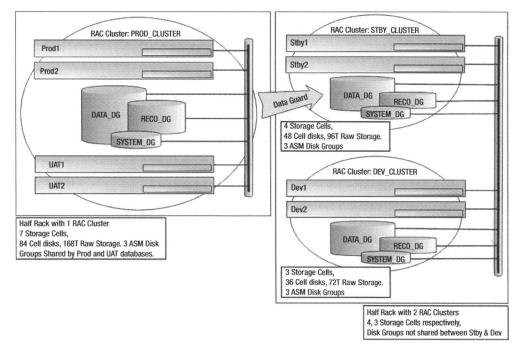

Figure 15-3. A typical configuration

Exadata Clusters

Exadata's ability to scale out doesn't end when the rack is full. When one Exadata rack doesn't quite get the job done for you, additional racks may be added to the cluster, creating a large-scale database grid. Up to eight racks may be cabled together to create a massive database grid, consisting of 64 database servers and 2,688 terabytes of storage. Actually, Exadata will scale beyond eight racks, but additional InfiniBand switches must be purchased to do it. Exadata links cabinets together using what Oracle calls a *spine switch.* The spine switch is included with all half rack and full rack configurations. Quarter rack configurations do not have a spine switch and cannot be linked with other Exadata racks. In a full rack configuration, the ports of a leaf switch are used as follows:

- Eight links to the database servers

- Fourteen links to the storage cells

- Seven links to the redundant leaf switch

- One link to the spine switch

- Six ports open

Figure 15-4 shows an Exadata full rack configuration that is not linked to any other Exadata rack. It's interesting that Oracle chose to connect the two leaf switches together using the seven spare cables. Perhaps it's because these cables are preconfigured in the factory, and patching them into the leaf switches simply keeps them out of the way and makes it easier to reconfigure later. The leaf switches certainly do not need to be linked together. The link between the leaf switches and the spine switch doesn't serve any purpose in this configuration, either. It is only used if two or more Exadata racks are linked together.

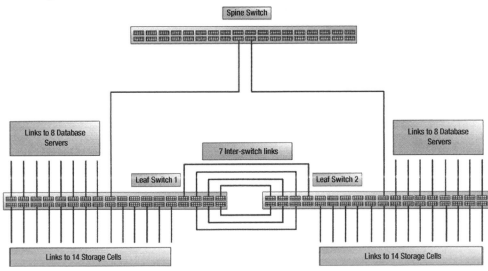

Figure 15-4. An Exadata full rack InfiniBand network

The spine switch is just like the other two InfiniBand switches that service the cluster and storage network. The diagram may lead you to wonder why Oracle would make every component in the rack redundant except the spine switch. The answer is that redundancy is provided by connecting each leaf switch to every spine switch in the configuration (from two to eight spine switches).

To network two Exadata racks together, the seven inter-switch cables, seen in Figure 15-4, are redistributed so that four of them link the leaf switch with its internal spine switch, and four of them link the leaf switch to the spine switch in the adjacent rack. Figure 15-5 shows the network configuration for two Exadata racks networked together. When eight Exadata racks are linked together, the seven inter-switch cables seen in Figure 15-4 are redistributed so that each leaf-to-spine-switch link uses one cable (eight cables per leaf switch). When you're linking from three to seven Exadata racks together, the seven inter-switch cables are redistributed as evenly as possible across all leaf-to-spine-switch links. Leaf switches are not linked to other leaf switches, and spine switches are not linked to other spine switches. No changes are ever needed for the leaf switch links to the compute nodes and storage cells.

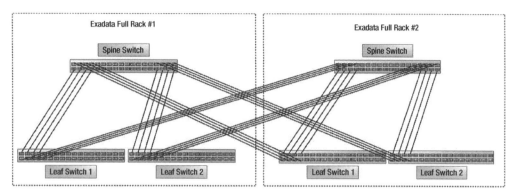

Figure 15-5. A switch configuration for two Exadata racks, with one database grid

Summary

Exadata is a highly complex, highly configurable database platform. In Chapter 14, we talked about all the various ways disk drives and storage cells can be provisioned separately, or in concert, to deliver well balanced, high-performance I/O to your Oracle databases. In this chapter we turned our attention to provisioning capabilities and strategies at the database tier. Exadata is rarely used to host standalone database servers. In most cases it is far better suited for Oracle RAC clusters. Understanding that every compute node and storage cell is a fully independent component is important, so we spent a considerable amount of time showing how to provision eight standalone compute nodes on an Exadata full rack configuration. From there we moved on to an Oracle RAC provisioning strategy that provided separation between three computing environments. And finally, we touched on how Exadata racks may be networked together to build massive database grids. Understanding the concepts explored in Chapter 14 and 15 of this book will help you make the right choices when the time comes to architect a provisioning strategy for your Exadata database environment.

CHAPTER 16

Unlearning Some Things We Thought We Knew

"It ain't what you don't know that gets you into trouble.

It's what you know for sure that just ain't so."

~ Mark Twain

Oracle does some things very differently when running on Exadata than when running on non-Exadata platforms. The optimizations provided by Exadata are designed to take a different approach than Oracle has traditionally followed. This change means that we need to attack some problems with a completely different mindset. That is not to say that everything is different. In fact, most of the fundamental principles remain unchanged. After all, the same database software runs on Exadata that runs on other platforms. But there are some things that are just fundamentally different.

This chapter focuses on how we should change our thinking when running databases on Exadata.

A Tale of Two Systems

The way we think about systems running on Exadata largely depends on the workload being executed. OLTP-oriented workloads tend to focus us on using flash cache for speeding up small reads. But frankly, this type of workload is not able to take advantage of most of the advantages provided by Exadata. DW-oriented workloads tend to focus us on making use of Smart Scans at every opportunity and trying to use all the available resources (CPU resources on the storage and database tiers, for example). This is where Exadata's built-in advantages can have the most impact. Unfortunately, most systems exhibit characteristics of both DW and OLTP workloads. These "mixed Workloads" are the most difficult and ironically the most common. They are the most common because it is rare to see an OLTP-oriented system that doesn't have some reporting component that produces long-running, throughput-sensitive queries. It's also quite common to see DW-oriented workloads that have OLTP-like trickle feeds. These combination systems require the most difficult thought process because, depending on the issue at hand, you will have to be constantly resetting your approach to managing performance. They are also difficult because DW workloads are generally constrained by the data-flow dynamics that control throughput, while OLTP systems are usually constrained by latency issues. So for mixed workloads you basically need to train yourself to evaluate each scenario and categorize it as either latency-sensitive or throughput-sensitive. This evaluation of workload characteristics should be done prior to beginning any analysis.

OLTP-Oriented Workloads

There is little to say about running OLTP workloads on Exadata. Since Exadata runs standard Oracle database software, you should not have to adjust your basic approach significantly. There are only a handful of points to keep in mind with this type of system.

Exadata Smart Flash Cache (ESFC)

The key component of Exadata when it comes to OLTP workloads is Exadata Smart Flash Cache (ESFC), which can significantly reduce disk access times for small reads. For that reason, it is important to verify that ESFC is working correctly. For this type of workload you should also expect that a large percentage of physical I/O operations are being satisfied by ESFC. This can be inferred fairly easily by looking at the average single-block read times. A single-block read should take around 0.5 ms if it is satisfied by flash cache. By contrast, single-block reads take on average around 5 ms if they are satisfied by actual disk reads. Standard AWR reports provide both average values and a histogram of wait events. If the average single-block read times are well above the 1 ms range, you should be looking for a systemic problem, like flash cards that are not working or a critical table has been defined to never be cached, using the CELL_FLASH_CACHE NONE syntax. The histograms should be used as well to verify that the average is not covering up a significant number of outliers. Here's the cellcli syntax to check the status of the flash cards:

```
CellCLI> list flashcache detail
     name:                 dm01cel03_FLASHCACHE
     cellDisk:
FD_00_dm01cel03,FD_01_dm01cel03,FD_02_dm01cel03,FD_03_dm01cel03,FD_04_dm01cel03,FD_05_dm01cel0
3,FD_06_dm01cel03,FD_07_dm01cel03,FD_08_dm01cel03,FD_09_dm01cel03,FD_10_dm01cel03,FD_11_dm01ce
l03,FD_12_dm01cel03,FD_13_dm01cel03,FD_14_dm01cel03,FD_15_dm01cel03•
     creationTime:         2010-03-22T17:39:46-05:00
     id:                   850be784-714c-4445-91a8-d3c961ad924b
     size:                 365.25G
     status:               critical
```

Note that the status attribute on this cell is critical. As you might expect, this is not a good thing. On this particular system, the flash cache had basically disabled itself. We noticed it because the single block read times had slowed down. This example is from an early version of cellsrv. The later versions include a little more information. Here is an example from cellsrv 11.2.2.3.1:

```
CellCLI> list flashcache detail
     name:                 enkcel03_FLASHCACHE
     cellDisk:
FD_14_cell03,FD_08_cell03,FD_13_cell03,FD_11_cell03,FD_02_cell03,FD_04_cell03,FD_01_cell03,FD_
00_cell03,FD_15_cell03,FD_03_cell03,FD_12_cell03,FD_10_cell03,FD_05_cell03,FD_09_cell03,FD_07_
cell03,FD_06_cell03
     creationTime:         2011-03-27T07:51:04-05:00
     degradedCelldisks:
     effectiveCacheSize:   365.25G
```

```
id:          7f60871e-d5f2-4990-b7e5-30c4a238de12
size:        365.25G
status:      normal
```

Notice the new attribute `degradedCelldisks`. Also notice that the flash cache on this cell shows a `status` of `normal`. Monitoring storage software behavior is covered in more detail in Chapter 12.

Scalability

Another thing to keep in mind when dealing with OLTP workloads is that the Exadata platform provides exceptional scalability. Upgrading from a half rack to full rack doubles the number of CPUs at both the database layer and the storage layer. The amount of ESFC is also doubled, as is the available memory. This allows Exadata to scale in a nearly linear fashion for many systems.

▓ **Kevin Says:** The authors are correct that doubling from a half rack to a full rack is perfect hardware scale-up. I urge caution, however, in presuming that the software—specifically Real Application Clusters (RAC)—will scale linearly with all applications. RAC has been around for over ten years, so let's not throw away our understanding of its scalability characteristics when considering Exadata. There is nothing about Exadata architecture that changes the intrinsic RAC scalability characteristics.

Write-Intensive OLTP Workloads

Write-intensive workloads are a subset of OLTP-oriented systems. There are some systems that just bang away at single-row inserts. These systems are often limited by the speed at which commits can be done, which often depends on the speed with which writes to the log files can be accomplished. This is one area where Exadata competes with other platforms on a fairly even playing field. There are no major enhancements that make Exadata run orders of magnitudes faster for systems that are bottlenecked on write operations. This means that there is no magic bullet, and traditional methods of tuning, such as minimizing commits, are appropriate for these types of systems.

▓ **Kevin Says:** Write-intensive workloads warrant deep thought. The authors point out that there are no *major enhancements* that make Exadata perform orders of magnitude better than Oracle systems connected to conventional storage. There are, in fact, no attributes of Exadata that favor write-intensive workloads as of the publication date of this book. The V2 and X2 models are capable of servicing over 1 million random single-block reads per second—from Exadata Smart Flash Cache on the full rack configuration. Random writes, on the other hand, have to go to spinning disks, of which there are 168 in the full rack configurations. The high-performance SAS drives can service roughly 300 random write IOPS—as long as the seeks are short. However, writes must be redundant, and thus the net random write bandwidth available to databases is roughly 25,000 IOPS. To scale an application to 1 million read IOPS on Exadata, the imposed read:write ratio is 40 to 1. That is, Exadata is 40-fold more read-capable than write-capable for random I/O. Applications that lean heavy on random writes will be the first to suffer this inherent imbalance. This imbalance is the reason some deployments require the flash assets of the cells to be provisioned as flash grid disks. Committing flash capacity in the static grid disk fashion, however, eats into the value proposition of Exadata. Every byte of storage committed to flash grid disk is less capacity available for the dynamic, intelligent flash cache algorithms. Deploying Oracle is often a balancing act—even in the Exadata environment. This book should equip readers with sufficient skills to use Exadata assets wisely.

DW-Oriented Workloads

Exadata was designed to speed up long-running queries against large volumes of data. So it should come as no surprise that data warehousing is where it's important that we change some of our basic thought processes. Of course, one of the major techniques is to be constantly looking for opportunities to allow Exadata optimizations to kick in. This means making sure that the application can take advantage of Smart Scans.

Enabling Smart Scans

The most important concept to keep in mind when dealing with DW-oriented workloads is that long-running statements should usually be offloaded. The steps to follow are:

1. Determine whether Smart Scans are being used.

2. If Smart Scans are not being used, fix things so that they will be used.

These points seem so obvious that we shouldn't need to repeat them. A large portion of the optimizations built into Exadata work only when Smart Scans are used. So one of the first changes you need to make in the way you think is to train yourself to be constantly considering whether Smart Scans are being used appropriately or not. This means you need to have a good understanding of which statements (or parts of statements) can be offloaded and be able to determine whether statements are being offloaded or not. We have covered the requirements for Smart Scans and some of the techniques that can be used to verify whether they are being performed or not throughout the book. But at the risk of being repetitive, we'll mention them again here.

There are two main requirements that must be met in order for Smart Scans to occur. The first is that the optimizer must choose to do a full scan of a table or a materialized view, or the optimizer must choose to do a fast full scan of an index. Note that Smart Scans are not limited to queries or even to subqueries. The optimizer can also choose to use full scans for DELETEs and UPDATEs when a large percentage of the rows will be affected. However, if your application is doing this, you might want to consider modifying it to do something like a truncate and rebuild.

The second requirement for Smart Scans is that the scans must be performed using the direct path read mechanism. Note that we intentionally didn't mention the optimizer in the description of the second requirement. This is because the optimizer does not make the decision about whether to use direct path reads or not. It is a heuristic decision that is made after the plan has been determined. As such, it is not directly exposed by any of the tools like explain plan type tools. What this means in practice is that it's easy to verify that the first requirement has been met, but more challenging to verify the second requirement.

On most Exadata implementations, a fairly high percentage of long-running queries are offloaded. You can check to see what percentage of your long-running SQL statements have been offloaded by selecting all the statements from v$sql (or from the AWR table DBA_HIST_SQLSTAT) that have an average run time of over some number of seconds, or that have an average logical I/O value that is greater than some reasonable value. Actually, the logical I/O is a better metric to use, as some of the offloaded statements will run very quickly and may not meet your minimum time criteria, which will give you a distorted perspective on the percentage of statements that are being offloaded. Here's an example (note that the scripts are included in the online code repository):

```
SYS@SANDBOX1> @offload_percent
Enter value for sql_text:
Enter value for min_etime:
Enter value for min_avg_lio: 500000

    TOTAL  OFFLOADED OFFLOADED_%
------------------------------
      13         11      84.62%

SYS@SANDBOX1> /
Enter value for sql_text: SELECT%
Enter value for min_etime:
Enter value for min_avg_lio: 500000

    TOTAL  OFFLOADED OFFLOADED_%
------------------------------
      11         11        100%
```

The listing makes use of the offload_percent.sql script, which calculates a percentage of statements currently in the shared pool that have been offloaded. We initially used it to evaluate all statements that had over 500,000 logical I/Os. We then ran it a second time and limited our investigation to statements that begin with the word SELECT. In the next listing we've made use of a script (fsxo.sql) that allows us to see the actual statements that contribute to the OFFLOAD_% calculated in the previous listing.

```
SYS@SANDBOX1> @fsxo
Enter value for sql_text:
Enter value for sql_id:
Enter value for min_etime:
Enter value for min_avg_lio: 500000
Enter value for offloaded:

SQL_ID          EXECS  AVG_ETIME OFFLOAD IO_SAVED_% SQL_TEXT
-------------------------------------------------------------------------------
0bvt5z48t18by       1       .10 Yes         100.00 select count(*) from skew3 whe
0jytfr1y0jdr1       1       .09 Yes         100.00 select count(*) from skew3 whe
12pkwt8zjdhbx       1       .09 Yes         100.00 select count(*) from skew3 whe
2zbt555tg123s       2      4.37 Yes          71.85 select /*+ parallel (a 8) */ a
412n404yughsy       1       .09 Yes         100.00 select count(*) from skew3 whe
```

```
5zruc4v6y32f9      5      51.13 No               .00 DECLARE job BINARY_INTEGER :=
6dx247rvykr72      1        .10 Yes           100.00 select count(*) from skew3 whe
6uutdmqr72smc      2      32.83 Yes            71.85 select /* avgskew3.sql */ avg(
7y09dtyuc4dbh      1       2.87 Yes            71.83 select avg(pk_col) from kso.sk
b6usrg82hwsa3      5      83.81 No               .00 call dbms_stats.gather_databas
fvx3v0wpvxvwt      1      11.05 Yes            99.99 select count(*) from skew3 whe
gcq9a53z7szjt      1        .09 Yes           100.00 select count(*) from skew3 whe
gs35v5t21d9yf      1       8.02 Yes            99.99 select count(*) from skew3 whe

13 rows selected.
```

The fsxo.sql script provides the same limiting factors as the offload_percent.sql script, namely a minimum average elapsed time and a minimum average logical I/O. It also optionally allows you to limit the statements to only those that are offloaded or those that are not offloaded. Please refer to the scripts for further details and keep in mind that these techniques can also be applied to the data recorded by AWR for a historical perspective.

In the next section we'll discuss some issues that can complicate your efforts to enable Smart Scans.

Things that Can Cripple Smart Scans

There are several common coding "techniques" that either disable Smart Scans completely or cause them to be much less effective than they could be. Some of the techniques are just bad practices regardless of whether you are on the Exadata platform or not. Others don't carry as significant a penalty on non-Exadata platforms, but when run on Exadata they can prevent the storage software from doing all that it could do. We've discussed many of these issues throughout this book. Here are a few that you should keep in mind because of the fundamentally different behavior on the Exadata platform.

Functions in WHERE Clauses

Oracle provides a large set of functions that can be applied directly in SQL statements. As we discussed in Chapter 2, not all of those functions are offloadable. Knowing which functions are not offloadable is important because the use of those functions in WHERE clauses disables predicate filtering that may otherwise provide a massive reduction in the amount of data to be transferred back to the database layer. Obviously, custom-written PL/SQL functions fall into the category of "non-offloadable" functions as well.

This issue is somewhat counterintuitive, since we are often doing full table scans anyway with data warehouse systems. On non-Exadata platforms, applying a function in a WHERE clause of a statement that is executed via a full table scan does not impose much of a penalty with regard to the amount of data that must be returned, because the database must already return all blocks from the table to the database server. With Exadata, though, applying a function that can disable predicate filtering can impose a huge performance penalty. By the way, using custom PL/SQL functions in a WHERE clause is generally also a bad idea on non-Exadata platforms, because additional CPU will be required to process PL/SQL for each row, as opposed to the optimized functions, based on C code, provided by Oracle.

⬛ **Note:** You can query V$SQLFN_METADATA to see which functions are offloadable.

Furthermore, "offloadable" functions can also impose large performance penalties. Here's a very simple example showing the negative effect of an offloadable function in a WHERE clause:

```
SYS@SANDBOX1> select count(*) from kso.skew3 where col2='KSO';

  COUNT(*)
----------
         9

Elapsed: 00:00:00.13
SYS@SANDBOX1> select count(*) from kso.skew3 where upper(col2)='KSO';

  COUNT(*)
----------
         9

Elapsed: 00:00:13.16
SYS@SANDBOX1> @fsx4
Enter value for sql_text: select count(*) from kso.skew3 where%KSO%
Enter value for sql_id:

SQL_ID          CHILD OFFLOAD IO_SAVED_%  AVG_ETIME SQL_TEXT
--------------------------------------------------------------------------------
0u8gnxmm7cbdk       0 Yes        100.00        .12 select count(*) from kso.skew3 where col
37t7fzkajz2fc       0 Yes         99.99      13.16 select count(*) from kso.skew3 where upp

Elapsed: 00:00:00.08
```

So UPPER is an offloadable function. Yet when we used it in the WHERE clause of this particular statement, the result was a large degradation in performance. If you've been following along on-screen, you may already have a pretty good idea why.

```
SYS@SANDBOX1> select name, value from v$mystat s, v$statname n
  2  where n.statistic# = s.statistic#
  3  and name like '%storage%';

NAME                                                                        VALUE
--------------------------------------------------------------------------------
cell physical IO bytes saved by storage index                                   0

SYS@SANDBOX1> set timing on
SYS@SANDBOX1> select count(*) from kso.skew3 where upper(col2)='KSO';
```

```
  COUNT(*)
----------
         9

Elapsed: 00:00:13.29
SYS@SANDBOX1> select name, value from v$mystat s, v$statname n
  2  where n.statistic# = s.statistic#
  3  and name like '%storage%';

NAME                                                                  VALUE
--------------------------------------------------------------   ----------
cell physical IO bytes saved by storage index                             0

Elapsed: 00:00:00.01
SYS@SANDBOX1> select count(*) from kso.skew3 where col2='KSO';

  COUNT(*)
----------
         9

Elapsed: 00:00:00.10
SYS@SANDBOX1> select name, value from v$mystat s, v$statname n
  2  where n.statistic# = s.statistic#
  3  and name like '%storage%';

NAME                                                                  VALUE
--------------------------------------------------------------   ----------
cell physical IO bytes saved by storage index                   15998312448

Elapsed: 00:00:00.01
```

Storage indexes are disabled by functions, just like regular indexes. This is not too surprising, but again, when we're already doing a full scan, we've trained ourselves to not worry about functions in the WHERE clause that could disable indexes. Exadata is different.

Chained Rows

This is a very broad generalization, but basically any Oracle processing that requires reading an extra block to complete a row causes the Exadata storage software to revert to block shipping, or *pass-through* mode. We have discussed this in several places in the previous chapters. A simple example is a chained row, but there are other situations that can cause Oracle to revert to pass-through mode. What this means in practice is that some operations that cause slight delays on non-Exadata platforms can severely impact performance on Exadata. The primary diagnostic symptom of this issue is the presence of many single-block-read wait events in combination with cell Smart Scan wait events. In such situations, you may find that you are better off not using offloading for the statements in question. Here is an example showing where Oracle spends its time when selecting from a table with chained rows:

```
SYS@SANDBOX1> select num_rows, chain_cnt, avg_row_len from dba_tables
  2  where table_name = 'T_CHAINED2';

   NUM_ROWS    CHAIN_CNT  AVG_ROW_LEN
------------------------------------
     100000       100000        12037

1 row selected.

SYS@SANDBOX> alter system flush buffer_cache;

System altered.

SYS@SANDBOX> select avg(length(c)) from tanel.t_chained2;

AVG(LENGTH(C))
--------------
          4000

1 row selected.


Execution Plan
----------------------------------------------------------
Plan hash value: 1927022845

-----------------------------------------------------------------------------------
| Id  | Operation                  | Name       | Rows  | Bytes | Cost (%CPU)| Time     |
-----------------------------------------------------------------------------------
|   0 | SELECT STATEMENT           |            |     1 |  4000 | 47533   (1)| 00:08:43 |
|   1 |  SORT AGGREGATE            |            |     1 |  4000 |            |          |
|   2 |   TABLE ACCESS STORAGE FULL| T_CHAINED2 |  100K |  381M | 47533   (1)| 00:08:43 |
-----------------------------------------------------------------------------------


Statistics
----------------------------------------------------------
          0  recursive calls
          0  db block gets
     332688  consistent gets
     332683  physical reads
          0  redo size
        341  bytes sent via SQL*Net to client
        448  bytes received via SQL*Net from client
          2  SQL*Net roundtrips to/from client
          0  sorts (memory)
          0  sorts (disk)
          1  rows processed
```

```
==== tkprof Output ====

SQL ID: 3upcma5nsnbcd Plan Hash: 1927022845

select avg(length(c))
from
 tanel.t_chained2


call     count     cpu   elapsed     disk    query   current     rows
------- ------- ------- --------- -------- -------- --------- ----------
Parse        2    0.00      0.00        0        0         0          0
Execute      2    0.00      0.00        0        0         0          0
Fetch        4   23.39    110.56   332683   665392         0          2
------- ------- ------- --------- -------- -------- --------- ----------
total        8   23.39    110.56   332683   665392         0          2

Misses in library cache during parse: 1
Optimizer mode: ALL_ROWS
Parsing user id: SYS
Number of plan statistics captured: 2

Rows (1st) Rows (avg) Rows (max)  Row Source Operation
---------- ---------- ---------- ---------------------------------------------
         1          1          1  SORT AGGREGATE (cr=332696 ...
    100000     100000     100000    TABLE ACCESS STORAGE FULL T_CHAINED2 (cr=332696 ...


Elapsed times include waiting on following events:
  Event waited on                         Times   Max. Wait  Total Waited
  -------------------------------------   Waited  ---------- ------------
  SQL*Net message to client                  4       0.00        0.00
  SQL*Net message from client                4       0.10        0.21
  cell single block physical read       166208       0.05       93.25 <== wow!
  reliable message                           1       0.00        0.00
  enq: KO- fast object checkpoint            2       0.00        0.00
  cell smart table scan                    256       0.01        0.11
********************************************************************************
```

In this example we ran a query against a table in which every row was chained (admittedly a bit of an extreme example). We generated a 10046 trace during the execution of the statement and then ran tkprof on the trace file, which produced the list of wait events just shown. Notice that the statement had an elapsed time of almost 2 minutes (110 seconds), of which more than 93 seconds was spent doing single-block physical reads. The statement used a full table scan and was clearly offloaded, as indicated by the cell smart table scan wait events, but it spent most of its time doing single-block reads. Of course, the single-block reads were a result of the chained rows. The next listing shows the difference between running the query with offloading and without offloading.

```
==== turn off smart scans

SYS@SANDBOX1> alter session set "_serial_direct_read"=true;

Session altered.

Elapsed: 00:00:00.01
SYS@SANDBOX1> alter session set cell_offload_processing=false;

Session altered.

Elapsed: 00:00:00.00
SYS@SANDBOX1> alter system flush buffer_cache;

System altered.

Elapsed: 00:00:01.99
SYS@SANDBOX1> select avg(length(c)) from tanel.t_chained2;

AVG(LENGTH(C))
--------------
          4000

Elapsed: 00:00:08.78 <== chained rows, direct path reads, no smart scan


==== turn off direct path reads

SYS@SANDBOX1> alter session set "_serial_direct_read"=false;

Session altered.

Elapsed: 00:00:00.01
SYS@SANDBOX1> alter system flush buffer_cache;

System altered.

Elapsed: 00:00:00.14
SYS@SANDBOX1> select avg(length(c)) from tanel.t_chained2;

AVG(LENGTH(C))
--------------
          4000

Elapsed: 00:00:09.35 <== chained rows, single block reads, no smart scan

==== turn on smart scans

SYS@SANDBOX1> alter session set "_serial_direct_read"=true;
```

```
Session altered.

Elapsed: 00:00:00.00
SYS@SANDBOX1> alter session set cell_offload_processing=true;

Session altered.

Elapsed: 00:00:00.00
SYS@SANDBOX1> alter system flush buffer_cache;

System altered.

Elapsed: 00:00:00.08
SYS@SANDBOX1> select avg(length(c)) from tanel.t_chained2;

AVG(LENGTH(C))
--------------
          4000

Elapsed: 00:01:59.24 <== OUCH! smart scan is not good for lots of chained rows

SYS@SANDBOX1> @fsx4
Enter value for sql_text: select avg(length(c)) from tanel.t_chained2
Enter value for sql_id:

SQL_ID          CHILD OFFLOAD IO_SAVED_% AVG_ETIME SQL_TEXT
------------------------------------------------------------------------------------
3upcma5nsnbcd       0 Yes       -27.41     159.24 select avg(length(c)) from tanel.t_chain

Elapsed: 00:00:00.06
```

Notice that the statement was offloaded and that the IO_SAVED_% calculation produced a negative number. This shows that more bytes were returned by the storage cells than the total number of bytes that the table occupies. It's clear from this example that chained rows can be much more detrimental to performance when attempting to make use of Exadata's Smart Scans than to queries that are handled in normal block-shipping mode. It's worth noting that this is an extreme example, as every row was chained. In fact, many of the records spanned three blocks. In this extreme case, it is clear that avoiding offloading actually improves the performance significantly. Of course, eliminating the chained rows would be the best solution.

Very Busy Cells

When a storage cell becomes very busy with CPU operations, it is possible for the storage software to begin refusing to perform offload activities on some portion of the requests. That is, if a particular cell becomes extremely busy and is getting offloadable requests from a database server that is not particularly busy, it may decide to send some data back to the database server that has not been processed or has only partially been processed. In some cases column projection may be done but not filtering, in other cases, cellsrv may revert to shipping entire blocks back to the database layer. So while this issue does not result in a complete shutdown of offloading, it can reduce the amount of work that is done on the storage tier.

This is an extremely complex topic, and it is difficult to observe the behavior directly. The goal of the feature is to utilize available CPU resources regardless of whether they are on the database tier or the storage tier. This behavior was introduced relatively recently, in cellsrv version 11.2.2.3.1 with databases running 11.2.0.2 with bundle patch 6 or later. There is a statistic called cell physical IO bytes pushed back due to excessive CPU on cell in 11.2.0.2 with BP 6 and later that shows this is happening. Note that the statistic name may change in a future version to something referring to "balancing CPU usage." The feature is designed to improve throughput on very busy systems, but it may also cause some degree of instability in the performance of certain statements. It is possible to disable this feature if your cellsrv is erroneously deciding it is too busy to take on additional work; but in general, if you observe this behavior, you are probably getting close to the limits of the system. Adding additional resources at the storage layer (more storage cells) may be a viable option.

■ **Kevin Says:** The authors are correct in their description of this new "feature." However, there is one point I cannot stress enough, and that is that the most compute-intensive work in query processing *must* occur in the database grid; yet there are significantly fewer processors there than in the storage grid (for example, 1:1.75 in the X2-2 and 1:1.31 in the X2-8 models). In the end, the only thing that matters is whether the users' experience is satisfactory. However, diagnosing an unsatisfactory user experience may prove difficult when this feature is invoked. The feature has the propensity to pass as much as 40% of the physical I/O payload to the cells either completely unprocessed or only lightly processed (as in, for example, EHCC projection). So, there are some scenarios I would be particularly concerned about. Allow me to explain.

We are no longer living the "*good life*" of the 1990s, when Unix systems were physically constrained by card slots for memory and CPU. We have systems with vast amounts of memory (a rapidly increasing trend) and ample CPU. We are no longer living the "*good life*" of "ample CPU" bottlenecked by front-side-bus limitations. In short, the industry is delivering to us huge, fast, balanced systems. The servers in the Exadata Database Machine are no exception. The significant cost of Exadata includes a feature known as *in-memory parallel query* and other features that can service users' needs without touching storage in the cells. I'm referring to features that lean heavily on host-tier resources and, in fact, rely very little on offload processing. If your Exadata system hosts an application that exhibits bursts of database-tier, CPU-intensive processing intermixed with use cases that drive cells to processor saturation, I urge close monitoring of this push-back (aka pass-through) feature. Heuristics that govern the "when" and "how much" for such a feature are very difficult to get right. If the heuristics are triggering this feature, the performance of certain applications may suffer—probably at a time when you really aren't in the mood for dealing with unpredictable system performance. However, as the authors point out, there are metrics available, and the feature can be tuned—or even disabled if necessary.

With this feature in the mix I know the first thing I'd check should users complain about response time, because when this feature is triggered you should expect your database grid processors to ratchet up to complete saturation. If your normal host CPU utilization level is not 100% when users are happy, then perhaps a little deductive reasoning will go a long way toward figuring out what has gone wrong should the complaints come in. Having said all that, let's not forget for a moment that DW/BI workloads *must* burn CPU. That is the nature of the beast as it were. Life is a never-ending series of choices.

CASE Statements

CASE statements (and their older cousin the DECODE function) are often used to avoid repeated scans of the same table. Generally speaking this is a reasonable technique, although analytic functions now provide another way to deal with this issue. Nevertheless, it is quite common to see code that applies this trick. The whole idea is to replace WHERE clauses with CASE statements. This is perfectly reasonable when all the blocks must be shipped back to the database server to be evaluated. But with Exadata's ability to do filtering at the storage layer, this technique may not be the best solution. Here's a quick example:

```
SYS@SANDBOX1> alter session set cell_offload_processing=false;

Session altered.

Elapsed: 00:00:00.00
SYS@SANDBOX1>-- Without Smart Scans
SYS@SANDBOX1> select /*+ full(a) */ count(*) from kso.skew a where col1 =1;

  COUNT(*)
----------
   3199971

Elapsed: 00:00:11.04
SYS@SANDBOX1> select /*+ full(a) */ count(*) from kso.skew a where col1 = 999999;

  COUNT(*)
----------
        32

Elapsed: 00:00:10.52
SYS@SANDBOX1> select sum(case when col1 = 1 then 1 else 0 end) how_many_ones,
  2                 sum(case when col1 = 999999 then 1 else 0 end) how_many_nines
  3   from kso.skew;

HOW_MANY_ONES HOW_MANY_NINES
------------- --------------
      3199971             32

Elapsed: 00:00:12.83
```

So you can see that without offloading, combining the statements basically cuts the elapsed time in half. This is what we're used to seeing on a non-Exadata platform. Now let's see what happens when we enable Smart Scans:

```
SYS@SANDBOX1> alter session set cell_offload_processing=true;

Session altered.

Elapsed: 00:00:00.00
SYS@SANDBOX1> alter session set "_serial_direct_read"=true;

Session altered.

Elapsed: 00:00:00.00
SYS@SANDBOX1>-- With Smart Scans
SYS@SANDBOX1> select /*+ full(a) */ count(*) from kso.skew a where col1 =1;

  COUNT(*)
----------
   3199971

Elapsed: 00:00:01.06
SYS@SANDBOX1> select /*+ full(a) */ count(*) from kso.skew a where col1 = 999999;

  COUNT(*)
----------
        32

Elapsed: 00:00:00.08
SYS@SANDBOX1> select sum(case when col1 = 1 then 1 else 0 end) how_many_ones,
  2                  sum(case when col1 = 999999 then 1 else 0 end) how_many_nines
  3   from kso.skew;

HOW_MANY_ONES HOW_MANY_NINES
-------------------------------
      3199971             32

Elapsed: 00:00:04.33
```

Offloading completely reverses the results. The total elapsed time to run the two individual statements (1.14 seconds) is about 25% of the time required to complete the combined statement (4.33 seconds). Notice also that the combined statement runs in a quarter of the time it took without offloading, but the individual statements completed in roughly one-tenth the time that was required without offloading. The combined statement was not as effective as the individual statements, since the CASE statement causes each record in the table to be returned to the database server for evaluation. So while the statement does benefit from column projection, it does not benefit from predicate filtering or storage indexes. Just to be clear, CASE statements don't disable Smart Scans, but they are often used in a way that reduces their effectiveness by eliminating the opportunity to filter rows at the storage layer.

Hinted Code

Hints are very useful for coercing the optimizer to do what you want it to do. Unfortunately, hints are not well documented and even less well understood. In many cases, hints are used to resolve a problem that is caused by some misconfiguration of the database. Their intended purpose is to allow humans to help the optimizer make the right choices in situations where it just can't do the job effectively (or consistently) on its own. This happens in situations where the optimizer is just not smart enough (yet) to arrive at the best execution plan in a specific situation. However, even when hints are used appropriately and are generating the expected behavior, they can prevent Exadata from taking advantage of some of its built in abilities. So the best approach when migrating to Exadata is to allow ample time for testing. And if your application makes use of hints, one of the important steps in the test plan should be to test its behavior without the hints. This can easily be accomplished by setting the hidden parameter `_optimizer_ignore_hints` to true.

Indexes

This may seem like a strange topic, but indexes can work against Smart Scans as well. The optimizer will try to use indexes if they are available. In a true data warehouse environment, indexes may not be necessary at all. We'll have more to say about indexes in the next section on mixed workloads, but it is important to understand that index usage often means that offloading is less likely to occur.

Row-at-a-Time Processing

It is amazing how often we see row at a time processing in very large data sets. This type of coding is rarely a good idea on non-Exadata platforms, and it is definitely not a good idea on Exadata. In fact, the differences in performance can be even more dramatic on Exadata because of the optimizations built into the platform.

Other Things to Keep in Mind

There are a few other things that you should keep in mind when working with DW systems: the use of Exadata Smart Flash Cache, compression, and partitioning.

Exadata Smart Flash Cache: Keep

Exadata Smart Flash Cache (EFSC) is thought of primarily as providing benefit to latency-sensitive SQL statements. It's important to remember that it can dramatically improve scan performance as well. By default, Smart Scans will ignore ESFC and will only scan disks. However, if an object is defined with the `CELL_FLASH_CACHE` attribute set to `KEEP`, Smart Scans will use both the disks and the ESFC for scanning. Obviously, overriding the default caching behavior for a large object will require some thought and testing, but this is definitely something worth considering. Here's an example:

```
SYS@SANDBOX1> alter session set cell_offload_processing=false;

Session altered.
```

```
SYS@SANDBOX1> select count(*) from kso.skew3;

  COUNT(*)
----------
 384000048

Elapsed: 00:00:50.11
SYS@SANDBOX1> alter session set cell_offload_processing=true;

Session altered.

Elapsed: 00:00:00.06
SYS@SANDBOX1> select count(*) from kso.skew3;

  COUNT(*)
----------
 384000048

Elapsed: 00:00:26.12

Elapsed: 00:00:00.04
SYS@SANDBOX1> alter table kso.skew3 STORAGE (CELL_FLASH_CACHE KEEP);

Table altered.

Elapsed: 00:00:00.07
SYS@SANDBOX1> select count(*) from kso.skew3;

  COUNT(*)
----------
 384000048

Elapsed: 00:00:28.74
SYS@SANDBOX1> select count(*) from kso.skew3;

  COUNT(*)
----------
 384000048

Elapsed: 00:00:09.46
SYS@SANDBOX1> /

  COUNT(*)
----------
 384000048

Elapsed: 00:00:08.06
SYS@SANDBOX1> alter table kso.skew3 STORAGE (CELL_FLASH_CACHE DEFAULT);

Table altered.
```

```
Elapsed: 00:00:00.21
SYS@SANDBOX1> select count(*) from kso.skew3;

  COUNT(*)
----------
 384000048

Elapsed: 00:00:26.10
```

In this example we turned off Smart Scans and did a query without a WHERE clause. The query took 50 seconds. We then enabled Smart Scans and ran the query again. This time the query took only 26 seconds. Next we altered the table, telling Oracle that we wanted ESFC to be more aggressive in caching this table (CELL_FLASH_CACHE KEEP). We then executed the statement again; this did not result in an improvement in performance, because the table's blocks were not stored in ESFC at that point. The subsequent executions, though, took only 8 to 9 seconds, showing the benefit of the caching. Finally, we disabled the aggressive caching and the statement execution returned to 26 seconds. This short example shows that making use of ESFC for offloaded queries can have a significant impact on performance.

Compression

Exadata's HCC is a big step forward in its ability to reduce the size of data stored inside of Oracle databases. The compression ratios that are achievable with HCC turn the concept of information lifecycle management on its head. HCC makes it practical to consider using compression instead of tiered storage or archiving and purging strategies. Because partitions of a table can be defined to use different compression methods, the combination of partitioning and compression can provide a much more robust solution for "archiving" data than actually purging it from the database.

You should remember, though, that HCC it is not appropriate for data that is being actively updated. A better approach is to partition data such that HCC can be applied to data that is no longer being changed. This leads us to the next topic, partitioning.

Partitioning

Partitioning is still a very key component for data warehousing systems. The optimizations provided by Exadata do not alleviate the need for a well-thought-out partitioning strategy. Of course, date-based strategies are very useful from a management standpoint. Being able to use more aggressive compression on older data is often a good approach. But partition elimination is still a technique that you will want to use. And of course, storage indexes can work well with partitioning, providing behavior comparable to partition elimination on additional columns.

You should keep in mind that the sizes of partitions can affect Oracle's decision to use Smart Scans. When performing a serial scan on a partitioned object, the decision to do direct path reads is based on the individual partition size, not the overall size of the object. This can result in situations where scans of some partitions are offloaded, while scans of others are not.

Mixed Workloads

There is a third type of system that is a combination of the other two. In fact, we could argue that the other two (OLTP and DW) rarely exist in the real world. There are many systems that don't fall neatly into the two main categories we've already described. In fact, most systems display characteristics of both.

Combining long-running, throughput-sensitive queries with fast, latency-sensitive statements definitely introduces some additional issues that must be dealt with. One of the main issues in systems of this type is how to deal with indexes.

To Index or Not to Index?

One of the biggest debates we've had during Exadata implementations is whether to drop indexes or not. Access paths that use indexes are generally not able to take advantage of Exadata-specific optimizations. We say generally, because offloading can occur in cases where the optimizer chooses to execute a Fast Full Scan on an index, but this is not the most common usage pattern for indexes. The more common pattern is to use them for retrieving relatively few records from a table using an Index Range Scan, and this operation is not currently offloadable. Generally speaking, we want to use index range scans on selective predicates, but since Exadata is so effective at scanning disk, in many cases the index-based access paths are no longer faster than the scan-based access operations. It's really a case of getting our bearings all over again with respect to when we want to use indexes and when we would expect a full scan to perform better.

One of the things we commonly heard when Exadata was first starting to appear at customer sites was that indexes were no longer necessary and that they should be dropped. For pure data warehouse workloads, this may actually be pretty good advice. However, we rarely see anything pure. Most systems have a mix of access patterns, with one set of statements hoping for low latency and another set hoping for high throughput. In these cases, dropping all indexes just will not work. This is why we saved this discussion for this section. The problem with mixed workloads, where it is necessary to keep indexes for specific sets of statements, is that the optimizer is not as well equipped to choose between using and ignoring them as one might hope. We'll discuss the optimizer's limitations next.

■ **Kevin Says:** I know the origin of the mistaken notion that indexes are not necessary with Exadata. You see, Oracle Database enjoyed majority market share of the world-wide data warehousing market (as per industry analysts) *before* Exadata came to market. The methodology required to coerce Oracle Database into delivering adequate performance in the pre-Exadata era required an immense amount of "index trickery." Oracle's competition (most notably Netezza [now IBM] and Greenplum [now EMC]) focused their marketing message on this "Achilles heel." However, this over-indexing phenomenon (with all the associated complexities) was never an Oracle database weakness per se. Before the original release of Exadata in 2008, customers did not have the richness of systems technology available for configuring a high-bandwidth, balanced DW/BI system. Imbalance and low bandwidth drove the need to avoid doing physical I/O. The only way to avoid physical I/O in that era was to fall into the "index death-spiral," as it became known in certain cliques within Oracle. While Exadata certainly addresses the I/O bottlenecks, there remains one all-encompassing truth: It is always faster *not* to do something than to do something fast. To that end, Exadata administrators need to remember that some of the tools their company has paid for include on-disk indexing technology. Always use the right tools for the job at hand.

To close this train of thought I'd like to put something into perspective. The software that put Oracle in the market leadership position for DW/BI prior to Exadata was Oracle Database 10g Release 2. If you were to deploy Oracle Database 10g Release 2 on the same number of processor cores you used in the pre-Exadata timeframe (circa 2007), you could easily enjoy as much as a tenfold performance increase for process-intensive use cases. And, since the methodology for deploying Oracle for DW/BI use cases in that timeframe used every trick in the book to avoid physical I/O, it is fair to presume that those systems were generally CPU-bound. Indeed, systems that are neither CPU-intensive nor I/O-intensive are probably not considered critical.

In our day-to-day work as IT professionals it is easy to miss just how rapidly technology is advancing all around us—particularly when we are naturally conservative about migrating production applications to state-of-the-art technology, and the state of the art—with or without Exadata—has been advancing at a phenomenal pace.

The Optimizer Doesn't Know

We've made the point several times that the optimizer is not aware that it is running on Exadata (yet). In general, the principles that guide the optimizer decisions are sound regardless of the storage platform. The fact that the code on the database tier is identical regardless of whether it's running on Exadata or not means that an application will behave similarly on Exadata in terms of plan selection. So you shouldn't expect any application to experience a large number of changes in the plans caused simply by moving to Exadata. This is a good thing from a stability standpoint.

The downside is that the optimizer is not aware that Exadata has optimizations that can cause full scans to perform much better than on other platforms. So mixed-workload systems that have many indexes make the optimizer's job more challenging. In fact, as you might expect, the optimizer will tend to pick index-oriented plans in preference to scan-based plans in situations where indexes are available, despite the fact that the scan-based plans are often much faster.

There are several ways to deal with the optimizer's tendency to prefer index access over full table scans. System statistics, optimizer parameters, and hints all come to mind as potential solutions.

▓ **Kevin Says:** Although the authors are correct to point out the current lack of Exadata-aware optimizer code, I do expect that to change. There should certainly be Exadata-aware optimizer improvements showing up over time.

System Statistics

System statistics provide the optimizer with additional information about the "system," including how long it takes to do a single-block read (typical of index lookups) and how long it takes to do a multi-block read (typical of full table scans). This may appear to be an ideal mechanism to manipulate the optimizer by giving it the additional information it needs to make the right decisions. Unfortunately, Smart Scans are not based on multi-block reads and in fact, Smart Scans can be orders of magnitude faster than multi-block reads. So modifying System Statistics is probably not the best option in this case.

▨ **Note:** The issue of whether to gather system statistics on Exadata comes up fairly often. System statistics are designed to provide additional information to the optimizer about the behavior characteristics of the hardware. In particular, they provide values for average single-block and average multi-block read times. Since Exadata often avoids actually performing multi-block reads, using Smart Scans instead, it seems counterintuitive to provide information to the optimizer about an operation that will seldom be used, particularly when this is one of the main inputs into the optimizer's cost calculations. If that argument is not enough for you, then please review MOS Note 1094934.1, which specifically states:

Note: It is currently not necessary to gather system statistics on the database machine.

Optimizer Parameters

There are a couple of initialization parameters that can push the optimizer toward or away from index usage. The parameters OPTIMZER_INDEX_CACHING and OPTIMIZER_INDEX_COST_ADJ can both be used for this purpose. While these are big knobs that can affect the core functionality of the optimizer, they were designed for the very purpose of making indexes more or less attractive to the optimizer. Using the parameters in a limited way, such as with an alter session command before running large batch processes, is a viable approach in some cases. These parameters can also be set at the statement level using the OPT_PARAM hint. Here's a very simple example:

```
SYS@SANDBOX> @bloom_join2.sql

COL2                            SUM(A.COL1)
----------------------------------------
asddsadasd                        153598416
2342                                    144

Elapsed: 00:03:21.39
SYS@SANDBOX> alter session set optimizer_index_cost_adj=10000;

Session altered.

Elapsed: 00:00:00.07
SYS@SANDBOX> @bloom_join2.sql
```

```
COL2                            SUM(A.COL1)

----------------------------------------
asddsadasd                        153598416
2342                                    144

Elapsed: 00:01:08.64
SYS@SANDBOX1> @dplan
Enter value for sql_id: 09m6t5qpgkywx
Enter value for child_no:

PLAN_TABLE_OUTPUT
----------------------------------------------------------------------------------
SQL_ID  09m6t5qpgkywx, child number 0
----------------------------------------
select /*+ bloom join 2  use_hash (skew temp_skew) */ a.col2,
sum(a.col1) from kso.skew3 a, kso.skew2 b where a.pk_col = b.pk_col and
b.col1 = 1 group by a.col2

Plan hash value: 466947137
```

Id	Operation	Name	Rows	Bytes	Cost (%CPU)
0	SELECT STATEMENT				37239 (100)
1	PX COORDINATOR				
2	PX SEND QC (RANDOM)	:TQ10002	2	66	37239 (1)
3	HASH GROUP BY		2	66	37239 (1)
4	PX RECEIVE		2	66	37239 (1)
5	PX SEND HASH	:TQ10001	2	66	37239 (1)
6	HASH GROUP BY		2	66	37239 (1)
* 7	HASH JOIN		1706	56298	37238 (1)
8	BUFFER SORT				
9	PX RECEIVE		142	1562	131 (0)
10	PX SEND BROADCAST	:TQ10000	142	1562	131 (0)
11	TABLE ACCESS BY INDEX ROWID	SKEW2	142	1562	131 (0)
* 12	INDEX RANGE SCAN	SKEW2_COL1	142		3 (0)
13	PX BLOCK ITERATOR		384M	8056M	37020 (1)
* 14	TABLE ACCESS STORAGE FULL	SKEW3	384M	8056M	37020 (1)

```
Predicate Information (identified by operation id):
-------------------------------------------------

   7- access("A"."PK_COL"="B"."PK_COL")
  12- access("B"."COL1"=1)
  14- storage(:Z>=:Z AND :Z<=:Z AND SYS_OP_BLOOM_FILTER(:BF0000,"A"."PK_COL"))
      filter(SYS_OP_BLOOM_FILTER(:BF0000,"A"."PK_COL"))

SQL_ID  09m6t5qpgkywx, child number 1
-------------------------------------
```

```
select /*+ bloom join 2  use_hash (skew temp_skew) */ a.col2,
sum(a.col1) from kso.skew3 a, kso.skew2 b where a.pk_col = b.pk_col and
b.col1 = 1 group by a.col2

Plan hash value: 2628392092
```

```
-----------------------------------------------------------------------------
| Id  | Operation                      | Name      | Rows  | Bytes | Cost (%CPU)|
-----------------------------------------------------------------------------
|   0 | SELECT STATEMENT               |           |       |       | 49465 (100)|
|   1 |  PX COORDINATOR                |           |       |       |            |
|   2 |   PX SEND QC (RANDOM)          | :TQ10002  |     2 |    66 | 49465   (1)|
|   3 |    HASH GROUP BY               |           |     2 |    66 | 49465   (1)|
|   4 |     PX RECEIVE                 |           |     2 |    66 | 49465   (1)|
|   5 |      PX SEND HASH              | :TQ10001  |     2 |    66 | 49465   (1)|
|   6 |       HASH GROUP BY            |           |     2 |    66 | 49465   (1)|
|*  7 |        HASH JOIN               |           |  1706 | 56298 | 49464   (1)|
|   8 |         PX RECEIVE             |           |   142 |  1562 | 12357   (1)|
|   9 |          PX SEND BROADCAST     | :TQ10000  |   142 |  1562 | 12357   (1)|
|  10 |           PX BLOCK ITERATOR    |           |   142 |  1562 | 12357   (1)|
|* 11 |            TABLE ACCESS STORAGE FULL| SKEW2|   142 |  1562 | 12357   (1)|
|  12 |         PX BLOCK ITERATOR      |           |  384M |  8056M| 37020   (1)|
|* 13 |          TABLE ACCESS STORAGE FULL | SKEW3 |  384M |  8056M| 37020   (1)|
-----------------------------------------------------------------------------
```

```
Predicate Information (identified by operation id):
---------------------------------------------------

   7- access("A"."PK_COL"="B"."PK_COL")
  11- storage(:Z>=:Z AND :Z<=:Z AND "B"."COL1"=1)
      filter("B"."COL1"=1)
  13- storage(:Z>=:Z AND :Z<=:Z AND SYS_OP_BLOOM_FILTER(:BF0000,"A"."PK_COL"))
      filter(SYS_OP_BLOOM_FILTER(:BF0000,"A"."PK_COL"))
```

So in this simple example, pushing the optimizer away from indexes with the alter session caused the optimizer to pick a plan that was considerably faster. The plans show that the improvement in elapsed time was a result of doing a full table scan, instead of using the index.

Hints

Of course hints can also be used to help the optimizer make the right choices, but that is somewhat of a slippery slope. Nevertheless, telling Oracle that you would prefer to do a hash join or ignore a specific index is an option. As mentioned in the previous section, the OPT_PARAM hint can also prove useful for setting some initialization parameters that can influence the optimizer's decisions.

Using Resource Manager

It's a commonly held belief that Oracle databases can't be configured to adequately handle both DW and OLTP workloads at the same time. And in truth, keeping them on separate systems does make them easier to manage. The downside of this approach is that it is expensive. Many companies dedicate the majority of their computing resources to moving data between platforms. The power of Exadata makes it tempting to combine these environments. Keep in mind that Exadata has additional capabilities for dividing resources between multiple databases that are not available on other platforms. IORM can prevent long-running DW queries from crippling latency-sensitive statements that are running on the same system. Having a good understanding of Oracle's resource management capabilities should change the way you think about what is possible in a mixed-workload or consolidated environment. Resource management is covered in depth in Chapter 7.

Summary

Exadata is different. To make the best use of it you'll need to think differently.

APPENDIX A

CellCLI and dcli

CellCLI is a command interpreter through which you can manage a storage cell. It is to a cell what SQL*Plus is to a database instance. dcli is a utility by which you can send a single command to all your database servers and/or storage cells in one go. We describe both utilities briefly in this appendix.

CellCLI Command Syntax

Exadata storage software uses the CellCLI utility as its command-line interface. Unfortunately, although the documentation set that comes with Exadata does have many examples of CellCLI commands, and even a chapter dedicated to CellCLI, it does not include any reference material on the syntax itself (particularly the LIST command). So we thought we would include a few of the things we learned while working with it.

It's interesting that Oracle chose to write an entirely new command-line tool for managing the storage cell. They could have used SQL*Plus, which has become the most well-known tool for managing databases and ASM. Be that as it may, CellCLI is the tool you will use for managing the storage cells. The syntax is somewhat different from SQL*Plus, but there are similarities, particularly with the LIST command. LIST is used to execute queries, and it looks very similar to the SELECT command that DBAs have become accustomed to. Like SELECT, it has WHERE and LIKE keywords that allow you to filter out unwanted information from the output.

Following is our top-ten list of things you should know about CellCLI:

1. CellCLI does implement a handful of SQL*Plus commands (START (@), SET ECHO ON, SPOOL, DESCRIBE, and HELP).

2. SELECT is replaced by LIST, and it must be the first keyword on the command line.

3. There is no FROM keyword (the LIST keyword must be immediately followed by the ObjectType, which is equivalent to a table name).

4. There is a DESCRIBE command, which displays the attributes (columns) that make up an ObjectType (table),

5. Column names are specified with the ATTRIBUTES keyword followed by the columns you wish to be displayed.

6. There is a default set of columns for each *ObjectType* that will be returned if the ATTRIBUTES keyword is not specified.

7. There is a WHERE clause that can be applied to any attribute and multiple conditions can be ANDed together; however, there is no support for OR.

8. There is no ORDER BY equivalent.

9. The DETAIL keyword can be appended to any LIST command to change the output from column oriented to row oriented.

10. The LIKE operator works, but instead of the standard SQL wildcard, %, CellCLI uses regex, so % becomes the .*

Getting Familiar with CellCLI

A good way to begin to get familiar with CellCLI is to explore its help interface. Following is an example of invoking online help:

```
CellCLI> help

 HELP [topic]
   Available Topics:
       ALTER
       ALTER ALERTHISTORY
       ALTER CELL
       ALTER CELLDISK
       ALTER GRIDDISK
       ALTER IORMPLAN
       ALTER LUN
       ALTER THRESHOLD
       ASSIGN KEY
       CALIBRATE
       CREATE
       CREATE CELL
       CREATE CELLDISK
       CREATE FLASHCACHE
       CREATE GRIDDISK
       CREATE KEY
       CREATE THRESHOLD
       DESCRIBE
       DROP
       DROP ALERTHISTORY
       DROP CELL
       DROP CELLDISK
       DROP FLASHCACHE
       DROP GRIDDISK
       DROP THRESHOLD
       EXPORT CELLDISK
       IMPORT CELLDISK
       LIST
       LIST ACTIVEREQUEST
       LIST ALERTDEFINITION
       LIST ALERTHISTORY
       LIST CELL
       LIST CELLDISK
       LIST FLASHCACHE
```

```
        LIST FLASHCACHECONTENT
        LIST GRIDDISK
        LIST IORMPLAN
        LIST KEY
        LIST LUN
        LIST METRICCURRENT
        LIST METRICDEFINITION
        LIST METRICHISTORY
        LIST PHYSICALDISK
        LIST THRESHOLD
        SET
        SPOOL
        START


CellCLI> help list

  Enter HELP LIST <object_type> for specific help syntax.
    <object_type>:  {ACTIVEREQUEST | ALERTHISTORY | ALERTDEFINITION | CELL
                    | CELLDISK | FLASHCACHE | FLASHCACHECONTENT | GRIDDISK
                    | IORMPLAN | KEY | LUN
                    | METRICCURRENT | METRICDEFINITION | METRICHISTORY
                    | PHYSICALDISK | THRESHOLD }

CellCLI> help list FLASHCACHECONTENT

  Usage: LIST FLASHCACHECONTENT [<filters>] [<attribute_list>] [DETAIL]

  Purpose: Displays specified attributes for flash cache entries.

  Arguments:
    <filters>:  An expression which determines the entries to be displayed.
    <attribute_list>: The attributes that are to be displayed.
                      ATTRIBUTES {ALL | attr1 [, attr2]... }

  Options:
    [DETAIL]: Formats the display as an attribute on each line, with
              an attribute descriptor preceding each value.

  Examples:
    LIST FLASHCACHECONTENT DETAIL
```

As you can see, the help system allows you to see a bit of the syntax for each command. You may also have noticed a couple of SQL*Plus carry-overs. SET, SPOOL, and START work pretty much as expected. Note that the @ character is equivalent to the SQL*Plus START command and that the only things you can use SET for are ECHO and DATEFORMAT. Now, here are a few examples of queries using the LIST command:

```
CellCLI> describe flashcachecontent
        cachedKeepSize
        cachedSize
        dbID
```

```
            dbUniqueName
            hitCount
            hoursToExpiration
            missCount
            objectNumber
            tableSpaceNumber

CellCLI> set echo on

CellCLI> @fc_content

> CellCLI> list flashcachecontent -
        where dbUniqueName like 'EXDB' -
          and hitcount > 100 -
          attributes dbUniqueName, objectNumber, cachedKeepSize, cachedSize, -
            hitCount, missCount
        EXDB    2       0       4194304         600     208
        EXDB    40      0       2424832         376     60
        EXDB    224     0       1802240         115     80
        EXDB    267     0       458752          128     9
        EXDB    383     0       2547712         157     27
        EXDB    423     0       1867776         180     41
        EXDB    471     0       4071424         552     85
        EXDB    472     0       1277952         114     22
        EXDB    474     0       13246464        286     326
        EXDB    475     0       5914624         519     124
        EXDB    503     0       5308416         669     455
        EXDB    5710    0       3735552         363     90
        EXDB    6207    0       393216          112     9
        EXDB    6213    0       3842048         359     147
        EXDB    6216    0       1245184         184     29
        EXDB    6373    0       3481600         222     61
        EXDB    56085   0       4194304         822     129
        EXDB    66849   0       438763520       1221    3322
        EXDB    71493   0       5636096         302     127
        EXDB    71497   0       1351680         320     22
        EXDB    71573   0       2760704         101     37
        EXDB    71775   0       1801412608      34994   46315

CellCLI> list flashcachecontent where dbUniqueName like 'EX.?.?' -
          and hitcount > 100 -
          attributes dbUniqueName, objectNumber, cachedKeepSize, cachedSize

        EXDB    2       0       4194304
        EXDB    18      0       1179648
        EXDB    37      0       622592
        EXDB    40      0       2424832
        EXDB    63      0       524288
        EXDB    104     0       688128
        EXDB    224     0       3407872
        EXDB    267     0       458752
        EXDB    383     0       2670592
```

```
                    EXDB    420     0       1507328
                    EXDB    423     0       1867776
                    EXDB    424     0       720896
                    EXDB    471     0       4071424
                    EXDB    472     0       1277952
                    EXDB    473     0       2351104
                    EXDB    474     0       13574144
                    EXDB    475     0       5521408
                    EXDB    503     0       5308416
                    EXDB    5702    0       262144
                    EXDB    5709    0       2416640
                    EXDB    5710    0       3735552
                    EXDB    6207    0       393216
                    EXDB    6210    0       131072
                    EXDB    6213    0       4227072
                    EXDB    6216    0       1245184
                    EXDB    6373    0       3579904
                    EXDB    56085   0       4194304
                    EXDB    66849   0       438763520
                    EXDB    71493   0       5636096
                    EXDB    71497   0       1351680
                    EXDB    71573   0       2801664
                    EXDB    71775   0       1801412608

CellCLI> list flashcachecontent -
        where dbUniqueName like 'EX.?.?' and hitcount > 100 -
          and objectNumber like '.*775'

          2356637742      6       71775

CellCLI> list flashcachecontent -
        where dbUniqueName like '.*X.?.?' -
          and objectNumber like '.*775' detail

          cachedKeepSize:          0
          cachedSize:              1801412608
          dbID:                    2356637742
          dbUniqueName:            EXDB
          hitCount:                34994
          missCount:               46315
          objectNumber:            71775
          tableSpaceNumber:        6

CellCLI> list flashcachecontent -
        where dbUniqueName like 'EX.?.?' -
          and hitcount > 100 -
          and objectNumber like '.*775'

          2356637742      6       71775

CellCLI> list flashcachecontent -
        attributes objectNumber, hitCount, missCount -
```

```
      where dbUniqueName like 'EX.?.?' -
        and hitcount > 100 -
        and objectNumber like '.*775'

      71775    34994    46315
```

The DESCRIBE verb works similarly to the way it does in SQL*Plus, but it must be fully spelled out; you can't use the familiar DESC as an abbreciation. Notice that there are no headings for column-oriented output. As you can see, you can execute scripts that contain CellCLI commands using the @ character, and use SET ECHO ON to display the commands in the scripts that you execute. Many of the LIST commands were strung across multiple lines by using the continuation operator (-). The LIST commands look a lot like SQL, except for LIST being used instead of SELECT and the regex expressions for matching when using the LIKE keyword. Also notice that in the last command a number was matched with a regex expression, implying a data type conversion, although all data may be treated as text. You can see that the ATTRIBUTES and WHERE keywords can be anywhere on the command line after the LIST ObjectType keywords. In other words, these two keywords are not positional; either one can be used first. Finally, the DETAIL keyword turns the output sideways. Or as the help says, "Formats the display as an attribute on each line, with an attribute descriptor preceding each value."

Sending Commands from the Operating System

In addition to running CellCLI interactively as you've seen in these examples, you can specify the -e option to pass in CellCLI commands from your operating system prompt. For example the following listing shows how the -e option can be used to query the status of cellsrv directly from the OS command line:

```
[exacel05:root] /root
> cellcli -e "list cell detail"
        name:                exacel05
        bmcType:             IPMI
        cellVersion:         OSS_11.2.0.3.0_LINUX.X64_110520
...
        cellsrvStatus:       running
        msStatus:            running
        rsStatus:            running
```

Among other things, the –e option is helpful when you want to invoke CellCLI from within an operating system shell script.

Configuring and Managing the Storage Cell

CellCLI is also used in a number of ways for configuring everything from disk storage to cell alerts. You can also use CellCLI for management tasks such as startup and shutdown. Following are a few examples of how to use CellCLI to configure and manage the storage cell.

Cell Services can be shut down one at a time or all at once. The following commands are used to shut down cell services:

```
-- Shutdown cell services one at a time --
CellCLI> alter cell shutdown services cellsrv
CellCLI> alter cell shutdown services ms
```

```
CellCLI> alter cell shutdown services rs

-- Shutdown all cell services --
CellCLI> alter cell shutdown services all
```

Cell services may also be started up one by one, or all at once. Note that the RS process must be started first or CellCLI will throw an error such as the following:

```
CellCLI> alter cell startup services cellsrv

Starting CELLSRV services...
CELL-01509: Restart Server (RS) not responding.
```

The following commands are used to start up cell services.

```
-- Startup cell services one at a time --
CellCLI> alter cell startup services rs
CellCLI> alter cell startup services ms
CellCLI> alter cell startup services cellsrv


-- Startup all cell services --
CellCLI> alter cell startup services all
```

The following commands shut down and restart the cell services.

```
-- Bounce cell services one at a time --
alter cell restart services cellsrv
alter cell restart services rs
alter cell restart services ms

-- Bounce all cell services --
alter cell restart services all
```

To show the current status of cellsrv, use the LIST CELL DETAIL command as follows:

```
CellCLI> list cell detail
        name:                   exacel05
        bmcType:                IPMI
        cellVersion:            OSS_11.2.0.3.0_LINUX.X64_101206.2
        cpuCount:               24
        fanCount:               12/12
        fanStatus:              normal
        id:                     1105FMM0J5
        interconnectCount:      3
        interconnect1:          bondib0
        iormBoost:              0.0
        ipaddress1:             192.168.12.9/24
        kernelVersion:          2.6.18-194.3.1.0.3.el5
        locatorLEDStatus:       off
        makeModel:              SUN MICROSYSTEMS SUN FIRE X4270 M2 SERVER SATA
        metricHistoryDays:      7
```

```
notificationMethod:      mail
notificationPolicy:      critical,warning,clear
offloadEfficiency:       139,935.6
powerCount:              2/2
powerStatus:             normal
smtpFrom:                "Exadata"
smtpFromAddr:            exadata@ourcompany.com
smtpPort:                25
smtpPwd:                 ******
smtpServer:              smtp.ourcompany.com
smtpToAddr:              all_dba@ourcompany.com,all_sa@ourcompany.com
smtpUser:
smtpUseSSL:              FALSE
status:                  online
temperatureReading:      27.0
temperatureStatus:       normal
upTime:                  37 days, 18:22
cellsrvStatus:           running
msStatus:                running
rsStatus:                running
```

Several of the settings you see in this listing can be set using the ALTER CELL command. These settings may be configured one at a time or together by separating them with a comma. For example:

```
-- Configure notification level for alerts --
CellCLI> ALTER CELL notificationPolicy='critical,warning,clear'


-- Configure the cell for email notifications --
CellCLI> ALTER CELL smtpServer='smtp.enkitec.com', -
                 smtpFromAddr='Exadata@ourcompany.com', -
                 smtpFrom='Exadata', -
                 smtpToAddr='all_dba@ourcompany.com,all_sa@ourcompany.com', -
                 notificationPolicy='critical,warning,clear', -
                 notificationMethod='mail'
```

By the way, if you haven't already stumbled across this feature, CellCLI stores a command history similar to the Bash shell. You can scroll up and down through your history and edit commands using the arrow keys. And regex also provides a very powerful pattern-matching capability. The CellCLI syntax will be something new to system administrators and DBAs alike, but once you understand the syntax, it really isn't difficult to master.

dcli Command Syntax

dcli is a tool by which you can execute a single command across all cells. Having worked on various clustered systems over the years, we've come to appreciate the importance of keeping scripts (and some configuration files) identical across all nodes. It's also very handy to have a facility for executing the same command consistently across all nodes of a cluster. Oracle provides the dcli command to do just that. Among other things, the dcli command allows you to:

- Configure SSH equivalency across all storage cells and/or database servers

- Distribute a file to the same location on all servers/cells in the cluster

- Distribute and execute a script on servers/cells in the cluster

- Execute commands and scripts on servers/cells in the cluster

dcli uses SSH equivalency to authenticate your session on the remote servers. If you do not have SSH equivalency established across servers/cells, you can still use it, but it will prompt you for a password for each remote system before executing the command. dcli executes all commands in parallel, aggregates the output from each server into a single list, and displays the output on the local machine. For example, the following listing shows the pmon processes running on all database servers:

```
[enkdb02:root] /root
> /usr/local/bin/dcli -l root -g dbs_group ps -ef | grep ora_pmon | grep -v grep
enkdb01: oracle     4973    1   0 Jun09 ?        00:00:16 ora_pmon_DEMO1
enkdb01: oracle     9917    1   0 Jun06 ?        00:00:15 ora_pmon_BL16K1
enkdb01: oracle     9929    1   0 Jun06 ?        00:00:20 ora_pmon_TEST1
enkdb01: oracle    10325    1   0 Jun06 ?        00:00:15 ora_pmon_SANDBOX1
enkdb01: oracle    32630    1   0 Jun06 ?        00:00:17 ora_pmon_DBFS1
enkdb02: oracle      715    1   0 Jun09 ?        00:00:16 ora_pmon_DEMO2
enkdb02: oracle     3718    1   0 Jun06 ?        00:00:15 ora_pmon_DBFS2
enkdb02: oracle     9531    1   0 Jun06 ?        00:00:20 ora_pmon_EXDB2
enkdb02: oracle    10072    1   0 Jun06 ?        00:00:10 ora_pmon_SNIFF
enkdb02: oracle    10085    1   0 Jun06 ?        00:00:20 ora_pmon_TEST2
enkdb02: oracle    10087    1   0 Jun06 ?        00:00:13 ora_pmon_BL16K2
enkdb02: oracle    10136    1   0 Jun06 ?        00:00:14 ora_pmon_SANDBOX2
enkdb02: oracle    23494    1   0 Jun06 ?        00:00:10 ora_pmon_SCRATCH
```

dcli is particularly usefull when you want to collect information from all storage cells using the CellCLI commands. The following example shows how dcli and CellCLI commands can be used together to report the status of all storage cells in a half rack cluster.

```
[enkdb01:root] /root
> dcli -g /root/cell_group -l root cellcli -e "list cell"

enkcel01: enkcel01        online
enkcel02: enkcel02        online
enkcel03: enkcel03        online
enkcel04: enkcel04        online
enkcel05: enkcel05        online
enkcel06: enkcel06        online
enkcel07: enkcel07        online
```

You may have recognized the /root/cell_group parameter in this example. This file is generated during the Exadata installation procedure (see Chapter 8 for more details). There are actually several of these "group files" that are useful for running distributed commands using dcli. These files may be described as follows:

> **dbs_group:** This file contains the management hostnames for all database servers in your Exadata configuration. It provides a convenient way to execute dcli commands on the database servers.

cell_group : This file contains the management hostnames for all storage cells in your Exadata configuration. It provides a convenient way to execute dcli commands limited to the storage cells.

all_group: This file is a combination of the dbs_group and cell_group files and contains a list of the management hostnames for all database servers and storage cells in your Exadata configuration. Using this file, you can execute dcli commands on all database servers and storage cells.

Any of the CellCLI commands we've discussed in this appendix may be executed from a central location using dcli. In fact the only restriction is that the command cannot be interactive (requiring user input during execution). For example, the following listing illustrates collecting all the current performance metrics from the storage cells.

```
dcli -l root -g /root/cell_group cellcli -e "LIST METRICCURRENT  ATTRIBUTES name, objecttype,
metricObjectName, metricValue, collectionTime"
```

The output from this command is much too verbose to show here. But with a simple script it can be formatted and distributed as needed. In fact, we used this script in Chapter 7 to collect IORM performance metrics and report on them through an external table definition in the database. Scheduling a report such as this to run daily would be a very convenient way to monitor I/O at the storage-cell level.

Summary

There are many more uses for dcli and CellCLI than we've covered here. System administrators will also find it useful for creating new user accounts on the database servers using the useradd and groupadd commands, for example. DBAs will find dcli useful for distributing scripts and other files to other servers in the cluster. And using dcli and CellCLI together provides a convenient way of managing, extracting, and reporting key performance metrics from the storage cells.

APPENDIX B

Online Exadata Resources

This appendix details some helpful online resources for DBAs managing Exadata. Oracle Support creates a good many of what are termed *support notes*. We list some of the most helpful, and you can read them—if you are a licensed user— by going to Oracle's support site. In addition, we list a few helpful blogs. The list of blogs is small, but growing. We list four that we particularly like and endorse.

Exadata MOS Support Notes

Listed here are several good online notes for managing the Exadata platform on My Oracle Support (MOS). Some of these notes are living documents, meaning they are continually updated as new software versions and patches become available. MOS Note 888828.1 is a must-read for anyone responsible for administering the system. It contains critical information about supported software releases. Some of the MOS Notes listed here, such as 757552.1, are simply placeholders for dozens of other important documents you will want to be aware of. Obviously this is not a comprehensive list, and there are many more good technical documents for Exadata on MOS. But we hope you find this list helpful in getting you started off in the right direction.

Helpful Exadata MOS Support Notes

Flashback Database Best Practices ....MOS Note: 565535.1
Database Endian Conversion ....MOS Note: 732053.1
RDS/OFED ....MOS Note: 745616.1
Exadata Best Practices ....MOS Note: 757552.1
11gR2 SCAN Explained ....MOS Note: 887522.1
Exadata Storage Server 11gR2 Supported Versions ....MOS Note: 888828.1
DBFS ....MOS Note: 1054431.1
Exadata Healthcheck Script ....MOS Note: 1070954.1
Exadata V2 Diagnosability and Troubleshooting Best Practices ....MOS Note: 1071220.1
Bare Metal Restore Procedure for Compute Nodes ....MOS Note: 1084360.1
Monitoring Exadata ....MOS Note: 1110675.1
Steps to shut down or reboot an Exadata storage cell without affecting ASM MOS Note: 1188080.1
Master Note for Oracle Database Machine and Exadata Storage Server ....MOS Note: 1187674.1
Exadata Patching Overview and Patch Testing Guidelines ....MOS Note: 1262380.1
Exadata Critical Issues ....MOS Note: 1270094.1
Exadata X2-2 Diagnosability and Troubleshooting Best Practices ....MOS Note: 1274324.1
Troubleshooting InfiniBand Switch Problems on Exadata ....MOS Note: 1286263.1
11.2.0.1 to 11.2.0.2 Database Upgrade on Exadata Database Machine ....MOS Note: 1315926.1

Exadata Bulletins and Blogs

Following are some helpful blogs. Some focus on Exadata alone. Others, such as Tanel Poder's blog, are more wide-ranging and cover the gamut of Oracle Database technologies.

Expert Oracle Exadata Blog:
http://www.ExpertOracleExadata.com

Kerry Osborne's Oracle Blog:
http://kerryosborne.oracle-guy.com

Tanel Poder's Blog:
http://blog.tanelpoder.com

Andy Colvin's Blog:
http://blog.oracle-ninja.com

Diagnostic Scripts

We've used several diagnostic scripts in this book. While the contents of many of them are displayed in the body of the book, some of them are lengthy enough that we decided not to print their contents in the listings. These scripts are all available online at www.EpertOracleExdata.com. Table C-1 in this appendix contains a list of the scripts along with a brief description of each one.

Table C-1. Diagnostic Scripts Used in This Book

Script Name	Description
as.sql	AS is short for Active SQL. This script shows all active SQL statements on the current instance as shown by V$SESSION. Note that you may need to execute it several times to get an idea of what's happening on a system, as fast statements may not be "caught" by this quick-and-dirty approach.
calibrate_io.sql	This script provides a simple wrapper for the DBMS_RESOURCE_MANAGER.CALIBRATE_IO procedure. The procedure must be run before Oracle will allow you to enable Auto DOP.
check_px.sql	This script contains a simple query of V$PX_PROCESS_SYSSTAT to show how many parallel server processes are currently in use.
comp_ratio.sql	This is a simple script that computes a compression ratio based on an input value (the original table size).
create_display_raw.sql	This script creates the display_raw() function, which translates raw data-type values into various other data-types (originally written by Greg Rahn).
dba_tables.sql	This is a simple script to query DBA_TABLES. It shows the number of rows, number of blocks and default degree of parallelism.
desc.sql	This script produces output similar to the SQL*Plus DESCRIBE command.

Script Name	Description
display_raw.sql	This is a simple script to translate a raw value into a specified data-type format such as NUMBER or VARCHAR2. It depends on the display_raw() function created by the create_display_raw.sql script.
dplan.sql	This script shows the actual execution plan for a SQL statement in the shared pool. This is a very simple script that prompts for a SQL_ID and CHILD_NO and then calls dbms_xplan.display_cursor.
dump_block.sql	This script dumps a data block to a trace file using ALTER SYSTEM DUMP DATAFILE. It prompts for fileno and blockno.
esfc_hit_ratio.sql	Useless script for calculating an incorrect Edxadata Smart Flash Cache hit ratio.
esfc_keep_tables.sql	This script displays objects that have the CELL_FLASH_CACHE attribute set to KEEP.
flush_pool.sql	This script uses ALTER SYSTEM FLUSH SHARED_POOL to flush all SQL statements from the shared pool.
flush_sql.sql	This script uses DBMS_SHARED_POOL.PURGE to flush a single SQL statetement from the shared pool. It only works with 10.2.0.4 and later.
fs.sql	This script allows you to search through V$SQL using a bit of SQL text or a SQL_ID. (FS is short for Find SQL) The script reports some statistical information, such as average Elapsed Time and average LIOs.
fsx.sql	FSX stands for Find SQL eXadata. This script searches the shared pool (V$SQL) based on the SQL statement text or a specific SQL_ID and reports whether statements were offloaded or not and, if offloaded, what percentage of I/O was saved. Note that there are several alternate versions of this script used in the book (fsx2.sql, fsx3.sql, and fsx4.sql). These versions reduce the width of the output to something more easily printed in the limits imposed by the printed book format.
fsxo.sql	This script is similar to the fsx.sql script but can be used to identify long-running statements and report on whether they have been offloaded or not. It can be used in conjunction with the offload_percent.sql script to drill into the individual statements contributing to it's calcualted offload percentage.
gather_table_stats.sql	This is a simple script to gather table statistics using the DBMS_STATS.GATHER_TABLE_STATS procedure.

Script Name	Description
get_compression_ratio.sql	This script is a wrapper for the built in compression advisor functionality (DBMS_COMPRESSION.GET_COMPRESSION_RATIO). It prompts for a table name and a compression type and then estimates the expected compression ratio by actually compressing a subset of the table's rows.
get_compression_type.sql	This script provides a wrapper for the DBMS_COMPRESSION.GET_COMPRESSION_TYPE procedure. It can be used to identifiy the actual compression type used for a specific row. It prompts for a table name and a rowid and returns the actual compression type for that row as opposed to the compression type assigned to the table.
mystats.sql	This is a simple script for querying V$MYSTATS.
old_rowid.sql	This script creates the old_rowid() function. The old_rowid() function accepts a rowid and returns the fileno, blockno, and rowno (the old rowid format).
obj_by_hex.sql	This script translates an object_id in hex format into an object name. The hex value is contained in block dumps.
offload_percent.sql	This script can be used to provide a quick check on whether statements are being offloaded or not on Exadata platforms. It allows all statements over a minimum time or a minimum number of LIOs to be evaluated and calculates a percentage of statements that have been offloaded.
parms.sql	This script displays database parameters and their current values. Includes a switch to show or suppress display of hidden parameters.
parmsd.sql	This script displays database parameters and their descriptions. Includes a switch to show or suppress display of hidden parameters.
part_size2.sql	This script shows the sizes of partitions as reported by DBA_SEGMENTS.
pool_mem.sql	This script provides a simple query against V$SGASTAT, showing memory assigned to various "pools."
queued_sql.sql	This simple script queries V$SQL_MONITOR for statements that are queued by the parallel statement queuing feature.
report_sql_monitor.sql	This is a script to call DBMS_SQLTUNE.REPORT_SQL_MONITOR.
si.sql	This script displays the current value for the statistic Cell Physical IO Bytes Saved by Storage Index from V$MYSTATS. It provides a quick way to check storage index usage.

Script Name	Description
snapper.sql	This is far and away the most robust script used in the book. It is really more like a monitoring program that can report on an extremely wide range of information about active sessions. Documentation can be found on Tanel's blog.
ss_off.sql	This script turns off Smart Scans via alter session (that is, it sets CELL_OFFLOAD_PROCESSING=FALSE).
ss_on.sql	This script Turns on Smart Scans via alter session (that is, it sets CELL_OFFLOAD_PROCESSING=TRUE).
table_size.sql	This script shows sizes of objects as reported by DBA_SEGMENTS. There is another version (table_size2.sql) that is basically the same script with a reduced number of output columns.
valid_events.sql	This script displays a list of wait events that match a text string.
whoami.sql	This script displays current session information, including SID, Serial#, Previous SQL Hash Value, and OS Shadow Process ID.

Index

Made in the USA
Lexington, KY
09 October 2012